INTRODUCTION TO THE COUNSELING PROFESSION

FOURTH EDITION

INTRODUCTION TO THE COUNSELING PROFESSION

DAVID CAPUZZI

Johns Hopkins University
Professor Emeritus, Portland State University

DOUGLAS R. GROSS

Professor Emeritus, Arizona State University

New York ■ San Francisco ■ Boston
London ■ Toronto ■ Sydney ■ Tokyo ■ Singapore ■ Madrid
Mexico City ■ Munich ■ Paris ■ Cape Town ■ Hong Kong ■ Montreal

Executive Editor: *Virginia Lanigan*
Series Editorial Assistant: *Scott Blaszak*
Marketing Manager: *Tara Whorf*
Composition and Prepress Buyer: *Linda Cox*
Manufacturing Buyer: *Andrew Turso*
Cover Coordinator: *Joel Gendron*
Editorial-Production Coordinator: *Mary Beth Finch*
Editorial-Production Service: *Shepherd, Inc.*
Electronic Composition: *Shepherd, Inc.*

For related titles and support materials, visit our online catalog at http://www.ablongman.com

Library of Congress Cataloging-in-Publication Data

Introduction to the counseling profession / [edited by] David Capuzzi, Douglas R. Gross.—
  4th ed.
    p. cm.
  Includes bibliographical references and index.
  ISBN 0-205-41067-7
  1. Counseling—Textbooks. I. Capuzzi, Dave. II. Gross, Douglas R.

  BF637.C6I535 2004
  158'.3—dc22

                                       2004049321

Printed in the United States of America.

10 9 8 7 6 5 4 3 2 1   09 08 07 06 05 04

CONTENTS

CHAPTER ONE
Early Historical Perspectives   3

HARRIET L. GLOSOFF, PH.D.
Associate Professor, Counselor Education
The University of Virginia
Charlottesville, Virginia

CHAPTER TWO
The Helping Relationship   56

SUSAN E. HALVERSON, PH.D.
Assistant Professor, Counselor Education
Portland State University
Portland, Oregon

RUSSELL D. MIARS, PH.D.
Associate Professor, Counselor Education
Portland State University
Portland, Oregon

MONICA I. ISHIKAWA, M.ED.
Doctoral Student
University of Oregon
Eugene, Oregon

ROLLA E. LEWIS, ED.D.
Associate Professor, Counselor Education
Portland State University
Portland, Oregon

DAVID CAPUZZI, PH.D.
Johns Hopkins University
Professor Emeritus, Portland State University
Portland, Oregon

DOUGLAS R. GROSS, PH.D.
Professor Emeritus
Arizona State University
Tempe, Arizona

ELLEN HAWLEY MCWHIRTER, PH.D.
Associate Professor, Counseling Psychology
University of Oregon
Eugene, Oregon

KAREN N. PAEZ, M.S.
Doctoral Student
University of Oregon
Eugene, Oregon

PAUL T. CEASAR, ED.D.
Assistant Professor and Coordinator, Counselor Education
Our Lady of Holy Cross College
New Orleans, Louisiana

JUDITH G. MIRANTI, ED.D.
Professor and Dean, Division of Humanities and Education
Our Lady of Holy Cross College
New Orleans, Louisiana

ANN VERNON, PH.D.
Professor and Coordinator, Counselor Education
University of Northern Iowa
Cedar Falls, Iowa

LARRY C. LOESCH, PH.D.
Professor, Counselor Education
University of Florida
Gainesville, Florida

LINDA H. FOSTER, PH.D.
Middle School Counselor
McAdory High School
Birmingham, Alabama

LINDA SELIGMAN, PH.D.
Professor Emeritus, Counseling and Development
George Mason University
Fairfax, Virginia

PART III   COUNSELING IN SPECIFIC SETTINGS   331

CHAPTER FOURTEEN
School Counseling   333

SUSAN KEYS, PH.D.
Associate Professor, Counselor Education
Johns Hopkins University
Baltimore, Maryland

ALAN G. GREEN, PH.D.
Assistant Professor, Department of Counseling and Human Services
Johns Hopkins University
Baltimore, Maryland

CHAPTER FIFTEEN
Counseling in Mental Health and Private Practice
Settings   357

REBECCA T. BROWERS, ED.D.
Associate Professor, Counselor Education
Eastern Washington University
Cheney, Washington

PART IV   COUNSELING SPECIAL POPULATIONS   381

CHAPTER SIXTEEN
Counseling the Older Adult   383

DOUGLAS R. GROSS, PH.D.
Professor Emeritus
Arizona State University
Tempe, Arizona

DAVID CAPUZZI, PH.D.
Johns Hopkins University
Professor Emeritus
Portland State University
Portland, Oregon

HANOCH LIVNEH, PH.D.
Professor, Counselor Education
Portland State University
Portland, Oregon

ELIZABETH WOSLEY-GEORGE, PH.D.
Associate Professor, Counselor Education
Portland State University
Portland, Oregon

PREFACE

The profession of counseling is best described as one through which counselors interact with clients to assist individuals in learning about and dealing with themselves and their environment and the roles and responsibilities inherent in this interactive process. Individuals exploring counseling as a career choice need to be aware of the personal, professional, and societal demands that are placed on the professional counselor. The role of the professional counselor calls for individuals who are skilled and knowledgeable in the process and theory that undergird the profession, who are able and willing to reach deeper levels of self-understanding, and who are able to integrate this skill, knowledge, and self-understanding to provide the effective counseling interaction to which clients are entitled. Individuals attempting to decide whether this is the right career choice for them will find the information contained in this text helpful in the decision-making process.

The book is unique both in its format and in its content. The contributed-authors format provides state-of-the-art information by experts in their respective fields. The content provides readers with areas not often addressed in introductory texts. Examples of these include a chapter devoted to counseling from a rehabilitative perspective, a chapter devoted to brief therapies, a chapter devoted to client diagnosis and assessment that includes an introduction to the DSM-IV, a chapter that takes a comprehensive look at mental health counseling, and a number of chapters that discuss counseling special populations. In addition, this fourth edition of our text contains chapters on research and writing in counseling, technology and counseling, and spirituality counseling. Both format and content enhance the readability of the book and should increase student interest in the material.

The book is designed for students who are taking a preliminary course in the counseling field and who are trying to determine if they are well matched to the profession of counseling; it provides an orientation to the profession and can be used by CACREP accredited and CACREP equivalent programs to help meet the professional orientation standard. The book presents a comprehensive overview of the major aspects of counseling as a profession and provides its reader with insight into the myriad of issues that surround not only the process of counseling and its many populations but also the personal dynamics of the counselor that have an impact upon this process. We know that one text cannot adequately address all the factors that make up this complex profession. We have, however, attempted to provide our readers with a broad perspective on the profession of counseling. The following overview highlights the major features of the text.

OVERVIEW

The format for this coedited/coauthored text is based upon the contributions of authors selected for their expertise in various areas of counseling. With few exceptions, each chapter contains information specific to a topic and uses case examples to demonstrate the various concepts within the chapter. The text is divided into the following four sections: Part One: Counseling Foundations, Part Two: Counseling Skills, Part Three: Counseling in Specific Settings, and Part Four: Counseling Special Populations.

Part One—Counseling Foundations (Chapters 1 through 5)—begins with information dealing with the philosophical and historical perspectives that serve as the foundation of the counseling profession and builds on this foundation providing the reader with current information regarding legislation, professional associations, certification, licensure, accreditation, and current issues and trends related to counseling. Chapters entitled The Helping Relationship, Ethics and the Beginning Counselor: Being Ethical Right from the Start, Research and Writing in Counseling, and Technology and Counseling are included.

Part Two—Counseling Skills (Chapters 6 through 13)—presents information relative to the skills counselors must acquire through a combination of education, supervision, and practice. These chapters discuss Individual Counseling: Traditional Approaches, Individual Counseling: Brief Approaches, Group Counseling, Career Counseling: Counseling for Life, Counseling and Spirituality, Creative Approaches to Counseling, Counseling Uses of Tests, and Diagnosis in Counseling. All of these chapters provide overviews and introduce readers to roles that cut across a variety of work settings.

Part Three—Counseling in Specific Settings (Chapters 14 and 15)—presents information relative to counseling in not only school counseling settings but also mental health and private practice settings. These chapters, School Counseling and Counseling in Mental Health and Private Practice Settings, highlight specific processes and procedures that have applications to these diverse settings.

Part Four—Counseling Special Populations (Chapters 16 through 20)—covers the wide spectrum of clients who present for the services of the counselor. Included in this section are special approaches for dealing with the elderly; couples and families; gay, lesbian, and bisexual clients; minorities; and clients with disabilities. Each chapter includes not only a discussion of the special needs of these populations but also specialized approaches and techniques that have been found to be effective with these groups.

Every attempt has been made by the editors and contributors to provide the reader with current information in each of the twenty areas of focus. It is our hope that *Introduction to the Counseling Profession* (4th ed.) will provide the neophyte with the foundation needed to make a decision regarding future study in the professional arena of counseling.

ACKNOWLEDGMENTS

We would like to thank the authors who contributed their time, expertise, and experience to the development of this textbook for the new professional. We would also like to thank our families, who provided the support to make our writing and editing efforts possible, as well as Phyllis Edmundson, Dean of the Graduate School of Education, and the Counselor Education faculty at Portland State University. Our thanks are also directed to Virginia Lanigan and other staff of Allyn & Bacon for their creativity, encouragement, and editing skills.

Special recognition is given to Mark Stauffer, research assistant at Portland State University, and recent graduate of the Couples, Marriage, and Family specialization of the Counselor Education Masters program. His competent work and coauthorship of the ethical/legal chapter helped make this fourth edition a reality. We wish him the very best as he enters the doctoral program at Oregon State University and moves closer to his goal of becoming a counselor educator.

We are grateful to the following reviewers whose comments provided valuable guidance in our work on the 4th edition:

Mary H. Jackson—Georgia Southern University
J. Trevor Milliron—Lee University
James J. Bergin—Georgia Southern University
John K. Miller—University of Oregon
Beverly A. Farrow—Marshall University Graduate College
Marilyn Pasquarelli—Marietta College
Charles Pryor—University of Louisiana at Monroe

MEET THE AUTHORS

Rebecca T. Browers, Ed.D., N.C.C., L.P.C., has been a counselor educator since 1986 and has recently retired from Counselor Education at Eastern Washington University, where she served as Coordinator of the Mental Health track. As an adjunct faculty member at Eastern Washington University and Gonzaga University, she currently teaches courses in theory, community counseling, group counseling, career development and supervision. Her research focuses on issues in aging. She is a nationally certified counselor.

Malachy Bishop, Ph.D., is an assistant professor in the Rehabilitation Counseling Program in the Department of Special Education and Rehabilitation Counseling at the University of Kentucky, Lexington, Kentucky. He received his M.S.Ed. in Rehabilitation Counseling from Portland State University, and his Ph.D. in Rehabilitation Psychology from the University of Wisconsin-Madison. His research interests include the application of quality of life research in counseling and psychology, and the process of adaptation to disability, particularly among persons with epilepsy and other chronic neurological conditions.

Paul T. Ceasar, Ed.D., is an associate professor of Counselor Education at Our Lady of Holy Cross College, New Orleans, Louisiana, who has published on the topic of integrating spirituality and counseling in the counseling process. He holds leadership positions at the state and national levels and has presented papers, workshops, and seminars on the topic of spirituality and counseling. He is on the Licensed Professional Counselor Board of Examiners in the state of Louisiana.

Bessie Chuang, M.Ed., has had ample opportunities to work with diverse populations in her roles as an Intergroup Dialogue Facilitator in Michigan's Program on Intergroup Relations, the Program Assistant for Dialogues on Diversity, and the Assistant Director of Student Activities. These enriching experiences complement the theoretical knowledge that she has developed through her undergraduate and graduate studies in psychology, counseling and higher education administration.

Teresa M. Christensen, Ph.D., is currently an associate professor of Counselor Education at the University of New Orleans and has a part-time private practice where she specializes in counseling with children, adolescents, and families. Dr. Christensen teaches courses and conducts research related to child and adolescent counseling, play therapy, child abuse and trauma, group work, clinical supervision, and qualitative research. She is also a Licensed Professional Counselor-Board Approved Supervisor in Louisiana, a Nationally Certified Counselor, and a Registered Play Therapist-Supervisor.

Cass Dykeman, Ph.D., is an associate professor of counseling at Oregon State University. Dr. Dykeman received a master's degree in counseling from the University of Washington and a doctorate in counselor education from the University of Virginia. He holds national certification in addictions counseling and school counseling. Dr. Dykeman is a past president of the Western Association for Counselor Education and Supervision. He has authored numerous books, book chapters, and research articles. Dr. Dykeman teaches doctoral research methods courses at Oregon State University.

Linda H. Foster, Ph.D., is a middle-school counselor at McAdory High School in Birmingham, Alabama, a licensed mental health counselor, a National Certified Counselor, and a National Certified School Counselor. She was the recipient of the Chi Sigma Iota (International) 2001 Outstanding Practitioner Award. She is a member of the National Board for Certified Counselor's school counselor credentialing committee and served as NBCC's liaison to the National Board for Professional Teaching Standards. She has published articles and/or made presentations on a variety of topics in the counseling profession including single-subject research, professional credentialing, cinematherapy, classroom guidance, and spirituality.

Harriet L. Glosoff, Ph.D., L.P.C., A.C.S., is an associate professor and director of Counselor Education at the University of Virginia (UVA). Her professional background includes extensive experience in clinical supervision and in the provision of counseling services in diverse settings such as community agencies, in- and outpatient psychiatric facilities, public schools, private practice, and university settings. She also served as the assistant executive director for Advocacy for the American Counseling Association (ACA) (1992–1994) and remains active in leadership positions within ACA and its divisions at the state, regional, and national levels. Her recent clinical practice has focused primarily on treatment of depression, eating disorders, anxiety, and issues related to loss and bereavement. Her current research interests are primarily in the areas of ethical practice and cultural issues in counseling, clinical supervision, and counselor education.

Alan G. Green, Ph.D., is an assistant professor and coordinator for the School Counseling Program at Johns Hopkins University. He is the principal investigator of Project Inspiration, a federally funded grant for the development and refinement of an urban elementary school counseling model being implemented in the Baltimore City Public School System of Maryland. Previously, Dr. Green was a research assistant and adjunct professor at the Metropolitan Center for Urban Education at New York University. Here he worked as project director of a federally funded Safe and Drug Free Schools data collection project with New York City Public Schools. Dr. Green's research interests are in urban education, academic underachievement among African Americans, and the use of data to improve schools.

Melinda Haley, M.S., N.C.C., is a nationally certified counselor and doctoral student at New Mexico State University. At NMSU, Melinda teaches Educational Psychology and conducts research regarding the cultural factors that affect attitudes toward inmates. Melinda has numerous publications in many different counseling subject areas, and her current research interests include, but are not limited to, personality disorders and personality development over the life span; criminology; the psychology of repeat offenders and variables that contribute to individual perceptions of inmates; multicultural issues in counseling, including racial bigotry; the psychology of ethnic cleansing; and posttraumatic stress disorders and the efficacious factors in trauma counseling.

Susan E. Halverson, Ph.D., is an assistant professor in the Counselor Education program at Portland State University. Dr. Halverson received her Ph.D. from the College of William and Mary in Williamsburg, Virginia, where she was the director of the New Horizons Family Counseling Clinic. Susan is licensed by the Commonwealth of Virginia as a Professional Counselor (L.P.C.) and a Marriage and Family Therapist (L.M.F.T.). She is also a Nationally Certified Counselor (N.C.C.) and a Nationally Certified School Counselor (N.C.S.C.). Her current research interests include cognitive development (moral, ethical, and conceptual) and counselor self-efficacy.

Reese M. House, Ed.D., is a nationally recognized counselor educator. He is Professor Emeritus at Oregon State University where he focused on preparing school counselors to be proactive change agents and advocates for social, economic, and political justice. He has experience as a school counselor, community activist, and HIV/AIDS educator. He currently works at the Education Trust in Washington, DC, as director of the National Center for Transforming School Counseling.

Monica I. Ishikawa, M.Ed., is a doctoral student in the counseling psychology program at the University of Oregon. She has a master's degree in counseling and guidance and a bachelor's degree in business administration with an emphasis in human resource management from the University of Hawaii at Manoa. Her experience includes working with at-risk minority students and an internship in the Governor's office in Hawaii. Her interests include child abuse prevention, program evaluation, and group work.

Susan Keys, Ph.D., has been active in the field of school counseling as a graduate student, school counselor, consultant, and counselor educator for over twenty-five years. She has worked as a school counselor in rural and urban settings and has experience working with a variety of culturally diverse populations. At present Dr. Keys is associate professor in the Department of Counseling and Human Services at Johns Hopkins University. Her research interests include innovative practices in school counseling and counselor education, models for collaborative school-family-community mental health teams, and interdisciplinary training for general educators, special educators, school administrators, and school counselors.

Courtland C. Lee, Ph.D., is a professor and director of the Counselor Education Program at the University of Maryland, College Park. He is the editor or coeditor of four books on multicultural counseling and the author of three books on counseling African American males. In addition, he has published numerous articles and book chapters on counseling across cultures. Dr. Lee is also a past president of the American Counseling Association.

Rolla E. Lewis, Ed.D., N.C.C., is an associate professor of Counselor Education at Portland State University, where he serves as coordinator of the school counseling specialization in the Counselor Education master's program. He has taught and counseled diverse students in alternative and public school settings. He was awarded the Civic Engagement Award at Portland State for creating a university-community collaboration with a local school district. The Oregon Counseling

Association presented Dr. Lewis with the Leona Tyler Award for outstanding contributions to the profession of counseling.

Hanoch Livneh, Ph.D., is professor of Counselor Education and coordinator of the Rehabilitation Counseling Specialization at Portland State University, Portland, Oregon. He received his M.A. and Ph.D. degrees in rehabilitation counseling psychology from the University of Wisconsin at Madison. Before joining the faculty at Portland State University, he served as the director of the rehabilitation counseling program, Department of Counseling and Educational Psychology, at Rhode Island College, Providence, Rhode Island.

Larry C. Loesch, Ph.D., is a professor and interim coordinator of the school counseling program in the department of Counselor Education at the University of Florida, a National Certified Counselor, and a research and evaluation consultant for the Center for Credentialing in Education. He was a corecipient of the 1983 APGA Research Award, the 1985 AMECD Exemplary Practices Award, and the 1992 AACD Arthur A. Hitchcock Distinguished Professional Service Award. He is a past president of the Florida Association for Counseling and Development, the Association for Measurement and Evaluation in Counseling and Development, Chi Sigma Iota (International), and the Southern Association for Counselor Education and Supervision. He was a Fulbright Scholar in the Slovak Republic.

Ellen Hawley McWhirter, Ph.D., is an associate professor in the Counseling Psychology program at the University of Oregon. She received her B.A. from the University of Notre Dame and her master of counseling and Ph.D. in counseling psychology from Arizona State University. Dr. McWhirter is the author of *Counseling for Empowerment* (1994, American Counseling Association) and coauthor of *Youth at Risk: A Comprehensive Response,* 3rd ed. (2004, Brooks/Cole). Her teaching interests include career counseling, research seminar, and clinical practica, and her scholarly interests focus on ethnic minority and female adolescent career development and on promoting empowerment through counseling and counselor training.

Benedict T. McWhirter, Ph.D., is an associate professor of Counseling Psychology at the University of Oregon and for most of his tenure there has served as director of doctoral training. He received his Ph.D. in counseling psychology from Arizona State University in 1992. His research interests include studying the effectiveness of small group interventions among adolescents at risk for problem behaviors. Among his publications is the text, *At Risk Youth: A Comprehensive Response* (3rd ed., 2004, Brooks/Cole) written with J. Jeffries McWhirter, Ellen Hawley McWhirter, and Robert J. McWhirter. Benedict's research interests also include studying college student development, loneliness, and connectedness. He links these two primary areas by examining the internal cognitive mechanisms and interpersonal skills that play a contributing or preventive role in social isolation and risk behavior among adolescents and young adults. For each of the past eight years Benedict has visited and worked in Santiago, Chile, where, with his spouse Ellen, he conducts training workshops for couples on conflict resolution, family communication, and group leadership and facilitation skills. Benedict was named as a Fulbright Scholar, through the U.S. State Department, to teach and conduct research in Chile during 2004.

Russell D. Miars, Ph.D., is associate professor in the Counselor Education program at Portland State University. Previously, Dr. Miars was director of the Counseling and Student Development Center and adjunct associate professor in Clinical Psychology at Indiana University of Pennsylvania. His research and scholarly interests include counselor supervision, legal and ethical issues, life span human development, and assessment in counseling. An emphasis in all his work is translating theory and research into effective clinical practice.

Jennie L. Miller, Ph.D., has been involved in many endeavors involving the counseling profession. She has been involved in teaching counseling skills and theory to others; practiced as a counselor for individuals, families, and couples; and advocated for various social justice issues. She has a special interest in gay, lesbian, bisexual, and transgendered issues, especially as they relate to adolescents and their development.

Judith G. Miranti, Ed.D., is dean of Graduate Studies and professor of Counselor Education at Our Lady of Holy Cross College. She is vice chair of the Council for the Accreditation of Counseling and related educational programs. She has published texts and textbook chapters and articles on the topic of spirituality and religion in counseling.

Karen N. Paez, M.S., is a doctoral student in the Counseling Psychology program at the University of Oregon, Eugene, OR. She received her B.A. in psychology from Auburn University and her M.S. in counseling and family human services from the University of Oregon. Karen's teaching and supervision interests include counseling diverse populations and crisis intervention. Her research interests focus on multicultural competency training of counselors and human service professionals in training, as well as identity development of biracial adolescents.

Sharon E. Robinson Kurpius, Ph.D., received her Ph.D. in counseling and in research methodology from Indiana University in 1978. At that time she accepted an assistant professor position in the Counseling Psychology program at Arizona State University. As a professor at ASU, she has pursued her interest in ethics and critical issues in the counseling profession. Her areas of research include academic retention of women and minority students, health psychology, and at-risk youth. She teaches and writes about professional ethics.

Linda Seligman, Ph.D., is a writer, professor, and practicing psychologist. She is author of nine books including *Technical and Conceptual Skills for Mental Health Professionals, Selecting Effective Treatments, Diagnosis and Treatment Planning for Mental Health Professionals,* and *Systems, Strategies, and Skills of Counseling and Psychotherapy.* She also has written over seventy-five professional articles and book chapters. Dr. Seligman is a licensed psychologist, as well as a licensed professional counselor. She has a private practice in Fairfax, Virginia, where she specializes in counseling people with depression and anxiety as well as people coping with chronic and life-threatening illnesses. Linda Seligman also is Professor Emeritus at George Mason University where she was a full professor, codirector of the doctoral program in Education, and coordinator of the Counseling and Development Program and the Community Agency Counseling Program. She is currently a faculty associate at Johns Hopkins University and a faculty member at Walden University. Dr. Seligman served as editor of the *Journal of Mental Health Counseling* and president of the Virginia Association of Mental Health Counselors. The American Mental Health Counselors Association selected her as Researcher of the Year. In addition, she has served as consultant to many professional organizations including the American Counseling Association, the American Mental Health Counselors Association, Sage Publications, the Department of Health and Human Services, and others.

Mark D. Stauffer, M.S., is a doctoral student in the Counselor Education Program at Oregon State University. He graduated from the Counselor Education Program at Portland State University where he served as a research assistant. Mark was a 2003 Chi Sigma Iota International fellow. In addition to authoring book chapters on counselor education, he is currently co-editing a career counseling textbook with David Capuzzi. Mark has worked in the Portland metro area at crises centers and other non-profit organizations providing counseling to individuals, couples and families. His areas of professional interest are death and dying, spirituality, and couples, marriage and family counseling.

Ann Vernon, Ph.D., L.M.H.C., N.C.C., is professor and coordinator of Counseling at the University of Northern Iowa where she teaches primarily in the school counseling program. In addition, she has a private practice where she specializes in working with children and adolescents. Dr. Vernon has written numerous articles, book chapters, and books, including *Thinking, Feeling, Behaving, What Works When with Children and Adolescents: A Handbook of Individual Counseling Techniques*, and *Counseling Children and Adolescents.* Dr. Vernon is vice president of the Albert Ellis Board of Trustees and has held leadership positions in several professional counseling associations. Dr. Vernon conducts workshops in the United States, Canada, as well as in other countries, on a variety of topics, including creative counseling techniques.

Elizabeth Wosley-George, Ph.D., is an associate professor and former coordinator of Counselor Education at Portland State University in Portland, Oregon. She was formerly director of Emergency Services of North Central Mental Health in Columbus, Ohio, and continues to consult for the Providence Health Systems Emergency Services in the Portland, Oregon area. She has teaching and research interests in the areas of diagnosis and treatment planning, psychopharmacology, multicultural perspectives in counseling, managed care, and behavioral health service delivery systems. Dr. Wosley-George has extensive community involvement and experience with individuals who have psychiatric disabilities. She also served on boards of agencies that serve the mentally ill population.

MEET THE EDITORS

David Capuzzi, Ph.D., N.C.C., L.P.C., is past president of the American Counseling Association (formerly the American Association for Counseling and Development) and is a Counselor Educator at Johns Hopkins University. He is Professor Emeritus and former coordinator of Counselor Education in the Graduate School of Education at Portland State University in Portland, Oregon.

From 1980 to 1984, Dr. Capuzzi was editor of *The School Counselor*. He has authored a number of textbook chapters and monographs on the topic of preventing adolescent suicide and is coeditor and author, with Dr. Larry Golden, of *Helping Families Help Children: Family Interventions with School-Related Problems* (1986) and *Preventing Adolescent Suicide* (1988). In 1989, 1996, 2000, and 2004, he coauthored and edited *Youth at Risk: A Prevention Resource for Counselors, Teachers, and Parents;* in 1991, 1997, and 2001, *Introduction to the Counseling Profession;* in 1992, 1998, and 2002, *Introduction to Group Counseling;* and in 1995, 1999, and 2003, *Counseling and Psychotherapy: Theories and Interventions* with Douglas R. Gross. *Suicide Across the Life Span: Implications for Counselors* (2004), *Approaches to Group Work: A Handbook for Practitioners* (2003), and *Sexuality Issues in Counseling*, the latter coauthored and edited with Larry Burlew, are his three latest texts. He has authored or coauthored articles in a number of ACA-related journals.

A frequent speaker and keynoter at professional conferences and institutes, Dr. Capuzzi has also consulted with a variety of school districts and community agencies interested in initiating prevention and intervention strategies for adolescents at risk for suicide. He has facilitated the development of suicide prevention, crisis management, and postvention programs in communities throughout the United States; provides training on the topics of "youth at risk" and "grief and loss"; and serves as an invited adjunct faculty member at other universities as time permits. He is the first recipient of ACA's Kitty Cole Human Rights Award and also a recipient of the Leona Tyler Award in Oregon.

Douglas R. Gross, Ph.D., N.C.C., is a Professor Emeritus at Arizona State University, Tempe, Arizona, where he served as a faculty member in Counselor Education for 29 years. His professional work history includes public school teaching, counseling, and administration. He is currently retired and living in Three Rivers, Michigan. He has been president of the Arizona Counselors Association, president of the Western Association for Counselor Education and Supervision, chairperson of the Western Regional Branch Assembly of the American Counseling Association, president of the Association for Humanistic Education and Development, and treasurer and parliamentarian of the ACA.

Dr. Gross has contributed chapters to seven texts: *Counseling and Psychotherapy: Theories and Interventions* (1995, 1999, 2003); *Youth at Risk: A Resource for Counselors, Teachers, and Parents* (1989, 1996, 2000, 2004); *Foundations of Mental Health Counseling* (1986, 1996); *Counseling: Theory, Process and Practice* (1977); *The Counselor's Handbook* (1974); *Introduction to the Counseling Profession* (1991, 1997, 2001); and *Introduction to Group Counseling* (1992, 1998, 2002). His research has appeared in *The Journal of Counseling Psychology; The Journal of Counseling and Development; The Association for Counselor Education and Supervision Journal; The Journal of Educational Research, Counseling and Human Development; The Arizona Counselors Journal; The Texas Counseling Journal;* and *The AMHCA Journal.*

Dr. Gross provides national training for certification in the areas of bereavement, grief, and loss.

PART I

COUNSELING FOUNDATIONS

Counseling as a profession has an interesting history and encompasses a number of basic premises and foundational perspectives in which the counselor needs to be educated. This section provides the beginning counseling student with an overview of both the historical context of counseling and the philosophical basis on which the counselor operates. This section introduces the counseling student to not only the process of counselor-client interaction, the helping relationship, but also information dealing with ethical and legal considerations. It also provides the student with important information on research and writing in counseling as well as technology and counseling.

The development of counseling as a distinct profession is outlined in Chapter 1, "Early Historical Perspectives." The roots of counseling are traced from the vocational guidance movement at the beginning of this century to the current status of professional associations, legislation, certification, licensure, accreditation, and current issues and trends related to counseling.

Chapter 2, "The Helping Relationship," presents to students the characteristics and qualities that distinguish helping professionals. Personal qualities that effective helpers possess are described, as well as such basic skills as the counselor's reflecting and listening skills, attention to nonverbal cues, and the ability to observe and follow perceptively a client's patterns of speech and behavior. These core skills provide a foundation for the beginning counselor to both understand the counseling process and become more self-aware about his or her own interpersonal interactions.

The relationship between the client and the counselor does not exist in a vacuum; rather, it is ingrained in the personal, legal, and ethical context of our society. Counselors are often called upon to make decisions regarding clients in which the "correct" mode of action may not be immediately clear. There may be two contradictory obligations—for example, the obligation to respect the confidentiality of a client and the obligation to protect that client from self-harm or the harming of others. When faced with situations such as this, the counselor cannot rely simply on personal judgment but, instead, needs to act from the basis of the professional guidelines and codes of ethics of the counseling and human development professions. Chapter 3, "Ethics and the Beginning Counselor: Being Ethical Right from the Start," provides an overview of the ethical and legal guidelines on which counselors must base their decisions. It discusses the role of personal values versus professional ethics; the question of counselor competence, clients' rights, confidentiality (including HIPAA and the "Privacy Rule"), and informed consent; and the practicalities of dealing with legal issues and client-related litigation. The chapter also reflects the increasing commitment among members of the profession to respect the diversity that our clientele represent. Such concepts are essential for the beginning counselor to understand and incorporate in gaining a sense of the professional status of the counselor.

Research and writing are major components of the experience of counselor education students in graduate programs all over the country. The fourth chapter in this text, "Research and Writing in Counseling," provides the beginning student with invaluable information about the integration of research, practice and theory, the definition of research, how to access databases, the differences between and value of both quantitative and qualitative research, guidelines for writing a term paper and developing thesis and dissertation proposals, and the ethics of writing and conducting research. This chapter is critical to the future success of all those working toward the completion of an advanced degree.

The use of technology in counseling and the possibilities for information retrieval presented by the World Wide Web is a topic of growing importance to counselors in all settings. Chapter 5, "Technology and Counseling," overviews information related to technology and its applications to counseling: cyber counseling/distance counseling, computer-assisted counseling, using technology in assessment and diagnosis, technological aids for client interventions, technologically based resources for counselors and clients, using technology for client/therapist referrals, technology in counselor supervision, technology and continuing education unit, technology aided counselor communication, and the paper work and scheduling applications. The content of this chapter underscores the importance of technology to the success of the counseling practitioner; it also addresses positives, negatives, and ethical issues connected with the counseling applications of technology.

CHAPTER ONE

EARLY HISTORICAL PERSPECTIVES

HARRIET L. GLOSOFF, PH.D.
University of Virginia

HISTORICAL AND FORMATIVE FACTORS

If one assumes that counseling is advising, counselors have existed since people have appeared on earth. Mothers, fathers, friends, lovers, clergy, and social leaders all provide such counsel—whether sought after or not. The idea of a professionally trained counselor is relatively new. This idea did not, however, emerge due to the recognition of a "deep need within human development" (Stripling, 1983, p. 206). The counseling profession evolved in response to meet the demands made by the industrialization and urbanization of the United States. At the turn of the twentieth century, America faced a confluence of social and economic problems such as the proper distribution of a growing workforce, dealing with an increasingly educated population, meeting the needs of immigrants, and the preservation of social values as family connections were weakened (Aubrey, 1982; Herr, 1985).

A representative democracy demands an educated citizenry taking responsibility for the government itself. As the new democracy developed, so did the ideal of education for all citizens. Toward the end of the nineteenth century, the curriculum of schools began to change and choices among school subjects became available. Help with such choices was necessary. Jessie Davis, one of the pioneers in counseling, declared in his autobiography that he had graduated from school "fairly well prepared to live in the Middle Ages" (Davis, 1956, p. 57). His experiences led directly to the establishment of guidance and counseling services in schools. Other factors were providing pressures that made the evolution of professionally training individuals to help people make choices inevitable. The industrial revolution and its attendant job specialization and technologic advances were some of those pressures. There was also an increase in democracy after the Civil War ended in 1865. If the

3

United States had continued to exist as a slave society or a closed class society, there likely would have been little need for the development of counseling services.

The population of the country was on the increase, and the census of 1890 revealed that the frontier was essentially closed. Larger cities were growing increasingly more crowded, and immigrants to the United States and other citizens could no longer move westward or eastward without regard for others. "Free" land was all but gone. It became necessary to remain near the cities to work, to live, and to get along with one's neighbors. Providing assistance in the choices necessary to live in the large industrially based cities became necessary.

During the twentieth century, the development of professional counseling in the United States was influenced by a variety of factors. The newly developed science of psychology began, and continued, studying the differences among individuals. Instruments for appraising people were in their infancy but were known to pioneers in the field, who noted the need for counseling services. As these tools developed more sophistication, they were adapted and/or adopted by counselors. Other factors contributing to the evolution of counseling included the work of leaders of the early settlement house movement and other social reformers; the mental hygiene movement; the extent to which Americans value personal success; the emphasis placed on the awareness and use of one's talents, interests, and abilities; the ongoing industrialization of the country; the continued growth of career education and career guidance; the development of psychology as a profession; and the rapid changes in all fields due to increased availability of technology (Shertzer & Stone, 1986).

Pressures from various socioeconomic factors also led to the kaleidoscope we know as counseling today. The history of counseling has continued the thread of individual choice in a society that prizes freedom to choose as an ideal. Like a kaleidoscope, the form, emphasis, and brightness of various aspects of counseling have changed as society changes. This chapter examines the following select facets of that kaleidoscope that have shaped the counseling profession:

- The vocational guidance movement
- The mental health counseling movement
- The development of professional identity
- The influence of federal legislation
- The history of the American Counseling Association
- Credentialing and the "professionalization" of counseling

The chapter concludes with a brief review of current issues and trends in the counseling profession.

BEGINNINGS OF THE VOCATIONAL GUIDANCE MOVEMENT

Perhaps the earliest notion of professional counseling in response to societal pressures was that of Lysander S. Richards. In 1881, Richards published a slim volume titled *Vocophy*. Vocophy was considered by Richards to be a "new profession, a system enabling a person to name the calling or vocation one is best suited to follow" (Richards, 1881). His work has been dismissed because there is no documented proof that he actually established the services he advocated. Nevertheless, his ideas fore-shadowed what was to come. He called his counselors "vocophers" and urged that they study occupations and the people they counseled.

Richards (1881) included letters from various famous people of the day in his book *Vocophy.* He believed that aspirants to particular occupations should consider what successful people had to say about the qualifications for success in that field. Letters from Grant, Longfellow, Westinghouse, and others, which described the ingredients for success in their occupations, were included.

Later, a series of pamphlets published by the Metropolitan Life Insurance Company in the 1960s and used widely by school counselors asked the question, "Should your child be a ———?" A famous person in a field would describe what was necessary for success in that field. Using successful people to provide career information is a technique employed by counselors today as well.

Richards also seemed advanced for his time regarding his views of women and youth, and their work. He said that if a woman could do the work "though at present solely followed by man, there can be no objections, whether normally or religiously considered, to her following it" (Richards, 1881, preface). He deplored the drifting of youth from job to job without consideration of what would be best for them and for society.

Whether Richards influenced those who followed is speculative. Influence is the quicksilver of history. He was active in the literary societies in the Boston area, as was Frank Parsons. Did they meet? debate? Richards's *Vocophy* was in the Harvard Library in the 1890s. In an article published in the later 1890s, Parsons (1894) expressed ideas similar to those of Richards. Brewer (1942) noted that Meyer Bloomfield, a colleague of Parsons at the Breadwinners Institute, mentioned Richards in his Harvard courses, as did Henry C. Metcalf of Tufts and Frank Locke of the YMCA in Boston.

Frank Parsons

Regardless of who influenced whom, the need for counseling about vocational choice seems to have permeated American society of the late nineteenth and early twentieth centuries. There is no question of the credit given to Frank Parsons for leading the way to vocational guidance. Parsons had a long history of concern for economic and political reforms that would benefit people. He published books and articles on a wide variety of topics, including taxation, women's suffrage, and education for all people. Of all his endeavors, Parsons was most interested in social reform and especially in assisting people to make sound occupational choices. Other pioneers in the field credited him with being the first counselor (Davis, 1914; Reed, 1944), and he has often been referred to as the "father of guidance." Parsons alone, of those individuals who had some direct connection with the organization and extension of guidance services, had a definite, well-thought-out, and organized social philosophy, which he articulated often and at length (Rockwell, 1958).

Parsons was one of the many, in the late nineteenth and early twentieth centuries who were striving to make the world a better place in which to live. These people saw in the growth of large private fortunes, based on industrial might and the resultant political power, a clear danger to the realization of a more perfect society based on the brotherhood of all humankind. They were humanitarians all, each seeking the good things in life for the individual within society. Parsons found himself in the company of such notables of this movement as Henry D. Lloyd, Edward Bellamy, Phillip Brooks, and Benjamin O. Flower (Rockwell, 1958). Parsons believed it was better to select a vocation scientifically than to drift through a variety of vocations, perhaps never finding one that would be best for the person and thus make society a better place in which to live. Meyer Bloomfield, director of the Civic Service House in Boston, asked Parsons to establish such a service within the Civic Service House. Thus, Parsons became director of what was called the Breadwinners Institute from 1905 through 1907 (Brewer, 1942).

Parsons developed a plan for individualized counseling and opened the Vocational Bureau of Boston in January 1908. He served as its director and vocational counselor. The primary goal of the bureau was to develop the potential of Boston's growing immigrant population. Although Parsons was but one of many who were seeking social reforms at this time, he was able to secure the support of the leaders of powerful groups in business, labor, education, and politics. His report to the members of the board controlling the Vocational Bureau was the first recorded instance of the use of the term "vocational guidance." (Brewer, in 1942, published the report as an appendix to his *History*.) Parsons's report emphasized that counseling was not designed to make decisions for counselees. "No attempt is made, of course, to decide FOR (sic) the applicant what his calling should be; but the Bureau tries to help him arrive at a wise, well-founded conclusion for himself" (Brewer, 1942, p. 304). According to Williamson (1965), this was consistent with the moral and intellectual atmosphere of that time. He traced the growth of counseling before Parsons's work to the concept of "vocational freedom of choice" (p. 3). He noted that the climate of the late 1800s stimulated practical application of vocational choice or individuals' freedom to pursue choice in personal development.

Parsons also developed a plan for the education of counselors. His plan was outlined in his book, *Choosing a Vocation* (1909), published posthumously. Parsons's prescriptions for how counselees should examine themselves and their lives reflected his political and social philosophy (Rockwell, 1958).

Early Ties Between Vocational Guidance and School Counseling

Many see educational settings as the first homes to the profession of counseling, especially in terms of vocational guidance. At about the same time that Parsons opened the Vocational Bureau, Jesse Davis began advising students about educational and vocational matters in 1898 (Aubrey, 1982). Jessie B. Davis had been unsure of what he wanted to do with his life throughout his educational career. He was questioned thoroughly by Charles Thurber, one of his professors at Cornell University, and that left a lasting impression on him. He began to use the professor's methods in his work with students at the Central High School in Detroit and attempted to incorporate guidance into the normal educational experience of students. In 1907, Davis became principal of the Grand Rapids, Michigan Central School and was able to implement his ideas of self-study, occupational study, and examination of self in relation to the chosen occupation throughout the seventh through twelfth grades (Brewer, 1942). This was done primarily through essays written in English classes. Essay topics varied from self-examination of values and ideals to the selection of a vocation by the twelfth grade. Throughout the topics, social and civic ethics were emphasized (Davis, 1914). Just five years later (1912), Grand Rapids established a citywide guidance department.

Grand Rapids was not the only city in the early 1900s that housed newly developed vocational guidance services. Both Anna Y. Reed in Seattle and Eli Weaver in New York established counseling services based on Social Darwinian concepts (Rockwell, 1958). Similar to Darwin's biological theory of "survival of the fittest," Social Darwinism contends that certain groups in a society become powerful because they have adapted best to the evolving requirements of that society. Reed decided that counseling services were needed for America's youth through her study of newsboys, penal institutions, and charity schools. She emphasized that business people were the most successful and that counseling should be designed to help youth emulate them. She equated morality and business ideals and was much concerned that whatever course of action was taken on any social question, it be taken on the basis of social research, of economy, and of how it would be accepted by the business world. Reed urged that schools keep children focused on the potential for making money, which she believed every pupil could understand (Reed, 1916).

The guidance services that Reed developed were similar to those of modern placement agencies that focus on an individual's acceptability to employers. Other programs, she said, "savored too much of a philanthropic or social service proposition and too little of a practical commercial venture" (Reed, 1920, p. 62).

Eli Weaver also believed in working within the framework of the existing society and looked on counseling as a means of keeping the wheels of the machinery well oiled. He was chairman of the Students' Aid Committee of the High School Teachers' Association of New York in 1905. In developing the work of his committee, Weaver concluded that the students were in need of advice and counsel before their entrance into the work-a-day world. He had no funds or active help from school authorities, but was able to secure the volunteer services of teachers to work with young people in New York. By 1910, he was able to report teachers actively attempting to help boys and girls discover what they could do best and how to secure a job in which their abilities could be used to the fullest advantage (Brewer, 1942; Rockwell, 1958).

Counselors in the school systems of Boston and New York during the 1920s were expected to assist students in making educational and vocational choices. It was during the 1920s that the certification of school counselors began in these two cities. It was also during that decade that the Strong Vocational Interest Inventory was first published (1928) and used by counselors setting the stage for future directions in career counseling (Shertzer & Stone, 1986).

The Creation of the National Vocational Guidance Association

The early pioneers in counseling clearly reflected society's need for workers who were skilled and happy in what they did. A distinct influence in early counseling was the vocational education movement. In 1906, the National Society for the Promotion of Industrial Education (NSPIE) was formed. People who were advocates of vocational counseling served on its board and later on the board of the Vocation Bureau established by Parsons. Ralph Albertson, an employment supervisor at William Filene's Sons Company and confidant of Frank Parsons, became secretary of the board of trustees of the Vocation Bureau (Stephens, 1970). Frank Snedden, a vocational educator from Massachusetts, is given credit for suggesting that a vocational guidance conference separate from the NSPIE be held (Brewer, 1942). Such conferences were held in 1911 and 1912.

At a third national conference in 1913, the National Vocational Guidance Association (NVGA) was formed in Grand Rapids, Michigan (Norris, 1954). Frank Leavitt became the first president and noted the economic, educational, and social demands for guidance and the counseling it entailed. He also felt that it was necessary "for the very preservation of society itself" (Norris, 1954, p. 17). Counseling in regard to career choice remained an integral part of the movement.

BEGINNINGS OF THE MENTAL HEALTH COUNSELING MOVEMENT

The economic, educational, and social reform forces that led to the organization of NVGA also led to other movements, which were later incorporated into the kaleidoscope we call counseling today. In the early 1800s, American reformers such as Dorothea Dix advocated for the establishment of institutions that would treat people with emotional disorders in a humane manner. Although these reformers made great strides in accomplishing their goals, following the Civil War there was a rapid decline in the conditions related to the humane treatment of institutionalized individuals (Palmo & Weikel, 1986).

Clifford Beers, who had suffered harsh treatment for mental illness in several psychiatric institutions, published *A Mind That Found Itself*, an autobiography about his experience (Beers, 1908). Publication of this book served as a catalyst for the mental hygiene movement and studies of people with emotional and behavior problems. Early studies of children with emotional problems supported the concept of providing counseling for all children in schools. Beginning at about the same time as vocational guidance, the mental hygiene movement and the field of psychology have had equally strong influences on the development of professional counseling. In 1908, the same year Frank Parsons opened the Vocational Bureau, William Healy, M.D., established the first community psychiatric clinic. The Juvenille Psychopathic Institute was founded to provide services to the young people in Chicago who were having problems. The institute used testing, modified psychoanalysis, and involvement of family members. In 1909, leaders of Cook County, Illinois, deciding that counseling services would benefit children, established countywide child guidance clinics. It was this same year that the U.S. Congress founded the National Committee on Mental Hygiene.

Early Psychologists

Wilhelm Wundt must be credited with establishing, in the late 1870s in Germany, the first experimental psychology laboratory. One way that Wundt endeavored to study how the mind is structured was by using a form of introspection or asking subjects to use self-reflection and to verbalize what they were experiencing (Belkin, 1988).

In the United States, William James modified Wundt's approach and tried to discover the functions of the mind, rather than focusing primarily on its structure. James believed that individuals functioned as holistic beings who use thoughts, reasoning, emotions, and behaviors. James and his followers are referred to as "functionalists," and they developed experimental designs to facilitate the understanding of why human beings' minds function as they do (Belkin, 1988). James's interest in the ideas of "adaptive functioning," "free will," and the conscious functioning of individuals is clearly pertinent to the development of the counseling profession. A scientific approach to social problems had become popular in the late nineteenth and early twentieth centuries. Granville Stanley Hall founded what many consider the first psychology laboratory in the United States at Johns Hopkins University in 1883 where he focused on collecting data on the mental characteristics of children (Belkin, 1988). His efforts in studying the development of children's mental and physical abilities continued under his tenure as president of Clark University, where he emphasized graduate study and research. The scientific approach to social problems was based on the assumption that the answer to a social problem could be discovered through objective research. Many consider G. Stanley Hall the "father of American psychology" (Belkin, 1988, p. 15). Even though his work itself has not endured, in addition to founding one of the first psychology departments, G. Stanley Hall was also the primary person to organize the American Psychological Association (APA) and he bestowed the first doctorates in the field of psychology. Of course, the early behaviorists such as John Watson and B. F. Skinner, and experimental psychologists, such as Max Wetheimer and Wolfgang Kohler, are also associated with the development of the field of psychology.

David Spence Hill, who organized the first guidance and counseling services in New Orleans, was a graduate of Clark University during the presidency of G. Stanley Hall. As director of research for the New Orleans schools, he discovered a need for guidance while researching whether there was a need for a vocational school in his district (Rockwell, 1958). He concluded that there was a need for such a high school, and he also believed it necessary to assist youth in assessing their abilities and in learning about the opportunities that would best help them use those skills. He was aware of the appraisal work being done by Binet and attempted to use the Binet tasks in helping the students in the New Orleans schools. He realized the need for counseling because of his belief that the education of an individual must be of the highest order. Counseling based on scientific research would help secure the best education for each pupil. If counselors were to help youth know themselves and match their characteristics with qualifications for jobs, it was necessary to have some means of measuring individual characteristics. Counselors relied a great deal on questioning youth about their abilities and their desires. There was the implicit assumption that counselees know themselves and could reason about their reported skills and their qualifications for jobs. A counselor's task was to help them in this process by using greater maturity and objective judgment. The development of tests and appraisal instruments lent a scientific air to the process.

During the late 1800s and early 1900s, the testing movement was also taking hold. In the 1890s, James Cattell was the first person in this country to focus on ways to measure intelligence. In 1984, he introduced the first mental abilities test, which was administered to freshmen entering Columbia University (Goldenberg, 1973).

At the turn of the twentieth century, the Binet-Simon Test was introduced in France (1905). In 1916, L. M. Terman of Stanford University released a revised version of the Binet-Simon Test he had developed, titled the Stanford-Binet Test. With the release of the Stanford-Binet Test, the term *intelligence quotient* or *IQ* was first used. Although the development of the Stanford-Binet certainly helped spearhead the testing movement in the United States, it was World War I that truly gave flight to the development and use of standardized instruments (Baruth & Robinson, 1987).

Influences of World War I and the Development of Testing

World War I influenced the counseling profession's roots in both the vocational guidance and mental health arenas. The Army, in order to screen personnel, commissioned the development of psychological instruments, including the Army Alpha and Beta IQ tests of intelligence. In the period following World War I, the number and variety of such instruments proliferated, and even though counselors were not the major creators of the instruments, they became users. Counselors began to use standardized instruments as tools for use in military, educational, and clinical settings. These screening tools also supported the development of aptitude and interest tests used by counselors in business and educational settings (Aubrey, 1982). Quantifying a person's intelligence, aptitude, achievement, interest, and personality gave a great deal of credibility to a counselor's judgment about the person (Ginzberg, 1971).

After World War I, psychological testing became pervasive in industrial personnel classification, in education, and in counseling offices. Knowledge about and skill in using standardized tests became part of the education of a counselor. Data derived from appraisal instruments were used to make better judgments about counselees and to advise them about what was the wisest decision to make. Large commercial producers of psychometric devices emerged. The process of developing and marketing tests to industry, education, government, and counselors in private practice became quite sophisticated. Counselors were expected to be experts in selecting and using appropriate instruments from a myriad of those offered. Their use in the counseling process became such that testing and counseling were often considered synonymous.

The practice of using tests in counseling was not without controversy. Criteria for psychometric instruments used in decision making were not published until 1954, with the publication of the American Psychological Association's *Technical Recommendations for Psychological Tests and Diagnostic Techniques* (Stephens, 1954). Publications such as *Testing, Testing, Testing* (Joint Committee on Testing, 1962), *The Educational Decision-Makers* (Cicourel & Kitsuse, 1963), and *The Brain Watchers* (Gross, 1962) are examples of many voices questioning the reliance on test data by counselors and others.

BEGINNINGS OF PROFESSIONAL IDENTITY

The Great Depression and the Continuation of the Career Guidance Movement

There was continued progress in the development of career counseling during the 1930s. The Great Depression, with its loss of employment for millions of people, demonstrated the need for career counseling to assist adults as well as youth to identify, develop, and learn to market new vocational skills (Ohlsen, 1983). At the University of Minnesota, E. G. Williamson and colleagues modified the work of Frank Parsons and employed it in working with students. Their work is considered by some to be the first theory of career counseling and it emphasized a directive, counselor-centered approach known as the "Minnesota point of view." Williamson's approach continued to emphasize matching individuals' traits with those of various jobs and dominated counseling during most of the 1930s and 1940s. The publication of the *Dictionary of Occupational Titles* in 1938 provided counselors with a basic resource to match people with occupations for which they were theoretically well suited (Shertzer & Stone, 1986).

The concept that society would be better if individuals and their occupations were matched for greater efficiency and satisfaction continued to shape the vocational guidance movement. There was a plethora of organizations dedicated to this end. In 1934, a number of them met to form the American Council of Guidance and Personnel Associations, or ACGPA (Brewer, 1942, p. 152), including the American College Personnel Association, the National Association of Deans of Women, the National Federation of Bureau of Occupations, the National Vocational Guidance Association, the Personnel Research Foundation, and the Teachers' College Personnel Association. By 1939 the name was changed to the Council of Guidance and Personnel Associations (CGPA), and other groups were added: the Alliance for the Guidance of Rural Youth, the International Association of Altrusa Clubs, the National Federation of Business and Professional Women's Clubs, the Western Personnel Service, the American Association of Collegiate Registrars (withdrew in 1941), the Institute of Women's Professional Relations, the Kiwanis International, and the Association of YMCA Secretaries met with the group from time to time.

Brewer (1942) stated that the October 1938 issue of *Occupations*, the publication of the NVGA, listed ninety-six organizations interested in furthering vocational guidance among the young people of the nation. Counseling, per se, was coming to the forefront of concerns within the vocational guidance movement. All groups seemed dedicated to placing "square pegs in square holes" through the use of tests.

During the 1950s, the U.S. government was particularly interested in issues related to vocational guidance or career guidance. In response to the Soviet Union's successful space program (for example, the launching of *Sputnik*), the government became concerned with identifying young people with scientific and mathematical talent. To this end, they passed the National Defense Education Act (NDEA) in 1958. Some contend that the impact of NDEA goes well beyond funding of vocational guidance programs. Hoyt (1974) stated that NDEA "had a greater impact on counselor education than any other single force" (Hoyt, 1974, p. 504). NDEA funded the training of guidance counselors at both the elementary and secondary levels, and NDEA training programs were established to produce counselors qualified for public schools (Herr, 1985). Although the legislation established counselor education programs specifically to train professionals to identify bright children and steer them into technical fields, these counselors were also trained in other domains of counseling as well.

Influence of World War II

World War II strongly influenced the confluence of the vocational guidance and mental health movements, along with that of rehabilitation counseling. The U.S. government continued to rely on standardized instruments and classification systems during World War II. The government requested that psychologists and counselors aid in selecting and training specialists for the military and industry (Ohlsen, 1983). Before and during World War II, millions of men and women were tested and assigned to particular duties according to their test scores and their requests. The armed forces stationed counselors and psychologists at many induction and separation centers. Picchioni and Bonk (1983) quote Mitchell Dreese of the adjutant general's office as saying that counseling, "is essentially the same whether it be in the home, the church, the school, industry, business, or the Army" (p. 54). The process was certainly an extensive use of the scientific approach to counseling. Society, through its representatives in government, had become embroiled in what counseling should be and what it should become. Society has not relinquished that sense of involvement through all the forms, shapes, and colors of the kaleidoscope counseling has become.

The use of standardized tests is not the only reason World War II had a tremendous influence on the counseling profession. Personnel were also needed on the front lines and in aid stations to help soldiers deal with "battle neuroses." This was accomplished through minimum training and what seemed to be an "overnight" credentialing of new medical school graduates and research-oriented clinical psychologists. Even though minimally trained, their interventions resulted in a significant reduction of chronic battle neuroses (Cummings, 1990).

In 1944, the War Department established the Army Separation-Classification and Counseling Program in response to the emotional and vocational needs of returning soldiers. The Veterans Administration (VA) also established counseling centers within their hospitals (Shertzer & Stone, 1986). The VA coined the term *counseling psychology* and established counseling psychology positions and training programs to fill these positions. The National Institute of Mental Health (NIMH) was established just after World War II and established a series of training stipends for graduate programs in professional psychology. NIMH reinforced the VA's standard of the doctorate being the entry level into professional psychology by setting up Ph.D. training stipends. The American Psychological Association (APA) was asked to set standards of training for the new programs in university graduate schools. Although the goal of the VA and NIMH was to train counseling psychologists for the public sector, more and more trained psychologists chose to enter private practice.

In addition, during the 1940s a trend toward working with the psychological problems of "normal people" emerged. In reaction to the Nazi movement and World War II, humanistic psychologists and psychiatrists came from Europe to the United States. Their work gradually influenced the strong quantitative leanings in counseling and contributed to the work of well-known psychologists such as Rollo May, Abraham Maslow, and Carl Rogers.

Carl Rogers and the Continuation of the Mental Health Movement

In reviewing a history of what has happened, it is often difficult to know whether events have shaped a leader of an era or whether a person has influenced events. There seems little doubt that Carl R. Rogers, his ideas, and his disciples affected counseling from its core outward. Rogers's idea was that individuals had the capacity to explore themselves and to make decisions without an authoritative judgment from a counselor. He saw little need to make diagnoses of client problems or to provide information or direction to those he called *clients*. He emphasized the importance of the relationship between the counselor and client. In his system, the client rather than the counselor was the most important factor. Since there was no advice given or persuasion used to follow a particular course, Rogers's system became known as *nondirective counseling*. Rogers became interested in the process of counseling and pioneered the electronic recording and filming of counseling sessions, an unheard-of idea at that time. Working in the academic environment of The Ohio State University and the University of Chicago, Rogers published his ideas in *Counseling and Psychotherapy: Newer Concepts in Practice* in 1942 and *Client-Centered Therapy* in 1951.

It is not the purpose of this chapter to delineate all the postulates of what became known as *client-centered counseling*, and later, *person-centered counseling*. It is important to note, however, the impact that approach had on counseling has continued to the present day. The rise to prominence of Carl Rogers's theory was the first major challenge to the tenets of the Minnesota point of view. In fact, many programs at counseling conventions debated the issue of client-centered versus trait factored counseling.

Rogers himself remained within the scientific approach to counseling. His concern was to learn what went on in the counseling process, to learn what worked (for him) and what did not. His was a search for necessary and sufficient conditions under which effective counseling could take place. Whenever research about client-centered counseling was reported by Rogers, it was supported by psychometric data. Certainly one of the effects of Rogers on the profession was to emphasize understanding the counseling process and the need for research. The ensuing debates about the primacy of feeling or rationality as a proper basis of counseling stimulated professional counselors to research their processes and techniques. Theories were refined, and new instruments for determining their efficacy were developed. Counselors-in-training became as familiar with recording devices as they were with textbooks.

Aubrey (1982) noted, "without doubt, the most profound influence in changing the course and direction of the entire guidance movement in the mid and late 1940s was Carl Rogers" (p. 202). Rogers built on the humanistic and individualistic foundations of the education guidance movement in which he was trained at Columbia University by formulating the nondirective client-centered approach to counseling. He brought a psychologically oriented counseling theory into the guidance movement, thus grounding the counseling profession in the broad disciplines of education and psychology (Weikel & Palmo, 1989).

FEDERAL LEGISLATION AND ITS INFLUENCE ON THE COUNSELING PROFESSION

The Great Depression prompted the development of government-sponsored programs that included a counseling component with an emphasis on classification. Both the Civilian Conservation Corps (CCC) and the National Youth Administration (NYA) attempted to help youth find themselves in the occupational scene of the 1930s (Miller, 1971). In 1938, the George-Dean Act had appropriated $14 million for vocational education, and by 1938 the Occupational Information and Guidance Services was established. The federal government became influential in the field of counseling and remains so today.

The following list exemplifies how the federal government has influenced the development of the counseling profession by offering *examples* of governmental actions and legislation. Primary sources of this information include ACA legislative briefing papers available from the ACA Office of Public Policy and Information; Barstow (personal communication, August 25, 2003); Baruth & Robinson, 1987; Humes, 1987; Vacc & Loesch, 1994; and Zunker, 1994. This is not meant to be an exhaustive listing of all legislation that has influenced professional counseling and counseling services.

1917   The Smith-Hughes Act created federal grants to support a nationwide vocational education program.

1933   The Wagner-Peyser Act established the U.S. Employment Services.

1936   The George-Dean Act continued the support established by the Smith-Hughes Act.

1938   The U.S. Office of Education established the Occupational and Information Guidance Services Bureau that, among other things, conducted research on vocational guidance issues. Its publications stressed the need for school counseling.

1944   The Veterans Administration established a nationwide network of guidance services to assist veterans. The services included vocational rehabilitation, counseling, training, and advisement.

1944   The U.S. Employment Service was begun under the influence of the War Manpower Commission. Fifteen hundred offices were established, and employment "counselors" were used.

1946   The George-Barden Act provided government support for establishing training programs for counselors. The emphasis was on vocational guidance and established a precedent for funding of training for counselors.

1946   The National Institute of Mental Health (NIMH) was established just after World War II, and the National Mental Health Act was passed in 1946 authorizing funds for research, demonstration, training, and assistance to states in the use of effective methods of prevention, diagnosis, and treatment of people with mental health disorders.

1954   The Vocational Rehabilitation Act (VRA) recognized the needs of people with disabilities. The VRA was a revision of earlier vocational rehabilitation acts and was prompted, in part, by the government's attempts to meet the needs of World War II veterans. It mandated the development of counselors who specialized in assisting persons with disabilities and allocated funds for the training of these counselors.

1955   The Mental Health Study Act of 1955 established the Joint Commission on Mental Illness and Health.

1958   As noted previously, the emphasis of the National Defense Education Act (NDEA) was on improving math and science performance in our public schools; counseling in the schools was seen as an important function in helping students explore their abilities, options, and interests in relation to career development. Title V of this act specifically addressed counseling through grants to schools to carry out counseling activities. Title V-D authorized contracts to institutions of higher education to improve the training of counselors in the schools.

1962   The Manpower Development Training Act was enacted and established guidance services to individuals who were underemployed and/or economically disadvantaged.

1963   The Community Mental Health Centers Act, an outgrowth of the Mental Health Study Act, was passed. It is considered by many to be one of the most crucial laws dealing with mental health that has been enacted in the United States. The act mandated the creation of more than 2,000 mental health centers and provided direct counseling services to people in the community as well as providing outreach and coordination of other services. The Community Mental Health Centers Act also provided opportunities for counselors to be employed outside of educational settings.

1964   The Amendment to the National Defense Education Act of 1958 continued to impact counseling through the addition of counselors in the public schools, especially elementary schools, aimed at reducing the counselor-student ratio.

1965   The Elementary and Secondary Education Act (ESEA) did much to develop and expand the role of the elementary school counseling program and the services provided by the elementary school counselor.

1972   Title IX of the Education Amendments to the 1964 Civil Rights Act mandated that no one be discriminated against or excluded from participating in any federally funded educational program or activity on the basis of sex. It also prohibited sex-biased appraisal and sex-biased appraisal instruments.

1975   Public Law (P.L.) 94-142, also known as the Education for All Handicapped Children Act, mandated guidelines for the education of exceptional children in public schools. It declared that all children, regardless of their disabilities, were entitled to an appropriate free public education. Counselors became instrumental in designing, implementing, and evaluating the individualized education plans that were required for each student with special needs.

1976   P.L. 94-482 was enacted, extending and revising the Vocational Education Act of 1963 and its 1968 amendments. P.L. 94-482 directed states to develop and implement programs of vocational education specifically to provide equal education opportunities to both sexes and to overcome sex bias and stereotyping. It also specified that funds must be used in vocational education for individuals who are disadvantaged, had limited English proficiency, and/or had handicapping conditions.

1977   Sections 503 and 504 were added to the civil rights law typically known as the Rehabilitation Act of 1973. Section 503 mandates all employers conducting business with the federal government (meeting specific criterion) to take affirmative action in the recruitment, hiring, advancement, and treatment of qualified persons with disabilities. Section 504 notes that no qualified person (spanning all age ranges) who is disabled may be discriminated against in any federally assisted program.

1977   President Carter established the President's Commission on Mental Health.

1979   The Veterans' Health Care Amendments called for the provision of readjustment counseling and related mental health services to Vietnam-era veterans.

1980   The Mental Health Systems Act was passed, stressing the need for balancing services in both preventive and remedial mental health programs. The act required the development of new services for children, youth, minority populations, older people, and people with chronic mental illness. The act was repealed during the same year it was passed because of the severe federal budget cuts for social programs during the first year of President Reagan's term in office.

1981   The Older Americans Act was enacted to improve the quality of life for many individuals who are 60 years of age or older by authorizing a comprehensive social services program. The act provides assistance for creation and implementation of services, including counseling.

1984   Carl D. Perkins Vocational Education Act amended the Vocational Education Act of 1963. Its primary purpose was to help the states develop, expand, and improve vocational education programs. The act sought to include previously underserved people such as those with disabilities, adults in need of both training and retraining, and single parents, to name a few. The legislation indicated that career guidance and counseling functions should be performed by professionally trained counselors. In addition, the entire act was filled with language that showed how important legislators believed counseling and career development services to be.

1990   Americans with Disabilities Act (ADA) prohibited job discrimination against people with disabilities. It also mandated that individuals with disabilities have the same access to goods, services, facilities, and accommodations afforded to all others.

1990   Carl D. Perkins Vocational Education Act was reauthorized setting directions for state and local agencies to develop vocational and applied education programs. It targeted single parents, displaced homemakers, and single pregnant women, noting that states were to use a certain percentage of their funds to provide basic academic and occupational skills and materials in preparation for vocational education and training to provide these people with marketable skills. In addition, states were required to use funds to promote sex equity by providing programs, services, and comprehensive career guidance, support services, and preparatory services for girls and women.

1994   The School-to-Work Opportunities Act set up partnerships among educators, businesses, and employers to facilitate the transition of those students who plan on moving from high school directly to the world of work.

1995   Elementary School Counseling Demonstration Act allocated $2 million in grant money for schools to develop comprehensive elementary school counseling programs.

1996   The Mental Health Insurance Parity Act (enacted in 1996 and became effective January 1, 1998) prevents health plans that cover mental health services from placing unequal caps on the dollar amount covered (either annually or on a lifetime basis) for the provision of mental health services if these same caps are not placed on the coverage of other medical services. Although this act has several limitations, it was a major step toward parity of insurance coverage for mental health services. Some of these limitations include that health plans are not required to provide mental health benefits. Additionally, it does not prohibit health plans from requiring higher deductibles and copayments for mental health services or from placing strict limits on the number of days of treatment covered for mental health conditions. Further, health plans that experience a 1 percent increase in premiums as a result of the parity provision as well as businesses with fewer than fifty employees are exempt from the provision. (ACA Office of Public Policy and Information, 1996)

1996   Health Insurance Portability and Accountability Act (HIPPA, Public Law 104-191) included language to promote "administrative simplification" in the administration of health care benefits by establishing national standards for the electronic transmission of health information, for the use and disclosure of personally identifiable health information, and for the security of information. Although the standards do not contain any counselor-specific provisions, they have an impact on all counselors, both as providers of mental health services and as health care consumers.

1997   The Balanced Budget Act included provisions that prohibit Medicaid managed care plans from discrimination against providers on the basis of the type of license they hold. This did not extend to fee-for-service plans administered through Medicaid.

1998   Higher Education Act Amendments reauthorized higher education programs into law for another five years. In addition to dropping student loan interest rates and increasing Pell Grant awards, the act created the *Gaining Early Awareness and Readiness for Undergraduate Programs* (GEAR-UP), which provides grants for establishing partnerships between colleges, schools, and community organizations. The provisions included payment for counseling services to certain at-risk and low-income students and other elementary, middle, and secondary school students. These services were specified to include counseling on financial aid, college admissions and achievement tests, college application procedures, and efforts to foster parental involvement in the encouragement of students' interest in college education. In addition, the amendments allow for personal counseling, family counseling, and home visits for students with limited English proficiency. The act also sent a clear message against the use of drugs. It declared that students who are convicted of any state or federal offense for the possession or sale of a controlled substance will not be eligible to receive any grant, loan, or work assistance under the Higher Education bill. (ACA Office of Public Policy and Information, 1998a)

1998   The Health Professions Education Partnerships Act (HPEPA) is a landmark piece of legislation. It recognizes professional counselors under health professional training programs. Specifically, education programs, counseling students and graduates, and counselor educators stand to be made eligible for a wide range of programs operated by the federal Health Resources and Services Administration (HRSA) and the federal Center for Mental Health Service (CMHS) to the same extent as other master's-level mental health professions. Where the term "graduate programs in behavioral and mental health practice" is referenced in these programs, the provisions passed in HPEPA include graduate programs in counseling. (ACA Office of Public Policy and Information, 1998b)

1998   The Workforce Investment Act (WIA) revamped all job training programs in the country as well as reauthorized the Rehabilitation Act. According to the ACA Office of Public Policy and Information (1998c), the WIA streamlined requirements for the major federal grant programs which support training and related services for adults, dislocated workers, and disadvantaged youth. Under the WIA, all adults, regardless of income or employment status, became eligible for core services. These services include skills assessments, job search assistance, and information on educational and employment opportunities.

The WIA mandated that states and local governments set up and maintain networks of "one-stop centers" in which consumers are afforded a single point of entry to federal job training and education programs, job market information, unemployment insurance, and other federal and state services and programs. The WIA required that training services for adults be delivered through vouchers. In addition, it was determined that the programs be administered at the state level by a board. These boards, in turn, designate local service areas. The provisions call for existing JTPA (Job Training Partnership Act) service delivery areas with populations greater than 200,000 to be designated as service areas (as long as they met JTPA performance standards during the previous two years).

1998   Reauthorization of the Rehabilitation Act. As noted, the WIA reauthorized the Rehabilitation Act for another five years. The act funds state-administered vocational rehabilitation services for people with disabilities. In addition, the act funds research on rehabilitation and disabilities, training for rehabilitation counselors, independent living centers, advocacy services, and other initiatives that facilitate the employment of individuals with disabilities. The act upheld previous requirements that state agency professionals meet state or national certification or licensure requirements. This means that professional rehabilitation counselors need to hold a master's degree in rehabilitation counseling or a closely related field. The act extended this requirement to private contractors with state agencies. In addition, the act renamed Individualized Written Rehabilitation Plans as Individual

Plans for Employment and expanded consumer choice and participation in the these plans. (ACA Office of Public Policy and Information, 1998c).

1999   Medicare, Medicaid, and SCHIP Balanced Budget Refinement Act (Public Law 106-554) included a section requiring the Medicare Payment Advisory Commission (MedPAC) to conduct a study on the appropriateness of establishing Medicare coverage of licensed professional counselors and other non-physician providers, including marriage and family therapists and pastoral counselors. MedPAC issued a weakly written report recommending *against* covering licensed professional counselors, marriage and family therapists, and pastoral counselors in June of 2002. Although MedPAC came to a negative conclusion, the language in P.L. 106-554 calling for the report marked the first time that Congress and the President had enacted legislation referencing licensed professional counselors with respect to Medicare.

Since the enactment of P.L. 106-554, legislation was introduced in both the House and the Senate—in both the 107th and 108th Congresses—which would establish Medicare coverage of licensed professional counselors. Most recently, language establishing Medicare coverage of state-licensed professional counselors and marriage and family therapists was included in S. 1, the Medicare prescription drug legislation passed by the Senate in the summer of 2003.

1999   The Elementary School Counseling Demonstration Act was approved as part of the Omnibus Spending Package for FY 2000. The act allocates $20 million for schools to hire *qualified* school counselors. These funds will be available to school districts that are awarded three-year grants by the Department of Education (ACA, 1999a).

1999   The Work Incentives Improvement Act (WIIA) may be considered the most significant federal law enacted for people with disabilities since the Americans with Disabilities Act passed in 1990 (ACA, 1999b). The WIIA removes many of the financial disincentives that have prevented millions of people with disabilities from working. For example, it changes out-dated rules that end Medicaid and Medicare coverage when people with disabilities enter or reenter the workplace. Among several provisions, the WIIA allows people to buy into Medicaid when their jobs pay more than low wages but when they may not have access to private health insurance. It also allows people with disabilities to keep their Medicaid coverage even though their medical condition has improved as a result of the medical coverage. In addition, it extends Medicare Part A coverage for people on Social Security disability insurance who return to work for another four and a half years. This will result in a difference between monthly premiums of almost $350 (the cost of purchasing Part A and B coverage) and $45.50.

The WIIA also makes major changes in the employment services systems for people with disabilities. People receiving SSI or SSDI benefits will be allowed to choose among participating public and private providers of vocational rehabilitation and employment services. These providers will be paid a portion of the SSI or SSDI benefits if the person goes to work and achieves "substantial earnings" (to be further determined through regulations not yet promulgated at the time this chapter was written).

2001   Department of Defense Authorization Act (Public Law 106-398) included language requiring the Tricare Management Authority to conduct a demonstration project allowing mental health counselors to practice independently, without physician referral and supervision. Licensed professional counselors are the only nationally recognized mental health professionals that Tricare requires to operate under physician referral and supervision. The demonstration project is expected to be concluded at the end of 2003, with a report to Congress by the Department of Defense to follow. Physician referral and supervision requirements for both marriage and family therapists and clinical social workers were removed by Congress following similar demonstration projects (Scott Barstow, personal communication, August 25, 2003).

2001   No Child Left Behind Act (NCLB, Public Law 107-110) was a massive reauthorization of the federal education programs contained in the Elementary and Secondary Education Act and included language renaming the Elementary School Counseling Demonstration Program the Elementary and Secondary School Counseling Program (ESSCP). This language both removed the "demonstration" tag from the program, and expanded it to secondary schools. Under the NCLB language, the first $40 million appropriated for the program in any year must be devoted to supporting counseling programs and services in elementary schools.

CONTINUING DEVELOPMENT OF PROFESSIONAL IDENTITY

History of the American Counseling Association

Vacc and Loesch (1994) noted that one way to understand the evolution of a profession is to study the history of a representative professional organization. The American Counseling Association (ACA) has a rich history that exemplifies its representation of professional counselors. The philosophical development of the counseling profession can even be seen by simply reviewing the three names by which ACA has been known along with the times those name changes occurred. From its founding in 1952 until 1983, ACA was known as the American Personnel and Guidance Association (APGA). From 1983 until 1992, it was called the American Association for

Counseling and Development (AACD). In 1992, the governing body of the association renamed it the American Counseling Association. For purposes of simplicity, the association will be referred to as ACA regardless of the time reference.

Although its official inception is noted as 1952, ACA can trace its organizational beginnings to the turn of the twentieth century with the formation of one of its founding divisions, the then National Vocational Guidance Association. Having roots in vocational guidance, education, and psychology have made for an interesting, rich, and often rocky evolution of counseling as a profession unto itself, even before the founding of ACA. The NVGA had considered changing its name at least five times between 1922 and 1948 to better reflect the concern members had about the total adjustment of their clients (Norris, 1954). Members of the American Council of Guidance and Personnel Associations, a federation of associations, were also considering whether it was wise or efficient to attempt to belong to several organizations doing essentially the same thing. Groups belonging to the federation had the practice of meeting in conventions at the same time and place. By the late 1940s, groups had established their identities in work settings, and members had begun to see commonalities of purpose and function. The name of the federation had changed from the American Council of Guidance and Personnel Associations (ACGPA) to the Council of Guidance and Personnel Associations (CGPA) in 1939, so there was precedence for a name change.

In 1948 Daniel Feder, as chair of CGPA and president of NVGA, urged consideration of forming a national organization to include individuals as well as associations. A Committee on Unification was appointed to develop a plan for such an organization. Its plan was presented at the 1950 convention and forwarded to the organizations concerned (McDaniels, 1964). Both the NVGA and the American College Personnel Association approved the plan and arranged their constitutions to join the new organization as divisions in 1951. At this time the Personnel and Guidance Association (PGA) was born. The following year, 1952, PGA changed its name to the American Personnel and Guidance Association (APGA) so as not to be confused with the Professional Golfers Association (PGA). APGA is now known as the American Counseling Association (ACA). Table 1.1 presents highlights of the ACA's development since its founding.

Professionalism: A Developmental Perspective

The mission of the American Counseling Association is "to enhance the quality of life in society by promoting the development of professional counselors, advancing the counseling profession, and using the profession and practice of counseling to promote respect for human dignity and diversity" (ACA, 2003b). A review of Table 1.1 indicates not only the developmental nature of the ACA during the past fifty-one years but also the evolving diversity of its divisions and its membership. The concept of unification was a common theme in this country in the 1950s (Vacc & Loesch, 1994). This trend may have been an influencing factor in the four independent founding organizations: NVGA (now NCDA), ACPA (now ACCA), NAGSCT (now ACES), and SPATE (now C-AHEAD) coming together to work as one federation. The basic

TABLE 1.1   Organizational Chronology of the American Counseling Association

YEAR	DIVISION NAME	EVENT
1951	PGA	The Personnel and Guidance Association was formed.
1952	APGA	American Personnel and Guidance Association became the new name for PGA.
1952		*The following divisions became founding partners of APGA:*
	ACPA	American College Personnel Association
	NVGA	National Vocational Guidance Association
	SPATE	Student Personnel Association for Teacher Education
	NAGSCT	National Association of Guidance Supervisors and College Trainers
		The following divisions became part of ACA or changed their names:
1953	ASCA	American School Counselors Association became a division.
1958	DRC	ACA added the Division of Rehabilitation Counseling.
1961	ACES	Association for Counselor Education and Supervision replaced the former NAGSCT.
1962	ARCA	American Rehabilitation Counseling Association became the new name for the former DRC.
1965	AMEG	Association for Measurement and Evaluation in Guidance was established.
1966	NECA	National Employment Counselors Association became a division.
1972	ANWIC	Association for Non-White Concerns in Personnel and Guidance was formed.
1973	ASGW	Association for Specialists in Group Work was established.
1974	NCGC	National Catholic Guidance Conference became a division.
	POCA	Public Offender Counselor Association was established.
1975	AHEAD	Association for Humanistic Education and Development replaced the former SPATE.
1977	ARVIC	Association for Religious Values in Counseling replaced what had been known as NCGA.
1978	AMHCA	American Mental Health Counselors Association became a division.
1983	AACD	American Association for Counseling and Development became the new name for what had been called APGA.
1984	AMECD	Association for Measurement and Evaluation in Counseling became the new name for the former AMEG.
	NCDA	National Career Development Association became the new name of the former NVGA.
	AMCD	Association for Multicultural Counseling and Development replaced the former Association for Non-White Concerns in Personnel and Guidance.
1984	MECA	Military Educators and Counselors Association became an organization affiliate of AACD.
1986	AADA	Association for Adult Development and Aging was formed.
1989	IAMFC	International Association of Marriage and Family Counselors was established.

(continued)

TABLE 1.1   Continued

YEAR	DIVISION NAME	EVENT
1990	IAAOC	Association of Addiction and Offender Counselors replaced the former POCA.
1991	ACCA	American College Counselors Association was formed to replace ACPA, which was in the process of withdrawing from ACA.
1992	ACPA	American College Personnel Association disaffiliated from ACA.
1993	ASERVIC	Association for Spiritual, Ethical and Religious Values in Counseling became the new name for ARVIC.
	AAC ·	Association for Assessment in Counseling became the new name for AMECD.
1995	ACEG	Association for Counselors and Educators in Government became the new name for MECA.
1996	AGLBIC	Association of Gay, Lesbian, and Bisexual Issues in Counseling became an organizational affiliate.
1997	AGLBIC	AGLBIC achieved division status.
1998	ACEG	ACEG became a division.
1999	CSJ	Counselors for Social Justice became an organizational affiliate.
	C-AHEAD	AHEAD changed its name to the Counselor Association for Humanistic Education and Development.
2002	CSJ	CSJ became a division.
2003	AACE	AAC changed its name to the Association for Assessment in Counseling and Education.

format of autonomous divisions working within an umbrella organization has continued to the present time. Divisions have been added as members' interests or counselor work settings changed due to changes in the socioeconomic milieu. Table 1.2 indicates the divisional structure of ACA as of September, 2003.

Change is very much reflected in reviewing the chronological evolution of ACA. For example, the parent organization, APGA, changed its name twice over a forty-year period. Before 1983, APGA began to feel pressures from its membership for a name change that would accurately reflect the purposes and work activities of its members. The terms *guidance* and *personnel* were onerous to some members. In addition to describing the profession better, the term *counseling* was more prestigious and understood by the public. By 1983, several of the divisions already recognized the terms *counseling* or *counselor* in their titles (ASCA, ARCA, ACES, ARVIC, POCA, NECA, and AMHCA). To appease its growing and diverse membership, to have a clearer identity with counseling, and to attract new members in a changing society, APGA became the American Association for Counseling and Development (AACD).

TABLE 1.2   Divisions of the American Counseling Association as of September 2003

AACE	Association for Assessment in Counseling and Education**
AADA	Association for Adult Development and Aging
ACCA	American College Counseling Association**
ACEG	Association for Counselors and Educators in Government
ACES	Association for Counselor Education and Supervision
AGLBIC	Association of Gay, Lesbian, and Bisexual Issues in Counseling
AMCD	Association for Multicultural Counseling and Development
AMHCA	American Mental Health Counselors Association**
ARCA	American Rehabilitation Counseling Association**
ASCA	American School Counselors Association**
ASERVIC	Association for Spiritual, Ethical and Religious Values in Counseling
ASGW	Association for Specialists in Group Work
C-AHEAD	Counseling Association for Humanistic Education and Development
CSJ	Counselors for Social Justice
IAAOC	International Association of Addictions and Offenders Counselors*
IAMFC	Internal Association of Marriage and Family Counselors**
NCDA	National Career Development Association*
NECA	National Employment Counseling Association**

*ACA membership is required for professional members only (not required for affiliate, regular student, and/or retired members).

**ACA membership is not required.

Nine years later in 1992, the name was again changed to the American Counseling Association, removing the word *development* from its title.

Such change was not limited to the parent organization. As can be seen in Table 1.1, five divisions (NVGA, NAGSCT, ANWIC, POCA, and MECA) changed their names at least once and three divisions (AMEG, NCGC, and SPATE) changed their names twice since they were formed. Such changes reflected not only the changing nature of the work of the divisions and their members but also brought the divisions' names more in line with the name changes that had occurred within the parent organization.

Beginning in 1952 with four divisions, the first new division to join the parent organization was the American School Counselors Association (ASCA) in 1953, which quickly became one of the two largest ACA divisions. After World War II, there was a growing recognition in America that people with disabilities had counseling needs. At the same time that the Veterans Administration was attempting to meet the needs of returning World War II servicemen and women, there were a number of ACA members becoming involved in rehabilitation counseling. These factors resulted in the organization of the second new division to join ACA, the American Rehabilitation Counseling Association (ARCA) in 1957 (known as the Division of Rehabilitation Counseling from 1957 to 1962).

Seven years passed before the addition of two new divisions. In 1965, professionals who used psychometric instruments in their settings needed an organization to help them improve the use of such instruments and to communicate among themselves. The Association for Measurement and Evaluation in Guidance (AMEG, now the Association for Assessment in Counseling and Education) was organized to serve this purpose, although not until 1968 was it formally incorporated as an ACA division. The continued interest in vocational counseling at that same time is evident in the formation of the National Employment Counselors Association (NECA) in 1966. NECA members, who came from both the private and public sectors of counseling, had a strong interest in vocational counseling and focused specifically on employment counseling.

The number of divisions in ACA again remained static for seven years, but the 1970s saw the formation and acceptance of several new divisions. There was increasing concern about minority representation with the structure of ACA. That concern, along with the general social consciousness movement in the 1960s and early 1970s, prompted the development of an interest-based division entitled the Association for Non-White Concerns in Personnel and Guidance (ANWIC), which was added in 1972.

In 1973, based on the growing use of groups as a form of counseling intervention, the Association for Specialists in Group Work (ASGW) became the tenth division of ACA. The following year, 1974, the National Catholic Guidance Conference (NCGC) became the eleventh division of ACA and brought to the parent association its first division with a strong religious orientation. During the last two decades, the focus of this division changed from that of a Catholic-based organization to a broader examination of spirituality, religious values, and ethical considerations in the field of counseling (Bartlett, Lee, & Doyle, 1985). This shift in focus is reflected in NCGC changing its name to the Association for Religious Values in Counseling (ARVIC) in 1977, and later (1993) to the Association for Spiritual, Ethical and Religious Values in Counseling (ASERVIC).

In 1974, the Public Offender Counselor Association (POCA) became the twelfth division and brought into the organization people involved with juvenile and adult probation and those who worked with or within our prison systems. The creation of POCA is one example of how responsive the counseling profession has been to the complex social problems faced by our society. During the 1980s, the correlation between addictive and criminal behaviors became quite clear. Many POCA members became interested in broadening the focus of POCA, and it became the International Association of Addictions and Offenders Counselors (IAAOC) in 1990.

As the demand for school counselors diminished in the early and mid-1970s, a need for counselors in a variety of community agencies developed and counselors found themselves in a variety of noneducational work settings. More nonprofit organizations and services such as crisis centers, hot lines, drop-in clinics, shelters for battered women, rape counseling centers, and clinics for runaway youth emerged. More agencies began to be funded by local governments and began to hire people with master's degrees and experience to run these centers. The profession responded, and in 1978 the American Mental Health Counselors Association (AMHCA) became the thirteenth division of ACA. Between 1976 and the early 1980s, AMHCA's membership expanded more quickly than probably any other mental health organization's (Weikel, 1985). It became the largest division within ACA and, along with ASCA, remains one of the two largest groups affiliated with ACA.

As noted previously, it was in 1983 that APGA changed its name to the American Association for Counseling and Development (AACD). The change symbolized the evolving professional orientation among the association's members, the fact that these members were being found more and more in noneducational work settings, and the concept that what members "did was counseling, not guidance" (Herr, 1985, p. 395).

In 1986, as a reflection of an increasingly larger aging population and problems attendant on growing older in a youth-oriented society, the Association for Adult Development and Aging (AADA) became the fourteenth division of what was now called the American Association for Counseling and Development. The strongest emphasis of AADA has been on gerontological counseling, midlife development, and preretirement planning, but its members have broadened their focus to include the counseling needs of persons across the adult life span.

In 1989, based on the growing emphasis on marriage and family counseling and the fact that many ACA members were involved in providing marriage and family counseling, the International Association of Marriage and Family Counselors (IAMFC) became the fifteenth ACA division.

During the later part of the 1980s, ACPA members who served a wide variety of student development needs on college campuses became unhappy with the increasing deemphasis of guidance and personnel issues in ACA and began movement to disaffiliate from ACA. The withdrawal of ACPA in 1992 led to the formation of its successor, the American College Counseling Association, with a more focused emphasis on counseling college students. At this time AACD became the American Counseling Association.

Members of ACA, recognizing the growing numbers of counselors who serve clients dealing with issues associated with their sexual orientation, lobbied for a specialty division that would focus on the needs of these clients and counselors. In April 1996, the Association of Gay, Lesbian, and Bisexual Issues in Counseling (AGLBIC) became an *organizational affiliate* of ACA. An organizational affiliate was defined before 1998 as an interest group with fewer than 1,000 members. In March of 1998, the ACA Governing Council voted to amend the ACA bylaws so that 500 or more members were required to achieve or maintain division status and in March of 2003, voted to reduce that number to 400. AGBLIC's membership quickly grew and it achieved status as a division in 1997.

In 1998, the Association for Counselors and Educators in Government (ACEG) became a division of ACA. This professional group was originally formed as an organizational affiliate in 1984 under the title of Military Educators and Counselors Association (MECA). Members of this division have primary professional affiliations to some branch of the military establishment or various levels of government.

Finally, in 1999, Counselors for Social Justice (CSJ) was formed as the newest organizational affiliate. This group was formed to help address issues related to social justice, oppression, and human rights within the counseling profession and the community at large. CSJ became an ACA division in 2002.

It should be noted that the American Counseling Association is much more than a collection of divisions. There is also a geographical regional structure composed of the following four regions: (1) *North Atlantic* (Connecticut, Delaware, the District of Columbia, Maine, Maryland, Massachusetts, New Hampshire, New Jersey, New York, Pennsylvania, Rhode Island, Vermont, and the Virgin Islands; (2) *Southern* (Alabama, Arkansas, Florida, Georgia, Kentucky, Louisiana, Mississippi, North Carolina, South Carolina, Tennessee, Texas, Virginia, and West Virginia); (3) *Midwest* (Illinois, Indiana, Iowa, Kansas, Michigan, Minnesota, Missouri, Nebraska, North Dakota, Ohio, Oklahoma, South Dakota, and Wisconsin); and (4) *Western* (Alaska, Arizona, California, Colorado, Hawaii, Idaho, Nevada, Montana, New Mexico, Oregon, Washington, Wyoming, and Utah). Each region, representing ACA state branches, was established to provide leadership training, professional development, and continuing education of branch members following the strategic plan adopted by the association.

Through its ACA Press, the association provides its membership with a plethora of books, scholarly journals, and monographs on topics of interest to counselors. Its workshop and home study program and regional and national conventions provide intensive training opportunities that allow members to keep up to date and earn continuing education units necessary in maintaining licensure or certification. Its *Code of Ethics and Standards of Practice* (1995) provides members and its public with both professional direction and guidance. Its legislative arm not only alerts members to current legislation that is either helpful or harmful to counseling but also gives members a voice in policy development at the federal, state, and local levels.

In 2004, with eighteen national divisions, fifty-six state and territorial branches, four regional assemblies, a myriad of divisional affiliates in each of the branches, and a membership of approximately 52,000, the American Counseling Association remains the strongest organization representing counselors on the national scene. It is not, however, without problems. ACA developed from a "group of groups" and throughout the 1990s was faced with ongoing organizational challenges that stem from the continued desire for groups to have independence while working under an umbrella structure. At the time this book went to press, ACA was still undergoing organizational upheaval. In October 1997, the Governing Council voted to amend the ACA bylaws so that, effective July 1, 1998, ACA members were no longer required to also belong to a division and division members were no longer required to also belong to ACA. This freedom of choice for members has led to some interesting developments. As of December 1999, fourteen divisions (77.8 percent) opted to require their professional members (typically defined as members with a master's degree in counseling) to belong to ACA in addition to their division. As of September 2003, only eleven of the divisions (61.1 percent) required professional members to also join ACA while seven divisions (AACE, ACCA, AMHCA, ARCA, ASCA, IAMFC, NECA) (38.9 percent) did not require ACA membership. Membership for all groups except for AMHCA and ASCA are processed through ACA. AMHCA and ASCA collect their own fees. It is not yet known how policy makers (e.g., legislators) may view this development. To date, a "strength in numbers" philosophy has facilitated the passage of legislation that has been important to the provision of counseling services and the recognition of professional counselors. It appears that ACA continues to be seen as the *primary* voice on national legislation. It is not clear, however, if ACA's current governing structure is the most effective or efficient way to serve the parent organization or the divisions. Different strategies to reorganize ACA have been reviewed and rejected by its Governing Council but this has not yet been resolved. The struggle of coming from a group of groups appears to remain in issues related to professional identity and to the governance of the profession.

CREDENTIALING AND THE "PROFESSIONALIZATION" OF COUNSELING

The most commonly noted criteria used to evaluate whether an occupation has evolved to the status of a profession include (1) a specialized body of knowledge and theory-driven research, (2) the establishment of a professional society or association, (3) control of training programs, (4) a code of ethics to guide professional behavior, and (5) standards for admitting and policing practitioners (Caplow, 1966; Glosoff, 1993). Given these criteria, no historical perspective of the counseling profession can be considered complete without a discussion of the development of standards related to the preparation and practice of professional counselors.

The counseling profession has met the majority of conditions just noted. There is an evolving body of knowledge and systematic theories and a body of literature to provide a forum for such information. ACA serves as the primary professional association for counselors. There are standards for training programs, professional preparation, and ethical behavior (see Chapter 3). Accredited counselor-training programs have been established, and credentials are granted to individuals demonstrating professional competencies (Glosoff, 1993; Remley, 1991). It should be noted that great progress has been made in establishing licensure and certification regulations, legally validating the profession.

The term *credentialing* was created to represent a broad array of activities pertaining to the establishment of professional training standards and regulations for practice (Bradley, 1991). This term most typically covers three major professional activities: academic program accreditation, certification, and licensure (Loesch, 1984).

Accreditation

Accreditation is one means of providing accountability. The licensed professions in this country began the process of regulation and quality control by developing standards for training programs. One definition of *accreditation* is provided by Altekruse and Wittmer (1991) as follows:

> [a] process by which an association or agency grants public recognition to a school, institute, college, university, or specialized program of study that has met certain established qualifications or standards as determined through initial and periodic evaluations (p. 53).

The development of standards of preparation for counselors began approximately forty years ago when a joint committee of the ACES and ASCA, divisions of ACA, began two major studies in 1960. More than 700 counselor educators and supervisors and 2,500 practicing counselors participated in the studies over a five-year period (Altekruse & Wittmer, 1991). The results facilitated the creation of the "Standards for Counselor Education in the Preparation of Secondary School Counselors," the first set of standards sanctioned for counselor education, in 1964. After a three-year trial, they were officially adopted by ACES in 1967 (Association for Counselor Education and Supervision, 1967). Shortly after, the "Standards for Preparation of Elementary School Counselors" (APGA, 1968) and "Guidelines for Graduate Programs in the Preparation of Student Personnel Workers in Higher Education" (APGA, 1969) were established.

The Council on Rehabilitation Education (CORE) was incorporated as a specialized accrediting body with a focus on rehabilitation counseling in 1972 and was a forerunner in setting educational standards and graduate program accreditation in counseling (Sweeney, 1991). The leaders responsible for the creation of the Council for Accreditation of Counseling and Related Educational Programs (CACREP) used CORE as a model. Both councils' basic counseling curricula, which are not focused on specialties, are similar. In addition to ARCA, the following four professional organizations were represented on the first CORE board: ARCA; Council on Rehabilitation Educators (now the National Council on Rehabilitation Education, NCRE); Council of State Administrators of Vocational Rehabilitation (CSAVR); International Association of Rehabilitation Facilities (now American Rehabilitation Association, ARA); and the National Rehabilitation Counseling Association (NRCA). CORE's current membership is composed of two public members and individuals appointed from the following sponsoring organizations: NRCA, ARCA, NCRE, CSAVR, and the National Council of State Agencies for the Blind (NCSAB).

According to Altekruse and Wittmer (1991), the "Standards for Entry Preparation of Counselors and Other Personnel-Service Specialists" was developed by ACES in 1973. This document, which merged earlier guidelines, was officially adopted by the ACA governing body in 1979. At that time, ACES was the only association accrediting body using the standards of training. Not until 1981 did ACA's board of directors adopt a resolution to formally oversee the responsibilities of the ACES National Committee on Accreditation. This led to the establishment of the Council for Accreditation of Counseling and Related Educational Programs (CACREP). CACREP was formed as an independently incorporated accrediting body, separate from ACA but sponsored by ACA and several divisions (CACREP, 1987). Since its inception, CACREP has conducted reviews of its accreditation standards. After the initial flurry of changes to the 1981 standards, CACREP declared a five-year time period during which only minor changes would be allowed (Altekruse & Wittmer, 1991). There have been three significant revisions made to the 1981 standards adopted by CACREP, in 1988, 1994, and 2001. These revisions are necessary to keep up with the continually evolving field of counseling. In addition to attempting to address technological changes in the delivery of higher education (such as distance learning programs), the 2001 standards presented some significant changes in the types of programs to be accredited and some minor changes in the eight common core curricular areas.

In addition to providing for accreditation of doctoral-level programs in counselor education and supervision, the 1994 CACREP standards provided for accreditation of master's degree programs in community counseling, with and without specialization in career counseling or gerontological counseling, marriage and family counseling/therapy, mental health counseling, school counseling, student affairs practice in higher education (with college counseling or professional practice emphases), and doctoral degree programs in counselor education and supervision (CACREP, 1994). The current CACREP standards (CACREP, 2001) provide for accreditation of doctoral programs in counselor education and supervision and master's degree programs in the following specialty area: career counseling (separate from community counseling), college counseling (no longer listed as an emphasis area under student affairs), community counseling, gerontological counseling (accredited separately from community counseling), marital, couple, and family counseling/therapy (instead of "marriage and family counseling/therapy"), mental health counseling, school counseling, and student affairs.

As of April 2003, CACREP had 434 accredited programs (CACREP, 2003). Of these 434 programs, 45 are doctoral-level and 389 are master's programs in 176 institutions. The majority of the master's programs are in the areas of school counseling (150) and community counseling (129). In addition, there were 45 accredited student affairs programs (33 in student affairs with an emphasis in college counseling and 12 with an emphasis in professional practice, administrative, or developmental emphases), 26 accredited marriage and family counseling/therapy programs, 29 accredited mental health counseling programs, 6 accredited career counseling programs, 2 accredited gerontological counseling programs, and 2 college counseling programs (accredited under the 2001 standards) (CACREP, 2003).

All academic programs accredited by CACREP, regardless of specialty designation, share a common core of curricular requirements. According to the 2001 CACREP *Accreditation Standards and Procedures Manual* (CACREP, 2001), all accredited programs must address the following eight curricular areas: professional identity, social and cultural diversity, human growth and development, career development, helping relationships, group work, assessment, and research and program evaluation. Supervised practica and internships also are required across all program areas. In addition to these common core areas, CACREP-accredited programs must also offer specific types of curricular experiences related to the specialty accreditation, such as community counseling, school counseling, and mental health counseling.

As of October 2003, CORE had accredited 94 master's programs offering a degree in rehabilitation counseling (Sue Denys, CORE staff, personal communication, October 3, 2003). Since its creation, CORE has reviewed and revised the standards for the accreditation of master's program in rehabilitation education on a regular basis. The first major standards revisions in 1981 were followed by revisions in 1988 and 1997. The most recent revisions in the CORE standards are available online and become effective with programs applying for accreditation after August 2004. The 2004 standards present some significant changes in the language used to describe curricular areas required. Based on the 1997 CORE *Manual* (1997), all CORE-accredited programs are expected to include courses in the following areas of study: foundations of rehabilitation counseling, counseling services, case management, vocational and career development assessment, job development and placement, and research. Effective August 2004, all CORE-accredited programs will be expected to address the following curricular areas of study: professional identity; social and cultural diversity issues; human growth and development; employment and career development; counseling and consultation; group work; assessment; research and program evaluation; medical, functional, environmental, and psychosocial aspects of disability; rehabilitation services and resources; foundations of rehabilitation counseling; counseling services; case management; vocational and career development, assessment, job development, and placement; research; and practicum and internship experiences (CORE, 2003). Supervised practicum and internship experiences are required under both the 1997 and 2004 standards.

Another professional organization that accredits counseling-related programs is the American Association for Marriage and Family Therapy (AAMFT). Along with CACREP, AAMFT accredits counselor education programs that emphasize marriage and family therapy. Unlike CACREP, however, AAMFT also accredits academic programs in departments of social work and home economics, and nonacademic programs such as agency-based training programs (Hollis, 2000).

Certification

It has been noted that *certification* is one of the most confusing of the credentialing terms (Brown & Srebalus, 1988). It is used in reference to (1) the process of becoming qualified to practice in public schools, (2) state laws passed in the same ways as licensure laws, and (3) recognition bestowed on individuals by their professional peers (such as certified public accountants).

Certification is often referred to as a "title control" process because it grants recognition of competence by a professional group or governmental unit but does not confer authority to the holder to practice a profession (Forrest & Stone, 1991; Loesch, 1984). As befits the confusing nature of the term *certification*, there is one exception to this rule. A designated state agency, most typically a state department of education, certifies school personnel. Professional counselors holding positions as public school counselors must be certified by the state to do so. Therefore, school counselor certification regulations are actually practice acts, because they control who may and may not practice as a school counselor (Loesch, 1984).

Types and Purposes of Certification

Certification in Schools. As noted, state boards or departments of education, by authority of state legislatures, establish certification standards for teachers, counselors, administrators, and other school personnel. Certification of school counselors first began in Boston and New York in the 1920s, but not until the National Defense Education Act (NDEA) was passed in 1958 did this type of certification take hold nationwide. By 1967 more than 24,000 guidance counselors were trained under NDEA funding. The NDEA also mandated the establishment of criteria that would qualify schools to receive funds for the services of school counselors, which led to the rapid growth of certification (Sweeney, 1991).

National Board Certification.   Many professional groups have initiated credentialing efforts at the national and the state levels that encourage excellence by promoting high standards of training, knowledge, and supervised experience. These standards promulgated by professional organizations may or may not be considered by governmental agencies, such as state departments of education or mental health, in relation to hiring and promotion requirements (Sweeney, 1991).

The first counseling-related national certification addressed the specialty of rehabilitation counseling. During the late 1960s rehabilitation counselors belonging to the National Rehabilitation Counselors Association and American Rehabilitation Counselors Association (an ACA division) began to work together toward establishing certification for rehabilitation counseling specialists (Forrest & Stone, 1991). Their efforts bore fruition in 1973 when the Commission on Rehabilitation Counselor Certification, known as CRCC, began to certify rehabilitation counselors (Forrest & Stone, 1991; Sweeney, 1991). More than 14,800 rehabilitation counselors were designated as CRCs as of October of 2003 (S. Gilpin, CRCC CEO, personal communication, October 3, 2003). Until recently, in addition to the general certification in rehabilitation counseling (CRC), CRCC offered specialty certification in addictions counseling and in clinical supervision. CRCC is no longer accepting new applications for certification in these specialties; however, individuals currently certified in these specialties who meet the continuing education requirements may apply for certification renewal.

CRCC divides the criteria for certification as a CRC into several categories. Depending on the category under which the applicant is seeking certification, requirements include either a master's degree in counseling (nonspecified) or a master's degree specifically in rehabilitation counseling. In addition to the requirement of a master's, CRCs are required to have relevant supervised professional experience as a rehabilitation counselor (if the applicant did not graduate from a CORE-accredited program), and successful completion of the CRCC examination (CRCC, 2003). The supervised experience requirement varies depending on the type of degree earned by the applicant. As noted, graduates of CORE-accredited programs are not required to have employment experience. Those who graduate with a master's in rehabilitation counseling from a non-CORE accredited program must demonstrate twelve months of acceptable employment experience under the supervision of a CRC. People with a master's degree in rehabilitation counseling from a program that was not fully accredited by CORE and do not meet the internship requirement must have twenty-four months of acceptable employment experience including a minimum of twelve months under the supervision of a CRC (CRCC, 2003).

There are also four categories of eligibility for individuals with master's degrees in counseling with an emphasis other than rehabilitation counseling. CRCC staff reviews applicants' transcripts to determine that they have had required courses.

The employment requirements vary for these applicants depending on the number of required courses they have taken. For example, applicants who have had one graduate course in counseling theories and at least one course in each of the following four areas: (1) assessment, (2) job placement or occupational information, (3) medical or psychosocial aspects of disabilities, and (4) community resources or delivery of rehabilitation services, must also have thirty-six months of acceptable employment experience including twelve months under the supervision of a CRC. A person with only two courses in the four areas noted is required to have forty-eight months of acceptable employment experience with a minimum of twelve months under the supervision of a CRC (CRCC, 2003).

In 1979, the National Academy of Certified Clinical Mental Health Counselors (NACCMHC) was the next national counselor certifying body to be established. The NACCMHC merged with the National Board for Certified Counselors (NBCC) in 1992. Basic requirements to become a Certified Clinical Mental Health Counselor (CCMHC) include: (1) completion of a minimum of sixty graduate semester hours; (2) graduation with a master's or higher degree from an accredited counselor-preparation program encompassing at least two years of post-master's professional work experience that included a minimum of 3,000 client-contact hours and 100 clock hours of individual supervision by a CCMHC, or a professional who holds an equivalent credential; (3) submission of an audio- or videotape of a counseling session; and (4) successful completion of the CCMHC's Mental Health Counselor Examination for Specialization in Clinical Counseling (NBCC, 1995). Weikel and Palmo (1989) noted that the stringent requirements to become a CCMHC may be one reason that there were only slightly more than 1,000 National Certified Clinical Mental Health Counselors (NCCMHCs) in 1985.

NBCC is probably the most visible and largest national counselor-certifying body (Sweeney, 1991). As of October, 2003, NBCC certified 34,488 National Certified Counselors, or NCCs (Melanie Wrenn, personal communication, October 1, 2003). The founding of NBCC offered the public a way to identify professional counselors who meet knowledge and skills criteria set forth by the counseling profession in the general practice of counseling. This was especially important given the paucity of counselor licensure laws at that time. The concept of a general practice of counseling is in line with CACREP's belief that there is a common core of knowledge that is shared by all professional counselors, regardless of any specific area of specialization. It is assumed that all counselors, regardless of their specialty area(s), must have a shared knowledge base and be able to perform some of the same activities (Forrest & Stone, 1991).

In order to be certified by NBCC as a National Certified Counselor (NCC), applicants must: (1) hold a minimum of a master's degree or higher with major study in counseling including a minimum of forty-eight semester or seventy-two quarter hours in graduate coursework; (2) demonstrate that their graduate coursework includes at least one course in each of the core curriculum areas delineated in the CACREP accreditation standards; (3) have successfully completed two academic terms of supervised field experience in a counseling setting, or one year with an additional year of post-master's supervised experience (1,500 additional hours of counseling experience including fifty extra hours of face-to-face supervision) beyond the required two years of post-master's supervised experience; (4) provide two professional endorsements; and (5) successfully pass the National Counselor Examination (NCE). Counselors who have not graduated from a CACREP-accredited program must also document the completion of a minimum of two years of post-master's supervised counseling experience (NBCC, 1999).

Once counselors have earned the designation of NCC, they can then qualify for specialty certification as an Approved Clinical Supervisor (ACS), National Certified School Counselor (NCSC), Certified Clinical Mental Health Counselor (CCMHC), Masters Addiction Counselor (MAC), Certified Gerontology Counselor (CGC), and/or National Certified Career Counselor (NCCC). There are currently 1,369 NCSCs, 1,334 CMHCs, 381 ACSs, 667 MACs, 729 NCCCs, and 195 CGCs (Melanie Wrenn, NBCC staff, personal communication, October 1, 2003). The NBCC board of directors decided to stop taking new applications for the CGC specialization area because of the low number of people who had pursued the credential (Schmitt, 1999a).

NBCC and CRCC are not, however, the only bodies that certify specialists in counseling and counseling-related specialties. For example, IAMFC, in addition to being an ACA division, is an affiliate of the National Academy for Certified Family Therapists, which offers five different options for certification of family therapists. The option most relevant for professional counselors requires professionals who are already NCCs or licensed as professional counselors to document professional training, supervision, and experience in working with couples and families (Smith, Carlson, Stevens-Smith, & Dennison, 1995). The American Association of Marriage and Family Therapy (AAMFT) also certifies its own members who meet certain criteria and has done so since the 1970s (Everett, 1990). AAFMT's credential is granted to members who have Clinical Member status. The International Certification Reciprocity Consortium (ICRC), the National Association of Alcoholism and Drug Abuse Counselors (NAADAC), NBCC and the CRCC (as previously noted) all offer specialty addictions certification. Finally, professionals specializing in the treatment of sexual dysfunction can be certified by the American Association of Sex Educators, Counselors and Therapists. Having multiple certifications offered by different associations in the same specialty areas may prove confusing for both professionals and consumers of mental health services.

Licensure

Brown and Srebalus (1988) define a license as "a credential authorized by a state legislature that regulates either the title, practice, or both of an occupational group" (p. 232). Although states enact licensure laws as a means to protect the public from incompetent practitioners, such laws also provide benefits for the profession being regulated. The very fact that a state considers a profession important enough to regulate may lead to an enhanced public image and increased recognition for that profession. Among several types of credentials presented to 1,604 professional counselors surveyed, a license as a professional counselor (or similar title) was considered the most important to hold (Glosoff, 1993). Likewise, licensure has been espoused by many as the most desirable of the different types of credentials in regard to securing recognition by insurance companies, governmental and private mental health programs, and consumers; being given preferred status in job hiring; and adding to the qualifications necessary to be seen as an expert witness (Foos, Ottens, & Hills, 1991; Glosoff, 1993; Remley, 1991; Sweeney, 1991; Throckmorton, 1992).

Just as certification can be confusing, so too can the concept of licensure. Since licensure laws typically delineate a "scope of practice" connected with the profession under consideration, licensing acts are often known as "practice acts" (Shimberg, 1982). States, with such laws in place, require people to be licensed or to meet criteria for exemption of licensing noted in those laws to engage in specified counseling activities. There are, however, licensing laws that dictate who may identify themselves as "licensed counselors" or use other counseling-related titles but do not regulate people who are not licensed. These laws are typically referred to as "title acts." Sweeney (1991) pointed out that it is essential to examine specific state laws and their accompanying regulations to determine the implications for practice. ACA assists counselors in this process by providing information about licensure requirements in each state and the District of Columbia on its website (*http://www.counseling.org*). ACA also typically publishes an annual list of counseling regulatory boards in the November/December issue of the *Journal of Counseling and Development*. In addition to using the resources provided by ACA, this author strongly encourages practitioners in those states with counselor licensure laws to ask the regulatory boards if they need a license to practice, and what they may and may not call themselves.

Licensure of counseling practitioners, separate from psychologists, can be traced to the early 1970s. Before 1976, no state law defined or regulated the general profession of counseling. This left the profession in a state of legal limbo—although counseling was not expressly forbidden (except where the laws regulating psychology specifically limited activities of professional counselors), it was not legally recognized as a profession, either (Brooks, 1986). At that time, the American Psychological Association began to call for stringent psychology licensure laws that would preclude other professionals from rendering any form of "psychological" services. In Virginia, this resulted in a cease-and-desist order being served to John Weldon, a counselor in private practice in 1972 (Hosie, 1991; Sweeney, 1991). The Virginia State Board of Psychologist Examiners obtained a court order restraining Weldon from rendering private practice services in career counseling (*Weldon v. Virginia State Board of Psychologist Examiners*, 1972). The Board claimed that Weldon was in fact practicing psychology, even though he presented himself as providing guidance and counseling services. In October 1972, Weldon was found to be practicing outside of the law but the court also ruled that the Virginia legislature had created the problem by violating his right to practice his chosen profession of counseling. The court proclaimed that personnel and guidance was a profession separate from psychology and should be recognized and regulated as such (Hosie, 1991). In response to the Weldon case, the Virginia legislature passed a bill certifying Personnel and Guidance Counselors for private practice in March 1975 (Swanson, 1988). This law was amended by the Virginia legislature in 1976 and became the first general practice act for professional counselors.

At about the same time, Dr. Culbreth Cook, an Ohio counselor, faced a challenge similar to that of Weldon. Cook, well known and respected in his community, was employed at a two-year college and provided private educational assessment on a part-time basis. Cook's education and training qualified him to offer the assessment services he rendered, but he was arrested on the felony charge of practicing psychology without a license (Hosie, 1991; Swanson, 1988). Dr. Carl Swanson, an attorney, counselor educator, and ACA Licensure Committee co-chair testified on Cook's behalf (Sweeney, 1991). The Cleveland Municipal Court judge refused to provide a restraining order against Cook, noting that even attorneys used the tools of psychology (*City of Cleveland, Ohio v. Cook*, 1975).

ACA has focused on licensure since the 1970s. It was 1973 when the first ACA licensure committee was created by the Southern Association for Counselor Education and Supervision (Hosie, 1991; Sweeney, 1991). The next year ACA published a position statement on counselor licensure and, in 1975, appointed a special Licensure Commission. The Commission distributed an action packet in 1976, including information about counselor licensure, the fourth draft of model state legislation, and strategies to pursue licensing (APGA, 1976).

Model legislation offers a prototype for counselors in states that do not have licensure laws, which are in the process of revising their current laws, and in which credentialing laws face sunset or legislative review (Glosoff, Benshoff, Hosie, & Maki, 1995). It also facilitates the development of uniform standards for the preparation and practice of professional counselors across the United States.

Since the first model legislation for licensed professional counselors was created, ACA has revisited and amended its model in order to reflect changes in standards within the profession and experiences in states that have implemented counselor licensure laws. An underlying philosophy of ACA's model legislation is that state licensure laws legalize the general practice of counseling within each state, whereas the credentialing of counseling specialists remains under the purview of professional credentialing organizations such as CRCC and NBCC.

The rate of licensure for counselors during the two decades between the time Virginia passed the first counselor licensure law and the endorsement of ACA's 1994 model legislation is seen by some to be painstakingly slow and by others as quite rapid. Brooks (1986) noted that "legislative successes were distressingly slow in the years following 1974" (p. 253). During the early 1980s, licensure took off when fifteen states passed some form of credentialing acts between 1981 and 1986, fourteen passed laws between 1987 and 1989, and seven passed laws between 1990 and 1994 (Glosoff, 1993; Glosoff et al., 1995). Having counseling licensure laws enacted at that rate is exceptional when compared with the twenty years it took the first eighteen state psychology laws to be passed (Brooks, 1988). Since 1994, in addition to the enaction of five new licensure laws, a number of states passed amendments that brought existing credentialing laws more into line with ACA's model legislation (for example, changing title acts to practice laws, expanding the scope of practice of professional counselors to include diagnosis and treatment of people with mental disorders, and increasing educational and experience requirements).

CURRENT ISSUES AND TRENDS IN COUNSELING

Counselors continue to respond to pressures from various socioeconomic factors—some of which led to the kaleidoscope we know as counseling today, others that will shape the future of the profession. These pressures cut across the various specialty areas of counseling and cannot be categorized or delineated as neatly as in a historical review of the profession. For organizational purposes, the current issues and trends will be briefly examined as they relate to the following topics: work settings, diverse clientele, licensure, recognition and reimbursement of professional counselors, and managed care. In addition to these areas, it is important to recognize how technology such as the Internet has, and will continue to influence the delivery of counseling services and clinical supervision. The proliferation of websites that offer psychoeducational information and counseling services has grown exponentially in a short period of time. The use of the Internet for counseling and counseling-related information offers potential benefits and drawbacks for clients and practitioners. To assist counselors in sailing in these uncharted waters, both ACA and NBCC have developed ethical standards for Internet or online counseling (see ACA, 1999d and NBCC, 1998). Readers are referred to Chapter 5 of this text for further exploration of technology and counseling.

Work Settings.   Counselors are employed in a wide variety of work settings. They provide services to people who exhibit a full range of functioning from healthy adaptation to pathology—from those seeking assistance with self-exploration to those individuals who are dysfunctional enough to require hospitalization. There is not enough space to comprehensively explore all those work settings and types of services, but I will attempt to briefly review some of the major trends related to work settings where counselors are employed.

School Counseling Services.   The establishment of comprehensive, developmental school counseling programs has progressed in a roller coaster way over the past century, following societal trends. School counseling started off strong in the 1920s, faced mobilized attacks against progressive education in the 1930s, rallied in the late 1950s and 1960s due to the National Defense Education Act, and continued to grow in the 1970s and early 1980s. Recently, Hollis (2000) noted that the most frequently offered master's program noted by respondents to his 1998 survey is school counseling. Of the 428 counselor education departments that submitted data on their degree programs, 314 (73 percent) offer a school counseling graduate program.

Although the value of having counselors in schools, kindergarten through secondary, has become widely recognized, budget cuts and lack of understanding about what school counselors do and do not do, have recently presented challenges for the counseling profession. Counselors often are faced with heavy caseloads and inadequate resources making it difficult for them to attend to their primary duties (Baker & Gerler, 2001). According to the ACA Office of Public Policy and Information (2002b), data from the National Center for Education Statistics' 2001 annual report indicated that the national average caseload for counselors in the school has grown to

536 students. This is more than double the maximum recommended student-to-counselor ratio of 250 to 1 set forth by ASCA and ACA. Heavy caseloads can greatly interfere with counselors' effectiveness (ACA, 1999c).

The lack of clarity on the part of other school personnel and that of the lay public regarding the role and function of school counselors has often led to counselors spending their time on noncounseling-related activities. There appears to be a lack of consensus among school counselors regarding their own professional identity. A pertinent question asked by many in examining this issue is the same one facing the entire profession—"Are we professional counselors first and specialists second or the other way around?" In the September 2003 issue of *Counseling Today*, this question was tailored specifically to school counseling and reframed as, "Are school counselors counseling professionals or educators first?" Brown and Kraus (2003) presented arguments that school counselors are counselors who have, through their training, specialized in "meeting the needs of school students, preschool through college" (p. 14). They contended that counseling and education are two separate professions and that moving from being a teacher to being a school counselor requires a "complete paradigm shift" (p. 14). Stone (2003) in a "counterpoint" argument, stated that school counselors are "educators who understand that they are uniquely positioned to touch all the students in their school through their skills; not just the most at-risk students, as would be the limitation if we [school counselors] practiced or defined ourselves just as therapists" (p. 15). In a related issue, school counselors will soon have an interesting choice regarding national board certification. As noted earlier in this chapter, NBCC has offered certification in the specialty of school counseling for many years. Recently, the National Board for Professional Teaching Standards (NBPTS) announced that they, too, are ready to certify school counselors. NBCC participated in negotiations with NBPTS for quite some time to arrive at joint standards (similar to the MAC standards adopted by both NBCC and NADAAC). Negotiations recently broke down and NBPTS is moving forward with plans. One major problem in developing mutually agreed upon standards is that NBPTS proposes certifying school counselors who do not hold a master's degree in counseling. This has been a core criterion for all NBCC credentials. It is unclear what this may mean for how school counselors perceive themselves first as counselors or as educators and how having national certification offered by both NBCC and NBPTS will influence the public's perceptions of counselors.

The lack of a unified professional identity, in my opinion, is a strong contributing factor in lack of resources and high ratios challenging school counselors. It also contributes strongly to the lack of uniformity in the training and experience requirements in licensure and certification standards set forth by state departments of education. For example, according to the ACA Office of Public Policy and Information (2002a), forty-one states and the District of Columbia require a master's degree in counseling and guidance or closely related field to be licensed or certified as a school counselor. Of the states that specified a minimum number of credit hours of graduate study, the number ranged from eighteen to thirty-nine. Some states require completion of a supervised practicum and/or internship while others do not. In 2002, approximately half of the states required applicants to have one to three years of previous teaching or related experience (ACA Office of Public Policy and Information, 2002a).

To assist with problems stemming from a lack of uniform identity and standards, ASCA developed a "national model" to provide a framework for school counseling programs (ASCA, 2002). The ASCA standards, as they are often called, refer to school counselors as educators with specific expertise in child and adolescent development. Although this point is still being heavily debated, the ASCA standards offer counselors and school administrators a guide for what counselors should be expected to do and not do. The "national model" recommends that school counselors spend 80 percent of their time in direct service to students and further suggests that all noncounseling activities be reassigned whenever possible.

School counseling programs have also been threatened throughout the history of public education by well-intentioned individuals and groups who have questioned or challenged the philosophy, content, and practices of counseling programs and materials. In recent years, the number of such challenges has increased, often resulting in censorship of counseling and guidance materials, activities, and programs. Concern has been raised by several parent groups that counseling usurps parental rights and teaches students to make independent decisions and that counselors use "New Age" techniques such as guided imagery. Again, this speaks to a lack of understanding about counselors and the techniques that are used.

It is clear that counselors must be able to document that their programs are based on a body of research if they are to combat fears generated by some of the negative literature being distributed by various groups (Marino, 1995). It is crucial to show the connection between students' psychological well-being and academic performance. In addition, it is critical to recognize that many people do not understand the nature of counseling in general or school counseling specifically. The idea of techniques such as guided imagery can be frightening, evoking thoughts of hypnosis and mind control. Counselors bear the responsibility to communicate effectively and systematically with parents, administrators, and their communities about the services provided by school counselors and their influence on students' learning, behaviors, and relationships with their parents.

Other challenges faced by counselors in school settings are similar to those of counselors in other settings. For example, it is essential that school counselors be able to demonstrate the effectiveness of their services in ways that policy makers and administrators can understand (ASCA, 2002; Baker & Gerler, 2001). In order to do this, there needs to be clearly stated goals and objectives associated with school counseling programs before counselors can determine the types of data they need to collect. This is especially important given the emphasis in the No Child Left Behind Act (2001) on results of standardized testing. School counselors need to be able to demonstrate how their services influence children academically. At the same time, in the climate of high stakes associated with standards of learning and standardized testing, school counselors are often asked to assist in the scheduling arrangements and to help students prepare for tests, which is not an appropriate or effective use of their time. To combat this, counselors will need to continue to advocate for themselves and for comprehensive developmental school counseling programs.

Baker and Gerler (2002) stated that counselors in schools, like in most settings, will be responsible for providing services to increasingly diverse student populations.

This requires that counselors be competent in the delivery of culturally sensitive and effective counseling services. They further discussed the need to learn to become successful social activists for all students (e.g., combating racism and sexism, providing for needs of sexual-minority youth). This means being active outside of the counseling office. Finally, school counselors have the challenge to effectively and ethically use sophisticated computer-based technology.

Community-Based Services.   Since the passage of the Community Mental Health Centers Act of 1963, master's- and doctoral-level counselors have found employment in community-based agencies. Many people think only of community mental health centers, typically funded through state and local government dollars, as the primary community-based employer of master's-level counselors. Counselors, however, are employed in a wide variety of government and privately funded agencies. Gladding and Ryan (2001) stated that these settings range from "group homes to telephone hotlines" (p. 344). Common community-based settings in which counselors are employed include child abuse agencies, domestic violence facilities (for both victims and perpetrators), homeless shelters, residential and outpatient substance abuse programs, programs for people who are HIV positive or have AIDS, vocational rehabilitation facilities, halfway homes, retirement communities, and crisis intervention programs (Gladding & Ryan, 2001; Vacc & Loesch, 1994).

Remediation of existing mental health problems remains the focus of the counseling services provided in most community mental health centers. In the past decade, however, preventive services have played a greater role. Health maintenance organizations (HMOs) offer a series of preventive workshops emphasizing everything from deterring back pain to establishing a healthy frame of mind. Because most counselors are trained in group counseling, education, and psychotherapeutic processes, they seem well suited to working in primary and secondary prevention programs such as those offered by HMOs. Similarly, there are increasingly more counselors working in behavioral medicine facilities (Vacc & Loesch, 1994). Mental health counselors have the training to assist individuals in understanding how their own behavior influences health and disease.

Business and Industry.   Business and industry settings offer counselors increasing opportunity for employment, most especially in employee assistance programs (EAPs), organizational career development programs, and consultation and training. In 2000, there were approximately 14,000 EAPs in the United States (Gladding & Ryan, 2001). EAPs emphasize very short-term treatment and referral of employees to help them address problems that may influence their job performance. Counselors working in EAPs most typically work on issues such as substance abuse, family concerns, financial problems, stress, and interpersonal difficulties that affect the work setting (Hosie & Glosoff, 2001). Counselors may be an EAP program administrator or be employed as a counselor directly by a corporation and have an office within a company. It is also not unusual for counselors to work on a contractual basis to provide counseling services to workers at a particular business (Hosie & Glosoff, 2001). For example, Gladding & Ryan (2001) found that after the bombing of the Federal

Building in Oklahoma City in 1995, the Kerr-McGee Corporation (housed only two blocks from the Federal Building) contracted with an external company to employ eighteen counselors. These counselors worked on-site with Kerr-McGee employees providing individual and group counseling.

As a result of new technology, economic fluctuations, and shifts in services and products, many companies have been forced to lay off or reassign employees. Many counselors also have been hired to provide career counseling with an emphasis on training and retraining, outplacement, and relocation services to those employees (Hosie & Glosoff, 2001). In addition, EAP counselors often provide crucial services in developing and implementing orientation programs for new employees as well as helping employees deal with issues related to retirement.

Many businesses have also focused on the effective use of their employees. Counselors have been hired or contracted to serve as consultants on organizational development and training issues, both of which typically require strong assessment and group process skills. Team building, stress management, preretirement planning, conflict management, and supervision are just a few examples of the types of training provided by counselors in business and industry (Lewis & Hayes, 1988).

Private Practice.   Brooks, in 1991, wrote that there were 10,000 ACA members who reported being in private practice. He purported that this was probably only a fraction of the total number of practitioners in either full- or part-time private practice. In a 1993 study, 29 percent of the ACA member participants reported private practice as their primary work setting (Glosoff, 1993). If the 1,604 participants were representative of the full ACA membership, this would equate to between 16,000 and 17,000 counselors in private practice. Although the exact number of counselors in private practice is hard to ascertain, it is clear that this number has increased significantly in the past decade. For example, according to a report published by the ACA Practice Research Network (2002), 42 percent of the 603 participants who completed the National Counselor Questionnaire reported that they worked at least some time each week in a private practice.

The increase is due, at least in part, to the success of counselors in passing counselor credentialing laws in forty-seven states and the District of Columbia. These laws have added to counselors being recognized as competent professionals who have the state's "blessing" to independently offer services to the public. The services offered by counselors in private practice are varied and focus on working with individuals, couples, families, and groups on issues as broad as career and personal adjustment to substance abuse, eating disorders, and sexual abuse (Hosie & Glosoff, 2001). Many of these counselors are also involved in consulting and training activities.

Although the number of private practitioners has been increasing, the pitfalls faced by these practitioners have also increased. In addition to the feelings of isolation expressed by many private clinicians, the stress of generating and maintaining a paying clientele may be rising as counselors deal more and more with insurance companies. Many clients cannot afford to pay for counseling services out of their own pockets and must rely on insurance benefits. Even those people lucky enough to have comprehensive insurance policies may discover that outpatient mental health therapy is not covered or is covered at only 25 to 50 percent versus the traditional 80 percent reimbursement for physical health services. Many insurance policies do not pay for marital or family counseling, nor do they pay if the person receiving services is not considered to have a mental disorder. Finally, many HMOs and preferred provider plans do not recognize master's or doctoral-level counselors, licensed or not.

The problems associated with insurance and managed care may drive many private practitioners, including counselors, to seek employment within agencies and hospitals. According to Psychotherapy Finances (1995), however, private practice is alive and well, with median fees and total incomes holding steady, and direct-pay clients still accounting for a large portion of private practice income. Those persons choosing to stay in private practice may do best in group practice settings where they can share administrative and marketing costs and the responsibility for being available to handle client emergencies.

Diverse Clientele

The types of clients served by professional counselors are as diverse as the work settings in which counselors are employed. Following are a few examples of the types of clients receiving increasing attention from counselors.

The frequency of abuse of all kinds in our country is astounding. Today's counselors are increasingly serving individuals who are abused, including very young children, adolescents, adults, and elderly clients—both men and women across all racial and ethnic groups. In addition, there has been a greater focus of late on treatment of the abuser. This often involves working with people who have been incarcerated for sexual assault, domestic violence, or pedophilia, or those who are on parole. Counselors working with people who are abused, and with those who abuse others, most typically do so in collaboration with other professionals such as attorneys, social workers, and law enforcement personnel (Vacc & Loesch, 1994).

Another client group receiving increased attention from mental health professionals, including counselors, are people who are HIV positive or have AIDS. There is probably not a community in the country that has gone untouched by the AIDS epidemic. The emotional and psychosocial ramifications of this epidemic are staggering for those afflicted, their families and friends, and the communities in which they live. Fear of people with HIV or AIDS may lead to a strong sense of isolation, increasing the already difficult task of living with a terminal illness. Counselors are needed to help ease this difficulty, but many may not have the training needed to specialize in assisting people with chronic and terminal diseases. Working with persons who are HIV positive or have AIDS also brings up new ethical dilemmas around confidentiality and the application of the duty-to-warn concept. For example, the 1995 ACA *Code of Ethics and Standards of Practice* specifically notes that counselors working with clients with communicable and fatal diseases are "justified in disclosing information to an identifiable third party, who by his or her relationship with the client is at a high risk of contracting the disease . . ." (ACA, 1995, p. 5).

There has also been a marked increase in counseling services targeted to older individuals. This makes sense, given the "graying of America" or the steadily increasing average age of the population. In response to the needs of older people, gerontological counseling has, and will continue, to grow as an area of specialization for professional counselors (Vacc & Loesch, 1999). Another facet of the graying of America or the aging of baby boomers is that there are increasingly large numbers of individuals who are ready to retire or have done so already. These individuals may not fall under the purview of gerontological counseling and appear to be an underserved population (Gladding & Ryan, 2001). Given our strong roots in the career development area, this seems to be an excellent market for professional counselors.

People with addictions (such as substance abuse problems, gambling, and sexual addictions) comprise yet another group being served by increased numbers of professional counselors. These services focus on the delivery of both prevention and remediation of addictive behaviors with counselors being employed by community mental health agencies, residential treatment programs, schools, and EAPs (Gladding & Ryan, 2001). The expansion of services in this area can be seen in the numbers of professional organizations offering certification to people who specialize in the delivery of addictions counseling.

Although counselors have traditionally worked with well-functioning individuals, they are increasingly serving people with severe and chronic mental illness in hospital and community settings. Counselors with both master's and doctoral degrees are expected by agencies to provide a variety of assessment and diagnostic services with clients who exhibit a wide range of clinical disorders (Hosie, West, & Mackey, 1993; West, Hosie, & Mackey, 1987; West, Hosie, & Mackey, 1988).

Regardless of the functioning level of clients, a "wellness" orientation remains the basis for the work of most counselors. Counselors are working with clients who seek achieving greater physical and mental health by making positive lifestyle choices. As presented earlier, these counselors are working in a variety of settings such as behavioral medicine clinics, HMOs, community centers, and EAPs, delivering a wide range of services from individual and group counseling to workshops on smoking cessation and stress management. Unfortunately, many preventive and wellness-oriented programs have focused more on physical than on mental well-being. This is a ripe area for counselors if they choose to market their services in assisting existing wellness programs to expand the mental health component of their interventions (Vacc & Loesch, 1994).

Multicultural Counseling.   One of the most significant trends in relation to clients being served by professional counselors is that they reflect the diversity seen in today's society in terms of age, race, ethnicity, gender, and sexual orientation. Sue (1991) wrote that "We are fast becoming a multicultural, multiracial, and multilingual society" (p. 99). He reported that one example of this trend was that 75 percent of people entering the labor market at that time were minorities and women. According to D'Andrea and Daniels (2001), the 1998 U.S. Bureau of the Census indicated that 71 percent of the total U.S. population come from non-Hispanic, White European backgrounds. They further presented that researchers predict that by

2020, only 64 percent of the U.S. population will come from non-Hispanic, White European backgrounds.

These demographic changes have had a notable impact on society in general as well as on the counseling profession. Many leaders in the field consider multiculturalism to be the *fourth force* in the profession (Pedersen, 1991b). This force calls for the reexamination of assumptions that are inherent in the delivery of traditional counseling services. The leaders of ACA also realized the importance of addressing the assumptions inherent in the ACA *Code of Ethics* (ACA, 1995). ACA has regularly reviewed and revised its *Code of Ethics*. In 2002, ACA leaders appointed an Ethics Revisions Task Force to review the 1995 code. A key charge assigned to the Task Force members was to specifically review the revision of the 1995 *Code of Ethics* from a culturally sensitive lens. The Task Force members anticipated presenting a draft of the revised *Code of Ethics* at the 2004 ACA conference.

It is more likely than not that counselors will work with clients who have different cultural backgrounds from their own. Although people from all cultures may encounter problems that counselors are trained to address, these problems are experienced within a cultural context that may not be understood by counselors. The profession must determine the applicability of traditionally taught theories to diverse clientele, as well as explore the effectiveness of *how* services are delivered (for example fifty-minute sessions, in counselors' offices, that focus on intrapsychic phenomena).

Pedersen (1991a) contended that counselors need to develop an increased awareness and understanding of cultural factors if they are to effectively provide services to a pluralistic clientele. In addition, counselor educators must help prepare the next generation of counselors to work from multicultural perspectives. Further, counseling-related research will need to include recognition of cultural differences and ensure that findings adequately reflect the cultural influences of research participants. Finally, Pedersen asserted that counselors need to "translate the skills, strategies, and techniques of counseling appropriately to many culturally different populations so that the counselor is prepared to match the right approach to each culturally different population" (p. 250). Although Pedersen presented no small challenge, it is clearly one that counselors and counselor educators must accept and make progress on.

The ACA *Code of Ethics and Standards of Practice* (1995) requires counselors to develop and maintain cross-cultural effectiveness. Standards related to diversity and cross-cultural counseling are infused throughout the code. For example, the preamble states that we "recognize diversity in our society and embrace a cross-cultural approach." In addition, the code states that ethical counselors make active attempts at understanding different cultural backgrounds, are aware of their own values, and avoid imposing their values on their clients. Further, both CACREP and CORE standards mandate that accredited programs address social and cultural foundations. Kiselica and Ramsey (2001) anticipated that multicultural training will become more infused throughout counselor education curricula and offer some suggestions for ways to do this. One major development was the publication of specific competencies associated with counseling clients from diverse populations by AMCD. These competencies were later adopted by ACA and several ACA divisions. Fong (1998), however, pointed out that these competencies have not been empirically validated. This is yet another challenge for the counseling profession—to conduct effective research in this area.

Licensure

In the twenty-five years since the passage of the Virginia certification law, a total of forty-seven states and the District of Columbia (jurisdictions) have enacted some form of counselor credentialing legislation. It appears that counseling has made great progress in gaining recognition as a profession. For example, in 1996, only seven years earlier, twenty-three (53.5 percent) of the then forty-three counselor credentialing laws regulated both the practice of counseling and the use of related titles ("practice acts") while 46.5 percent of the credentialing laws provided protection only in reference to the use of counseling-related titles (Espina, 1999). In 1999, thirty-four of the then forty-six counselor credentialing laws were practice acts (Espina). In 2003, according to the information provided on the ACA website, forty-six of the forty-eight jurisdictions (96 percent) were practice acts.

The model legislation endorsed by ACA's governing body in 1994 is clearly a practice act and establishes a comprehensive scope of practice for licensed professional counselors (LPCs). This scope of practice represents the broad continuum of services provided by professional counselors in the general practice of professional counseling and across specialty areas (Glosoff et al., 1995). The broadness of the scope is not meant to imply that all LPCs are experts in the provision of all services. Including a comprehensive scope of practice does, however, legally protect LPCs who are practicing within their scope of expertise. Without this protection, LPCs practicing within their scope of training (for example, career counseling, crisis intervention, or assessment) may find themselves, like John Weldon, legally prevented from rendering the very services for which they have been trained (Glosoff et al., 1995).

The 1994 ACA model legislation for LPCs includes the following requirements for licensure: (1) completion of a minimum of 60 graduate semester hours in counseling from a regionally accredited institution of higher education, including an earned master's degree in counseling, or an earned doctoral degree in counseling. The master's degree must consist of a minimum of 48 semester hours. Applicants graduating from programs offering at least 48 graduate semester hours but less than 60 can become licensed upon completing post-master's course work to meet the 60-hour requirement; (2) applicants must document that their 60 semester hours consisted of study in each of the following areas: (a) helping relationships, including counseling theory and practice; (b) human growth and development; (c) lifestyle and career development; (d) group dynamics, processes, counseling, and consultation; (e) assessment, appraisal, and testing of individuals; (f) social and cultural foundations, including multicultural issues; (g) principles of etiology, diagnosis, treatment planning, and prevention of mental and emotional disorders and dysfunctional behavior; (h) marriage and/or family counseling therapy; (i) research and evaluation; and (j) professional orientation and ethics; (3) a minimum of 3,000 hours of supervised experience in professional counseling performed over a period of not less than two years under the supervision of an approved supervisor; (4) documentation that the 3,000 supervised hours included at least 1,200 hours of direct counseling with individuals, couples, families or groups and a minimum of 100 hours spent in direct (face-to-face) supervision with an approved supervisor; and (5) successful completion of a written examination as determined by the counseling regulatory board.

Although a great deal has been achieved in the licensing arena and ACA's model legislation has provided counselors with much guidance in the development of counselor-credentialing laws, the statutes are far from uniform in their scope and requirements. This may be due, in part, to the revisions of ACA's model legislation for licensed professional counselors over the years. Licensure laws passed in the 1980s mirror the education, training, and supervision standards that were endorsed by the profession at that time, whereas those passed recently tend to be more comprehensive in the scope of practice and impose more stringent requirements than earlier licensure laws.

According to information provided by ACA (2003a), twenty-three of the forty-eight counselor-credentialing laws in place (47.9 percent) in 2003 mandated that applicants complete sixty graduate semester hours in counseling or a closely related field (as suggested by ACA's 1988 and 1994 models). Education requirements, however, range from a master's degree with no specified number of hours, to sixty semester hours. It should be noted that four of the states on ACA's chart did not specify the number of semester hours required in the laws enacted but may in their regulations. Some argue that most master's-level professional counselors do not have sixty semester hours, yet close to half (46 percent) of the 1,604 ACA members who participated in a 1993 study reported having earned a minimum of sixty graduate semester hours in counseling (Glosoff, 1993). Hollis (2000) predicted a trend in counselor education programs increasing the required credit hours for graduation to insure that their graduates will meet state licensure requirements.

Supervision and experience requirements also vary. Although the majority of jurisdictions (81.25 percent) require a minimum of two years of post-master's supervised experience for licensure, some jurisdictions do not specify how many years work experience are required whereas others designate the number of years but not the number of practice or direct supervision hours needed (ACA, 2003a). Even the titles granted to professional counselors by the regulatory boards vary. "Professional Counselor" is the most frequently used title (used in 62.5 percent of the jurisdictions). Sixteen jurisdictions (33.3 percent) use titles specifically referencing mental health counseling such as "Mental Health Counselor," "Clinical Professional Counselor," and "Clinical Counselor" (ACA). This lack of uniformity in titles used by state-credentialed counselors has proven to be detrimental to credentialed counselors in their ongoing efforts to gain the same recognition afforded to psychologists and clinical social workers.

Requirements for counselors to continue their education once they are licensed also vary from jurisdiction to jurisdiction. According to Sattem (1997), in 1997, the majority of jurisdictions (67.4 percent) with counselor-credentialing laws mandated continuing education. Based on information provided by ACA (2003a) and by professional counseling boards via their websites, as of September 2003, forty-two of the forty-eight jurisdictions with counselor-credentialing laws (87.5 percent) required some continuing education for counselors to renew their licenses. Information was not available regarding the continuing education requirements in six states. The number of continuing education hours required ranged from four to twenty every two years with more than half (52.1 percent) of the jurisdictions requiring twenty hours annually.

I believe that continuing education requirements for counselors to renew their licenses increased, and will continue to increase, for three reasons. First, most professions require members to stay abreast of current information in their fields after graduation. Requiring continuing education is one way to inspire confidence in professional counselors and this will be important in the profession's continuing efforts to gain recognition from legislators, other policy makers, and the public. Second, NBCC and CRCC both require one hundred clock hours of approved continuing education during each five-year period. Third, requiring continuing education to renew licensure supports the professional standards set forth in the 1995 ACA *Code of Ethics*, which specifically directs counselors to maintain their level of competence in the skills they use and to keep a reasonable level of awareness of scientific and professional information.

In addition to lack of uniformity, or maybe because of it, there have been legal challenges regarding what professional counselors can and cannot do as part of their scope of practice. For example, licensed counselors in several states have found themselves embroiled in legal battles over their ability to use a variety of standardized assessment instruments (Schmitt, 1999b). This is ironic given the strong roots that the counseling profession has in testing and assessment. The challenges are driven by efforts on the part of state psychological associations to proclaim that the use of most tests comes under the sole purview of doctoral-level psychologists. These tests run the gamut from personality to psychoeducational and career-related measures.

Counselors will continue to fight for their right to administer and interpret those tests based on education and training rather than on the name of the degree they earned. Legislation proposed by several state psychological associations may serve to bring together master's- and doctoral-level counselors, social workers, marriage and family therapists, and speech therapists who may all find themselves unable to legally provide testing services for which they are trained. In response to proposed legislation that seeks to limit the use of tests solely on degrees or licenses held, the National Fair Access Coalition on Testing (FACT) was created in 1996. FACT represents more than 500,000 counseling and mental health professionals. The organization has taken an active role in challenging proposed and enacted legislation and in court cases against mental health professionals who are charged with practicing psychology without a license based on their use of standardized instruments for which they have been adequately trained.

This same type of challenge has been put forth as to counselors' abilities to diagnose and treat clients, especially those with mental disorders. These efforts to restrain trade require that counselor licensure laws include language similar to the 1994 ACA model legislation which specifically states that counselors "(c) conduct assessments and diagnoses for the purposes of establishing treatment goals and objectives. . . . Assessment means selecting, administering, scoring and interpreting psychological and educational instruments designed to assess achievements, interests, personal characteristics, disabilities, and mental, emotional and behavioral disorders"

(Glosoff et al., 1995, p. 211). According to ACA (2003a), although all jurisdictions allow credentialed counselors to treat people with emotional disorders (noted on the ACA website as Tx in bold), only thirty-three (68.75 percent) specifically include the diagnosis of emotional disorders (noted on the ACA website as Dx in bold) in the scope of practice of credentialed counselors. This does, however, represent gains made by the counseling profession in this area. In 1999, although the majority of jurisdictions (82.6 percent) specifically allowed credentialed counselors to treat people with emotional or mental disorders, only 40 percent specifically included diagnosis in the scope of practice of credentialed counselors (Espina, 1999). As presented earlier, laws passed in the 1980s tend to be less comprehensive in the scope of practice afforded to counselors. Rather than try to enact new laws, some states have attempted to broaden their requirements and scope of practice through changes in regulations.

Finally, the struggle to enact counselor licensure laws in the final three states (California, Hawaii, and Nevada) will be crucial. The primary opposition to counselor licensure has traditionally been, and remains, psychologists. They have often, however, been joined in their opposition by licensed social workers and by groups of paraprofessionals (for example, baccalaureate-level addictions workers). Although I have discussed the need to pass comprehensive practice acts, it should also be noted that practice acts, especially those with strong scopes of practice, are perceived by other professional groups as more threatening than title protection acts, and, therefore, are more strenuously opposed (Glosoff, Benshoff, Hosie, & Maki, 1995).

RECOGNITION AND REIMBURSEMENT OF PROFESSIONAL COUNSELORS

Credentialing has far-reaching ramifications for the hiring and reimbursement of professional counselors. Contrary to popular belief, credentialing affects the reimbursement of those professionals in settings other than private practice. Administrative rules used by several federal, state, and local agencies specify that only state-licensed practitioners can be employed by these agencies. These same rules often stipulate that only licensed workers can supervise mental health services, and call specifically for licensed psychologists. In the late 1970s, Alabama eliminated all counselor position titles because of this type of thinking. This is also true at many university counseling centers that will only hire licensed psychologists. These are just a few examples of how credentialing has become strongly related to employment opportunities for counselors. There is an increasing trend in this direction (Glosoff, 1993).

Reimbursement for services rendered has played a strong part in the licensure movement for all mental health practitioners. A motivating force in psychological licensing of the late 1960s and early 1970s was to secure third-party reimbursement and to be included in national health insurance (Hosie, 1991). To facilitate these two goals, in 1975, APA established the *National Register for Health Service Providers in Psychology* as a means of identifying qualified practitioners of psychological services. Since January 1, 1978, to be listed in the *National Register* one was required to have obtained a doctoral degree in psychology from a regionally accredited educational institution. Even though it has been argued that proficiency can be developed just as well in a counselor education department as in a psychology department, criteria for inclusion in the *National Register* clearly does not allow anyone who was trained outside of a psychology department to take the examinations for licensure or certification as psychologists in most states (Rudolph, 1986). This had direct economic consequences for many doctoral-level professional counselors who were previously eligible to be licensed as psychologists.

Even though insurance companies traditionally used inclusion in the *National Register* as a criterion for reimbursement eligibility, that has changed, and counselors have met with some success in their efforts to be recognized as eligible providers. Professional counselors are included in some federal legislation and federally funded programs. For example, licensed counselors and CCMHCs are recognized by the Office of the Civilian Health and Medical Program of the Uniformed Services (known as TRICARE) as meeting standards for third-party payment. Unfortunately, TRICARE only reimburses for services provided by mental health counselors if the clients are referred by a physician and if the physician provides ongoing supervision of the counseling services. These limitations are not placed on services provided by clinical psychologists, clinical social workers, psychiatric nurses, and marriage and family therapists. ACA and AMHCA have been working for several years to enlist Congressional support for parity between counselors and other TRICARE mental health service providers (Barstow, 1999). The Department of Defense Authorization Act (Public Law 106-398), enacted in fiscal year 2001, and discussed earlier, addresses this issue.

Another example of counselors' success in their efforts to be recognized as qualified providers under federal legislation is that in October of 1998, one of ACA's top legislative priorities was accomplished with the enactment of the Health Professions Education Partnerships Act (HPEPA). According to the American Counseling Association Office of Public Policy and Information (1998b) HPEPA revised the Public Health Services Act (PHSA) by including counselors under the definition of mental health professionals. In addition, the HPEPA provisions directly influence the ability of counselor education programs to compete for clinical training grants by having graduate programs in counseling included in the HPEPA term "graduate program in behavioral and mental health practice." The act did not include a specific authorization level for any programs. Therefore, the passage of HPEPA does not, in itself, guarantee that counselors will be made eligible for any specific program. For example, although HPEPA added "counseling" to the current list of mental health professionals eligible for the CMHS clinical traineeship program, at the time HPEPA was enacted, the staff of the CMHS indicated that they did not expect any new clinical traineeships to be granted.

The passage of HPEPA also sets the stage for counselors to be included in the National Health Service Corps and its loan repayment program (ACA Office of Public Policy and Information, 1998b). This program provides financial assistance in repaying student loans in exchange for working in health professions in underserved areas for two to four years following graduation (for example, serving in public inpatient mental institutions or federal or state correctional facilities or as members of the faculties of eligible health professions). Other programs influenced by HPEPA provide for grants to schools to identify, recruit, select, and financially support people from disadvantaged backgrounds for education and training in health and behavioral and mental health fields, and grants to aid in the establishment of centers of excellence in health professions education for underrepresented minority individuals.

At the beginning of the twenty-first century, however, counselors were not yet included as recognized providers of Medicare or mental health services paid for through Federal Employee Health Benefit Plans (FEHBP). The PHSA *was not* enacted to determine which professional practitioners would be recognized as providers of health or mental health services. Federal and state laws and regulations related to Medicare, Medicaid, and the Federal Employee Health Benefit Plans, however, used the list of disciplines included in the PHSA as a guideline when developing criteria for reimbursable providers of mental health services. This indirectly led to counselors being excluded as reimbursable providers of service covered through public and private insurance programs. It is important to note that the enactment of HPEPA does not equate to the attainment of "core provider status" in other federal programs such as Medicare, Medicaid, or the Federal Employees Health Benefits Program. The inclusion of counselors as mental health providers under HPEPA hopefully will, however, change the precedent that has been used in determining provider eligibility for reimbursement purposes under other laws.

There have also been attempts made by the ACA, AMHCA, and ACA's state branches to change the laws and regulations that have excluded professional counselors as eligible providers of services paid for through Medicare and Federal Employee Health Benefit Plans. Because professional counselors are not included as Medicare providers in the federal statute, they have been unable to "sign off" on the delivery of mental health services through Medicare. This, in turn, may deter administrators from hiring professional counselors. Many people are not aware that the Medicare policy on the coverage of partial hospitalization services furnished in Community Mental Health Centers (CMHCs) allows for services to be provided by professionals *other than* physicians and psychologists. This has been used to have CMHCs and other state agencies write regulations and policies to include LPCs as employees. Even so, the law itself needs to be amended to specifically include LPCs *or* do away with the list of providers and include a statement that covered services include "individual and group therapy provided by any licensed mental health professional."

As noted earlier in this chapter, the Medicare Payment Advisory Commission (MedPAC) conducted a study on the appropriateness of establishing Medicare coverage of licensed professional counselors and other non-physician providers, including marriage and family therapists and pastoral counselors. MedPAC issued a weakly written report recommending *against* covering licensed professional counselors, marriage and family therapists, and pastoral counselors in June of 2002. Although Med-PAC came to a negative conclusion, the language in 1999 Medicare, Medicaid, and SCHIP Balanced Budget Refinement Act (P.L. 106-554) calling for the report, marked the first time that Congress and the President had enacted legislation referencing licensed professional counselors with respect to Medicare. Since the enactment of P.L. 106-554, legislation was introduced in both the House and the Senate that would establish Medicare coverage of licensed professional counselors. Most recently, language establishing Medicare coverage of state-licensed professional counselors and marriage and family therapists was included in S. 1, the Medicare prescription drug legislation passed by the Senate in the summer of 2003.

Although FEHBP is regulated by a federal law, group policies are written across the country by various insurers—most often Blue Cross/Blue Shield. At present, mental health services provided by psychologists but not licensed counselors are covered. Although the enactment of HPEPA does not result in attainment of "core provider status" in FEHBP, the inclusion of professional counselors as mental health professionals in the HPEPA provisions may help in counselors' legislative efforts to make changes in FEHBP.

Medicaid, which is a federal program, is implemented through state regulations. Once again, most states have used the list of core disciplines from the PHSA in determining which mental health practitioners are eligible to provide reimbursable services. The enactment of the 1997 Balanced Budget Act included provisions that prohibit Medicaid managed care plans from discriminating against providers on the basis of the type of license they hold. The act, however, did not extend to fee-for-service plans regulated through Medicaid and most states have traditionally used fee-for-service programs. This is changing, however, and many states have moved to managed Medicaid care plans. Even with the passage of the 1997 Balanced Budget Act and the inclusion of professional counselors as recognized mental health professionals through HPEPA, the battle to include professional counselors as recognized Medicaid providers has been fought primarily at the state level.

Major criteria for acceptance as reimbursable practitioners, set forth by most sources of third-party reimbursement, include educational degrees and the possession of a license, which allows the mental health provider to practice independently (Bistline, 1991; E. Bongiovanni, personal communication, April 27, 1993; Throckmorton, 1992). State licensure is also a prerequisite to becoming eligible for third-party reimbursement by insurance companies via any state mandates regulating insurance codes. Research indicates that LPCs do receive reimbursement from some insurance companies in states that do not legally mandate this (Throckmorton, 1992; Zimpfer, 1992). However, without a state mandate, there are no guarantees that LPCs or their clients will be reimbursed for services rendered.

A number of states have legislated mandates, often called "freedom of choice" (FOC) laws that require the reimbursement for services provided by specific professionals, such as LPCs, if these services are covered by a health plan. FOC laws increase consumers' choice of providers, thereby expanding the markets for mental health providers. These laws, however, do not regulate managed care companies, employers that set aside money to pay for the medical claims of their employees, or publically funded (state or federal) insurance programs. Licensed counselors are included as clinicians and as administrative staff in managed mental health systems (Throckmorton, 1992).

Managed Care

Licensed counselors have gained ground in their efforts to be included as clinicians and as administrative staff in managed mental health systems (Throckmorton, 1992). In fact, the National Board for Certified Counselors received a $25,000 grant from the United States Department of Health and Human Services' Center for Mental Health Services (CMHS) to conduct a nine-month research study on the short- and long-term influence of managed care on the training for and provision of mental health services. The inclusion of representatives from NBCC and ACA on this type of federal study is a strong indicator of the recognition that professional counseling gained during the last twenty years. Inclusion in managed care organizations themselves, such as preferred provider organizations (PPOs) and health maintenance organizations (HMOs) is helpful to counselors and their clients in that it allows for reimbursement of services. It is also important to realize that managed care does much more than influence practitioners' income. The strong movement toward establishment of managed care companies is influencing the practices of most mental health practitioners. The majority of 1,700 professional counselors, psychologists, psychiatrists, social workers, and marriage and family therapists, surveyed in 1995, reported changing their practices in the following ways: (1) adopting time-limited therapy techniques, (2) attending training workshops on brief therapy, (3) shortening the length of therapy, and (4) having to deal with an increased number of disallowed insurance claims (Psychotherapy Finances, 1995).

This emphasis on brief therapy must be addressed by counseling education programs, many of which continue to teach the application of traditionally based theories. This has ethical implications for both training programs and practitioners. It is considered unethical for practitioners to use modes of treatment for which they are untrained. Counselor educators have a responsibility to provide adequate training appropriate for the work settings in which their graduates will most likely be employed. Readers are referred to Chapter 7 of this text for more information on brief therapy modalities.

Working within managed care organizations also raises many other issues. Counselors have expressed several concerns about dealing with managed care companies including time limits or caps placed on the number of sessions approved, increased paperwork, decreased flexibility in treatment planning, dealing with the gatekeeper system, and lack of qualified personnel acting as gatekeepers (Glosoff, 1998). It is also common for counselors to find themselves up against ethical dilemmas in their attempts to balance their obligations to both managed care systems and their clients. Typically, these dilemmas are related to matters of informed consent; confidentiality; termination, referral, and abandonment; financial incentives or fees; diagnosis/assessment; competence; limited client choice of diverse providers; and teaching, training, and supervision of practitioners and students (Danziger & Welfel, 2001; Glosoff, 1998).

Technology

The use of computer-based technology in counseling, supervision, and counselor education has continued to grow over the past two decades and will likely continue to do so. Computer-based applications have helped counselors with tasks such as scheduling and maintaining client records. Counselors also use computers on a regular basis to facilitate activities associated with student affairs and services such as orientation and judicial affairs (Sampson & Bloom, 2001), and with career planning programs. It is not uncommon for counselors to use electronic mail to communicate with clients and colleagues or to use the World Wide Web to explore resources for themselves and their clients. Although many counselors may argue against it, counseling services are being offered on the Internet. Finally, there has been an increased use of technology associated with both distance learning and supervision in counselor education programs. While there may be advantages to using computer technology to assist in the delivery of counseling services, it also raises some serious ethical concerns. The profession has begun to address these concerns through the development of standards related to the use of technology in counseling and counselor education. For example, the Technology Interest Network of the Association for Counselor Education and Supervision adopted a set of competencies for counselor education graduate students in 1999. Readers may access these competencies online at *http://www.acesonline.net/competencies.htm*. In addition, the American Counseling Association adopted ethical standards for Internet counseling that readers can access online at *http://www.counseling.org/site/PageServer?pagename=resources_internet*. The National Board for Certified Counselor provides ethical standards for the practice of Internet counseling. Readers may access these online at *http://www.nbcc.org/ethics/webethics.htm*. A challenge for professional counselors is to learn to effectively and ethically use the technological resources available. Readers are referred to Chapter 5 in this book for further information.

SUMMARY

The roots of counseling are deeply embedded in a variety of disciplines that have come together and created different emphases at various points in time. These emphases have led to the development of counseling specialties, counselors working in a wide variety of settings and offering a broad range of services, and the profession struggling with the formation of an identity.

Counselors in the United States, regardless of work setting or theoretical orientation, are linked by the common belief that a person has the capacity and right to choose directions and activities that are most personally satisfying. Choices must be made within the bounds of social and moral value systems that will not bring harm to self or to others. The counselors who were pioneers and the counselors who work now were/are dedicated to helping individuals find their way in an increasingly complex society.

Counselors are active in dealing with a great number of social problems that affect the populations with which they work. Society is in turmoil trying to deal with the use of illegal drugs, changing family structures, the effect of technology on education, occupations and employment, immigration issues, and complex pluralism, leading to the development of special populations at risk of being inundated by the majority. There is not space here to discuss each issue and the role of counselors in addressing these. Counselors must work to ensure that through their systematic, scientific, and professional efforts individuals and groups will be served well.

Acknowledgments

I would like to extend my gratitude and appreciation to Perry Rockwell, Jr., Ph.D., and Professor Emeritus of Counselor Education at the University of Wisconsin at Platteville. His pioneer work in the area of the historical underpinning of guidance and counseling in the United States formed the basis for the first edition of this chapter. I also would like to thank Michael Mason, a doctoral student at the University of Virginia for his assistance in updating the information on credentialing and licensure laws and Scott Barstow, Director of Public Policy for the American Counseling Association, for information on federal legislation enacted since the last edition.

CHAPTER TWO

THE HELPING RELATIONSHIP

SUSAN E. HALVERSON, PH.D.
RUSSELL D. MIARS, PH.D.
Portland State University

THE PROFESSIONAL HELPING RELATIONSHIP[1]

Most people find themselves engaged in some type of helping relationship nearly every day. Some helping occurs informally while other helping happens in a more formal way. Friends and family usually help one another in a reciprocal, informal way while helping professionals such as counselors, psychologists, or social workers help their clients within a formal, unidirectional relationship. In a friendship, people share concerns and give each other information, advice, and support. Professional helping, in contrast, places much more responsibility on the helper, who must strive to be objective and helpful in a more directed, purposeful way. The professional helping relationship is unique in that a more independent, mature, fully functioning individual emerges as a result of the helping relationship.

This chapter focuses on the characteristics, knowledge, and skills needed by the counselor to build effective counselor-client helping relationships. The first section describes the helping relationship and the following sections review what research has shown to be the characteristics of effective counselors and the skills needed to be a good helper or counselor. Throughout the skills sections, you will find examples taken from conversations between a counselor and client; we have added these exam-

---

[1]The senior author of this chapter in the first edition was Art Terry, Ph.D., Associate Professor in the Graduate School of Education at Portland State University. Dr. Terry died in September of 1993. We wish to acknowledge the contribution he made to the content of the original version of this chapter.

ples to demonstrate, more clearly, specific techniques you might use when working with clients. A description of the case from which these excerpts were drawn can be found on page 59. As you read through this chapter, think about yourself and how closely you fit the description of an effective counselor.

WHAT IS THE HELPING RELATIONSHIP?

In the helping relationship, individuals work together to resolve a concern or difficulty and/or foster the personal growth and development of one of the two people. Rogers (1961) defined a helping relationship as one "in which at least one of the parties has the intent of promoting the growth, development, maturity, improved functioning and improved coping with life of the other (party)" (p. 39). The goals of any counselor-client relationship, whether in educational, career or personal counseling, can be put into four basic goal areas: changes in behavior and lifestyle, increased awareness or insight and understanding, relief from suffering, or changes in thoughts and self perceptions (Brammer & MacDonald, 1996).

An important aspect of the helping relationship is that it is a process that enables a person to grow in directions chosen by that person. It is the counselor's job to make the client aware of possible alternatives and encourage client acceptance of responsibility for taking action on one or more of these alternatives.

The helping relationship minimally can be broken down into three phases—that of relationship building, that of challenging the client to find ways to change, and that of facilitating positive client action (Egan, 2002). In the first phase, the goal is to build a foundation of mutual trust and client understanding. Once trust and understanding have been established, the helper, in the second phase, challenges the client to "try on" new ways of thinking, feeling, and behaving. In the final phase, the counselor facilitates client actions that lead toward change and growth in the client's life outside the counseling relationship.

Most helping occurs on a one-to-one basis, and studies of the quality of the counseling relationship have shown that it is more the collaborative attitudes and feelings of the counselor, rather than the specifics of theoretical orientation, that are important for positive outcome (Sexton & Whiston, 1994; Sexton, Whiston, Bleuer, & Walz, 1997). Specific procedures and techniques are much less important than the alliance between counselor and client. It is important to understand that it is the way in which the counselor's attitudes and procedures are perceived by the client that makes a difference, and it is the client's positive perception that is crucial to a good helping relationship (Rogers, 1961; Sexton, Whiston, Bleuer, & Walz 1997).

The ultimate goal of a professional helping relationship should be to promote the development of more effective and adaptive behavior in the client. The specific goals for a given client are determined collaboratively by the counselor and the client as they interact in the helping relationship. In the next section we will examine the characteristics of individuals who serve as effective and competent counselors.

WHAT ARE THE CHARACTERISTICS
OF EFFECTIVE COUNSELORS?

Effective counselors have specific personal qualities and are able to convey those qualities to the people they help. There is an increasing amount of evidence supporting the concept that helpers are only as effective as they are self-aware and able to use themselves as vehicles of change (Okun, 1996). As you read through this section, you might think about each quality or trait and see how it fits for you.

Combs (1986) summarized thirteen studies that looked at helpers in a variety of settings. These studies supported the view that there are differences in the beliefs of effective and ineffective person-centered helpers. Effective counselors are interested in and committed to an understanding of the specialized knowledge of the field and find it personally meaningful. As such, they are challenged to remain current in their knowledge and skills. They also believe that the people they help are capable, adequate, trustworthy, dependable, and friendly. Effective counselors focus on positive self-beliefs and have confidence in themselves, their abilities, and their worth. They like people and have a feeling of oneness with others. Effective counselors use interventions that focus on the individual's perception of self and expand the individual's view of life rather than narrowing it. They are committed to freeing rather than controlling the client and are able to be objectively involved with, rather than alienated from, their clients.

The term "self-actualized" has been used by Patterson (1985) to describe a constellation of characteristics that effective counselors possess. Aware and accepting of self, they are individuals who are likewise aware of their environment and interact with it in a reality-oriented way. In living, they are open to a full range of experiences and feelings, are spontaneous, and have a sense of humor. When interacting with others, they are able to be involved, yet remain somewhat detached (Cormier, Cormier, & Cormier, 1997). They are empathic, compassionate, and believing of the client's world. In the process of dealing with problems and issues, they are able to help clients clearly see their own worlds while adding a fresh perspective to the issues. Respected by others, these individuals are authentic (Pietrofesa, Hoffman, Splete, & Pinto, 1978), perceived as trustworthy (Strong, 1968), and abide by ethical standards of the profession (Gladding, 2000).

Counseling is demanding work, and effective counselors often display high energy levels (Carkhuff, 1986). Intense focusing with another individual, trying to hear clearly, often needing to tolerate ambiguity (Pietrofesa, Hoffman, Splete, & Pinto, 1978), and taking appropriate risks can put heavy demands on the counselor's energy. Therefore, a challenge to individuals pursuing the counseling profession is to have good self-care strategies (see Brems, 2000).

Rogers (1958) identified four conditions that he believed all counselors should provide in the context of a helping relationship. These necessary, but not necessarily sufficient, core conditions were (1) unconditional positive regard for the individual, (2) genuineness, (3) congruence, and (4) empathy. Later, Carkhuff and Berenson (1967) added two additional traits or skills to the list: respect and concreteness. Thirteen years later, Ivey and Simek-Downing (1980) labeled these traits "communications skills," and added warmth, immediacy, and confrontation to the list.

The sections on helping skills that follow the case study are intended to help you gain a better understanding of the traits and skills needed to be an effective counselor.

CASE STUDY

On the intake form, Lisa described herself as 33 and married with three children. She came to counseling because she was feeling desperate and needed to talk her problem over with someone. Concerns about her marriage and her children were at an all-time high. Her husband, Peter, was to come to counseling with her, but backed out at the last minute, hoping that she wouldn't go either.

Peter and Lisa first met when they lived in California; she worked as a waitress in a restaurant where he often came to eat. They started dating, and it wasn't long until they were serious about each other. In Lisa's view, the only obstacle to their marriage was that he was not yet divorced. Peter told her that it would take time but there was no question he would get a divorce.

They talked about what it would be like to be together. He said she was such a contrast to his wife, whom he described as really crazy. One day he happened to mention that he had two kids—a boy and a girl. They were with his wife, but he'd like to get them before they too became crazy. Soon they were talking about all living together; she would take care of the kids until the divorce was final. This sounded wonderful to Lisa, because she didn't want to be a waitress all her life.

Peter, Lisa, and the children had been living together for three years when they moved to the Chicago area. Peter was tired of his current job and had heard that there were great opportunities there. When they got there, the only work he found that paid a decent wage was that of a night watchman at a big plant. He liked the title of "security officer" but really didn't like working nights. This turned out to be a very difficult time for Lisa because she found out that she was pregnant and she had to keep the kids quiet during the day while Peter slept.

When she came to counseling, Lisa's most immediate concern was that they had just purchased a house, representing themselves as husband and wife. At the time she wasn't worried because she knew that they would soon be married. But several weeks later, she proposed to Peter that they now should legalize their relationship, especially since they had a 2-year-old daughter. Lisa was absolutely appalled when he told her that he had never initiated any divorce action.

As time went on, Lisa became more aware of problems in their relationship. Peter drank too much and became more demanding and threatening. He had hit her only once, but his attitude and the gun he carried made her feel very intimidated and threatened. She didn't want to stay with him, but she had no place else to go.

She was concerned about leaving him because of the children. If she took only their daughter, what might happen to the other two children? She'd grown to love them, but didn't want to be accused of kidnapping. She also wasn't certain that she could support herself, let alone three more!

The intimidation and verbal abuse by her husband escalated, as did the drinking. He forbade her to go to counseling. She knew she must leave him, but didn't know where to go.

Epilogue

With the counselor's help, Lisa explored the alternatives available to her. She called the legal aid service for advice about the children. One evening, he became extremely physically abusive with her and she had to call the police to restrain him. The next day Lisa took the children and moved into a domestic shelter.

BASIC SKILLS AND CONCEPTS

According to Ivey (1998), the aim of counseling is personal and social development. He has described a hierarchy of microcounseling skills that define what the counselor does in an interview to achieve specific results. Ivey's hierarchy rests on a foundation of attending behaviors and basic listening skills. Our list of skills is based on Ivey's model with additional information taken from Cormier, Cormier, and Cormier (1997), Egan (2002), and Ivey (1998).

Attending Skills

Attending behavior, including eye contact, body language, vocal quality, and verbal tracking, is one of the most powerful of the communication skills (Ivey, 1998). In the counseling relationship, counselors communicate through body language and words that their full attention is on the client's nonverbal and verbal behaviors. Eye contact, facial expressions, and body posture are the physical fundamentals that indicate to others that you are either carefully attending or not attending to them.

Eye Contact.   Good eye contact is not an unwavering stare, but an intermittent, yet frequent, looking into the eyes of the client. It tells the other person that you are interested in them and what they have to say. Effective eye contact occurs more frequently when there is a comfortable distance between counselor and client, when topics being discussed are not too threatening, when neither person is trying to hide something, when there is adequate rapport between counselor and client, and when one is listening rather than talking. Cultural differences abound in what is considered appropriate eye contact (Ivey, 1998). The counselor should first consider cultural differences if eye contact seems strained or awkward in the relationship.

Attentive Body Language.   Body orientation can encourage or discourage interpersonal interactions. In our culture, a slight forward body lean and a relaxed, comfortable posture are usually received favorably and indicate interest in the client. Egan (2002) uses the acronym SOLER to describe this attentive body posture. The letters stand for *Squarely*—face the client, *Open*—body posture, *Lean*—forward slightly, *Eye*—contact, and *Relaxed*—manner.

Distance.   The distance between counselor and client also affects communication. There is an optimal "comfort zone" for conversing that is largely controlled by cultural influences. It is about an arm's length in American culture. It is imperative that the counselor be aware of the level of comfort or discomfort that the client is experiencing with the distance and adjust it if necessary.

The distance between counselor and client may become so close that it involves *touch*. Counselors should always be sensitive to the therapeutic value of touch. This involves a consideration of the client issues and sensitivity to the role that touch has played in creating the issue, and what professionals who are considered experts recommend as best practice. For example, it is not recommended that counselors working with individuals traumatized by physical abuse utilize touch as part of their therapeutic behavior.

Humanistic models suggest that touch that is genuinely felt may help create within the client a willingness to be open and share. Driscoll, Newman, and Seals (1988) found that college students observing videotapes felt that counselors who touched their college-age clients were more caring than counselors who did not. Suiter and Goodyear (1985) found that counselors who used a semi-embrace with clients were seen as less trustworthy than counselors who either did not touch, or only touched their clients' hands or shoulders. There was also greater acceptability of touch when female counselors initiated it. It must be emphasized, though, that touch without genuine feeling behind it may be more harmful than helpful. The type of touch that is generally considered acceptable is one that is long enough (1–3 seconds) to make contact yet does not create uncomfortable feelings. Most professionals who do touch believe that appropriate touching is contact of the counselor's hand or forearm with the client's hand, arm, shoulder, or upper back, and recognize that gender differences may influence how such contact is interpreted.

While there are many things counselors can do to convey an interest in their clients, certain mannerisms are distracting. Behaviors such as gum chewing, cigarette smoking, or continual change of body position may seriously affect any interpersonal interaction and convey a sense of counselor disinterest.

Vocal Tone.   Another aspect of attending behavior is voice tone. A warm, pleasant, caring voice strongly indicates an interest and willingness to listen to the client. The pitch, volume, and rate of speech can convey much of one's feeling toward another person or situation. Scherer (1986) has shown that the use of specific paralinguistic cues can convey either high or low levels of self-confidence. High levels of confidence are conveyed when you speak in a caring voice that is neither hesitant nor rapid, but which projects inner qualities of warmth, respect and compassion for the client. These cues of self-confidence can affect client perceptions of counselor expertness, attractiveness, trustworthiness, and associated satisfaction with the counseling relationship (Barak, Shapira, & Fisher, 1988).

Verbal Tracking.   Even when the client engages in long irrelevant discourses, the counselor often needs to remain relaxed and follow the client's topic and logic. The counselor can choose to either attend or ignore certain portions of the client's statements—this is termed *selective attention.* The portions of the client's statements to which a counselor attends depend upon the counselor's theoretical orientation and professional beliefs. It is imperative that counselors be aware of their own patterns of selective attention, for the topics their clients focus on will tend to be partially determined by those topics to which the counselor unconsciously attends.

Silence is another important part of verbal attending behavior. The counselor's ability to remain silent while clients are silent facilitates clients listening to themselves and/or the counselor more carefully. Remaining silent is often an excellent tactic to start a reluctant client talking because silence is perceived by many clients as a demanding condition that must be filled with a response. However, the meaning of silence is culturally based (Murphy & Dillon, 2003). The challenge for beginning counselors is learning to be comfortable enough with silence to use it effectively.

The Basic Listening Skills

Active listening is an extremely important dimension of counselors' work (Egan, 2002). Counselors need to be sure that they are hearing the client accurately and clients must know that the counselor has fully heard them, seen their point of view, and felt the world as they experience it. The basic listening skills that facilitate active listening include client observation; noticing client nonverbal behavior; the use of encouraging, paraphrasing, and summarization statements; the reflection of client feelings; and the use of open and closed questions. The outcome of using these basic listening skills in combination is the establishment of an empathic relationship with the client (Carkhuff, 1969). The overall purpose of empathy is to " . . . understand the situation of another person from that person's perspective" (Berger, McBreen, & Rifin, 1996, p. 210).

Client Observation.   Simply observing the client provides the counselor with a rich source of "silent information." Noticing and paying attention to the *physiological cues* expressed in another person's appearance and physique provide a way to identify the internal emotional responses of the other person. Bandler and Grinder (1979) have identified four cues—changes in skin color, lip size, muscle tone, and/or breathing—that can reflect the internal emotional processes and the physiologic changes occurring within the client. These physiologic messages are difficult to hide because they are generally involuntary reactions of the autonomic nervous system. Observing subtle changes in these areas can silently reveal the moments of emotional change for a client.

The points during the interview at which eye contact is broken, the voice changes, skin color changes, shifts in body posture occur, or when changes in muscle tension or facial expression take place may indicate moments when important information is being revealed. Observations of discrepancies between nonverbal behavior and what is being said should be checked out with the client by the use of such questions as "Are you aware that you are smiling as you talk about the sadness you feel?"

Verbal Behavior.   In addition to nonverbal behavior, one can also learn a great deal from the client's verbal behavior. At the most basic level, the counselor should note *topic changes* or *topic exclusions* and any *key words* that appear again and again. For example, when the client continues to use "should" or "ought" statements, it may indicate a lack of control in those areas and should be explored further.

Sentence structure is an important clue to how the client views the world. Is the client the subject or the object of the sentence? Specifically, does the client feel he or she does the acting, or is acted on? Are concerns portrayed as being in the past, the present, or the future? Are there key words and descriptions that give a clue to the client's worldview? Hearing certain patterns of words and ideas gives clues to a client's typical thought processes and self perceptions.

Incongruities, discrepancies, and *double messages* are nearly universal in counseling interviews. They are often at the root of a client's immobility and inability to respond creatively to difficult life situations (Egan, 2002). The "Freudian slip" is an example of such an incongruity. When counselors notice such incongruities, they may either choose to hold back and say nothing or try to bring the discrepancy into the client's awareness. The emotional state of the client and the impact upon the relationship should be the main consideration when making this decision. In time-limited counseling, or within certain theoretical frameworks such as Gestalt, immediate confrontation may be the preferred intervention.

Encouraging, Paraphrasing, and Summarizing.   The skill of *encouraging* includes the use of both "encouragers" and "restatements," both of which punctuate the interview and provide a smooth flow. Using encouragers such as head nods, an interested facial expression, or verbal utterances such as "umm" or "uh-huh" is an active way to let clients know that they have been heard and understood. Encouragers can be used to influence the direction taken by the client and are part of selective attention as described above.

One powerful type of encourager is for the counselor to respond with a restatement of a "key word" or a short phrase from the client's statement, often in a questioning tone of voice.

Lisa: I often feel afraid around him.

Counselor: Afraid of him?

The *paraphrase* always uses some of the same key words from the client's statement, but might add some counselor observations. It is an encapsulated rephrase of the content of the client's message in the counselor's words. The strength of the paraphrase is that the counselor is giving of self, yet is paying primary attention to the client's frame of reference. This skill is frequently very helpful in letting clients clarify issues that may have been cloudy as well as letting them know that they have been heard accurately.

A good paraphrase has four main parts:

1. Noting some aspect of the client's mode of receiving information (visual, auditory, kinesthetic)
2. Key words and constructs used by the client

3. A summary of the essence of what the client has said
4. A checking out of the counselor's accuracy in hearing, such as, "Is that right?" or "Is that close?"

To illustrate the elements of a good paraphrase, consider the following example:

> **Lisa:**   I'd like to run away and never come back, but what would happen to the kids?
>
> **Counselor:**   It sounds like you're feeling trapped and confused. If you only had yourself to think about, you'd know what to do, but you really care about the children.
>
> **Lisa:**   You're right! I do feel trapped and confused!

Summarizations are similar to paraphrasing, except that they "paraphrase" a longer period of conversation. They gather together a client's verbalizations, facts, feelings, and meanings, and restate them for the client as accurately as possible. Summarizations frequently give the client a feeling of movement as ideas and feelings are explored (Brammer & MacDonald, 1996).

Summarizations may be useful in the beginning of a session to warm up a client or at other times to bring closure to discussion on a theme. They can be used to add direction and coherence to a session that seems to be going nowhere (Egan, 2002). Summarizations are also valuable to counselors as a check on the accuracy of their understanding of the information that has just been gathered.

Here is an example of a summarization in an interview with Lisa:

> **Counselor:**   You're feeling overwhelmed because so many things seem wrong—you're feeling the need to be protective of the kids and yourself. You're less certain you'll ever be married or even want to be married to Peter.

Reflection of Feelings.   Besides hearing the words of the client accurately, the counselor must uncover and recognize the emotions underlying those words. Reflecting client feelings is very similar to paraphrasing except that the paraphrase is associated with content (such as facts and information), while reflection of feelings is associated with the emotions related to the content. This skill is used to discover and sort out positive and negative client feelings and can best be done by using concise statements that connect the client's feelings with the causes of those feelings (Egan, 2002; Evans, Hearn, Uhlemann, & Ivey, 1993). It is important for the counselor to have learned how to recognize and accurately label emotions such as anger, gladness, sadness, fear, or being scared before trying to reflect these emotions in others.

A reflection of feelings consists of five basic parts:

1. A sentence stem using the client's method of receiving information (auditory, visual, kinesthetic)
2. Use of the pronoun "you"

3. A feeling label or emotion stem
4. A context or setting for the emotion
5. The correct tense of the reflection (frequently it is the present tense; e.g., "Right now, you are angry")

You may also want to check to see that the reflection is accurate; for example:

Lisa: I just don't know what to do.

Counselor: It sounds like with all these responsibilities, you're feeling trapped, confused, and immobilized. You're not certain which way to turn. Is that how you feel?

Questions.   The use of questions can open communication. In the helping relationship, effective, open communication is especially necessary from the counselor. It facilitates moving the client from self-exploration through increased understanding and finally commitment to appropriate action. By using specific verbal leads, the counselor is able to bring out the major facts, feelings, and self-perceptions that a client brings to the session. Effective use of open and closed questions can encourage the client to talk more freely and openly.

Open questions are considered by some to be the most valuable of the attending skills. Open questions usually begin with "what," "how," "could," or "would" and require the client to provide a longer, more expansive response than simply "yes" or "no." Open questions are used to begin interviews; to encourage clients to express more information; to elicit examples of particular behaviors, thoughts, or feelings; and to increase the client's commitment to communicate. Some examples might be:

Counselor: What would you like to discuss today?

Counselor: How did that make you feel?

Counselor: Could there be other reasons for the way you acted?

Sometimes a client is very talkative and rambles or jumps from topic to topic. In such a case, *closed questions* can be used to gather information, give clarity, gain focus, and narrow the area of discussion. These closed questions usually begin with the word "is," "are," "do," or "did." One must use caution though, because extensive use of closed questions can hinder conversation (Egan, 2002). A questioning counselor can appear to have all the power in the relationship, and this inequality can destroy the counselor-client alliance, especially during initial encounters.

Clients from some cultures are rapidly turned off by counselor questions, as are those clients who have not developed trust in their counselors. Frequently, the same information can be obtained by asking the client what goals they have, how they feel about those goals, and how they plan to attain them. (Note that asking too many questions at once can confuse clients.) "Why" questions are especially troublesome because they may put clients on the defensive or leave them feeling they must provide a logical explanation for their behavior.

Because questions may cause resistance with some clients, the skills of encouraging, paraphrasing, summarization, and reflection of feeling may be used to obtain similar information yet seem less intrusive to the client.

Self-Attending Skills

Counselors who are aware of their own values, beliefs, and assets are much more likely to find it easier to "be with" clients, help clients explore personal issues, and facilitate client action. Therefore, the self-attending skills are extremely important for each person who wishes to be an effective counselor. There are several components to the self-attending process. Shulman (1979) referred to these counselor components as "tuning-in." The first component in the "tuning-in" process is self-awareness.

Self-Awareness.   The personal knowledge and understanding that the counselor has of self and the counseling setting are extremely important to the self-attending process. Practically speaking, the counselor should not consciously rehearse how counselors are "supposed" to be. The effective counselor acts professionally, but does not put on a professional front, play acting some imaginary expert counselor. Effective counselors know their strengths as well as their weaknesses, and by understanding themselves are able to overcome self-consciousness and devote fuller attention to what the client is trying to disclose.

In the process of learning counseling skills, there may be times when using the skills seems awkward and uncomfortable. The learning cycle for trainees recognizes that learning counselor skills can sometimes be an unsettling process. Unlearning competing behaviors and relearning new ones in their place take time, a great deal of concentration, and practice. Counselor self-awareness is crucial throughout this process.

Centering and Relaxing.   *Centering*, or getting "in touch" and then "in-tune" with one's person (Brammer & MacDonald, 1996) is an important skill for the counselor to develop. By becoming centered the counselor is able to show more social-emotional presence (Egan, 2002) in the counseling relationship and to give the client his or her undivided attention. With a keener focus than is common in most human interaction, the counselor is better able to empathically understand the client's problems and concerns. Similarly, a significant level of relaxation (both physical and psychological) in the counselor will help clients relax as they face the stress and challenges of the counseling process itself.

Humor.   The counselor who can enjoy and use *humor* effectively has an invaluable asset. The healing power of humor has long been valued, but its place in therapy is only slowly gaining respect (Keller, 1984). Although counseling is serious business, there are many truly humorous dimensions to the human condition and when humor appears as a natural outgrowth of the counselor-client relationship it should be attended to (Prochaska & Norcross, 2003). Humor can provide a means of connecting with clients, and counselors need to affirm any humor presented by their clients. Laughter and joking can release built-up tensions and laughing at one's self can be extremely therapeutic—since it requires seeing one's problems in a whole new perspective.

Nonjudgmental Attitude Toward Self.   Counselors need to have a broad awareness of their own value positions. They must be able to answer very clearly the questions, "Who am I?" "What is important to me?" "Am I nonjudgmental?" (Brammer & MacDonald, 1996).

This awareness aids counselors in being honest with themselves and their clients and in being free from judgments about themselves. In addition it helps the counselor avoid unwarranted or unethical use of clients to satisfy personal needs. Although counselors may have opinions about traits of people they like and want to associate with, one characteristic of effective counselors is that they try to suspend personal judgments about their clients' lives.

Nonjudgmental Attitude Toward Others.   This attitude is one of respect for a client's individuality and worth as a person and is very similar to Rogers' (1961) concept of "unconditional positive regard." It allows clients to be open and to be themselves, because they know that the person they are in a relationship with (the counselor) will not be judging them or what they say. The counselor conveys this nonjudgmental attitude by being warm, accepting, and respectful toward the client; this is especially important in the early phases of the relationship.

Respect describes the helping attitude and skill that communicates this acceptance of the client as a person of worth and dignity (Rogers, 1957). In utilizing this skill, the counselor demonstrates a belief in the client's ability to deal with his or her problems in the presence of a facilitative person. Often counselors express this respect by what they do not do, rather than what they do—such as not giving advice (for example, see Egan, 2002). Respectful counselors use communication skills to actualize the power, ability, and skills already possessed by the client. In other words, the counselor believes in the problem-solving ability of the client. These skills and attitudes are very important in facilitating an effective helping relationship. They communicate a willingness to work with the client and an interest and belief in the client as a person of worth (Cormier et al., 1997).

The way you nonverbally attend to the client is one way you express respect (Egan, 2002). Respectful behavior conveys the message "I'm glad I'm here, I'm glad you're here." Respect is also expressed through appropriate warmth, understanding, and caring.

Communicating respect entails suspending judgment of the client (Cormier, Cormier, & Cormier, 1997; Egan, 2002). Rogers (1967) has effectively described this kind of respect as the ability of the counselor to "communicate to his client a deep and genuine caring for him as a person with potentialities, a caring uncontaminated by evaluations of his thoughts, feelings or behaviors" (p. 102).

> **Lisa:**   I am really feeling very helpless. I like staying home and taking care of the kids. Going back to work isn't something I want to do.

Counselor: The dilemma you face is complicated by something that you like to do and something you don't really want to do.

Respect is rarely found alone in communication. It usually occurs in combination with empathy and genuineness.

Genuineness.   When counselors relate to clients naturally and openly, they are being genuine. Being a counselor is not just a role played by the individual. Instead, it is the appropriate revelation of one's own feelings, thoughts, and being in the counseling relationship. Egan (1975) cautions "being role free is not license; freedom from role means that the counselor should not use the role or facade of counselor to protect himself, to substitute for effectiveness, or to fool the client" (p. 92).

The effective use of genuineness reduces the emotional distance between the counselor and client (Cormier, Cormier, & Cormier, 1997). It breaks down the role distance and links the counselor and client together, allowing the client to see the counselor as human, and a person similar to him or her. The genuine counselor is spontaneous, nondefensive, and consistent in relationships.

Lisa: Do you think I'm as crazy and mixed up as I feel?

Counselor: Your confusion and indecisiveness make you wonder whether I see you as crazy. I really don't experience you that way.

Concreteness.   In the process of exploring problems or issues, a client often presents an incomplete representation of what has happened. The goal of concreteness is to make the information and awareness gained through self-exploration more specific and concrete (Meier & Davis, 1993). It is the task of the counselor to help the client clarify the pieces of the puzzle and fit them together so that the whole makes sense to the client. This clarification increases the likelihood that an organized, specific, workable action plan can be implemented and accepted by the client. When encouraging concreteness, one attempts to focus very specifically on the situation at hand, and tries to make clear all facets of the issue, including the accompanying behaviors and feelings.

There are several ways to help clients become more concrete and focused. When a client makes a vague statement, the counselor can reflect in a more concrete way. At times, a rambling client may need to be focused. The effective use of concreteness in such situations may feel like interrupting, but should lead to increased counselor-client interaction. When counselor invitations to be more concrete or specific are necessary, leads such as "what" and "how" rather than "why" will usually produce more relevant and specific information (Egan, 2002).

Lisa: I'm really confused about what to do.

Counselor: You're feeling stuck and confused because you always thought you'd be married and now you're not so certain he wants that to happen.

or

Counselor: What specifically has happened that has led to the confusion?

or

Counselor: Help me to understand what events are most closely related to this confusion you're feeling.

Effective use of concreteness keeps the counseling session productively focused and aims at making vague experiences, behaviors, and feelings more specific. The more specific the information, the better the understanding and the more effective future choices and actions will be.

ADVANCED SKILLS AND CONCEPTS

The first goal of helping is to help clients tell their story in an understandable way (Egan, 2002). This involves the facilitation of client self-understanding. Such exploration helps both the counselor and client understand the client's problems and concerns. Clients begin to focus and see more clearly the puzzles of their life and are led skillfully to identify the missing pieces and blocks. This exploration involves a look at the real self, and related issues. The process leads to insightful self-understanding that invites the client to change or take action.

Once the beginning counselor is adept at using the basic counseling skills, advanced skills and concepts can be added to the repertoire. These skills and concepts are more action oriented and allow the counselor to facilitate deeper client self-understanding, change, and eventual termination of the helping relationship. The advanced understanding and challenging skills include advanced empathy, self-disclosure, confrontation, and immediacy (Egan, 2002).

Advanced Understanding and Challenging Skills

Advanced Empathy.   *Primary empathy* forms the foundation and atmospheric core of the helping relationship (Gladding, 2000). It involves listening for basic or surface messages with frequent, but brief, responses to those messages. The skills of paraphrasing and reflection of feeling serve the counselor well in establishing an empathic base of understanding the client (Carkhuff, 1969). The counselor sees the world from the client's frame of reference and communicates that it has been understood. The goal is to move the client toward identifying and exploring crucial topics and feelings. During this early self-exploration phase, the counselor must be sensitive to signs of client stress or resistance and try to judge whether these arise from lack of accurate response or from being too accurate too quickly. As the counselor moves the client beyond exploration to self-understanding and action, advanced skills become more necessary.

Primary empathy gets at relevant feelings and meanings that are actually stated; the skill of *advanced empathy* gets at feelings and meanings that are hidden or beyond the immediate reach of the client (Egan, 2002). The most basic form of advanced empathy is to give expression and understanding to what the client has only implied. It challenges the client to take a deeper look at self.

Advanced empathy includes the identification of themes presented by the client. Feeling, behavioral, experiential, or combined themes may occur. Once the counselor recognizes the themes, the task is to communicate the relevant ones to the client in a way that will be heard and understood. The themes must be based solidly on an accurate understanding of the client's feelings, experiences, and behaviors and communicated as concretely as possible using the client's experiences and communication style.

The act of bringing together in a summary way relevant core material that the client has presented in only a fragmented way is part of advanced empathy. The counselor helps the client fill in the missing links in the information. When it becomes apparent that two aspects of client information are closely linked, this information should be shared, but the counselor must guard against premature speculation or unfounded linkages.

As the counselor explores the deeper, underlying meaning of an experience of the client, the skill of reflection of meaning can be used. It provides a way for the client to develop a new worldview and interpret old situations or information in new ways. Because information is always subject to individual interpretation (Gelatt, 1989), the counselor needs to reframe the situation, belief, or experience to help the client view it from a different perspective and also check out that the interpretation is correct.

Advanced empathy gets at more critical, deeper, and delicate issues and, therefore, puts the client under additional stress. To avoid overwhelming the client and evoking resistances, the counselor's empathetic responses should be tentative and cautious. Leads such as "From what you have said . . . ," "Could it be that . . . ," or "It seems like . . . ," may be most helpful.

Counselors may find it helpful to reflect back to clients what they see as the meaning of an experience.

Lisa: Finding out about his kids was somewhat of a surprise.

Counselor: It seems as if finding out about the children didn't matter as long as the two of you were together. Could it be that now the accumulation of surprises and your growing feelings of uneasiness are making you wonder about the relationship?

Self-Disclosure.   Hendrick (1988) and Peca-Baker and Friedlander (1987) have found that clients want to have information about their counselors. Sharing oneself can be a powerful intervention for making contact with clients, but it should not be an indiscriminate sharing of personal problems with clients (Egan, 2002; Sexton, Whiston, Bleuer, & Walz, 1997).

Self-disclosure is defined as any information counselors convey about themselves to clients (Cormier, Cormier, & Cormier, 1997; Cozby, 1973). It can generate a more open, facilitative counseling atmosphere, encourage client talk and additional trust, and create a more equal relationship. In some instances, a self-disclosing counselor may be perceived as more caring than one who does not disclose. At times, counselor self-disclosure can present a model for clients to increase their own levels of disclosure about events and feelings (McCarthy, 1982).

The use of self-disclosure as a skill involves consideration of timing, goals, genuineness, and appropriateness. Effective self-disclosure does not add another burden to an already burdened client (Egan, 2002), and it should not distract the client from his or her own problems (Sexton, Whiston, Bleuer, & Walz, 1997). The counselor must consider how the client will be able to benefit from the information shared.

Perhaps the most important type of self-disclosure is that which focuses on the relationship between you and your client. If you are having a difficult time listening to a client, for example, it could be useful to let them know that it is difficult. However, it helps to only describe your own feelings and reactions and not judge the client. It may be fairly easy for the counselor to self-disclose, but making the disclosure relevant to the client is the important and more complex task (Ivey, 1999). The counselor's self-disclosure should be genuine and fairly close in mood and content to the client's experience. As a counselor, you must remember that self-disclosure is appropriate only when it is genuine, benefits the client, and adds to client movement or understanding, and does not interfere with the counseling process or contribute to raised levels of client anxiety (Cormier, Cormier, & Cormier, 1997). For example,

> **Lisa:** I can't believe I was so dumb and gullible.
>
> **Counselor:** It seems like you shouldn't have been so trusting. I've found when I get in these situations that it is easy to beat myself up. I've learned instead to think of ways to be gentle on myself.

How willing are you to engage in appropriate and relevant self-disclosure? You become vulnerable when you share your own experiences, feelings, and reactions, yet can you expect your clients to become vulnerable in front of you if you rarely show them anything of yourself? Good self-disclosure is a kind of sharing that clients can use to grow, and it lets them know how you're perceiving and experiencing them (Sexton, Whiston, Bleuer, & Walz, 1997).

Most evidence indicates that a moderate amount of self-disclosure has more impact than too little or too much. Counselors who disclose very little risk being seen as aloof, weak, and role-conscious (Egan, 2002), whereas the counselor who discloses too much may be seen as lacking in discretion, being untrustworthy (Levin & Gergen, 1969), seeming preoccupied (Cozby, 1973), or needing assistance.

Confrontation.   Confrontation is a skill that is used when there are discrepancies, conflicts, or mixed messages being sent by the client. The mixed messages may occur between the verbal and nonverbal messages sent by the client or between two contradictory verbal messages. Egan (1975) describes confrontation as "the responsible unmasking of the discrepancies, distortions, games and smoke screens the client uses to hide both from self-understanding and from constructive behavioral change" (p. 158).

When confronting a client, the counselor must always exercise concern for the client's understanding of the challenge so that there will be client progress, not denial and flight. To do this effectively, the counselor must accurately reflect the situation. Using a tentative reflection is important, especially if it is early in the relationship. Consideration should also be given to the state of the client; an already distressed, confused, or disorganized client will not benefit from a confrontation. In fact, confrontation with such clients may add to their distress or confusion.

> **Lisa:**   I was really hurt when he told me that he hadn't filed for a divorce at all. All along I thought it had been done three years ago . . . I just can't leave him.
>
> **Counselor:**   You're feeling really torn. You're not legally married to him, yet something is keeping you in the relationship.

Confrontation should be done with care and may be more effective if done gradually. A gradual confrontation will give the client time to assimilate information. Good counselor practice demands a careful balance between confrontation followed by support in the form of primary empathy, positive regard, and respect (Ivey, Ivey, & Simek-Downing, 1987).

Immediacy.   The phenomenon of immediacy involves the counselor's sensitivity to the immediate situation and an understanding of what is occurring at the moment with clients (Pietrofesa, Hoffman, & Splete, 1984). It involves the ability to discuss directly and openly with another person what is happening in the "here and now" of an interpersonal relationship (Egan, 2002). This is sometimes referred to as "you-me" talk.

The use of immediacy combines the skills of confrontation and self-disclosure and requires the counselor to reveal feelings and/or challenge the client to deal more openly with his or her feelings. The purpose of immediacy responses is to help clients understand themselves more clearly, especially what is happening at that moment and how they are relating to the counselor in the session. The focus can be on the client, the relationship, or the clinician's own feelings and reactions (Murphy & Dillon, 2003). As interviews move more to the present tense, the counselor's presence in the interview becomes more powerful and important (Ivey, 1998), and the counselor is modeling a kind of behavior that clients can use to become more effective in all their relationships.

Counselors usually know what is happening in a session, but do not always act on it. Acting on what is happening at the moment is part of the phenomenon of immediacy. When either counselor or client has unverbalized thoughts or feelings that seem to be getting in the way of progress, the counselor should bring it up for discussion.

> **Lisa:**   I'm not exactly certain how to tell you about all the other messes in my life.
>
> **Counselor:**   It sounds like something is getting in the way of your trusting me to understand everything that's happened in your life.

There are many areas or issues in which the skill of immediacy might be used: trust, differences in style, directionless sessions, dependency, counterdependency, and attraction are areas where "you-me" talk might pay off (Egan, 2002). Other areas might include concern for the client's welfare, lack of follow-through on homework, and the client questioning the value of counseling.

Carkhuff (1969) suggests that the counselor ask, during the course of the interview, "What is the client trying to tell me that he or she can't tell me directly?" The answer lies embedded in the verbal and nonverbal behavior of the client. The skilled helper can uncover it and make it an "immediacy" topic.

In considering whether to use immediacy, the counselor should decide whether it is appropriate to focus the relationship on here-and-now concerns at this specific time. If so, then counselor-initiated leads will focus on the identification and communication of feelings. The counselor must seriously consider word choice; as in many other cases, a tentative statement may be more inviting of a client response.

ACTION SKILLS

The goal of counseling is to have a client come away from the process changed. This growth or change often entails the counselor and client working together on an action plan appropriate to the client's stated goals. These action plans should grow out of the counseling work itself and be based in part on the theoretical orientation of the counselor and what is considered the standards for practice in the profession. For instance, a behaviorally oriented counselor will be more inclined to use behavioral contracts and/or systematic desensitization. A transactional analysis therapist, in contrast, will focus on such concepts as ego states, game playing, and life scripts (Gladding, 2000).

It is important for the counselor to remember that the theoretical orientation is secondary to the development of effective core helping skills. These skills seem to be shared by all effective helpers and really address the quality of the interaction between the counselor and the client. With respect to the action phase, for example, Egan (2002) has suggested that the counselor must have skills to help clients choose effective strategies for change and maintain action-based change programs.

Termination Skills

The ending of a helping relationship can be either one of the most gratifying or one of the most difficult and frustrating aspects of the relationship. Termination may occur either by mutual agreement or prematurely (i.e., before all goals of counseling are met). When counselor and client agree that the goals of counseling have been accomplished, they may mutually agree that it is time to terminate. Sadness about parting and some client anxiety may be expected, but by exploring and sharing such feelings, each person is more likely to leave with a sense of growth and accomplishment because goals have been achieved. This process also gives them time to prepare for the future (Murphy & Dillon, 2003). It is important to leave time to discuss feelings about ending and, for a smooth termination, it is important for both individuals to know when the last session will occur (Meier & Davis, 1993).

Either the counselor or the client may initiate premature termination. When counselor-initiated termination occurs, the client needs to be informed as early as possible or reminded that only a limited number of sessions are available. Frequently, counselors may be in the position of terminating counseling prematurely in schools and agencies with session limits. On rare occasions, it may occur because of irreconcilable differences or perceived lack of commitment by the client. When the counselor does terminate the sessions, the reasons must be specified to the client. Most counselors agree that early termination by the counselor violates the premise that clients are in charge of solving their own problems, and early termination may lead to feelings of personal rejection in the client. These feelings should be dealt with before termination is complete. Referring the individual to another agency and/or keeping the door open for future sessions are sometimes helpful.

When the client prematurely terminates the sessions, the counselor should try to explore with the client the reasons for termination. Letting clients know that they are in charge of the decision to return in the future can be beneficial, as is the exploration of possible referral resources.

When termination is mutual or initiated by the counselor, several steps can benefit the outcome of the relationship (Ward, 1984). There should be discussion and evaluation of the goals that have already been reached. Closure issues and feelings need to be discussed and clients need to be prepared for similar happenings in the future. Clients should be prepared for self-reliance and continued self-help. Finally in the last session, discussion is likely to be lighter and more social. Okun (1996), for example, often shares a poster with the client that symbolizes the significance of the client's journey. The termination process should not focus on the generation of new problems or issues, but rather on an appreciation of the growth that has already occurred.

SUMMARY

The helping relationship consists of three relatively distinct phases: building the relationship, challenging the client to find ways to change, and facilitating positive action. Effective counselors have a number of similar characteristics, including high levels of self-awareness, empathy, genuineness, and respect for others, and an ability to use themselves as vehicles of change.

Effective counselors use attending skills (eye contact, body language, and vocal tone) and basic listening skills (client observation, encouraging, paraphrasing, summarizing, reflection of feeling, and open/closed questions) throughout the helping relationship. Counselor self-attending skills emphasize the importance of the person of the counselor in mediating the communications skills necessary in the helping relationship.

Counselors also need primary and advanced empathy skills as well as the challenging skills of confrontation, self-disclosure, and immediacy. These skills deepen the helping relationship and move the client toward therapeutic change. Counselor action skills facilitate behavior change around the client's stated goals for counseling. Finally, termination skills are needed to bring closure to, and end, the helping relationship.

ETHICS AND THE BEGINNING COUNSELOR

Being Ethical Right from the Start

MARK D. STAUFFER, M.S.
Oregon State University

SHARON E. ROBINSON KURPIUS, PH.D.
Arizona State University

Here you are, beginning your coursework in counseling as a new master's degree student. If you are like most of your classmates, you are feeling overwhelmed with all you have to learn to be a competent counselor. While excited about your first counseling session and about being helpful to clients, you realize that there is much you do not know about making good professional decisions based on ethical standards and state and federal law. The purpose of this chapter is to introduce you to the basic ethical concepts and legal guidelines that will influence your behavior as a counselor. In the end, it is up to counselors to integrate new knowledge and insight into their counseling practices. With that goal in mind, we hope to challenge preconceived notions and stimulate new understandings regarding right and wrong, moral and immoral, ethical and unethical, and legal and illegal.

This chapter is organized into several sections. First, a brief background is given, followed by an exploration of how motivations to enter the counseling profession influence behavior. The body of this chapter, however, is concerned with client rights and welfare, diversity in ethical considerations, confidentiality, and other real-life legal and ethical issues.

BACKGROUND: BASIC CONCEPTS

First, it will help to clarify what the word "ethics" means. MacKinnon (1998) stated that ethics is a branch of philosophy, specifically moral philosophy, and it "asks basic questions about the good life, about what is better and worse, about whether there is any objective right and wrong, and how we know it if there is" (p. 5). According to the *New Oxford American Dictionary* (2001), ethics are "moral principals that govern a person's or group's behavior." (p. 583). Another definition provided by the *American Heritage College Dictionary (2002)* states that ethics are, "The rules or standards governing the conduct of a person or the members of a profession" (p. 480). Whether spoken or unspoken, codified or not, individuals and groups have beliefs about what is right and wrong, about what is ethical and unethical. These beliefs motivate our day-to-day behaviors. On personal, familial, communal, and societal levels, ethics exist as part of the complex way humans create interpersonal boundaries and make choices. Ethical dilemmas arise that are not easily solvable because of the multifaceted nature of life. If you consider current debate on life and death issues such as abortion, capital punishment, and euthanasia, it is easy to understand that ethical practice is not a formula for behavior carved in stone but rather an arena in which dilemmas arise.

The dictionary definitions of ethics previously mentioned address those behaviors that are considered ethical by some group, such as a professional group. Joining and identifying as a member of a group usually signifies that you agree to adhere to the ethical standards established by the group. In the mental health profession, that group could be the American Counseling Association (ACA), the American Psychological Association (APA), or the National Board of Certified Counselors (NBCC), just to name a few. In this chapter, the discussion of ethics will be based on the guidelines provided by professional codes of ethics such as the ACA *Code of Ethics and Standards of Practice* (1995) (hereafter referred to as ACA *Code of Ethics*), and the APA *Ethical Principles of Psychologists and Code of Conduct* (2002) (hereafter referred to as APA *Ethical Principals*).

Another relevant distinction is the difference between mandatory ethics and aspirational ethics (Remley & Herlihy, 2001). Mandatory ethics are influenced and shaped in conjunction with legal standards. Aspirational ethics, as the name implies, promote ethical behavior based on broad-spectrum aspirations such as justice and respect for the rights and dignity of persons. Principles and virtues generally fall under aspirational ethics, though a difference does exist between the two. Virtue ethics derive from aspirations, so importance is placed on one's internal moral process and on "who one is." Principle ethics is concerned with "what one does" and implies a certain level of obligation to act in certain ways (Sim, 1997, p. 31). Meara, Schmidt, and Day (1996) suggested that integrating both virtue and principle ethics into professional ethical standards would improve counselor competence, especially in multicultural settings in which flexibility is a necessity.

Law enters into the picture when public safety, health, and welfare are jeopardized in some way. "Legal standards represent the minimum behavior society will tolerate of a professional" (Remley & Huey, 2002). There are criminal laws concerning specific actions that are crimes (e.g., statutory rape, fraud, tax evasion) and civil laws for disputes of personal interest to individuals, groups, or organizations, including the government. Three important types of law are legislative, constitutional, and common law. Law and legislative standards of conduct can be unclear, let alone "broad and open to situational interpretation" (Cottone & Tarvydas, 2003, p. 45). Legal statutes are created by legislative bodies of government and are interpreted by court systems. Such situational interpretations found in court verdicts become a type of guidepost or precedent for future cases. The creation, interpretation, and enforcement of laws are not separate from cultural values and biases and fluctuate with political tides. Law and judicial interpretation on the federal, state, district, and territorial level are most often in agreement with one another, but in some situations they do not agree. This is true for laws affecting the counseling profession.

Malpractice torts, a form of common law, are of particular importance to professional counselors. The United States is influenced by English common law, a type of law that validates commonly held principles that are difficult to codify and allows judges to rule over actions. An example is tort law that allows an individual to receive compensation for injury inflicted by others. Through an ad hoc judicial process, tort law establishes standards for appropriate behavior and assigns responsibility for wrong done to others. This usually applies to injurious actions caused by carelessness or neglect. A tort is not a crime. A malpractice tort, a law based on a general principle that holds professionals responsible for practices that harm clients, empowers judicial systems to establish what is unacceptable conduct for the professional (Remley & Herlihy, 2001).

Informed counselors also understand the relationship between what is ethical and what is legal. Dilemmas often arise because differences exist between ethical standards and law. Should one follow or break a law that is unethical by one's personal and professional standards? Counselors are sometimes forced to answer such questions with immediate action and then bear the consequences of their choices. At other times law and ethics do not interact directly for example, when an ethical standard is alegal, in other words no law covers the standard. This is true because law establishes the minimum requirements for counselor behavior. Examine the following categorical graph as an exploration of the possible interplay between law and ethics. Can you add a few of your own examples?

	LEGAL	**ILLEGAL**	**ALEGAL**
Unethical	Advertising as having unusual talents	Unwarranted disclosure of confidential information	Attempts to enhance "professional" skills at the expense of the client
Ethical	Reporting child abuse	Refusing to testify to prevent client harm	Providing some service to the profession without profit

It is best to stay up-to-date and aware of state and federal law, state licensing board requirements, and the ethical standards of professional counseling organizations. As a new practitioner, this may seem daunting and perhaps threatening; however, it helps to remember that these standards exist to protect both the counselor and the client. They foster higher standards for the professional practice of counseling.

CHOOSING TO BE A COUNSELOR: AN ETHICAL BEGINNING

What are your motivations for becoming a counselor? These motivations are often the root sources of a counselor's behavior, whether or not such behavior is legal or ethical. In 1972, Max Hammer in his classic chapter entitled "To Students Interested in Becoming Psychotherapists," discussed motivations for entering the helping profession. Hammer believed that persons often had wrong reasons, such as the need to be dominant, to be needed and loved, to be a voyeur on other's lives, to be an omnipotent healer, to escape one's own life, and to cure themselves by curing others. Corey, Corey, and Callahan (1998) indicate that the therapeutic process could be blocked when therapists use clients to fulfill their own needs to nurture others, to feel powerful or important, or to win acceptance, admiration, respect, or awe. Acknowledging that therapists have their own needs, Corey et al. remind us that "therapists should be aware of the danger of working primarily to be appreciated by others instead of working toward the best interests of their clients" (p. 36).

It is unethical when counselors use the counseling relationship to meet their own needs. The ACA's (1995) *Code of Ethics* states under A.5. Personal Needs and Values that "in the counseling relationship, counselors are aware of the intimacy and responsibilities inherent in the counseling relationship, maintain respect for clients, and avoid actions that seek to meet their personal needs at the expense of clients." It also stipulates that "Counselors refrain from offering or accepting professional services when their physical, mental or emotional problems are likely to harm a client or others." The APA *Ethical Principles* (2002) state, "Psychologists exercise reasonable judgment and take precautions to ensure that their potential biases, the boundaries of their competence, and the limitations of their expertise do not lead to or condone unjust practices" (Principle D: Justice).

Clients are often harmed by counselors who are meeting their personal needs through "multiple relationships" with their clients. Multiple relationship means that a counselor relates to a client in a professional role and concurrently or sequentially occupies several other professional or nonprofessional roles with the client (e.g., friend, intimate partner, peer, member in the same association). While not all multiple relationships are harmful or unethical, some can be devastating to clients.

The most devastating effects tend to occur when a counselor engages in some type of sexual relationship with a client, one type of multiple relationship unequivocally considered unethical in the counseling profession. Having a sexual relationship with a client is the most consistently violated ethical standard among psychologists and the second most frequently claimed violation against counselors (Herlihy & Corey, 1992; see also ASPPB, 2001). All codes for ethical professional behavior stress that sexual intimacies with clients are unethical. "Counselors must not engage in any type of sexual intimacies with current clients and must not engage in sexual intimacies with former clients within a minimum of two years after terminating the counseling relationship" (ACA, 1995, A.7. Sexual Intimacies with Clients). Two years may not be sufficient. In fact, a task force of the ACA Ethics Committee, which recommends code revisions to the ACA Ethics Committee and Governing Council for consideration of approval, has been discussing the possibility of a five-year minimum (M. Kocet, personal communication, July 24, 2003). At present, "counselors who engage in such a relationship after two years following termination have the responsibility to thoroughly examine and document that such relations did not have an exploitive nature" (ACA, 1995, A.7. Sexual Intimacies with Clients). As Robinson Kurpius (1997) pointed out, regardless of the reason for becoming involved intimately with a client, it is always unethical and often illegal. A client advocacy website posted the following comments from a client who was victimized by a therapist:

> It's really hard to explain how powerful the therapist seems to the client. He is supposed to be the expert, the trusted person who knows what is best for you. I wish I hadn't ignored my uneasiness and confusion when he started touching me. I guess I wanted him to take my pain away and to take care of me. It turned out that I was taking care of his needs most of the time. I was someone for him to confide in, to hold, to be flattered by. (Public Education Work Group, 1988, p. 1)

Counselors who are emotionally healthy do not need to engage in sexual relations with a client nor do they meet such types of personal needs through the counseling relationship. When sexual contact becomes part of a therapeutic relationship, the expectation of trust that is essential to the process of therapy is violated (Thoreson, Shaughnessy, Heppner, & Cook, 1993).

Research has demonstrated that a therapeutic alliance, also known as a working alliance, is one of the preeminent factors in therapeutic efficacy and outcome (Bordin, 1994; Hovarth & Symonds, 1991; Lustig, Strauser, Rice, & Rucker, 2002). An effective therapeutic alliance rests on the personal well-being and mental health of the counselor, which allows for bonding, collaborative goal setting, and task accomplishment. Emphasizing the personhood of the counselor, Hammer (1972) stated that, "the kind of person that the therapist is will be the primary determinant of whether or not there will be therapeutic results" (p. 3). Furthermore, he suggests that the client "probably cannot grow beyond the level of emotional health and maturity achieved by his [her] therapist" (p. 21). Hammer urged that,

> . . . to be really effective, the therapist needs to know from *personal experience* what the "path" is that leads from internal conflict and contradiction to liberation. If you do not know how to liberate yourself from an internal conflict, fear or pain, then you are not in a position to help others do it either. . . . What right does the therapist have to ask the patient to face his [her] rejected truths and anxiety and to take risks in terms of exposing himself [herself] and making himself [herself] vulnerable, if the therapist is not willing or able to do so? (p. 12)

Your first ethical responsibility is to be as emotionally healthy as possible, to be continually aware of how your own "unfinished business" could potentially influence your attempts to be helpful to others, and to seek professional help as soon as you are aware that some aspect of your own life may be infringing on your work as a counselor. Your competence is limited by your own self-awareness and psychological health and maturity (Corey et al., 1998; Robinson, 1988).

Counselors integrate and use principles as a way to monitor and reflect upon internal motivations and behaviors that guide action, especially when difficulties arise. Professional literature and organizations suggest that certain principles serve as guideposts for how counselors are expected to behave. Upon review of professional literature, Remley and Herlihy (2001) suggested six principles for counselors to consider:

1. Beneficence—do good, promote well-being and health
2. Nonmaleficence—do no harm, prevent harmful actions and affects
3. Autonomy—recognize and respect independence and self-determination
4. Justice—promote fairness and equality in dealings
5. Fidelity—be responsible to clients and honor agreements
6. Veracity—be truthful and honest in dealings

The APA *Code of Ethics* (2002) incorporates these foundational principles into its ethical code:

Principle A: Beneficence and Nonmaleficence

Principle B: Fidelity and Responsibility

Principle C: Integrity

Principle D: Justice

Principle E: Respect for People's Rights and Dignity

PROFESSIONAL RESPONSIBILITY

Counselors have a fiduciary responsibility to their clients. In the counseling relationship, counselors must be accountable for client welfare and rights. Furthermore, counselors have a responsibility to the public, to other professionals, to agencies and institutions in which they work, as well as to the counseling profession. Counselors must be competent, respect client rights, maintain confidentiality, promote welfare, and respect differences in clients.

The Importance of Multiculturalism in Ethics

Although EuroAmerican and "mainstream" values have thus far dominated our profession, our ethical standards are shifting toward a reflection of the diverse society within which we live. A revision of the ACA *Code of Ethics* is likely to occur in the near future. Kocet (personal communication, November 5, 2003), who is the head of the task force described earlier in this chapter, was asked about the central areas for consideration that influence the taskforce's recommendations to the ACA Ethics Committee and Governing Counsel. He stated that, "The multicultural component of the revision process is central to our work. We infuse cultural sensitivity to many different areas, such as counselor education/teaching, diversity in programs, dual and multiple relationships, etc." Multiculturalism "is the main charge of the code revision taskforce given to us by former ACA President David Kaplan." Continual effort on the part of professional organizations, educational institutions, counseling professionals, and students is necessary in order to represent, respect, and appropriately serve the diverse world within which we practice counseling.

A challenge in creating ethical standards is finding a set of standards that is specific enough to highlight proper behavior and yet broad enough so that the codes are neither myopic nor unrepresentative. Ibrahim (1996) suggested that the counseling profession seek a universalistic approach to ethical standards; that is, having ethical codes that reflect what is common across cultures while honoring the ethics of each individual culture (as cited in Atkinson, 2004). As of now, most ethical codes have aspirational goals related to multiculturalism that are broad and require the counselor to act from what the code implies rather than from specific behavioral guidelines. Cottone and Tarvydas (2003) commented that, "implied ethical standards are not enforceable in grievance processes, which limits the profession's ability to protect consumers from being harmed by incompetent multicultural practices" (p. 211).

Almost all beginning counselors understand that cultural insensitivity, racism, oppression, and discrimination are *wrong*. However, what often remains unclear is how such problems manifest in subtle ways in ordinary activity. For example, the guiding principles mentioned earlier may indeed be useful guideposts for behavior, and yet, if counselors assert autonomy as a core value when working with a client whose worldview holds collectivism as a central value, incompetent and harmful counseling may be the result. Also, a beginning counselor may not be aware of how much work and effort is truly necessary to be a culturally competent counselor.

There are several passages in both the APA (2002) Ethical Principles and the ACA (1995) Ethical Codes that state or convey the message that it is unethical to discriminate, harass, or demean clients on the basis of age, gender, gender identity, race, ethnicity, culture, color, marital status, national origin, spirituality/religion, sexual orientation, disability/ability, language, and socioeconomic status (APA, 2002; ACA, 1995). It is important to examine closely the above list. Ethical codes have made it clear that discrimination is not acceptable for any reason; however, listing is necessary to make clear the basis by which individuals discriminate. When considering each of these categories, what is your experience and that of others? What are your preconceived notions? What are your discriminatory tendencies? When looking at this issue it is important to recognize the issue on an individual, group, and universal level (see Sue & Sue, 2003). For example, we can recognize pain as a human phenomenon, but we must also try to understand how specific groups and individuals experience pain differently. Ethics codify bases by which counselors must not discriminate, but counselors should strive to understand and validate the variation, complexity, and severity of the underlying issues. There are individuals and groups who are yet to be acknowledged in their need for social justice. How is the above list not complete? For example, one form of discrimination that is often unrecognized is discrimination based on body fat/size. The following exemplifies why respect and awareness of difference is important:

> Sandy McBrayer, the 1995 national Teacher of the Year, tells of visiting an elementary school that was proud of its ethnic diversity and the integration achieved within the school's social milieu. The principal walked her to the newly built multipurpose "cafetorium" and ceremoniously pulled open the doors to reveal children of all colors eating, talking, and laughing together. As she entered, a contrasting scene near the door caught her eye. Separated from the rest of the student body were two large children who sat at a table eating their lunches in silence, staring directly ahead. They were not laughing. They were not talking. They were just bringing their forks to their mouths and down again, trying to be inconspicuous and to finish quickly. This day, they were too slow. As other children finished their meals and exited the cafetorium, they threw their uneaten food at the two children. (Loewy, 1998)

Based on a study of fifty-two professionals, Loewy (1994/1995) found that mental health counselors were no less biased than the general public in that they stereotyped fat persons negatively and thin people positively (as cited in Loewy, 1998). The list by which we discriminate grows as we recognize ways in which counselors think and behave in hurtful and harmful ways. So, one task of the counselor is to stop malevolent action and take responsibility for harmful behavior.

Beginning in the late 1960s, concern was raised over counseling someone who was of a different ethnicity without being competent to do so. According to Atkinson (2004), professional competence is still the quintessential ethical issue regarding multicultural counseling. Sue and Sue (2003) note, "From our perspective, mental health professionals have seldom functioned in a culturally competent manner. Rather, they have functioned in a monoculturally competent manner. . . . We submit that much of the current therapeutic practice taught in graduate programs derives mainly from experience and research with middle- to upper-class White folks" (pp. 9–10). This critique is not new to the field of counseling and comes from within the community of counselors. It is a statement that we hope challenges us to improve.

Though it will be discussed in more detail in Chapter 19, multicultural counseling competence involves many aspects of growth and training. Simply put, three components exist: (a) an awareness of one's cultural values and biases, (b) cultural awareness of your client's worldview, and (c) using culturally appropriate counseling practices (ACA, 2002). A skilled counselor will proactively grow, study, receive trainings, and seek supervision in order to become better able to meet the needs of diverse clients. Part of a counselor's job is to become secure with his/her own cultural identity, which many correlate with greater openness and acceptance of different cultural backgrounds (as noted in Semans & Stone Fish, 2000). Self-examination and becoming secure regarding one's heritage is hard especially when it means being aware of shortcomings and requires accountability for intolerance, oppression, racism, and elitism. A counselor is also called on to be "aware of and respect, cultural, individual, and role difference" (APA Principle E: Respect for People's Rights and Dignity). In order to move from being unaware to aware, it is important to have didactic and experiential knowledge of individual and group difference, especially in areas where most harm occurs and awareness is critically needed.

Is it ethical to apply counseling theories, techniques, and even ethical standards without consideration for a client's cultural background? It may be easy to answer "no" to this question; however, to truly practice such consideration is another task. Would your religious convictions or conceptualization of "appropriate" counseling prevent you from collaborating with a client's traditional healer?

The client's culture may also influence the boundaries of the counseling relationship. In some cultures, for example, sharing food or small gifts is a sign of respect. The APA *Code of Ethics* (2002) states, "A psychologist refrains from entering into a multiple relationship if the multiple relationship could reasonably be expected to impair the psychologist's objectivity, competence, or effectiveness in performing his or her functions as a psychologist, or otherwise risks exploitation or harm to the person with whom the professional relationship exists. Multiple relationships that would not reasonably be expected to cause impairment or risk exploitation or harm are not unethical" (3.05a, Multiple Relationships). The important point is that a skilled counselor considers client welfare and culture when using counseling interventions and applies consistent efforts to be competent.

Counselor Competence

This naturally brings us to the topic of counselor competence. The notion that it is unethical to practice beyond the limits of one's competence is widely accepted. Here are some important points drawn from the ACA *Code of Ethics* (1995) regarding competence:

1. Boundaries of competence:
   a. Provide only those services for which you are qualified.
   b. Represent accurately your professional qualifications.
2. Continuing education:
   a. Grow professionally through involvement in continuing education.
3. Qualified for employment:
   a. Only accept employment for which you are qualified.
   b. Hire for professional counseling positions only those that are qualified.
4. New specialty areas of practice:
   a. Practice in new specialty areas only after appropriate education, supervision, and experience.
   b. Take steps to insure nonmalefecience in using the new specialty area.
5. Impairment:
   a. Seek assistance in solving personal issues.
   b. Refrain from your professional services if a client may be harmed by your physical, mental, or emotional problems.

6. Ethical issues consultation:
   a. Consult with colleagues and other relevant professionals regarding ethical issues.
7. Monitor effectiveness:
   a. Make continual efforts to monitor and improve efficacy and outcomes. (C.2 Professional Responsibility)

To this list, we would add your responsibility as counselors-in-training to learn basic and advanced skills, to integrate academic study with supervised practice, to develop self-understanding and awareness, to receive training in multicultural competency, and to become intimately familiar with ethical codes of practice (ACA, 1995, C.1 Standards Knowledge; APA, 2002, Introduction and Applicability) and relevant laws influencing the profession.

As a student, it is your professors' responsibility not only to foster your learning of these aspects of competence but also to be aware of the "academic and personal limitations of students and supervisees that might impede performance." Counselor educators "assist students and supervisees in securing remedial assistance when needed, and dismiss from the training program supervisees who are unable to provide competent service due to academic or personal limitations" (ACA, 1995, F.2. Counselor Education and Training Programs). As a student, your competence is a shared responsibility between you and your training program. However, after you graduate and enter the professional world, it is your professional and ethical responsibility to remain competent.

In order to work within your boundary of competence, it is essential to recognize your strengths and weaknesses. Defining your areas of competence occurs through both subjective and external evaluation. The subjective component involves some self-evaluative measure, usually this includes critical and honest self-examination. Calling this subjective component an internal perspective, Robinson Kurpius and Gross (1996) cautioned counselors to do everything possible to gain the skills and knowledge basic to the profession. Counselors need to stretch their skills continually by reading and attending to new and developing trends, through attaining postgraduate education, and through attending seminars and workshops aimed at sharpening and increasing both knowledge and skill bases.

The objective component helps solidify your identification with the profession and verifies to the profession and the public that you have achieved some level of competence. The objective component typically includes completing appropriate graduate training, acquiring certifiable supervised direct-client counseling hours, and passing professional and state credentialing exams. One exam many choose to take is the National Counselor Examination (NCE) produced by the National Board for Certified Counselors (NBCC). The NCE is meant "to assess knowledge, skills, and abilities viewed as important for providing effective counseling services. The NCE is designed to be general in nature. It is intended to assess cognitive knowledge which should be known by all counselors regardless of their individual professional specialties" (NBCC, 2001a, p. 1).

The NCE (NBCC, 2001a, p. 1) tests the following content areas:

1. Human growth and development
2. Social and cultural foundations
3. Group work
4. Helping relationships
5. Career and lifestyle development
6. Appraisal
7. Research and program evaluation
8. Professional orientation and ethics

While taking an exam might indicate that you have a minimum knowledge base in the profession, it is not enough. The ACA *Code of Ethics* (1995) clearly states that "Counselors must practice only within the boundaries of their competence, based on their education, training, supervised experience, state and national professional credentials, and appropriate professional experience" (C.2.a., Boundaries of Competence). The APA *Ethical Principles* (2002) makes a similar statement and adds that

> Psychologists provide services, teach, and conduct research with populations and in areas only within the boundaries of their competence, based on their education, training, supervised experience, consultation, study, or professional experience. (Principle 2.01a, Boundaries of Competence)

Although APA requires training *or* experience, we would prefer to err on the conservative side and stress that both training and experience are essential for you to claim competence.

The ethical standards are quite clear regarding what you should do if you are not competent to treat a certain client problem. You are responsible for the welfare of the client; therefore, it is your professional duty to obtain for that client the best services possible—be it from you or from a professional colleague. Clients are not subjects for your trial-and-error learning but deserve the best professional care possible. Remember, your primary ethical obligation is nonmalificence—do no harm (Welfel & Kitchener, 1995). Here is a rough step-by-step procedure to assist you when you recognize that your competency is insufficient.

1. Limit your services and refer your client to other helping professionals that can meet the needs of your client in the given area and consider expanding your competence base. (NOTE: Refer to more than one professional so that the client has options and does not feel obligated to receive services from a specific professional.)
   or
2. Suspend your services and refer to several appropriate professionals while you receive sufficient training and supervision in the specialty area.
   or
3. Terminate professional responsibilities and make appropriate referrals.

   4. If there is no one to whom you can refer (which would be an exception rather
   than a common occurrence):
      a. Educate yourself with professional literature on the presenting problem.
      b. Seek supervision of your work with the client.

To be competent, continuing education is a never-ending requirement. The
words of this doctoral graduate are admirable, "When I decided that I was really
going to be a psychologist and do therapy, I attended every training seminar, conference, and workshop I could so that I could be really good at what I do." Like so
many graduates, be it from a master's or a doctoral program, he was not a finished
product upon receipt of his degree. In order to become truly proficient at what he
had chosen to do, he had to seek all the advanced didactic and experiential input he
could get. Only by continually growing himself is he comfortable offering his services to others.

One area of training for which students are often not adequately prepared is diagnosis. Typically, insurance companies will not pay for service unless the client has
a DSM-IV diagnosis. The ability to diagnose has been the subject of debate and
court proceedings. In Arizona, a social worker diagnosed a client as paranoid, a diagnosis which was confirmed by a consulting psychiatrist (*Cooke v. Berlin*, 1987). When
the client later killed a man and was diagnosed with atypical psychosis, the social
worker was sued by the victim's widow. Although the case was eventually settled out
of court, it left important questions unanswered. What is the appropriate scope of
practice of various mental health professionals? Had there been competent diagnosis,
would there have been an assessment of dangerousness resulting in a duty to warn?
When can one professional, especially an unlicensed one, provide information to another without the risk of malpractice? These questions all center on knowing the
limits of one's competence and behaving within the boundaries of professional training and experience.

A final area of professional competence that must be discussed is ethically presenting your services and credentials to the public. Most codes of ethics warn professionals against making false claims regarding expertise and qualifications and hold the
professional responsible for correcting misrepresentation of their qualifications by
others (ACA, 1995, C.4.a., Credentials Claimed). For example, if you are called "doctor" and you do not hold a doctoral degree in counseling or a related field, you must
correct this misrepresentation immediately. In advertising services, counselors "may
only advertise the highest degree earned which is counseling or a closely related field"
(ACA, 1995, C.3.a., Accurate Advertising). One cannot claim that he or she is a "can-
didate for" a degree. When trying to build a practice, client testimonials must be
avoided as well as implying unusual or one-of-a-kind abilities (Koocher & Keith-
Spiegel, 1998). Athough the ACA *Code of Ethics* (1995) does not mention use of media
to advertise services, the APA *Principles* (2002) state that a paid advertisement must be
acknowledged or "clearly recognizable" as such (5.02c, Statements by Others).

The Federal Trade Commission has granted considerable freedom for advertising as a result of the *Goldfarb v. Virginia State Bar* (1975) ruling. How and if you
advertise your services will require you to weigh carefully what is legally permitted

with what is ethically acceptable. Regardless of the area of service being discussed, you are the first-line judge of your professional competence. Although credentialing bodies, professional organizations, and state legislative bodies may set standards for practice, you must be the most critical evaluator of your ability to provide service. This often becomes quite a challenge when one's living depends on having clients who will pay for service. Remaining ethical is not always the easy choice.

CLIENT RIGHTS AND WELFARE

When clients enter a counseling relationship, they have a right to assume that you are competent. In addition, they have certain rights, known as client rights, as well as responsibilities. These rights have their foundation in the Bill of Rights, particularly the First and Fourth Amendments of the Constitution of the United States, which are freedom of religion, speech, of the press, and right of petition and freedom from unreasonable searches and seizures, respectively. The concepts of confidentiality, privileged communication, and informed consent are based on the Fourth Amendment, which guarantees privacy. Privacy has been defined as "the constitutional right of an individual to decide the time, place, manner, and extent of sharing oneself with others" (Corey et al., 1998, p. 158).

Privacy and Confidentiality

Confidentiality and Privileged Communications.   The concept of privacy is the foundation for the client's legal right to privileged communication and the counselor's responsibility to hold counseling communications confidential. Confidentiality is a professional concept. Privileged communication is a legal term referring to a right held by clients to prevent therapeutic information from entering into a legal proceeding. This means that clients, not counselors, have control over who has access to what they have said in therapy and that they are protected from having their communication disclosed in a court of law. Confidentiality is so important that both the APA (2002) *Ethical Principles* and the ACA (1995) *Code of Ethics* devote an entire section to privacy and confidentiality. However, a client's confidential communications may not be privileged in a court of law unless the mental health professional is legally certified or licensed in the state in which he or she practices.

Some states grant the clients of state certified or licensed mental health professionals (i.e., psychologists, professional counselors, marriage and family therapists) the right of privileged communications. Some states grant clients this right only when engaged in therapy with certain helping professionals (e.g., psychologists but not professional counselors). On a federal level, in 1996, the U.S. Supreme Court ruled in *Jaffee v. Redmond* that communication was indeed privileged communication for "psychotherapists," a term which places emphasis on a professional providing a type of counseling rather than on a professional title (i.e., psychologist, social worker, professional counselor). It is a landmark case in that it was liberal in its application of the term psychotherapist. Since then, privileged communication was given to a client of a licensed clinical social worker (see Cottone & Tarvydas, 2004). HIPAA's Privacy Rule, discussed later in this section, may eventually influence a definition of who is a psychotherapist because of its widespread acceptance. It defines the term "psychotherapy notes" as, "notes recorded (in any medium) by a health care provider who is a mental health professional documenting or analyzing the contents of conversation during a private counseling session or a group, joint, or family counseling session and that are separated from the rest of the individual's medical record" (USDHHS, 2003, p. 9). As of now, much is still uncertain regarding privileged communication for clients who seek services of certain mental health professionals in various states.

Outside of eligibility concerns, in order for communication to be privileged, four conditions must be met.

1. Communication must originate in confidence that it will not be disclosed.
2. Confidentiality must be essential to the full and satisfactory maintenance of the relationship.
3. In the opinion of the greater community, the relationship must be one that should be sedulously fostered, or in other words, noted by care and persistent effort.
4. Injury to the relationship by disclosure of the communication must be greater than the benefit gained by the correct disposal of litigation regarding the information. (Schwitzgebel & Schwitzgebel, 1980)

If, as a counselor you can claim these four conditions and your professional licensure or service makes your clients eligible, your clients' communications are not only confidential, but also they are privileged and, therefore, are protected from being disclosed in a court of law. One must remember, however, that there is always a balance between a client's right to privacy and society's need to know.

In spite of the importance given to confidentiality and privileged communication, Pope, Tabachnick, and Keith-Spiegel (1987) reported that 62 percent of psychologists in a national survey indicated that they had unintentionally violated a client's confidentiality and 21 percent had intentionally violated a client's confidentiality. These alarming statistics suggest that mental health professionals are at risk for violating this core ethical principle. Therefore, adept mental health professionals are acutely aware of the professional standards regarding confidentiality and of their state's laws governing privileged communication. For example, in most states, if personnel working in the mental health professional's office breach a client's confidentiality, the professional is guilty of breaching the confidentiality. Secretaries and other staff who have access to client records are considered extensions of certified/licensed mental health professionals.

HIPAA and the "Privacy Rule."   In the late 1990s, debate and concern over the privacy of health services has increased because of advances in technology and the shift to managed health care. For example, service providers faxing entire health records to insurance agencies pose threats to insured patients. The U.S. Department of Health and Human Services created the Health Insurance Portability and Accountability Act (HIPAA). It affects the job task requirements of counselors, especially those working with health insurance companies. This complex federal initiative was produced by the U.S. Department of Health and Human Services (USDHHS). The primary motivation for the enactment was to ensure the privacy of those that seek health services while at the same time allowing for client information to move freely to provide the best level of care for individuals seeking professional help. This mandate also sought to improve how consumers understand and manage their use of personal health information (USDHHS, 2003).

The Department of Health and Human Service's "Privacy Rule," formally titled *standards for privacy of individually identifiable health information*, focuses on the use and disclosure of client information termed, "protected healthcare information (PHI)." This is information on any past, present, or future mental or physical health including payment information of clients. Since its final revision in 2002, movement toward compliance has posed new legal and ethical considerations for counselors and other helping professionals. Certain health service providers under the umbrella of this health regulation are called "covered entities"; often helping professionals such as counselors, psychologists, and social workers fall into this category when, "they hold or transmit [PHI] . . . in any form or media, whether electronic, paper, or oral" (USDHHS, 2003, p. 3).

As a division of the Department of Health and Human Services, the Office of Civil Rights (OCR) has the responsibility for HIPAA implementation through the encouragement of voluntary compliance and enforcement through civil monetary penalties (USDHHS, 2003). Currently, agencies including individual providers of mental health services rely or consult with "HIPAA experts" on how to conduct business. Futhermore, the widespread adoption of these privacy standards will affect all groups of helping professionals. The nuances involved in operationalizing HIPAA are extensive; for this reason a detailed and thorough explanation is beyond the scope and purpose of this chapter. Some important aspects of the privacy rule are presented, however.

The privacy rule applies to information that might identify or could be used to identify a person. A counselor may disclose information to a client or to other entities with client authorization. Difficulty arises when the disclosure of information poses potential harm to the client. For example, if a client wants to release psychotherapy notes to an unqualified and untrained helper. There are also specified uses and disclosures of identifiable information without authorization (e.g., treatment, payment, health operations (e.g., scheduling), quality assurance). However, in all cases, use and disclosure of health information should be limited to the "minimum necessary" to provide services (USDHHS, 2003, p. 10). So, it may mean counselors only transmit sections; for example, parts of pages or pages where information has been blacked out in the copying process.

The Privacy Rule addresses protected information related to counseling and psychotherapy. Except in certain circumstances, individuals have the right to review and obtain a copy of their protected health information in a counselor's "designated record set." The designated record set is that group of records that is "used to make decisions about individuals" (USDHHS, 2003, p. 12). The rule makes an exception for "psychotherapy notes." A psychotherapy note is descriptive of a relatively smaller portion of most mental health records. It does not include the following: "medication prescription and monitoring, counseling session start and stop times, the modalities and frequencies of treatment furnished, results of clinical tests, and any summary of the following items: diagnosis, functional status, the treatment plan, symptoms, prognosis, and progress to date" (USDHHS, 2003, p. 9). Agencies should have policies to distinguish a psychotherapy note from other records and should have separate storage for each type of record. A counselor must obtain client authorization for specific uses and disclosures of psychotherapy notes. Some important exceptions exist: for use in treatment whereby the originator of the note is the sole user; to conduct training programs in order to instruct and supervise students, interns, and other trainees; to defend oneself in legal proceedings activated by a client; to facilitate HHS checks for compliance; to avert a "serious and imminent threat to public health or safety; and for lawful oversight of a counselor by a health oversight agency" (USDHHS, 2003, p. 9).

The privacy rule requires professionals to inform, if not educate, clients about their privacy rights and about privacy procedures and practices used in the counseling agency. Professionals inform clients by notice. Notices explain and provide examples of how protected information is used, disclosed, amended, inspected, and copied including exceptions and prohibitions. Notices also inform clients regarding their right to restrict, revoke, and receive an accounting of disclosures. So a client may request that an authorization be valid for only ten days and that he or she be informed if the transmission is completed. A general notice should also be posted in reasonably clear view on the counseling premises. Furthermore, notices are given to clients upon intake, promptly mailed to clients when initial communications are by phone, or sent electronically (in a proper format) when providing services online. In the case of emergency situations, a privacy notice is given as soon as practicably possible. Written notices have headings similar to this example: NOTICE OF PRIVACY PRACTICES: THIS NOTICE DESCRIBES HOW INFORMATION ABOUT YOU MAY BE USED AND DISCLOSED AND HOW YOU CAN GET ACCESS TO THIS INFORMATION. PLEASE REVIEW IT CAREFULLY. Agencies with websites should post a notice of their privacy practices on the site. Furthermore, counselors make a "good faith" effort to obtain from clients in writing an acknowledgment that they received a privacy notice and document efforts made when written acknowledgment is not possible (USDHHS, 2003).

Authorization forms for use and disclosure of information should be in specific terms and allow the client to understand their privacy rights. "All authorizations must be in plain language, and contain specific information regarding the information to be disclosed or used, the person(s) disclosing and receiving the information, expiration, right to revoke in writing, and other data." (USDHHS, 2003, p. 9). According to Robinson Kurpius (1997), when clients give authorization, they should be informed about what exact information is being released, to whom, for what purpose, and the time period for which the signed consent for release is valid. This is in keeping with both APA and ACA ethical guidelines. Under the privacy rule, an agency providing covered health services must also set up procedures for the use of forms for "routine" disclosure and create criteria to follow when unusual, non-routine disclosures of information are required. Counselors may not demand that clients give authorization for the release of information in order to receive treatment, except in certain limited circumstances (USDHHS, 2003).

HIPAA stipulates that training on privacy practices should be an ongoing procedure for the entire agency *workforce.* This covers how information is handled and who should handle what types of protected information. The privacy rule requires that classifications of personnel related to information access be clarified on the basis of workplace role and then operationalized. For example, an agency database should not allow an office manager access to psychotherapy notes; he/she should only be able to access the minimum information necessary to effectively perform his or her job (e.g., schedule clients, bill insurance). Agencies should also appoint or identify a "privacy officer," incorporate privacy protocol and safeguards, and instruct clients on greivance procedures (USDHHS, 2003, p. 14).

In addition to the above information related to privacy, Snider (1987) makes some very practical and useful suggestions for protecting written material such as case notes and test data. He stresses that the absolute minimum storage is a locked file cabinet—not just a locked office door. If a mistake is made while writing case notes, a single line should be drawn through the written text and initialed and dated by the counselor. Text should never be erased or whited out.

Exceptions to Confidentiality.   There are three global issues that require one to breach confidentiality. In cases of minors, counselors have both a legal and ethical responsibility to protect them from " . . . future harm of continued abuse or neglect and to protect children who are insufficiently autonomous to act on their own behalf" (Sattler, 1990, p. 105). Minors are usually all individuals under the age of 18; however, some states recognize emancipated minors who are 16 or older. Counselors should know their state laws that apply to minors and breaching confidentiality (Lawrence & Robinson Kurpius, 2000). Every state has passed a law mandating the reporting of child abuse. Regardless of the counselor's personal feelings about helping a client to overcome his or her abusive behavior, the abuse must be reported. Society has deemed that knowing of and stopping the child abuse outweigh the abuser's right to privacy. Differences exist among states, so counselors should check with their state protective service for information on what is specifically meant by abuse.

Many states also require that counselors report instances of abuse, neglect, or exploitation of incapacitated and vulnerable adults. In Arizona, incapacitated is defined as "an impairment by reason of mental illness, mental deficiency, mental disorder, physical illness or disability, advanced age, chronic use of drugs, chronic intoxication, and other causes to the extent that the person lacks sufficient understanding or capacity to make or communicate responsible decisions" and a vulnerable adult is defined as, "an individual who is eighteen years of age or older who is unable to protect himself from abuse, neglect or exploitation by others because of a physical or mental impairment" (Arizona Revised Statute 46–451).

Finally, privilege is automatically waived when a client presents a "clear and imminent danger" to self or others (ACA, 1995, B.1.c. Exceptions). A well-known court case that established such mandatory disclosure is *Tarasoff v. Board of*

Regents of the University of California (1974, 1976). In this case, a young graduate student, Poddar, had been working with a university psychologist regarding his depression and anger resulting from being rejected by a female peer, Tatiana Tarasoff. He told the psychologist about his intent to buy a gun. The psychologist notified the campus police both verbally and in writing about his concerns that Poddar was dangerous and should be taken to a community mental health facility. The police interviewed Poddar and released him from custody. The psychologist's supervising psychiatrist decided that the letter to the police and selected case notes should be destroyed. Shortly thereafter, Poddar shot and stabbed Tatiana to death. The California Supreme Court held that "once a therapist does in fact determine, or under applicable professional standards reasonably should have determined, that a patient poses a serious danger of violence to others, he bears a duty to exercise reasonable care to protect the foreseeable victims of that danger" (Tarasoff, 1976). This has been interpreted as the duty to protect or the duty to warn. In these instances, it is the counselor's overriding responsibility to protect an intended, identifiable victim from harm that could result from a client's actions.

Other instances when the privilege is typically lost include when a client introduces his or her mental condition as an element in a court case, when the mental stability of either spouse is introduced in a child custody case, when the counselor is working for the court such as in conducting a court-ordered examination, when the client is suing the counselor, and when the counselor believes that the client is in need of immediate hospitalization for a mental disorder. It is strongly suggested that at the onset of therapy, counselors inform clients about the limits of confidentiality and the specific instances when confidentiality must be breached. Clients can then make informed decisions about what they say in therapy.

Confidentiality and HIV.   Controversy exists in the general public over the right of confidentiality of AIDS patients. Counselors face a dilemma between protecting the right of confidentiality and a duty to warn when working with clients who do not inform their sexual partners of their medical condition. The APA (1991) took a leadership role in this area, and at the 1991 annual meeting, the Council of Representatives passed the following resolutions:

1. A legal duty to protect third parties from HIV infection should not be imposed.
2. If, however, specific legislation is considered, then it should permit disclosure only when the provider knows of an identifiable third party who the provider has a compelling reason to believe is at significant risk for infection; the provider has a reasonable belief that the third party has no reason to suspect that he or she is at risk; and the client/patient has been urged to inform the third party and has either refused or is considered unreliable in his/her willingness to notify the third party.
3. If such legislation is adopted, it should include immunity from civil and criminal liability for providers who, in good faith, make decisions to disclose or not to disclose information about HIV infection to third parties.

This resolution provides concrete guidelines for breaching the confidentiality of clients with AIDS. The ACA *Code of Ethics* (1995, B.1.d. Contagious, Fatal Diseases) addresses this same issue,

> A counselor who receives information confirming that a client has a disease commonly known to be both communicable and fatal is justified in disclosing information to an identifiable third party, who by his or her relationship with the client is at a high risk of contracting the disease. Prior to making a disclosure the counselor should ascertain that the client has not already informed the third party about his or her disease and that the client is not intending to inform the third party in the immediate future.

Robinson Kurpius (1997) points out that "unless there is an identifiable victim and the client refuses to behave in a manner that protects this person, the covenant of confidentiality should not be broken" (p. 10). As Koocher and Keith-Spiegel (1998) noted, in cases such as this, good clinical judgment is essential in making decisions regarding duty to protect.

Confidentiality and Subpoenas.   It would be remiss not to discuss subpoenas and how counselors should respond to them in an attempt to protect a client's confidentiality. Here is an important point to consider when dealing with legal involvement related to counseling: if you are not trained as a legal professional then seek legal counsel. For example, how will you know whether a subpoena is valid or not? When a counselor divulges information inappropriately in what seems to be a valid circumstance, he or she is still responsible for breaches of confidentiality even when done with good intention. If you are feeling unsure about a legal matter, seek help from a trusted or highly recommended legal expert.

Regardless of the type of subpoena received—whether it is a (typical) subpoena that requires your presence at court or for a deposition or it is a subpoena duces tecum that requires you to bring your records with you—you should initially claim the privilege for your client (Schwitzgebel & Schwitzgebel, 1980). This forces the court or your client's attorney to require you to breach confidentiality. You then have the option of refusing to testify or to produce your records, in which case you will most likely be ruled in contempt and have to go to jail. In these rare instances, you need to find a personally acceptable balance among what the law requires, what is ethically appropriate, and what you find to be morally correct. Again, this is a personal decision that only you can make because you will be the one experiencing the consequences of your decision.

Informed Consent

This brings us to a discussion of informed consent. According to Everstine et al. (1980) three elements must be present for informed consent to be legal.

1. Competence—requires that the person granting the consent is able to engage in rational thought to a sufficient degree to make competent decisions

about his or her life. Minors cannot give informed consent, and consent must be sought from their parents or legal guardian. Minors give informed assent.

2. Informed—requires that the individual is given the relevant information about the procedures to be performed in a language that he or she can understand.

3. Voluntariness—requires that consent is given freely by the client. All three elements must be present for consent to be informed.

The ACA (1995) *Code of Ethics* is very specific with respect to what should be disclosed to clients in order for them to give informed consent:

> When counseling is initiated, and throughout the counseling process as necessary, counselors inform clients of the purposes, goals, techniques, procedures, limitations, potential risks and benefits of services to be performed, and other pertinent information. Counselors take steps to ensure that clients understand the implications of diagnosis, the intended use of tests and reports, fees, and billing arrangements. Clients have the right to expect confidentiality and be provided with an explanation of its limitations, including supervision and/or treatment team professionals; to obtain clear information about the case records; to participate in the ongoing counseling plans; and to refuse any recommended services and be advised on the consequences of such refusal. (A.3.a., Disclosure to Clients)

The APA (2002) *Ethical Principles* requires a fourth element—that "Psychologists appropriately document written or oral consent, permission, and assent" (3.10.d., Informed Consent).

If you are asked by a client to disclose to a third party information revealed in therapy, have the client sign an informed consent form before making any disclosure. You may be surprised to learn that counselors are not even permitted to respond to inquiries about whether they are seeing a person in therapy—even the client's name and status in counseling are confidential, unless the client has granted permission for this information to be released.

One exception is when your services are being paid through an insurance company or health maintenance organization (HMO). This automatically grants the insurance company or HMO limited access to information regarding the client. The client needs to be made aware of the parameters of the information that will be shared prior to beginning therapy. Again, it is evident how important it is to have potential clients sign an informed consent form before they become clients. Finally, HIPAA guidelines are to be considered in how information is handled by counselors and office staff when dealing with clients using insurance benefits to retain services.

Right to Treatment

Having clients sign informed consent forms implies that they have a right to receive or refuse treatment. Many court cases have been based on the right-to-treatment issue. In the early 1970s, *Wyatt v. Stickney* (1974) was the first case in which the right to treatment was ruled a constitutionally protected right. The case was filed against the state of Alabama on behalf of mentally disabled institutionalized patients who were being kept confined under conditions of psychological and physical deprivation. There was one physician for every 2,000 patients, making adequate care impossible. The court ruled that involuntarily committed patients have a constitutional right to receive "such individual treatment as will give each of them a realistic opportunity to be cured or to improve." In addition, the court required the institution to have individualized treatment plans developed by qualified mental health professionals for each patient. Furthermore, committed patients have the right to their own clothing, to receive minimal pay for labor performed, to receive mail, to exercise several times per week, and to have an appropriate physical environment in which to live.

In *Rogers v. Orkin* (1980) and in *Rennie v. Klein* (1981), courts ruled that clients have the right to refuse treatment. In *Rogers*, the court ruled that the "power to produce ideas was fundamental to our cherished right to communicate." The court indicated that the right to refuse medication and seclusion was a Fourth Amendment right but cited several state interests that can overrule a person's right to this privacy: police power—the right of the state to protect others from harm; *parens patriae*—the duty of the state to prevent the patient's condition from deteriorating; and consideration of the financial costs of operating facilities that may result from extended hospitalization (Levenson, 1989). *Rennie* held that the right to refuse medication could only be overruled under due process, except in an emergency. All of these court cases have provided us with parameters for client rights with respect to treatment issues. Counselors should be constantly alert to the legal issues surrounding this very important client right.

Client Welfare

The preceding discussion rests on the premise that the counselor's primary obligation is to protect the welfare of the client. The ACA (1995) *Code of Ethics* states that "the primary responsibility of counselors is to respect the dignity and to promote the welfare of clients" (A.1.a., Primary Responsibility). A similar statement is made in the *Preamble* to the APA (2002) *Ethical Principles*, specifically stating that it has "as its goals the welfare and protection of the individuals and groups." Inappropriate multiple relationships, counselors' personal needs, and conflicts between employing institutions and client needs all influence client welfare. Inappropriate multiple relationships and counselor needs have already been discussed; therefore, attention needs to be given to the third concern.

Employer policy and client needs may contrast drastically. For instance, suppose you work in a prison setting and an inmate tells you that he or she is using drugs, which is against all prison rules. What are you going to do? Or imagine that you are a school counselor and a 15-year-old tells you that he or she is using drugs. What is in the best interests of each of these clients? How will your behavior affect your relationship with each client, with your future clients, and your position within the institution? Similar conflicts may arise when you are employed by a business or industry and the needs of the employee/client may not be in agreement with the goals of the business (Newman & Robinson, 1991). To whom do you owe loyalty? To the employer who signs your paycheck or to the employee/client? These questions are not easy to answer nor is there always one right answer. In cases such as these, you must decide what is ethical based on the most current ethical guidelines and what is right or wrong for you personally.

Thus far, the discussion has focused on individual clients. An additional set of guidelines come into play when you are doing group work or working with a couple or family. In a group setting, special issues include qualifications of the group leader, informed consent when more than the group leader will be participating in therapy, the limits to confidentiality and to privileged communication when third parties are present in therapy, and understanding how individuals will be protected and their growth nurtured in a group situation. Unlike individual counseling, clients who want to be involved in a group experience need to be screened before being accepted into a group. This screening not only ensures that the client is appropriate for the group but also protects other group members from a potentially dysfunctional group member.

It is evident that client welfare, whether in individual therapy or in group work, rests squarely on the shoulders of the counselor. The counselor must be cognizant of the various aspects of the counseling relationship that can jeopardize the client's welfare and take the steps necessary to alleviate the situation. Robinson Kurpius and Gross (1996) offer several suggestions for safeguarding the welfare of each client:

1. Check to be sure that you are working in harmony with any other mental health professional also seeing your client.
2. Develop clear, written descriptions of what clients may expect with respect to therapeutic regime, testing and reports, record keeping, billing, scheduling, and emergencies.
3. Share your professional code of ethics with your clients and prior to beginning therapy discuss the parameters of a therapeutic relationship.
4. Know your own limitations and do not hesitate to utilize appropriate referral sources.
5. Be sure that the approaches and techniques utilized are appropriate for the client and that you have the necessary expertise for their utilization.
6. Consider all other possibilities before establishing a counseling relationship which could be considered a harmful dual relationship.
7. Evaluate the client's ability to pay and when the payment of the usual fee would create a hardship. Either accept a reduced fee or assist the client in finding needed services at an affordable cost.
8. Objectively evaluate client progress and the therapeutic relationship to determine if it is consistently in the best interests of the client.

We would be remiss if we ended the discussion of client welfare without mentioning the problems that arise from our technological society. In this age of computers and the Internet, client confidentiality is continually at risk because anyone sophisticated in computer hacking can tap into insurance records, university records, and so on. Testing by computer has become popular. More and more computer-based interventions are being developed to address issues such as career indecision, lack of assertive behaviors, and irrational beliefs. The question that must be raised, however, is how secure are individual results and personal information? We must also ask ourselves whether computer testing and even computer interactive counseling are best for our clients. What about the all-important human element? Again, these questions are not easy to answer. Each of us must struggle with what we are told in the ethical guidelines, our own comfort level with the privacy afforded or not afforded by using computers, and how all of this affects client welfare.

The increasing use of the Internet to provide counseling interventions compounds such ethical questions. Indeed, the "information highway" poses many new ethical concerns that were not present just a decade ago (Cottone & Tarvydas, 2003). In 1999, the ACA Governing Council approved guidelines for computer use. Here are a few important points conveyed in the council's document:

1. Counselors must consider the appropriateness of online counseling and explain the potential limitations of such services.
2. Counselors must explain the limits of confidentiality particular to online counseling.
3. Counselors must explain and notify clients about certain aspects of how confidential information is handled (e.g., who has access to the counselor's computer).
4. Counselors must only use "secure" sites for confidential information and may either use secure or insecure sites for general information.
5. "Professional counselors identify foreseeable situations in which confidentiality must be breached in light of the law in *both* the state in which the client is located and the state in which the professional counselor is licensed" (A4).
6. "Professional counselors identify clients, verify identities of clients, and obtain alternative methods of contacting clients in emergency situations" (B3).
7. There are certain circumstances in which a client must waive a right to priviledged communication because of the nature of online services.

Client Rights—Summary.   The rights of your clients are many and varied. Perhaps one of the best statements regarding client rights can be found at the National Board for Certified Counselors Web Site. The NBCC (2001b) lists the following client rights and responsibilities:

YOUR RIGHTS AS A CONSUMER
- *Be informed of the qualifications of your counselor: education, experience, professional counseling certification(s), and license(s).*
- *Receive an explanation of services offered, your time commitments, fee scales, and billing policies prior to receipt of services.*
- *Be informed of the limitations of the counselor's practice to special areas of expertise (e.g., career development, ethnic groups) or age group (e.g., adolescents, older adults,).*
- *Have all that you say treated confidentially and be informed of any state laws placing limitations on confidentiality in the counseling relationship.*

- *Ask questions about the counseling techniques and strategies and be informed of your progress.*
- *Participate in setting goals and evaluating progress toward meeting them.*
- *Be informed of how to contact the counselor in an emergency situation.*
- *Request referral for a second opinion at any time.*
- *Request copies of records and reports to be used by other counseling professionals.*
- *Receive a copy of the code of ethics to which your counselor adheres.*
- *Contact the appropriate professional organization if you have doubts or complaints relative to the counselor's conduct.*
- *Terminate the relationship at any time.*

YOUR RESPONSIBILITIES AS A CLIENT

- *Set and keep appointments with your counselor. Let him or her know as soon as possible if you cannot keep an appointment.*
- *Pay your fees in accordance with the schedule you pre-established with the counselor.*
- *Help plan your goals.*
- *Follow through with agreed upon goals.*
- *Keep your counselor informed of your progress toward meeting your goals.*
- *Terminate your counseling relationship before entering into arrangement with another counselor.*

Notice that the consumer/client responsibilities require the counselor to have provided the client with informed consent at the beginning of therapy. Also note that the client cannot behave unethically—only counselors can make that mistake.

SUMMARY

Before you know it, you will be graduating and entering the professional world of counselors, fondly known as the "real world." If you are like most mental health professionals, you will quickly find yourself involved in situations in which you will be uncertain as to what is ethical and what is not. This is not unusual, and the best advice we can give you is to know the ethical guidelines, seek supervision, and consult with colleagues, professional ethics committees, and your ethics professor.

Some situations which typically cause confusion, according to research by Pope et al. (1987), include: performing forensic work for a contingency fee; accepting goods (rather than money) as payment; earning a salary which is a percentage of client fees; avoiding certain clients for fear of being sued; counseling a close relative or friend of a current client; sending holiday greeting cards to your clients; giving personal advice on the radio or television program; engaging in a sexual fantasy about a client; limiting treatment notes to name, date, and fee; inviting clients to an office open house; and allowing a client to run up a large, unpaid bill. From the information provided in this chapter, you should now have some idea about the ethical approach to each of these. But often the ethical answer is not crystal clear and surrounding circumstances need to be considered.

Robinson and Gross (1989) surveyed 500 members of the American Mental Health Counselor's Association and found that those who had not had a course in ethics had a particularly difficult time recommending ethical behaviors in response to a series of case vignettes. As a result, Robinson and Gross strongly recommend increased graduate-level education focusing on professional ethics. Just knowing the codes is not enough; students need experience applying the ethical guidelines to case scenarios and need to discuss the moral reasoning behind their decision making.

More and more clients are suing their counselors and psychologists for malpractice. Insurance rates for mental health professionals are soaring, and insurance companies/HMOs often want to settle out of court rather than endure the costs of fighting to prove your innocence. This may leave you in a vulnerable position. Your best defense is to behave as ethically as possible while doing everything in your power to promote the best interests of your client.

Most of you have entered this profession in order to help others while earning a living for yourself. We believe counseling is a noble profession, especially if you give your best to each of your clients by being aware of when you are burned out, stressed, or just plain tired and by limiting your contact with clients when your personal problems could interfere with the quality of your help. If you keep the ethical codes in mind at all times; strive to be as mentally, emotionally, spiritually, and physically healthy as possible; obtain a thorough graduate education that emphasizes both knowledge and practice; and seek advanced training and supervision when you are in the "real world," then you should be a benefit to your clients and to your profession. With those last tidbits of advice, we welcome you to your journey and evolution as a counselor.

CHAPTER FOUR

RESEARCH AND WRITING IN COUNSELING

TERESA M. CHRISTENSEN, PH.D.
University of New Orleans

What is research? How does research apply to counseling? How do I, as a beginning counseling student, incorporate research into what I am learning about counseling and my writing? What steps do I take to effectively search databases, construct literature reviews, and conduct research? At first glance, answers to these questions may seem rather simplistic and obvious; however, such issues often lead to high levels of anxiety, apprehension, and hours of wasted time spent by students who initially struggle with research and writing in their graduate studies (Galvan, 1999; Rechtien & Dizinno, 1997; Szuchman, 2002).

Numerous authors and presenters have addressed issues concerning how to conduct research in counseling (e.g., Creswell, 1994; Herman, 1997; Merchant, 1997; Stockton & Toth, 1997). Szuchman (2002) supplied a new method for counseling students and professionals about how to write research papers in APA (Publication Manual of the American Psychological Association). Szuchman's book provides hands-on skills and instructions about how to construct papers that report research and incorporates concepts from recent literature that pertain to selecting research topics, accessing resources, reviewing literature, critiquing research, and writing a literature review in social sciences (e.g., Coelho & La Forge, 1996; Galvan, 1999; Nicol & Pexman, 1999; Nisenoff & Espina, 1999). Despite these authors' efforts to illuminate issues that pertain to research and writing in counseling, Szuchman (2002) is the first to devote an entire text to this topic. Few have directly addressed issues specific to different methodological approaches and the process of planning and initiating a literature review and research project that pertains specifically to the field of counseling.

Of that which does exist, literature related to this topic suggests that many master's and some doctoral students may be hesitant, defensive, and lack knowledge and confidence about their ability to understand, apply, and integrate research as a result of various factors (Nicol & Pexman, 1999; Rechtien & Dizinno, 1997; Szuchman, 2002). Such factors are considered to be multidimensional and include issues such as counseling students' confusion surrounding professional journals and APA guidelines. Some students have difficulty distinguishing between literature that reports original empirical research with anecdotal reports, theoretical articles, literature reviews, and descriptions of programs, practice strategies, or standards (Galvan, 1999). In particular, Galvan (1999) attributed students' apprehensions to their lack of previous training regarding how to: (a) search databases for reports of original research and related theoretical literature, (b) analyze these particular types of literature, and (c) synthesize them into cohesive essays. Furthermore, novice students may find it difficult to conceptualize how research relates to the theory and practice of counseling. Szuchman (2002) added that most advanced undergraduate and beginning graduate students are in need of training specific to writing research papers in the style described by the APA publication manual.

This chapter will attempt to incorporate various perspectives and ideas about: (1) the integration of research, practice, and theory; (2) the definition of research; (3) literature reviews and conducting research; (4) legal and ethical considerations in research; and (5) program evaluations.

INTEGRATION OF RESEARCH, PRACTICE, AND THEORY

Many professionals in counselor education believe that research is the backbone of counseling practice and theory. Some authors go as far as to suggest that practice, research, writing, and publishing are the obligations of the professional counselor (Coelho & La Forge, 1996; Szuchman, 2002). Furthermore, advocates of research contend that it defines the profession of counseling, builds on old and generates new thinking and theory, sheds light on practice strategies that are effective and ineffective, and creates a forum for communication between various professionals in the field (Coelho & La Forge, 1996; Herman, 1997; Loesch & Nicholas, 1996; Stockton & Toth, 1997). Some experts have insisted that counselors provide a service when they become more involved in the practice of doing research (Herman, 1997). Essentially, many believe that counseling is informed and directed by research.

DEFINITION OF RESEARCH

For the purposes of this chapter, attention is directed toward original research existing in academic journals and other professional resources. Research reports are considered to be original (primary sources) when they highlight initial results, including details about methodology, findings, implications, limitations, and conclusions (Galvan, 1999). Whereas secondary sources of research are generated by someone other than the researcher and often include general descriptions of findings with only minor details about methodology. Most of the research found on the Internet, in summaries included in textbooks, magazines, newspapers, and on television and radio are examples of secondary sources of research. To avoid misinterpretation or distortion of research methodology and findings, it is wise to rely predominately on primary research.

Quantitative Versus Qualitative

In terms of methodological procedures, research can be defined as quantitative or qualitative. Some researchers use a combination of the two, but for the purpose of this chapter, each methodology will be explained separately. There have been many controversial discussions and open debates regarding the usefulness of quantitative and qualitative methodology in counseling. Recently, many experts have contended that both methodologies are important as the profession of counseling is in a state of transition in which the eclectic and subjective nature of humanity is appreciated (Herman, 1997). Accordingly, counseling students need to be familiar with the strengths and limitations of both types of research and must be able to accept quality research as informative and important, regardless of its methodological underpinnings. Meaning that, continuous dialogue regarding quantitative and qualitative research is encouraged and essential. Therefore, these two methodological approaches will be introduced and explored throughout the remainder of this chapter in terms of how they relate to each other, their unique attributes, and aspects related to the quality and credibility of each approach.

Quantitative Research.   Quantitative research involves a systematic, logical, reductive, and empirically focused manner of interpreting information (Creswell, 1994). Researchers who use quantitative methodology utilize their worldview to develop hypotheses and test relationships of clearly defined variables that can be measured (Morse & Field, 1995). The goal is to gather information, reduce it through valid and reliable instrumentation, and produce numerical results in the form of statistics. Such numerical results possess differing meanings including averages, percentages, frequency of occurrence, and so on. The goal of many statistical operations is to test the hypotheses and determine whether there is a relationship between variables (Morse & Field, 1995). In general, quantitative researchers seek a statistical way to determine whether a cause and effect relationship exists between two or more variables (Lincoln & Guba, 1985).

In order to infer causal relationships, quantitative researchers believe that it is possible to extrapolate their personal values from the research process (Morse & Field, 1995). Furthermore, these researchers attempt to isolate specific factors, focus their investigations on predetermined variables, and control other variables that may interfere with the research process or alter researchers' hypotheses. When working with human beings and focusing on social sciences, it can be difficult to control for all factors of the human experience and isolate variables. However, many researchers and professional journals in the field of counseling prefer research based on quantitative inquiry (Merchant, 1997; Sexton, 1996).

Coincidently, much of the training in research for undergraduate students in psychology and sociology and many graduate students in counseling rely primarily on the positivistic, linear, and reductionistic methods of quantitative research (Hoshmund, 1989; Merchant, 1997). Despite a history of remarks supporting the notion that reductionistic science or quantitative research is not adequate to capture the richness and diversity of human experience, support for quantitative research persists (Merchant, 1997). In a recent review of articles in the *Journal of Marriage and Family*, it was noted that of 527 publications from 1989 to 1994, 517 (98.1 percent) were entirely or primarily quantitative (Ambert, Adler, Adler, & Detzner, 1995). More recently, Sexton (1996) found that of 344 current outcome studies published in 116 professional journals from 1988 to 1994, more than 95 percent were quantitative. Merchant (1997) suggested that professionals in psychology and counseling may be relying primarily on quantitative research methods in the attempt to seek validation from those who practice research in the hard sciences.

Qualitative Research.   Despite the efforts of Freud, Piaget, and other theorists in the early 1900s who used qualitative methods to construct developmental theories, research in counseling has predominantly neglected the use of naturalistic methodology (Merchant, 1997). Yet over the last fifteen years, there have been several attempts to value and incorporate qualitative research into the field of counseling (Ambert et al., 1995; Creswell, 1994; Lincoln & Guba, 1985; Merchant, 1997; Morse & Field, 1995; Polkinghorne, 1991; Sexton & Griffin, 1997; Strauss & Corbin, 1998). Flick (1998) stated, "Qualitative research is establishing itself in the social sciences and in psychology" (p. 1). Furthermore, Merchant (1997) devoted an entire monograph to the use of qualitative research in counseling and specifically highlighted the "relevance/fit of qualitative research" to many counselors' theoretical beliefs about human beings, ways of being with clients, and values about the process of counseling (p. 12). Most recently, Shank (2002) described how qualitative research is a "personal skills approach" (p. 1).

Qualitative research includes various nonnumerical methods of investigating human experience and behavior (Denzin & Lincoln, 1994; Shank, 2002). Various terminologies such as naturalistic inquiry, ethnography, fieldwork, observation, and systematic inquiry into meaning often accompany qualitative research (Polkinghorne, 1991; Shank, 2002). Philosophically speaking, qualitative researchers believe that knowledge is contextual. Therefore, the researcher and reader must understand the overall process and see meaning in context (Lincoln & Guba, 1985; Rubin & Rubin, 1995; Sexton, 1996; Shank, 2002). Qualitative research is process-oriented, looks to explore why and how people behave, think, and make meaning as they do, and is conducted through an intense and/or prolonged contact with a life situation (Ambert et al., 1995; Merchant, 1997; Miles & Huberman, 1994; Shank, 2002). Such situations are commonly based on reflections of everyday life of individuals, groups, societies, and organizations.

Researchers attempt to capture data based on the perceptions of those being investigated. This is accomplished through a process of deep attentiveness, empathic understanding, and suspending or "bracketing" preconceptions about the topics under exploration (Miles & Huberman, 1994, p. 6). Qualitative data analysis is done primarily with words and entails a process through which information is explicated from narratives describing a particular setting, way of life, action, process, or manner of accounting for and managing one's life (Miles & Huberman, 1994; Shank, 2002). Qualitative research is inductive in that researchers build on existing knowledge, discover and explore areas about which little is known, and construct concepts and theories as they emerge from the data (Lincoln & Guba, 1985; Maxwell, 1992; Shank, 2002; Strauss & Corbin, 1998).

In general, the objectives of good qualitative research are to: (1) develop theory that is based on rich description resulting from documentation, description, and identification of patterns and relationships between concepts; (2) identify the essence of experience; (3) describe process; (4) understand meaning, context, and process; (5) develop causal explanations; (6) explore and identify phenomena; (7) create theoretical explanations of reality; and (8) describe theory and practice (Denzin & Lincoln, 1994; Lincoln & Guba, 1985; Maxwell, 1992; Miles & Huberman, 1994; Morse & Field, 1995; Shank, 2002). The overall purpose of qualitative research is to produce vivid, dense, full, and integrated descriptions in the natural language of an experience or situation under investigation (Polkinghorne, 1994). Such objectives are accomplished through exploring the phenomena under investigation in its natural setting. This includes using words, dialogue, narratives, and personal reflections as data. Accordingly, the researcher is viewed as the primary instrument for data collection (Ambert et al., 1995; Lincoln & Guba 1985; Maxwell, 1992; Shank, 2002; Strauss & Corbin, 1998). Qualitative research puts social science researchers in a position to design unique ways to explore and analyze concrete cases through the use of people's expressions and activities in their daily living (Flick, 1998; Shank, 2002).

Based on the assumption that significant contributions to the literature can be made by using any methodology that answers the research question, provided the methods are applied correctly, counseling courses must provide information about both forms of research. Furthermore, research and writing in counseling course work should be designed to enhance students' understanding of human experience, thus producing exposure to diverse methodological procedures. Counseling students involved in reviewing, reading, and designing research projects are encouraged to seek meaningful answers to their questions. Therefore, they are urged to review publications that inform them about human nature through the use of both quantitative and qualitative research (Herman, 1997; Merchant, 1997; Stockton & Toth, 1997; Szuchman, 2002).

LITERATURE REVIEWS AND CONDUCTING RESEARCH

Whether it be for a term paper, program evaluation, or thesis, intense anxiety can accompany students' thoughts about reviewing literature, planning and carrying out a research project, and producing a coherent essay (Galvan, 1999; Szuchman, 2002). Anxiety can be diminished and the task of conducting research can best be completed through a thorough review of existing literature and a careful plan for the project. Students' perceptions may change if they shift from conceptualizing research as a complicated and overwhelming project, to a process with various phases and tasks. As students expose themselves to literature, research becomes more manageable and less anxiety provoking. Based on these assumptions, this chapter provides a five-phased process for conducting a literature review and generating a plan for doing research. This process includes: (1) selecting a topic and searching for literature, (2) organizing literature, (3) analyzing literature, (4) structuring a written review of literature and developing a comprehensive essay, and (5) designing a plan for conducting research.

Many phases include steps that build from others and procedures that transfer to other parts of the writing and research processes. When doing projects, students are encouraged to carefully generate a time line with a list of important due dates, specific guidelines, and any regulations that may affect their progress. These activities are designed to assist students in preparing themselves and in gaining a clear purpose for what they are attempting to accomplish. For example, if students are concerned with a thesis or dissertation, they must become aware of proposal and defense dates, university and departmental guidelines, and potential boundaries or resource issues that may interfere with their projects.

Specific guidelines to be aware of before beginning a project include, but are not limited to, local, state, government, and university regulations regarding the use of human subjects in research. Other guidelines can be located through specific counseling departments, university research offices, and the appropriate publication manuals (i.e., the fifth edition of the Publication Manual of the American Psychological Association [2001]), as utilized by most counseling-related departments. Committee members, faculty advisors, and other instructors can also provide information about resources and issues related to the processes of writing and conducting research.

PHASE ONE—SELECTING A TOPIC AND SEARCHING FOR LITERATURE

Obviously, the first step in conducting a search is to determine a specific topic about which to review and write. When doing term papers and sometimes in the case of master's theses, a topic is predetermined or limited by an instructor. If this is the case, students should clarify requirements regarding data searches and use of specific journals. For example, some instructors provide a list of detailed topics to choose from and specify the use of professional journals related to the field of counseling.

If not predetermined by course instructors, the selection of a topic can be difficult for beginning and advanced counseling students. Students are advised to pick a topic that can be kept narrow, is well defined, and within an area that sparks personal interest. Ideas can be generated from classroom lectures, discussions, textbooks, or current issues prevalent in the field of counseling. Begin a search for literature immediately in order to clarify or report potential problems. Personal interest is important for those beginning a thesis or dissertation because they will spend time and energy on this topic and must be able to consistently maintain focus, desire, and interest to complete the project.

Choosing a topic, narrowing and broadening that topic, and searching for literature often coincide. Constructing a literature review begins with a thorough, yet manageable search of current publications in professionally prepared journals and database systems. It is wise to utilize resources related to other fields such as psychology and sociology. Students are also encouraged to use information obtained from professional conferences, presentations, and organizational monographs.

Narrowing the Topic.   A successful search for literature begins with a well-defined topic, yet often a topic cannot be defined until foundational information is known. Students are encouraged to start with an idea or concept that they are interested in learning more about. As students conduct searches of various databases related to their topics, they should attempt to narrowly define and specify exactly what they are exploring. Ways to limit the topic and search include using only those articles that are presented in professional journals, within a specified time frame (the last seven to ten years), related to a specific course, and within a particular theory or area of practice. Another way to limit the topic may be to conduct a preliminary search for literature related to a topic and then attempt to generate the first draft of a topic statement (Galvan, 1999; Szchman, 2002). A topic statement is a well-thought-out sentence that describes what a student is going to write about and/or research.

Case Example.   If interested in counseling children, this topic can be limited by: (1) specifying the topic to counseling with children who have been abused, (2) using only journal articles published in the last five to seven years, (3) focusing on issues related to small group counseling with children who have been abused, and (4) focusing on articles that address cognitive-behavioral group counseling with children who have been abused. A topic statement could be: Implications of cognitive-behavioral group counseling with children who have been abused.

As previously inferred, defining a topic and conducting database searches work simultaneously. Based on information collected through searches of existing data, students may find themes that become interesting to them. They may think of questions for which they want answers. These are all great reasons to narrow searches on a topic that supplies an adequate avenue for literature reviews.

Searching Counseling-Related Databases.   Based on advances in the counseling profession, society, and technology, there are several methods to identify and utilize current literature. Reviewing literature in counseling can best be accomplished by searching varying databases and utilizing multiple methods to gather relevant information. Those interested in learning about a specific topic can gain a diversified and complete cluster of information by reviewing professional journals sponsored by or affiliated with the American Counseling Association (ACA) and the American Psychological Association (APA), searching the Internet, connecting to specific websites, accessing computerized database programs in counseling and other related fields, and attending professional conferences or seminars. Specific suggestions regarding database searching follow.

The word *database* refers to a constellation of information and resources arranged according to specialized topics and ease of retrieval. Each library has a unique organizational system that utilizes a multitude of online electronic database search options. Therefore, students must familiarize themselves with searching features and computer resources in their libraries. Many libraries provide workshops, handouts, and attendants that can inform others about effective ways to conduct electronic searches, yet many students can figure out how to operate computers and gain familiarity with electronic search devices and library resources on their own. With the abundance of database options, some students may be unclear about how to access those that are specific to counseling. The following is a list of databases that are appropriate for counseling-related projects (Galvan, 1999; Szuchman, 2002).

Basic Biosis—information related to life science and human behavior

CINAHL—content focused on nursing, allied health, biomedical, and consumer health

Dissertation Abstracts—primary research from doctoral dissertations on a range of academic subjects

ERIC—information related to education, counseling, and related fields

Medline—topics related to public health, medicine, and psychiatry

NCJRS—information regarding corrections, drugs, crime, juvenile justice, and victims

PAIS International—content specific to social, economic, political, and public policy issues

PsycINFO—numerous articles related to psychology, counseling, and psychiatry

PsycLit—a subset of PsycINFO including only books and journals related to mental helath

SERLINE—a subset of Medline with articles related to public health, medicine, nutrition, etc.

Social Sciences Abstracts—articles related to sociology, psychology, anthropology, etc.

Sociological Abstracts—information related to sociology, counseling, and psychology

Social Work Abstracts—articles focused on sociology, social work, counseling, and social sciences

Sport Discus—information on sports medicine, physical education, psychology, nutrition, etc.

Online databases highlight abstracts from numerous publications including journal articles, doctoral dissertations, professional presentations and papers, books, newspapers, and government documents. Similar information can also be obtained through various websites.

The Internet.   With recent advances in our technological capabilities, volumes of information can be accessed via the Internet. Specific websites and other online links offer a quick and cost-efficient means for gathering a multitude of information.

While accessibility to great quantities of information is useful, it is pertinent to realize the shortcomings of such resources. In many situations, summaries and excerpts from journal articles or professional papers on web pages and listserves can be incomplete, even inaccurate. It is better to rely on original work created by primary authors and researchers, rather than secondary sources such as a websites, which often include a mere synopsis of important information from a journal article. Students cannot be cautioned enough to be mindful of the validity, content, and implications suggested by sources derived from the Internet. As adapted from Nisenoff and Espina (1999), a list of various websites and listservs focused on issues related to counseling and mental health can be found at the end of the chapter.

Professional Journals.   In the hope of exposing students to professional publications in counseling, some instructors in counselor education require that students utilize journals supported by or affiliated with the ACA. Such professors may include a list of specific journals to be used or merely make reference to ACA-affiliated journals. These journals are numerous and cover a wide range of issues affiliated with counseling. Most notably is the *Journal of Counseling and Development* (JCD), the official publication for the American Counseling Association. This journal is printed quarterly (Winter, Spring, Summer, and Fall) and illuminates various areas directly related to research, theory, and practice in counseling.

Other journals serve as official publications for specialized divisions within the ACA. Specialized divisions focus on a particular issue, population, or phenomena related to counseling and, therefore, provide journals that illuminate information related to the specialized area at hand. Based on trends in the field of counseling and social sciences, divisions of the ACA sometimes split into independent associations, expand their focus, merge with other divisions, or cease to exist. Some of the ACA journals are selectively available and frequently change names. Thus, it can be quite difficult to provide a comprehensive list of all journals affiliated with the ACA. Consequently, the goal of this section is to introduce some of the most commonly utilized journals affiliated with the ACA and other organizations related to counseling.

1. *Adultspan*—Published twice a year (Spring and Fall), an official publication of the Association for Adult Development and Aging (AADA), and highlights articles on current research, theory, and practice in the area of adult development, aging, and implications for counseling.

2. *Counseling and Values*—Published three times a year in January, April, and October, an official publication of the Association for Spiritual, Ethical, and Religious Values in Counseling (ASERVIC), and includes articles about the relationship among psychology, philosophy, religion, social values, and counseling.

3. *Counselor Education and Supervision*—an official publication of the Association for Counselor Education and Supervision (ACES) (published quarterly in September, December, March, and June), and includes articles on research, theory development, and program applications in the area of counselor education and supervision.

4. *Measurement and Evaluation in Counseling and Development*—Published quarterly in January, April, July, and October, an official journal of the Association for Assessment in Counseling and Education (AACE), and includes articles about measurement specialists, counselors, or other personnel in schools, public and private agencies, businesses, industries, and government.

5. *Journal of College Counseling (JCC)*—Published twice yearly (Spring and Fall), an official journal of the American College Counseling Association (ACCA), and addresses issues specific to college counselors.

6. *Journal of Counseling and Development (JCD)*—Published Quarterly (Winter, Spring, Summer, and Fall), an official journal of the American Counseling Association (ACA), intended to publish archival material as well as research-related counseling.

7. *Journal of Employment Counseling*—This journal is published four times a year in March, June, September, and December, an official publication of the National Employment Counseling Association (NECA). Articles highlight theory, research, and practice in employment counseling and vocational issues.

8. *Journal for Humanistic Counseling Education and Development*—an official journal of the Counseling Association for Humanistic Education and Development (C-AHEAD) (published twice a year in the Spring and Fall), and includes articles for educators and counselors interested in humanistic education and practices.

9. *Journal of Mental Health Counseling*—Published four times a year in January, April, July, and October, an official publication of the American Mental Health Counselors Association (AMHCA), and includes articles on issues related to mental health counseling with various populations.

10. *Journal of Multicultural Counseling and Development*—Published quarterly in January, April, July, and October, an official publication of the Association for Multicultural Counseling and Development (AMCD), and includes articles on multicultural and ethnic minority interests in counseling.

11. *Journal of Professional School Counseling*—Published five times a year in October, December, February, April, and June, an official publication of the American School Counselor Association (ASCA), and includes articles that address counseling in elementary and secondary schools.

12. *Journal for Specialists in Group Work*—Published quarterly in March, June, September, and December, an official publication of the Association for Specialists in Group Work (ASGW), and includes articles on research, practice, and theory related to group work.

13. *Rehabilitative Counseling Bulletin*—Published four times a year in September, December, March, and June, an official publication of the American Rehabilitation Counseling Association (ARCA), and includes articles related to rehabilitative counseling.

14. *The Career Development Quarterly*—Published quarterly in March, June, September, and December, an official publication of the National Career Development Association (NCDA), and includes articles regarding career development and occupational resources.

15. *The Family Journal: Counseling & Therapy for Couples and Families*—Published four times a year in January, April, July, and October, an official publication of the International Association of Marriage and Family Counselors (IAMFC), and includes articles on couples and family counseling.

16. *The Journal of Addictions and Offender Counseling*—Published twice a year in October and April, an official publication of the International Association of Addictions and Offender Counselors (IAAOC), and includes articles on attitudes and behaviors of addictions and offender counselors as well as theoretical and philosophical rationales for specific programs in these areas.

In addition to books, journals, professional papers, and newspapers, students may also attain important information from monograms, video and audio productions, personal interviews, and professional presentations at conferences. Journals in related fields such as psychology and sociology may also serve as excellent resources for literature reviews and research projects.

Students should start with the most recent publication and work backwards. If they find an article that is relevant to their topic, students are encouraged to focus on the article's reference list or bibliography. Many ideas and additional literature can be discovered through the review of articles previously used to explore any subject matter. Students are also encouraged to search for theoretical articles regarding their topic because these manuscripts often highlight key elements. Students should keep an eye out for existing reviews conducted on a topic relevant to their topic because previously published review articles are an excellent source for identifying additional information and expanding the scope of literature in a field of study. Finally, it is important that students identify the most prominent studies on their topics.

After following numerous leads, spending hours at the library, quarters at the copy machine, and frustrating nights in periodicals at the library, students are now prepared to analyze and review the literature they have gathered.

PHASE TWO—ORGANIZING LITERATURE

Once students have secured a significant amount of literature regarding a chosen topic, they are faced with the task of organizing various pieces of information into one comprehensive essay. This can seem overwhelming and impossible to beginning counseling students. In many ways, students have already begun to unconsciously familiarize themselves with current topics during their perusal of titles, abstracts, and journals. The next step involves a more detailed review as students are encouraged to read the first few paragraphs of each article in order to gain an overview of the research designs and writing styles of various authors. Students should note different researchers' perspectives and approaches to inquiry including their purposes for conducting the research, and reasons for reporting their findings.

To become even more oriented to the literature, students should explore the hypothesis section of the article and focus on researcher hypothesis, research questions, and purpose. In the event that the article is not specifically related to research, readers are advised to scan the article for the conceptual framework or the author's rationale for creating the specific manuscript. Then students should continue to scan the remainder of the article, making note of headings and subheadings.

To group information into categories, cluster all articles into separate stacks that appear to correspond with common themes emerging from the information collected. Based on unique manners of organizing information, students may select any method that fits for them, but a common practice is to organize based on topics, subtopics, and chronological order (Galvan, 1999; Szuchman, 2002). Once students have loosely organized the articles, it is time to prepare for a thorough reading and analysis of the information.

Now students should revisit their organizational schema and begin to organize in greater detail. By reading the entire article, students can begin to summarize key points and become familiar with what the article is attempting to tell its readers. Students can develop a personalized format for recording notes and build a conceptual map that highlights common themes throughout all of the articles. Being consistent and dogmatic about their personal system of review, students can prevent disorganized or repetitive procedures. This will pay off later when they start writing the literature review (Galvan, 1999; Szuchman, 2002).

When organizing, it is also important that students focus on explicit definitions and terms used by the authors. Questions about whether these definitions and terms match others' perceptions are important. Students are encouraged to note differences and similarities of opinion among various authors.

Next, it is time to explore methodological strengths and weaknesses in these terms: (1) Did the author provide enough information and clarify his or her purpose for conducting the study? (2) Is the study quantitative or qualitative? (3) How does the author use his or her findings to support or reject previous findings and perspectives? and (4) Does the research provide new insight regarding the topic? "Students must make sure that they understand the difference between the author's empirical evidence and his or her interpretations or assertions" (Galvan, 1999, p. 34). To avoid mistaking authors' assertions for actual findings, students should be aware of and avoid making statements that are not substantiated by the research they have reviewed unless they are clearly labeled as assertions (Galvan, 1999).

Students should focus on major trends, themes, or patterns in the results of the literature that they review. They should identify and explore gaps that exist and highlight such discoveries in their write-ups, particularly when conducting a literature review for a thesis or dissertation. Due to human nature and the obstacles for researchers in the field of counseling, gaps in research can be catalysts to new and innovative approaches to practice, research, and theory. If there is a lack of relationship among studies on the same topic, discuss reasons for divergent thoughts. For example, two articles may focus on the same topic, but from different theoretical frameworks. Explanations and assertions as to why such differences exist are important.

Other issues to address in literature reviews include ways that specific manuscripts inform the reader about their topic. If students experience a complete lack of research directly related to their topic, they may need to explore other avenues of research or literature. For example, if a student was going to conduct a literature review of group supervision with child counselors, but found nothing on that topic, it would be permissible to explore publications on group supervision, training child counselors, individual supervision of child counselors, and so on. If an article is included that does not explicitly connect to the topic at hand, a writer must provide a clear rationale describing reasons for its inclusion. Once information is read and organized, it is time to reevaluate references and ensure that a complete collection of timely, significant, and viable data exists with which to construct a well-thought-out review. As Galvan (1999) and Szuchman, (2002) contend, a literature review should represent the latest work done in the subject area, present an historical overview of the topic, and explicitly communicate reasons for including articles that are not directly related to the topic. Coelho and La Forge (1996) added that, "One should read extensively inside and outside the profession to ensure that the proposed contribution to the literature is a genuine one rather than merely repeating something that has already been written about" (p. 18).

At this point in the writing process, students should generate a preliminary list of references and citations. Oftentimes, throughout the writing process, students can get caught up in other organizational aspects and forget to keep track of references and appropriate citations. This can lead to extreme frustration near the end of the writing process, because students can easily find themselves in a desperate search for a specific article or citation that is missing from the volumes of information they have collected.

PHASE THREE—ANALYZING LITERATURE

During their organization of literature, students are encouraged to briefly explore the methodological section of the manuscripts collected. This includes an analysis of the methodology in terms of data collection and analysis procedures. As previously explored, methodological approaches utilized in counseling can be qualitative, quantitative, or a combination of these two methodologies. Based on philosophical and procedural differences between these two approaches, the following discussion will examine pertinent issues from each.

Quantitative Research.   By reducing information to averages, percentages, and correlation coefficients, quantitative researchers utilize statistics and numbers to represent relationships. Readers can easily identify quantitative investigations by merely looking at the results section of an article and noting whether or not the researchers used statistics and numbers to present findings of their study. Quantitative research has dominated social sciences for most of the 1900s; therefore, the majority of literature in the area of counseling illuminates quantitative rather than qualitative results (Galvan, 1999; Merchant, 1997).

To analyze a quantitative study, students are encouraged to orient themselves to common themes in literature regarding effective use of quantitative methodology. Based on the following premises, students can explore method sections in quantitative reports and determine whether researchers adhere to basic guidelines. According to Creswell (1994) and Galvan (1999), at a minimum, effective quantitative methodology should:

1. State a researcher's hypotheses at the onset of the investigation. Research hypotheses should not change throughout the study and should be evaluated only after all data are collected and analyzed.

2. Quantitative researchers serve as nonbiased individuals who can measure various aspects of human nature and counseling. Therefore, these researchers should remain objective throughout the entire investigation.

3. Use random selection in attaining research participants from a sample of the population that is said to represent the norm. This means that participants should be randomly picked out of a larger group of representative subjects.

4. Include rather large sample sizes—between one to two hundred or a thousand, depending on the topic and resources of the researcher.

5. Indicate that specific variables of human nature were isolated, controlled for, and measured through quantifying procedures that produce numbers for data analysis.

6. Give detailed descriptions of data collection and analysis procedures. Measurements are taken with instruments that are believed to be scored objectively and deemed to be reliable and valid.

7. Present results using statistics. Use these statistical results to make inferences to correlations and relationships between variables and among groups of variables.

8. Indicate the reliability and validity of findings and address causality. Researchers must make generalizations between the study group and the general population. Researchers should never state results in terms of causes, but correlations.

Qualitative Research.   Instead of adhering to the assumptions of the physical sciences as with quantitative researchers, qualitative researchers, much like counselors, focus on assumptions that address the complex nature of human experience (Sexton & Griffin, 1997). To understand the phenomenology of such naturalistic researchers, Hill and Gronsky (1984) proposed the following assumptions: (1) there is not one truth, but multiple truths or realities, depending on the perspective; (2) clinical phenomena are elusive and reactive; (3) clinical problems are deeply rooted and difficult to predict and manipulate in a controlled and rigid environment; (4) humans should be studied holistically and systematically rather than in isolated, restrictive, and incremental fashions; (5) systematic or circular models of causality may be more appropriate and useful than linear causality when exploring humans and their unique experiences.

Much like quantitative investigations, qualitative research can be identified by the titles of the articles. Titles often contain words such as naturalistic, exploration, or phenomenology and authors usually indicate that their study is qualitative in the abstract, introduction, or rationale for conducting the investigation. The results section of a qualitative article will be presented in terms of a narrative describing categories, themes, and trends that are usually supported by quotations and comments from the actual research participants.

Similar to quantitative research, good practice in qualitative research must address questions of reliability and validity, yet these terms are replaced with parallel terms including dependability, trustworthiness, and authenticity in qualitative research (Lincoln & Guba, 1985; Shank, 2002). Literature on how to conduct qualitative research and how to ensure appropriate qualitative procedures emphasize several aspects. Students are encouraged to familiarize themselves with the following qualitative concepts. They can then compare such issues with methodological reports in the qualitative literature that they have collected. Denzin and Lincoln (1994), Lincoln and Guba (1985), Maxwell (1992), Shank (2002), and Strauss and Corbin (1998) suggested that qualitative research include:

1. A statement of a general purpose without imposing rigid, specific goals and hypotheses to guide a study. Throughout the processes of data collection and analysis, this general purpose may emerge, and it is subject to change as additional data are collected.

2. Disclosure of the researcher's philosophical orientation and personal biases regarding the social and cultural context of the investigation.

3. Purposive and theoretical sampling procedures to select research participants who are accessible and appropriate for the research and topic. Purposive and theoretical sampling is a technique in which the sites, events, and participants being studied are deliberately chosen based on the purpose of the investigation and the phenomena being explored. Accordingly, sample sizes may include as few as one participant to as many as thirty or forty.

4. The researcher is the primary means of data collection by using relatively unstructured instruments such as interviews, observations, questionnaires, focus groups, existing documents, and so on to gather information.

5. Detailed descriptions of the internal process of the investigation as researchers select participants, gather data, analyze data, and report their findings.

6. Prolonged engagement of the investigators with the material/people being studied. This includes spending extended periods of time with the participants to gain in-depth insights into the phenomena under investigation. Emphasis is often placed on how participants are experiencing themselves and the situation in which they are placed.

7. Movement between interpretation and observation in a cyclical process, thus allowing one aspect to inform the other.

8. Results presented predominately or exclusively in words, narratives, or stories with an emphasis on understanding research participants' experiences and perspectives.

9. Rich descriptions so that researchers are able to ground their interpretations in the data by illustrating concepts through interview excerpts or describing relationships of data to theoretical concepts.

10. A focus on "what and how" rather than "why" when analyzing and presenting data.

11. Use of triangulation procedures to confirm and verify findings. Triangulation refers to utilizing multiple sources of information, interpretation, and theory to support, challenge, clarify, and verify findings. Such sources may include, but are not limited to, existing literature, more than one researcher, experts in the field being explored, and divergent theories.

12. For more information, review Shank (2002) "The seven deadly sins of qualitative research" (p. 180).

Through exploring both quantitative and qualitative research and comparing the two methodologies, differences between the two seem blatant. Yet, both methodologies possess characteristics and procedures to ensure the credibility of findings. Differences between methodologies and unique measures to ensure trustworthiness of findings are important and must be understood in order to effectively evaluate the strengths and weaknesses of a study (Galvan, 1999).

Other important aspects to consider when addressing the quality of a quantitative or qualitative study include:

1. Determining if the study is experimental, meaning is the purpose of the study to assess the effectiveness of something, such as an innovative counseling technique or a new drug? If so, note how the researcher selected participants, assigned treatment conditions, and measured outcomes.

2. Note if the study is nonexperimental (meaning that participants' traits are measured without attempting to change anything). Be conscious of attempts to extrapolate correlations between outcomes and findings generated by the investigation.

3. Determine if researchers directly addressed issues related to measures of validity (Does the instrument or results seem accurate or correct?) and reliability (Would the instrument be consistent or would the same results occur over time?) for quantitative research. For qualitative research, are findings credible, trustworthy, thorough, and comprehensive (Did researchers provide a detailed explanation or a brief description of what they did to ensure issues of validity, reliability, credibility, and trustworthiness?). Readers should attempt to make their own assessments of whether the measures were appropriate given the purpose of the research.

4. Pay attention to the sampling procedures. In the case of a quantitative study, usually the more participants the better and only through random sampling can researchers generalize their findings to the overall population. In qualitative investigations, participants are purposely selected and described in detail. The number of participants is directly related to the topic at hand and may not necessarily be a factor.

5. Understand that when quantitative researchers imply that there is statistical significance, they are suggesting that there is a difference between two variables, and that the difference is significantly greater than might be expected by chance alone. Because small differences can be classified as statistically significant in some studies, researchers should make note of the size of the differences.

6. Realize as Peshkin (1988) contends, "Beginning with the premise that subjectivity is inevitable, . . . researchers should systematically seek out their subjectivity, not retrospectively when data have been collected and analysis is complete, but while their research is actively in progress" (p. 17). Essentially, researchers should be aware of and communicate to the reader how their personal biases might have shaped their study and its outcomes (Peshkin, 1988).

7. Note (Galvan, 1999) that all empirical studies are subject to errors. Readers should refrain from assuming that an investigation provides absolute truths or definitive answers to a given research problem. Furthermore, researchers should examine and discuss flaws of their investigations. Limitations to specific studies can often shed light on important aspects related to the topic being explored, as well as serve as ideas for future research.

8. Consider that implications about how the study informs the profession about the topic being explored and suggestions for future research are also essential aspects in both quantitative and qualitative research. From a qualitative perspective researchers should discuss the transferability and quantitative researchers should address the generalizeability of their findings.

PHASE FOUR—STRUCTURING A WRITTEN REVIEW OF LITERATURE AND DEVELOPING A COMPREHENSIVE ESSAY

It is finally time to explore ideas about how to conceptualize and synthesize review findings and writers' beliefs about literature. Students are encouraged to look at the development of a literature review as a process with a planning phase, a construction phase, and a refining phase. This section serves as an overview of key aspects to consider when creating a literature review.

Structuring the Literature Review.   Before integrating literature into the form of a literature review, students need to clarify their purpose, choice of voice, and the audience to whom they are writing. If the literature review is for a class assignment or term paper, there may be specific guidelines that instructors provide. For example, they may provide an outline, specify page limitations, or determine the focus of the review. When choosing the voice in academic writing, many suggest that the first person, "I," be avoided and that third person or facts be allowed to speak for themselves (Galvan, 1999). Students must also take into consideration who will be reading their literature reviews. If the review is part of a thesis or dissertation, various committee members and reviewers will be reading students' work and in most cases, literature is used to establish a framework and build a rationale for a study. Accordingly, information regarding methodology, suggestions for future research, gaps in research and literature, and other important details should be highlighted.

After clarifying the purpose and audience of the literature review, students are then faced with the task of organizing their ideas into an outline or structured plan. Such a plan gives direction to the information that students have obtained throughout their review of the literature. It also allows students a forum to creatively articulate their thoughts or judgments about the research that they have reviewed (Coelho & La Forge, 1996; Galvan, 1999). This means that students should have formed judgments about the topic based on their analysis and synthesis of the research literature (Galvan, 1999). The task of creating an outline that exhibits the integration of information and communicates students' thoughts and judgments can be accomplished in a few basic steps.

First, students must integrate various sources into a comprehensive summary and then clarify how all of this information is related. Next, students are encouraged to articulate their assertions, contentions, or propositions regarding the literature and research they have reviewed. Once students have established an argumentation for the reader, they should design their outlines around this set of beliefs. This includes reorganizing notes and ideas according to their assertions, contentions, or propositions.

Now that students have a detailed outline, they should begin connecting their beliefs to topic headings in the outline that emerged as they reviewed the literature. Students should focus on building a comprehensive and clear discussion of their line of argumentation under subheadings in the outline to define and describe each concept, clarify interrelationships among concepts, discuss connections to the topic, and discuss relationships among various studies or sources. Subheadings also address obvious gaps or areas needing further attention or research, ideas about how individual studies relate to and enhance theory, and innovative concepts that clarify misconceptions about the topic.

Writing the Literature Review.   Once students have developed a detailed outline including specific headings, subheadings, and concepts, they are ready to construct the first draft. This first draft is intended to serve as a rehearsal and an opportunity to explore initial attempts at articulating the context and arrangement of information and ideas (Coelho & La Forge, 1996). If students have done their work in formulating a well-organized and specific outline, they simply transfer concepts from that outline into a narrative with transitions, continuity, and appropriate grammar.

Students are encouraged to introduce their topic with the identification of the broad area under review. They should avoid global statements and instead move from a general topic to specific concepts and ideas. This includes giving details about what the topic is and how it relates to other aspects related to the field of counseling.

For example, when discussing group counseling with children affected by abuse, it may be logical to begin with a brief introduction to research about group work with children. Then get more specific and address issues related to counseling children who have been abused. Finally, discuss the specific topic of group work with children who have been abused.

Students should indicate the importance of the topic and comment on the timeliness in terms of a specific context. They need to identify their reasons for conducting a review of the literature and discuss why it is being done at this time. For example, when conducting a literature review for a thesis or dissertation, students may indicate that their research will address a gap in existing research. In this example, students would also need to explain why the topic is important and issues currently faced by the field of counseling as a result of the topic. Students must remember to always justify their comments regarding how they determined a gap in literature and why they believe the topic is of importance now.

When students are citing a classic or landmark study, attempting to replicate it, or hoping to elaborate on it, they should indicate so. Landmark studies are those that are pivotal and influential in the historical development of the published literature and topic under investigation (Galvan, 1999; Szuchman, 2002). Such studies stimulate additional research in many instances, thus provide a solid foundation for students to build upon.

Students are also encouraged to discuss other literature reviews related to the topic being explored and make reference to reviews on issues related to the topic (Szuchman, 2002). In the case that earlier reviews were published about the same topic, writers are encouraged to incorporate a discussion about such reviews by focusing on how they are different, adequate, and worthy of readers' attention (Galvan, 1999). While students should cover their topic in great detail, they may find that related concepts printed in previous reviews are important, but not worthy of extended exposure. In this situation, students should simply make reference to other reviews when it may be useful to readers. On the other hand, if students locate research with an inconsistent or widely varying discussion, they should cite these manuscripts separately and indicate the effect on their topic and the field of counseling.

When writing a thesis, dissertation, or article for publication, students are encouraged to cite all relevant references in the literature review before they proceed to reporting original research. In this situation, students will use their review to justify and provide a rationale for conducting their studies. They should refrain from including long lists of nonspecific references within their text. Students are encouraged to cite only those references that provide direct quotations or essential facts needed for the text. Students should avoid the overuse of direct quotations and attempt to summarize whenever possible. Yet, it is vital that students give credit where credit is due. They should use references whenever they need to provide proper credit to an author or creator and to demonstrate the coverage given in a manuscript (Galvan, 1999). A brief discussion of legal and ethical implications follows.

Noting the Legal and Ethical Implications of Writing. Students must be aware that copyright protection begins at the creation of a work, regardless of registration with the U.S. Copyright Office. Copyright laws acknowledge that individuals own ideas once they have created them (Remley & Herlihy, 2001). Students must give credit to sources via proper referencing and citation when they use the words and creations of others. Due to the ethical and legal implications of proper referencing, when in doubt, students should review guidelines in the most recent edition of the American Counseling Association's (ACA) *Code of Ethics and Standards of Practice* (1995) and the American Psychological Association's (APA) style manual (currently 5th edition [APA], 2001).

Depending on the source and the manner in which it is used, the APA manual (2001) specifies guidelines about how to properly cite the work of others. Published and unpublished sources that require citation include journal articles, books, professional presentations, personal interviews, videos, material from the Internet, and so on. Detailed descriptions and guidelines for appropriate citation and referencing are clarified and issues regarding manuscript organization, style, and format are included in the APA manual (2001).

Creating a Comprehensive Essay.   Since first drafts are seldom, if ever, complete, clear, and coherent, once students have completed the first draft, they must begin the process of refining their work. Although it is often easy to get discouraged, students should be prepared to rewrite at least two or three times after the first draft is finished. Szuchman (2002) indicated that the writing process inherently includes the following process of revision: (a) first draft, (b) first rewrite, (c) second rewrite, (d) third inspection—not a rewrite, and (e) the final touches. Others have indicated that there are usually at least two rewrites throughout the process of revising a research paper or manuscript. As Zinsser (1990) so appropriately commented, "Writing is hard work. A clear sentence is no accident" (p. 13).

When available, allowing peers or others to proof first and subsequent drafts can be extremely helpful. Students are encouraged to seek others who are willing and able to read and critique their work. Feedback is the most effective way for writers to gain perspective and enhance quality. If unable to receive feedback from others, students are encouraged to challenge themselves and their writing as they proofread their own manuscripts. During this self-editing process, students should compare their draft with their topic statement and outline; avoid using synonyms for recurring words; spell out all acronyms when they first appear in the text; avoid the use of contractions; set off coined terms in quotations; avoid slang expressions, colloquialisms, and idioms; and avoid plagiarism (Galvan, 1999). In addition, students must look for typical errors in typing, writing, spelling, and grammar. Students must edit and revise the first draft as many times as necessary to clarify, solidify, and edit flaws related to their work.

Since many authors understand that the writing process can be overwhelming, they have offered the following suggestions. Writers should develop a process of writing that is unique to them. A unique writing process takes into consideration writers' personalities and different writing styles. This can include the selection of a specific time of day to enable authors to write while they are fresh (Creswell, 1994). Coelho and La Forge (1996) stated that writers must avoid writing binges, but should focus on writing in small, yet regular amounts. Writers are also encouraged to understand that writing is a slow and tedious process requiring time, patience, and persistence. Writers may want to schedule daily writing tasks, generate goals for each day, keep daily charts of writing progress, select others to proofread who will provide supportive and corrective feedback, and try to work on two to three writing projects at once (Creswell, 1994). Coelho and La Forge (1997) asserted that writing is in a constant state of evolution; therefore, writers must be flexible and open to new ideas that occur while writing. This will allow writers to fill in gaps and elaborate relationships between concepts throughout the entire process of creating an essay or manuscript for publication.

PHASE FIVE—DESIGNING A PLAN FOR CONDUCTING RESEARCH

Theses and Dissertations.   At the conclusion of a literature review, those interested in conducting research need to consider their plans for carrying out research agendas (Cone & Foster, 1995). When writing a thesis or dissertation, this can be an ideal opportunity for students to solidify their research purposes and agendas and meet with faculty advisors. Students may find that they need to reexamine specific characteristics of their research plan, including the initial research question, hypotheses, and data collection and analysis procedures. This process can often lead to a revision of the initial research plan. For example, based on suggestions regarding methodology, students may find that they need to review and incorporate additional literature regarding the use of a specific methodological approach or alter their research plan to fit a particular mode of data collection and analysis.

This is also an excellent time for masters and doctoral students to coordinate with their advisors and develop detailed and specific plans for the remainder of their investigations. It is crucial that those embarking on theses or dissertations take ample time to decide how, when, where, and with whom they will conduct their research. Students must address specific details regarding the sample population, their research purpose, specific research questions, methodological procedures, and potential barriers. A tentative time line of events and procedures must be developed before the research process can be initiated.

LEGAL AND ETHICAL CONSIDERATIONS IN RESEARCH

According to ethical guidelines, studies must be rigorously and carefully designed or they may be considered to be unethical due to the waste of time and potential harm they can pose to participants and researchers (Remley & Herlihy, 2001). Therefore, students must take various legal and ethical considerations into account in the initial phases of planning their investigations. Of highest priority, researchers must protect research participants from harm. This includes voluntary participation, informed consent, ensuring confidentiality, and paying attention to issues of diversity.

Remley and Herlihy (2001) have discussed several of the ethical mandates pertaining to research that are supported by legal requirements. For example, any institution that receives federal funds must maintain a system to review research proposals with the intent to protect the welfare of research participants (Remley & Herlihy, 2001). Most universities and government affiliated organizations require that research including human subjects be reviewed and approved by a committee prior to the onset of data collection. Consequently, if students do not plan studies that integrate legal and ethical requirements, they will not receive approval from such review committees. This would more than likely delay students' research and could cause serious problems for students and research participants. For this and other reasons, students must familiarize themselves with ethical guidelines in conducting and reporting research prior to embarking on a research plan. A full discussion of such issues is provided in the ACA's *Code of Ethics and Standards of Practice* booklet (1995).

PROGRAM EVALUATIONS

Up to this point, this chapter has been directed toward students concerned with constructing literature reviews and conducting research for a thesis or dissertation. However, there are other reasons that counseling students may do research, such as program evaluation. Program evaluations are based on whether the goals for implementation of a counseling program are being met and whether clients are getting what they need from the counseling experience. In many schools and agencies, counselors are asked to be accountable and produce evidence indicating the effectiveness of their practice. Novice and experienced counselors are faced with program evaluations and often struggle with how to accomplish this task. Such requests can be met by counselors if they simply begin to gather data and record information about their activities and efforts throughout their daily lives as professional counselors.

Counselors are encouraged to utilize data collection procedures outlined in both quantitative and qualitative methodologies to attain various forms of information that testify to their effectiveness. Depending on the unique styles and settings of counselors, they should select methodological procedures that fit their individual, school, and agency needs. For example, a school counselor may simply begin keeping track of students they meet with on a weekly basis. They could develop a chart and tally specific issues that they address with various students and specific interventions or techniques that they used. At the end of a semester, these school counselors could analyze their data and produce a report highlighting numerical results of their efforts. Such research would provide a record of accountability regarding what school counselors have done over a specific period of time. This information would address issues of program effectiveness for principals, school board officials, and other school-related personnel.

SUMMARY

This chapter addressed issues related to writing and research in counseling. Concepts and ideas were directed toward novice and experienced counseling students who are currently encountering assignments ranging from essays, term papers, and literature reviews to theses and dissertations. Specific attention was placed on the role of research in the profession of counseling. Concepts included the importance of research, the definition of research, how to use research and literature in counseling, how to construct a comprehensive essay or literature review, legal and ethical implications for writing and research, and how to use research in program evaluations.

CHAPTER FIVE

TECHNOLOGY AND COUNSELING

MELINDA HALEY, M.S., N.C.C.
New Mexico State University

The use of technology in counseling has been apparent in some form or another for the last five or six decades. In the 1950s, Dr. Joyce Brothers used radio to reach millions of listeners and provide services (Pergament, 1998). Interactive video therapy began in the late 1950s at the University of Nebraska where client and therapist were connected by television for the counseling session (McCarty & Clancy, 2002). Telephones have been employed for such services as suicide hotlines and 24-hour counseling services (McCarty & Clancy, 2002; Riemer-Reiss, 2000a, 2000b) and students and counselor educators have been using audiotapes in supervision for decades while more recently videotapes have been utilized. When we speak of technology today, it is not often audiotapes or even fax machines we think of, but rather we tend to identify with the computer age. In the past decade, this type of technology has burgeoned. Computerized hi-tech innovations have invaded nearly every aspect of modern life from how we do our banking to how we stay in touch with loved ones.

This type of technology has also affected the way counselors perform their job tasks. In 2001, a Delphi survey found that 40 percent of counselors relied on computer related technology to complete 59 percent of their daily job related tasks such as record keeping, assessment, and administration of tests. Present estimates are by the year 2008, 90 percent of counselors will be using some form of computer related technology in 92 percent of their work (Cabaniss, 2001).

Technology in counseling services is varied and includes: software to aid in report writing; spreadsheets for recording client data; statistical analysis packages for analyzing client data; publishing software for marketing and client recruitment; and software for assessment and testing. E-mail and listservs are used for personal and professional communication as well as for consultation, supervision, referral, and professional development. The World Wide Web (WWW) is used for client information (professional and informational websites), advertising of services and provision of counseling services, marketing, and a host of other purposes (Hackerman & Greer, 2000).

In fact, current estimates are that several thousand counselors use Internet websites to advertise their counseling services (Heinlen, Welfel, Richmond & Rak, 2003).

The realization that the technological age has profound significance for counseling has spurred great debate and controversy within the profession regarding how technology will be used. Professional associations and governing agencies have scrambled to provide counselors with guidelines, competencies, and ethics to regulate usage and provide protection to clients. This has been important for many new technological arenas, such as Internet counseling, as there have been no preceding laws, regulations, or codes of conduct to guide counselors (Gould, Munfakh, & Lubell, 2002; National Board of Certified Counselors (NBCC), 2001; Sands, 2000).

The technological age in counseling has come upon us so quickly that many of us are still trying to catch our breath from thinking about all the exciting possibilities. This chapter will explore many of the current technological innovations counselors are using in their work today. An emphasis will be placed on discussing the benefits, consequences, considerations, and ethical implications for using these technologies in counseling.

CYBER COUNSELING/DISTANCE COUNSELING

Cyber counseling is a growing modality of providing counseling services. A Harris poll conducted in 2001, found the following: 24 million Americans have sought help or mental health information online, 200 websites exist offering mental health information or advice, and 350 to 800 counselors and mental health specialists provide some or all of their services online (Blair, 2001; Goedert, 2003; Kalb, 2001; LeBeau, 2001). Online mental health services are not only prolific, but also are here to stay (Grohol, 1997). This new modality of mental health service has sparked some of the greatest controversy within the counseling profession.

Internet behavioral health services have been called by many names: cyber counseling, telehealth, cyber-consultations, virtual couch therapy, cyber psychology, and cyber therapy, to name just a few (Hackerman & Greer, 2000). In this chapter, this form of therapy will be referred to as cyber counseling. A further distinction needed for this section is that cyber counseling is counseling that is performed strictly with the use of computers via the Internet (e.g., e-mail, websites or chat rooms), whereas distance counseling can use a variety of mediums in addition to the computer, such as the telephone, television satellite hookup, or video- and audiotape. Counseling utilizing both these forms can be done with individuals, couples, or groups (Cabaniss, 2001). In addition, there are generally two types of counseling available (Stover, 1993):

1. Single question, single answer, single fee counseling, where the "counseling" between counselor and therapist is conducted in a single interaction, and
2. Continuous, ongoing counseling.

When counseling is not performed face-to-face, it can be either synchronous or asynchronous. Synchronous counseling occurs when there is little or no gap between the responses of the counselor and the client and the interaction resembles a dialogue (Cabaniss, 2001). Synchronous counseling might be delivered utilizing the telephone or a satellite hookup. Asynchronous counseling occurs when there is a gap in time between the response of the counselor and the client (Cabaniss, 2001). Asynchronous counseling uses mediums such as e-mail. For example, the client asks the counselor a question through e-mail and the response might come back the next day versus instantaneously as in face-to-face counseling or counseling done through a telephone hotline.

There are various forms of cyber counseling and distance counseling currently available. These include:

1. *Telephone Counseling:* These generally are crisis lines and 24-hour counseling lines.
2. *Radio Counseling:* This method has been made famous with such personalities as Dr. Joyce Brothers, Dr. Laura, and Dr. Sue Brown.
3. *E-mail Counseling:* The counseling experience consists of e-mails sent between counselor and client.
4. *Bulletin Board Counseling:* Users post questions to an online bulletin board. Clients generally use an identity pseudonym for confidentially (e.g., Mickey Mouse). The mental health professional posts an answer for all users to see.
5. *Chat Room Counseling:* This allows for synchronous counseling as counselor and client(s) can engage in text communication in real time. Chat room counseling is popular for group counseling as several people can communicate at the same time.
6. *Web-Telephony Counseling:* This allows for real-time speaking over the Internet using a microphone and speakers.
7. *Videoconferencing:* This is real-time (synchronous) counseling using audio and video technology and provides distance counseling but in a face-to-face manner. Generally, this is done with a camera, monitor, and computer processor (Stamm, 1998). A new technology called CU-SeeMe uses camera equipment, software, real-time, and audio-visual communications. This technology allows group counseling to take place simultaneously with up to six people (Powell, 1998).
8. *Computer Assisted or Simulated Counseling:* These are generally computer generated answers to questions or concerns through software programs such as Eliza, the computer therapist (see the list of websites at the end of the chapter for more information). The client does not receive help through a live person although a live person may oversee the program (Barak, 1999; Rogers, 2001).
9. *E-coaching:* This is a human guided interactive module series for such issues as depression or anxiety. Each module might consist of eight or nine interactive applications that the client would complete on his or her own. Once finished, the client sends the completed application to an e-coach for process, feedback, and homework redirection (Blair, 2001).

Discussion of each of these modes of cyber or distance counseling would be too lengthy and take up more space that this chapter allows. However, a brief discussion on videoconferencing will aid the reader in understanding this concept of counseling service. Videoconferencing requires both counselor and client to have a Web cam that can transmit images and sound via the Internet. In this way, counseling takes place synchronously. Both participants can see and hear each other simultaneously although each participant may live in different geographical locations and time zones.

Counselors have used videoconferencing technology to treat such issues as depression, suicidal ideation, mood disorders, eating disorders, and attention deficit disorder to name a few (McFadden, 2000). Some studies suggest that counselors are just as effective at building rapport and a working relationship using videoconferencing as in face-to-face counseling and have been similarly effective in treating some disorders such as schizophrenia and obsessive-compulsive disorder (Stamm, 1998).

However, research also shows that counselors need to be more aware of physical appearance when using this medium. For example, some colors in clothing do not transfer well and can affect client perceptions of the counselor (Stamm, 1998). On the other hand, communicating using the Internet transcends physical location, professional or socioeconomic status, and demographic differences between sender and recipient. Engstrom (1997) discusses research that found participants who felt themselves unattractive were inclined to be more vocal and confident when using the Internet as a form of communication.

Positives.   Cyber counseling or distance counseling is often more convenient for both counselor and client. This is especially true for asynchronous counseling using store it-and-forward technology such as e-mail. Store and forward systems take various types of data (e.g., text or psychological test data) and store it on a computer, which can then be forwarded to another computer to be seen by another person. Because the information is actually "stored" at both the sender and receiver ends, the parties need not be present simultaneously (Stamm, 1998). This can be beneficial as counseling can occur without a cumbersome synchronizing of counselor/client schedules.

This form of counseling can eliminate many barriers that might keep an individual from using counseling services such as inability to access a counselor's office due to geographical location or a disability. When services are provided via e-mail, both counselor and client can respond at his or her own convenience rather then at a prescribed time (LeBeau, 2001). In addition, while face-to-face counseling typically occurs no more than once per week, cyber counseling usually occurs with much more frequency (Barak, 1999).

One additional benefit to this type of counseling is all communication is written and therefore automatically documented. Both client and counselor can refer back to the communication at any time for clarification. This can also aid in the counselor's supervision as counseling exchanges are recorded verbatim (Barak, 1999). However, this written record also causes some ethical concerns regarding confidentiality, which will be discussed momentarily.

Distance counseling whether via the computer or other technological means also appears to reduce client anxiety or embarrassment toward the counseling process (Sands, 2000). This may be especially true for certain personality types such as schizoid (Hackerman & Greer, 2000). Another benefit for the counselor is that distance counseling and cyber counseling circumvent the quagmire that has become managed care. A counselor can offer services as a provider without having to be governed by managerial systems. However, what is an advantage for the counselor is often a drawback for the client. These services are not usually covered by insurance.

Some forms of cyber counseling have been found to be more beneficial in some cases then typical face-to-face counseling. For example, in couples therapy when the couple is interacting in an emotionally reactive way, having the communication slowed down via e-mail and forcing the couple to express themselves in written form without gestures or facial expressions, has been found to be both effective and cathartic for them. In addition, having them write their story seemed to make them more reflective and obtain better understanding (Sands, 2000).

Counseling performed via chat rooms offers the client a measure of anonymity that cannot be found in face-to-face counseling (Sands, 2000). However, client anonymity can also produce profound problems for the counselor such as when a client discloses intentions of self-harm or child abuse.

Negatives.   It is difficult for counselors to build rapport and show genuine positive regard with clients in the same manner that rapport is nurtured in face-to-face counseling (Barak, 1999; Hayes, 1999; Ingram, 1998). In addition, the counselor cannot assess a client's nonverbal behaviors, which give a counselor additional data upon which to confer hypotheses and diagnoses as well as identify incongruent communication and behaviors (e.g., client says s/he is angry yet is smiling). It may also be difficult to address deep clinical issues (Hackerman & Greer, 2000). Using this medium, it is more likely that miscommunication will take place because visual and auditory cues are missing (Childress, 1998).

Another drawback to using a computer in counseling is the hypothesis postulated by Suler (1998) who believes transference can occur from the user onto the computer just as a client often transfers onto the counselor. However, the counselor cannot help a client work through this transference as readily as can occur when the client is transferring onto the counselor and the counseling is face-to-face (Childress, 1998).

Additionally, there are many websites on the Internet that purport to be therapeutically inclined but are not regulated in any way. For many sites the service provided is by someone other than a mental health specialist (Barak, 1999). It is a "buyer beware" market. Only counselors that are certified or licensed can be held to ethical standards and guidelines. If a "counselor" is not a member of a regulating board (e.g., American Counseling Association, American Psychological Association, or National Board of Certified Counselors), complaints for violations cannot be filed.

Some sites are legitimate but offer services in such a way that could cause harm to clients (Carr, 2000). For example, while most cyber counseling sites prohibit counseling suicidal clients and mandate the referral of such clients for help within their communities, some sites do work with suicidal clients via technological means (e.g., e-mail and Internet). Analyses of one such site found that the average first response to a client in crisis usually occurred as late as 36 hours after the initial contact and counselors typically responded by e-mail, snail-mail (regular postal letters) or by telephone (Powell, 1998). For a client seriously at risk for a suicide attempt, the delay in receiving any intervention may cost the client his or her life.

Ethical Issues.   As can be imagined there are a plethora of ethical concerns with both cyber counseling and distance counseling. Confidentiality is certainly at the forefront of these (Alexander, 1999). How does a counselor insure client confidentiality? Currently, technology allows for the encryption of communication between computer systems (NBCC, 2001). However, this is not a failsafe method. In addition, how does a counselor certify confidentiality if the communications are then to be saved on the computer? Many computer systems have passwords that must be utilized to gain access to files or enter computers. This too is not foolproof.

Other ethical concerns pertain to client safety. How can a client ascertain that the person on the other end of the telephone or computer is actually a counselor? How does a client find out the counselor's credentials? The National Board of Certified Counselors Standards of Practice (2001) stipulate that a counselor's website have all the links necessary for a client to ascertain that counselor's certification and/or licensure. However, even if a counselor's credentials are verified, how does the client know that a counselor is trained for the given issue brought forth by the client? If the counselor states he or she is receiving supervision, how can the client accurately verify this?

If the client resides in a different state than the counselor and a problem does arise, which state has jurisdiction? If elder abuse is disclosed by the client but the client's home state does not require the counselor report it, however the counselor's home state does, then what? Which state has jurisdiction? What if the client resides in a different country? How are multicultural concerns satisfied? As demonstrated there are a plethora of safety and ethical concerns regarding this form of counseling. Counselors are obligated to fully disclose any risks associated with a counseling modality. Cyber counseling is no different. Counselors must allow clients to make informed choices and therefore, counselors providing this type of service need to be well versed in the benefits and costs to this type of counseling (Childress, 1998; Goedert, 2003).

The National Board of Certified Counselors has provided standards for the ethical practice of Internet counseling (NBCC, 2001). These standards specifically address Internet counseling and do not duplicate other standards set by the NBCC for other forms of counseling. Internet counseling standards should be used in combination with the most current ethical codes. These standards can be obtained online at *http://www.nbcc.org/ethics/wcstandards.htm*. The American Counseling Association (ACA) has also published standards: *http://www.counseling.org/site/PageServer?pagename =resources_internet* and the American Psychological Association (APA) has published guidelines and standards for services provided by telephone, teleconferencing, as well as the Internet. These can also be accessed online at *http://www.apa.org/ethics/ stmnt01.html*. Because technology is ever expanding these standards and codes should be viewed frequently for changes and updates.

The standards and guidelines established by the different counseling organizations address ethical concerns such as:

- How to verify the identity of a client by using code words
- How to identify minor clients and gain permission and informed consent by a parent or guardian

- How the client can contact the counselor
- When and how e-mail messages will be looked at and answered
- What will be done in the event of a technological failure

For more information regarding the different coalitions regulating cyber counseling contact the ACA Center for Effective Counseling Practice at *http://www.cecp@counseling.org* or visit the website of one of the above organizations.

COMPUTER-ASSISTED COUNSELING

Computer-assisted counseling utilizes computer software to provide assessment, intervention, and specific counseling techniques to clients (Bower, 1990). The category of computer-assisted counseling can include any computer-based application that aids the counselor in his or her work. This can include software packages for assessment or treatment planning; psychoeducational software packages to provide clients information about disorders such as depression; and computer-assisted counseling whereby the computer actually provides a type of counseling service to clients.

Computers as Counselors

The first computer counselor prototype was developed more than thirty years ago by Joseph Weizenbaum, who wrote a computer application named "Eliza." The program simulated natural language comprehension and approximated a nondirective counseling session by using preprogrammed responses when cued by a client (Computers, a Sympathetic Shoulder, 1999). Essentially "Eliza," in semi-Rogerian fashion, rephrased and reflected back remarks made by the client in such a way as to cause the client to think deeper about his or her issues. Today "Eliza" is utilized mostly for entertainment purposes; however, based upon that idea numerous applications have been created to help clients with mental health issues. Eliza, can be accessed online at *http://www.manifestation.com/neurotoys/eliza.php3*. There are several different "Elizas" and additional versions can be found by entering the search terms "computers" and "Eliza."

Voice-Activated Computer Systems

There are many ways computers can assist in the counseling and support of a client. For example, Isaac Marks from Bethlem-Maudsley Hospital Institute of Psychiatry in London developed BTSTEPS (Computers, a Sympathetic Shoulder, 1999). This is a computer-based, voice activated telephone system that helps clients with obsessive-compulsive disorders. Client's can obtain prerecorded advice on such topics as exposure therapy. This program can give specific replies based on client information, such as behavioral targets to aim for and feedback on client progress.

In addition, computerized virtual reality systems have been used to help those with phobias by providing a form of systematic desensitization (Viire, 1997). The client is exposed to his or her hierarchy of anxiety provoking stimuli by computer simulation. Once the client has mastered his or her hierarchy then in vivo exposure can begin. However, by that time the client's anxiety regarding his or her phobia has been greatly diminished.

Other systems have been used to provide specific counseling techniques for specific disorders such as depression. For example, these computer programs might use well-known cognitive behavioral techniques, such as thought stopping exercises, to help clients evaluate their cognitions and reduce depression (Bower, 1990). Studies conducted have shown these software systems are just as efficacious as face-to-face therapy for treating mild depression (Bower, 1990).

Other counselor-assisted computer innovations include Roger Gould's Therapeutic Learning Program (TLP) to help clients deal with stress (Smith, 2001a, 2001b). Gould's computer program is said to systematically explore a client's issue within ten sessions. More information on this software can be found at: *http://www.masteringstress.com*. In addition, many counseling agencies and managed care organizations have set up online interactive consumer services, including self-help and health education programs to aid clients (Amig, 2001).

There are many applications that fall under computer-assisted counseling too numerous to mention here. Every counseling specialty, from school counseling to mental health counseling, has access to software programs to aid the counselor in nearly every aspect of the counseling process. Computer software programs are being used more than ever to perform some of the more perfunctory aspects of counseling work to free up valuable counselor time to spend on more pertinent client issues.

Positives.   The use of computer-aided counseling can help clients when they cannot afford frequent sessions or can be used between sessions to supplement or reinforce the therapeutic gains made by face-to-face counseling. Supplementing face-to-face counseling by using computer-guided self-treatment can substantially cut therapy costs for the client. In addition, since some systems can be accessed by the telephone and are often voice-activated, clients do not necessarily have to have a computer. These systems can also be made available 24 hours per day. Therefore, clients can access these systems for support when a flesh-and-blood counselor cannot be reached.

Negatives.   Computers are fallible and programs are only as good as those people who programmed them. Systems also have to be maintained and updated. This can sometimes be difficult, time consuming, and expensive. In addition, computers cannot build a relationship with a client nor notice the nuances of a client's speech. Computers are literal and can only process what is typed into them and cannot, at least at this time, respond in a spontaneous human way nor show empathy, emotion, or understanding of nonverbal cues. Computers cannot assess and diagnose a client, create a treatment plan, or monitor a client's progress without human input, nor should they.

Computer software packages that help with data collection, assessment, interpretation of tests, and so on are also imperfect. Computer generated interpretations of assessment inventories may not be correct or may not consider individual client circumstances. Software can become corrupted and information can be lost. Counselors can become lackadaisical and become overly dependent upon computers to perform job tasks.

Ethical Concerns.   The dangers come when a counselor uses computer-assisted counseling as a primary means of intervention instead of using it as a counseling aid. Since many of the applications deal specifically with depression or severe anxiety, it would be unethical not to personally monitor a particular client and assess for suicidal ideation. With voice-activated systems, a client might be in serious trouble with no human counselor available to make an assessment. Computer-assisted counseling should be used as a supplement and not as the main provision of services.

TECHNOLOGY IN ASSESSMENT AND DIAGNOSIS

Assessment can be defined as the accumulation of knowledge about a person from a variety of sources for purposes of providing some kind of intervention, diagnosis, or treatment for an individual seeking services. Regardless of counselor specialty, technology can be used in the assessment process. One burgeoning technological innovation used for assessments is the Internet.

Online Testing

A survey given to members of the Association for Assessment in Counseling (AAC) seeking knowledge of counselor technology use in assessment revealed that the majority of those surveyed (n = 153) used the Internet in their assessment practices (Ludberg & Cobitz, 1999). Counselors have access to a wide variety of assessment instruments through Internet sites that can be appropriate for a wide variety of diverse clients who may vary by ethnicity, gender, or age and many of these can be provided to the client cost free (Wittmer, 2000). These tests and assessments can measure specific factors such as level of IQ, a specific aptitude, level of emotional intelligence, or a certain attitude; while others are more general and evaluate various personality characteristics or help with vocational interests (Barak, 1999; O'Halloran, Fahr & Keller, 2002). For example, to see an online Emotional Intelligence test, an online Culture Fair Intelligence Test, or examples of online Verbal or Spatial Intelligence Tests visit *http://www.queendom.com/tests/iq*. Other sites assess client interests and personalities. For example (Career Keys) *http://www.careerkey.org/english* and the (Keirsey Temperament Sorter) *http://www.keirsey.com* are just a couple of those available. Some websites offer these services free while others require payment. Some enable retrieval of test results immediately while others will e-mail the results at a different time (Barak, 1999). Again, it is a "buyer beware" market as some sites are better than others. This author does not endorse any of the websites listed within the chapter. Websites are provided simply as examples of the types of services offered.

Test Interpretation and Scoring Software

In addition, computer-based test interpretation programs (CBTI) have been available since the 1950s (Aiken, 2000; Wyatt, 1991). Hundreds of these programs and services are available and include programs that can score and interpret the results of tests for anything from neuropsychological functioning to cognitive abilities and personality traits (Aiken, 2000). Generally, these interpretations are a result of either data ensuing from the clinical experiences of many psychodiagnosticians or from an accumulation of statistical data that define the relationships between questions answered on an inventory and a specific typology (Aiken, 2000). In addition, computers can aid in the entry of test data as information can be processed quickly using optical scanning. Some assessments such as the Minnesota Multiphasic Personality Inventory (MMPI) and the Millon Behavioral Health Inventory come with answer sheets that can be directly scanned into a computer (Block, 1994). There are also software packages available that will print out narrative testing reports for clients.

Databases

Databases can also be used in the assessment process. For example, The Dangerous Assessment Database contains information that aids experts in deciding whether to release potentially dangerous psychiatric patients (Davidson, 1991). This program consists of statistical information that is used to predict the likelihood that a released psychiatric patient would be a danger to society. The database system works by requiring input on 1,000 different questions in such areas as family background, childhood behavior, and response to therapy. The information is then weighted for reliability on a scale from unconfirmed reports, at the low end, to certified reports where there have been attempts to corroborate evidence (Davidson, 1991). Bias is accounted for by requiring input from the expert assessors to ascertain any underlying factors, which might influence judgment (Davidson, 1991).

Databases such as these could be used for a variety of important concerns in addition to decision making in psychiatric release, such as helping counselors assess for self-harm and suicidality. There are also computer programs that aid in clinical decision making by presenting a step-by-step sequence of decisions for diagnoses and symptomology (Wyatt, 1991). In addition, the Government Information Locator Service (GILS) can be useful in obtaining needed information concerning disorders, psychotropic drugs, and treatments. GILS is similar to the World Wide Web and is used for cataloging federal information resources (Houser, 1995). Information seekers need not be licensed or have credentials to access the GILS system such as might be the case for comparable websites. For example, Houser (1995) explains the difference between finding information on the Web and the GILS system using the website for the Center for Disease Control and Prevention as an example. This organization primarily disseminates to the medical community reports on outbreaks of infectious diseases and generally, only medical personnel have access to the information. In contrast, the GILS user may not be a member of the medical community but can still access the same information. For more information on GILS see *http://www.usgs.gov/gils/index.html.*

Other uses of technology for assessment purposes include: databases for maintaining assessment results, desktop spreadsheets (e.g., Excel or Lotus), or mainframe statistical packages (e.g., SAS or SPSS) for recording and analyzing information; use of assessment programs that incorporate multiple computerized instruments; electronically recorded patient tracking software with pre- and post-treatment measures; computerized biofeedback assessment; video, audio, floppy disc or CD-ROM to store data; and e-mail and fax to transmit data (Lundberg & Cobitz, 1999).

Technology has also been used in the process of diagnosis with some success. McCarty and Clancy (2002) discussed a study conducted at the Medical Center of Central Massachusetts concerning the reliability and validity of conducting diagnoses through teleconferencing methods. The study compared diagnoses for acute psychiatric patients who were involuntarily admitted. Half the group was diagnosed face-to-face while the other half was diagnosed through teleconferencing. Results showed that the "telediagnoses" had a perfect correlation, one with another, and had a .85 correlation with the face-to-face diagnoses. Similar results were found between teleconferencing and face-to-face assessments using the Mini-Mental Status Exams, Yale–Brown Obsessive-Compulsive Scale, the Hamilton Depression Scale, and the Hamilton Anxiety Scale (McCarty & Clancy, 2002).

Positives.   Barak (1999) describes several advantages to using technology for assessment purposes especially if provided by professionals in combination with ongoing counseling. Using computerized testing gains a counselor access for fast, accurate, highly accessible testing and scoring. Because the test is scored electronically, the process is nearly errorless. Data are accessible as soon as the respondent finishes the test and the data are stored in electronic form for easy transfer to a statistical package for analysis or to be incorporated into a databank. The counselor and the user have immediate access to instructions, test items, scoring techniques, and so on, and these can be easily updated as needed. Data from testing can be electronically submitted to a central location so norms can be updated frequently. Testing can be convenient for both counselor and client as tests can be taken nearly at any place, at any time. Assessment and testing can be conducted even when counselor and client are geographically separated, by using electronic transfer of data or by using the Internet. Finally, there are no expendable materials as everything is done electronically.

Negatives.   Barak (1999) also noted several disadvantages to using technology in assessments. Many tests put on the Internet may not meet the American Psychological Association's psychological testing standards. Counselors using tests from the Internet often cannot verify the validity or reliability of the tests they are using. In addition, counselors may not be present when testing is conducted, and therefore, cannot ascertain whether the client understood the test instructions. If the client did not understand, the whole test could be invalidated. Often test results and interpretations are not presented with clear explanations for the client. This could be problematic such as when a client receives a low IQ score or has been assessed in a negative way. The counselor also has no way to verify if the client actually took the test or had an accomplice take the test for him or her.

Ethical Concerns.   Ethics in the use of technology for assessment is an issue of broad concern, with access to information being the most commonly identified problem area. It may be difficult to verify the authenticity of electronic information (e.g., fraudulent transcripts or inaccurate Internet data) (Lundberg & Cobitz, 1999). When items are faxed, e-mailed, or otherwise electronically transmitted, fraud can be difficult to ascertain.

In addition, any time information is electronically transmitted, the sender has no control over the information once sent. As mentioned previously, confidentiality may be compromised with cyber transfers. Testing conducted via the Internet may have data collected by the website controlling the test (Barak, 1999). These website owners are not held to any ethical standards. In addition, in order to send information electronically, the information must be saved in an electronic format on a hard drive or floppy disk. These mediums must also be secured with passwords or be locked in secure locations to protect the information within.

Paper-and-pencil tests formatted for the Internet may not retain their psychometric properties. Changing the test format to fit electronic needs may compromise an otherwise acceptable test when originally constructed to be taken in paper-and-pencil form. Just because the original test had good reliability and validity, changes made to provide it in electronic form may change the test in an important way that would compromise these measures. It would be prudent for a counselor to seek information regarding these concerns for any test conducted electronically. Some tests are available from large testing companies such as the Strong Interest Inventory, the Myers-Briggs Type Indicator, and the Self-Directed Search. These companies provide counselors with the online validity and reliability information (O'Halloran, Fahr, & Keller, 2002).

However, do not assume that a test found on the Internet is the electronic form of a proven paper-and-pencil assessment unless it is from a reliable source. Some of the tests online are not the original tests but have been purposefully altered to prevent or bypass copyright violation. Alterations such as these significantly damage the utility for using these tests due to reliability, validity, and ethical concerns (Barak, 1999). It is important for a counselor to verify any test he or she decides to use from the Internet for its validity and reliability coefficients. If the site gives none, it is best not to use those tests and assessments. Reputable sites give these coefficients for the electronic version offered. Counselors should use caution and informed consent when using assessment instruments from the Internet.

In addition, clients need to understand the limits of confidentiality when using tests online. When using tests that are not offered from reliable sites, the client should also be informed that these tests are exploratory in nature and results should be presented as hypotheses due to the invalidated nature of most online assessments (O'Halloran, Fahr, & Keller, 2002).

TECHNOLOGICAL AIDS FOR CLIENT INTERVENTIONS

Again, computers and the Internet have become a well-used resource for counselors in many areas of their professional duties. Many counselors have found an endless source of inspiration and resources available to be used for interventions from online sources. Wittmer (2000) discussed some ways counselors have utilized the Internet and computer software to print out materials to be used therapeutically with clients. Counselors have used sites such as those that offer puppet patterns or art materials. These materials can be used with children or trauma victims to create a virtual world in order to describe difficult situations. For an example of such a site, see *http://www.kn .pacbell.com.* Desktop publishing, paint, or animation software has also been used so that clients can draw for art therapy or to express themselves in new ways. Some software can even be used to help clients create dramas complete with set design, wardrobe, scripts, and so on. There is an abundance of sites that can be used by counselors such as NickJr at *http://www.nickjr.com* that provide many games and other tools for counselors to use when working with children. One only has to jump online to find endless resources, possibilities, and materials that can be used therapeutically.

PowerPoint software can be used for psychoeducational presentations for groups or for individual clients with issues such as substance abuse, domestic violence, anger management, grief counseling, conflict resolution, sexual harassment, assertiveness training, or any other subject. Of course, counselors have been using videotapes and audiotapes for many decades to aid clients in counseling for educational purposes or to present vignettes to practice client skills or therapy applications.

Positives.   The Internet makes it possible for counselors to access many materials for free that might otherwise be cost prohibitive to use in their counseling practice. The possibilities are endless for its applicability for counseling work. In the expressive domain, with paint and art programs, computer animated skits that can be created, or puppets that can be downloaded and colored, a plethora of possibilities exist. All of these ideas can be used to aid a child or adult in greater expression of emotion or concerns, or actually aid in the practice of new skill sets. Scenarios can be created and clients can use these programs in the same way as role-play to work through issues.

Computer software can be expensive but once bought it becomes an inexhaustible resource that the counselor can use with clients repeatedly and many programs have printable materials that can be given to a client. The counselor does not have to buy these materials redundantly, but can simply print them from the software program each time as needed.

Negatives.   As these materials are all supplemental, there are not many negatives associated with them. However, some software programs can be expensive and Internet sites come and go. A counselor may find a site that fits his or her needs perfectly and then find that the site became discontinued.

Ethical Concerns.   Counselors need to be careful that the materials fit the client's needs and will be therapeutically beneficial. If the counselor becomes adamant about using materials from the Internet and selects materials that are not appropriate for the client's issue simply because the counselor is excited about using technology or if the counselor insists upon using these materials even though the client does not want to use them, then ethical problems will exist. Counselors must be careful not to be blindsided by the excitement of using technology and, therefore, use materials that do not therapeutically benefit the client. However, if used properly, the Internet, computer software programs, and audio/videotapes can greatly aid a counselor in the intervention process.

TECHNOLOGICALLY BASED RESOURCES FOR COUNSELORS AND CLIENTS

Today, research and informational resources are as close to the counselor and client as a mouse click. The Internet has created an increased number of sources from which counselors can access and learn about counseling research and obtain information to help their clients. Counselors can access professional journals, professional organizations, such as the American Counseling Association and the American Psychological Association, and electronic databases containing psychological research articles.

Online Databases

Many counseling journals are offered through online databases either free or for a cost. A counselor can type in his or her search terms and, instantaneously on the computer screen, see every article listed within that database pertaining to that subject. Numerous online databases offer journals that provide hundreds of full-text articles available to be printed, saved on disc or hard drive, or e-mailed right to the counselor's home or office. One example of such a database is PsycINFO, which contains over 800,000 abstracts and covers about 1,300 journal titles (Stover, 1993).

Counselors can access the latest information on nearly any counseling topic. Most university or public libraries subscribe to databases that provide access to these professional journals, newsletters, or magazines at no cost to the user as long as that user belongs to that institution. However, an individual counselor can subscribe to them as well for a fee. One example of a hard copy publication offered in electronic form is the American Counseling Association's *Counseling Today* (see *http://www.counseling.org/ctonline* for more information).

Many of the online journal databases simply offer an electronic version of the hard copy journal article. A counselor can still go to the library and access the same article on the shelf if he or she prefers. However, more frequently journals are being created that have no hard copy equivalent and are only available online in electronic form. Two examples of these are the e-journals and h-journals. Members of the American Counseling Association may be familiar with one e-journal, which is the

American Counseling Association's eNews. This is a news and practice bulletin, made available to subscribers (Baltimore & Jencius, 1999). These e-journals are made available online or else are e-mailed directly to the subscriber.

The h-journals, on the other hand, are hypermedia journals that only appear online. As per their name, hypermedia journals generally have audio or video clips that can be accessed within the article and hyperlinks to take a reader into other sites to gather additional information (Baltimore & Jencius, 1999). In addition, many of the reference articles have links so a reader can access and read them immediately. (see the *Journal of Technology in Counseling* (JTC) in the websites listed at the end of the chapter for an example of this type of h-journal).

Information Services and Forums

The Internet houses a plethora of information important to the work of counselors. Numerous websites provide information on etiology, medications, the latest therapeutic treatments, and ways for clients to cope for a variety of mental health disorders or other counseling issues (Rogers, 2001). For an example of these types of available sites, see the Online Dictionary of Mental Health at *http://www.human-nature.com/odmh/index.html* (Barak, 1999).

There are many such sites available to counselors too numerous to list here. Some websites are collection points of information to aid clients in finding counselors in their communities who specialize in that client's particular issue or concern. Sites such as MagellanAssist also offer hundreds of self-education tools to help with the early stages of change when clients are considering making behavioral modifications (Blair, 2001). Other sites are specialized to address specific issues such as sexual abuse, sexual problems, relationship issues, alcohol and drug abuse, eating disorders, or gay and lesbian issues (Powell, 1998). Some sites cater to the professional counselor and expect a certain level of education and prior training when accessed, whereas some sites cater to the public and expect the user to have no experience or training and, therefore, are more simplistic.

Counselor informational forums, such as PsychNet, are a valuable resource for counselors and offer a multitude of information and services for the counselor who subscribe. These include (Stover, 1993):

1. Information regarding licensure requirements by individual state
2. Bulletin boards to provide access to consultants, equipment, private practices for sale, job openings, etc
3. Access to computer services, computer consultants, and computer shareware
4. Opportunities for earning continuing education units through online courses as well as information regarding continuing education courses, seminars, and workshops held elsewhere
5. Access to database libraries such as KNOWLEDGE INDEX and PsychSearch
6. Upcoming events notification and calendar

7. Access to financial services (e.g., electronic insurance billing, malpractice insurance, collection services.)
8. Listings of employment opportunities and job openings by state
9. Psychological testing with results returned by e-mail
10. Access to a psychopharmacology database and a forum whereby counselors can ask questions and receive answers.
11. Access to a research grants database that lists grant opportunities
12. Access to special interest groups such as feminist psychology or psychology and the law

PsychNet offers more services too numerous to mention here but, hopefully, the reader gains a sense of what a valuable resource these information services and forums can be to a counseling practitioner or educator. However, often these types of services are membership driven and when membership lags information may not be updated in an expedient manner.

Virtual Self-Help Groups

There are also many Internet based virtual self-help groups conducted online as well as those conducted through chat rooms or e-mail that can provide additional support for individuals seeking change (Delmonico, Daninhirsh, Page, Walsh, L'Amoreaux, & Thompson, 2000). Subsequently, there are sites that aid a client through the self-help process by providing guidance, assessment of the problem, evaluation of the severity of the problem, information on background and development of the issue at hand; offering suggestions for change; and aiding in goal making. The site might also offer suggestions on books, videos, or other instructional materials that will aid an individual in working through his or her issue (Barak, 1999).

There are also sites online developed by individuals who have faced an experience such as abortion, or deal with an illness such as AIDS, which serve to bring people with like issues together for support and information (Barak, 1999; Swiss AIDS, 1999). These are not professional sites but can lend a client additional emotional support by conversing with others with the same issues. These sites can be accessed 24 hours per day. Some sites offer virtual communities whereby people with like issues, such as addiction, can exchange ideas, information, and coping mechanisms by posting messages on electronic bulletin boards or by sending e-mail (King, 1994).

Positives.   There are numerous resources available online or through computer software that can be downloaded and printed. Internet research is easier than ever with easy-to-use search engines and hypertextual indexed links that allow counselors and clients to access information on nearly any topic within seconds at any time of the day or night and in relative privacy. Professional psychological information banks are generally an accurate, easily accessed, frequently updated resource that can be used by counselors and clients alike at any time of the day or night. Counselors can research information on specific disorders, access the most current journal articles regarding treatment or theory, or converse with supervisors or colleagues, all from the convenience of home or office.

Negatives.   It is not always easy to ascertain the accuracy of information found on the Web. Both counselors and clients are cautioned to use information from authentic sites such as the American Counseling Association or American Psychological Association to be certain information is correct and updated regularly. Many websites are individually owned and operated and are not peer reviewed or authenticated. The Internet is not a stable entity and is subject to rapid change and a lack of uniformity. Websites may change addresses, shut down or change contents (Gale & McKee, 2002). Material may fail to download or may not be credible. However, websites that have endings such as (gov., edu, .org) generally are more reliable because these endings denote government, educational, or professional organizational websites and are authorized by the Internet Corporation for Assigned Names and Numbers (Gale & McKee, 2002).

Online professional journal databases are generally reliable and accurate but unless a counselor has access to them, through his or her organization, the cost for subscription could be prohibitive. Therefore, access to peer reviewed, scholarly sources of counseling research may be limited. Even if the counselor belongs to the American Counseling Association and has access to that organization's database, access is limited to American Counseling Association journals. In comparison, many universities give students and faculty access to many different databases, each of which provide access to ten to fifty journals. Two databases deemed useful for counselors and provided on the Internet for free are *ERIC* and *Ingenta* (Gale & McKee, 2002). However, these only provide abstracts and not the full text article.

Counselor use of electronic journals also requires a computer and an Internet hookup and the associated skills to access the journal and perform a search of the database. If the Internet connection is not reliable, the computer processor is slow, or the counselor does not have the skills to conduct an effective search, the downloading of articles can be a frustrating process.

Ethical Concerns.   Counselors must verify that information they receive or use is correct. It might be prudent to crosscheck information found on the Internet with other journal sources unless it is from a recognized professional source such as the American Counseling Association, PsychNet, or accessed through a university or other reputable organization's database.

CLIENT/THERAPIST REFERRALS

Technology has aided in the referral process for both counselors and clients. Today, there are many websites designed to provide information to individuals and provide guidance as to whether that individual should seek counseling (Barak, 1999). Sites such as the American Psychological Association's "Talk To Someone Who Can Help" *http://helping.apa.org* offers information regarding how counseling can help, what counseling modality works for different issues, and lets the consumer know information that will aid him or her in counseling decisions.

Other sites such as Psyfidential at *http://www.psyfidential.com* allow the consumer to enter geographical information, preferred counseling modality, and counselor practice specialties and then receive a list of counselors who meet those specifications from which the consumer can choose (Barak, 1999). These sites perform a service to both clients and counselors by providing resources and information that provide the best match for the client.

In addition, many counselors advertise online through websites. A general search for "counseling" or "counselors" will give a consumer multiple listings from which to choose. Information on these sites generally includes information about counseling modality or counselor specialties, location of the office, contact information, operating hours, services provided, and fee schedules. Most of these sites provide the consumer with an e-mail address through which a potential client can converse and ask questions.

Positives.   These online referral sources can save a client valuable time and provide a more efficient method of finding appropriate services. In minutes, a client can enter information and obtain a list of counselors in his or her area from which to choose. Counselors also can effectively advertise services and provide a client with more information than could be placed in a telephone book ad. Internet websites can often be low cost. The counselor can also utilize web links to provide intake forms for a client to fill out and bring to the first session or to provide the client with the counselor's disclosure statement. A link can even be provided discussing the limits of confidentiality and other pertinent information. This can save valuable time if the client has already read and signed these documents prior to arrival. The counselor can then answer questions and ascertain client understanding once these topics have been introduced.

Negatives.   Not all counselors advertise online nor will all counselors in a given area come up in a general Internet search. Therefore, only certain types of counselors can be found online to the exclusion of other types. This may limit a client's choices. In addition, often a client really benefits from a face-to-face visit so the client can ascertain if a particular counselor will be someone with whom he or she can form a strong working relationship. It is difficult to get a sense of someone through an ad or an e-mail conversation. However, if the client feels a particular counselor is not a good fit for him or her, he or she is always free to terminate the relationship and find another, although this can become time consuming for the client.

Ethical Concerns.   Clients might provide too much information on websites and, therefore, hinder confidentiality. Clients are cautioned when filling out online assessments for counselor referral to provide neutral information (Barak, 1999). In addition, counselors using these website referral mechanisms need to make sure the information being provided to potential clients is valid and accurate. It is unethical to represent oneself falsely. If the counselor has someone else design his or her web page, the counselor needs to make sure there are no errors in representation. Counselors need to frequently update their websites or referral information and make sure their specialty areas, level of education, counseling modalities, and training are reflected accurately.

TECHNOLOGY IN COUNSELOR SUPERVISION

Counseling students have long used audio- or videotapes to record their sessions for later perusal by their supervisor (Pelling & Reynard, 1999). These forms of technology have been beneficial but the counseling session is already over before the supervisor gets a chance to view the work that has been done. This is of course only if the student is not getting live supervision such as a supervisor viewing the session via a one-way mirror and/or using the "bug in the ear" (e.g., supervisor uses a radio transmitter while the supervisee has an earphone) or uses a telephone to transmit feedback and suggestions (Casey, Bloom, & Moan, 1994; Smith, Mead, & Kinsella, 1998).

Many universities use such one-on-one live supervision. However, newer approaches eliminate the "bug in the ear," which can be highly disruptive to student trainees, and utilize instead networked computers which allow the supervisor to type in messages that can be viewed on the trainee's computer screen (Casey, Bloom, & Moan, 1994). Some systems, instead of using text messages, simply present the trainee with a graph line on a computer monitor located behind and above the client's head. The graph line represents the trainee's counseling behaviors or techniques. Therefore, the supervisor can indicate trainee performance simply by moving the graph line up or down (Smith, Mead, & Kinsella, 1998). This is far less intrusive then the traditional "bug in the ear" or text on a computer screen that the counselor has to read but is not as informative an intervention. The trainee might know his or her performance is under par, but have no idea how to correct it.

Even though the VCR seems near extinction as a supervision tool and because of more technological advances, the VCR has not been replaced but rather this technology has been enhanced to include dual track recording. This allows a supervisor to record his or her own comments on the videotape track while the session's original soundtrack is preserved on the original tape (Casey, Bloom, & Moan, 1994). Therefore, when the counselor in training plays back the enhanced version, the supervisor's comments are superimposed on the sound track over and above the student's and client's voices. This technique is especially useful in distance supervision where student and supervisor are not viewing the tapes together.

Other ways old technology has been enhanced for supervision include using enhanced observation labs that provided video camera and VCRs for each room, an intercom system and a master video monitoring system that enables a supervising professor to view all counseling sessions simultaneously enabling live supervision of multiple students at the same time (Braggerly, 2002). Enhanced features allow the supervising professor to increase the audio sound for one individual room, use the intercom system to intervene if a problem develops that needs immediate attention, or to alert all students to important information such as time remaining for the session.

One exciting innovation takes this concept one step farther and uses web cams on the student trainee's computer. For example, Michael Armendariz at New Mexico

State University is now implementing a program in that university's training center. Once installed, counselors in training will use these cameras to record counseling sessions or transmit the session live via the Internet to the supervisor's office computer. This technology allows the student immediate feedback during and after a session as well as immediate intervention from the supervisor should client or counselor safety become compromised. In addition, these digitized images can be saved for later viewing with the student.

Computers are also used in training by providing counselors with interactive, multimedia simulations of counseling sessions in which the trainee can practice when a "live" client is not available or when counselors want to practice skills for crisis situations (Casey, 1999). For example, the computer simulation can be a scenario of a suicidal client. Students can then practice their skills without risking the safety of a real client.

Another technology used for supervision has been the use of electromyography (EMG) machines, which allow supervisors to infer the supervisee's emotional state during the session by monitoring skin conductance levels (SCL) and skin temperature. Casey, Bloom, and Moan (1994) report that this is done using two video cameras, one taping the counseling session and one filming the psychophysiological readings. This gives the supervisor objective data regarding the emotional state of the counselor trainee. This technology can aid supervisors in enabling student counselors to use themselves as a counseling tool by attending to their own feelings and intuitions.

Remote counseling supervision for those students on internship has also been utilized by using compressed video (Casey, Bloom, & Moan, 1994). The University of Wyoming launched such a program in the early 1990s. Supervisors at the university coordinate a video telephone conference at a prescribed meeting time. This is synchronous communication and occurs in real time with all participants on the telephone simultaneously. Mentoring using this format or via the Internet is also an option (Knouse, 2001). Both supervision and mentoring help beginning counselors develop skill and competence.

Technology has also made supervision easier for counselors who are not in university training programs. Often counselors, who have already graduated from their counseling programs and are licensed or certified, find themselves in need of supervision. Ethically when working with a counseling issue or an ethnic population for which the counselor has not previously worked, supervision or referral is warranted. If a counselor wants to add a specialization, counseling modality, or work with a diverse population, the counselor will need someone trained in that area to supervise him or her until that counselor reaches a level of competence in the new area.

Supervision can be provided via the Internet in various ways. Communication via e-mail enhances availability and access between counselor and supervisor. Instruction or recommendations are given in writing so a counselor can have documentation of consultations. A supervisor can utilize different websites to provide a counselor with more information regarding topic areas or populations of interest.

Stamm (1998) discussed a case study of distance supervision conducted by the Veterans Affairs Cooperative Study Program. In this study, supervisors from three sites in Providence, Rhode Island, Los Angeles, California, and White River Junction, Vermont, supervised counselors in Boston, Massachusetts, Miami, Florida, Minneapolis, Minnesota, New Orleans, Louisiana, Palo Alto, California, Providence, Rhode Island, San Diego, California, San Francisco, California, Seattle, Washington, and West Haven, Connecticut. For every supervisor there were twenty supervisees all located at some distance from the supervisor location. Supervision was conducted via audio- and videotape, weekly telephone conversations, and with daily, or as needed, e-mails. One-third of the way into the study the following transmissions were counted between supervisor and counselor: 20,000 e-mails, 1,800 hours of individual phone supervision, 500 hours of group phone consultations, 450 secured fax information forms, 10,000 hours of audiotaped sessions, and 3,500 hours of psychotherapy videotape. Supervision conducted in this manner was deemed a success establishing that supervision, like counseling, can be done from a distance (Stamm, 1998).

Positives.   One benefit of using the Internet for supervision is that the counselor and supervisor do not have to reside within the same geographical location. This opens up many possibilities for counselors when choosing a supervisor (Clark & Stone, 2002). The positive attributes for audio, video, or digital taping of sessions has been noted by Pelling and Reynard (1999) in that they offer a high level of accuracy of observation, provide the supervisor a high level of objective detail regarding client/counselor interaction, as well as enable accessibility of reflection for the student.

Negatives.   There may be instances when a counselor needs a supervisor to be accessible in person. Distance supervision would make this difficult. In addition, the same concerns exist as mentioned in other sections of this chapter regarding confidentiality. Once client information leaves a counselor's hand via the Internet there is no guarantee that client confidentiality can be maintained. Furthermore, unless the supervisor is well known in the field it may be more difficult to ascertain the supervisor's expertise or credentials when he or she is located a great distance from the counselor.

Negatives associated with video or audio taping of sessions is that equipment can fail. Tapes can be accidentally erased or be "eaten" by the VCR or audiotape player. Tapes can also be misplaced or lost, which compromises client confidentiality. However, as long as due care is taken, these forms of technology greatly enhance a supervisor and trainee's ability to analyze each session for strengths and growth areas. Often, we forget important details of our sessions especially when they are rich in emotion or information. Capturing it on video- or audiotape maintains the integrity of the work for evaluation.

Ethical Concerns.   Both counselor and supervisor need to show care when communicating via e-mail or the Internet so identifying details of a client are not given in order to protect client confidentiality. E-mail is often not secure although we might think that it is. When we have to provide a user identification and password to access it within our own office or home we can become lulled into a false sense of security. Many counselors try to offset risk by providing a disclaimer on e-mail transmissions warning of the confidential nature of the communication such as the following:

> The information contained in this e-mail message may be privileged, confidential, and protected from disclosure. If you are not the intended recipient, any dissemination, distribution, or copying is strictly prohibited. If you think that you have received this e-mail message in error, please reply to the sender to that effect.

However, such a disclaimer does not erase the damage done to a client if pertinent or identifying information regarding a client falls into the wrong hands.

In addition, before committing to distance supervision, counselors should check with licensing agencies and state law to ascertain if the state the counselor lives in or organization through which the counselor is licensed or credentialed accepts such practices (Stamm, 1998). Some states and agencies may have stipulations regarding working across state lines.

CONTINUING EDUCATION UNITS (CEUS)

Every counselor is aware that upon graduation, certification, or licensure, a counselor's education does not end. To maintain certification and/or licensure, counselors must engage in a certain number of continuing education units or credits. Technology has made meeting this requirement much easier. Although there is still some resistance to using computers and online instruction in the counseling field, distance education has enabled people all over the world to receive an education or continue building upon that education using computers (Quinn, Hohenshil, & Fortune, 2002).

Distance education can be defined as "a structured teaching and learning method that uses a wide spectrum of technologies, including computer networking, audio/video conferencing, and paper-based materials, to reach learners at a distance" (Woodford, Rokutani, Gressard, & Berg, 2001, p. 1). Increasingly, counseling programs are offering more courses, seminars, and workshops online (Clark & Stone, 2002). These courses can be used to satisfy continuing education credits.

Online education is burgeoning and current estimates are that 7 million people are educated online each year (McFadden, 2000). The American Council on Education (ACE) has recognized at least 300 distance learning programs offered by education institutions including some prestigious ones such as Stanford, Purdue, and Duke universities (McFadden, 2000). A minimum of 900 educational institutions within the United States offer full-degree programs (McFadden, 2000).

Methods for providing distance education include (National Center for Education Statistics, 1997–1998):

- *Asynchronous Internet instruction:* The student does the assignment and e-mails it to the instructor. The instructor grades the assignment and gives feedback to the student. Tests are also conducted online.

- *Two-way interactive video or satellite hookup:* Instructor and students can see each other via a video link or satellite hookup. Instruction is given in real time, therefore, the students and teacher can interact during instruction.
- *One-way prerecorded video:* The instructor video tapes a lecture and provides it to students.

Woodford, Rokutani, Gressard, and Berg (2001) and Jones and Karper (2000) reviewed the research literature regarding the efficacy of distance learning. Their findings indicate:

- Distance education is as effective as traditional face-to-face instruction as long as the method and technologies used are appropriate to the instructional tasks, student-to-student interaction is available, and instructor feedback to students is done in a timely manner.
- Distance education is effective as long as effectiveness is measured by the achievement of learning, by the attitudes of students and teachers, and by return on the investment.
- The instructional format in and of itself is not important as long as all students have equal access to resources and the delivery technology is appropriate to the content taught.

Positives.   There are many benefits for counselors to engage in distance learning in fulfillment of their CEUs or to further their education. Counselors who live in rural areas can easily access educational materials through accredited programs that will fulfill continuing education requirements (Woodford, Rokutani, Gressard, & Berg, 2001). Counselors can take advantage of course offerings via computer from prestigious institutions such as Stanford or Duke or from many countries around the world. For example, distance education is offered in China, most of Europe, Austria, Canada, Israel, the Sudan, Ethiopia, Kenya, Zambia, India, and most of Latin America (McFadden, 2000). Therefore, counselors are not limited to obtaining classes within their own geographical area or country.

When the distance educational course offers asynchronous instruction, the counselor can then access materials, complete tests, send in papers, and so on at any convenient time. This gives the counselor a lot of flexibility to incorporate pertinent class work into his or her schedule. Sometimes counselors are in need of CEUs and have tight schedules and, therefore, may be forced by time constraints to choose educational opportunities that fit a certain time frame or geographical location. Distance learning frees the counselor from these constraints and allows him or her to choose where and when he or she receives instruction.

Negatives.   Technology is not foolproof. Internet servers go down. Computer viruses wreak havoc. Distance education is relatively new and many things periodically can and do go wrong. These types of glitches can seriously undermine the educational advances such technology brings to counselors. In addition, students need to be computer literate. Many students today are computer literate but some are not.

Some older students who did not grow up in the computer age might have a disadvantage in comparison with a younger student who grew up with computers. Both types of students may theoretically have the same access to class materials but one student might be able to utilize materials easier or more effectively. It is hard to ensure then, the criteria of equal access.

Ethical Concerns.   Counselors need to be aware of classes offered online and make sure the National Board of Certified Counselors (NBCC) recognizes them for CEUs. There are many unaccredited classes offered online as well as those that meet NBCC standards for continuing education (Sands, 2000). As always it is a "buyer beware" market and counselors considering distance learning as a method of meeting continuing education units should check with the appropriate licensing or credentialing agency to make sure such classes meet requirements. Many online classes will advertise if they do meet CEU requirements and if so for which groups (e.g., social workers, psychologists, counselors). Do not make the assumption if CEUs are offered that they meet NBCC criteria. Many professions require continuing education and not all credentialing or licensing agencies agree on what is appropriate for continuing education.

TECHNOLOGY AIDED COUNSELOR COMMUNICATION

Counselor communication has also become enhanced using technology. Counselors have been using technology to communicate for decades via the telephone and more recently, facsimile machines, but through computer technology and the Internet, communication between client and counselor, or counselor and supervisor/colleague, has never been faster or more efficient.

Electronic Transmission and Storage

Computers can be linked into vast networks whereby files and information can be shared and accessed by any individual within the network who holds the proper password. Electronic mail can be sent and received in mere seconds anywhere in the world as opposed to the several days it takes to send a paper letter through the U.S. postal service (also known as snail mail). Some organizations even allow clients and counselors to make and cancel appointments via e-mail or a website on the Internet.

In addition, information can be put onto a 3.5" floppy disk to be stored or mailed. CD-ROM drives can save entire filing cabinets full of information that normally take up an inordinate amount of office space and contain it all in an area approximately six inches by three inches (CD-ROM record storage, 1995). When needed, this information can quickly be uploaded onto the computer screen and then e-mailed to anywhere in the world.

Listservs

Counselors can also use e-mail discussion lists, "listservs," to communicate and receive information (Pelling, 2002). To subscribe, an e-mail is sent to the listserv master and then the subscriber is added to the list. Once a counselor is added to the list, he or she can send and receive messages to and from the entire group. Listservs are intended to link like-minded individuals to inform, promote, and stimulate discussion and debate on a particular issue (McFadden, 2000). Normally, these discussions are specific to the users of the listservs. This is a great communication source and allows counselors to consult with colleagues all over the world who hold expertise or knowledge in different specialty areas of interest.

For example, counseling graduate students can join a discussion listserv, communicate with counseling students from all over the world, and compare programs, ethics, or any other aspect of counselor education. Some organizations such as the American Counseling Association sponsor these types of listservs for counseling students. Two examples of group specific listservs include CESNET-L for counselor educators and COUNSGRADS for graduate students in counselor education (McFadden, 2000).

Some listservs may also be subject specific such as ADA-LAW (*listserv@ listserv.nodak.edu*), which centers on discussion regarding the Americans with Disabilities Act. Therefore, counselors interested in certain subject areas can join specific listservs and exchange information.

Synchronous Communication

Communication can also be conducted synchronously. Synchronous communication can be conducted via "chat rooms" or videoconferencing. These communications take place in real time, and therefore demand synchronization of sender and receiver. There are two different types of chat environments: text-only and multi-media. Multi-media chat rooms are known as GMUKS (Graphical Multi-User Konversations) in which users choose an actual character to represent themselves onscreen (Sands, 2000). This adds a visual dimension that can mimic physicality and movement and typically are in the shape of animals, cartoon characters, or celebrities (Sands, 2000). In addition, "emoticons" can be used to simulate expression. The "emoticon" is an ASCII glyph used to indicate an emotional state in an e-mail or transmission. Examples include (Sands, 2000):

1. The smiley face :-)
2. The winking face ;-)
3. The frowning face :-(

For a dictionary of "emoticons" available for online emotional expression, see *http://www.chirpingbird.com/netpets/html/computer/emoticon.html*.

Videoconferencing is more complicated and costly than mere chat room communication but is advantageous when the people communicating desire to see each other visually. Videoconferencing is the "next best thing to being there" and can be used even when individuals are on opposite sides of the world (Braggerly, 2002). Even though videoconferencing is more expensive than chat room communication, technological advances within the last few years have made the hardware and software to support this medium increasingly economical. For example, Riemer-Reiss (2000) points out that most new computers already include sound cards and digital cameras can be added to a computer system for under $250.00. Software can also be inexpensively purchased that allows sound and moving pictures to be transmitted over the Internet, simply by the initiator typing in the receiver's web address. Once the two computers have established an Internet link, interactive communication can begin.

Wittmer (2000) discusses many types of electronic tools counselors can use for supervision or collaboration purposes. Many of these are free such as NetMeeting at *http://www.microsoft.com/widows/netmeeting/* or the Cu-SeeMe technology mentioned earlier. These applications allow counselors to communicate with both audio and video, exchange graphics on an electronic whiteboard, transfer files, use text-based chat rooms, and collaborate on any Windows-based program (Engstrom, 1997).

Computer and Internet technology has even revolutionized faxing through websites such as Fax4Free (*www.fax4free.com*). With this site, a counselor can send faxes anywhere in the United States, Canada, or Australia free of charge with many more countries becoming available in the near future. In addition, some websites can aid in translation when working with a client or sending or receiving information in a foreign language. AltaVista has an online language translator (*http://babelfish.altavista.com/cgi-bin/translate?*), which allows a user to paste in text and choose the appropriate translation. This application will also allow a web address of a foreign site typed into the window and the application will translate the entire web page for the user (Wittmer, 2000).

Positives.   Wittmer (2000) and Jedlicka and Jennings (2001) discussed many advantages and disadvantages of using technology in communication. When using fax, computer, or Internet-based forms of communication, the sender and receiver can communicate at any time, day or night, without having to synchronize times such as would be needed when communicating by telephone. Another advantage is a person can thoroughly think through a communication before sending it.

These types of communication are also cost and time efficient. For example, e-mail is generally free as long as one has an Internet hookup; when a counselor needs to communicate with many people he or she can send a "bulk" e-mail with no more effort or time required than it takes to send out a single e-mail, simply by clicking on multiple addresses for the recipient. Files can be attached to the e-mail, therefore long prewritten information need not be typed twice or printed. Huge amounts of information can be sent in this manner saving large amounts of money for postage and handling or long-distance fees for sending faxes.

Negatives.   Most communication via computers, fax, or the Internet must be typewritten. This may be a hardship for some who do not have typing skills or who are disabled. Written communication cannot convey nonverbal subtleties, such as hand gestures, facial expression, or tone of voice. Some people do not write clearly and if the recipient does not understand, clarity cannot be gained immediately but another communication must be sent. Counselors might receive numerous e-mail messages, which must be read, and perhaps responded to; this can be time consuming. Often, e-mail users get "spammed," which is the equivalent to receiving online junk mail. It can be difficult to ascertain which communications are "junk" and cannot be discarded until the counselor opens the e-mail. In addition, viruses can be sent through e-mail via word attachments. These can infect the counselor's computer causing disruptions and headaches.

Ethical Concerns.   There are certain protections in place when using the U.S. postal service for communication purposes that are not found when communicating electronically. For example, it is a felony to open another person's "snail mail" whereas e-mails and faxes can be intercepted and read by other individuals with minimal or no penalties. Therefore, as discussed before, confidentiality cannot be guaranteed when using electronic mediums. This can cause ethical issues for counselors using this form of communication if great care is not used to protect the identity of the client.

In addition, concerns regarding videoconferencing in relationship to confidentiality have been addressed by the America Psychological Association (APA), the American Counseling Association (ACA), the National Board of Certified Counselors (NBCC), and the International Society for Mental Health Online (ISMHO), all of whom have composed formulized statements regarding the use of such technology in counseling (McFadden, 2000). Contact these organizations or access their websites for specific information regarding these formulized statements.

PAPERWORK AND SCHEDULING APPLICATIONS

In days of old, counselors had to use manual typewriters or typewriters with limited memory (capacity of a paragraph or so) to type up progress notes, treatment plans, case conceptualizations, or other numerous documents that counselors always need to write. When errors were made, entire documents might have to be typed over onto new paper. Today, word processing programs have made this job much simpler. Counselors can theoretically produce error free documents utilizing such features as spell check and thesaurus and have the ability to move entire sentences or paragraphs to new locations within a document, printing only when the document is in its final state.

If later upon inspection, the counselor does notice an error within the document, he or she can go back into the document and change the error, thus printing out a new copy rather then retyping the entire document or defacing it with white-out. In addition, if the counselor finds out new information about a client that was not previously included in a document, these additions can be quickly added. CD-ROM, floppy disks, or the counselor's hard drive can store such documents minimizing the need for multiple hard copies (CD-ROM record storage, 1995).

Client records can also be maintained on computers limiting bulky files. This considerably reduces the office space needed for file storage. One type of electronic storage system available is optical disk storage. This system offers such innovations as automated indexing and automated searching and creates hard copies only when necessary (Carroll, 1995; Wintrob, 1995). Therefore, if a counselor needs a client file, he or she can enter the client's name and a date and the optical system will instantaneously locate the file. However, optical disk files often won't work on another optical disk drive, at least not with any high rate of success, so this can be problematic if disk drives need to be changed (CD-ROM record storage, 1995).

Even if the technological advances ended there, it would be enough, but technology has produced many more innovative features to make paperwork and organization easier for counselors today. Software programs are available to aid in writing treatment plans, progress reports, and nearly any other ongoing document needed for a client's file. Case conceptualization forms can be stored on hard drives so the counselor can access and simply place check marks in the categories that apply.

Counselors can also use "personal information managers," which is a software application for a computer that can help counselors organize information. According to Wittmer (2000), the utility of personal information managers is that it allows an individual to enter information such as textual notes, appointments, reminders, lists, dates, and so forth and the computer program links these random bits of information in meaningful ways. This software can alert counselors to such things as scheduling conflicts and remind counselors of impending appointments. These personal information managers can be installed on home or office computers, handheld devices, or even accessed online. Examples of such online devices can be found at *http:// www.emailaddresses.com/email_pim.htm.*

Positives.   All of this technology can significantly reduce the amount of time it takes a counselor to organize, schedule, and complete paperwork, which frees more time for client contact hours. Reports are neat and nearly error free with diligent proofing. Counselors no longer need to rely on a dictionary to check spelling but can have the computer do it for them. Documents can be printed or saved and sent in electronic form. Old documents that still need to be saved can be scanned into a computer and saved, minimizing space needed to maintain old client files similar to the old microfiche systems.

Negatives.   Computers are not always secure and many people may have access to them. Hackers can break into seemingly secure systems and upload confidential materials. Password protected systems are not fail proof but often neither are the office doors or filing cabinet locks in counselors' offices. Conversely, better operating systems are being developed with enhanced security options to ensure protection for users from outside tampering (Locking down, 2003).

Counselors must be computer literate to take full advantage of software programs that streamline paperwork as some software programs do not come with illustrative directions (Wong, 2000). Computers and technology can be wonderful when they are working but very frustrating when they are not. Software and files can become corrupted and important information lost.

Ethical Concerns.   Ethical concerns mirror those discussed earlier, primarily concerns regarding confidentiality. However, are paper records any more safe than electronic records? It is up to individual counselors and organizations to ensure client safety and confidentiality. The same guidelines exist for electronic file storage as it does for paper file storage. Records need to be kept in locked devices (e.g., filing cabinets) within locked offices and facilities. Computers with sensitive client data should be password protected. Only pertinent employees should have access to these security codes. See the guidelines established by the American Counseling Association, American Psychological Association, and the National Board of Certified Counselors for more information regarding electronic data storage.

SUMMARY

Counselors need to build their technological knowledge and skills in order to use these tools in their work. Many counselor education programs are not training graduates in the use of current technology (Edwards, Portman, & Berthea, 2002; Hines, 2002). Currently, there is a call to the profession to integrate technology into the curriculum of counselor education programs (Baltimore, 2002). The Association for Counselor Education and Supervision (ACES) has composed twelve counselor education technological competencies that graduates should master upon leaving any program (Haley & Carrier, 2002). However, when ACES surveyed its membership regarding technological proficiency in these twelve competency areas the results showed that members felt the highest level of competence with e-mail, listservs, and audiovisual equipment and felt the lowest level of competency for computerized testing, knowledge of web counseling, and use of computerized statistical packages such as SAS and SPSS (Myers & Gibson, 2003). In other words, members felt comfortable with the older, more rudimentary forms of technology and had less comfort with the more current innovations.

Technology is advancing so fast that by the time this chapter is in print, parts of what is talked about here may already be obsolete. There may also be innovations that are not covered in this chapter. If counselor education programs are not training future counselors to use the technology currently available, these counselors will fall behind other mental health service workers who are using this technology. There is no choice today as to whether a counselor will use technological advances in his or her practice. It is more a matter of which technology the counselor chooses. A new world has opened to counselors within the last few decades. A world that at times can be frightening and exciting, simultaneously. There are so many choices from which to consider as technology can be utilized in some form or another to aid in nearly every aspect of a counselor's work. Counselors need to think about the benefits, the drawbacks, and the ethical considerations when implementing technology into their work.

While there can be a plethora of concerns regarding the use of technology in a "paperless" society, many such concerns are only more modern versions that faced the standard paper society. For example, counselors have used videotapes and audiotapes for years for supervision and documentations purposes. The electronic versions of these, CD-ROM or floppy disk, require no more consideration. All such devices should be locked up in a secure location, such as a locked drawer or filing cabinet, in addition to being locked within an office. What is a concern, however, is when these devices are uploaded onto a computer hard drive. With VCRs and audiotape players, one can listen to or watch a counseling session, with no fear that remnants of that session remain behind on the equipment used to play it. With computers, there is a concern that client information might be inadvertently left behind.

Counselors must use more caution and diligence to ensure that technology does not breach client safety or confidentiality. Counselors must also weigh the cost and benefits of using such technology for clients. The consideration for implementing any technology should be on providing improved client services and should not be implemented merely to satisfy the curiosity of the counselor. However, there are many technological innovations that can streamline paperwork and other time-consuming tasks, which will free a counselor to attend to more pertinent client issues. Using some of the technology discussed within this chapter is still controversial among some counseling professionals. However, regardless of how one feels about the issue of technology in counseling, one thing is certain: technology is here to stay.

PART II

COUNSELING SKILLS

The responsibilities of counselors, regardless of the setting in which they implement their roles, require that they be competent to provide clients with a variety of services. These services cannot be implemented unless counselors have mastered a number of core knowledge and skills areas. This section of the text provides the reader with an overview and introduction to the counseling skills, and associated knowledge base, that become the focus of much of the counselor education and supervision experience.

Chapter 6, "Individual Counseling: Traditional Approaches," provides information on approaches to working therapeutically with individual clients, including more in-depth descriptions of differing approaches such as Freudian, cognitive-behavioral, and Rogers's person-centered approach. Mechanisms of change within the individual are discussed, as well as rationales for understanding how individual problems develop. Chapter 7, "Individual Counseling: Brief Approaches," describes and discusses models for brief therapies. This topic is an important one to the role of the counselor given the impact of managed care and emphasis on cost containment and the chapter presents an excellent overview for the beginning professional.

Chapter 8, "Group Counseling," presents the basic components of group counseling, including a discussion of the history of group counseling, types of group work, qualities of the effective group leader, stages of group life, and common myths that beginning counselors and therapists often hold about the nature of group work.

Counseling as a profession had its roots in the vocational guidance movement of the early part of this century, and working with career and vocational issues remains a significant part of many counselors' roles today. Chapter 9, "Career Counseling," provides an introduction to the different theories and styles of career counseling. It also outlines the stages of career exploration and tools and interventions that the career counselor can use to assist the client in such a search. The authors describe the major vocational tests that a counselor might use to gain more information about a client's career and vocational needs.

Spirituality counseling is a topic of increasing importance to counselors all over the country as more and more clients seek the assistance of the professional counselor with issues related to their spirituality. The authors of Chapter 10, "Counseling and Spirituality," discuss issues relating to support for the inclusion of spirituality by the counseling profession, models addressing the spiritual dimensions and the counselor's role, ways to assess for spiritual dimensions, characteristics of healthy spiritual development and implications for counselors, and research findings and their implications for training and practice.

Counselors need to remain open to new innovative methods and theories that may increase their professional effectiveness. Chapter 11, "Creative Approaches to Counseling," which describes a number of alternative approaches to working with clients, is an important chapter. Many of these approaches are becoming more well known as their effectiveness has been demonstrated. Such alternative therapies include music and art therapy, movement therapy, and the creative use of guided imagery. Such interventions are exciting in the possibilities they present for the counselor wishing to assist clients in self-expression and personal growth; such approaches are becoming more widely used.

The role of testing and use of assessment instruments within the counseling profession are described in more depth in Chapter 12, "Counseling Uses of Tests." The author presents a number of key terms and concepts and describes various categories of tests that a counselor might have occasion to use with a client.

Chapter 13, "Diagnosis in Counseling," provides a comprehensive outline of the major categories in the DSM-IV currently used by the therapeutic community in providing accurate diagnosis and assessment. The importance of diagnosis to the overall counseling process is described, as well as benefits and risks inherent in the process of diagnosis.

CHAPTER SIX

INDIVIDUAL COUNSELING: TRADITIONAL APPROACHES

BENEDICT T. MCWHIRTER, PH.D.
MONICA I. ISHIKAWA, M.ED.
University of Oregon

While the history of counseling and psychotherapy are rich with diverse approaches to understanding and resolving human problems, the primary goal of counseling remains in its ability to foster optimal human functioning and development (Walsh, 2003). For the purposes of this chapter, we present three traditional theoretical orientations in counseling that seek to promote psychological healing and well-being (Hansen, 2002). The three approaches that we focus on are psychoanalysis and the psychodynamic approach that represents psychodynamic theory (Freud, 1915–1917, 1949); rational-emotive therapy, as a cognitive-behavioral approach that represents cognitive-behavioral theory (Ellis, 1962, 1995); and person-centered therapy, an approach to counseling that reflects the humanistic tradition (Rogers, 1951).

Since this chapter is designed to present a fairly simple overview of the three traditional approaches to counseling, you should be aware that our discussion is fairly restricted. Similarly, current meta-analysis of counseling outcome studies shows that no particular counseling approach is most effective for all persons (Hansen, 2002). It is important to keep in mind that the objective of counseling and psychotherapy, regardless of the therapeutic approach used, is to benefit the client (Driscoll, 1994), and at the core of any type of counseling approach is the counselor's empathy toward the client (Walsh, 2003). Empathy and involvement are critical in both developing

In D. Capuzzi & D. Gross (Eds.) *Introduction to the Counseling Profession.*

positive therapeutic relationships and in promoting effective outcomes in counseling and psychotherapy (Walsh, 2003).

The field of counseling is constantly being redefined by new findings, changing values, and contemporary issues (Garfield & Bergin, 1994). The human experience is so complex and multi-faceted that current literature reflects a strong bias toward "eclectic" or "integrative" models and approaches to counseling, or a "best fit" model, whereby counselors fit interventions to the specific needs and background of each client they work with (Petrocelli, 2002). This assumption suggests that the appropriateness of any particular theoretical orientation or intervention is dependent on the individual client, and it allows the counselor to draw upon a wider range of knowledge, rather than specifying one particular school of thought, in selecting appropriate interventions (Driscoll, 1994). As such, a review of any single theoretical approach or individual strategy, as we do in this chapter, must be read critically and with an understanding of how contemporary literature and practice comment on each of the approaches we present. At the same time, to further assist you in your in-depth pursuit to study the three approaches to counseling we discuss here, we have included a Suggested Reading list at the end of this chapter. In that list we also present other approaches that are similar to each of these major approaches.

THE STORY OF SALLY

Sally is a 36-year-old European-American woman who entered counseling hoping to deal with a variety of issues and concerns that had been bothering her and getting in the way of her leading a fulfilling life. She expressed the desire to improve her interactions with significant others, coworkers, and acquaintances. She reported being troubled by intense feelings of depression and loneliness, as well as feelings of anger and resentment that she harbors toward people in her past and present. Sally hoped to decrease what she referred to as her "bitchy" behavior, to stop interpreting messages and situations in a consistently self-critical way, and to put closure on a two-year dating relationship.

Sally described a very difficult childhood in which her father's family (aunts, uncles, cousins) continuously criticized and ridiculed her. She pointed out that her parents never defended her and even restricted her from protesting against her relatives' verbal abuse. She felt that from a very early age she experienced rejection and loneliness. Sally reported that her intimate relationships as an adult have mirrored her relationships with her relatives as a child. In other words, Sally believed that she has consistently involved herself with people who are similar to those family members who have caused her so much emotional pain in the past. She was married and divorced three times, and described each of these relationships as being very destructive: her first husband beat her, her second husband was a drug addict, and her last husband "wanted a mother." She explained that her marriage relationships reflected her need to win people over and gain their approval, especially people who remind her of past relatives who never approved of her and were so "emotionally abusive" toward her.

Sally expressed concern that she now gives herself the same negative messages that she has heard all her life. She reported that she does not understand why she continues to "kick herself" in spite of the fact that she now lives a thousand miles away from her family. She stated that at times she really hates herself. She expressed strong fears of being mistreated and rejected in the future, as she has been in the past. She expressed frustration with her behavior, but tended to avoid an in-depth disclosure of her feelings, which were very intense and difficult for her to manage. Sally began counseling with an expressed desire to change or better manage these complex emotions and issues in her life.

Now we turn to the three counseling approaches to discover how each would identify the development of Sally's problems and intervene to modify her affect, cognition, and behavior so that she would be able to lead a more productive and satisfying life.

THE PSYCHODYNAMIC APPROACH

Most psychological theories have three basic dimensions that involve how a client thinks (cognition), feels (emotions), and acts (behavior) (Worell & Remer, 2003). Differences among the various approaches to counseling, whether it be psychodynamic, cognitive-behavioral, or humanistic in orientation, depend on how much analysis is given to one or more of these areas (Worell & Remer, 2003). A thorough understanding of these differences is necessary in understanding how we as practitioners systematically choose to perceive our clients' behaviors, interpret their experiences, and provide the appropriate intervention to fit their needs. The purpose of this section is to present an overview of psychodynamic psychology and the theoretical constructs that may be useful to beginning therapists. The psychodynamic approach discussed here is not pure Freudian psychotherapy. Although based on traditional psychoanalytic theory, this presentation is influenced by contemporary trends in psychodynamic thought; see Kohut (1985), Robbins (1989), and Stolorow (1992) for excellent discussions on more recent directions in the use of psychoanalytic theory in counseling.

In recent years, many others have expanded the scope of traditional psychoanalytic and psychodynamic theory to include a range of applications. Literature has focussed on the overlap between psychodynamic and attachment theories. See Becker and Schmaling (1991) for a discussion about the interpersonal aspects of depression from the two perspectives, and Dozier and Tyrrell (1998) for a discussion about the role of attachment in therapeutic relationships. Refer to Lionells (1995) for an overview of some contemporary implications and uses of interpersonal-relational psychoanalysis. See Benjamin (1998) for a discussion of psychoanalysis and feminist theory, and Wheeler and Izzard (1997) for their comments on integrating difference (sexual identity, race, and culture) into psychodynamic counselor training. Lanyado and Horne (1999) provide an excellent discussion of the development and practice of psychoanalytic psychotherapy with children and young people. Finally, see Frank (1999) for a discussion on the possibility of a rapprochement between psychoanalysis and cognitive-behavior therapy, while grounded in a contemporary relations perspective.

Finally, for any theory, examining how and why the theory was developed and to what extent the sociopolitical environment of the theorist's time influenced the theory conceptualization or of the theorist's view of human suffering itself are critical to understanding the theory and its limits (Worrel & Remer, 2003). For example, psychoanalysis was born in Europe during a time when Europeans needed a psychotherapy that complimented their view of their often tragic lives (Hansen, 2002). Although this chapter does not focus on multicultural or feminist perspectives, all three counseling approaches in this chapter were originally developed for and by White European and European Americans. In examining research on the effectiveness of psychotherapy, Sue and Constantine (2003) caution that practitioners balance universal findings of a study (i.e., empirical studies using dominant culture populations) with culture specific findings of a study (i.e., empirical studies using ethnic minority populations) as they relate to optimal human functioning. In other words, in an effort to facilitate human functioning and development among diverse populations, the practitioner must often critically examine and question the appropriateness of the counseling approach they choose, and how this fits into the worldviews and life experiences of the diverse clients they serve. Currently, a challenge in the field of counseling and psychotherapy is to examine the effectiveness of various theoretical approaches to counseling with many different populations and cultural/ethnic groups.

Rationale: How Problems Evolve

The psychodynamic approach seeks to explain how an individual's personality expresses itself through the behavior he/she displays in various situations. When an individual is considered to be functioning in a healthy manner, the individual possesses a high degree of psychological insight into his or her functioning and his or her behaviors reflect an increased level of awareness, or consciousness (Gelso & Woodhouse, 2003). Conversely, when an individual's behavior is driven by unrecognized defense mechanisms and levels of anxiety, the individual is often said to be driven by his or her incongruent state of unconsciousness.

The psychodynamic approach stresses the influence of genetic impulses or instincts, the concept of life energy or libido, the influence of the client's life history—psychosexual and psychosocial development—on personality formation and the irrational, unconscious sources of human behavior (Robbins, 1989). Freud (1949) viewed people as inherently instinctual creatures, driven by their striving for infantile gratification. Throughout life, the individual is strongly motivated to seek out satisfaction of one of two primitive instinctual drives: sex and aggression. Therefore, a conflict is engendered between instinctual desires and the control of these emotions that must be maintained in the social world of "reality." To cope with this conflict, defense mechanisms, some conscious and others unconscious, are used that deny, falsify, and/or distort reality. As a consequence, the ego is protected from intrusive thoughts and instinctual energy or psychic energy is re-channeled into socially approved outlets. However, one's emotional awareness and perceptions of self and others are often inhibited by the defense mechanisms used.

Freud's (1915–1917) conceptualization of the unconscious and different levels of awareness are probably the most significant contributions of psychoanalysis to the field of psychology. Freud held that three different levels of consciousness influence personality development and functioning: the conscious, the preconscious, and the unconscious. The conscious level consists of those thoughts of which the individual is aware at the moment. The preconscious includes information that can be brought to the conscious level with relative ease. In traditional psychoanalytic theory, the third level of awareness, the unconscious, is the most important component of the mind because it largely determines human behavior.

Some unconscious information cannot readily be brought to the conscious level because it is too anxiety provoking to one's ego. Indeed, resistance to acknowledging its existence is blocked by employing ego defense mechanisms. For example, a person may truly hate his or her father, yet be unaware that these feelings exist and/or unable to accept that they do. In psychoanalytic theory, the importance of these unconscious feelings is that they constantly strive to become conscious, and the individual then expends considerable psychic energy to keep them in the unconscious. Thus, people are in a perpetual state of internal conflict, often unaware of the cause of this struggle to prevent unacceptable, anxiety provoking feelings and emotions from entering their consciousness.

The conflict at the unconscious level is postulated as being an ongoing battle for control of psychic energy among the three structural components of the personality. These are known as the id, the ego, and the superego. The id is the original system of personality, present at birth, that is characterized as the primary source of psychic energy (libido) and is the place where instincts reside; it is driven by the pleasure principle—an infantile need for immediate gratification. The second structural component of the personality is the ego, which functions to maintain an individual's contact with the external world or reality; it is governed by the reality principle—realistic and logical thinking designed to satisfy needs in a socially acceptable manner. The ego serves as a mediator between the superego and the id. In traditional Freudian theory, the ego is sometimes seen as being at the mercy of the other two competing forces. In more modern theory, however, the task of the therapist is seen as helping the ego decide and balance id and superego (Kohut, 1985). The third component of the personality is the superego, which serves as the person's moral code of conduct. Analogous to the popular concept of "conscience," the superego results from the social mores and parental moral attitudes that are internalized by the child during development.

Anxiety is a state of tension that serves as the motivating force within the person, and frequently results from the constant conflict among the id, ego, and superego. For example, negative emotions develop from unconscious memories of past childhood experiences, from frightening impulses driven by the id (such as aggressive desires that may be forbidden), from guilt derived from an overly self-critical superego, or from the inadequacy of the ego to resolve these internal conflicts. Anxiety serves as a warning to the ego that it is in danger of being overwhelmed, and, therefore, anxiety may be repressed by the ego defense mechanisms. However, ego defense mechanisms also tend to deny, falsify, or otherwise distort reality (Freud, 1936). Consequently, the individual's personality development is impeded, and realistic problem-solving strategies can also remain underdeveloped.

The complex task of the counselor is to help the client uncover the structure of anxiety of that personality so that reconstruction can begin. In the case of Sally, the psychodynamically oriented counselor believes that the origin and solution to her problems lie deep within her unconscious. For example, her excessive anxiety and depression might well be explained by the conflict between her angry, hostile feelings toward her parents and her superego, which continues to insist that parents are to be loved. Her ego defense mechanisms of turning against self and identification with the aggressor force her to expend considerable energy hiding the conflicts from herself and contribute to her self-defeating behavior.

A primary therapeutic task is to help Sally become more aware of her style of handling her anxiety and the underlying causes of her depression. Subsequently, more personally satisfying and socially approved ways of resolving these tensions and conflicts are discovered, helping Sally to develop more mature ways to use her psychic energy and to become more aware of problematic behaviors that result from unconscious impulses.

Mechanisms of Change

The goal of psychodynamic counseling with Sally is to make her conscious of unconscious material. Therefore, the counselor's goal is to help the client recognize unconscious personality characteristics that influence consistent behavior patterns across various situations. The two means by which this is done is through transference and a working alliance. Gelso and Carter (1985, 1994) provide an in-depth discussion of these components of the counselor-client relationship. The scope of this chapter only allows us to explore briefly here the dynamics and importance of these change processes in psychodynamic theory.

Transference.   Transference occurs when the client re-experiences, in therapy, emotions and attitudes originally present in earlier relationships, often the parent-child relationship (but others as well), and focuses these past feelings and emotional and behavioral reactions on the counselor. In the case of Sally, transference expressed itself in Sally's negativistic attitude about the perceived lack of help she was receiving from the counselor. In discussions with her about her early childhood psychosocial development (see Erikson, 1968), it became clear that this aspect of her personality was developed in her relationship with her cousins. Eventually she was able to work through her unresolved conflicts with her cousins by means of the transference relationship.

The counselor interpreted the transference relationship in order to help Sally understand how she was misperceiving, misinterpreting, and misresponding to the counselor, and to other people outside the counseling relationship, as a consequence of experiences in her earlier relationships with her cousins. The transference relationship helped her achieve a corrective emotional experience by means of abreaction, or "reliving" the original tension-evoking emotional experience. This "new" emotional experience provided a catharsis or release of tension and anxiety resulting from the process of bringing repressed ideas, feelings, wishes, and memories of the past into consciousness.

Working Alliance.   The interpretation of the transference experience and Sally's acceptance of it were based on the therapeutic alliance developed between the counselor and Sally. Conceptually, the working alliance construct has its foundation in

Freud's emphasis on the client-therapist collaboration in treatment (Connor-Greene, 1993). The primary focus of early writings emphasized the "therapeutic alliance" detailing the client's identification with the therapist, focusing on the more affective aspects of the client's collaboration in therapy. It was not until Greenson's (1967) writings that the therapeutic alliance was more comprehensively described as a working alliance, suggesting that the client's motivation and ability to work in the treatment situation were crucial for treatment success.

A more contemporary conceptualization of the working alliance identifies both the client-therapist relationship and the client's collaborating in the tasks of treatment as central to positive therapeutic outcome (Gaston, 1990; Lambert & Bergin, 1994). In fact, recent empirical work on social perception has recognized the existence and importance of countertransference processes within the therapeutic context (Andersen, Glassman, Chen, & Cole, 1995). Countertransference occurs when a counselor's reaction to her or his client is based on a past conflict with a parent or other significant person (Gelso & Hayes, 1998); that is, countertransference involves the counselor's personal characteristics and their impact on the counseling relationship. Others have suggested that the counselor represents a secure attachment figure for adult clients (Dozier & Tyrrell, 1998; Farber, Lippert, & Nevas, 1995). From the attachment perspective, the counselor provides the client with the secure base necessary for exploring repressed feelings and impulses and bringing them into consciousness.

Bordin (1976) took the working alliance concept out of its psychoanalytic context and reframed it from a more pantheoretical viewpoint. He built on Greenson's (1967) earlier work but separated the working alliance from its attachment to the process of transference. His focus was on the conscious partnership of the client and the therapist working together to bring about change. Although Bordin perceived the working alliance as an integrated relationship, he defined three constituent components that in combination define the quality and strength of the working alliance. These three elements were tasks (in-counseling behaviors and cognitions), goals (outcomes), and bonds (the complex network of positive personal attachments between the client and the counselor).

Horvath and Greenberg (1989) stated that the significant departure for Bordin (1976) from previous theorists was to conceptualize the client-therapist interdependence along the dimension of mutuality. Bordin's concepts of task, goal, and bond involve collaboration and depend on the degree of concordance and joint purpose between the counselor and client. In other words, the client is much more a problem solver and the counselor becomes more directive in the approach to therapy (Bergin & Garfield, 1994). The counselor and the client agree on which in-therapy and outside-therapy tasks will be helpful in obtaining the goals of counseling. In the case of Sally, the working alliance was nourished by the counselor to facilitate a more positive counseling outcome.

Summary of the Psychodynamic Approach

A counselor using the psychodynamic approach tends to concentrate on the effects of past experience on shaping patterns of behavior through particular cognitions (defenses) and interpersonal styles of interaction and perception (transference) that have become repetitive and that interfere with health (Ursano, Sonnenberg, & Lazar, 1991). In the history of this approach, conceptualization of a dysfunctional personality, or psychopathology, was given the most attention, while methods of treatment were given nominal attention (Gelso & Woodhouse, 2003). In other words, the therapist often spent more time focusing on making the unconscious conscious, rather than other methods (i.e., focusing on client strengths) to effect change. Likewise, what was considered optimal human functioning and development at the time this approach was conceived, was originally contrasted against White, European males, and so it is essential for the counselor to understand the implicit and explicit limitations of this theoretical orientation when working with other populations (i.e., women, ethnic minorities, gays and lesbians), and how to properly address them in practice. Conversely, in order to be effective with their clients, counselors using a psychodynamic approach need to recognize that there are intrapsychic forces motivating people that are not entirely conscious. They must understand the significance of childhood experiences and use the concept of transference in the counseling relationship. They need to know how people defend themselves from external and internal threats with ego defense mechanisms and other methods of resistance. Finally, a counselor using this approach needs to effectively create a working alliance that facilitates the counseling process. In so doing, transference dynamics can be interpreted for clients so that they can experience an abreactive catharsis of their debilitating past history.

THE COGNITIVE-BEHAVIORAL APPROACH

The history of cognitive-behavior therapy has evolved through various theoretical positions. Some of the important stages of that evolution include behavior modification (Skinner, 1938, 1953) and its expansion into applied behavioral analysis (Michael, 1991; Morris, 1992), and imaginal systematic desensitization (Wolpe, 1982). Each of these approaches represents traditional reinforcement theories whose primary focus, although not exclusive focus, is to modify observable behaviors, without addressing intervening variables.

With the advent of cognitive-behavioral therapies such as rational-emotive behavior therapy (Ellis, 1962, 1995), social learning theory (Bandura, 1977) and social cognitive theory (Bandura, 1991, 1993), cognitive therapy (Beck, 1976), and cognitive-behavior therapy (Meichenbaum, 1977), internal self-regulatory variables became pivotal determinants of behavior. It would be helpful for you to keep in mind that the list of cognitive-behavioral therapeutic approaches given here is only representative and not exhaustive. The emphasis on the cognitive mediated aspects of behavior has facilitated a focus in therapy on client attributions, appraisals, expectations, and belief systems. These intrapsychic variables are viewed as integral cognitive processes in their effects on emotions and behaviors.

Albert Ellis is considered one of the most influential theorists in the field of cognitive-behavioral approaches to counseling. We will use his system of rational-emotive behavior therapy, or REBT (Ellis, 1995, 1999a) (formerly known as RET [Ellis, 1962, 1993a]) to illustrate one cognitive-behavioral approach and will apply

REBT in conceptualizing therapeutic interventions for Sally. Ellis has applied REBT to working with elderly people (1999b), treating obsessive-compulsive disorder (OCD) (Ellis & Dryden, 1997), and counseling for stress (Ellis, Gordon, Nennan, & Palmer, 1997). Several contemporary articles and books provide comprehensive illustrations of the practice and goals of REBT (Ellis, 1997; Ellis & MacLaren, 1998).

Rationale: How Problems Evolve

Rational-emotive behavior therapy (REBT), the fundamentals of which were developed by Albert Ellis in 1955, is based on the premise that emotional disturbance has several important cognitive, emotive, and behavioral sources. Although emotional disturbance or "neurosis" does not develop entirely from cognition or thinking, the etiology of unhealthy behaviors is heavily influenced by the process of an internal dialogue that is negatively affected by the individual's irrational beliefs. According to Ellis, human beings develop strong preferences for achievement, approval, comfort, and health, which are life goals. Due to a human innate propensity to construct absolutist demands, preferences can easily be transformed into irrational beliefs, which are dogmatic musts, shoulds, and thoughts that become the standard by which social situations are measured. The interaction between irrational beliefs and social stimuli creates debilitating emotional reactions for the individual. In short, an underlying principle of REBT is that a person feels what he or she thinks (Ellis, 1993a, 1999a).

Rational-emotive behavior therapy is based on a humanist and constructivist approach to conceptualizing human agency (Ellis, 1993c). REBT is concerned with the individual's systemic, phenomenological field and suggests that people strive to achieve life goals that are usually centered on remaining alive and being reasonably happy, such as attaining success, love, and comfort. The path to achieving these goals, however, is regularly blocked by interpersonal or environmental adversities that Ellis calls activating events. Ellis proposed the ABC model of emotional disturbance (1993a) and the more recently expanded ABCDE model (Ellis, 1995, 1999a) to describe this process.

During the process of maturation, the individual develops characteristic beliefs (B's) that are used to interpret and take action in response to these adversities or activating events (A's). An individual's belief system consists of rational beliefs, which are preferences that create appropriate emotional and behavioral consequences, and irrational beliefs, which are dogmatic musts and absolutist demands that create inappropriate and dysfunctional consequences. Therefore, cognitive, emotive, and behavioral consequences (C's) are created by the imposition of the individual's belief system (B's) on the activating events (A's). Thus, when a preponderance of irrational beliefs compared to rational beliefs comprises the individual's belief system, emotional disturbance and unhealthy behaviors will result (Ellis, 1993a).

When RET (Ellis, 1962) was first practiced an emphasis was placed on ego disturbance—that is, self-induced emotional disturbance created by self-denigrating irrational or illogical thinking. However, it was soon recognized that people also had discomfort disturbance or low frustration tolerance (LFT), again caused by irrational beliefs that are especially characterized by the individual's belief that other people and external conditions absolutely must be a certain way (Ellis, 1993b). As a consequence, Ellis added to the idea of ego disturbance the idea of discomfort disturbance, or LFT. Throughout his writings, Ellis (1993a) has maintained that ego and discomfort disturbance often occur simultaneously and significantly interact to cause severe neurotic problems.

In short, Ellis (1993a) maintains that emotional disturbance is the result of irrational and illogical thinking that occurs in the form of internalized sentences or verbal symbols that are generated from an irrational system of beliefs. Thus, according to REBT, people are largely responsible for their emotional disturbances resulting from their irrational thinking. Ellis recognizes that emotions reflect a complex mode of behavior that is intricately tied to a variety of sensing and response processes and states. Nevertheless, the process of behavior change is built on the premise that people need to change their way of thinking (cognitive restructuring) in order to correct their irrational belief systems. Therefore, REBT takes an active directive approach in disputing (D) a client's antiempirical and overgeneralized self-statements—the client's irrational beliefs. The objective is "to persuade and teach clients to vigorously, powerfully, and persistently think, feel, and act against their demandingness and to return to their preferences" (Ellis, 1993c, p. 199). Next we consider each of these components of REBT—A, B, and C—separately and how they might relate to Sally's concerns and behaviors. Later in this discussion of REBT, we will discuss the notion of disputing (D) the old belief system and experiencing new behavioral and emotional effects (E) as a result of increased rational thinking.

Activating Event.   Usually a precipitating activating event or adversity is what motivates a person to enter counseling. In the case of Sally, her recent volatile breakup with a man she had been dating for two years brought on a great deal of stress and depression. The relationship, and the manner in which it ended, led Sally to begin to recognize her pattern of entering into destructive relationships, and the need to seek help to alter her typical interpersonal patterns of behavior.

Beliefs.   The events that brought Sally to counseling were partially a realization that her emotional reactions within the relationship were not successful in eliciting either the desired responses from her partner or permitting Sally to maintain an emotional equilibrium. She became aware that her own emotions, thoughts, and behaviors within the relationship contributed to its termination, as well as to other problems in her life. Her system of irrational beliefs about relationships and her negative beliefs about herself led her to feel depressed. Her beliefs were characterized by self-statements such as "I absolutely need to be loved by this person in order to be happy and whole" and "Since I made mistakes in the relationship, I am to blame for its failure." Sally's failure to understand the causes of her dysfunctional life, and the impact of her belief system, are what prompted her to begin counseling.

Consequences.   For many clients, the negative emotions of guilt, anger, depression, and anxiety are emotional consequences that appear to be directly caused by the activating event. REBT posits that these emotional consequences are actually caused by clients' beliefs about the activating event. In Sally's case, she strongly believed that her feelings of rejection, sadness, and depression were directly related to the emotional turmoil in her relationship with her father and his family and not simply in her current relationship. Sally felt that she was repeatedly rejected and indirectly told that she was a terrible person. She communicated these feelings by disclosing in counseling that her parents would not allow her to "fight back" when her relatives criticized and "verbally abused" her. These past events, augmented by similar current events in her life, appear to be at the root of her own belief system about herself and the world around her. But in REBT, it is precisely this belief system that mediates the link between the activating event and the emotional consequence and not just the event itself, such as the ending of her two-year relationship, that creates turmoil. Therefore, REBT focuses on changing a client's system of irrational and illogical beliefs.

Mechanisms of Change

Belief System.   Identifying the client's belief system is a major focus of REBT and is a key mechanism of change (Ellis, 1993a). The belief system is the mediating variable between the activating event and inappropriate consequences or emotional disturbance. Since most people draw a direct connection between activating events (A's) and consequences (C's), the main goal of the REBT counselor is to help clients identify their irrational beliefs (B's) and thinking that underlie the emotional disturbance. Ellis (1962) originally identified ten irrational beliefs that all humans have that inevitably lead to pervasive dysfunctional behavior. Although he later added to the original list of irrational beliefs (Ellis & Whiteley, 1979), Ellis (1993a) has recently concluded that all these beliefs can be synthesized into three general categories of irrational beliefs, each including a rigidly prescribed must, should, or demand:

1. "I (ego) absolutely must perform well and win significant others' approval or else I am an inadequate, worthless person."
2. "You (other people) must under all conditions and at all times be nice and fair to me or else you are a rotten, horrible person!"
3. "Conditions under which I live absolutely must be comfortable, safe, and advantageous or else the world is a rotten place, I can't stand it, and life is hardly worth living!" (p. 7)

Two main tenets of REBT counseling are to (1) demonstrate to the client that self-talk is a primary source of emotional disturbance, and (2) help the client to restructure internal sentences in order to eliminate the underlying irrational beliefs. Sally felt that she had always been the object of abusive jokes, criticized incessantly, and told in a variety of ways that she was a worthless, unlikable person. She also made self-deprecating statements during her counseling sessions, such as "I need to prove to myself that I'm acceptable"; "The most I could hope for is to be stuck with losers and to be victimized"; and "I guess I need to be lectured to; I don't like yelling at myself, but that's what I end up doing." Following the two main tenets of REBT, the counselor helped Sally clarify how she perceived events and interpreted messages from others as well as from herself, and helped her dispute her beliefs. As a consequence of this process, Sally was able to acknowledge her irrational beliefs concerning her need to be accepted and approved by others in all situations or feel that she was worthless as a person. Furthermore, she recognized that she was not able to perform perfectly in all situations, but nevertheless remained a "good" person.

Dispute.   The real work of rational-emotive behavioral counseling involves the disputing of the client's irrational beliefs. The counselor actively challenges the client's existing belief system with the intent of eliminating the irrational beliefs and helping the client to develop and internalize a set of more positive and rational beliefs. Therefore, the process of uncovering the illogical, irrational nature of Sally's internal messages was the primary focus of counseling. As noted, the counselor provided new, supportive, and logical self-statements such as "I can be disliked by certain people and still be a good and worthwhile person."

In counseling sessions, the illogical need to be loved by everyone at all times was consistently disputed. This strategy had a very positive effect as Sally began to realize that her self-critical, irrational belief system intensified her depression and anger, contributing to other problems in her relationships. By changing her belief system, she began to recognize more effective and positive ways of seeing herself and of relating with others. Homework was assigned with the intent of practicing her newly acquired rational beliefs. Whenever she felt that she was being disliked or rejected by someone, she was instructed to repeat three times to herself the following sentence: "I am still a good and worthwhile person, even if this person does not appreciate me." Again, the objective was to develop both socially and personally appropriate preferences, supported by rational beliefs, and to eliminate absolutist demands.

Effect.   Changing the client's irrational belief system is not a straightforward process. The focus on disputing irrational beliefs typically produces changes in behavior and diminishes discomfort disturbance, but does so over time and as the client is able to integrate new information. Nevertheless, the client is encouraged to notice these changes and to celebrate their emergence. For example, as Sally noticed the cognitive and behavioral changes related to her irrational beliefs, she began to experience a new effect (E) or emotional consequence. Thus, in working with Sally, the REBT counselor would proceed through the process of evaluating and explaining the ABCDEs of Sally's behaviors in order to have her thoroughly incorporate a new rational belief system.

Summary of the Cognitive-Behavioral Approach

The cognitive-behavioral approach tends to highlight the importance of irrational or dysfunctional beliefs in the creation of emotional disturbance; furthermore, this approach typically uses a range of cognitive, emotive, and behavioral strategies of challenging and changing these beliefs for more functional ones (Ellis, 1999b). As such, the basic assumption of the REBT approach to counseling is that most people in our society develop many irrational ways of thinking. These irrational thoughts lead to inappropriate behavior and disturbing emotional reactions that create ego and discomfort disturbance. REBT counseling is structured to facilitate clients' recognition of their irrational beliefs and alter their interpersonal patterns of behavior so that they are based on more functional, logical beliefs. The accomplishment of this goal requires an active/directive counselor who is at once supportive and at the same time has the capacity to actively engage and challenge the client (Ellis, 1993c).

THE PERSON-CENTERED APPROACH

In this section, we discuss person-centered therapy, one of the major theoretical approaches in the humanistic framework. This approach, developed by Carl Rogers (1951, 1957), has been known during its evolution as nondirective, client-centered, Rogerian, and person-centered therapy. The present use of the term person-centered therapy reflects an expanding scope of influence, including Rogers's interest in how people obtain, possess, share, or surrender power and control over others and themselves (Corey, 1991). Indeed, themes embedded in the person-centered approach have been applied to a range of settings, involving care of people with Alzheimer's disease (Zeman, 1999), work in the cases of conflict resolution (Joyce, 1995), and therapy in Japan (Hayashi, Kuno, Morotomi, Osawa, Shimizu, & Suetake, 1998). Other counseling approaches, such as "relationship-centered counseling" (Kelly, 1997), have evolved out of the person-centered tradition. Some of the fundamental assumptions underlying a person-centered approach to therapy have also been examined from feminist (O'Hara, 1996) and multicultural perspectives (Brodley, 1996). Some have suggested that the approach risks "colluding with prevailing oppression and hierarchies if it fails explicitly to challenge implicit power structures within our society" (Hawtin & Moore, 1998, p. 91), while others have recommended replacing client-centered counseling with "culture-centered counselling" (Laungani, 1997, p. 343). As can be seen from this continued broad and diverse application, the person-centered approach to counseling is widely practiced.

Rationale: How Problems Evolve

A central issue in person-centered therapy is how the individual perceives the world. What the individual perceives in his or her phenomenological field is more important than the "actual" reality. In other words, what the individual perceives to be occurring is the reality. Thus, a consistent effort to understand and experience as far as possible the unique qualities of each client's subjective world is fundamental to person-centered therapy. The focus is not primarily with past causes of behavior; rather, person-centered therapy focuses on current experiences, feelings, and the interpersonal relationships of the individual.

Person-centered counseling is based on a belief that people act in accordance with their self-concept. One's self-concept is heavily influenced by experiences interacting with others and the environment. In order for a healthy self-concept to emerge, a person requires unconditional positive regard, such as love, support, respect, acceptance, and nurturing.

Often in childhood, as well as later in life, a child is given conditional positive regard by parents and significant others in his or her life. In other words, parents and others communicate to the child, either directly or indirectly, exactly what the child must be or how the child must act in order to receive positive regard. Feelings of self-worth develop if the person behaves in accordance with these prescribed emotional and behavioral patterns because acceptance and approval are thereby achieved. Sometimes, however, children may have to deny or distort their perception of a given situation when their personal needs conflict with the expectancies of someone that they depend on for approval.

The individual is thus caught in a dilemma because of the incongruence between personal growth needs and needs for positive regard. On the one hand, if a person does not do as others wish, he or she is not valued and accepted. On the other hand, if a person conforms, he or she disregards personal needs to evolve a self-concept predicated on internally derived goals. In this case, the ideal self that the person is striving to become is thwarted. The larger the discrepancy between the real self and the ideal self, the more incongruence a person experiences. In other words, conflict arises when individuals must choose between personal needs for self-actualization and the approval that significant others provide that is conditional to certain behaviors, thoughts, or feelings.

One's self-concept is a learned attribute, starting from birth and progressively developing through childhood, adolescence, and adulthood. In Sally's case, she experienced a conflict between the conditions of receiving positive regard, or validation, that were placed on her as a child and the experience of evolving as a person who had unique needs and goals. For example, she received messages from her parents that she should not "fight back" or confront her cousins and other relatives for being verbally abusive toward her. Her parents communicated to her, "You're better than they are, you don't need to fight back." Much of Sally's present negative interpersonal interactions with others reflect a self-concept that has attempted to incorporate messages such as this example. But this message is contradictory to her need to feel safe, assertive, and protected. Therefore, Sally harbors a great deal of anger and resentment toward her family and toward others who remind her of her family that consistently frustrated her self-actualizing potential. She frequently uses inappropriate anger, lashing out at people in current relationships because they "remind" her of family members against whom she was never able to "fight back."

Sally's poor self-concept resulted in part from a long history of negative and/or mixed messages from others that have been internalized. In addition, the conflict between how she should be and act in order to be a "good," acceptable person, and how she, in fact, behaves toward and thinks about others exacerbates the incongruence between her real self and her ideal self. For a long time, Sally has given herself the message that she is an undesirable, unacceptable person. Unfortunately, Sally's self-concept was formed on this premise, and she now finds it difficult to respond to others and to herself in a caring and accepting way. Her marriage relationships validated her negative self-image because they have "proven" to her that she is a "failure," a "victim," and will "always be stuck with losers."

Mechanisms of Change

Self-Actualization.   Within the humanistic framework, the self-actualizing tendency is the primary motivating force of the human organism. Self-actualization is an
inherent tendency in people to move in directions described by words such as
growth, adjustment, socialization, independence, self-realization, and fully functioning. Thus, in the humanistic philosophy that underlies the person-centered approach, humans have an innate capacity to interact with their environment in ways
designed to maintain and enhance their self-concept. Rogers (1951) emphasized that
the client's natural capacity for growth and development is an important human
characteristic on which counseling should focus. For example, in spite of the negative
experiences that Sally has had in her life and her subsequent emotional pain, anger,
and self-defeating behaviors, she has an innate predisposition to be self-actualized.
This predisposition can be nourished and drawn out, given a facilitative psychological climate.

Core Conditions for Constructive Personality Change.   In his classic article,
Rogers (1957) identified the core conditions that must exist in order for constructive
personality change to occur:

1. The first two persons are in psychological contact.
2. The first, whom we shall term the client, is in a state of incongruence, being
    vulnerable or anxious.
3. The second, whom we shall term the therapist, is congruent and integrated in
    the relationship.
4. The therapist experiences unconditional positive regard for the client.
5. The therapist experiences an empathic understanding of the client's internal
    frame of reference and endeavors to communicate this experience to the client.
6. The communication to the client of the therapist's empathic understanding and
    unconditional positive regard is to a minimal degree achieved. (p. 96)

Rogers identified three personal characteristics, or attitudes, of the therapist
that are essential before a therapeutic relationship can be established: (1) genuineness, or congruence, (2) unconditional positive regard, and (3) empathy. These characteristics offered by the counselor to the client result in a therapeutic climate that
allows the client's self-actualizing tendency to flourish. Due to the centrality of their
importance to person-centered therapy, we will describe each of these characteristics.

Genuineness.   Genuineness or congruence, is the counselor's capacity to be "real"
in the relationship. Thus, genuineness is used to denote honesty, directness, and sincerity, and an absence of a professional façade. Rogers (1961) defines genuineness as
follows: "By this we mean that the feelings that the counselor is experiencing are
available to his awareness, that he is able to live with these feelings, be them in the
relationship, and able to communicate them if appropriate. . . . It means that he is
being himself, not denying himself" (p. 417). Genuineness, then, is the counselor's

ability to be psychologically open and present with the client in therapy. The counselor is "real" in the relationship, demonstrating a consistency between her or his own feeling/experience at the moment and her or his verbal and nonverbal communications to the client.

In Sally's case, the counselor's willingness to be genuine in the relationship with her provides Sally with a psychological climate that can be trusted, thereby facilitating her self-disclosure. The counselor's genuineness and openness to being present with Sally are crucial elements contributing to her change process. They allow her to be real and to come into psychological contact with her counselor, expressing her feelings with the knowledge that she is and will be supported.

Unconditional Positive Regard. This counselor characteristic has also been referred to as "nonpossessive warmth" and "regard" and is equivalent to respect, appreciation, and acceptance of another person. It can be described as the counselor's ability to experience an acceptance of every aspect of the client's personality. "Nonpossessive" or "unconditional" implies that the counselor does not qualify his or her acceptance of the client, but accepts the client fully as a separate person with a right to his or her own thoughts, words, actions, and feelings.

Unconditional positive regard is a crucial component of the counseling relationship with Sally, especially in light of the fact that Sally's self-worth has previously been validated only when she has responded and behaved in an explicitly defined and prescribed manner. The counselor offers positive regard with no conditional stipulations. This caring, accepting attitude of Sally's individuality emerges from the belief that she can discover within herself the necessary resources for her own growth. Eventually, Sally will come to understand that she is capable of taking charge of her own life.

Empathy. Empathic understanding, or empathy, may be defined as an active, immediate, continuous process of living another's feelings, their intensity, and their meaning instead of simply observing them. The accuracy of a counselor's empathic understanding and sensitivity to the client's feelings and experiences, as they are revealed during the moment-to-moment interaction of the counseling session, conveys the counselor's interest in appreciating the client's phenomenological world. The counselor strives to sense fully and accurately the inner world of the client's subjective experience. The concept of accurate empathy, like the other counselor attributes, has evolved over the years in the direction of freeing the counselor to be a more active participant in the therapeutic encounter. High levels of accurate empathy go beyond recognition of obvious feelings to an exploration of and communication about perceptions of underlying client messages.

In one interview, Sally said that her depression and feelings of resentment typically drove her to do things to others that pushed them away or kept them from getting close to her. Sally expressed how she behaved, but failed to indicate her feelings about the consequences of her behavior. The counselor focused on these unspoken feelings, assisting Sally's process of making contact with them and, ultimately, with the more intimate aspects of her inner self. When the counselor asked Sally to describe her loneliness, she began to cry. Since loneliness was the result of her behaviors toward others, but a feeling she had never previously identified, helping her to recognize and deal with her loneliness was a major factor in her continuing growth.

Summary of the Person-Centered Approach

A major assumption of the person-centered theoretical approach is the belief in the individual's innate motivation toward self-actualization and in the individual's potential to be a fully functioning person. A person will generally seek help in therapy when a significant incongruence between his or her real self and ideal self develops. The main intent in counseling is to develop a relationship between the counselor and the client that will facilitate the client's capacity for understanding his or her unhappiness and moving on to constructive personal growth. Crucial to the creation of this relationship are the counselor's characteristics of genuineness, unconditional positive regard, and accurate empathy. Therefore, creating and maintaining a nonthreatening, anxiety-free relationship in which client growth can take place is an essential component of person-centered therapy.

SUMMARY

Three counseling theories within the psychodynamic, cognitive-behavioral, and humanistic traditions in psychology are Freudian-based psychoanalytic and general psychodynamic theory, Ellis's rational-emotive behavior therapy, and Rogers's person-centered therapy. Individual therapy from the psychodynamic perspective focuses on unconscious intrapsychic forces, childhood experiences, ego defense mechanisms, and the notion of transference and countertransference in the therapeutic relationship. Building a working alliance in therapy in order to interpret and confront transference dynamics and defense mechanisms is critical to successful counseling. Individual counseling from Ellis's approach focuses on the role of irrational thinking that people maintain about the world and self that leads to inappropriate behavior and to disturbing emotional reactions. Confronting irrational beliefs and learning more functional, logical beliefs about interpersonal patterns are central to the therapy process. Person-centered therapy is based on the belief that people have an innate motivation toward self-actualization, have the capacity for understanding their unhappiness, and can become fully functioning. Counseling focuses on developing the relationship between the client and counselor, marked by counselor genuineness, unconditional positive regard, and accurate empathy. Maintaining this nonthreatening, anxiety-free relationship is an essential component of successful person-centered therapy. Each of these traditional theoretical approaches has made enormous contributions to the process of counseling individuals toward achieving positive change, growth, and self-understanding. The case of Sally illustrates these contributions.

To aid you in putting the three approaches presented in this chapter within their theoretical and practical context, the following list contains other approaches that are similar to the three selected approaches:

PSYCHODYNAMIC
Psychoanalysis (Freud)
Analytic theory (Jung)
Contemporary psychoanalytic theory (Erikson)
Individual psychology (Adler, Dreikurs)
Interpersonal theory of psychiatry (Sullivan)
Neurosis and aggression (Horney)
Social psychology (Fromm)
Personality (Murray)
Organismic theory (Goldstein)

BEHAVIORAL (COGNITIVE-BEHAVIORAL)
Rational-emotive behavior therapy (Ellis)
Transactional analysis (Berne)
Reality therapy (Glasser)
Operant conditioning (Skinner)
Social modeling (Bandura)
Reciprocal inhibition (Wolpe)
Cognitive behavior modification (Meichenbaum, Beck)

HUMANISTIC
Person-centered (Rogers)
Gestalt therapy (Perls)
Logotherapy (Frankl)
Psychology of being (Maslow)
Existential (May, Binswanger, Yalom, Jourard)

CHAPTER SEVEN

INDIVIDUAL COUNSELING: BRIEF APPROACHES

ROLLA E. LEWIS, ED.D.
Portland State University

There is no singular or simple generic approach to brief counseling. There are numerous brief approaches that flow from diverse traditions. "Brief counseling" is an umbrella term that covers a wide array of brief approaches, each with its own history, literature, cheerleaders, and detractors. Students interested in brief counseling should recognize that there are over four hundred different forms of counseling and therapy, and that over 50 approaches are covered by the brief counseling umbrella. Surveying all the literature regarding brief counseling would be too broad and have little value to students trying to develop an understanding about what brief counseling is and how brief counseling helps clients. Even with those limitations, numerous brief theories and methods compete for space in this introductory chapter, and there is not time nor space to cover all 50 plus brief approaches.

This short chapter will concentrate upon a few collaborative, competency-based brief approaches that recognize and begin with utilizing client strengths and resources within orientations that are explicitly intentional about being effective and efficient. These brief approaches fall under a variety of names but this chapter will refer to them as competency-based or strength-based brief counseling. Although the chapter will speak about differences, there will be a tendency to lump rather than split strength-based approaches. To give strength-based approaches a fair hearing, it might be helpful to view each approach as a dialect of the same language; the language of effective and efficient change. By concentrating upon strength-based brief counseling approaches, the goal in this chapter is to help introductory students appreciate a cluster of brief approaches and methods that can be viewed as expressing diverse dialects emerging from a common language concerned with helping clients construct more satisfying lives for themselves enhancing their ability to choose, and utilizing their competencies and resources. The dialect analogy drawn from linguistics could help free counselors from falling into the trap that there is a singular and correct dialect that all must speak. The English dialects spoken in Jamaica, England, the Midwest, the South, and in African American communities are all English but some dialects are privileged because they are spoken and written by those in power. Linguists point out to uptight language police that all dialects have consistent grammars that enable speakers to express themselves and experience the world in unique and culturally appropriate ways (Lakoff & Johnson, 1999; McWhorter, 2001). If you are a student, just use a nonstandard dialect in writing a paper and see what happens to your grade. Similar to dialects that are judged as less than by speakers of privileged dialects, brief counseling is viewed by some as a nonstandard, less than, and not as "deep" as other long-term forms of counseling. Obviously, we use agreed upon dialects to insure an intellectual lingua francas within education, politics, and the workplace, and long-term counseling has been the lingua francas within the counseling community. If only to maintain contact with third-party payers, counselors are finding that they must be able to hang "Brief Counseling Spoken Here" next to whatever sign they are putting on their practice. In terms of the brief counseling dialects analogy, regardless of the dialect spoken, the goal in brief counseling is not about treatment duration, it is about doing what works effectively and efficiently.

What works is of great concern to therapists and counselors (Hubble, Duncan, & Miller, 1999). Therapeutic treatment works for 80 percent of all clients. At least 50 percent of clients can benefit from five to ten counseling sessions, and 20–30 percent require treatment lasting more than twenty-five sessions (Asay & Lambert, 1999). Lambert (1992) defined four broad common therapeutic factors influencing successful counseling: client and extratherapeutic factors, therapeutic relationship, expectancy and placebo effects, and therapeutic technique factors. Client and extratherapeutic events accounted for 40 percent of clients' counseling and therapeutic improvement. The therapeutic relationship accounted for 30 percent, expectancy and placebo effects accounted for 15 percent, and therapeutic technique accounted for 15 percent of clients' improvement in counseling and therapy. The strength-based approaches in this chapter draw on what works and the common factors illustrating what facilitates clients' improvement. The common factors strongly influence the brief approaches shared in this chapter because each approach presupposes clients bring strengths and competencies into the therapeutic process.

Based on the choice to limit the number of brief approaches addressed in this chapter, students may want to explore the richness and variety of diverse brief counseling approaches not covered or merely touched upon in this chapter. For instance, Adlerian, rational-emotive behavior therapy, reality therapy, narrative, health realization, and psychodynamic practitioners have developed brief counseling theory and interventions that guide counselors seeking time efficient pathways for helping others. Shulman (1989) finds similarities between Adlerian psychotherapy and some forms of brief therapy by pointing out that rapid assessment, flexibility, and active interpretation of emotions and goals are part of the Adlerian approach. Ellis (1989, 1990, 1996) proposes rational-emotive behavior therapy as a briefer and better form of therapy. Ellis states the ABC method is probably the most effective brief method for changing fundamental "disturbance-creating attitudes." Palmatier (1990, 1996) links reality therapy to brief approaches. Narrative therapists offer theory that guides practice intended to help clients move from problem-saturated stories to more hope-filled alternative stories (Monk, Winslade, Crocket, & Epston, 1997; White & Epston, 1990; Winslade & Monk, 1999). By focusing on the nature of mind, consciousness, and thought, health realization offers a psychoeducational approach as a new paradigm for brief treatment (Pransky, 1998; Pransky, Mills, Sedgeman, & Bleven, 1997). Still, those of a psychodynamic bent, may want to refer to the literature that concentrates on helping clients address maladaptive interpersonal problems and related neurotic disturbances (Binder, Strupp, & Henry, 1995; Levenson, 1995; Mann, 1981, 1991; Worchel, 1990). To aid students in this self-exploration, interested students should refer to sources cited throughout this chapter and to the following supplemental brief counseling sources (Bertolino & O'Hanlon, 2002; Cooper, 1995; DeJong & Berg, 2002; Friedman, 1993; Hart, 1995; Hoyt, 1994, 1996, 2000; Hubble et al., 1999; Koss & Shiang, 1994; Lipchik, 2002; Matthews & Edgette, 1997; Miller, 1997; Miller, Hubble, & Duncan, 1996; Rosenbaum, Hoyt, & Talmon, 1990; Strupp, 1981; Walter & Peller, 1992, 2000; Wells & Giannetti, 1990; Zeig & Gilligan, 1990).

A CULTURAL CONTEXT AND BRIEF BACKGROUND

Brief counseling approaches have been forwarded in the profession for a number of reasons. For instance, time and cost are critical factors that have facilitated the proliferation of brief therapies, and when managed care approves a limited number of visits for mental health care, mental health counselors are forced to adopt short-term approaches (de Shazer, 1985; Hoyt, 2000). A simplistic dualistic argument can follow; evil and greedy corporations verses selfless professionals who care only about client well-being. But look at the issue from differing perspectives. Many practitioners complain managed care companies have rejected lengthy counseling and adopted "quick fix" approaches merely due to cost. At the same time, although it is accurate to say that many corporations focus on costs over people, studies have also found that the vast majority of clients are not long term and that the majority of clients benefit from brief treatments (Asay & Lambert, 1999; Hoyt, 2000; Koss & Shiang, 1994; Lambert, 1992; McKeel, 1996). Only 20–30 percent of clients require treatment lasting over twenty-five sessions (Asay & Lambert, 1999). Counselors want to advocate for necessary treatment for those clients needing more than twenty-five sessions and they want to be aware sometimes therapy goes beyond what is necessary. Efran, Lukens, and Lukens (1990) go so far as to say that some of the therapists complaining about decreasing the duration of treatment are concerned primarily with their own incomes. Exploring such issues is beyond the scope of this chapter, and such arguments should be placed in a cultural context.

Culturally, Westerners quantify time; we measure and count the passage of time, and recognize our lives have a limited duration, of unknown length that makes knowing when we are going to die uncertain, and makes life planning not quite as effective as the expiration date on milk containers. In the West's technological culture, clocks fetter the invisible passage of time and our lives. Clocks have influenced how we see and live in the world, creating a metaphor that we live in a *machina mundi,* "world machine," that influences our very being (Crosby, 1997). Time is ticking away. To waste time is sin. Time is money. Step back briefly and consider that the philosopher Henryk Skolimowski (1994) argues that our cultural understanding of time takes on ontological and epistemological dimensions. How we understand time influences how we see reality and how we construct knowledge. For instance, stop reading briefly and think about how you are spending your time. How are you organizing your time you need to read this chapter? What do you have to give up? What do you hope to gain by "spending" your time reading this? How does your own relation with time influence how you view (and construct) reality and knowledge? Claxton (1997) points out, "Within the Western mindset, time becomes a commodity, and one inevitable consequence is the urge to 'think faster': to solve problems and make decisions quickly" (p. 5). In the West, we have a tendency to force the quick answer and instant solution, but some challenges in life cannot be met by seeking a quick or instant answer; some challenges require patience, intuition, and relaxation. Sometimes slowing down will get you where you want to be more prepared. Some brief counseling approaches are efficient and effective because they draw upon this wisdom. Brief counseling is culturally congruent. Efficient and effective interventions save time because they are designed to insure that clients attend "not one more session than is necessary" (Hoyt, 2000). Parsimonious interventions that are efficient and effective certainly save money and time for clients and managed care systems.

The move to brief approaches did not occur overnight or come upon the professional scene as a postmodern intellectual fashion statement. During World Wars I and II, the desire to get soldiers back to the battlefront as quickly as possible led to short-term therapeutic interventions rather than long explorations of neurotic or psychotic problems (Fisch, 1994). The therapeutic goal (if it can be called that) was to insure the mental stamina of fighting forces. In order to serve the "military's institutional need for a steady supply of dependable human resources" during World War II, clinicians devised a "menu of creative psychotherapeutic alternatives and shortcuts" in order to insure that the maximum number of soldiers could be returned to the active theater in the minimum of time (Herman, 1995, p. 112). More recently, managed care has been attracted to brief approaches because their focus on symptom relief and increased function seems pragmatic and cost effective (Hoyt, 1995).

The overemphasis on length of treatment may take those interested in brief counseling approaches down the wrong path. For the most part, brief therapists argue that the short duration of therapy results from using effective and efficient therapies (Bertolino & O'Hanlon, 2002; Cade & O'Hanlon, 1993; DeJong & Berg, 2002; Hoyt, 2000; Matthews & Edgette, 1997; Zeig & Gilligan, 1990). "Indeed, the actual number of hours logged in psychotherapy is much less important . . . than is the significance of the experiences that transpire during that time" (Mahoney, 1997, p. 34).

Even with an emphasis on effective and efficient therapy, there is some debate about how long brief counseling should be. For Hoyt (1995), "no magic number" of sessions for brief therapy exists, whereas Sharf (1996) offers three to forty sessions as a range. Although debatable, brief therapy generally ranges from one to twenty-five

sessions. Some consider twenty-five the maximum number of sessions for brief therapy (Koss & Butcher, 1986). Using any specific, pre-set number of sessions is arbi-
trary and may not be in the best interest of the client. For the purposes of this chapter Hoyt (1995) will serve as a guide; brief therapy is not defined by "a particular
number of sessions but rather the intention of helping clients make changes in
thoughts, feelings, actions in order to move toward or reach a particular goal as time-
efficiently as possible" (p. 1). In essence, the goal of brief therapy is not to minimize
treatment but to provide effective services to those seeking help. Brief counseling
does not seek to create Madison Avenue instant cures for those seeking therapeutic
help but rather to facilitate meaningful change effectively and efficiently for the
clients being served.

Given the wide variety of different brief approaches, it is important to consider
possible common ground, where the diverse approaches can be lumped together
rather than split apart. In order to provide some sense of common ground, Cooper
(1995) offers eight technical features common to the various forms of brief counseling that are adapted here:

1. Maintain a clear and specific treatment focus.
2. Be conscious and conscientious about how you use time.
3. Limit goals and clearly define counseling outcomes.
4. Emphasize the present, and here-and-now.
5. Make your assessment rapidly and integrate assessment into treatment.
6. Review progress frequently and discard ineffective interventions.
7. Maintain a high level of therapist-client collaboration.
8. Be pragmatic and flexible when using techniques.

In a similar vein, like Cooper's (1995) eight technical features, Fisch (1994) offers counselors four principles many brief approaches have in common:

1. Narrow the database regarding what counselors focus upon with clients.
2. Use interactional rather than intrapsychic concepts.
3. Influence change by having a task orientation rather than an insight orientation.
4. Define goals in order to know when to stop therapy.

Cooper's (1995) common technical features and Fisch's (1994) principles illustrate a common ground that reveals how brief counselors have overlapping core values.

More importantly, research regarding the efficacy of brief approaches and the
assertion that there are common factors determining therapeutic outcomes helps
brief counselors to concentrate on what works in counseling (Asay & Lambert, 1999;
Bertolino & O'Hanlon, 2002; Hubble et al., 1999; Koss & Butcher, 1986; Koss &
Shiang, 1994). Brief counselors embrace pragmatism and parsimony in their therapeutic approach. They see human change as the inevitable and build on client resources and competence. Brief counselors use homework, recognize that significant
change occurs outside of therapy, and believe that life outside of counseling is more
important than counseling itself. In addition, brief counseling practitioners recognize

that there are times when therapy does not help, and counseling is best when it is focused upon specific contexts and problems (Bertolino & O'Hanlon, 2002; Cade & O'Hanlon, 1993; Cooper, 1995; Durrant & Kowalski, 1993; Hoyt, 2000; Wells & Giannetti, 1990).

The rest of this chapter will introduce students to strength-based brief approaches that find roots in the work of Gregory Bateson, Milton Erickson, and others who shifted counseling from concentrating on deficits to looking for strengths, from exploring problems to creating solutions, and from fixation on the past to active construction of a preferred future (Bertolino & O'Hanlon, 2002; Hoyt, 2000).

COMPETENCY AND STRENGTH-BASED BRIEF APPROACHES

This section will focus upon three separate brief approaches that emerge from a common history rooted in client competencies and strengths (Bertolino & O'Hanlon, 2002; DeJong & Berg, 2002; Fisch, 1994; Hoyt, 1994, 1996, 2000). Using the dialect analogy, brief problem-solving, solution-focused, and solution-oriented approaches can claim roots within the same strength-based language of counseling, but each continues to evolve and lay claim to its own uniqueness. Even today, the strength-based approaches explored in this chapter continue to be informed by and influenced by each other and find that their therapeutic dialects are now being changed and influenced by other emerging strength-based theories, such as narrative therapy.

For all their differences, each brief approach shared in the remainder of this chapter draws upon client strengths in solving problems, finding solutions, or discovering possibilities to altering how they might overcome their presenting problems. The strength-based approaches do not embrace a normative model that prescribes what is normal and healthy or abnormal and deviant; the approaches move away from viewing clients as pathological and resistant, and concentrate on working with clients to find out what works in their own lives.

FOCUS ON PROBLEM SOLVING

The brief therapy model developed at the Mental Research Institute (MRI) is referred to as the MRI brief therapy approach, brief problem-solving therapy, and brief problem-focused therapy (Cooper, 1995; Fisch, 1990; O'Hanlon & Weiner-Davis, 1989). Don Jackson, in 1958, founded MRI in Palo Alto, California. A separate research group from Menlo Park, California, influenced the innovative experimental attitude at MRI. Lead by Gregory Bateson from 1952 to 1962, the group included collaboration and consultation with John Weakland, Jay Haley, Don Jackson, William Fry, Jr., and Virginia Satir.

Haley notes of Bateson's group, "Data of various types were used in the research: Hypnosis, ventriloquism, animal training, popular moving pictures, the nature of play, humor, schizophrenia, neurotic communication, psychotherapy, family systems and family therapy" (quoted in Cade & O'Hanlon, 1993, p. 2). During the ten-year project, Bateson's group investigated a variety of topics such as cybernetics, communication, paradox, and logical types. Throughout the project's history, the Bateson group members consulted with the psychiatrist Milton Erickson, who used hypnosis, indirect suggestion, stories, metaphors, and riddles to help his clients change (Cooper, 1995; Haley, 1973; O'Hanlon, 1987, 1990; Zeig & Gilligan, 1990). The various connections involving Bateson's Palo Alto group and MRI are remarkable and would keep a counseling soap opera going for years. Bateson's Palo Alto group studied with Jackson, Haley, Weakland, and Satir. The connection with Erickson and Satir led to Bandler and Grinder's study of the practices of Fritz Perls, Erickson, and Satir and the creation of neurolinguistic programming. Haley, who was affiliated with MRI, went to Philadelphia to work with Salvador Minuchin. Haley's (1973) own work moved toward strategic or problem-solving therapy. Steve de Shazer (1985) studied at MRI and went off to develop solution-focused therapy. O'Hanlon and Weiner-Davis (1989) moved from solution-focused therapy to create solution-oriented therapy, which with O'Hanlon (1999) has evolved into possibility therapy. Even White and Epston (1990), in Australia and New Zealand, were influenced by inquisitive openness demonstrated by Bateson's group, MRI, and the different practitioners who were making connection on the West Coast. The connection with others, sharing ideas, open, and experimental approach created a supportive context where practitioners openly explored innovative ways to find out what would work to help people with problems.

With as many techniques that they developed, the essence was not in the techniques. Weakland asserted that there was a fundamental principle in Erickson's work, stating in an interview, "the Ericksonian essence . . . has nothing to do with technique. It has nothing to do with theory. It mainly had to do with Erickson being very curious" (Hoyt, 1994, p. 12). Curiosity must be emphasized because the Erickson and the Bateson group's open and experimental approach clearly influenced the members at the Mental Research Institute in how they intervened with people and understood behavior change.

In 1966, Richard Fisch opened the Brief Therapy Center at MRI to see what therapeutic results could occur in a strictly limited period of a maximum of ten one-hour sessions that focused on the main presenting complaint, using active techniques to promote change, and searching for the minimum change required to resolve the presenting problem (Fisch, Weakland, & Segal, 1982). The MRI approach made no attempt to develop insight because problems were considered interactional in nature. The therapeutic goal for the brief problem-solving approach was to resolve the presenting problem as it occurs between people. The emphasis was on change and outcomes, not knowledge, insight, or other such concerns. It was assumed that change would be easier if people did something differently.

Fisch et al. (1982) cite four reasons for a client coming to therapy:

1. Clients have concern about behavior, actions, thoughts, or feelings of themselves or someone with whom they are significantly involved.
2. The problem or concern is described as deviant in the sense of being unusual or inappropriate and "distressing or harmful, immediately or potentially, either to the behaver . . . or to others." (p. 11)

3. Clients reported their efforts or those of others about stopping or changing the behavior have been unsuccessful.
4. Clients or those concerned about them seek professional help in changing the situation because they have not been able to make the change on their own.

Clients enter therapy because they want change. In MRI's problem-focused brief therapy, problem formation and problem maintenance are seen as parts of a vicious circle process where clients' attempts to change the problem have been mishandled, leaving clients stuck (Watzlawick, Weakland, & Fisch, 1974). Because people create problems by misinterpreting ordinary life difficulties, clients' attempts to change the problems were viewed as sometimes aggravating the problem. Clients (and for that matter, therapists) can get stuck because of the way they view and behave around the problem. "We are talking only of views, not of reality or of truth, because we believe that views are all we have, or ever will have" (Fisch et al., 1982, p. 10). Thus, the therapeutic goal in problem-focused brief therapy is to interrupt the vicious circle and initiate resolution of the problem. Counselors assess where clients are stuck, what they are doing to get unstuck, and how to influence them to stop doing what they regard as logical or necessary (Fisch, 1990). The MRI approach to helping clients get unstuck has been used in a variety of contexts, including as a feminist intervention with victims of domestic violence (McCloskey & Fraser, 1997).

Helping clients get unstuck sometimes involves reframing the problem. "To reframe . . . means to change the conceptual and/or emotional setting or viewpoint in relation to which a situation is experienced and to place it in another frame which fits the 'facts' of the same concrete situation equally well or even better, and thereby changes its entire meaning" (Watzlawick et al., 1974, p. 95). The technique, drawn in large measure from the work of Milton Erickson, seeks to infuse new meaning into a situation (O'Hanlon, 1987). Watzlawick et al. (1974) cite the example of Tom Sawyer's reframing the drudgery of whitewashing the fence into something fun and attractive, and then having his friends accept the "reality" that whitewashing can be pleasurable.

The Therapeutic Process

Assessment.   During the initial stages of treatment, the brief problem-solving therapist must gather adequate information seen as basic to every case. The assessment should include:

1. A clear understanding of the essential complaint. Who does the problem belong to? "Who is doing what that presents a problem, to whom, and how does such behavior constitute a problem?" (Fisch et al., 1982, p. 70). The questioning is persistent, firm, and polite.
2. A complete and precise understanding of just what "solutions" have been attempted, especially any efforts being made currently. The basic thrust and details regarding these "solutions" should be identified.
3. A determination of the client's minimal goals and the criteria for evaluating the achievement of those goals.

4. The use of the client's position, language, and values in the assessment. "However questionable or undesirable an aspect of the client's life may seem, we are disinclined to intervene unless the client has some complaint about it" (Fisch et al., 1982, p. 122).
5. A determination of who is most invested in change. Who is the customer? Who is the complainant? Fisch et al. (1982) state, "Get the 'window shopper' down to business" (p. 43).

Therapist Maneuverability. It is one thing to know how to best proceed, and it is quite another to have the freedom to move in the direction one thinks is best. Since clients are viewed as often hindering therapeutic efforts out of desperation or fear that things will get worse, it is critical for therapists to keep their options open. Several tactics suggested by Fisch et al. (1982) include:

1. Avoid taking definite positions prematurely. Taking firm positions may be aversive to the clients' sensibilities and values.
2. Take time. Defer implicit pressure to perform as therapists.
3. Help clients commit to a position. This limits clients' maneuverability. Therapists should use qualifying language to avoid making a commitment to a position. At the same time, therapists should get clients to be specific.
4. Take a one-down position and ask the client for help. The one-down position puts clients at ease and allows therapy to proceed like two people having a conversation.
5. Work with the complainant(s). Determine who is discomfited by the problem. Is it the client or another person?

Intervention. Because clients' "attempted solutions" are viewed as maintaining and perpetuating the problem, the interventions planned by the therapist will be directed toward helping clients depart from their solutions. This may be accomplished by either interdicting the problem-maintaining behavior or by altering clients' view of the problem so that it is no longer viewed as a problem. Problem-solving brief therapists view problems as arising from five basic attempted solutions clients maintain. Interventions arise from therapists' responses to problems being maintained by these five basic solutions:

1. Attempting to force something that can only occur spontaneously. Clients' concerns with bodily functioning, personal and sexual performance, and so forth fall into this category. Clients become "enmeshed in the painful solution of trying to coerce a performance that can only occur spontaneously" (Fisch et al., 1982, p. 130). In one example of a client complaining of obsessive ruminations, the therapist suggests that the client begin controlling the obsessive thoughts by setting a time for them to begin. Instead of resisting the ruminations, the client is given the opportunity to control them by bringing the thoughts forth at a prescribed time of day when the thoughts were normally not occurring.

2. Attempting to master a feared event by postponing it. These are usually self-referential complaints regarding shyness, creative blocks, performance blocks

(stage fright), and so on. Clients basically attempt to prepare for the feared event in such a way that the event will be mastered in advance, and avoid the actual doing. The intervention involves exposing the client to the task while requiring non-mastery. One shy male client was directed to go to a public place, like a bar or skating rink, and approach the most desirable-looking woman with the introduction, "I would like to get to know you better but I am very shy talking with women" (Fisch et al., 1982, p. 139). The client was directed further to expect possible rejection, and not to go out with the woman, because the assignment was designed to deal with rejection, not to meet women. The essential strategy involves exposing the client to the feared task while restraining the client from successfully completing it.

3. Attempting to reach accord through opposition. These problems involve conflict in an interpersonal relationship that centers on issues requiring mutual cooperation. These problems include marital disputes, employee disputes, and other conflicts commonly referred to as power struggles. "Complainants with these problems engage in the attempted solution of haranguing the other party to comply with their demands . . . and demand that the other party treat them with respect, care, or deference" (Fisch et al., 1982, p. 140). The brief problem-solving solution in this case is to get the complainant to take a "one-down" position.

4. Attempting to attain compliance through volunteerism. These problems result from the perceived inability or abhorrence to asking something of another. "The common thread involves one person attempting to gain compliance from another while denying that compliance is being asked for" (Fisch et al., 1982, p. 154). The overall strategy here is to get the person with the problem to ask directly for what he or she wants.

5. Confirming the accuser's suspicions by defending oneself. These problems result from one person suspecting another of an act both parties view as wrong. Usually one accuses the other of infidelity, excessive drinking, dishonesty, delinquency, and the other, by the act of denying the accusation, actually confirms the accuser's suspicions. It places both in an accuser/defender role. One technique for breaking up this interaction is to agree with the accuser. Fisch et al. (1982) share the story of an elderly couple who had been playing the game for over thirty years. The wife accused the husband that "he was no fun" and the husband denied it. After he began agreeing with her, she stopped accusing him and the game ended.

Additional General Interventions. Coupled with the five approaches previously listed are four other general interventions. One, "Go slow" is an intervention that is used with clients whose main attempted solution is trying too hard. The authors recommend against any overt optimism, or assuming a worried expression if there is any acknowledgment of good news. Two, dangers of improvement might be considered an extension of "Go slow" because the client is asked to recognize the possible dangers in resolving the problem. If clients lose weight, they may have to buy a new wardrobe, or if they improve their sexual performance, their partner might not be able to keep up with them. Three, making a

"U-turn" is a shift to an opposite direction because the directive or strategy is not working. This tactic is especially effective when the therapist has inadvertently taken the wrong position with a client. Four, how to worsen the problem is used when advising clients to continue the ineffective approach they are using. It is generally used with clients who are having difficulty changing what they are doing (Fisch et al., 1982).

Termination Is Done Without Fanfare.   Generally, goals are assessed and the client is given a simple goodbye. In fact, according to Fisch et al. (1982) it may be important to terminate with a "doubtful and cautionary note" (p. 179).

FOCUS ON SOLUTIONS

Solution-focused therapy is the model of brief therapy developed at the Brief Family Therapy Center (BFTC) in Milwaukee, Wisconsin, by Steve de Shazer and Insoo Kim Berg. Characterized as MRI's younger sibling, the solution-focused brief counseling approach looks closely at the pattern of interaction around the complaint, approaches for changing the pattern, and creating outcomes (Lipchik, 2002). Like MRI, the BFTC draws on Gregory Bateson's theoretical ideas and Milton Erickson's clinical work. Like MRI, solution-focused therapy has been criticized for its apparent faith in technique, and some practitioners have moved beyond atheoretical techniques toward developing a solution-focused theory that integrates language and emotion (Lipchik, 2002; Parry & Doan, 1994).

The major difference is that solution-focused therapy offers a shift in therapeutic focus away from problems and toward solutions. Solution-focused counseling can be viewed as building upon the MRI approach, but the essential shift is on client strengths, solutions, as well as still using whatever the client brings to the session that can promote healthy change. The counseling conversation changes from concentrating on problems to finding solutions. For solution-focused counselors, the solution-finding process holds therapeutic promise, and the therapeutic task entails helping clients to develop expectations of change and solutions. Solution-focused counselors pay relatively little attention to the details of the complaint, and instead highlight how the client will know when the problem is solved. For solution-focused brief counselors, the key to brief therapy is using what clients bring to meet their needs in such a way that clients will be able to find satisfactory solutions to problems (de Shazer, 1985, 1990, 1991; DeJong & Berg, 1998, 2002; Hoyt, 1994, 1996; Lipchik, 2002; Matthews & Edgette, 1997; Miller et al., 1996; Walter & Peller, 1992, 2000).

More than assessing how problems are maintained or how to solve them, solution-focused counseling asserts that helping people involved in troublesome situations requires getting them to do something different, even if it seems irrational, irrelevant, bizarre, or humorous (de Shazer, 1985). No problem occurs all of the time, and using clients' strengths and resources for bringing about change is crucial. One goal involves getting clients to envision their future without the presenting problem. When clients are able to do that, the problem is diminished (de Shazer, 1990).

The Therapeutic Process

Assessment.   The BFTC group assumes clients want to change. "Resistance" is not an issue for solution-focused therapists because they attempt to connect the client's present with the future, complimenting clients on what they are already doing that is useful, and suggesting something for them to do that might be good for them. De Shazer (1985) offered twelve building blocks of complaint and six basic assumptions for viewing and changing clients' complaints.

The twelve complaints usually include:

1. A bit or sequence of behavior
2. The meanings ascribed to the situation
3. The frequency with which the complaint happens
4. The physical location in which the complaint happens
5. The degree to which the complaint is involuntary
6. Significant others involved in the complaint directly or indirectly
7. The question of who or what is to blame
8. Environmental factors such as jobs, economic status, living space, and so on
9. The physiological or feeling state involved
10. The past
11. Dire predictions of the future
12. Utopian expectations (de Shazer, 1985, p. 27)

The six basic assumptions that de Shazer (1985) offers to help therapists draw maps of client complaints and construct solutions are:

1. Constructing complaints to involve behavior that is brought on by the client's worldview.
2. Complaints are maintained by clients thinking the decision they made about the original problem was the only thing to do, and thus getting trapped into doing more of the same.
3. Understanding that minimal changes are necessary when initiating change. There can be a "ripple effect." Once change is initiated, additional changes will be generated by the client to solve the complaint.
4. Using the clients' view of what reality would look like without the complaint, solution-focused therapists generate ideas for what to change.
5. Suggesting a new frame or new frames of reference and new behavior based on this new view, resolution of the problem can be promoted.
6. Viewing change holistically, a change in one part of the system will likely effect changes in other parts of the system.

Intervention.   Solutions, not problems, are the primary focus in solution-focused therapy. Emphasis placed on problems moves the client in the wrong direction and is based on a faulty assumption. Solution-focused brief therapy is cooperative and oriented toward change, solutions, the present, and the future.

Because solution-focused therapy assumes that therapists and clients co-construct perspectives on the problem, establishing rapport and promoting cooperation are crucial initial moves in therapy. Change is an interactional process and it is essential that therapists "fit" into the worldview of clients in order to jointly construct a problem that can be solved. If done effectively, therapists shape and change the process so clients can solve their own problems in therapy.

The presession change question technique involves seeking exceptions to the problem or exploring the solutions clients have been attempting. The goal is to create an expectation for change, emphasize the active role and responsibility of clients, and demonstrate that change happens outside of counselors' offices. Counselors simply ask, "Since the last time we met, have you been noticing some changes in yourself or discovering a new way of looking at the problem?"

Another technique involves searching for exceptions. Finding exceptions to when clients feel stuck helps to clarify the conditions for change by reorienting clients to the hope of finding a solution, implying clients have strengths and ability to solve problems, providing tangible evidence of resolution, and helping clients discover forgotten personal resources. Exceptions might include therapists' questions such as:

"When did you manage this problem in the past? What did you do differently?"

"Tell me when things were just a little better."

De Shazer (1985) describes working with a couple who were complaining about arguing. He asked them to describe what life would be like after they quit arguing. After the couple described what life would be like after these arguments, they no longer had an investment in arguing. Life would be better when they stopped fighting.

The miracle question is another technique that helps clarify goals and highlight exceptions to the problem by stimulating the client to imagine a solution and remove constraints to solving the problem, and building hope for change. With this technique clients are asked, "Suppose that one night, while you were asleep, there was a miracle and this problem was solved. How would you know? What would be different?" (de Shazer, 1991, p. 113). Such questions allow clients to envision their lives without the problem.

Scaling questions is another technique designed to make the abstract concrete by quantifying intangibles, placing power with clients, and demonstrating change. Clients are asked, "On a scale of 1 to 10, where 1 means you have no influence over your problem, and 10 means you have total influence, where would you place yourself today?" To support the initial question, therapists add further questions such as "Where would others place you on this scale?" and "What do you need to move a fraction of a point up the scale?"

These brief examples show how each technique attempts to induce doubt regarding the severity and dominance of the problem by helping clients find exceptions to the occurrence of the problem and toward helping clients understand their lives are not constantly dominated by the problem. Finding that the problem is not always occurring in their life or that they can imagine a future without the problem enables clients to define goals that concentrate on constructing solutions. As the name suggests, solution-focused therapy concentrates using techniques and interventions that create the expectation that solutions exist or are imminent.

SOLUTION-ORIENTED
AND POSSIBILITY THERAPY

Solution-oriented brief therapy is the approach developed by Bill O'Hanlon and Michele Weiner-Davis that changes direction from both MRI and BFTC. Milton Erickson's influence is central. Solution-oriented brief counseling focuses on people's competence, with therapists cocreating solvable problems with clients. The approach has evolved into O'Hanlon's (1999) possibility therapy. The solution-oriented approach has a future goal orientation focused on bringing about small but positive outcomes for clients. Both solution-oriented and possibly therapy "emphasize the importance of client's internal experience" (Bertolino & O'Hanlon, 2002, p. 7). Like Rogerian counseling, clients must feel heard and understood during the counseling process if change is going to occur.

Influenced by both the MRI and BFTC approaches, solution-oriented counselors added that clients are stuck not just by how they are "doing" the problem but also how they are "viewing" the problem. Views, actions, and context became crucial in solution-oriented counseling, and solution-oriented practitioners were encouraged to attempt three actions:

1. Changing what clients are doing in regard to their actions and interactions around the situation perceived as problematic
2. Changing the clients' frames of reference and their view of the situation viewed as problematic
3. Evoking resources, solutions, and strengths to bring to the situation perceived as problematic (O'Hanlon & Weiner-Davis, 1989)

Solution-focused and solution-oriented therapies both utilize self-reinforcing patterns of thought and behavior. O'Hanlon and Weiner-Davis (1989) point out, "If the client walks into a behaviorist's office, he will leave with a behavioral problem. If clients choose psychoanalysts' offices, they will leave with unresolved issues from childhood as the focus of the problem" (p. 54). O'Hanlon and Weiner-Davis (1989) explain that clients' complaints are negotiated and "cocreated" with therapists, and the solution-oriented approach begins the therapeutic process by looking for clients' strengths, solutions, and competence. One intention in separating the two approaches is to show the continuing drift in solution-oriented and other practices away from purist thinking and toward integrating diverse ideas found in literature using a variety of terms, such as constructivist, narrative, postmodern, collaborative, competency-based, interactional, and more (Bertolino, 1999; Bertolino & O'Hanlon, 2002; Cade & O'Hanlon, 1993; Cooper, 1995; DeJong & Berg, 2002; Friedman, 1993; Hoyt, 2000; Matthews & Edgette, 1997; Neimeyer & Mahoney, 1995; O'Hanlon, 1999; Parry & Doan, 1994; Walter & Peller, 1992, 2000).

Solution-focused and solution-oriented therapy are frequently confused, and the confusion resulted in O'Hanlon describing his approach as possibility therapy. Possibility therapy has three essential differences from solution-focused therapy: one, validating emotional experience; two, being flexible rather than formulaic with clients; three, being mindful of political, historical, and gender influences upon problems clients bring into counseling. O'Hanlon's possibility therapy is not purist nor pushing allegiance to a single model for counseling but is open to using ideas and perspectives from differing approaches, such as Ericksonian, strategic, behavioral, solution-focused, and narrative (Bertolino & O'Hanlon, 2002; O'Hanlon, 1999).

O'Hanlon (1999) offers three principles that guide the work of possibility therapists:

1. Acknowledge and validate the client's perceptions and experience.
2. Facilitate clients in shifting how they view things and/or do things.
3. Recognize client resources, expertise, experiences and collaborate with them about the direction counseling is going.

The Therapeutic Process

Assessment and Interventions.   Assessment is viewed as directly tied to therapists' metaphors and assumptions. "We have never had a client with an unresolved Oedipal conflict or an overactive superego. Just lucky, we suppose!" (O'Hanlon & Weiner-Davis, 1989, p. 54). Furthermore, solution-oriented therapists look at problems not as pathological manifestations but as ordinary difficulties encountered in life.

Assessment and intervention are not separated into distinct steps. In fact, the initial interviewing process is viewed as an intervention. Because interviewing utilizes solution-oriented techniques, "clients can experience significant shifts in their thinking about their situations during the course of the [first] session" (O'Hanlon & Weiner-Davis, 1989, p. 77). Solution-oriented therapists use presuppositional questioning, such as "What were the good things about the dinner?" rather than "Did anything good happen at the dinner?" Such approaches begin with the way clients perceive and talk about their problems. By looking for exceptions to the problem, solution-oriented therapists attempt to normalize or depathologize problems, making problems simply a natural response to life events.

O'Hanlon and Weiner-Davis (1989) offer eight techniques for changing patterns of doing or viewing problems:

1. The frequency or rate of the performance of the complaint could be changed. Have the client who goes on candy binges slowly eat candy when not on a binge.
2. The timing of complaint performance could be changed. Have depressed clients schedule their depression for a specific time of the day.
3. The duration of the performance of the complaint could be changed. Have the compulsive handwasher wash the left hand five minutes and the right hand thirty seconds.
4. The location of the performance of the complaint could be changed. The authors describe a situation where a wife and husband were directed to move their arguments into the bathroom with the husband getting undressed and laying down in the bathtub and the wife sitting fully clothed on the toilet. The couple's subsequent actions and laughter broke their pattern of chronic arguments.

5. The complaint pattern could have one or more elements added to it. Clients with eating disorders are told to put on their favorite shoes or dress before bingeing.
6. The sequence of components or events in the complaint pattern could be changed. A teen was directed to tape-record her father's lectures. Then, at the appropriate time when her father was about to lecture her again, the teen was told to play the lecture back and thereby beat her father to the punch.
7. The complaint pattern could be broken into smaller pieces or elements. Spouses were told to conduct their arguments on paper with each person taking turns to write five minutes, then to exchange their papers.
8. The complaint performance could be linked to the performance of some burdensome exercise. In this case, people who are chronically late may have to do something they hate to do for the same duration of time they are late. For instance, if they hate cleaning the bathroom, they must spend one minute cleaning the bathroom for each minute they arrive late.

In each instance, solution-oriented interventions are negotiated with the clients within a collaborative relationship where change is expected. The interventions are designed to help clients change their "doing" or "viewing" of problems, and the goal is to help clients look toward possibilities rather than problems. The approach involves using what is going right rather than focusing on what is going wrong.

Solution-oriented and possibility therapy theorists augment their work with narrative interventions and have been influenced by narrative thought (Bertolino, 1999; Bertolino & O'Hanlon, 2002). Solution-focused and possibility therapists are beginning to be informed by political, historical, and gender influence on clients' problems in the same way that narrative therapists are aware that domestic abuse is something the counselor should put on the table as a problem. Both possibility and narrative approaches view humans as actively engaged in a socially constructed process of making meanings and creating stories (Monk et al., 1997; Neimeyer & Mahoney, 1995).

Brief solution-oriented and possibility therapy encourage counselors to use stories, anecdotes, parables, and humor to help clients change. This practice has been influenced by the narrative therapists White and Epston (1990) who attempt to help clients move from problem-saturated stories to more hope-filled alternative stories. Like solution-oriented therapists, Epston and White (1995) believe clients have "personal solution knowledges" that help them move beyond "expert knowledges" and toward authoring the story of their own lives.

White and Epston's (1990) theory guides their practice helping clients achieve victory over problems that have become oppressive in their own lives; the techniques range from those designed to help clients view problems differently, to giving parties, certificates, ribbons, and therapy-ending rituals. The crucial point in narrative theory is that the person is never the problem, the problem is the problem. One technique, "externalization of the problem," has been embraced by solution-oriented and possibility therapists because the problem is redefined in such a way that the problem is placed outside the clients. For example, if clients' presenting problem involves depression, therapists might ask, "How long has the depression been pushing you around?" Thus, the depression becomes a controllable object outside of clients, rather than an internalized enduring condition within clients. The counselor can enlist the help of family members to unite with the identified client to fight back against the externalized problem.

AN INTERVENTION WITH AN ADOLESCENT

The separate brief approaches reveal the practical applications problem-focused, solution-focused, solution-oriented, and narrative approaches have for adolescent and school-age populations (Amatea, 1989; Bertolino, 1999; Durrant, 1995; Metcalf, 1995; Mostert, Johnson, & Mostert, 1997; Murphy, 1997; Selekman, 1993a, b; Sklare, 1997; Winslade & Monk, 1999). Durrant (1995), Metcalf (1995), Murphy (1997), and Sklare (1997) advocate changing the way professional helpers think about difficulties by encouraging helpers to focus energy on solutions and competencies rather than problems. Winslade and Monk (1999) locate problems in a cultural landscape that challenges counselors to consider their own cultural positioning and the need to help youth find their own competence and life story. Amatea (1989) offers an interpretation of problem-focused therapy for school behavior problems, whereas, Bertolino's (1999) possibility-oriented and Selekman's (1993a, b) solution-oriented offer an improvisational melding of all these approaches to address adolescent difficulties. Change comes from helping people (adults and adolescents) think and act differently about problematic situations. O'Hanlon (1999) offers possibility therapy as an approach that moves beyond liabilities by drawing upon strengths and encouraging clients to do one thing different. Such simple and pragmatic suggestions are at the heart of the strength-based approaches that work toward encouraging clients to change one small thing.

The Case of the Girl Who Knew She Was Stupid

Barbara, a 16-year-old female student, met with the school counselor regarding her class selection for the upcoming school year. Barbara was enrolled in a college prep program, and she had a 3.6 GPA on a four-point scale. Neither parent had completed college, but both encouraged Barbara to go to college in order to "get a good job" that would pay "good money." During an earlier session in the later part of the school year with the school counselor, Barbara expressed a sense of feeling stupid and a desire to drop a class needed to meet the college entrance requirements.

Barbara: I'm stupid. I want to drop German.

Therapist: Drop German. That's a big decision. Umm. When did stupidness start standing in your way?

Barbara: A long time ago.

Therapist: By looking at your GPA, I see that stupidness certainly hasn't blocked your way to good grades.

Barbara: You just don't know.

Therapist: Right, I might not know how hard you've worked. Here's what I do know. By looking at my computer screen, I see a college-prep student with a 3.6 GPA. That shows me you've outwitted stupidness and that you have a pretty full Smart Bank. It also shows me you have not let stupidness push you around or make you quit. You've pushed stupidness around.

Barbara: Maybe. I still want to drop German next year.

Therapist: Is it stupidness or German that's pushing you around?

Barbara: German. My teacher doesn't help me at all. She just passes us all along, and I'm not prepared for next year. I don't know a thing.

Therapist: Not a thing? On a scale of 1 to 10, how would you rate what you know now in German compared to what you knew before you took German?

Barbara: About a 5.

Therapist: We're halfway there. It's not a ten, but it's a solid start.

Barbara: Umm.

Counselor: As I see it, you have a pretty full Smart Account. Your 3.6 GPA is just numbers on my screen, but it indicates your hard work, resources, and wealth. I think you have other accounts elsewhere, like a Knowing What to Do Account. What made you come in here to see me?

Barbara: I don't know. I just wanted to figure things out.

Therapist: And here we are. It will take some planning and effort but together we'll make German work.

Barbara: Okay.

This case shows the use of externalizing the problem, scaling questions, and metaphor. The first step in this intervention was externalizing stupidness as an object that was standing in Barbara's way. Barbara then shifted the external problem to German and the German teacher. Obviously, the teacher may be part of the problem, but using scaling questions helped establish that Barbara was "halfway there" in her knowledge of German. The counselor pointed out the fact that Barbara made the appointment, revealing her own solution-finding skills. Two subsequent sessions focused on strategies for dealing with her German teacher, and developing a plan for continuing her success in meeting the requirements necessary to get into college.

ETHICAL CONCERNS

There are a number of ethical concerns raised about brief therapy; issues such as therapist influence, client welfare, not addressing the underlying problem, and abandonment are typically raised. Koss and Shiang (1994) state, "no evidence exists to suggest that brief psychotherapy produces any greater negative effects than long-term psychotherapy" (p. 689). Most people do not enter therapy to receive "overhauls." Surprisingly, given that the median therapeutic duration is six to eight sessions, it might be said that operationally all counseling is short term. Besides the pressure of third-party payments to reduce the cost of psychotherapy, most people want to be helped as quickly as possible without spending a great deal of time or money (Bergin & Garfield, 1994).

Traditional psychodynamic therapies have been directed toward helping clients achieve insight or awareness. Palmatier (1996) states, "Psychodynamic therapists believe their work targets the real problem, is intensive, and results in long lasting changes. They criticize pragmatic approaches as shallow and temporary toying with symptoms. Therefore, symptom relief per se is not a value in therapy" (p. 91). Most brief therapies have targeted symptoms by getting clients to see and do things differently. This active relationship raises questions for some. The problem-focused approach used at MRI is frequently described as manipulative and questioned on ethical grounds. Fisch (1990) argues that manipulation is unavoidable in therapy, and the real issue is facing up to how therapists acknowledge their manipulation and assessing the therapeutic outcome. Fisch states, "Ethical and responsible therapy involves working with the client's reality (frame of reference, worldview, etc.) rather than requiring clients to accept the therapist's reality" (1990, p. 430). Indeed, brief therapy may be more ethical than long-term care if we are evaluating treatment on the basis of effective and efficient outcomes. In brief therapy, treatment is collaborative, therapists take clients' presenting complaints seriously, clients determine the success of treatment, and it is consumer oriented (Cooper, 1995). Palmatier (1996) points to core problems regarding long-term therapy, "psychodynamic therapy is nebulous, long-term, and aims to elicit insight and not behavior change" (p. 91). (Given some of the ethical concerns regarding brief therapy, brief therapists should press the ethical question around prolonged long-term care but that is not the point.)

Professionals must advocate that clients receive adequate and effective treatment; some clients will take longer than others. Counselors are faced with the demands of third-party payers, research regarding the effectiveness of brief approaches, and clients who "do not seem to want to spend a great deal of time and money on their personal psychotherapy but prefer to be helped as quickly as possible" (Bergin & Garfield, 1994, p. 9). Models that focus on effectiveness and efficiency inform both long-term and brief approaches. Counselors may take on a role similar to a family doctor; the client might have a long-term relationship but does not see the doctor every week. Such practice is similar to using brief, intermittent psychotherapy throughout a person's life cycle (Cummings & Sayama 1995). Counseling is moving beyond metaphors of infectious disease and ideas of permanent "cures" and toward helping people find solutions to some natural problems that are part of living. In the end, ethics are not merely lists of prescriptive rules, but rather personal and professional perspectives that inform actions taken to help people seeking help (Hoyt & Combs, 1996). Counselors have a literature that points toward common factors influencing therapeutic outcomes (Asay & Lambert, 1999; Lambert, 1992). Ethical counselors look for what works to help clients.

SUMMARY

Common assumptions found in brief approaches to short-term therapy include pragmatism and parsimony, a view that human change is inevitable, that clients have resources and competence, that significant change occurs outside of therapy, and that life outside of therapy is more important than therapy itself.

The strength-based brief approaches point toward different forms of participation with clients, away from objectifying clients or facilitating insight, and toward collaborating with people in order to help them see and respond to problems differently. For strength-based brief therapists, problems are maintained by ineffective strategies for solving them. MRI facilitates clients in getting unstuck. Solution-focused counseling points clients away from problems and toward solutions. Solution-oriented therapy and possibility therapy are more concerned with cocreating with clients solvable problems or recognizing different options. Each draws on client resources and strengths.

Generally, brief therapies challenge the counseling profession to evolve. Third-party payers, research regarding the effectiveness of brief approaches, and clients who prefer to be helped as quickly as possible support continued research and experimentation with brief approaches. Although we caution against promoting any quest for instant cures, the thoughtful evolution toward therapies that are effective and efficient help counselors look deeply at the nature of their work and the impact it has upon the lives of their clients. In fact, brief therapy may press counselors to consider the deeper impact that the time variable has upon counseling designed to help clients define more meaningful and joyous lives for themselves. Indeed, some brief therapies teach clients to attend to their thinking in order to live more meaningful and joyous lives (Pransky et al., 1997). As the profession is pressed to focus on efficiencies, counselors and clients do not have time to talk about or explore meaning and joy, but merely day-to-day survival. Mere survival brings us to the larger question about the roles of counselors in our culture. Time may be money but people matter, and wasting time may be problematic but wasting our sense of wonder and appreciation are even more tragic. Indeed, as moment-to-moment experience and professional counseling practice are commodified in terms of productivity, time is taken away from pointing toward simply pondering or appreciating the wonders of life. A brief intervention here might include doing one thing different—taking time to be curious about flowers, looking at and smelling flowers with someone you love, leaving work early, extending the conversation at dinner, and so on. Brief or long, counselors have a role in helping individuals to reach their goals and in assisting their communities to evolve in a more just, compassionate, and beautiful direction.

CHAPTER EIGHT

GROUP COUNSELING

DAVID CAPUZZI, PH.D.
Johns Hopkins University
Professor Emeritus Portland State University

DOUGLAS R. GROSS, PH.D.
Professor Emeritus Arizona State University

The twenty-first century poses challenges and possibilities that should be of high interest to the beginning counselor enrolled in a counselor education program and considering becoming a group work specialist. If we believe that the 1950s may have symbolized "the individual in society," the 1960s "the individual against society," the 1970s "the individual's conflict with self," and the 1980s "the individual's integration into the family," the society of the 1990s and beyond may clearly be characterized as "the individual's integration with the machine" (Shapiro & Bernadett-Shapiro, 1985). Much of the work in education, employment, and day-to-day living situations will be done by computers; connections between colleagues, friends, and family members will be maintained by telephone lines, word processors, and modems. The replacement of consistent social contact with friends and coworkers by e-mail will create a much greater need for interpersonal communication on a person-to-person basis. Groups will provide an antidote to human isolation and more and more counselors and other human development specialists will be called upon to serve as group facilitators. The beginning counseling and human development specialist will experience an explosion of opportunities and escalating concomitant responsibilities as a group work specialist.

There are a number of reasons why the responsibilities of a group work specialist are so important to address. A facilitator must be skilled in catalyzing a therapeutic climate in a group and in monitoring therapeutic factors inherent in the group (Berg, Landreth, & Fall, 1998; Corey, 2004; Gladding, 2003; Ohlsen & Ferreira, 1994). Facilitators must also be able to assess which clients they can assist given the facilitators' level of skills, to describe their services and aspects of the group experience, to engender trust and confidence, and to answer questions about client rights and responsibilities, confidentiality, and expectations for change.

The purpose of this chapter is to provide an introduction to group work for those interested in pursuing follow-up education and experience in the context of master's and doctoral graduate preparation. The history of group work, types of groups, stages of group life, characteristics of group facilitators, responsibilities and interventions in groups, myths connected with group work, and issues and ethics of group work will be overviewed.

THE HISTORY OF GROUP WORK

Beginnings

As noted by Vriend (1985), the first half of the twentieth century was characterized by lively interest, experimentation, and research in the promising new field of group dynamics. Behavior in small groups, leadership styles, membership roles, communication variables, and so on were all examined and studied for their application to groups in a variety of settings (Hare, Borgatta, & Bales, 1967; Johnson & Johnson, 2000). J. H. Pratt (Boston), Jesse. B. Davis (Grand Rapids), J. L. Moreno, Alfred Adler, Samuel R. Slavson, Rudolf Dreikurs, Nathan Ackerman, Gregory Bateson and Virginia Satir were all well-known practitioners who pioneered early approaches to group work (Berg, Landreth, & Fall, 1998).

In 1947, a history-making conference in Bethel, Maine, was attended by a multidisciplinary group of researchers and practitioners from university and community settings throughout North America. The National Training Laboratory (NTL) in Group Development of the National Education Association held its first "laboratory session" at which T-groups (the "T" is for training) and the laboratory method were born (Bradford, Gibb, & Benne, 1964; Roller, 1997). First, using themselves as experimental subjects, participants at the conference created a laboratory situation in which the behavior of the participants was more important than any effort or technique employed. The situation created a safe place for group members to explore their own behavior, feelings, and the responses of others to them as people separate from social, work, and family roles. Under the direction of the NTL, such conferences continued each summer and the T-group movement grew and achieved national visibility.

As time passed, T-groups appeared on university campuses and in other settings. The T-group provided a fresh concept with tremendous appeal as opportunity was provided for group members to become more "sensitive," to "grow emotionally," and to "realize their human potential." The country began hearing about the "human potential movement" and of exciting developments in California, particularly at the Esalen Institute at Big Sur (Neukrug, 1999) and at the Center for the Studies of the Person founded by Carl R. Rogers and his colleagues. Soon there were a variety of marathon and encounter groups; it was an era of openness, self-awareness, and getting in touch with feelings.

The 1960s and 1970s

The 1960s were a time of social upheaval and questioning. There were riots on campuses and in cities as civil rights groups struggled to raise the consciousness of the nation about unfair discrimination and prejudice. Leaders such as John F. Kennedy and Martin Luther King, Jr., became the idolized champions and international symbols of a people's determination to change a society and to promote social responsibility. The nation united in grief-stricken disbelief as its heroes were martyred and determination to counter the human rights violations of the decades escalated. As the 1960s ended, the encounter groups movement, emphasizing personal consciousness and connection with others, reached its zenith, then gradually waned as events such as the Charles Manson killings, Watergate scandal, the first presidential resignation in the history of the United States, the group killings en route to the Munich Olympics, and the rise of fanatic cults made people in all parts of the country question the extent to which permissiveness and "human potential" should be allowed to develop (Janis, 1972; Rowe & Winborn, 1973).

For professionals in education and mental health, however, the 1960s and 1970s were decades of maintained interest in group work despite the highs and lows of societal fervor and dismay. Mental health centers conducted more and more group sessions for clients, and counselor education, counseling psychology, psychology, and social work departments on university campuses instituted more and more course work and supervised experiences in aspects of group work. In 1973, the Association for Specialists in Group Work (ASGW) was formed and by 1974 (Berg, Landreth, & Fall, 1998; Neukrug, 1999) it had become a division of the American Counseling Association (at that time named the American Personnel and Guidance Association). Similar developments took place in the context of other large professional groups such as the American Psychological Association and the National Association of Social Workers.

The 1980s

The 1980s witnessed increasing interest in group work and in working with special populations. Groups were started for alcoholics, adult children of alcoholics, incest victims, adults molested as children, persons who are overweight, underassertive persons, and those who have been victims of violent crimes. Other groups were begun for the elderly, for those dealing with death and other losses, for people with eating disorders, smokers, and the victims of the Holocaust (Neukrug, 1999; Shapiro & Bernadett-Shapiro, 1985). This increasing specialization brought with it an increasing need for higher standards for preparation of the group work specialist as evidenced by the development of training standards for group work specialists (ASGW, 1983, 1992) and the inclusion in the standards of the Council for Accreditation of Counseling and Related Educational Programs (CACREP, 1988) of specific group work specialist preparation guidelines for the graduate-level university educator to follow. At the same time, this increasing specialization has brought with it a reliance on self-help groups composed of individuals who share a specific affliction. Usually, such groups are not facilitated by a professional and this set of circumstances can be in conflict with the values and standards of professional group workers unless they have given some thought to how they might be involved (Corey, 2004).

The 1990s and Beyond

The escalating interest in group work and in working with special populations so evident in the decade of the 1980s continued into the last decade of the century. The 1983 ASGW standards for training of group counselors was revised and a new set of standards was adopted in 1991 (ASGW, 1991). Although the 1991 standards built on the 1983 standards emphasizing the knowledge, skills, and supervised experience necessary for the preparation of group workers, the newer standard broadened the conception of group work, clarified the difference between core competencies and specialization requirements, defined the four prominent varieties of group work, and eliminated the previously made distinctions among different kinds of supervised field experience (Conyne, Wilson, Kline, Morran, & Ward, 1993). In addition, CACREP, in its 1994 and 2001 revisions of accreditation standards, reemphasized the importance of group work by identifying principles of group dynamics, group leadership styles, theories of group counseling, group counseling methods, approaches used for other types of group work, and ethical considerations as essential curricular elements for all counselor education programs (CACREP, 1994, 2001). In addition, technology has taken the use of groups to computers through the use of chat rooms, computer conferencing, listservs, and news groups. Although the issues and ethics of group work will be overviewed at the end of this chapter, it should be noted that the practice of the group work professional will require increasing levels of expertise and an enhanced ability to participate in and apply the results of needed research. The history-making national conference for group work specialists, conceptualized and sponsored by ASGW in early 1990 in Florida and repeated during subsequent years in other parts of the country, symbolizes the importance of group work to the clients served by the counseling and human development professional.

TYPES OF GROUPS

Most textbooks for introduction-to-counseling courses begin the discussion of group work by attempting to make distinctions among group therapy, group counseling, and group guidance. In general, *group therapy* is described as being longer term, more remedially and therapeutically focused, and more likely to be facilitated by a facilitator with doctoral-level preparation and a more "clinical" orientation. *Group counseling* may be differentiated from group therapy by its focus on conscious problems, by the fact that it is not aimed at major personality changes, by an orientation toward short-term issues, and by the fact that it is not as concerned with the treatment of the more severe psychological and behavioral disorders (Corey, 2004; Gazda, Ginter, & Horne, 2001).

The term *group guidance* usually is descriptive of a classroom group in a K through 12 setting in which the leader presents information or conducts mental health education. In contrast to a group therapy or group counseling situation involving no more than eight to ten group participants, a group guidance experience could involve twenty to forty group participants, lessening opportunities for individual participation, and facilitator observation and intervention.

For the purposes of this chapter ASGW's definitions of the four group work specialty types are presented next as a point of departure for classifying groups (Conyne et al., 1993). The reader may wish to do additional reading relative to group "types" from sources such as Corey (1985, 2004), Dinkmeyer and Muro (1979), Gazda (1984), Gladding (2003), Neukrug (1999), or Ohlsen (1977).

Task/Work Groups

The group worker who specializes in promoting the development and functioning of task and work groups seeks to support such groups in the process of improving their function and performance. Task and work group specialists employ principles of group dynamics, organizational development, and team building to enhance group members' skills in group task accomplishment and group maintenance. The scope of practice for these group work specialists includes normally functioning individuals who are members of naturally occurring task or work groups operating within a specific organizational context. It is important to note that graduate course work for specialists in task and work groups should include at least one specialization course in organizational management and development. Ideally, course work should be taken in the broad area of organizational psychology, management, and development to develop an awareness of organizational life and how task and work groups function within the organization. In addition, a task/work group specialist might also develop skill in organizational assessment, training, program development, consultation, and program evaluation.

Clinical instruction for training in working with task and work groups should include a minimum of thirty clock hours (forty-five clock hours recommended) of supervised practice in leading or coleading a task/work group appropriate to the age and clientele of the group leader's specialty area(s) (such as school counseling, community counseling, mental health counseling, etc.).

Guidance/Psychoeducational Groups

The psychoeducational group specialist educates group participants. Such participants may be informationally deficient in some area (e.g., how to cope with external threats, developmental transitions, or personal and interpersonal crises). The scope of practice of psychoeducational group leaders includes essentially normally functioning individuals who are "at risk" for, but currently unaffected by, an environmental threat (e.g., AIDS), who are approaching a developmental transition point (e.g., new parents), or who are in the midst of coping with a life crisis (such as suicide of a loved one). The primary goal in psychoeducational group work is to prevent the future development of dysfunctional behaviors.

Course work for specialization in psychoeducational groups should include at least one specialization course that provides information about community psychology, health and wellness promotion, and program development and evaluation. Ideally, psychoeducational group specialists would also take course work in curriculum design, group training methods, and instructional techniques. Psychoeducational group specialists should also acquire knowledge about the topic areas in which they intend to work (such as AIDS, substance abuse prevention, grief and loss, coping with transition and change, and parent effectiveness training).

Clinical instruction for preparing to facilitate psychoeducational groups should include a minimum of thirty clock hours (forty-five clock hours recommended) of supervised practice in leading or coleading a psychoeducational group appropriate to the age and clientele of the group leader's specialty area(s) (such as school counseling, community counseling, mental health counseling, etc.).

Counseling Groups

The group worker who specializes in group counseling focuses on assisting group participants to resolve the usual, yet often difficult, problems of living by stimulating interpersonal support and group problem solving. Group counselors support participants in developing their existing interpersonal problem-solving competencies so that they may become more able to handle future problems of a similar nature. The scope of practice for their group work includes nonsevere career, educational, personal, interpersonal, social, and developmental concerns of essentially normally functioning individuals.

Graduate course work for specialists in group counseling should include multiple courses in human development, health promotion, and group counseling. Group counseling specialists should have in-depth knowledge in the broad areas of normal human development, problem identification, and treatment of normal personal and interpersonal problems of living.

Clinical instruction for counseling groups should include a minimum of forty-five clock hours (sixty clock hours recommended) of supervised practice in leading or coleading a counseling group appropriate to the age and clientele of the group leader's specialty area(s) (such as community counseling, mental health counseling, school counseling, etc.).

Psychotherapy Groups

The specialist in group psychotherapy helps individual group members remediate in-depth psychological problems or reconstruct major personality dimensions. The group psychotherapist differs from specialists in task/work groups, psychoeducational groups, or counseling groups in that the group psychotherapist's scope of practice is focused on people with acute or chronic mental or emotional disorders characterized by marked distress, impairment in functioning, or both.

Graduate course work for training in group psychotherapy should include multiple courses in the development, assessment, and treatment of serious or chronic personal and interpersonal dysfunction. The group psychotherapist must develop in-depth knowledge in the broad areas of normal and abnormal human development, diagnosis, treatment of psychopathology, and group psychotherapy. Clinical instruction for working with psychotherapy groups should include a minimum forty-five clock hours (sixty clock hours recommended) of supervised practice in leading or coleading a psychotherapy group appropriate to the age and clientele of the group leader's specialty area(s) (such as mental health counseling, community counseling, etc.).

STAGES OF GROUP LIFE

In an outstanding article, David G. Zimpfer (1986) pointed out that since the 1940s much has been written about the developmental phases or stages through which a small group progresses over time (Bales, 1950; Braaten, 1975; Golembiewski, 1962; Hare, 1973; Hill & Gruner, 1973; Thelen & Dickerman, 1949; Tuckman, 1965). He also noted that recent contributions to this topic range from descriptive, classificatory schemes (such as the initial, transitional, working, and final stages presented by Corey in 1985, 2004) to detailed analyses of a single phase of group development (such as the 1965 exploration of authority relations in T-groups presented by Reid). Zimpfer's recommendation to the group work specialist is to select the theory or model of small-group development that applies to the kind of group to be conducted. There are many additional resources that describe small-group development that can be read as a follow-up to this chapter and as a follow-up to Zimpfer's recommendation (Donigan & Malanti, 1997; Gladding, 2003; Goldstein & Noonan, 1999; Jacobs, Masson, & Harvill, 1998; MacKenzie, 1997).

After studying a variety of models and conceptualizations of the developmental stages of groups and calling upon our own collective experience, we propose a composite conceptualization (Capuzzi & Gross, 1992, 1998, 2002) of the stages of group life. In our view, the developmental process consists of four stages: (a) definitive stage, (b) personal involvement stage, (c) group involvement stage, and (d) enhancement and closure stage.

Definitive Stage

The length of time associated with this stage in group development varies with the group and is best explained in terms of the individual group member's definition of the purpose of the group, commitment, and involvement in it, and the degree of self-disclosure he or she is willing to do. Characterizing this stage of development are questions such as: Whom can I trust? Where will I find support? Will I be hurt by others knowing about me? How much of myself am I willing to share? These questions, and the lack of immediate answers, typify members in the definitive stage as increased anxiety, excitement, nervousness, and self-protective dialogue increase. The dialogue during this stage tends to be of a social nature (small talk) as the members test the waters of group involvement. To help group members deal effectively with the definitive stage, the group leader needs skills in dealing with issues such as trust, support, safety, self-disclosure, and confidentiality.

In the definitive stage in group development, individuals define, demonstrate, and experiment with their own role definitions; they "test" the temperament, personality, and behaviors of other group members; and they arrive at conclusions about how personally involved they are willing to become. The individual's movement through this stage can be enhanced or impeded by the group's makeup (age, gender, number, values, attitudes, socioeconomic status, and so on), the leadership style (active, passive, autocratic, democratic), the group's setting (formal, informal, uncomfortable, relaxed), the personal dynamics the individual brings to the group (shy, aggressive, verbal, nonverbal), and the individual's perceptions of trust and acceptance from other group members and from the group leader.

The definitive stage is crucial in group development because this stage can determine for the individual (and, therefore, for the group) future involvement, commitment, and individual, and group success or failure as the group progresses.

Personal Involvement Stage

Once individuals have drawn conclusions about their commitment and role in the group, they move into the personal involvement stage of group development. This stage is best described in terms of member-to-member interactions—the sharing of personal information, confrontation with other group members, power struggles, and the individual's growing identity as a group member. Statements such as "I am," "I fear," "I need," and "I care" are characteristic of this stage of group involvement. Through speech and behaviors, the individual member demonstrates the degree of personal sharing he or she is willing to invest and confirms the commitment made during the definitive stage. The personal involvement stage is one of action, reaction, and interaction. Both fight and flight are represented in this stage as individuals strive to create a role within the group. This creating process often involves intense member-to-member interactions followed by a retreat to regroup and become involved again. The interactions that ensue not only enhance the member's place within the group, but also aid in firmly establishing the group as an entity in its own right.

The personal involvement stage offers the individual the opportunity to try out various behaviors, affirm or deny perceptions of self and others, receive feedback in the form of words or behaviors, and begin the difficult process of self-evaluation. Individual involvement in this stage of group development is critical to the eventual outcome of the group.

Group Involvement Stage

As a result of the information about self gained in the personal involvement stage, group members move into the group involvement stage, characterized by self-evaluation and self-assessment of behavior, attitudes, values, and methods used in relating to others and also by members' channeling their energies to better meet group goals and purposes. During this stage the term *member* and the term *group* become somewhat more synonymous.

Degrees of cooperation and cohesiveness replace conflict and confrontation as members, now more confident in their role in the group, direct more of their attention to what is best for the group and all its members. This stage reveals increasing role clarification, intimacy, problem exploration, group solidarity, compromise, conflict resolution, and risk taking.

The group, with its purposes and goals, is merging with the individual purposes and goals of its members. Individual agendas are being replaced by group agendas and the members are identifying more with the group. Bonding is taking place between members as they join forces to enhance the group and, in turn, enhance self in relation to the group. References to "insider" and "outsider" differentiate the group and the member's life outside the group. Members grow protective of other group members and also of the group itself. The group and its membership take on special significance unique to those who are part of the process. This melding of member and group purposes and goals is necessary to the group's ongoing success.

Enhancement and Closure Stage

The final stage in a group's life is often described as the most exhilarating but also the saddest aspect of group work. The exhilaration stems from the evaluation and reevaluation that are so much a part of the final stage. The evaluative aspect consists of reevaluation of the group process and individual and group assessment of change, in conjunction with individual and group reinforcement of individual member change, and a commitment to continue self-analysis and growth. Members have an opportunity to share significant growth experiences during the group tenure, and they receive feedback, generally positive, from other group members and the leader. Members are encouraged to review the process of the group and to measure changes that have taken place since their first entering the group to this period just before closure. Member statements at this stage of group development tend to be along the line of: "I was . . . now I am," "I felt . . . now I feel," "I didn't . . . now I do," and "I couldn't . . . now I can."

The sadness in this final stage centers on leaving an environment that provided safety, security, and support and individuals who offered encouragement, friendship, and positive feedback. A major concern seems to be whether the individual will ever be able to replace what he or she found in the group and be able to take what was learned in the group and apply it elsewhere. The answer to both questions is generally yes, but the individual is too close to the experience to have this self-assurance. Our experience indicates that this stage often ends with members' unwritten agreement to continue group involvement and, more specifically, to continue contact with members of the present group. Most group members find, after distancing themselves from the group, that neither of these activities is essential. The gains they made from the group experience will serve them well as they move into other facets of their lives.

The movement from group initiation to group termination varies. Groups differ in this movement process for a myriad of reasons, and no one conceptualization has all the answers or addresses all the issues inherent in the group process. This framework can provide, however, guidelines for working with groups.

Characteristics of Group Facilitators

Many writers who are expert in group counseling have described the personal traits and characteristics of effective group counselors (Corey, 1985, 2004; Dinkmeyer & Muro, 1979; Gladding, 2003; Kottler, 1983). As expressed by Gerald Corey in 2004:

> Group leaders can acquire extensive theoretical and practical knowledge of group dynamics and be skilled in diagnostic and technical procedures yet be ineffective in stimulating growth and change in the members of their groups. Leaders bring to every group their personal qualities, values, and life experiences. To promote growth in the members' lives, leaders need to live growth-oriented lives themselves. To foster honest self-investigation in others, they need to have the courage to engage in self-appraisal. If they hope to inspire others to break away from deadening ways of being, they need to be willing to seek new experiences themselves. In short, the most effective group direction is found in the kind of life the group members see the leader demonstrating and not in the words they hear the leader saying. (p. 25)

We believe that there are characteristics that the effective group leader must possess in order to do an effective job of facilitating group process. The reader is directed to sources such as Arbuckle (1975), Carkhuff and Berenson (1977), Jourard (1971), Truax and Carkhuff (1967), and Yalom (1975) for earlier readings on this topic. Corey's 2004 presentation is summarized here as a constructive point of departure for the beginning counselor.

Presence. The leader's ability to be emotionally present as group members share their experience is important. Leaders who are in touch with their own life experiences and associated emotions are usually better able to communicate empathy and understanding because of being able to relate to similar circumstances or emotions.

Personal Power. Personal power comes from a sense of self-confidence and a realization of the influence the leader has on a group. Personal power that is channeled in a way that enhances the ability of each group member to identify and build upon strengths, overcome problems, and cope more effectively with stressors is both essential and "curative."

Courage. Group facilitators must be courageous. They must take risks by expressing their reactions to aspects of group process, confronting, sharing a few life experiences, acting on a combination of intuition and observation, and directing the appropriate portion of the group movement and discussion.

Willingness to Confront Oneself. It takes courage to deal with group members; it is not easy to role model, confront, convey empathy, and achieve a good balance between catalyzing interaction and allowing the group to "unfold." It also takes courage on the part of the group leader to confront self. As Corey (2000) so aptly stated:

Self-confrontation can take the form of posing and answering questions such as these:

- Why am I leading groups? What am I getting from this activity?
- Why do I behave as I do in a group? What impact do my attitudes, values, biases, feelings, and behaviors have on the people in the group?
- What needs of mine are served by being a group leader?
- Do I ever use the groups I lead to satisfy my personal needs at the expense of the members' needs? (p. 30)

Self confrontation must be an ongoing process for the leader because the leader facilitates the capacity of members in a group to ask related questions about themselves.

Sincerity and Authenticity.   Sincerity on the part of a group counselor is usually considered to be related to the leader's genuine interest in the welfare of the group and the individual group member. Sincerity also relates to the leader's ability to be direct and to encourage each member to explore aspects of self that could easily be distorted or denied completely. Effective leaders are able to be real, congruent, honest, and open as they respond to the interactions in a group. Authenticity means that the leader knows who he or she really is and has a sense of comfort and acceptance about self. Authenticity results in an ability to be honest about feelings and reactions to the group in a way that is constructive to individuals as well as the group as a whole.

Sense of Identity.   Group leaders often assist members of a group in the process of clarifying values and becoming "inner" rather than "outer" directed. If the leader of a group has not clarified personal values, meanings, goals, and expectations, it may be difficult to help others with the same process.

Belief in the Group Process and Enthusiasm.   Leaders must be positive and enthusiastic about the healing capacity of groups and their belief in the benefits of a group experience. If they are unsure, tentative, or unenthusiastic, the same "tenor" will develop among members of the group. As will be noted in a subsequent discussion of myths, the outcome of a group experience is not totally dependent on the leader; however, the leader does convey messages, nonverbally as well as verbally, that do have an impact on the overall benefit of the experience.

Inventiveness and Creativity.   Leaders who can be spontaneous in their approach to a group can often facilitate better communication, insight, and personal growth than those who become dependent on structured interventions and techniques. Creative facilitators are usually accepting of members who are different from themselves and flexible about approaching members and groups in ways that seem congruent with the particular group. In addition, a certain amount of creativity and spontaneity is necessary to cope with the "unexpected"; in a group situation the leader will continuously be presented with comments, problems, and reactions that could not have been anticipated prior to a given session.

GROUP FACILITATION: RESPONSIBILITIES AND INTERVENTIONS

Responsibilities

One of the most important responsibilities of counselors interested in becoming group work specialists is to have a thorough understanding of what elements or factors are important in making groups effective in helping those who participate. Even though the group approach is a well-established mode of "treatment," anyone interested in facilitating a group must ask and understand the question of what about groups makes them effective. One difficulty in answering such a question is that the therapeutic change that results from group participation is a result of a complex set of variables including leadership style, membership roles, and aspects of group process.

In a fascinating discussion of this topic, George and Dustin (1988) promote Bloch's (1986) definition of a therapeutic factor as "an element occurring in group therapy that contributes to improvement in a patient's condition and is a function of the actions of the group therapist, the patient, or fellow group members" (p. 679). Although this definition sounds somewhat "clinical," its application to all types of groups is apparent because it helps distinguish among therapeutic elements, conditions for change, and techniques. Conditions for change are necessary for the operation of therapeutic elements but do not, in and of themselves, have therapeutic force. An example of this is the fact that a sense of belonging and acceptance—a therapeutic element that enhances personal growth in groups—cannot emerge unless the "condition" of the actual presence of several good listeners in the group exists. Likewise, a technique, such as asking members to talk about a self-esteem inventory they have filled out, does not have a direct therapeutic effect but may be used to enhance a sense of belonging and acceptance (George & Dustin, 1988). Group work specialists have a responsibility to understand the research that has been done on therapeutic elements of groups so they can develop the skills to create a group climate that enhances personal growth. Corsini and Rosenburg (1955) published one of the earlier efforts to produce a classification of therapeutic elements in groups. They abstracted therapeutic factors published in three hundred pre-1955 articles on group counseling and clustered them into nine major categories:

1. *Acceptance:* a sense of belonging
2. *Altruism:* a sense of being helpful to others
3. *Universalization:* the realization that group members are not alone in the experiencing of their problems
4. *Intellectualization:* the process of acquiring self-knowledge

5. *Reality testing:* recognition of the reality of issues such as defenses and family conflicts
6. *Transference:* strong attachment to either the therapist or other group members
7. *Interaction:* the process of relating to other group members that results in personal growth
8. *Spectator therapy:* growth that occurs through listening to other group members
9. *Ventilation:* the release of feelings that had previously been repressed

In 1957, in an attempt to take the classification of therapeutic elements in groups further, Hill interviewed nineteen group therapists. He proposed the six elements of catharsis, feelings of belongingness, spectator therapy, insights, peer agency (universality), and socialization. Berzon, Pious, and Farson (1963) used group members, rather than leaders, as the source of information about therapeutic elements. Their classification included:

1. Increased awareness of emotional dynamics
2. Recognizing similarity to others
3. Feeling positive regard, acceptance, and sympathy for others
4. Seeing self as seen by others
5. Expressing self congruently, articulately, or assertively in the group
6. Witnessing honesty, courage, openness, or expressions of emotionality in others
7. Feeling warmth and closeness in the group
8. Feeling responded to by others
9. Feeling warmth and closeness generally in the group
10. Ventilating emotions

A very different set of therapeutic elements connected with group experience was proposed by Ohlsen in 1977. His list differs from earlier proposals in that it emphasizes client attitudes about the group experience. Ohlsen's paradigm included fourteen elements that he labeled as "therapeutic forces":

1. Attractiveness of the group
2. Acceptance by the group
3. Expectations
4. Belonging
5. Security within the group
6. Client readiness
7. Client commitment
8. Client participation
9. Client acceptance of responsibility
10. Congruence
11. Feedback
12. Openness
13. Therapeutic tension
14. Therapeutic norms

In what is now considered a landmark classification of "curative factors," Yalom (1970, 1975) proposed a list of therapeutic elements based on research he and his colleagues conducted:

1. Instillation of hope
2. Universality
3. Imparting of information
4. Altruism
5. The corrective recapitulation of the primary family group
6. Development of socializing techniques
7. Imitative behavior
8. Interpersonal learning
9. Group cohesiveness
10. Catharsis
11. Existential factors

It is not possible to present all the possibilities for viewing the therapeutic elements of a positive group experience. It is possible, however, to encourage the beginning counselor to study the research relating to these elements prior to facilitating or co-facilitating groups under close supervision.

In an interesting discussion of facilitator responsibilities Ohlsen and Ferreira (1994) discuss the topic from a very practical perspective. Understanding which clients can be helped through participation in a group; being able to describe a potential group experience to a client; understanding how to conduct an intake or pre-group screening interview; teaching group members how to be good clients and good helpers; mastering skills for structuring, norm setting, and feedback; and recognizing when to terminate a group and assist members to continue their growth after the group terminates are among the responsibilities Ohlsen and Ferreira (1994) address. We recommend further reading on this topic as the reader pursues information on the role of the group work specialist.

Just as the importance of understanding the responsibilities of a group facilitator cannot be stressed enough, the topic of interventions or techniques used by facilitators is important to consider.

Interventions

Numerous approaches to the topic of intervention strategies for groups can be found in the literature on groups. Corey (2004) approached the topic by discussing active listening, restating, clarifying, summarizing, questioning, interpreting, confronting, reflecting feelings, supporting, empathizing, facilitating, initiating, setting goals, evaluating, giving feedback, suggesting, protecting, disclosing oneself, modeling, linking, blocking, and terminating. Dinkmeyer and Muro (1971) discussed the topic by focusing upon promoting cohesiveness, summarizing, promoting interaction, resolving conflicts, tone setting, structuring and limit setting, blocking, linking, providing support, reflecting, protecting, questioning, and regulating. Bates, Johnson, and Blaker (1982) emphasized confrontation, attending behavior, feedback, use of questions, levels of interaction, and opening and closing a session. They also presented the four major functions of group leaders as traffic director, model, interaction catalyst, and communication facilitator.

Individuals new to the profession of counseling may better relate to the topic of intervention strategies by becoming familiar with circumstances during which the group leader must take responsibility for intervening in the group's "process." A helpful model (and a favorite of ours) is that presented by Dyer and Vriend in 1973 in terms of ten occasions when intervention is required:

1. *A group member speaks for everyone.* It is not unusual for a member of a group to say something like, "We think we should . . .," "This is how we all feel," or "We were wondering why. . . ." This happens when an individual does not feel comfortable making a statement such as "I think we should . . ." or "I am wondering why . . ." or when an individual group member is hoping to engender support for a point of view. The problem with allowing the "we" syndrome to operate in a group is that it inhibits individual members from expressing individual feelings and thoughts. Appropriate interventions on the part of the group leader might be, "You mentioned 'we' a number of times. Are you speaking for yourself or for everyone?" Or "What do each of you think about the statement that was just made?"

2. *An individual speaks for another individual in the group.* "I think I know what he means" or "She is not really saying how she feels; I can explain it for her" are statements that one group member may make for another. When one person in the group speaks for another it often means that a judgment has been made about the capacity of the other person to communicate or that the other person is about to self-disclose "uncomfortable" information. Regardless of the motivation behind such a circumstance, the person who is allowing another group member to do the "talking" needs to evaluate why this is happening and whether the same thing occurs outside the group. In addition, the "talker" needs to evaluate the inclination to make decisions and/or rescue others. Appropriate interventions include saying, "Did Jim state your feelings more clearly than you can?" or "How does it feel to have someone rescue you?" Statements such as "Did you feel that June needed your assistance?" or "Do you find it difficult to hold back when you think you know what someone else is going to say?" might also be possible.

3. *A group member focuses on persons, conditions, or events outside the group.* Often group counseling sessions can turn into "gripe sessions." Complaining about a colleague, friend, or a partner can be enjoyable for group members if they are allowed to reinforce each other. The problem with allowing such emphasis to occur is that such a process erroneously substantiates that others are at fault and that group members do not have to take responsibility for aspects of their behavior.
Possible interventions for the group leader include: "You keep talking about your wife as the cause of your unhappiness. Isn't it more important to ask yourself what contributions you can make to improve your relationship?" Or "Does complaining about someone else really mean you think you would be happier if he or she could change?"

4. *Someone seeks the approval of the leader or a group member before or after speaking.* Some group members seek nonverbal acceptance from the leader or another group member (a nod, a glance, a smile). Such individuals may be intimidated by authority figures or personal strength or have low self-esteem and seek sources of support and acceptance outside themselves. One possible intervention is for the leader to look at another member, forcing the speaker to change the direction of his or her delivery. Another possibility is to say something like, "You always look at me as you speak, almost as if you are asking permission."

5. *Someone says, "I don't want to hurt her feelings so I won't say what I'd like to say."* It is not unusual for such a sentiment to be expressed in a group, particularly in the early stages. Sometimes this happens when a member thinks another member of the group is too fragile for feedback; other times such reluctance is because the provider of the potential feedback is concerned about being "liked" by other group members. The group leader should explore reasons for apprehension about providing feedback, which can include asking the group member to check with the person to whom feedback may be directed to determine whether such fears are totally valid.

6. *A group member suggests that his or her problems are due to someone else.* Although this item overlaps with item three, this situation represents a different problem from a "group gripe" session. A single group member may periodically attribute difficulties and unhappiness to someone else. Interventions such as "Who is really the only person who can be in charge of you?" Or "How can other people determine your mood so much of the time?" are called for in such a case. We are not suggesting a stance that would be perceived as lacking empathy and acceptance. It is, however, important to facilitate responsibility for self on the part of each group member.

7. *An individual suggests that "I've always been that way."* Such a suggestion is indicative of irrational thinking and lack of motivation to change. Believing that the past determines all one's future is something that a group member can believe to such an extent that his or her future growth is inhibited. The group leader must assist such a member to identify thinking errors that lead to lack of effectiveness in specific areas. Such a member needs to learn that he or she is not doomed to repeat the mistakes of the past. Possible statements that will stimulate examination of faulty thinking and assumptions are "You're suggesting that your past has such a hold over you that you will never be any different" or "Do you feel that everyone has certain parts of their life over which they have no control?"

8. *Someone in the group suggests, "I'll wait, and it will change."* Often, group members are willing to talk about their self-defeating behavior during a group session but aren't willing to make an effort outside the group to behave differently. At times, they take the position that they can postpone action and things will correct themselves. A competent group leader will help members develop strategies for doing something about their problems outside the group and will develop a method of "tracking" or "checking in" with members to evaluate progress.

9. *Discrepant behavior appears.* Group leader intervention is essential when discrepancies occur in a member's behavior in the group. Examples of such discrepancies include a difference in what a member is currently saying and what he or she said earlier, a lack of congruence between what a member is saying and what he or she is doing in the group, a difference between how a member sees himself or herself and how others in the group see him or her, or a difference between how a member reports feelings and how nonverbal cues communicate what is going on inside. Interventions used to identify discrepancies may be confrontational in nature because the leader usually needs to describe the discrepancies noted so the group member can begin to identify, evaluate, and change aspects of such behavior.

10. *A member bores the group by rambling.* Sometimes members use talking as a way of seeking approval. At times such talking becomes "overtalk." The leader can ask other members to react to the "intellectualizer" and let such a person know how such rambling affects others. If such behavior is not addressed, other members may develop a sense of anger and hostility toward the "offender."

Johnson and Johnson (2000) also noted a number of situations that may require immediate intervention on the part of the group facilitator:

11. *A member responds with a rehearsed or often used statement.* Sometimes members don't know what to say after another member of the group has shared. This may be due to discomfort related to the speaker's topic, strong emotion precipitated by the sharing that has just taken place, "unfinished business" similar to that of speaker, or a number of other reasons. In an attempt to be responsive or fill a silence, the member may comment in a way that is similar to how he or she responds whenever discomfort or strong emotion is experienced. The comment may not fit the context and seem inappropriate, insensitive, or even unrelated. The leader may need to ask that member to clarify or respond differently so that the group can continue their work more effectively. This may even lead to some introspection and growth on the part of the member who misspoke.

12. *A member remains silent or non-participatory.* When a member remains silent while other group members actively participate in the group experience, it may encourage other group members to wonder why that member has chosen to be so inactive. Sometimes other members fantasize about what the silent member is like and begin to resent the silence and resent the group leader for allowing that member to be so nonparticipatory. Members can become so agitated that they may begin to make demands on the silent member and blame or scapegoat the member for things that occur in the group. It behooves the group leader to be invitational with such a member so that the silence is not misinterpreted by members of the group.

13. *A member's expectations for the group are not met.* Sometimes members enter groups with a preconceived idea of what the group will be like. When such expectations are not met, the member could respond in any number of ways: withdrawal, confrontation of the group leader, disagreements with other members of the group, ventilation of anger, and so on. The group leader will need to encourage the member to share the reasons behind the discontent; sometimes doing so can lead to a resolution of the difficulties being experienced by the member and enhance the quality of the group experience for all concerned.

14. *A member of the group wants all the "air time."* There are instances in which a high-need member of the group demands to be the sole focus of the attention of the group leader and the other group members. In such a circumstance it may be difficult for anyone else to participate unless the facilitator intervenes. Such an intervention would need to be done in a way that communicates respect for the needs of the member and, at the same time, lets other members of the group know they, too, are important. A statement such as "I know how important this is to you. Let me see if I can accurately summarize so we can come back to this after other members have a chance to participate" may be necessary on the part of the group leader. Otherwise, members of the group will start wondering if one member will be allowed to take up all the time and question the value of the group experience.

15. *A group member blocks the expression of intense emotions by other members of the group.* Sometimes strong emotion makes a member feel uncomfortable and unsure of what to say. This could happen because of what the member has been taught about what emotions are appropriately shared or even if they should be shared. This could also occur when the emotion and experience mirrors similar unresolved issues of the member attempting to cut off such expression. The group leader would need to respond to such attempts and encourage the member to be introspective and aware of the tendencies and reasons for such "blocking."

Berg, Landreth, and Fall (1998) and Jacobs, Masson, and Harvill (1998) are two sources of additional information on the topic of the leader's role in intervening in the group's "process" because of what individual members are doing or leaving unsaid.

In addition to the interventions described, the reader should be alerted to the necessity to be prepared to resolve resistance in groups. Clark (1992), Higgs (1992), Ohlsen and Ferreira (1994), and Ormont (1993) provide some excellent guidelines on this aspect of the group leader's role.

Myths Connected with Group Work

Counselors who are group work specialists are usually quite enthusiastic about the benefits for clients of participation in a small group. Indeed, the outcomes of a competently facilitated group experience can be such that personal growth occurs. Often the memory of such an experience has an impact on clients well into the future. On the other hand, group work, as with other forms of therapeutic assistance (such as individual or family), can be for better or for worse (Carkhuff, 1969). Many group workers follow a belief system that can be challenged by empirical facts.

Beginning counselors are well advised to be aware of a number of myths connected with group work so they don't base their "practices" on a belief system not supported by research (Anderson, 1985; Kalodner & Riva, 1997).

Myth #1: "Everyone Benefits from Group Experience"

Groups do provide benefits. The research on the psychosocial outcomes demonstrates that groups are a powerful modality for learning, which can be used outside the group experience (Bednar & Lawlis, 1971; Gazda & Peters, 1975; Parloff & Dies, 1978). There are times, however, when membership in a group can be harmful. Some research shows that one of every ten group members can be hurt (Lieberman, Yalom, & Miles, 1973). The research findings that seem to relate most to individuals who get injured in groups suggest some important principles for the beginning counselor to understand: (1) those who join groups and who have the potential to be hurt by the experience have unrealistic expectations, and (2) these expectations seem to be reinforced by the facilitator who coerces the member to meet them (De Julio, Bentley, & Cockayne, 1979; Lieberman, Yalom, & Miles, 1973; Stava & Bednar, 1979). Prevention of harm requires that the expectations members have for the group are realistic and that the facilitator maintains a reasonable perspective.

Myth #2: "Groups Can Be Composed to Ensure Effective Outcomes"

The fact is that we do not know enough about how to compose groups using the pregroup screening interview. In general, objective criteria (such as age, sex, socioeconomic status, presenting problem) can be used to keep groups homogeneous in some respects, but behavioral characteristics should be selected on a heterogeneous basis (Bertcher & Maple, 1977). The most consistent finding is that it is a good idea to compose a group in such a manner that each member is compatible with at least one other member (Stava & Bednar, 1979). This practice seems to prevent the evolution of neglected isolates or scapegoats in a group.

The essence of group process, in terms of benefit to members and effective outcomes is perceived mutual aid such as helping others, a feeling of belonging, interpersonal learning, and instillation of hope (Butler & Fuhriman, 1980; Long & Cope, 1980; Yalom, 1975).

Myth #3: "The Group Revolves Around the Charisma of the Leader"

It is true that leaders influence groups tremendously, but there are two general findings in the research on groups that should be noted. First, the group, independent of the leader, has an impact on outcomes. Second, the most effective group leaders are those who help the group develop so that members are primary sources of help to one another (Ashkennas & Tandon, 1979; Lungren, 1971).

As noted by Anderson (1985), research on leadership styles has identified four particular leader functions that facilitate the group's functioning:

1. *Providing:* This is the provider role of relationships and climate-setting through such skills as support, affection, praise, protection, warmth, acceptance, genuineness, and concern.

2. *Processing:* This is the processor role of illuminating the meaning of the process through such skills as explaining, clarifying, interpreting, and providing a cognitive framework for change or translating feelings and experiences into ideas.
3. *Catalyzing:* This is the catalyst role of stimulating interaction and emotional expression through such skills as reaching for feelings, challenging, confronting, and suggesting; using program activities such as structured experiences; and modeling.
4. *Directing:* This is the director role through such skills as setting limits, roles, norms, and goals; managing time; pacing; stopping; interceding; and suggesting procedures. (p. 272)

Providing and processing seem to have a linear relationship to outcomes: the higher the providing (or caring) and the higher the processing (or clarifying), the higher the positive outcomes. Catalyzing and directing have a curvilinear relationship to outcomes. Too much or too little catalyzing or directing results in lower positive outcomes (Lieberman et al., 1973).

Myth #4: "Leaders Can Direct Through the Use of Structured Exercises or Experiences"

Structured exercises create early cohesion (Levin & Kurtz, 1974; Lieberman et al., 1973); they help create early expression of positive and negative feelings. However, they restrict members from dealing with such group themes as affection, closeness, distance, trust, mistrust, genuineness, and lack of genuineness. All these areas form the very basis for group process and should be dealt with in a way that is not hampered by a large amount of structure. The best principle around which to plan and use structured exercises to get groups started and to keep them going can best be stated as "to overplan and to underuse."

Myth #5: "Therapeutic Change in Groups Comes About Through a Focus on Here-and-Now Experiences"

Much of the research on groups indicates that corrective emotional experiences in the here and now of the group increase the intensity of the experience for members (Levine, 1971; Lieberman et al., 1973; Snortum & Myers, 1971; Zimpfer, 1967). The intensity of emotional experiences does not, however, appear to be related to outcomes. Higher level outcomes in groups are achieved by members who develop "insight" or cognitive understanding of emotional experiences in the group and can transfer that understanding into their lives outside the group. The Gestaltists' influence on groups in the 1960s and 1970s (Perls, 1969) suggested that members should "Lose their mind and come to their senses" and "stay with the here-and-now." Research suggests that members "use their mind and their senses" and "focus on the there and then as well as on the here and now."

Myth #6: "Major Member Learning in Groups Is Derived from Self-Disclosure and Feedback"

There is an assumption that most of the learning of members in a group comes from self-disclosure in exchange for feedback (Jacobs, 1974). To a large extent, this statement is a myth. Self-disclosure and feedback per se make little difference in terms of outcomes (Anchor, 1979; Bean & Houston, 1978). It is the use of self-disclosure and feedback that appears to make the difference (Martin & Jacobs, 1980). Self-disclosure and feedback appear useful only when deeply personal sharing is understood and appreciated and the feedback is accurate (Berzon, Pious, & Farson, 1963; Frank & Ascher, 1951; Goldstein, Bednar, & Yanell, 1979). The actual benefit of self-disclosure and feedback is connected with how these processes facilitate empathy among members. It is empathy, or the actual experience of being understood by other members, that catalyzes personal growth and understanding in the context of a group.

Myth #7: "The Group Facilitator Can Work Effectively with a Group Without Understanding Group Process and Group Dynamics"

Groups experience a natural evolution and unfolding of processes and dynamics. Anderson (1979) labeled these stages as those of trust, autonomy, closeness, interdependence, and termination (TACIT). Tuckman (1965) suggested a more dramatic labeling of forming, storming, norming, performing, and adjourning. We suggested a four-stage paradigm earlier in this chapter. Two reviews, which include over two hundred studies of group dynamics and group process (Cohen & Smith, 1976; La Coursiere, 1980), revealed remarkably similar patterns (despite differences in the labels chosen as descriptors) in the evolution of group processes as a group evolves through stages. It is extremely important for group facilitators to understand group processes and dynamics to do a competent job of enhancing membership benefits derived from participation.

Myth #8: "Change Experienced by Group Participation Is Not Maintained over Time"

Groups are powerful! Changes can be maintained by group members as much as six months to a year later even when groups meet for only three or four months (Lieberman et al., 1973).

Myth #9: "A Group Is a Place to Get Emotionally High"

Feeling good after a group session is a positive outcome but is not the main reason for being in a group in the first place. Some group members have periods of depression after group participation because they don't find elsewhere, on a daily basis, the kind of support they received from other members of the group. Group members should be prepared for this possibility and assisted in their ability to obtain support, when appropriate, from those around them.

Myth #10: "A Group's Purpose Is to Make Members Close to Every Other Member"

Although genuine feelings of intimacy and cohesiveness develop in effective groups, intimacy is the by-product and not the central purpose of the group. Intimacy develops as individual members risk self-disclosure and problem solving and other group members reach out in constructive ways.

Myth #11: "Group Participation Results in Brainwashing"

Professional groups do not indoctrinate members with a particular philosophy of life or a set of rules about how each member "should be." If this does occur in a group, it is truly a breach of professional ethics and an abuse of the group. Group participation encourages members to look within themselves for answers and to become as self-directed as possible.

Myth #12: "To Benefit from a Group, a Member Has to Be Dysfunctional"

Group counseling is as appropriate for individuals who are functioning relatively well and who want to enhance their capabilities as it is for those who are having difficulty with certain aspects of their lives. Groups are not only for dysfunctional people.

ISSUES AND ETHICS: SOME CONCLUDING REMARKS

Although a thorough discussion of issues and ethics in group counseling is beyond the scope of this chapter, it is important for the beginning counselor to be introduced to this topic. The *Professional Standards for Training of Group Workers* (ASGW, 1991, 2000), *Boundary Issues in Counseling* (Herlihy & Corey, 1997), and *Ethical, Legal, and Professional Issues in Counseling* (Remley & Herlihy, 2005) are all excellent points of departure for the counselor interested in groups, as well as *Principles for Diversity-Competent Group Workers*, published in 1999 by the Association for Specialists in Group Work (ASGW). In addition, these resources serve as useful adjuncts to the *Code of Ethics and Standards of Practice* of the American Counseling Association (1995).

ASGW (1991, 2000) recommends that the group work specialist acquire *knowledge competencies* (for example, understanding principles of group dynamics, the roles of members in groups, the contributions of research in group work), *skill competencies* (diagnosing self-defeating behavior in groups, intervening at critical times in group process, using assessment procedures to evaluate the outcomes of a group), and *supervised clinical experience* (such as observing group counseling, coleading groups with supervision, participating as a member in a group). Interestingly, these very training standards have become an issue with some counselor preparation programs as they struggle to obtain a balance between the didactic and clinical components of the set of educational and supervisory experiences required to prepare an individual to do a competent job of group counseling. The clinical supervisory aspects of preparing the group work specialist are costly for universities, and often counselor educators are encouraged to abandon such efforts in favor of classroom didactics.

Another example of some of the issues connected with group counseling has to do with continuing education after the completion of masters and/or doctoral degree programs. Although the National Board for Certified Counselors (NBCC) requires those who achieve the National Certified Counselor (NCC) credential to obtain one hundred contact hours of continuing education every five years, there is no specification of how much this professional enhancement activity should be focused on aspects of group work if group work is the declared area of specialization of an NCC. In time, there may be a specific continuing education requirement for the group work specialist.

Readers should refer to ACA's *Code of Ethics and Standards of Practice* (1995) for ethical guidelines pertaining to groups. An interesting earlier document, *The Ethical Guidelines for Group Leaders* (ASGW, 1991), initially helped clarify the nature of ethical responsibilities of the counselor in a group setting. These guidelines presented standards in three areas: (1) the leader's responsibility for providing information about group work to clients, (2) the leader's responsibility for providing group counseling services to clients, and (3) the leader's responsibility for safeguarding the standards of ethical practice. One of the greatest single sources of ethical dilemma in group counseling situations has to do with confidentiality. Except for the few exceptions delineated in ACA's *Code of Ethics and Standards of Practice* (1995) counselors have an obligation not to disclose information about the client without the client's consent. Yet, the very nature of a group counseling situation makes it difficult to ensure that each member of a group will respect the other's right to privacy.

Other issues such as recruitment and informed consent, screening and selection of group members, voluntary and involuntary participation, psychological risks, uses and abuses of group techniques, therapist competence, interpersonal relationships among the members of a group, and follow-up all form the basis for considerable discussion and evaluation. In addition, these issues emphasize the necessity of adequate education, supervision, and advance time to consider the ramifications and responsibilities connected with becoming a group specialist.

Group experiences can be powerful growth-enhancing opportunities for clients, or they can be pressured, stifling encounters to be avoided. Each of us has a professional obligation to assess our readiness to facilitate or cofacilitate a group. Our clients deserve the best experience we can provide.

SUMMARY

The use of groups of all types is increasingly important to the role of the counselor in a variety of settings. As the decades have passed, emphasis has shifted from T-Groups to encounter groups to working with special populations. Self-help groups of all types are flourishing. The ASGW standards for the training of group counselors have received widespread acceptance.

ASGW's definitions of the four group work specialty types (task/work, guidance/psychoeducational, counseling, psychotherapy groups), information about stages of group life, and research on the characteristics of group facilitators have also enhanced the ability of the group work specialist to function in the best interests of clients in groups. In addition, the more group work specialists know about their responsibilities and the interventions they need to master, myths connected with group work, and issues and ethics associated with groups, the more competent they will be as facilitators of group experiences. The importance of broad-based education and carefully supervised group practicum and other clinical experiences for group work specialists cannot be overemphasized.

CHAPTER NINE

CAREER COUNSELING

ELLEN HAWLEY MCWHIRTER, PH.D.
KAREN N. PAEZ, M.S.
University of Oregon

Trying to eliminate her nervous fidgeting by clasping her hands under the table, the novice counselor watches as the cards are handed out.

Who will this first client be? Am I going to know what to say?

The anticipation builds as each member of the group is provided with demographics and a single phrase describing the client's main concern. She releases a hand to reach for the blue index card and quickly skims its contents. Female, OK, age twenty-three, great, concern. . . .

The counselor stifles a sigh of disappointment. No thrill, no challenge here. "Seeking career counseling."

Graduate students in counseling and counseling psychology (Heppner, O'Brien, Hinkelman, & Flores, 1996) and beginning counselors (Pinkney & Jacobs, 1985) have been found to have negative attitudes about career counseling, and are disinterested in spending counseling time engaged in career counseling activities. Some of these negative attitudes may be based on the impression that career counseling is no more than a process of going through endless inventories and reference material to find the right job for a rather dull, helpless person. Contrary to these impressions, however, career counseling is an intriguing and complex area of counseling that requires an in-depth knowledge of human nature and involves an active, collaborative relationship between the counselor and the client. Although there may be some distinctions between personal and career counseling, most authors agree that there is considerable overlap between the two (e.g., Betz & Corning, 1993; Croteau & Thiel, 1993; Pace & Quinn, 2000; Sharf, 2002). We hope that the information provided in this chapter will diminish any unfounded negative impressions the reader may have and illustrate the variety and challenge inherent in the tasks of career counselors.

Condensing the theory and practice of contemporary career counseling into a single chapter is a formidable task, and requires the elimination or scant coverage of many important aspects of career counseling. The purpose of this chapter is to introduce the beginning counselor to a developmental perspective of career counseling, and to introduce the basic components and activities that are considered the territory of the career counselor. In order to accommodate this purpose within space limitations, evaluation and critique of current theories and interventions will be minimized. Emphasis will be placed on description, with references provided for more detailed analysis of the history, theory, and research related to career counseling. The beginning counselor is urged to consult contemporary career textbooks such as those by Brown and Associates (2002), Isaacson and Brown (1999), Osipow and Fitzgerald (1995), Seligman (1994), Sharf (2002), and Zunker (2001), and journals such as the *Journal of Vocational Behavior*, the *Career Development Quarterly*, the *Journal of Career Assessment*, the *Journal of Counseling and Development*, the *Journal of Career Development*, and the *Journal of Counseling Psychology*.

Before proceeding with a discussion of career development theories, three definitions are in order. Recognition of the pervasive nature of work in human lives has led to broader and more developmental definitions of career than early in this century. Drawing from the National Vocational Guidance Association (1973), career is defined in this chapter as, "a time-extended working out of a purposeful life pattern through work undertaken by the individual." Career development refers to, "the total constellation of psychological, sociological, educational, physical, economic, and chance factors that combine to shape the career of any given individual" (NVGA, 1973). Finally, career counseling may be described as:

> . . . a series of general and specific interventions throughout the life span, dealing with such concerns as self-understanding; broadening one's horizons; work selection, challenge, satisfaction, and other intrapersonal matters; work site behavior, communication, and other interpersonal phenomena; and lifestyle issues, such as balancing work, family, and leisure. Thus, career counseling primarily involves career planning and decision making while encompassing many other matters, such as integrating life, work, family and social roles, discrimination, stress, sexual harassment, bias, stereotyping, pay inequities, and "tokenism." (Engels, Minor, Sampson, & Splete, 1995, p. 134)

Thus, presenting problems in career counseling might include difficulty responding to a homophobic workplace, marital dissatisfaction related to a dual-career situation, poor decision-making skills, lack of knowledge about wheelchair-accessible leisure options, role conflicts and poor stress management skills, or any of the more traditional issues brought to career counseling such as fear of interviews, lack of occupational information, need to develop a resume, or desire to choose or change a career.

The knowledge and skills required for competent career counseling have been specified in the context of preparation standards (Council for Accreditation of Counseling and Related Educational Programs, CACREP, 2001; National Career Development Association, NCDA, 1997). Along with the career counseling competencies of CACREP and NCDA, the beginning career counselor should be knowledgeable of the multicultural counseling competencies (Sue et al., 1998), applicable multicultural guidelines (American Psychological Association, APA, 2003), and the ethical codes for the American Counseling Association (1995).

THEORIES OF CAREER COUNSELING

John Krumboltz (1989) stated that while the purpose, emphasis, and vocabulary of the major theories of career counseling may differ, there are no fundamental disagreements between them. Comparing theories to maps, Krumboltz (1994) points out how they are similar: both represent an oversimplification of reality; both distort certain features; both employ symbols to depict reality and are intended to provide a big picture; and, finally, the usefulness of both maps and theories is dependent on the purpose for which they are used. The various career counseling theories represent different aspects of the same territory; no one theory covers the entire area, and the theories overlap. Although further development is needed in career theory, the ultimate goal is not to develop a "perfect" theory but theories that are "perfect" for given purposes.

Among the implications that might be drawn from Krumboltz' analogy is one very pertinent to the beginning career counselor. Theoretical viewpoints cannot be adopted or rejected on the basis of their "goodness" or "badness" without specifically considering their intended scope, emphasis, and purpose. A theory useful for understanding one aspect of the career development process may shed little light on another. Rigid adherence to one particular theory may, therefore, be detrimental to understanding the career process in its entirety. This is not to say that one should carry about a hodgepodge of unrelated concepts and explanations, but that theories should be used according to their intended purposes.

Some of the major theories of career development are briefly described here. Although only the most central concepts of each have been presented, more detailed reviews of each theory and critiques of the related research are available in the texts mentioned previously.

Trait-and-Factor Theory

Frank Parsons.   The trait-and-factor approach to career counseling was established in the work of Parsons (1909), and most authors credit the origin of vocational counseling to Frank Parsons. Although the turn of the century was witness to a variety of innovative guidance programs, Parsons conceptualized a model for career guidance that is still viable in contemporary formulations of career counseling. Parsons was concerned about the difficult social problems experienced by immigrants new to the United States and viewed assistance with vocational selection as one means of alleviating their impoverished status. Hawks and Muha (1991) argue that recommitment to the social change orientation characterized by Parsons is critical to optimizing the educational and occupational attainment of young people, and especially ethnic minority youth, in our still-stratified society. A special section of the *Career Development Quarterly* (2001, Vol. 50, No. 1) was devoted to discussing Parsons's contribution to the field of career development, including his commitment to social change

(O'Brien, 2001). Parsons's vision was highlighted recently at a national convention because of its ongoing relevance to career counseling professionals (Fouad, 1999).

Parsons proposed a three step model for helping individuals choose a vocation, summarized as follows: (1) develop knowledge about self, including aptitudes, interests, and resources; (2) develop knowledge about the world of work, including the advantages, disadvantages, opportunities, and requirements associated with different occupations; and (3) find a suitable match between the individual and the world of work (Parsons, 1909). His work stimulated increased interest in vocational guidance nationwide (Zunker, 2001), and elements of trait-and-factor theory can be found in most contemporary theories of career development (Isaacson & Brown, 1999).

A career counselor ascribing to the trait-and-factor approach would structure the counseling experience according to the three steps outlined by Parsons (1909). First, the counselor would generate information about the client's aptitudes, interests, goals, resources, and so on. Next, the counselor would use his or her knowledge of occupations to assist the client's exploration of possible career alternatives. After the client has accrued a sufficient amount of self- and occupational knowledge, the counselor would facilitate the client's choice of an occupation that is consistent with the identified personal qualities and interests.

John Holland.   The work of John Holland has been classified under both trait approaches to career development (Swanson, 1996) and personality-based theories of career (Sharf, 2002). Holland (1996a, 1996b, 1997) assumes that people develop relatively permanent sets of behaviors or personalities that they seek to express through occupational choices. In addition, he asserts that people project their views of themselves and of the work world onto occupational titles. Assessment of these projections serves to identify information about the occupational areas that might be most satisfying for an individual, as well as to illuminate relevant aspects of the individual's personality.

According to Holland's theory (1996a, 1996b, 1997) there are six basic types of work environments in U.S. society, and six corresponding modal personal orientations. Modal personal orientations are the way the person typically responds to environmental demands. People achieve the most work satisfaction when their work environment matches their modal personal orientation. For example, positions in education or social welfare are considered "social" occupational environments and would be most suited to "social" personal orientations, that is, people who perceive themselves to be sociable, skilled at dealing with others, and concerned with helping others and solving human problems. Some people are dominant in one particular orientation, while others exhibit a combination of orientations in their interactions with the environment. The six orientations are often referred to as "Holland's hexagon" because they are depicted in relation to one another such that the most similar orientations are adjacent and the most distinct are opposite each other on the hexagon. Recent research on the Strong Interest Inventory provides some evidence for the validity of Holland's hexagon with college women and men of diverse racial/ethnic minority backgrounds (Day, Rounds, & Swaney, 1998; Fouad, 2002; Lattimore & Borgen, 1999). There have also been a number of studies investigating the use of

Holland's theory cross-culturally (Leong, Austin, Sekaran, & Komarraju, 1998; Leung & Hou, 2001; Soh & Leong, 2001).

In addition to the "social" orientation described above are five other orientations: "realistic," "investigative," "conventional," "enterprising," and "artistic." "Realistic" persons are described as practical, concrete, and rugged, as interested in activities requiring physical strength, and as less likely to be sensitive and socially skilled. Corresponding work environments are found in the skilled trades such as plumbing or machine operation, and in the technical trades such as mechanics and photography.

"Investigative" persons are described as preferring to think rather than act, as intellectual, abstract, and analytical. Work environments most suited to the investigative orientation are scientific, such as those of the chemist or mathematician, as well as the technical environments of the computer programmer and the electronics worker.

"Conventional" persons are practical, well-controlled, conservative, and prefer structure and conformity to the abstract and the unique. Conventional environments are typified in those of the office worker, the bookkeeper, and the credit manager.

An "enterprising" individual is likely to prefer leadership roles, and to be aggressive, extroverted, persuasive, and dominant. Managerial positions in personnel and production, and positions in real estate, life insurance, and other sales areas correspond most closely to the "enterprising" work environment.

Holland's final personality orientation, "artistic," corresponds to persons who are imaginative, independent, expressive, and introspective; their preferred work environments include those of the artist, the musician, and the writer. Holland (1996b) and Blake and Sackett, (1999) provide detailed descriptions of the modal orientations, which may be helpful for the counselor interested in further exploration of these concepts.

Counselors grounded in Holland's approach will generally attempt to determine the client's modal personal orientation and then explore corresponding work orientations. In this sense, the trait-and-factor approach is represented. For a contemporary review of recent developments, a special issue of the *Journal of Vocational Behavior* (1999, Vol. 55, No. 1) focuses on Holland's theory. Several instruments are available for assessing modal orientations, the most common of which are probably the *Strong Interest Inventory* (Harmon, Hansen, Borgen, & Hammer, 1994) and Holland's *Self-Directed Search* (1991a, 1991b). Lofquist and Dawis's (1969, 1984) Work Adjustment Theory is another extension of trait-and-factor approaches to career counseling.

Social Learning Theory

Perhaps the foremost proponent of the social learning approach to career counseling is John Krumboltz (Krumboltz, 1994, 1996). Krumboltz identifies four types of factors; that influence career decision making: (1) genetic endowment and special abilities, (2) environmental conditions and events; (3) learning experiences; and (4) task-approach skills. He defines task-approach skills as the skills an individual applies to new tasks and problems, including cognitive processes, work habits, and values. Every individual is born into specific environmental conditions with certain genetic characteristics; these interact to influence the life experiences, opportunities, and learning of the individual. Learning experiences are followed by rewards or punishments that also influence the individual's development. According to Krumboltz, career choice is influenced by individuals' unique learning experiences in the course of their lifetimes.

Task-approach skills, self-observation generalizations, and actions are the result of an individual's learning experiences. Self-observation generalizations are the self statements made by individuals after assessing their performance or potential performance against learned standards. They are expressed in the form of interests. Actions are decision-related behaviors that emerge from the individual's task-approach skills and self-observation generalizations.

A counselor approaching career clients from a social learning perspective would be interested in the learning experiences that have influenced the client's career development. Often a client's inaccurate self-observations, maladaptive beliefs (Krumboltz & Vosvick, 1996), or deficient task-approach skills are a barrier to exploration of potential career choices and to making career decisions. The counselor's role may include a strong psychoeducational component, helping the client to revise faulty beliefs or observations and to learn new skills that will facilitate the career exploration and choice process, including decision-making skills.

Social Cognitive Career Theory

Lent, Brown, and Hackett (1994) proposed a theoretical model of career choice and implementation grounded in Bandura's (1986, 1997) general social cognitive theory. Their model emphasizes the importance of personal agency in the career decision-making process and attempts to explain the manner in which both internal and external factors serve to enhance or constrain this agency. Lent, Brown, and Hackett (1994, 2002) suggest that career interests directly influence career choice goals (e.g., career aspirations), which increases the likelihood of certain career choice actions (e.g., declaring an academic major). Contextual and social cognitive factors are hypothesized to directly influence the development of career interests, goals, and actions. Contextual factors include discrimination, socioeconomic status, job availability, educational access, perceived and real barriers, and other influential environmental factors. Lent et al. argue that the particular effect that contextual factors have on an individual's career choice often depends on her or his personal appraisal of and response to those factors. The social cognitive factors (Bandura, 1997) include self-appraisals such as self-efficacy expectations, or beliefs about one's performance abilities in relation to specific tasks, as well as outcome expectations, or beliefs about the likely consequences of given behaviors.

Lent et al. (1994, 2002) propose that contextual and social cognitive factors are responsible for shaping the experiences that lead to the development of interests and choices, as well as the relationship between interests and choices, and between career choices and attainments. Even if an individual possesses high levels of career self-efficacy, high outcome expectations, and interests that are congruent with those expectations, she or he may still avoid selection of a particular career if she or he perceives insurmountable barriers to career entry or career goal attainment. This model represents an important contribution to understanding career interests, choices, and implementation, because it integrates the social forces of racism, sexism, classism, and homophobia that shape the career development process of all individuals, as well as related contextual/environmental factors such as role models, socialization, and perceived opportunities and barriers. The growing body of literature on the career development of people of color (for example, see Arbona, 1990; Bowman, 1998; Byars, 2001; Flores & O'Brien, 2002; Fouad & Bingham, 1995; Leong & Hartung, 1997; Martin & Farris, 1994; McWhirter, Hackett, & Bandalos, 1998; Walsh, Bingham, Brown, & Ward, 2001) as well as the broader literature on counseling people of color (see Atkinson, Morten, & Sue, 1998; Comas-Diaz & Greene, 1994; Lee, 1997; Pedersen, 2000; Sue & Sue, 2002) consistently stresses the influence of contextual factors. Implications for career counseling include acknowledging and clarifying the role of environmental factors and cognitions in the career development process and providing opportunities to test and enhance self-efficacy and outcome expectations.

Developmental Theories

Developmental career theories view the selection and implementation of careers as part of a long-term developmental process that begins early in life and ends with death. Developmental theorists recognize the contributions of early experiences, life events and opportunities, and the maturation process on the development of interests, the exploration process, and career outcomes. Most contemporary theories of career choice incorporate elements of the developmental perspective. In this chapter, "career" has been defined from a developmental perspective in recognition of the widespread acceptance of career as an ongoing, lifelong process.

Ginzberg, Ginsburg, Axelrad, and Herma (1951) were among the first theorists to link the developmental theory with occupational choice. Their work, along with the work of Teideman and O'Hara (1963) and others, has been valuable in shaping developmental theories. Two developmental approaches are briefly discussed in this section. First, major components of the work of Donald Super are presented. Readers may wish to consult a special issue of the *Career Development Quarterly* (1994, Vol. 43, No .1) devoted to Super's tremendous contributions to career development theory. Next, Linda Gottfredson's (1981) theory of circumscription and compromise is presented.

Donald Super.   Super (1957, 1963, 1990) contended that individuals select occupations consistent with their self-concept. He argued that the manner in which people implement their self-concepts into occupational choices is a function of their developmental life stage. It, therefore, follows that vocational behaviors should be examined in the context of the particular demands of a person's developmental life stage. The vocational developmental stages formulated by Super are as follows: (1) growth (ages 0–14) is characterized by the development of interests, aptitudes, and needs in conjunction with the self concept; (2) exploration (ages 15–24) consists of a tentative phase of narrowing down options; (3) establishment (ages 25–44) is characterized by choosing and implementing a career and stabilization within that career; (4) maintenance (ages 45–64) involves the continued efforts to improve work position; and

(5) disengagement (ages 65 and above) is characterized by preparation for retirement and retirement itself. While providing age ranges, Super recognized individual variation in passage through the stages; he also noted that recycling of the stages often occurs during reconsideration of career plans or career changes. Each stage has a corresponding set of developmental vocational tasks.

Throughout the lifespan, individuals are called upon to fulfill the demands of a variety of roles, such as child, student, leisurite, citizen, worker, and homemaker. The life-career rainbow (Super & Neville, 1986) provides a physical representation of how these roles may overlap with and influence vocational development and behaviors. Career maturity is another important concept proposed by Super (1974) and refers to the readiness of individuals to make good vocational choices. Assessment of the client's career maturity often helps to set the stage for appropriate interventions (Levinson, Ohler, Caswell, & Kiewra, 1998; Sharf, 2002). Fouad and Arbona (1994) review the research on the applicability of Super's model to people of color. For a comprehensive analysis of Super's theory and its application to career counseling, the beginning counselor should review Osborne, Brown, Niles, and Miner (1998).

Linda Gottfredson.   Gottfredson's (1981, 1996, 2002) theory of circumscription and compromise incorporates elements of a social systems approach into a developmental perspective, and focuses on the influence of gender, social class, and intelligence upon career aspirations and choices. Her theory concerns the manner by which children "seem to re-create the social inequalities of their elders long before they themselves experience any barriers to pursuing their dreams" (p. 85). According to her theory, all people have a unique "zone of acceptable alternatives," consisting of the range of occupations acceptable for consideration and reflecting their view of where they fit in society. This zone is bounded by the greatest and least amount of effort individuals are willing to expend in order to attain that career, as well as by their willingness to pursue careers nontraditional for their gender. For example, an individual might consider a range of occupations perceived to be more prestigious than secretarial work, such as nursing or management, but not as demanding as becoming a physician or a lawyer. If the individual is male, he might automatically rule out nursing because it is a traditionally female profession and inconsistent with his perceived gender role.

Gottfredson postulates that as the self-concept develops, people become oriented to the implications of size and power (ages 3–5), gender roles (ages 6–8), social valuation (ages 9–13), and finally, as their interests emerge, they become oriented to or aware of their internal unique self (ages 14 and older). The zone of acceptable alternatives is narrowed (circumscribed) as age increases. That is, occupations that are perceived as incongruent with the child's view of appropriate gender roles are the first occupations to be eliminated, followed by occupations perceived as too low in prestige for the young person's social class, and finally, occupations requiring too much or too little effort are eliminated. When compromise in occupational choices is required, Gottfredson argues that people will first sacrifice their interests related to work, for example, their internal unique self, followed by prestige. Gottfredson (2002) provides a detailed summary as well as recent extensions of her theory. The extensions of her core theory include further attention to the impact of individual and group differences and a discussion of how biosocial theory best addresses these concepts. Under the umbrella of the nature-nurture partnership theory, Gottfredson (2002) highlights individual and group difference considerations for career counselors to utilize when working with clients.

Assumptions and Diversity

The majority of career counseling theories were developed based on the behaviors of able-bodied, heterosexual, middle- to upper-class white males. This is true of most traditional counseling theories. Hence, there are numerous, unspoken assumptions embedded in many contemporary approaches to career counseling. Our ability to work effectively as career counselors is contingent upon our awareness of these assumptions and willingness to critically reflect on the appropriateness of any theory, technique, or strategy with a given individual. Career interventions suited for white middle-class males will not necessarily be appropriate for or meet the needs of other individuals. Theoretical developments such as the social cognitive career theory (Lent, Brown, & Hackett, 1994) are critically important because they integrate critical factors shaping the reality of women, ethnic minorities, gay and lesbian individuals, and people with disabilities such as the influence of discrimination, perceived barriers, self-efficacy and outcome expectations, and environmental support. A small number of resources are offered below; this is by no means an exhaustive list and the reader is encouraged to explore far beyond these resources in developing competencies consistent with the needs of our diverse society.

Contemporary researchers have increased emphasis on women's career development in the last several decades. Society has come a long way since advice such as the following, on supervising women workers, was considered professionally acceptable: "General experience indicates that 'husky' girls—those who are just a little on the heavy side—are more even-tempered and efficient than their underweight sisters" (from *Transportation Magazine*, July, 1943). Nonetheless, considerable gender role stereotyping of occupations and gender stratification continue. Considerations and recommendations for career counseling with women are provided in special issues of the *Journal of Career Assessment* (1997, Vol. 5, No. 4; 1998, Vol. 6, No. 4) and the *Career Development Quarterly* (2002, Vol. 50, No. 4). Chapters and articles by Fitzgerald and Weitzman (1992), Cook, Heppner, and O'Brien (2002), and Crozier (1999) may also prove very helpful in identifying and addressing issues pertinent to female career counseling clients. Finally, classic texts such as Betz and Fitzgerald's (1987) the *Career Psychology of Women*, Walsh and Osipow's (1994) *Career Counseling for Women*, and more recently, Worell and Remer's (2003) *Feminist Perspectives in Therapy: Empowering Diverse Women* are excellent resources.

Resources for career counseling with ethnic minority clients have accumulated much more slowly. Texts by Osipow, Leong, and Barak (2001), Walsh, Bingham, Brown, and Ward (2001), Sharf (2002), and the chapter by Dillard and Harley (2002) address this topic with varying amounts of detail. Peterson and Gonzales (2000) integrate ethnic diversity and socioeconomic status throughout their text. The most comprehensive text to date is probably Leong's (1995) *Career Development and Vocational Behavior of Racial and Ethnic Minorities.* Sample articles addressing cultural issues in the context of career counseling include Brown (2002), Fouad and Arbona (1994), Hackett and Byars (1996), Ibrahim, Ohnishi, and Wilson (1994), Leong and Hartung (1997), Pearson and Bieschke (2001), Rivera, Anderson, and Middleton (1999), and McWhirter (1997), as well as a special issue of the *Career Development Quarterly* (1993, Vol. 42, No. 1).

The Americans with Disabilities Act (ADA) of 1990 has raised consciousness among employers, counselors, and to some extent, the general public about the rights of people with disabilities. The implications of this act for career counselors are numerous; Crist and Stoffel (1992) offer an excellent analysis of the ADA with respect to employees with mental impairments. Nagler's (1993) *Perspectives on Disability* is a helpful and comprehensive resource that includes a focus on the multidimensional impact of the ADA. Career counselors must be familiar with the ADA to properly serve their clients. Other resources addressing the career counseling needs of individuals with disabilities include Alston, Bell, and Hampton (2002), Dipeoulu, Reardon, Sampson, and Burkhead (2002), Enright, Conyers, and Szymanski (1996), Fabian, Lent, and Willis (1998), National Center on Secondary Education and Transition (2002), Reiff (1997), Szymanski and Parker (1996), and Wehman (2001).

Only quite recently has the literature addressed career counseling with gay, lesbian, and bisexual individuals. Issues related to coming out, workplace outing, fear of AIDS, job discrimination based on sexual orientation, workplace homophobia, as well as dual career and parenting versus career issues, illustrate the intersection between sexual orientation and career counseling. Hunt, Jaques, Niles, and Wierzalis (2003) describe a variety of career issues and concerns relevant to individuals with HIV/AIDS. Gelberg and Chojnacki's (1995) article on the process of becoming gay, lesbian, and bisexual affirmative career counselors offers a realistic perspective of the challenges this endeavor represents. Other helpful references include Chung (1995), Croteau, Anderson, Distefano, and Kampa-Kokesch (2000), Croteau and Thiel (1993), Morrow, Gore, and Campbell (1996), Prince (1997), and Ritter and Terndrup (2002). Gay/lesbian career development was the focus of a special issue of the *Career Development Quarterly* (1995, Vol. 44, No. 2) and the *Journal of Vocational Behavior* (1996, Vol. 48, No. 2).

Is it possible to be knowledgeable about all cultures and all types of disability? To fully understand the complexities of gender and sexual orientation as they interact with career development? Of course, the answer to this question is "no." It is certainly possible, and in fact a professional obligation, to develop an approach to all clients that explores and honors their individual differences. Such an approach requires continuous education through reading, consultation with colleagues, seminars and workshops, as well as ongoing critical self-reflection. Career counselors risk perpetuating disadvantage and discrimination when they fail to understand the dynamics of privilege and oppression, and the role of such environmental factors as poverty, access to education and health care, in the career development process (McWhirter, 1994, 2001; O'Ryan, 2003).

A FRAMEWORK FOR CAREER COUNSELING

The remainder of this chapter is devoted to presenting a simple schema for conceptualizing the career counseling process, with specific recommendations for counselors identified along the way. A three-step model of assessment, intervention, and evaluation provides a simple organizational framework for incorporating the wide range of activities that constitute career counseling (Kinnier & Krumboltz, 1984). In addition, Salomone (1988) contends that many career counselors operate under the assumption that there are three stages to career counseling: self-exploration, exploration of the world of work, and creating a satisfying match between self and work. Recall that these steps are rooted in the work of Parsons. What is missing from this model, argues Salomone, are two additional stages: implementation of educational and vocational decisions, and assisting clients to adjust to the new environment resulting from their career decision. It is often assumed that once a career choice has been made and steps toward achieving this goal identified, the counseling process is finished. However, for many clients, implementation of these steps represents a barrier equal to the original problem of making a career decision. Additionally, beginning a new job or an educational program may involve a variety of income, relationship, and general lifestyle adjustments. Consideration of these factors will enable the counselor to be responsive to the various developmental needs of their clients during different points in the counseling process. Each of Salomone's (1988) five stages can be incorporated into the intervention or second phase of counseling.

Assessment

The assessment phase of career counseling begins when the client walks through the door. As with personal counseling, the counselor should immediately begin gathering information via both nonverbal and verbal behaviors. The client's eye contact, posture, self-presentation, and manner of dress may all provide pieces of information that enhance the counseling process. For example, feedback about a client's tendency to mumble and avoid eye contact may prove extremely useful to the client with a string of unsuccessful interviews. Well-developed and acute powers of observation lead to feedback that is more concrete and potentially useful to the client.

Verbal assessment procedures must incorporate basic listening skills. Consistent use of listening skills will facilitate an atmosphere in which the client feels safe, understood, and accepted. The counselor should identify early in the session what the client is seeking in career counseling. As we have defined career from a developmental perspective, a wide array of problems and concerns fall under the rubric of "career," and an even wider range of goals may unfold in the assessment process. Counselors should view client goals as a function of the client's developmental stage and tailor interventions accordingly. By carefully establishing what the client hopes to get out of career counseling, the counselor can address misconceptions and unrealistic expectations right from the start. Direct and open-ended questioning, paraphrasing, and perception checking will facilitate this process.

Another component of the assessment phase is clarification of the counselor's style and approach to counseling and of the client's expectations of his or her role. Unfortunately, many clients perceive counseling as a process in which an expert answers and directs while clients passively absorb the counselor's expertise. Allowing clients to participate in this fashion not only puts an unrealistic burden on the counselor but also is a great disservice to the client. Establishing an active, collaborative relationship is an important component of facilitating the empowerment of clients, and increases the likelihood that clients will be prepared to deal with future problems and concerns (McWhirter, 1994, 2001). Throughout the process of assessment, the counselor actively lays the groundwork for establishing a positive working relationship with the client.

Finally, before moving to the intervention phase of counseling, it is important to establish the results of the client's previous efforts to resolve his or her career dilemma, to estimate a baseline of the behavior the client wishes to change or develop, and to assess the client's existing skills and resources. Keep in mind that clients' assessment of their own efforts may be inaccurate. A battered woman, for example, may have exercised great creativity and initiative in pursuing her career related goals, and yet she may dismiss those efforts because her partner has sabotaged them (Chronister & McWhirter, in press). In addition, presenting a list of skills and capabilities may violate the cultural norms of the client. Thus, counselors should be prepared to carefully explore and validate what the client has tried in the past. Knowing the client's initial goals and how far along the client is toward achieving those goals is an extremely important, and often neglected, prerequisite to evaluating the success of career counseling interventions. Readers will note that many of the interventions discussed below could also be considered components of the assessment phase.

Intervention

Once the nature of career counseling has been clarified and a specific goal or goals have been established, the intervention phase of career counseling may begin. Interventions will vary depending upon the specific needs of the client, the theoretical framework of the counselor, and the counselor's knowledge of available resources. The number of assessment instruments, references, and resources related to career development has expanded so rapidly in the past three decades that the beginning counselor may find the prospect of intervention a bit overwhelming. In this section, some of the most common intervention approaches and instruments will be presented.

Because most career interventions are useful across several theoretical frameworks, they will not be discussed in reference to specific theoretical orientations. This section is divided according to Salomone's five stages. This arrangement is more applicable to clients interested in career exploration and selection than those with concerns related to dual careers and other issues; however, it provides an efficient way to present, in a limited space, information central to career counseling. Readers should note that interventions discussed with respect to one stage will not always be associated with that stage of counseling in actual practice; individual client needs rather than adherence to a formula should influence the type and order of the interventions employed.

Stage 1: Knowledge About Self

Interests.   Because of the important relationship between interests and occupations, many career interventions incorporate a process of identifying and exploring the client's interests. A variety of approaches to interest measurement exist; Isaacson (1985) categorizes these approaches as qualitative and objective. Several qualitative approaches are presented first, followed by descriptions of several popular objective interest inventories. More detailed information about inventories and the other tests discussed in this chapter is available in the Buros's *Mental Measurements Yearbook* series, Kapes, Mastie, Whitfield's *A Counselor's Guide to Career Assessment Instruments* (2001), Zunker and Osborn's *Assessment Results for Career Development* (2001), and the *Journal of Career Assessment*. Finally, several microcomputer programs with an interest assessment component are described.

Qualitative approaches to interest assessment include structured interviews, such as the life career assessment, or the LCA, discussed in detail by Gysbers, Heppner, and Johnston (1997). Career genograms, the detailed analysis of a family's work-related history, may help the client to identify concrete areas of interest and how they developed (Brown & Brooks, 1991; Gysbers et al., 1997; Heppner, O'Brien, Hinkleman, & Humphrey, 1994; Okiishi, 1987). As there may be differences between the interests assessed by objective inventories and those verbally expressed by the client, measures such as the self-administered Vocational Card Sort (Slaney, 1978) have been recommended to identify career interests (McWhirter, Torres, & Rasheed, 1998; Peterson, 1998; Zunker & Osborn, 2001). Review of the client's previous jobs, activities, and accomplishments may provide another starting point for discussion of interests. The counselor must be sure to break down each experience into its component parts to avoid erroneous conclusions. For example, the client who volunteers at a nursing home may enjoy interacting with the elderly; on the other hand, attractive features of the job could be related to autonomy, being in charge of other volunteers, working in the kitchen, or a host of other possibilities. The counselor and client should attempt to draw up a highly specific list of interests, as this will facilitate the task of identifying potential options. Martin and Farris (1994) offer an excellent framework for qualitative, culturally appropriate career assessment with Native Americans. According to Goldman (1990), the advantages of qualitative assessment include a greater degree of adaptability with respect to individual characteristics such as gender and ethnicity. McMahon, Patton, and Watson (2003) note that while assessment is a fundamental part of career counseling, qualitative assessments have received little attention within the career counseling literature. They provide several suggestions as a guide for the career counselor developing qualitative assessments for use with clients.

Qualitative approaches may be used alone or in conjunction with formal or published inventories. The counselor should provide the client with information concerning the use of assessment instruments so that they can determine together if this is a desirable option. The decision to use objective assessment instruments should be carefully considered, for while they often save time, objective instruments typically require less activity on the part of the client, and may indirectly communicate to clients that they are not capable of identifying their own interests. In addition, indiscriminate reliance on instruments can lead to a "gas station" style of counseling: drive in, take test, explain, drive out, "thank you for shopping at the counseling center." Finally, objective assessment instruments have been plagued by gender and racial bias, and evidence of reliability and validity should be prerequisite for using such instruments with women and people of color. Career assessment with people of color is the focus of a special issue of the *Journal of Career Assessment* (1994, Vol. 2, No. 3); Walsh and Osipow (1994) include a chapter on gender bias in career assessment. Other valuable references include the career assessment chapters of the *Handbook of Multicultural Assessment* (Gainor, 2001) and *Career Counseling for African Americans* (Ward & Bingham, 2001) as well as articles pertaining to cultural issues in career assessment found in the special edition of the *Journal of Career Assessment* (2000, Vol. 8, No. 4) addressing career assessment in the new millennium. The counselor should employ a system of self-checks to assess continuously whether the client is receiving optimal service with the use of an objective instrument.

The Strong Interest Inventory.   The Strong Interest Inventory (SII) is among the most widely used interest inventories. It was created by Strong in 1927, and most recently revised by Harmon, Hansen, Borgen, and Hammer (1994). The results of the 317-item SII permit clients to contrast their interest patterns with those of people in over 100 different occupations. Separate scales exist for males and females to reduce bias related to gender differences. Contrary to many a client's hopes, the SII does not provide information concerning how successful a person might be in a chosen field, nor does it indicate a career area that a client should or should not pursue. What it does provide is a launching point for exploration of career options that have never been considered, and a point of departure for discussing why certain career interests are congruent or incongruent with those of persons employed in that field. The SII is organized according to Holland's (1973) typology of modal orientations, so the client can easily determine the orientations with which his or her interests most closely coincide. This may help the client to focus in on a particular group of careers to explore more thoroughly. Research investigating the validity of the SII with Latinos, African Americans, Native Americans, and Asian Americans has produced mixed findings; several reviews of this research are available in the special issue of *Journal of Career Assessment* noted previously, as well as in the 1994 Strong manual (Harmon et al., 1994). Recently, Chartrand, Borgen, Betz, and Donnay (2002) described use of the Strong to understand career goals.

Self-Directed Search.   The Self-Directed Search (SDS) was developed by John Holland (1991a, 1991b) and published by Psychological Assessment Resources. The SDS is a self-administered inventory that assesses an individual's activities, competencies, and career interests, and translates this information into matching career options. The results of the inventory correspond with Holland's occupational typology and are also cross-referenced with the *Dictionary of Occupational Titles* (DOT). The SDS is thorough and relatively easy to administer.

Kuder Occupational Interest Survey. The Kuder Occupational Interest Survey (KOIS) was developed by G. Frederick Kuder in 1966 and most recently revised by Zytowski (1985). The KOIS is published by Science Research Associates. Form DD provides interest comparisons to persons in a variety of occupations and college majors, making the inventory useful for high school and college students and out-of-school adults (Kapes et al., 2000). Form E focuses on the initial stages of self- and occupational exploration, and is most useful to students in grades eight through ten.

Microcomputing Programs.   There are several interactive microcomputer programs designed to facilitate a client's self-exploration of interests. Each program also contains other components, such as values assessment, occupational information, and skills assessment. A brief review of three such programs follows.

SIGI+ is an extension of SIGI, the System of Interactive Guidance and Information, which is described in a later section of this chapter. SIGI+ contains nine components, beginning with a system overview followed by a self-assessment section. In this section, users are guided through an inventory of their interests, values, and skills. Other sections of SIGI+ allow users to learn about careers that correspond to the results of their inventory, as well as providing advice on financial assistance, suggestions for decision-making, training requirements for specific occupations, and a large quantity of additional occupational information.

The Discover program, like SIGI+, contains interest, ability, and values inventories to facilitate the user's self-assessment. Strategies for identifying occupations, occupational information, and information about educational institutions are available with the Discover program. In addition, Discover contains a section that incorporates Holland's Self-Directed Search. A newer version of Discover, called Discover for Adult Learners, was developed for unemployed adults or those in the process of school or job market reentry or career changes. Among other developments, Discover for Adult Learners contains a skills inventory that incorporates the user's previous work experiences. Finally, Eureka's Micro SKILLS is a computer program that begins with a skills inventory similar to the process described in Bolles's *What Color Is Your Parachute? 2004* (2003). This inventory is useful for adults reentering the workforce or changing careers, owing to its focus on experiences as well as interests.

Aptitudes.   Gathering knowledge about the self should also include assessment of the client's aptitudes and skills. Knowing what the client does well facilitates the identification of career-related skills or careers at which the client may succeed. One common informal way to assess aptitudes is by reviewing grades in various subject areas. However, this presents only a limited amount of information. Clients should be encouraged to identify the specific types of class activities in which they were successful: oral presentations, group projects, detailed note-taking, debates, and so on. Work-related successes should also be noted: Was the client ever complimented for achievements in productivity, facility cleanliness, or record-keeping? Clients might be encouraged to interview others for additional information about their special talents or skills. As we noted earlier, be wary of the client who claims a general lack of proficiency, since such a claim may be more reflective of a low self-concept or low self-efficacy expectations than of actual performance. The counselor should be prepared to dig deeply and specifically to obtain information about aptitudes, since obvious signs of success such as grades and awards are often the only signs to which people attend. In addition to the informal information gathering, some circumstances may warrant the use of an aptitude test.

Differential Aptitude Test. The Differential Aptitude Test (DAT) was developed by Bennet, Seashore, and Westman. The DAT was most recently updated in 1990 and is published by the Psychological Corporation. Several forms have been developed and revised. The DAT is widely used across the country by schools and counseling services and has proven extremely useful to high school students trying to determine how they might fare in future educational endeavors. Counselors should be aware that while this instrument is useful in the prediction of general academic success, it is not useful for the prediction of success in specific academic areas, nor does prediction extend to the area of occupational success.

General Aptitude Test Battery. The General Aptitude Test Battery (GATB) was developed and published by the U.S. Employment Service in 1947, with periodic revisions since that time. A unique advantage of the GATB is that this test allows clients to compare themselves with actual workers in specific occupations with respect to nine aptitudes (e.g., motor coordination and clerical perception). The GATB has often been used to assist in job placement, and can be used in conjunction with the new Employment Service Interest Inventory to facilitate the exploration of job possibilities in the DOT and the Occupational Outlook Handbook (OOH) (Sharf, 2002). Zunker and Osborn (2001) note that concerns have been raised about test bias against racial and ethnic minority groups, as well as the need to update the test to reflect changes in technology. Additional aptitude tests are reviewed in the Buros's Mental Measurement Yearbook series.

Values. Values clarification is an important component of career counseling (Zytowski, 1994). In order to make realistic decisions about future occupational pursuits, an individual should have a good idea about the relative importance of values such as family time, income, prestige, autonomy, and a wide variety of other values that are affected by the nature of an occupation. For example, an individual who highly values family time is not likely to be satisfied with a traveling sales position, nor would someone valuing autonomy fare well in a job that involves constant scrutiny by a supervisor. Mael (1991) offers an excellent discussion of the factors influencing career-related behaviors of Observant Jews, illustrating the interaction of specific values and religious practices with the world of work.

Often clients begin career counseling without ever having considered the relationship between occupational choices and value satisfaction. The counselor must be prepared to initiate and accompany the client's exploration of values, as well as anticipate the potential value conflicts and means of satisfaction in the occupations under consideration. By bringing value exploration into the counselor-client interaction, the cultural factors underlying the career development process can be used as a tool for culturally appropriate intervention. Dominant culture values are embedded in many of the theories and practices of career counseling, limiting their appropriateness for use with those whose values are different than the dominant culture such as members of ethnic minority groups (Osipow & Fitzgerald, 1995). Hartung (2002) posits that the career counselor should examine cultural factors influencing values by (1) identifying sets of values that delineate the influence of broader cultural values on the individual, and (2) examining the individualistic and/or collectivistic cultural value orientations of the client. Leong and Gim (1995) and Shin (1999) provide a discussion of career-relevant personality characteristics and values among Asian Americans; exploration of such resources is especially important when working with an individual of a sociocultural background distinct from that of the counselor.

Changing values are not infrequently the impetus of a decision to seek career counseling. Loss due to death, divorce, or changes in health status may necessitate a reprioritization of values. In such a case, income may replace helping others, or job security may supersede autonomy in an individual's values hierarchy. Counselors should be sensitive to the changing nature of values over an individual's lifespan and the implications of value changes for career choices.

Kinnier and Krumboltz (1984) summarized the basic processes involved in many values clarification exercises. They found that most such exercises include one or a combination of the following: identification and analysis of the values issue; examination of past experiences, preferences, behaviors, and decisions that are related to the present issues; investigation of how others view the issue (by direct questioning or imagining what respected others would do in a similar situation); testing or self-confrontation about tentative choices, positions, or resolutions; finding personal environments that are conducive to clear thought about, or temporary escape from, the issue ("sleeping on it" or quiet meditation); and making the "best" tentative resolution and living in accordance with it, revising if needed. Counselors can use widely available strategies devised and published by others or create their own variations of values clarification techniques.

Some clarification exercises involve consideration of values in light of one's mortality. The "lifeline" exercise requires the client to imagine having a terminal illness and to review priorities from this mindset; "Epitaph" and "Obituary" exercises require clients to write down their own version of how they want to be remembered after they have died (Kinnier & Krumboltz, 1984).

The Work Values Inventory developed by Super (1970) is one example of an objective instrument for assessing work-related values. Other available instruments include the Work Environment Preference Schedule, the Salience Inventory, the Study of Values, and the Survey of Interpersonal Values. The latter two instruments are designed to explore both work-related and personal values.

The System of Interactive Guidance and Information (SIGI) is a microcomputer program primarily geared toward helping users clarify their most important values and providing information about careers consistent with the values identified.

There are ten values that the user must evaluate in terms of importance: income, prestige, independence, helping others, security, variety, leadership, interest field, leisure, and early entry. Peterson, Ryan-Jones, Sampson, and Reardon (1994) found that SIGI users report positive impact on their career exploration.

Stage 2: Knowledge About World of Work

Career counselors are responsible for introducing clients to resources for occupational information. More specifically, part of the counselor's job is to ensure that clients are able to obtain career-related information independently in the future. Occupational information is vast and constantly changing, and keeping up to date can be a staggering task. Fortunately, many resources are available that significantly reduce the amount of time and research required of both the counselor and the client. In this section, informal, formal, and microcomputer sources of career information will be presented.

Informal processes of obtaining career information can be interesting and rewarding for the client. The most direct way to find out about a career of interest is to talk to someone already doing it! The client can locate potential interviewees from a variety of sources including friends, relatives, and classmates; local alumni associations; service and professional organizations; and even the local phone directory. The counselor may help the client formulate a set of questions that will maximize the amount and value of the information yielded by the subsequent interview. "Shadowing," or following individuals on the job, is an option that provides an even more concrete idea of what a particular career involves.

College and university campuses provide another rich source of occupational information. Clients may wish to seek out instructors in their field of interest for insights into the nature of specific occupations. Libraries offer journals and magazines serving professional audiences; these resources will provide information on current developments and the cutting edge of research in the field. Additionally, libraries contain reference materials such as labor market statistics, occupational forecasts, and descriptive information. Some of these resources are further described below.

A number of excellent reference materials are typically found in counseling centers, career development centers, and libraries. The most recent version of the Occupational Outlook Handbook or the OOH, as of this writing, is the 2002–2003 edition, and an online edition is available at *http://www.bls.gov/oco./*. The Guide for Occupational Exploration (GOE, 2001), like the OOH, is updated regularly. In addition, the U.S. Department of Labor published the Dictionary of Occupational Titles from 1939 until 1991, and is now replacing this resource with a database called "O*NET" that can be accessed online at the following website: *http://online.onetcenter.org/*. O*NET provides information about careers, requirements, and a host of other services such as online skills assessments. The first state-based computerized career information system was Oregon Career Information Systems (Oregon CIS). Developed to provide Oregonians with integrated, timely, and comprehensive information useful in career development, planning, and decision making, there are now similar information systems in most states as well as a national CIS office located in Oregon. Resources such as the ones described here provide databases that are highly useful for individuals and organizations seeking information such as the nature of specific jobs, the skills and abilities required, how to prepare for entry into the field, forecasts for employment, and how to determine whether such work might be of interest to an individual. Counselors should be familiar with the particular classification system used in each source before introducing these references to clients, in order to maximize utility and minimize client confusion.

Computerized guidance programs are another source of occupational information. The Guidance Information System-III (GIS-III) allows the user to access information in any of six files: occupations, four-year colleges, two-year colleges, graduate schools, financial-aid information, and armed services occupations (Isaacson, 1985). The user simply enters the characteristics of interest into the computer and is provided with a listing of corresponding schools, programs, or occupations. For example, a client may be interested in pursuing a liberal arts degree at a private institution in the East or the Midwest. Using GIS, the client can enter these characteristics and receive a list of private Eastern and Midwestern schools that provide degrees in liberal arts. SIGI, CIS (the Career Information System) and Discover also have large amounts of occupational information. The relative ease with which computer files can be updated and accessed makes computers an invaluable source of current occupational information.

With the recent advances in technology, the Internet and the World Wide Web are fast becoming important and rich sources of information on the world of work. For individuals with access to computer technology, an abundance of websites providing information on careers and occupations exist. For example, the University of California at Berkeley Career and Education Guidance Library maintains a website of career exploration links *www.uhs.berkeley.edu/Students/CareerLibrary/Links/careerme.htm*. Other websites of interest include the U.S. Department of Labor (*www.dol.gov*), and websites for the state departments of education. To find more career-related Internet resources, conduct searches using the various web search engines available. For a review of the impact of the Internet and technological advances on career counseling and assessment, the beginning counselor is encouraged to read Gore and Leuwerke (2000), Isaacson and Brown (1999), and Oliver and Whitson (2000).

Stage 3: Creating a Match

For the client interested in choosing an occupation, this stage of career counseling refers to the process of deciding which occupations are consistent with the client's skills, interests, and values. Eventually, the client will have to narrow down the list of occupations, and career counselors often assist in the decision-making process.

Decision making is a part of life, but unfortunately many people lack the skills important for making effective decisions. Decision making within career counseling has been conceptualized in terms of four components: (1) conceptualization of the problem as one of choice, (2) enlargement of the response repertoire, (3) identification of discriminative stimuli, and (4) response selection (Olson, McWhirter, &

Horan, 1989). Enlargement of the response repertoire refers to the process of generating a large number of alternative actions. Identification of discriminative stimuli involves weighing the advantages and disadvantages of each potential course of action, as well as assessing the probable results of each. For example, while the advantages of writing a Pulitzer Prize-winning book are many, the probability of doing so is quite slim. Teaching clients this or other decision-making models provides them with a skill generalizable to a multitude of situations and helps ensure subsequent satisfaction with the decisions they make. It is important to integrate cultural values into the decision-making process. For example, the involvement of parents and other family members in career decision making varies quite a bit across cultures, and counselors should not assume that mainstream middle-class Western values such as "'independent' decisions" and "whatever makes me happy" are salient for a given client (e.g., see Sue et al., 1998; Yang, 1991).

Career decision making has been the focus of an enormous amount of empirical and conceptual literature. Some recent sample publications, including those that focus on career decision-making measures or instruments, include Albion and Fogarty (2002) (validation of the Career Decision Making Differences Questionnaire), Blanchard and Lichtenberg (2003) (an application of Gottfredson's theory to decision making), Brown (2000) (contextual influences on decision making), Chung (2002) (gender and ethnic differences in career decision-making self-efficacy), Cohen (2003) (existential theory applied to career decision making), Gati and Saka (2001) (a comparison of Internet-based vs. paper-and-pencil career decision-making measures), Krieshok (2001) (ways in which decision-making literature can inform practice), and Nauta, Saucier, and Woodard (2001) (sexual orientation and career decision making).

Stage 4: Implementation of a Decision

Salomone (1988) raises the issue that once a decision has been made, the task of the career counselor is not over. The client may lack specific skills, support, or information necessary for successful implementation of the decision. The counselor should be prepared to assist the client in developing these skills, locating sources of support, or obtaining the information in areas such as resume writing, interviewing, assertiveness, or communication. If part of the client's decision involves actions such as changing a behavior, developing a hobby, or participating in a new organization, the counselor can be a valuable source of support and encouragement. Oftentimes, the simple scheduling of tasks will be enough motivation for the hesitant client to follow through on decisions.

Transtheoretical models of counseling, such as the Stages of Change model (Prochaska & DiClemente, 1984, 1992; Prochaska, DiClemente, & Norcross, 1992) can be used to assess a client's readiness for decisions involving action and assist in the development of interventions tailored to the stage of change that the client is in. The Stages of Change model provides an understanding of the different stages that an individual must undergo in order to follow through with a particular change process. Individuals in the *precontemplation* stage have little or no awareness of the need or intention to change (an adult child, Chris, is living at home, without a job or source of income, and with no intention to seek education or employment). In the *contemplation* stage, this awareness of the need/desire for change surfaces; however, a commitment to change has not yet evolved (Chris's parents request that Chris either contributes to the household income or moves out, but Chris does not think that this "threat" is serious and has no plans for action). Once the individual reaches the *preparation* stage, the decision to make a change has been made (Chris accepts that getting a job is probably necessary and decides to begin seeking a job . . . within the next couple of weeks). The preparation stage prepares the individual to enter the *action* phase in which the behaviors necessary for change are enacted. In the action phase, Chris engages in job seeking. The final step is the *maintenance* phase, in which the change is maintained over time. If Chris discontinues job seeking without finding a job, or finds a job but is then fired or laid off, the cycle begins again. Prochaska, DiClemente, and Norcross (1992) explain that individuals may cycle through these stages a number of times before entering and sustaining maintenance of the change; the duration of any particular stage can vary widely. Effective career counselors will recognize that when clients enter career counseling, they may not be ready to change behaviors that become the focus of intervention. Understanding the nature of change processes can help the career counselor meet clients where they are and assist them in taking the next step toward change. When clients are not achieving their own goals, examining their process using the stages of change model can be very useful to both counselor and client.

Anxiety may interfere with the client's motivation to carry out a plan of action. Anxiety is often founded upon irrational beliefs or expectations. According to Krumboltz (1994), maladaptive or irrational beliefs are a common obstacle to career development, and he recommends cognitive restructuring as one means to address this problem. Cognitive restructuring involves identifying irrational beliefs and replacing them with rational and realistic thoughts. Nevo (1987) has identified a set of common irrational beliefs with respect to careers, for example, "There's only one perfect job for me." The counselor's familiarity with the world of work and with the client's skills and personality can be used to reduce anxiety and encourage action.

Stage 5: Adjustment to New Setting

Sometimes the goals established in career counseling will result in the client moving into a new environment. This may be the result of a job promotion, the start of a new job, enrollment in an academic program, a change of residence, or a combination of these and other changes. The client may be challenged to cope with a new set of demands and expectations, as well as to interact with unfamiliar groups and individuals. The new environment may be characterized by racism and sexual harassment, support and professional challenge, widespread demoralization, or may simply differ radically from the prior environment and require a major adjustment. Issues often perceived as the sole territory of personal counseling are commonly encountered in career counseling. Often clients are dealing with career concerns as a result of or in conjunction with developmental issues such as divorce, changes in ethnic identity status, children leaving home, coming out as gay or lesbian, changing financial circumstances, or changes in health.

Training in skills such as communication, human relations with diverse groups, and giving or receiving supervision may help the client interact in a healthy and productive way with new coworkers, supervisors, and acquaintances. Assertiveness training may help clients secure what they need from the environment and safeguard their rights without infringing upon the rights of others. Stress inoculation and relaxation training may assist clients to deal with the anxiety associated with these new situations. Strategies for dealing with loneliness, frustration, and feelings of inadequacy may also serve an important function at this time of transition.

At the close of this section, it is important to emphasize again that the arrangement of specific interventions with specific stages in career counseling is by no means set in stone. For example, cognitive restructuring may be called for as the client begins the self-assessment process and at a variety of other points in the career counseling process. In addition, career counseling interventions need not follow each and every one of the five steps identified by Salomone (1988). Rather, the process should be dictated by the nature of the client's concern and the plan that the counselor and client establish together.

Evaluation.   Evaluation is the third step in the career counseling framework. As indicated earlier, evaluation is a sorely neglected aspect of career counseling. While many career counselors are aware of the immediate outcomes of counseling, such as the choice of a college major or a reduction of job stress, in general practice, there is very little formal follow-up. In addition, it is good practice for counselors to end every counseling relationship with an evaluation of the process. Such an evaluation may be incorporated into one of the final sessions and may yield important information for both the counselor and the client. Potential closing topics to cover are similar to those of personal counseling: the relative helpfulness of the interventions, the degree of support experienced by the client throughout the process, the extent to which the client felt respected and understood, the extent to which the client felt like an active participant and collaborator, topics on which the client might have wanted to spend more or less time, and what the client might like to have done differently. Feedback for clients might include the counselor's perceptions of their relevant strengths and weaknesses, changes and progress noted by the counselor, and suggestions for future directions.

There is also a need in career counseling for more formal evaluations of the relative effectiveness of various interventions. Surprisingly little is known about how various career interventions affect the vocational development process. Brown and Krane (2000) describe the results of several meta-analyses of the effects of career interventions and noted five specific intervention components that appear to be associated with positive career counseling outcomes: written exercises, individualized interpretation and feedback, world of work of information, modeling opportunities, and attention to building support within a social network. Their review is a promising step forward in understanding the complexity of career counseling and vocational choices.

SUMMARY

Career counseling is a vital and dynamic area of counseling. While a variety of theoretical perspectives currently inform the career counselor, a developmental perspective has been emphasized in the definition and description of career counseling. The framework presented in this chapter may serve as an initial organizer for viewing the roles and activities of the career counselor, while the references listed may guide future, more in-depth exploration of career development theories and career interventions. We hope that beginning counselors will continue to pursue the vast resources of available information in the area of career counseling. Further exploration and utilization of these resources can make the process of career counseling a productive, challenging, and enjoyable experience for both the counselor and the client.

CHAPTER TEN

COUNSELING AND SPIRITUALITY

PAUL T. CEASAR, ED.D.
JUDITH G. MIRANTI, ED.D.
Our Lady of Holy Cross College

The evolving profession of counseling has as its roots a variety of disciplines and has long been influenced by secularism, rationalism, and agnosticism—the secularism of medicine, the rationalism of the scientific method, and the agnosticism of Sigmund Freud (Kelly, 1995). Because counseling is an evolving profession, counseling has seen the need to adhere to, conform to, and draw support from the various ideologies even if these ideologies seem to have undervalued the spiritual dimensions which counselors have come to admit are important dimensions of human life. It is as though, in its own right, the counseling profession must legitimize the place of and inherent value of this critical component.

The concept of spirituality has taken on a renewed interest within the helping professions. This resurgence has been due in part to an appreciation of the holistic approach to the person and the interconnectedness of mind, body, and spirit (Clinebell, 1995). In addition, research has indicated that the spiritual component in a person's life can have a significant impact on that person's capacity for overall wellness (Borysenko, 1987; Chandler, Holden & Kolander, 1992; Hickson, Housley, & Wages, 2000; Siegel, 1990; Weil, 1995).

The spiritual dimensions of counseling began to receive national recognition over the past decades as evidenced by the numerous publications on the topic (Burke & Miranti, 1995; Frame, 2003; Kelly, 1995; Richards & Bergin, 1997). Practitioners and counselor educators have been cautious and hesitant to incorporate spirituality and/or religion because of a lack of clear guidelines from the profession. Rather than take the risk and be in possible violation of the unwritten code, these professionals relied on the legal statutes of separation of church and state, the ethical codes of other professions, or their own personal biases.

As people express their questions regarding basic life issues and their struggles to make sense out of their lives, consideration of the spiritual dimension of the person becomes an important component in counseling (Aponte, 1996; Fukuyama & Sevig, 1997; Myers & Truluck, 1998). Moore (1992) stated that the emotional complaints of the current times, the complaints that counselors hear every day in practice, include issues of (a) emptiness; (b) meaninglessness; (c) vague depression; (d) disillusionment about marriage, family, and relationships; (e) a loss of values; and (f) the yearning for personal fulfillment. These issues are of a spiritual nature in that they suggest a search into areas which may involve relationships with a transcendent power (Clinebell, 1995) or access to those areas of the person requiring elements of self-transcendence (Chandler et al., 1992). Thus, if the task of the counselor is to understand the individual(s) in order to provide full facilitation of the counseling process, it is important that the spiritual realm be a part of the repertoire that the counselor brings to the session.

Counselors are challenged to be sensitive to spiritual issues, understand how best to help clients process their concerns, and be aware of their own personal stance related to the spiritual dimension (Aponte, 1996). Whereas at different times in the history of the helping profession the spiritual dimension to counseling was not considered explicitly a part of the counseling session, researchers are indicating that many counselors acknowledge the value and importance of spirituality within themselves and their clients (Bergin, 1991; Jensen & Bergin, 1988; Myers & Truluck, 1998).

This current recognition of the spiritual has been gradual and is in response to several factors in the current understanding of persons, their growth and development. These awarenesses include (a) a holistic point of view, (b) an appreciation of a wellness model for human development, (c) a greater appreciation of multicultural inclusiveness, and (d) having a viable place to deal with spiritual issues.

This chapter will provide a description of spirituality as formulated by the Summit on Spirituality (1995); support the practice of incorporating the spiritual dimension into the counseling process; address the counselor's role; provide criteria for healthy spirituality; suggest ways to assess for the spiritual dimension; utilize traditional and contemporary techniques and methods; and explore the implications for training and practice.

SUMMIT ON SPIRITUALITY

Reviewing ten years of writings on the topic of spirituality in journals of the American Counseling Association resulted in the edited publication *Ethical and Spiritual Values* by Burke and Miranti (1992). A second publication, *Counseling, the Spiritual Dimension* (Burke & Miranti, 1995), encouraged counselors and counselor educators to consider their own spirituality and to facilitate the enhancement of spiritual wellness for their students and clients. Authors cited in these publications along with other noted contributors on the topic of spirituality in counseling were invited to participate in the First Invitational Summit on Spirituality, which was held in Charlotte, North Carolina, on October 20–23, 1995. Twelve authors accepted the invitation and began the task of compiling a description of spirituality and a listing of needed competencies.

The proceedings of this summit can be found in *Counseling Today* (1995). Since then, the participants of the summit have published numerous books and articles on the spiritual dimensions of counseling and have significantly influenced the counseling profession.

Description of Spirituality

Language is an inadequate medium in which to express completely the essence of spirituality. A definition or description of spirituality is only a starting point that cannot fully represent the entire concept. Any definition or description must be accompanied by qualifications and the following reflections: Spirituality may be defined as the animating force in life, represented by such images as "breath," "wind," "vigor," or "courage." Spirituality is the infusion and drawing out of spirit in one's life. This is experienced as an active and passive process.

Spirituality is also described as the capacity and tendency that is innate and unique to all persons. This spiritual tendency moves the individual toward knowledge, love, meaning, hope, transcendence, connectedness, and compassion. Spirituality includes one's capacity for creativity, growth, and the development of a value system. Spirituality encompasses the religious, spiritual, and transpersonal (Summit on Spirituality, 1995, p. 30). The participants of the summit thought a description rather than a definition would provide a more global approach to the concept of spirituality, thus a working description was formulated.

There are a variety of ways in which spirituality has been defined or described. Clinebell (1995) stated that spirituality refers to the individual's search for meaning and value in life and relationship with a transcendent power.

Most agree that there are many definitions and interpretations regarding the terms religion and spirituality. Wilber (2000) offers several definitions of spirituality:

1. "Spirituality involves the highest levels of any of the developmental lines" (p. 129)
2. "Spirituality is the sum total of the highest levels of the developmental lines" (p. 130)
3. "Spirituality is itself a separate developmental line" (p. 130)
4. "Spirituality is an attitude (such as openness or love) that you can have at whatever stage you are at" (p. 133)
5. "Spirituality basically involves peak experiences" (p. 134)

Although spirituality may be experienced and expressed through religion which is defined as an organized system of faith, worship, cumulative traditions, and prescribed rituals (Ingersoll, 1994), spiritual issues that arise in counseling may or may not be associated with a religious belief system.

Competencies

The participants at the Summit on Spirituality recommended that in order for counselors to appropriately address the spiritual and/or religious concerns of clients, they need to be able to:

- Explain the relationship between spirituality and religion.
- Describe religious and spiritual beliefs and practices in a cultural context.
- Engage in self-exploration of one's religious and spiritual beliefs in order to increase sensitivity, understanding, and acceptance of one's belief system.
- Demonstrate sensitivity and acceptance of a variety of religious and/or spiritual expressions in client communication.
- Identify limits of one's understanding of a client's religious and/or spiritual expressions and demonstrate appropriate referral skills and possible referral sources.
- Assess the relevance of the religious and/or spiritual themes in the counseling process as befits each client's expressed preference.
- Use a client's religious and/or spiritual beliefs in the pursuit of the client's therapeutic goals as befits the client's expressed preference. (p. 30)

A Quest for Spiritual Expression

Many organized religions have seen a decline in membership. Thus, there is a sense of spiritual homelessness that Steere (1997) describes as:

> The spiritually homeless are those whose quest for meaning and wholeness has carried them away from their church home. They wander the streets in search of a place to house their thirst for healing and inner peace. They have a consumer mentality, which demands services they no longer find viable or satisfying in organized religious life. Those who are spiritually homeless seek two things. The first is spiritual direction that can bring meaning or purpose to their lives, a certain sense of inner fulfillment or satisfying devotion to something sacred. The second is healing, not simply physical and emotional healing, but wholeness and well-being that comes from facing our vicissitudes, coping with the estrangement that can overwhelm our personal relationships as couples, families, friends, and coworkers. This concern for wholeness, which is the root meaning of the word holy, is the driving force behind spiritual homelessness, which in turn, provides the background for a rapprochement between psychotherapy and spirituality. (p. 13)

Just as mental health professionals have recognized the importance of inquiring about ethnicity and other aspects of culture, they should routinely explore the spiritual dimension of clients' lives. It is essential to clarify whether spiritual beliefs are based in deeply held convictions or merely followed meaninglessly. The following questions suggest some lines of inquiry that can be useful.

- How important are spiritual beliefs and practices in the clients' lives?
- To what extent do the clients identify with a spiritual orientation?

- How do past or present spiritual beliefs and practices contribute to presenting problems or block healing and growth?
- How has adversity or trauma wounded the spirit?
- How might a spiritual void or disconnectedness from religious roots exacerbate suffering or alienation?

How can past, current, or potential spiritual resources be identified or drawn upon to ease distress, support problem-solving, help clients to accept what cannot be changed and foster healing? (Adopted from Walsh, 1999).

SUPPORT FOR THE INCLUSION OF SPIRITUALITY BY THE PROFESSION

Hickson et al. (2000) investigated the attitudes of Licensed Professional Counselors concerning spirituality in the therapeutic process and found that LPCs recognize the importance of being aware of their own spiritual beliefs. Spirituality was also viewed as a universal phenomenon that can act as a powerful psychological change agent.

A study of marriage and family counselors' beliefs about the appropriateness of addressing religious and spiritual issues in counseling found that 95 percent of the respondents believed in the relationship between spiritual and mental health (Carlson, Kirkpatrick, Hecker & Killmer, 2002).

Those who are opposed to the inclusion of the spiritual and religious dimensions of counseling have expressed concerns that counselors who address the spiritual dimension may be likely to violate ethical guidelines by imposing their values on clients. The revised code of the American Counseling Association, 1995; the American Association of Marriage and Family Therapy, 1985; and the American Psychological Association, 1992, have encouraged their members to respect individual differences in values and to be sensitive and respectful to the diversity of religious and spiritual traditions. According to Lee and Sirch (1994), to do otherwise would violate the ethical code of the counseling profession.

The *Code of Ethics and Standards of Practice* (1995) of the American Counseling Association addresses the religious and spiritual needs of clients. Counselors who choose to ignore these dimensions may be in violation of the Code which regulates the profession of counseling and may fail to promote the growth and development of their clients. Section A on the Counseling Relationship, A.2., "Respecting diversity," specifically mentions that "counselors do not condone or engage in discrimination based on . . . religion . . . ," "actively attempt to understand diverse cultural backgrounds of the clients with whom they work," and learn "how the counselor's own cultural/ethnic/racial identity impacts his or her values and beliefs about the counseling process." Ignoring spiritual and religious issues in counselor preparation runs the risk of inadvertently fostering some degree of counselor insensitivity to clients' spiritual and religious concerns as these are relevant to counseling (Hinterkopf, 1994).

Although not specifically recommending an extensive treatment of spirituality and religion, accreditation standards do refer to the spiritual/religious dimensions by including "religious preference" in curricular standards in the core area of Social and Cultural Foundations (Council for Accreditation of Counseling and Related Educational Programs, 1994). An article published in the *Journal of Counseling and Development*, "Spirituality, Religion, and CACREP Curriculum Standards" (1999, pp. 251–257), by Burke, Hackney, Hudson, Miranti, Watts, and Epp provides methods and examples for including spirituality and religion for each of the CACREP core curriculum areas. It was recommended by the authors that a balanced inclusion of the spiritual and religious dimensions at appropriate points in the CACREP curriculum is a reasonable step in helping counselor trainees acquire competencies necessary for incorporating these aspects into the counseling process.

Reluctance to Include the Spiritual Dimensions in Counseling

There are several reasons counselors may be hesitant to incorporate the spiritual dimension into the counseling process:

A fear of imposing personal values

The counselor's attitude toward religion or spirituality

A lack of knowledge of various religions or spiritual belief systems

A lack of theoretical models for incorporating the spiritual dimension

Bergin and Garfield (1994) contend that the continual influence of philosophical and theoretical biases against the spiritual perspective is one of the main reasons why this dimension is not more fully integrated into the practice of counseling. Another reason may be the counselor's own feelings about personal religious and/or spiritual beliefs. Some counselors may have had negative personal experiences that have not been resolved or their own biases and prejudices may have not been addressed.

A lack of knowledge of spiritual issues or of different religious traditions may keep a counselor from exploring the client's issues. This may present an opportunity for practicing professionals to attend workshops and seminars on the topic in order to enhance their skill base. Another possible reason for the hesitation may be the inability of the counselor to apply a theory or technique that would be appropriate to the presenting situation. Also, there is a belief that spiritual and religious issues should only be discussed with spiritual or ecclesiastical leaders (Wolf & Stevens, 2001).

Several authors have documented their success and have provided examples for incorporating this perspective (Chandler et al., 1992; Curtis & Davis, 1999; Frame & Williams, 1996; Hinterkopf, 1994; Prest & Keller, 1993; Smith, 1993).

Models Addressing the Spiritual Dimensions and the Counselor's Role

Models can be useful as they offer frameworks for understanding how clients may be experiencing their spiritual or religious concerns. They can also help in assessing where clients are in their religious or spiritual growth (Frame, 2003).

In applying spirituality within a counseling setting, there are several models that may be helpful in conceptualizing cases in which the spiritual dimension might be present. Steere (1997) mentions seven such models and provides descriptions of these models and ways in which the counselor may facilitate the client's progress within these models.

The Wellness Model

An appreciation of viewing the person from the perspective of a holistic wellness model has emerged as research on various levels of human behavior has taken place. Witmer, Sweeney, and Myers (1993) translated many of the wellness theoretical and research concepts into a holistic wellness model. The developmental constructs of this model came from empirical research in the fields of sociology, psychology, anthropology, religion, education, and behavioral medicine (Witmer & Sweeney, 1992). A major strength of the model is that it includes a broader perspective and wider range of factors contributing to holistic wellness than other contemporary models and provides measures to assess these factors (Hermon & Hazler, 1999).

The mind-body-spirit connection is seen as a way of viewing persons which offers a complete picture of individuals and what impacts persons. The wellness model views people as growing and developing throughout the life span. Spirituality is conceptualized as the core characteristic of healthy persons, the core of wellness (Seaward, 1995), and the source of all other dimensions of wellness (Chandler et al., 1992). Expanding on the Chandler et al. model, Hinterkopf (1998) incorporates a focusing method which may be used in helping client's with their spiritual issues.

The Developmental Model

The developmental model reflects an earlier description of spirituality as an inner attitude that emphasizes energy, creative choice, and a powerful force for living. Also, emphasized was a person's partnership with a power greater than the individual, a co-creatorship with God (Ingersoll, 1994). This description would coincide with a developmental model in which the individual is perceived as being in a process of growing and changing in life. The psychological growth in this model is seen as synonymous with spiritual growth (Genia, 1995; Helmeniak, 1987; Hinterkopf, 1994; Worthington, 1989). Within the periods of change and transition, the person may experience a period of confusion, uncertainty, and emotional distress. Thus, in these times of struggle, the spiritual reality may involve a concept of a higher being (God) who is present (consciously or unconsciously) as the person searches to clarify his or her next move in life. This imminent concept of God perceives God as a spiritual presence within the self as well as in all living beings.

One developmental model offers stages of spiritual or faith development similar to the stages of development which are presented within the realms of the psychosocial, cognitive, and moral dimensions of the person. Thus, as James Fowler (1981) offers his stages of faith development, the components of the stages coincide with those presented by Erikson, Piaget, Kohlberg, and others who have articulated stages of development. Consequently, as the counselor is aware of the level of development of the client and her or his struggle to move to an advanced stage, the corresponding spiritual awareness will need to be considered and adjusted.

What follows is an overview of the spiritual developmental model (Fowler, 1981):

1. *Undifferentiated Faith:* (ages 0 to 2) The dependence of the infant upon its nurturers tends to the development of trust; a primal sense of one's dependence on a caring being beyond oneself.

2. *Intuitive-Projective Faith:* (2–7 years) Without a system of logic, the developing child relies on its *intuitive* experience and its *imagination* to structure its world; thus images of God, both positive and negative, flow from the child's experience of the world and people around it, as projected onto God through imagination. These images may lead to feeling "good" or "shameful." (Some adults carry residues of this stage as part of their image of God.)

3. *Mythic–Literal Faith:* (7–12 years) Development of concrete thinking leads the child to want to know "how things really are," rather than relying on fantasy. This is most easily summarized in stories that give drama and mythical power to order the world, especially religious and biblical stories. However, because the child is unable to step back and evaluate these stories, they are taken *literally*. This is also the period of developing "fairness," for example, good is rewarded and bad is punished, even on the cosmic level. (Some adults may carry residues of this stage when they continue to take things literally rather than seek deeper meanings and when they deal with God as a rewarder and punisher with whom they must "bargain.")

4. *Synthetic-Conventional Faith:* (Adolescence) Development of abstract thinking leads one to explore ideals and possibilities. It also allows one to perceive another's view of oneself. Synthesizing others' views of oneself helps to form an identity. However, this identity is closely tied to being part of a group. Faith, then, is the shared faith of the groups to which one belongs. Since it is important to one's sense of belonging, it is often uncritical and tacitly accepted. (Many adults continue to approach faith as solely a group experience, for example "I believe what the community believes.")

5. *Individuative-Reflective Faith:* (Early Adulthood) This is the stage of geographically and emotionally "leaving home." This means critically examining the values and beliefs one was formed in and developing a personal set of values and beliefs. There is less reliance on external authority and the relocation of authority within the individual in order to take personal responsibility for how one thinks and acts. This is often a lengthy process which is full of conflict for the individual. (Normally this occurs during young adulthood but may not occur until the 30s or 40s, if at all.)

6. *Conjunctive Faith:* (Mid-Life) Based on Carl Jung's idea of "conjunction of opposites," at mid-life the complexities of existence no longer allow for clear, simple, rational explanations. One is both young and old; masculine and feminine; constructive and destructive; having a conscious mind and a shadow self. Since the truth is more complex, we are open to other worldviews and faith expressions and recognize a deeper reality that goes beyond any one formulation of truth, for example, a mysterious divinity with which we attempt to relate (communion with God).

7. *Sacrificial Faith:* (Older Adult) Realizing the universal value and unity of all people and living in deep communion with God, one begins to love like God loves, for example, self-emptying and without regard for power and personal security.

Another description of the stages of spiritual growth is developed by Peck (1987). The basic stages that he enumerates and which roughly fit the stages which Fowler (1981) offers are:

1. *Chaotic, Antisocial:* The stage of undeveloped spirituality which includes all children and one in five adults. The person in this stage is basically unprincipled with actions being basically self-serving.

2. *Formal, Institutional:* This is the stage of most churchgoers and believers. Faith at this level is more of a legalistic religion with an attachment to the forms and structures of religion. The concept of God is a punitive God, though at times loving.

3. *Skeptic, Individual:* The person is no longer dependent on the institution for governance. One's religious orientation is individualistic and may fall into the category of a "nonbeliever." However, the person is not antisocial and often is committed to social causes.

4. *Mystic, Communal:* This stage is marked by a sense of unity, connectedness, and a link with the larger cosmos. There is an awareness of the enormity of the unknown, but rather than fear, there is a desire to penetrate deeper into it. The peoples of the world are seen more in terms of community with an openness to dispel that which divides people.

As the client experiences changes in his/her life, the spiritual challenge may be present to move to a higher level of faith. Thus the role of the counselor is to walk the journey with the client. The caring presence of the counselor encourages and empowers the client to be patient with the changes, to search for strength for endurance until that time when things begin to take on a direction with which the client feels is the right course. The focus is on the here and now, getting in touch with the present awareness. The client may come to experience a renewed sense of commitment and meaning in his/her life. As mentioned earlier, the spiritual awareness is a deeper, inner presence of the source of life that is constant in all living processes. Aponte (1996) views spirituality in a broad context, which takes into account all the various influences in one's life. He writes:

> I suggest that this broader view also depicts spirituality as an active dynamic force that springs from within the core of a person, as well as from family and community. Consider spirituality as a complex dynamic in people's lives that develops, matures,

and evolves through life's triumphs and hurts, changes and growth; think of it as so much a part of life that no emotional pain, psychological distress, or relationship struggle can be understood in depth without accounting for people's spirituality. (p. 495)

Systemic Model

Another model of spiritual presence that Steere (1997) developed was that of the systemic model. He states:

> It follows upon the need to comprehend spiritual presence in the relational context of shared experience, which develops a common mentality, uniting and drawing together social units such as couples, families, extended families, and all sorts of other human communal groupings into living systems that operate as a whole. (pp. 219–220)

Many of the descriptions of spirituality point to the interconnectedness of peoples and the universe (Summit on Spirituality, 1995). Humans do not live in isolation but as an interactive body with an awareness of being part of a greater whole. The systemic model developed by Steere (1997) works on the concept that spiritual awareness comes through experiencing oneself "as part of a much larger and more intelligent process in which you and those with whom you join are growing and evolving" (p. 238). He continued that in the systemic model, spiritual presence emerges within ongoing relationships moving people to construct new ways of thinking and interacting so as to heal the members, overcome their impasses, or enhance their common meaning and purposes in concert with the larger environment of other living systems.

The hope in the process of counseling is to help the clients come to a deeper awareness and understanding (wisdom). The spiritual dimension is that this level of understanding is part of a greater and higher order of intelligence.

A Case Study.   James is a 46-year-old male who had reluctantly agreed to counseling on the prodding of his wife. James and Jennifer have two children, ages 16 (boy) and 14 (girl). James and Jennifer have been married for 18 years. James reported that he has been feeling listless and disinterested in everything. He has been successful in his work, but does not feel motivated. He says that he feels guilty that he is going through whatever this experience is in his life. He says that he should be more appreciative since life has been good to him. He says that he cares about his children and has been a good provider for them. He admits that he may have gotten overinvolved in his work and now that his children are teenagers, he does not feel a close part of their lives. He stated that he has always been a very responsible person. His family background was fairly strict and he has always done what was the right thing to do. He mentions that he does not want to divorce and leave his family, but that he is miserable. He says that there is not another woman in his life, but that he has fantasized about getting a fresh start in life.

How would spirituality fit into this situation? James is expressing a sense of meaninglessness in his life and a sense of being directionless and in some ways disconnected with himself and with others. In addition to the types of therapies which might be appropriate in working with James, the element of spirituality might be introduced by asking him what is or has been his spiritual experience. This may or may not include a belief in a God or a higher power. If it does, the counselor may invite him to talk about his notion of God and how God has been a part of his life. The counselor may then ask what his current concept of God is and try to determine in what way he is experiencing God's presence.

Applying the Developmental Model

As this search is part of the developmental model, the counselor is encouraging an awareness of a spiritual presence and may use techniques to help James experience such a presence, for example, relaxation, guided imagery, meditation. Part of James' demeanor has been a life of "doing," so part of the spiritual awareness is to help him balance his life with a sense of "being." This hopefully will help him create spaces to be open to a transcendent presence in his life. James may also be in the Eriksonian stage of Generativity vs. Stagnation and thus will be in a process of finding a new direction in his life. He is likewise at a mid-life point in his life where he is questioning his life structure (Levinson, 1978). Thus, he is seeking new meaning for his relationships and his work. Note that the counselor is not imposing his or her religious orientation, but is facilitating and accessing the presence of the spiritual dimension in James' life. The counselor enters this phase of James' journey and is present to him as he works through this transitional period of his life, guiding to gain hope from a deeper reality and presence.

A Case Study. The Martin family, consisting of a single mother (Judy), one teenage girl (Brandy), 14 years old, and one son (Josh), 12 years of age, comes for counseling. The identified client is Brandy who has run away from home on a couple of occasions and is constantly acting out at school and at home. The father (Mike) and Judy have been divorced for three years and Mike is currently living with his new wife. Even though they live in the same city, Mike does not see the children on a regular basis. The children have experienced rejection, hurt, and a significant change in lifestyle since the divorce. Brandy holds her mother responsible for the divorce saying that if she would have been a better wife, her dad would not have left. At times, she says that she wants to live with her dad, but he has not encouraged this union.

Whichever approach a family counselor might use in working with this family, the process of counseling might be enhanced by considering the spiritual dimension. In this setting, the counselor is aware that each member of the family is at a different developmental stage spiritually and each is experiencing a different awareness of understanding of the situation. The counselor is sensitive to the needs of each member for healing and for some type of reconnecting with one another in terms of trust, forgiveness, and care. Through the interactive process, the goal would be to have the members of this system (including the father and step-mother, if possible) participate in working toward an atmosphere enabling the system to function, allowing for growth in a healthy environment. For example, from a social constructionist perspective, this process would respect each member's perspective and through the mutual sharing, a greater wisdom would emerge providing a sense of being a part of a greater reality and intelligence than the limitations of each individual part (McAuliff & Eriksen, 1999).

After reviewing the work of several marriage and family counselors, Wolf and Stevens (2001) and Carlson et al. (2002) documented the appropriateness of including religious and spiritual issues in counseling, and Stander, Piercy, Mackinnon, and Helmeke (1994) concluded that it is possible to use existing marriage and family techniques and principles to address religious issues in counseling. The latter continued that the kinds of questions used to explore relationships with families can also be used to explore individual's spiritual relationships and resources. Narrative and constructivist approaches seem well suited for this exploration.

Other Models

As mentioned earlier, Steere (1997) offered other spiritual models such as the Empathic Model, the Sacred Model, the Crisis Model, the Expansive Model, and the Supernatural Model, each of which deals with some aspect of human behavior and counseling theories and incorporates a way to view these approaches with an eye toward spiritual presence. Some areas mentioned in those models are (a) dealing with the core meaning of life as based on our life stories (narrative, existential), (b) addressing the crisis concept (transformation) as used in AA settings, and (c) searching the unconscious (psychodynamic). Frame (2003) offered additional developmental models such as Allport, Oser, Genia, and Washburn.

Assessing the Spiritual Dimension

Spirituality and religion, similar to age, gender, and culture which are explicitly cited in the CACREP standards, are potentially significant aspects of a comprehensive assessment of clients (Malony, 1993). Career, personality, and wellness instruments are available that include spirituality and religion as a component. Several instruments are: Spiritual Wellness Inventory, Ingersoll, 1995; the CISS, Campbell, 1992; the WEL, the Wellness Evaluation of Lifestyle, Witmer, Sweeney, and Myers, 1994; the SWBS, the Spiritual Well-Being Scale, Ellison, 1994. When a more specific spiritual/religious assessment seems desirable, structured interview forms and instruments are available for obtaining a spiritual/religious case history (Faiver & O'Brien, 1993).

The counselor, in order to facilitate an understanding of the client's religious and/or spiritual issues that are relevant to the resolution of the concerns that the client brings to counseling, may administer and interpret appropriate assessment instruments. Formal and/or informal assessment results can be used for the purpose of assisting a client's decision making, self-exploration, understanding, and action planning (Kelly, 1995). In conducting an informal assessment, counselors would gather pertinent information that would assist them in understanding their client's spiritual worldview and also help them to decide if their client's spiritual and religious background is relevant to their expressed concerns and issues.

Chandler et al. (1992) offer three ways to assess the client's spiritual wellness. First of all, the counselor views the client in terms of that individual's current personal development (age and maturation level) and degree of health within that stage of development (including the level of functioning in each of the dimensions of wellness—(emotional, occupational, physical, intellectual, and social). Secondly, determine the client's spiritual wellness in relation to spiritual repression versus spiritual preoccupation. Thirdly, be aware of the client's level of spiritual development.

The following questions may be used in the intake interview to help determine the client's belief system (Burke & Miranti, 1998):

When you want to feel strength, where do you go, or whom do you see?

When you want to feel comfort, where do you go, or whom do you see?

How would you describe what gives meaning to your life?

What one goal do you have that is most important to you right now?

The following global assessment question, formulated by Richards and Bergin (1997) are suggestions that may help counselors understand the worldview and belief systems of their clients:

What is the client's metaphysical worldview (e.g., Western, Eastern, Naturalistic-Atheistic, Naturalistic-Agnostic)?

What was the client's childhood religious affiliation and experiences?

What is the client's current religious affiliation, if any, and level of devoutness?

Does the client believe his or her spiritual beliefs and lifestyle are contributing to the problems and concerns in any way?

Does the client have any religious and spiritual concerns/needs?

Is the client willing to explore his or her religious and spiritual issues?

Does the client perceive that his or her religious and spiritual beliefs are a potential source of strength and assistance?

Shafranske and Malony (1996) recommend that training programs should provide direct clinical training and supervision that includes assessment of spirituality and religion as variables in mental wellness and exposure to implicit and explicit models for addressing these issues in the counseling process. By remaining open to the religious and spiritual concerns of clients, the counselor can facilitate the exploration of these issues if presented by the client.

There are several assessment approaches. One such approach is the Spiritual Genogram (Frame, 2000), which is a map of several generations of a family including family structure and composition, symbols depicting members of the family, and biological and legal relationships to one another. The purpose is to discover patterns of behaviors, beliefs, and practices that may be affecting clients' religious/spiritual issues.

Frame (2003) in her book entitled *Integrating Religion and Spirituality into Counseling* describes several instruments that have been developed to measure a variety of aspects of spirituality and spiritual well-being. Also included are instruments used to assess harmful or pathological aspects of religion and spirituality. Ingersoll (1995) constructed and validated the *Spiritual Wellness Inventory*, which yields information regarding the client's religious and spiritual issues.

Characteristics of Healthy Spiritual Development

As mentioned previously, some assessment instruments offer aspects of a healthy spirituality. The Center for Human Development at the University of Notre Dame offers the following criteria for a healthy spirituality (Helmeniak, 1987, pp. 10–11):

1. A Developing Self-Concept—which includes an accurate self-perception and loving self-acceptance. Without this, paradoxically, surrender of the self to radical conversion is probably impossible.
2. A Responsible Self-Awareness—an ability to be present to one's needs, feelings, and emotions which may signal the movement of the spirit within.
3. A Sense of Autonomy or Inner-Directedness—a basic trust in the validity of one's own experience and values which can allow one to leave behind a conventional viewpoint and move toward a personally integrated faith.
4. An Appreciation of Genuine Authority—which mediates social interactions and balances individual experience with traditional norms.
5. A Principled Morality—based on self-chosen but universally valid principles ultimately reducible to one: Love. From this vantage point, laws derive their validity or are judged wanting.
6. A Person Orientation—in which one places highest priority on relating to another person as a "Thou" rather than an "It."
7. A Holistic View of Development—in which physical, emotional, and intellectual development is seen as intrinsically related to spiritual development.
8. A Present Centeredness—which allows one to live and encounter the richness and depth of reality as revealed in the sacrament of the present moment.
9. An Openness to the Transcendent—a readiness to find mystical experience in the reality of self, others, and the world.

This list might be compared to that of Clinebell (1992) who says that high-level wellness in our spiritual life comes from satisfying seven basic spiritual needs.

1. We all need to experience regularly the healing, empowering love of God.
2. We all need to experience renewing times of transcendence regularly.
3. We all need vital beliefs that give some sense of meaning and hope to our lives in the midst of our losses, tragedies, and failures.
4. All of us need to have values, priorities, and life commitments center in integrity, justice, and love, to guide us into personally and socially responsible living.
5. All of us need to discover and develop the inner wisdom, creativity, and love of our spiritual self.

6. All of us need a deepening awareness of our oneness with other people and with the natural world.

7. We all need spiritual resources to heal the painful wounds of grief, guilt, resentment, unforgiveness, and self-rejection. We also have a need for spiritual resources to deepen our feelings of trust, self-esteem, hope, joy, and love of life.

Implications for Counselors

Bergin and Jensen (1990) estimated that two-thirds of Americans believe that religious beliefs are important and that 85 percent of marriage and family counselors "try hard" to live according to their religious beliefs. Myers and Truluck (1998) conducted a similar survey of counselors and found that 57 percent reported participating in organized religious practices weekly and 63 percent reported engaging in individual religious practices daily. Thus, there is little doubt that the issue of God, religion, values, and spirituality will be either implicit or explicit in the lives of those participating in a counseling session. Thus, it is important that the counselor be aware of her or his background and present position regarding these issues.

Fukuyama and Sevig (1997) developed a course on counseling and spirituality for counselor training. The following questions were developed for personal exploration (writing), dyad sharing, and group discussions (p. 235):

1. What are some of your earliest childhood memories of religion, of God or a transcendent power, of the sacred or holy (such as beauty or mystery)?

2. What is your religious background, that of your parents and grandparents? Construct a family tree that represents your religious heritage.

3. Who influenced your beliefs about religion and religious values, and how did they influence you? Do you know people who are spiritual? What qualities embody your concept of spirituality?

4. How have your religious beliefs and spiritual experiences changed as you have moved through life stages such as adolescence, young adulthood, midlife, and elder years?

5. In some models of spiritual growth, there is a period of darkness or a "desert experience." Have you ever experienced this and if so, how was that a part of the journey?

6. Where and when were there other turning points on your journey, such as peak experiences, crises, and transitions that influenced your religious beliefs or spiritual growth?

7. Where are you now on the journey? Are you active in an organized religion? How does religion help or restrict your spirituality? What is your sense of spiritual or religious community like?

8. What has been frightening or confusing to you about spirituality? What has been joyful and energizing?

9. Recall a situation, event, or moment that you felt was spiritual and describe it.

Additional questions for the counselor to ask:

What is my own concept of spirituality and the worldview that it represents?

Where am I in my own spiritual development?

What might be my "growing edges" in challenging myself toward further spiritual growth?

Where am I spiritually in the present?

Are there obstacles which might impair my ability to help another in his or her spiritual development?

RESEARCH FINDINGS: IMPLICATIONS FOR TRAINING

A study conducted by Carlson et al. (2002) of family counselors' beliefs about the appropriateness of addressing religious and spiritual issues in counseling found that 95 percent of the respondents considered themselves to be a spiritual person; 94 percent indicated that spirituality was an important aspect of their personal lives; and 96 percent believed that there is a relationship between spiritual health and mental health. The study by Hickson et al. (2000) indicated that counselors recognized the importance of being aware of their own spiritual beliefs in the counseling process. This would necessitate counselor awareness and the development of skills needed to address spiritual issues with clients.

Affirming spirituality as an essential component of the counseling process necessitates continued research regarding the spiritual experiences of our clients across cultures. Present research involves the constructs of spirituality, spiritual well-being, spiritual wellness, religiosity, and transpersonal experiences.

The recent attention to diversity issues has underscored the need for inclusion of the spiritual perspective. Myers and Truluck (1998) replicated a study conducted by Jensen and Bergin (1988) using a sample of professional counselors. They posed two research questions: (1) Are professional counselors' perceptions of the relation of religion to mental health the same as those of other mental health professionals? (2) Are professional counselors' perceptions of the role of values in counseling the same as those of other mental health professionals?

The results of the Myers and Truluck (1998) replication study clearly indicated the need for counselor education programs to include the spiritual and religious dimension of counseling and to train counselors in the various models, techniques, and theoretical approaches in order to effectively address these dimensions. The researchers reported that counselors in fact did differ from other mental health providers in every area measured. In every instance, including both the perceptions of counselors regarding the importance of religious beliefs and values in their own lives and the perceived importance of those values in guiding the process of counseling with clients, professional counselors rated the items as being more important than did the other mental health providers (Myers & Truluck, 1998). The study concludes that clients with spiritual needs may have a greater chance of those needs being met if they choose a professional counselor rather than another mental health professional for their spiritual concerns.

According to Ingersoll (1994), spiritual wellness is a reflection of spiritual health. A study was conducted by Ingersoll (1998) to investigate the common dimensions of spiritual wellness agreed on by leaders from eleven spiritual traditions. This study was a part of a larger project to create a cross-traditional spiritual wellness inventory. The dimensions were developed with the help of a cross-cultural panel and they point toward universals in the spiritual experience that go beyond particular religious beliefs. The author concludes that perhaps the best use of such an inventory of spiritual dimensions is for individuals to assess their own spiritual state and not that of others. The dimensions can also be used in courses in counselor education that specifically address diversity issues because spiritual tradition is one variable of diversity (Ingersoll, 1998).

There is support in the literature for inclusion of the spiritual and religious dimensions in training programs and the development of competencies to address these dimensions (Pate & High, 1995; Richards & Bergin, 1997; Souza, 2002). If counselor educators fail to address these issues in a way that encourages counselors in training to explore their own belief systems, they will miss an opportunity to become aware of how individual belief systems might influence their work with clients, and how possible transference and counter transferences issues can surface.

Implications for Practice

Counselors, in order to effectively facilitate life-enhancing change, must be equipped with skills and competencies necessary to address the spiritual and religious needs of their clients. Issues of religion and spirituality are such an individual reality, it is important that the counselor remain open to the various components both of religious and spiritual beliefs. For example, the beliefs of people and religious groups would have a perspective on such issues as (a) the experience and description of God or a higher power; (b) the rituals; (c) death and afterlife; (d) purpose in life (including motivation to live a certain lifestyle); (e) roles of men and women; (f) morality; (g) the world of the spirit; and (h) prayer. One can see that each of these dimensions can have cognition, emotional, attitudinal, and behavioral consequences, affecting the approach and outcome of counseling.

Another sensitivity to the culturally diverse component is an appreciation of the varieties of religious and spiritual groups. Depending on the counselor's locale the counselor may experience such diversities as Jewish, Protestant sects, Catholicism, Hinduism, Muslim, and Buddhist traditions. Each will have it own unique approaches to the life issues mentioned earlier. The counselor must also take care not to presume that the clients maintain certain religious or spiritual practices which may dominate certain cultures. This would be, for example, presuming that all Indians are Hindus or all Hispanics are Catholic.

What follows is a listing of suggestions and recommendations by noted contributors in the field:

1. Affirm the importance of the client's spirituality in his/her life when it is expressed either directly or indirectly. A multicultural perspective respects religious and spiritual concerns as an important aspect of the client's culture (Pate & Bondi, 1992). What words might be used to affirm the client?

2. Invite exploration of spiritual issues with non-threatening questions, for example, In what ways does your faith or spirituality play a role in what you are going through right now? Note the difference between exploration and explanation in that the goal is to assist clients in understanding their own spirituality rather than attempting to educate them in religious beliefs or practices.

3. Attempt to enter the client's worldview by adopting his/her vocabulary and imagery without adopting his/her worldview. This will increase rapport for a working therapeutic alliance. Mattson (1994) points out that many religions are caught up in the concept of sin and judgment. He urges the counselor to be prepared to help them understand the concepts of grace and forgiveness as well. Borysenko (1990) presents some excellent distinctions between healthy and unhealthy guilt.

4. Exploration of spiritual issues may be facilitated by accepted counseling techniques such as meditation, guided imagery, mindfulness exercises, journaling, bibliotherapy, relaxation techniques, and other approaches from theories which may be tailored to a spiritual orientation (e.g., gestalt). These particular techniques access the innate spiritual dimension of the person. Grimm (1994) suggested that other spiritually related techniques might include intrapsychic techniques (prayer, scripture study, rituals), as well as family and social support methods (e.g., group support, communication, mutual participation, communal spiritual experience, group identification).

5. Be open to referring to or consulting with religious figures in the client's life.

6. Be open to referring to another counselor if necessary.

SUMMARY

For many average people who seek the help of counselors, spirituality and religion are significant aspects of their lives. When counselors, for whatever reason, fail to address or simply ignore a client's religious tradition or spiritual beliefs, they could inaccurately conceptualize the presenting problem, jeopardize the forming of an effective therapeutic relationship, and overlook appropriate intervention strategies in the process. A knowledgeable sensitivity to these aspects of the clients' lives and level of development builds on the respectful understanding that counselors are expected to show for clients' diversity.

The effective inclusion of spirituality and/or religion in the counseling curriculum will require counselor educators and students to question their own biases and prejudices and get in touch with their own spirituality—an expectation already common to diversity and multicultural courses.

Individuals will realize their full potential when all aspects of development are addressed. This holistic, wellness approach will enable the client to achieve balance and harmony in his/her life. The integration of religious and spiritual issues in the counseling process and the positive outcomes of a client's physical, emotional, psychological, and spiritual well-being far outweigh any barriers or possible negative consequences. Suggestions, recommendations, case studies, and approaches are included as a catalyst for exploring ways to incorporate spirituality into the counseling process.

CHAPTER ELEVEN

CREATIVE APPROACHES TO COUNSELING

ANN VERNON, PH.D.
University of Northern Iowa

INTRODUCTION

Effective counseling establishes a therapeutic relationship to help clients think, feel, and behave in more self-enhancing ways. This relationship enables clients to work through difficulties (Nugent, 2000). As Caple (1985) noted, "Clients come to counseling seeking a different potentiality, a way to find something better than they presently know" (p. 173). In effect, this occurs when the counselor helps clients develop more options for their lives and encourages them to accept more responsibility for their choices and actions (Kottler, 2004). Through counseling, clients become more aware, conceptualize their experiences differently, and see themselves and their ways of being more constructively. Wagner (2003) stressed that counselors should not only focus on eliminating problems, but also look for opportunities to facilitate optimal development. According to Thompson, Rudolph, and Henderson (2004), counseling is "a process in which people learn how to help themselves and, in effect, become their own counselors" (p. 22). This implies that the counselor won't "fix it" so that the client will feel and act better, but rather that a mutual "working together" process can help the client overcome the dysfunctional aspects that interfere with her or his life.

Counseling has basically been a mental arena, characterized by a predominately verbal orientation, according to Dunn and Griggs (1995). In their opinion, this verbal orientation is very limiting, especially for children and adolescents whose developmental needs are different and who may not be verbally proficient. Nickerson and O'Laughlin (1982) advocated action therapies that use nonverbal relationship modes as an alternative to the traditional verbal approaches. They stressed the importance of developing "a more relevant and effective means of helping people cope with psychological problems and life stresses" (p. 5). Gladding (1995) concurred with this viewpoint, stating that verbal techniques alone are not sufficient for reluctant or nonverbal clients. Gladding (1998) emphasized that effective counselors "are aware of the multidimensional nature of the profession and are able to work with a variety of populations by using appropriate interventions" (preface). In Gladding's opinion, one of the most effective approaches is to use the creative arts.

For many clients who seem relatively unaffected by the counseling process, standard techniques alone are inadequate. These clients may benefit more from approaches that combine theory and practice in more flexible, creative ways, while at the same time focusing on the unique as well as universal qualities of clients (Gladding, 1995). This is especially pertinent for children and adolescents, as well as clients from diverse cultural groups, according to Dunn and Griggs (1995).

In the 1980s, information about counseling for individual learning styles began to appear in the literature and seems to support Nickerson and O'Laughlin's (1982) contention that verbal approaches to counseling are often ineffective (Griggs, 1983, 1985; Griggs, Price, Kopel, & Swaine, 1984). Myrick (1997) concurred, noting that if counselors do not take learning styles into account, they may experience less success with some clients. He stressed that counselors must be "flexible, adaptive, and learn how to use different counseling approaches" (p. 111).

The term learning style refers to the way a person perceives and responds to the learning environment. Milgram, Dunn, and Price (1993) cited the following learning style elements: environmental stimuli such as light, sound, and temperature; emotional stimuli such as structure, persistence, motivation, and responsibility; sociologic stimuli such as peers, adults, self, and group; physical stimuli such as auditory, visual, tactual, kinesthetic, and time of day; and psychological stimuli such as cerebral dominance and global, analytic, impulsive, and reflective stimuli.

The learning style approach assumes that individuals have unique learning patterns that should be accommodated in the counseling process. If this is not done, some clients may feel inundated with words, since counseling is primarily a talking process, and feel overwhelmed, insecure, or lost (Myrick, 1997). Furthermore, the client may resist (Griggs, 1985). Dunn and Griggs (1995) emphasized that this resistance is due in part to the "mismatch between the counseling interventions, strategies, and techniques used by the counselor and the learning-style preferences of the counselee" (p. 29). Griggs (1985) identified counseling techniques in addition to verbal interaction that are compatible with different learning styles: art therapy, imagery, bibliotherapy, psychodrama, mime, and play techniques. Gladding (1992, 1998) cited the visual arts, writing, music, play, and literature as creative approaches that can be adapted to fit a variety of client needs and populations. All of these would be considered effective, action-oriented, creative therapies according to Nickerson and O'Laughlin (1982).

This chapter describes a variety of creative, specialized counseling approaches that may be used either as a complement to a predominately verbal orientation with a client, or as the primary therapeutic method. These approaches may be used with clients of all ages and in a variety of settings such as schools, hospitals, or mental health centers. As Nickerson and O'Laughlin (1982) noted, these therapies are relevant for nonverbal clients, and for anyone who "needs to explore and to integrate their behavior in a comprehensive and effective fashion" (p. 7). Gladding (1995) agreed with Nickerson and O'Laughlin, noting that creative approaches help clients as well as counselors see things from a different, more positive, perspective. According to Gladding, "Clients from all backgrounds can benefit from using a creativity approach regardless of whether the form is fixed, such as with some creative exercises, or spontaneous" (p. 4).

ART

Art therapy, derived from art and psychology, literally means using art in a therapeutic way (Jennings & Minde, 1993). Lev-Wiesel and Daphna-Tekoha (2000) noted that art therapy techniques allow the counselor to examine the client's inner language, which leads to increased insight, and Kwiakowska (2001) stressed that art facilitates expression and helps clients perceive themselves more clearly. Although art has been used since the beginning of history as a means of communication and healing, the use of art therapy, particularly with children, has increased during the past two decades (Dufrene, 1994; Jennings & Minde, 1993; Malchiodi, 1997). Vondracek and Corneal (1995) defined art therapy as "the use of art in a therapeutic setting to foster an individual's psychological growth and well-being" (p. 294). These authors referred to art within the therapeutic context as a means of bringing subconscious material into awareness, which in turn leads to perception and interpretation.

A distinction is made between using art techniques in counseling as opposed to pure art therapy, which focuses more on artistic eloquence as opposed to creating art and looking at the symbolism (Kramer, 1998). Typically, counselors focus on the latter. Gladding (1998) emphasized that art is effective because it is usually perceived as nonthreatening. One of the advantages of using art in therapy is that it is a way for clients to articulate thoughts and express experiences that they cannot put into words (Silver, 2001).

Although the majority of research on art therapy has focused on making the unconscious material explicit, art therapy can also be used to increase understanding of conscious material. For example, a client can be encouraged to express his or her anger resulting from a loss in a drawing, and the client and therapist can discuss what the drawing symbolizes and the feelings it evoked.

Rubin (1988) noted that "art, like talk, is simply a way of getting to know each other, another mode of communication" (p. 181). Cited as being particularly effective with reluctant, nonverbal clients, Bush (1997) stated that painting and drawing can facilitate growth and change as the counselor helps the client focus on symbolic areas of pain and growth in an accepting, understanding manner. Gladding (1998) indicated that art provides an emotional outlet for people who have difficulty expressing their needs, feelings, and desires and is an effective way to help them begin to understand their confusion. Catharsis and growth, as well as assessment, are the three major purposes of art, noted Brems (2002).

According to Vondracek and Corneal (1995), counselors use art in therapy with children, adolescents, adults, and the elderly. Silver (2001) described using art with various client populations such as abused, emotionally disturbed, hearing-impaired, or brain-injured individuals. Art therapy is used in a variety of settings, such as schools, prisons, rehabilitation centers, hospitals, and clinics. It is now not only being used to work with people who have problems (Landgarten & Lubbers, 1991), but also it is more prevalent in helping "normal" clients, where the emphasis is on growth and self-development (Vondracek & Corneal, 1995). Art also transcends cultural boundaries, so it is especially effective with diverse populations (Gladding, 1995).

The Process

Many art forms can be used to help clients gain self-awareness and work through emotional conflicts: painting, sculpting, modeling with clay, photography, drawing, printing/designing, collages, or graphic art. Gladding (1992, 1998) identified using already existing artwork as a means of introducing images that facilitate communication and understanding. In addition, Gladding (1992, 1998) discussed the use of body outlines and serial drawing as visual art forms that can be used with clients to help uncover troublesome issues.

According to Kenny (1987), the goal is communication between the helper and the client rather than mastery of art form or content. In the process, the client is encouraged to express feelings symbolically through an art form. As Allan (1982) noted, the counselor's role is basically that of a listener who responds to the client and allows him or her time and space to initiate interaction. After a given interval, the counselor might invite the client to share by issuing a simple invitation such as "Would you like to tell me what's happening in your picture?" If working with a more seriously disturbed client with whom art media is used in each session, Allan indicated that the counselor's role may change. After several sessions, the counselor might become more active by relating the art to what is occurring in real life as well as emphasizing positive aspects that indicate growth.

Art is an effective means of initiating contact with a client, as illustrated in the following example. Amanda, a third-grader, was referred by her teacher because she seemed preoccupied and unhappy. In the initial meeting, the counselor noted that Amanda seemed quite anxious and hesitant. To establish rapport and facilitate expression, the counselor put some modeling clay on the table and invited Amanda to play with it. At first Amanda just rolled the clay around without molding it. The counselor made no comment, but simply communicated an attitude of acceptance. Presently, Amanda began to shape the clay into a bridge. Next she made a car and attached small clay dots to the car. As she placed the car on the bridge, the bridge collapsed. At this point the counselor asked Amanda if she would like to tell her about what was happening. Amanda explained that the dots were people—her family. The counselor reflected that something must have happened to the family in the car, and Amanda began to talk about how her family had had an accident because her Dad and Mom were drunk. She shared her feelings of fright and how she took care of her brothers and sister after the accident. As she talked, she began to roll the clay and pound it, tears streaming down her cheeks. As the counselor supported her, it became apparent that the feelings Amanda needed to express would be more readily verbalized in future sessions as the counselor began to help Amanda deal with her painful situation.

Art media can be used in the manner previously illustrated, or in a more directed manner to facilitate a process. For example, clients could be instructed to draw their family, paint their life story or their dreams, or illustrate a book that describes a situation with which they are dealing. They could be asked to sketch and color themselves in moods that they experienced recently, or be invited to draw a picture representing something that they need in their life. Designing a T-shirt, a banner, or a bumper sticker with a motto they feel describes them are good ways to encourage personal growth and sharing, particularly with resistant adolescent clients.

Photography can also be used effectively to elicit feelings and create awareness. Amerikaner, Schauble, and Ziller (1982) outlined a method of using twelve client-created photographs describing how the client sees self to stimulate self-awareness. Gladding (1992, 1998) described using old photographs to help the elderly participate in a life review process, and Vernon (1993) explained how photographs were used with an adolescent to help her more realistically assess experiences with her peers. Photographs can also help clients assess what is blocking their personal effectiveness, as in the case of Tim.

Tim, a 35-year-old male, referred himself for counseling because he felt overwhelmed at work and under extreme stress. In the initial session, Tim described feeling overwhelmed by his obligations and commitments at work, home, and in the community. In the next session, the counselor handed Tim a Polaroid camera and asked him to take pictures of things, people, and places that were important to him and that he, perhaps at one time, had enjoyed. She also asked him to take pictures of things, places, or people that he thought were contributing to the stress and the feeling of being overwhelmed. He was instructed to put these pictures into two separate envelopes—one for the things that were important to him, and the other for the factors that he thought were contributing to the stress.

The following week, Tim returned with his pictures, which served as a springboard for a discussion about the events in his life that were taking precedence over the things that were important to him, and about his feelings of "have to" versus "want to." Tim was asked to go through his envelope of pictures that created stress and select some that he could eliminate from his life. By actually being able to "see" what his stressors were, Tim found it easier to identify what he could more readily eliminate. Then he and the counselor worked on strategies for dealing with the other sources of stress.

Implementation Considerations

In employing art, Rubin (1988) cautioned that experience and skill are necessary if working at a sophisticated level, but that specific training in art is not essential with simple expressive work and minimal interpretation. Brems (2002) emphasized that there are various approaches to the use of art and that it can be used exclusively or in combination with other strategies.

Rubin (1988) also noted that therapeutic work through art may be one way for clients to feel in charge when other parts of their life are overwhelming. As a trusting relationship is established, the counselor invites the client to share the meaning from his or her perspective. In essence, the counselor observes the client's work as it develops, attends to the nonverbal and verbal communication offered, and responds to clarify.

Kenny (1987) identified the following factors that may help the counselor understand clients' artwork by considering the larger context of their world:

1. In Western culture, dark colors or heavy shading generally indicate sadness, depression, or anger; excessive use of white may indicate emotional rigidity.
2. Small figures, particularly of self, may indicate insecurity, anxiety, or low self-esteem.
3. Sadness, violence, aggression, or other emotional disturbance are often represented with dark images, storms, accidents, fighting, or murder.
4. Texture of materials can provide insight: aggressive, angry clients might select bold or tough materials, whereas a nonassertive client might choose watercolors or something softer.
5. Clients with emotional disturbances tend to depict figures more grotesquely, stiff and rigid, or unintegrated, with some body parts being exaggerated. Excessive shading may indicate high anxiety.

The basic function of art therapy is to facilitate emotional expression from clients who do not communicate well verbally and to execute the counseling process more effectively through visual representation. Art therapy can be used to reduce resistance and put the client at ease during an initial session, can be used strategically in later sessions to help the client clarify and gain awareness, or can be used over a period of several sessions as the main vehicle to work through painful issues. Brems (2002) added that it is an effective means of introducing and discussing difficult topics or affects. Gladding (1992) emphasized that art helps awaken clients to "a new sense of self and deeper understanding of their intra- and interpersonal relationships" (p. 66). Bush (1997) noted that as clients "liken themselves to artists who can repaint canvases they do not like after the paint is dry, they can, in effect, learn to paint over their problems to attain new solutions" (p. 4).

Art Therapy: An Introduction (Rubin, 1998) and *Windows to Our Children* (Oaklander, 1988) are excellent resources for the professional interested in learning more about using art in a counseling relationship.

IMAGERY

The use of imagery, described as visualization or seeing with the mind's eye (Gladding, 1992, 1998) and as the "language of the unconscious mind" (Bourne, 1995, p. 241) has increased over the years, especially in career counseling, life planning, and personal counseling (Skovholt, Morgan, & Negron-Cunningham, 1989), as well as with children and adolescents (Plummer, 1999). According to Skovholt et al. (1989), imagery "allows the client and counselor to bring into awareness unconscious material that is already influencing choices . . . and allows the client to try on alternative roles" (p. 287). Witmer and Young (1987) noted that imagery facilitates awareness of personal values, emotions, goals, conflicts, and spiritual desires. Gladding (1992) emphasized that imagery is a "universal and natural modality for helping people engender change" (p. 42).

There is good rationale for using imagery in counseling. First of all, many clients already use imagery to help them learn new material or remember things (Gladding, 1992). Secondly, imagery can help people change behavior. Plummer (1999) noted that because the body cannot distinguish between a vivid mental experience and an actual physical experience, clients who use imagery may actually perform better. The use of imagery also teaches clients how to stimulate creativity and develop cognitive flexibility. In addition, because many client problems are connected to images of self and others, using imagery to change perspectives is helpful. Finally, imagery promotes a holistic approach (Gladding, 1992, 1998) and is especially effective with Native Americans, according to Dunn and Griggs (1995).

Although free daydreams are often cited as one form of imagery, this section describes the use of guided imagery and concrete images to help a client reconceptualize events and change behavior.

Guided Imagery

Guided imagery is a structured, directed activity designed to increase artistic expression, personal awareness, and concentration (Myrick & Myrick, 1993). In guided imagery, the counselor orchestrates a scenario for the client that consists of stimulus words or sounds to serve as a catalyst for creating a mental picture (Myrick & Myrick, 1993). Sometimes called guided fantasy, the process involves inducing relaxation, the actual fantasy, and processing the fantasy (Skovholt et al., 1989). The use of relaxation is important because it helps bridge the gap between prior activities and the imagery experience to move the client's focus from external to internal.

Myrick and Myrick (1993) identified the following guidelines when using guided imagery:

1. Create a scripted story. This is particularly helpful because it allows the counselor to select words that connote vivid textures and other senses.
2. Introduce the concept of guided imagery, and instruct the client to sit or lie in a relaxed position, focusing on breathing.
3. Read the script slowly, using a quiet and soothing voice to help create vivid images.
4. Bring closure to the experience by stopping at a pleasant place accompanied by positive feelings. Inform the client that you are getting ready to stop, and as you count to three slowly, have the client open her or his eyes and stretch.
5. Invite the client to discuss the experience, focusing on positive aspects of the activity as well as his or her experiences with obstacles and how he or she overcame them.

The following script was used with a middle-aged woman who suffered from anxiety and procrastinated about completing housework and other chores. After being instructed to relax by imagining a peaceful scene and engaging in deep breathing to release tension, Jana was invited to involve herself in this imagery experience.

> *Setting:* Imagine that it is next Monday. (pause) You are waking up in the morning. What time is it? (pause) You get up and eat breakfast. Who is there? (pause) You finish breakfast. You don't have to leave for work until noon. What needs to be done? What do you do first? (pause) How do you see yourself doing this task, and how long does it take? Is anyone helping you? If not, how are you feeling about that? (pause) You finish this activity. What do you do now? (pause) It is now time to get ready to leave for work. (pause)
>
> *Work:* You are now at work. Are you working alone, or are you interacting with others? What tasks are you doing? Are you enjoying them? (pause)
>
> *Home:* You have left work and are home again. Are you alone? (pause) If not, who is there? Do you interact with them? (pause) It is time to get dinner. Do you do this alone, or does anyone help you? (pause) Now it is after dinner. What do you do? Who is with you? (pause) Now it is time for bed. Tomorrow you will not work and will be at home all day. What will you do? How will you do it? (pause)
>
> *End:* You may open your eyes, and we will discuss your experience.

In processing the imagery exercise, Jana said that it was not difficult to see what needed to be done, but it was hard to visualize what she would do first. Once she did select a task, it wasn't too difficult to see herself taking the necessary steps to complete it. She saw herself alone in doing the housework and resented that. She described the work portion of her day, where she had no trouble completing necessary tasks, as basically enjoyable.

In reflecting on the exercise, it seemed helpful for Jana to list the chores that needed to be done each day so she wouldn't become anxious about deciding what to do. It was also appropriate to begin teaching her some assertiveness skills so that she could negotiate for equity with the housework. The guided imagery effectively helped the counselor and client clarify issues and pinpoint target areas for goal setting and skill development.

Guided imagery has also been used successfully in career counseling where clients are asked to image "A Day in the Future"; "The Opposite Sex," growing up as the opposite sex and holding a job usually held by the opposite sex; or "Mid-Career Change or Retirement," focusing on shifting from the present career focus (Skovholt et al., 1989). Omizo, Omizo, and Kitaoka (1998) suggested using guided imagery with children to help clarify problems, reduce anxiety, enhance self-concept, and make behavioral changes. Bourne (1995) described its usefulness with athletes to achieve peak performance and as a part of a treatment program for various diseases.

Use of Concrete Images

Images can also be used therapeutically in isolation to help stimulate thinking that can lead to more productive behavior. When using images this way, the counselor tries to relate the image to something familiar to the client or something that conveys a type of metaphor, as in the following example.

Eighteen-year-old Nat was in counseling for depression. Irrational beliefs in the form of exaggerations, overgeneralizations, and awfulizations contributed to his depression. In the session when the image was introduced, Nat was discussing an incident with his girlfriend. He assumed that because she didn't call him every day, she didn't care about him. He said he couldn't stand it if she found someone else.

In previous sessions, the counselor had helped Nat dispute these irrational beliefs, but they continued to be quite prevalent. As Nat and the counselor were working on these irrational beliefs in the present session, the counselor glanced out the window and noticed a bug zapper. She called it to Nat's attention and asked him to watch the zapper and describe how it operated. The counselor explained to Nat that he could image that his head was a zapper, too—when he started to think irrationally, he should visualize these irrational thoughts being deflected, just like the bugs were when they hit the zapper. Although this may seem simplistic, it helped Nat stop the irrational thinking more effectively because he could quickly recall the bug zapper image and use this to trigger his disputations before he felt the negative effects of the irrational beliefs.

In listening carefully to the client's problem, it is not difficult to think of helpful images. Children who have difficulty controlling impulsive behavior might be asked, when they start to feel out of control, to visualize a stop sign. Pairing the visualization with self-statements such as "I don't have to hit—I can walk away" increases the effectiveness of the image. A child who is reluctant to go to bed because she or he is afraid of monsters can visualize herself or himself in a scary Halloween costume, frightening away any monsters that might come into the room.

Gladding (1998) pointed out these benefits of imagery: it can be performed anywhere, it is an available resource that most clients already employ, it teaches clients how to use their imaginations to stimulate creative problem solving, it is a powerful type of mental practice, and it is holistic. In addition, many client problems, such as eating disorders, are connected to their images of self and others. Imagery helps clients learn about themselves, and although it might not work for everyone, it can be an extremely effective method to access information and resolve problems.

HYPNOTHERAPY

In hypnotherapy, hypnosis is used in conjunction with various forms of psychotherapy (Vondracek & Corneal, 1995). Havens and Walters (2002) stressed that in everyday life, everyone has experiences that resemble hypnosis. Consequently, professionals should utilize it in a therapeutic manner. Plummer (1999) asserted that hypnosis is an effective way to help clients become more aware of their inner experiences, to reexperience past events, and to envision new possibilities. Hypnotherapy also helps clients assume responsibility for healing themselves, noted Havens and Walters (2002). Olness and Kohen (1996) suggested that clients often feel passive and helpless over their problems, and that hypnotherapy can "teach an attitude of hope in the context of mastery" (p. 89).

Winsor (1993) cited three styles of hypnosis: directive, which is based on simple commands; Ericksonian, which relies on indirect methods such as stories, confusion techniques, and metaphors; and permissive, in which the client and hypnotherapist contract to help the client gain access to an altered state of consciousness.

Hypnosis is generally induced as part of counseling, or in conjunction with pain reduction. Havens and Walters (2002) contended that the common denominator of all problems presented in counseling is emotional pain. The presenting concern may be relationship issues, feelings of inadequacy, depression, or anxiety. In any case, the counselor's job is to help clients describe their specific pain, and counseling involves "replacing that suffering with comfort" (p. 6). Olness and Kohen (1996) cautioned against using hypnosis for "fun" (p. 95), using hypnosis if it could exaggerate existing emotional problems, or using this form of treatment if the real problem should be treated in another way.

Because hypnosis is used in conjunction with counseling, the specific procedures used in hypnotherapy depend on the theoretical framework of the counselor. Hypnotherapy is often used in conjunction with behavior therapy, eclectic therapy, and supportive therapies (Weitzenhoffer, 1989), as well as psychoanalysis (Vondracek & Corneal, 1995).

According to Olness and Kohen (1996), there are three broad categories of hypnotherapy: supportive, ego-enhancing methods; symptom-oriented methods; and dynamic, insight-oriented methods. The main goal of supportive, ego-enhancing methods is to help the client feel more capable of dealing with problems and challenges, more worthy, and better able to be in control of internal and external circumstances. This method might be particularly helpful for clients who have pervasive anxiety or who are afraid of surgery. Supportive phrases such as "I think you can get through this" are used to help the client gain control.

In the symptom-oriented method, the effort is directed at removing, changing, or alleviating physical or emotional symptoms. This method is especially useful for treating phobias, pain control, and habit control. Dynamic, insight-oriented methods are used for symptom relief and ego strengthening, but special methods are also used to help the client understand the issues that create and maintain the problem. In this method, they gain insight into and work through underlying conflicts.

The Process

There are four phases of hypnotherapy, according to Olness and Kohen (1996): the pre-induction interview, induction, hypnotherapeutic intervention, and arousal after the hypnotic state has been terminated. Wagner (2003) stressed the importance of developing a good relationship and exploring reservations about the procedure during the pre-induction interview before moving to the induction phase. During the induction phase, a variety of strategies can be used, according to Wagner: visual imagery (imagining a favorite place or activity), auditory imagery (imagining a favorite musical selection), ideomotor techniques (hand levitation), progressive relaxation, and eye fixation techniques. After the induction, the counselor proceeds to the intervention stage, using developmentally appropriate suggestions to facilitate symptom reduction. Kohen (1997) recommended having clients describe their experience when they are no longer in the trancelike state.

Cautions and Applications

Critics have raised questions about the use of posthypnotic suggestions and other hypnotic practices because they represent undue influence over the client's behavior or encourage antisocial behavior. Weitzenhoffer (1989) noted that under hypnosis, a client's defenses may be reduced before he or she is ready to deal with the repressed material. This author stressed the importance of proper training for practitioners who use hypnotherapy. When used appropriately, hypnotherapy has been used successfully with weight control, anxiety disorders, sexual dysfunction, eating disorders, obsessive compulsive disorders, substance abuse disorders, and smoking cessation (Sapp, 2000). It has also been used to treat common childhood problems such as nail biting, enuresis, encopresis, phobias, sleep disorders, and thumb sucking (LaBaw & LaBaw, 1990). Winsor (1993) stated that hypnosis has regained scientific credibility in the past fifty years and is used to treat a growing number of medical as well as psychological problems.

MUSIC

Music, which has played an important role in healing and nurturing for centuries, is another effective counseling approach to use with a variety of populations (Horden, 2000; Newcomb, 1994; Wigram, Pedersen, & Bonde, 2002). Gladding (1992) described music as a "therapeutic ally to the verbal approaches to counseling" (p. 14) and noted that music is a creative experience that can be used to initiate other counseling processes. Because most clients enjoy singing, dancing, or listening to music, this can be an ideal approach for clients who have difficulty expressing themselves verbally (Newcomb, 1994). It is important to distinguish between music therapy, which Peters (2000) described as "a planned, goal-directed process of interaction and intervention, based on assessment and evaluation of individual clients' specific needs, strengths, and weaknesses, in which music or music-based experiences are specifically prescribed to be used by specially trained personnel to influence positive changes in an individual's condition, skills, thoughts, feelings, or behaviors" (p. 2) and using music techniques in counseling. Gladding (1998) stated that music therapy is more direct and implemented by therapists who are specialists in music and human behavior.

Music has been used in individual as well as group settings to promote closeness within families (Miller, 1991), encourage healing (Clarkson, 1994) and wellness (Peters, 2000), reduce depression and increase self-esteem (Hendricks, 2000), and develop interpersonal relationship skills and a sense of purpose (Maas, 1982). Music has also been used successfully with the mentally challenged, institutionalized elderly, emotionally disturbed, sensory impaired clients, and with depressed clients in a hospital setting (Davis, Gfeller, & Thaut, 1999), as well as with physically and/or developmentally delayed clients (Wigram et al., 2002), and with behaviorally disturbed or socially maladjusted children and adolescents (Peters, 2000). Maranto (1993) recommended using music with the elderly and in treating stress disorders. Davis et al. (1999) stressed the importance of music therapy in treating individuals with psychological disorders, delinquent behavior, or drug addiction. Gladding (1992, 1998) discussed the effectiveness of music with children, adolescents, families and couples, and clients with chronic illnesses.

Music is a catalyst for self-expression and can result in a number of therapeutic changes, including heightened attention and concentration; stimulation and expression of feelings; and insight into one's thinking, feeling, and behavior (Thaut, 1990). It can be used to alleviate burnout (Peters, 2000), and plays an important role in preventive care and health maintenance (Guzzetta, 1991). Gladding (1998) noted that music is a versatile tool that can reduce anxiety, elicit memories, communicate feelings, develop rapport, and intensify or create moods. Music is energizing and also has a calming effect.

Although music can be used as the primary method of treatment, it can also be incorporated into the counseling experience to facilitate the process more effectively. Or music may be used to introduce or convey messages in classroom guidance sessions and to clarify issues as a "homework" assignment. Song lyrics or CDs are perhaps the most accessible form of music, but for improvisation purposes, a guitar, drum, shakers, xylophone, or keyboard are useful.

Applications

Music can effectively establish rapport, particularly with teenagers, who are often not self-referred. Having the radio softly tuned into a popular rock station when the client walks into the office can help facilitate communication and relaxation. Generally, it is best left to the client to initiate conversation about the music, but if she or he doesn't, the counselor might comment on the song, inquire whether or not the client likes to listen to music, and then ease into the traditional get acquainted phase of the session. After a first session, one teenager commented to me that he was surprised to hear the music and that it didn't make it seem like he was "going to a shrink." This helped establish trust by communicating to the client that the counselor had some understanding of where he was coming from.

To help clients get more in touch with what they are thinking and feeling, music can be a useful homework assignment. The client is invited to bring in CDs or record songs that illustrate how she or he is thinking or feeling that week. Clients can also find songs that express who they are, their conflicts, or their hopes. This is effective especially for teenagers, since music is such an important part of their life experience.

This approach was used with 14-year-old Annette, a depressed, nonverbal client who asked to see a counselor because of home conflicts. Despite the fact that she had initiated the counseling, it was difficult for Annette to express what was happening at home and why she was so upset. Annette was very willing to do the music assignment and came back the following week with several tapes. The counselor invited her to play the tapes, briefly reflected on what she thought was expressed through the music, and then encouraged Annette to share how the songs related to her experiences. Annette opened up some, which facilitated verbal exchange about the problems.

After several sessions of discussing and working through some of her difficulties, Annette was again asked to bring in songs that told more about her current feelings. This time the songs were less conflictual and more hopeful. The use of music homework had helped the counselor understand Annette's pain and confusion so they could begin dealing with it. The music also provided a useful way to determine therapy progress.

Vernon (2002) suggested using music in the counseling session and described having depressed adolescents "take a sad song and make it better," by selecting a song that conveyed elements of their own depression and rewriting the lyrics to convey a more hopeful outlook. She also developed the concept of "silly songs," where children take a familiar song and write silly lyrics to help them gain new perspective. For example, this song, sung to the tune of "Three Blind Mice" helps sad children develop different coping strategies:

> Three sad kids,
> Three sad kids,
> See how they cry,
> See how they cry,
> They all got tired of crying so much,
> They ran around and made faces and such,
> You've never seen these kids laughing so much,
> The three happy kids, the three happy kids. (Vernon, 2002, p. 129)

Newcomb (1994) described using songwriting to promote increased self-awareness and facilitate emotional release. She noted that song lyrics can be used to teach children about positive interpersonal relationships and suggested pairing children up and having them draw to music as a way to increase communication and cooperation. Peters (2000) indicated that music can be used to encourage team work.

Music can also be used with children in classroom guidance lessons (Bowman, 1987). Depending on the particular theme of the lesson, the songs selected could be hard rock lyrics that communicate useful messages, or songs from albums that contain guidance-oriented material, such as "Free to Be . . . You and Me" by Marlo Thomas (1979) or "Imagination and Me" by Joe Wayman (1974), or "If You Believe In You" by Dan Conley (1994). For example, with primary children, the song "I Worry" from the Dan Conley album can introduce a lesson on how everyone worries from time to time. After playing the recording, children can be invited to sing the song, and a discussion can follow about the main points in the song. Follow-up activities include making a "worry box," to contain the worries, writing advice columns about how to handle typical worries, or incorporating bibliotherapy.

Advantages

Because music is a popular medium and readily available, counselors are only limited by their creativity to specific applications. Music can easily be integrated into counseling sessions to help clients clarify issues, communicate problems, or monitor progress. It can also be used improvisationally to encourage risk taking, spontaneity, and creative expression. Clients might be invited to experiment with various musical instruments to create a piece of music that is meaningful to them. Putting words to the music adds yet another dimension. Improvisations can also be applied effectively in a group setting to encourage cooperation and cohesiveness. If clients respond to the use of music, it provides a pleasurable way to connect with them to stimulate personal awareness and growth.

WRITING

Writing offers a powerful way for clients to clarify feelings and events and gain a perspective on their problems. Bradley and Gould (1999) noted that writing contributes to personal integration and provides a cathartic experience. For many clients, seeing something in writing has more impact than hearing it.

Writing as a therapeutic experience can take numerous forms, and the reader is encouraged to experiment with the variations later described to meet a client's needs most effectively. Obviously, for very young children writing must be more simplistic, or the counselor may choose to serve as the recorder. In addition, some clients don't find certain forms of writing helpful, and, therefore, it is important to gear the assignment to what the counselor deems will be most useful for achieving the therapeutic goals. Therapeutic writing approaches range from structured to more open-ended. Examples of each are described in the following sections.

Autobiographies

Autobiographies are generally written one of two ways: describing a particular segment or aspect of one's life, or writing a chronicle that covers all of one's life history (Bradley, Gould, & Hendricks, 2004). How the autobiography is used depends on which approach most effectively assists the client to clarify concerns, express feelings, and work toward resolution. In either case, once the client provides the written material, the counselor helps the client clarify the issues by asking questions, probing for feelings, confronting discrepancies in the writing, identifying specific concerns, and setting goals for change.

In one case in which this approach was used, the counselor determined that because the client was struggling with a relationship with her spouse, it would help her to chronicle all past significant relationships and indicate how these relationships were established, what was meaningful about them, how they were terminated, and how the client felt. Having done this assignment, the client and counselor identified some patterns in the way that the client reacted to significant others. In other instances, it might benefit the client to write a more detailed account of her or his life to see how perceptions and values change over time and to develop some perspective about the future.

Correspondence

We typically think of correspondence as appropriate when face-to-face contact isn't possible. However, correspondence can also help clarify concerns and expression in other ways. White and Murray (2002) noted that letter writing can allow for self-exploration and change. For example, clients can be encouraged to write letters to themselves to give themselves positive feedback about an accomplishment or some advice about how to handle a particular problem. Or, correspondence can occur between client and counselor to elaborate on important points that occurred during the session (White & Murray, 2002).

Clients may also find it useful to write a letter (probably unsent) to a person with whom they are in conflict to help them express thoughts and clarify issues. This approach was used with an elderly client who was angry with his sister. To help him diffuse the anger and develop some perspective about the problem, he first put his thoughts on paper and then discussed his feelings with the counselor. The counselor helped him identify the behaviors that upset him and speculate on alternative viewpoints. As a homework assignment, the client rewrote the letter. When he brought it in the following week, the concerns were more succinctly expressed and the anger was more focused. The counselor showed the client ways to express the anger more assertively and how to dispute overgeneralizations and exaggerated thinking.

In this example, the client sent his letter, and it did not affect the relationship negatively, as the first letter might have. Instead, the first letter served as a valuable catharsis and a tool for the counselor to help the client clarify the problem and develop skills to address it more effectively.

In other cases, clients may not use the counselor as an editor, but may simply write a letter as a way of dealing with feelings. After they have written the letter, they may keep it, give it to the person with whom they are in conflict, or tear it up. It is important for clients to realize that an unedited letter that generally contains a lot of anger may create more problems when received. On the other hand, such a letter can serve as a springboard for getting problems out in the open.

Orton (1997) suggested that children write letters to a deceased loved one, describing both happy and sad memories. Writing a letter to one's disease, such as cancer or Chrohn's, is an exceptionally helpful form of catharsis for clients who suffer from illnesses but often keep their feelings to themselves.

Journaling

Journaling, either structured or unstructured, is a form of expressive writing that helps clients reflect on their personal experiences and discover how much growth has taken place (Gladding, 1998). When unstructured journaling is used, the client is invited to write down thoughts and feelings about events each day. The journal can then be used as catharsis. During each session, the counselor can invite clients to share anything from the journal that they felt was significant, anything they would like help with, or items they want to talk more about. With clients who are not very verbal, the journal can illuminate issues to encourage discussion. Journaling allows for self-expression and the acceptance of feelings, relieves emotional pain, and allows clients to start dealing with emotions on a cognitive and objective manner (Mercer, 1993). By recording thoughts and feelings, both client and counselor are better able to understand the dimensions of the problem and monitor behavior.

Journaling can also be more structured, however; for example, the counselor can present the client with a list of suggestions to guide the writing. These suggestions may include identifying events that were pleasurable or upsetting, goals that were accomplished, people whom they did or did not enjoy being with, and feelings about each of these topics. Often clients initially need these guidelines but don't generally rely on the structure for long. Regardless of the form, Gladding (1998) recommended reviewing the journal material on a regular basis to increase reflection and insight.

Structured Writing

Structured writing can be in the form of open-ended sentences, questionnaires, or writing in session. Hutchins and Cole (1992) cautioned that writing does not replace counselor-client interaction, but rather serves as a starting point for discussion as well as a way to help the client generate and synthesize data.

Open-ended Sentences.   Open-ended sentences may be used to establish rapport or to determine areas of concern to address during the counseling sessions. Children or adolescents, who are often more nonverbal, may readily respond to open-ended sentences, but they can also be very effective with adults, such as in couple counseling. Open-ended sentences can provide a valuable source of information and set the client at ease with a structure to which she or he can respond. With very young children, the counselor can serve as the recorder so the child doesn't have to labor over writing.

Open-ended sentences can be general starters such as these:

"I get upset when . . ."
"If I could change something in my life, it would be . . ."
"I am happy when . . ."
"In my free time I like to . . ."

Or the starters may be geared more specifically to an area of concern the client previously expressed such as:

"I wish my spouse would . . ."
"Three things I consider important in our relationship are . . ."
"I think my spouse should . . ."
"The thing I most appreciate about my spouse is . . ."

Both of these strategies effectively collect information about thoughts and feelings that can be used as the counselor helps the client sort through concerns. In employing open-ended sentences, it is important to gear the starters to the client's developmental level. It is not necessary to have a long list of starters—the real purpose is to elicit information that can be used in the counseling session, not simply to collect data.

Stories. Writing personal stories with different endings is an effective way to help clients of all ages make a decision when it is difficult to select an alternative. In using this strategy, the client is first invited to write the personal dilemma and is then encouraged to write several different endings to the same story. Dialog between the counselor and client should focus on the advantages and disadvantages of each ending, as well as consequences. This technique facilitates problem resolution.

Writing in Session. For many clients, seeing things in print has more impact than hearing them. For this reason, clients might be encouraged to take notes during the counseling session and refer to these notes during the interim to work on aspects of the problem. In working with young children or clients who labor over writing, the counselor may opt to record key ideas that might be useful to the client.

Poetry

Woytowich (1994) noted that "writing can help relieve pressure and help us to 'get on with life'" (p. 78), describing the effective use of poetry to help school-aged clients deal with depression and suicidal feelings. For Sloan (2003), poetry helps clients "sift through the layers of their lives in search of their own truths" (p. 35). With clients who are unsure about writing poetry, Woytowich suggested asking specific questions about the event. As clients tell their story, the counselor writes down what is shared and gives it back to them in the form of verses.

Gladding (1995) discussed the idea of prescribing a specific poem related to a client's problem. Reading the poem helps the client understand she or he is not alone in experiencing this emotion. After reading the poem, the client is encouraged to do her or his own writing for further self-expression. It is critical that the poem be pertinent or relevant to the client's situation, age, and culture.

Poetry can be a form of catharsis and can also provide a liberating, therapeutic effect that increases understanding and contributes to more accurate self-perceptions (Bates, 1993). In addition, poetry enables clients to use words to reconstruct reality. Bates described poetry as "a way of seeing and ultimately, a way of knowing" (p. 155).

Poetry can be used by counselors to help prevent their own burnout and promote self-renewal (Gladding, 1987). It can also be used as a catalyst for growth and healing in hospitals, nursing homes, prisons, adult education centers, and chemical dependency units (Hynes, 1990). Gladding (1998) described having elderly residents in long-term care facilities read poems aloud as a group and react to the content with their own opinions and emotions, which enhances self-concept and group cohesiveness.

Poetry can facilitate assessment as well as healing. The following poem was written by a sixteen-year-old girl who struggled with depression. It was often difficult for her to describe how she was feeling, so she accepted the invitation to write about her feelings through poetry, and this became the vehicle for discussing her pain.

WHAT IS HAPPINESS?
So many things, so many worries,
In a life where pain isn't a wonder,
Where happiness is unknown.
But I wonder most of all,
Is there such a thing as happiness,
Or is it just a word?
I see it in their eyes, as well as mine,
That anger, that darkness, that emptiness,
That eats you up inside.
But yet no one cares,
Because it is just a part of life,
Or is it?
Is there a better way; another world,
Where everything, everybody is happy,
And pain is unknown?
But what is happiness?
Is it worry, or wonder?
Does anybody know?
Is dying happiness?
I often think so,
No other way; no other world,
Out of this hell where happiness is unknown,
And you cry yourself to sleep every night,
But no one knows; no one is there.
And as I lie here, I wonder,
Am I the only one, or are there more?
And I dream, I dream of a place where I do not exist,
And that to me is happiness.

After a year of counseling, in which she typically described her feelings through her poetry, she began to feel better, as reflected in the following poem:

A finalizing day has yet to arrive.
Everyday the same obstacles,
But now we can overcome.
The shadow upon me is slowly drifting away,
To where I can actually see myself, and all that lies around me.
So this will all end
And I will finally get my wish of happiness,
Now and forever.

BIBLIOTHERAPY

The term bibliotherapy refers to a process designed to help individuals solve problems or better understand themselves through their response to literature or media (Doll & Doll, 1997; Pardeck, 1994). Jackson (2000) noted that literature has been used to establish relationships with clients as well as to promote their insight. According to Pardeck (1998), the goals of bibliotherapy include (1) providing information and insight about problems, (2) communicating new values and attitudes, (3) creating an awareness of how others have dealt with similar problems, (4) stimulating discussion about problems, and (5) providing solutions.

Bibliotherapy has been used to increase academic and emotional development with children with serious emotional disturbances (Bauer & Balius, 1995; Pardeck & Pardeck, 1993), to enhance self-esteem in learning disabled children (Gladding, 1998), and to help clients cope with stress and change (Pardeck, 1994). Nugent (2000) discussed using bibliotherapy as a way of helping clients deal with unfinished business and alleviate depression. Bradley & Gould (1999) described it as a helpful process for clients needing to work through grief, and Pardeck (1998) identified ways in which bibliotherapy increased socialization and self-actualization.

According to Gladding (1992, 1998), bibliotherapy can be practiced with disturbed clients, with clients who have moderate emotional and behavioral problems, and with a normal population to enhance development. Borders and Paisley (1992) also discussed the developmental approach, stressing the importance of using bibliotherapy in classroom guidance sessions with children.

Bibliotherapy is especially effective for clients who process things visually as opposed to auditorily. The author recalls working with a couple experiencing relationship difficulties. She was attempting to stop the cycle of blame and increase this couple's understanding of their communication differences and ways of perceiving the world. Since verbal efforts had not been successful, she suggested they read a book as a homework assignment. When the couple arrived for the next session, they were eager to share their insights. The information they had learned provided them with new perspectives and information they needed to move to the next level of problem solving regarding their relationship issues.

In addition to literature in print, such as fiction, non-fiction, poetry, self-help books, and fairy tales, movies can be used as a bibliotherapy tool. This approach is particularly effective with adolescents who spend a great deal of time watching movies, but who may not pick up a book. Movies that depict events or emotions similar to those of the client can facilitate insight and emotional catharsis in addition to identification of coping strategies.

The Process

Gladding (1992) noted that in the bibliotherapy process, "a triadic connection" is fostered (p. 83). This triad includes the piece of literature, the client, and the facilitator who helps the client process an insight and apply it to his or her own life. Before using bibliotherapy, it is important to have a relationship built on trust and rapport.

Also, the client and the counselor should agree on the presenting problem and complete some preliminary problem exploration (Pardeck & Pardeck, 1993).

In selecting books for treatment, it is important to consider the presenting problem. Also, the practitioner should select books that contain believable characters, situations that are relevant to the situation, and that offer realistic hope. The selections should be developmentally appropriate (Wagner, 2003) and reflect the client's culture, gender, and age. Pardeck (1994) noted that it is often more effective to suggest rather than prescribe books. This author also emphasized that discussion, counseling, and follow-up activities are an essential part of the bibliotherapy process.

PLAY

"Play therapy is an approach to counseling young children in which the counselor uses toys, art supplies, games, and other play media to communicate with clients using the 'language' of children—the 'language' of play" (Kottman, 2001, p. 4). Generally used with children ages 3 to 10, play provides a way for children to express their experiences and feelings through a natural, self-healing process (Landreth, 1993). Because children's experiences are often communicated through play, it becomes an important vehicle to help them know and accept themselves. Through play, children are able to act out confusing or conflicting situations, make choices (Thompson, Rudolph, & Henderson, 2004), learn and practice problem-solving and relationship building skills (Kottman, 2004), master their fears (Kottman, 2001), explore alternative perceptions of problems and difficult relationships (Kottman, 2004), and learn to communicate more effectively (Brems, 2002). According to Brems, "play is perhaps one of the most common techniques utilized by child therapists" (p. 248).

Play Therapy Approaches

Kottman (2004) described four approaches to play therapy: Child-Centered, Adlerian, Cognitive-Behavioral, and Theraplay. Child-centered play therapy is based on the philosophy that children have an innate capacity for growth and maturity and that they are capable of being constructively self-directing. In this form of play therapy, the therapist builds a warm, genuine relationship with the child to facilitate a strong therapeutic bond. The therapist is totally accepting of the child and respects the child's ability to solve problems. Although the therapist maintains an active role, he or she does not manage or direct the experience. Rather, the child-centered play therapist believes that by communicating acceptance and belief in the child, the child will tap into his or her innate capacity for solving problems.

In Adlerian play therapy, the play therapist utilizes the principles and strategies of individual psychology along with the skills and concepts of play therapy. The Adlerian play therapist develops an egalitarian relationship with the client, then uses play to gain an understanding of the child's lifestyle and how the child conceptualizes his or her world. Next, the therapist helps the child gain insight into his or her lifestyle by using stories, artwork, metaphors, and metacommunication. Finally, the therapist provides reorientation and reeducation for the client, which can involve learning and practicing new skills.

Cognitive-behavioral play therapy combines play therapy approaches with cogntive and behavioral strategies. The cognitive-behavioral play therapist involves the child in the therapeutic process through play and examines the thoughts, feelings, and environment of the child. Next, the therapist helps the child develop more adaptive thoughts and behaviors, along with more effective problem-solving strategies. This form of play therapy is problem-focused, structured, and directive. Specific behavioral and cognitive interventions that have been proven to be successful for particular problems are employed.

Theraplay is directive, intensive, and brief. This type of play therapy is a treatment method that is modeled on the healthy interaction between parents and their children. It actively involves parents as observers and later as co-therapists. Play therapists use activities and materials that facilitate structure, challenge, intrusion/engagement, and nurture to remedy problems that create problems for children. The therapist is in charge of the session and the sessions are predictable and structured.

Uses of Play

Play can be used in several different ways to meet the developmental needs of all children. Orton (1997) identified the following uses of play:

1. To aid in the assessment process. The counselor notes the child's interactions, inhibitions, preoccupations, perceptions, and expressions of feelings and ideas.

2. To establish a working relationship. For children who may be fearful, nonverbal, or resistant, the use of play can help establish an accepting relationship, as in the case of Ryan.

Ryan, age 6, was referred for inability to relate effectively to others. In the initial interview, he sat as far away from the counselor as possible and only shook his head in response to questions. Instead of continuing to talk, the counselor got out a can of shaving cream and squirted some onto a large tray. Then she started playing with it, shaping it into different forms. Ryan watched for a few minutes and then hesitantly approached the table and began to play. The counselor added more shaving cream and some food coloring. Ryan's eyes widened, and he began making pictures out of the cream and chatting about what he was creating. By initiating the play that stimulated Ryan to interact, the counselor was able to establish a working relationship.

3. To help children express their concerns. Frequently, children will not or are not able to verbalize feelings about events. Play can be used to facilitate verbalization as well as provide a means of dealing with the issue. In the following situation, the counselor used a dart game to elicit angry feelings.

Dan was a behaviorally disordered third-grader who was hostile and aggressive with other children and adults. After an angry confrontation with the principal, the teacher requested that the counselor work with Dan. Knowing that he would be defensive, the counselor set up a dartboard equipped with rubber-tipped darts. When

Dan entered the office, the counselor simply invited him to play darts. After several minutes of play, the counselor commented to Dan that he was really throwing the darts as if he were angry. Dan didn't comment, but simply continued to play. After a while he stopped and sat down. The counselor asked if there was anything he'd like to talk about, and he began to share situations in which other kids picked on him, he'd call them names and then got in trouble for name-calling. After discussing this for a while, the counselor asked Dan if he'd like to come back again to talk more about his anger and what he could do about it. He agreed to come, but expressed a desire to play darts again. Using the dartboard initiated verbalization and let Dan express his hostile, angry feelings.

4. To promote healing and growth. For example, 6-year-old Amelia was the youngest in her family. The teacher reported that several children had complained that every time Amelia played a game, she had to win. If she wasn't winning, she changed the rules. The counselor invited Amelia to play a board game, and when she tried to change the rules, the counselor commented on this. They discussed Amelia's need to win and what it said about her if she didn't win. After several sessions of this nature, the counselor invited several of Amelia's friends in to play. Amelia played the game without changing the rules. This experience seemed to successfully teach her alternative behaviors to help her interact more appropriately.

Regardless of how play is used, the therapeutic relationship is extremely important. Showing interest in what the child chooses to do and being patient and understanding are crucial.

Selection of Materials

Landreth (1993) discussed the importance of selecting play materials that facilitate (1) exploration of real-life experiences, (2) expression of a wide range of feelings, (3) testing of limits, (4) expressive and exploratory play, (5) exploration and expression without verbalization, and (6) success without prescribed structure. This author warned against using mechanical or complex toys or materials that required the counselor's assistance to manipulate. Kottman (2003) suggested that toys should represent five different categories: family/nurturing toys, scary toys, aggressive toys, expressive toys, and pretend/fantasy toys. Kottman (2003, 2004) listed specific examples of toys to facilitate exploration of family/nurturing, including dolls of different ethnicities, dollhouses and furniture, play dishes, and soft blankets. Examples of scary toys, which help children express their fears and how to cope with them, include rubber snakes, monsters, insects, and fierce animal puppets. Dart guns, play swords and knives, toy soldiers, and a pounding board or bop bag were identified as toys that allowed children to express anger and aggression. Crayons, clay, paints, pipe cleaners, chalk, and newsprint were cited as examples of materials to facilitate creative expression. Pretend/fantasy toys that help children express their feelings and explore roles and behaviors include masks, costumes, hats, jewelry, telephones, magic wands, and people figures.

Toys selected should be in good condition. It is also important not to have so many toys that the room is cluttered and junky. The specific use of the toys depends on whether the approach is structured, where the counselor selects the toys to fit the child's problem, or nondirective, in which the child has more freedom to choose materials.

Games

Board games provide another way to establish rapport, facilitate verbalization, release feelings, and teach new behaviors (Vernon, 2002). Bradley, Gould, & Hendricks (2004) noted that games are familiar and non-threatening and have diagnostic value. Schaefer and Reid (2000) cited their usefulness in addressing specific topics in counseling. Games allow clients to gain a sense of mastery and receive positive feedback. For preadolescents and adolescents in particular, board games can make counseling more enjoyable and thus more productive.

Games such as checkers or chess generally work well in establishing rapport, as do other commercial board games. Once rapport has been established, the counselor may want to develop or select games that specifically address the concerns with which the child is working. The case of Stephanie illustrates this point.

Stephanie, a fourth-grader, was frequently upset because she made assumptions about what her peers were thinking and, therefore, assumed that they didn't like her, were upset with her, or didn't ever want to be her friend. To help her recognize how she upset herself by mistaking what she thought for factual information, the counselor engaged Stephanie in a game called "Fights with Friends" (Vernon, 2002, pp. 225–227). They took turns drawing assumption cards and coping strategies cards, identifying whether the child in the situation was thinking rationally (not making assumptions) and was demonstrating effective behavioral coping strategies. If not, Stephanie or the counselor had to identify what the assumptions or ineffective coping strategies were and discuss how to change them before putting an X (client) or O (counselor) on the game board (like tic-tac-toe).

After the game was completed, the counselor asked Stephanie to identify the difference between a fact and an assumption, and how making assumptions negatively affected her relationships with her friends. She then invited her client to make a set of new assumption and coping strategies cards that pertained specifically to her situation. They were able to discuss Stephanie's tendency to mistake a fact ("My friend didn't sit by me in the lunchroom") from an assumption ("Because she didn't sit by me, there must be something wrong with me and she must not like me anymore"). The game was a concrete way of helping this fourth-grader work through her problem.

The value of play therapy is undisputed; research supports its use with a wide range of presenting problems (LeBlanc & Richie, 1999). Because the actual process of play therapy is complex and needs more explanation than this brief overview, the reader is encouraged to read *Play Therapy: Basics and Beyond* (Kottman, 2001), *The Play Therapy Primer* (O'Connor, 2000), or the *Handbook of Play Therapy, Volume II: Advances and Innovations* (O'Conner & Schaefer, 1994).

MORE CREATIVE APPROACHES

The number of creative approaches used in a counseling session is endless. The only limiting factors are the counselor's own creative abilities to develop effective methods of helping the client resolve issues. I have found the following approaches helpful in the process of working with clients.

Props

Using props during a session can stimulate thinking or elicit emotion about a problem. Props are a way, other than words, to reach the client. For example, a woman who was constantly pessimistic was given a set of old eyeglasses and four round circles of paper—two grey and two pink. She was instructed to tape the grey paper on the glasses and talk about her day from a "doom and gloom" perspective. Next, she was asked to substitute the pink paper and describe her day as if she were looking through "rose-colored glasses." She and the counselor then discussed the difference in the two perspectives and set some goals for developing a more optimistic perception of events.

In working with a young adult on her tendency to procrastinate, the counselor brought a pile of newspapers to the session. She invited her client to make a list of all the things she procrastinated about. Next, she asked her to lie on the floor and one by one, she read off the list of things about which the client procrastinated. As she read each one, she piled a bunch of newspapers on the client until the pile was quite high after all of the items on the list had been read. Next, they talked about how she felt with everything "all piled up," applying it to her personal experiences with procrastination. She then identified what she could do or say relative to each item on the list to help resolve the procrastination problems, and as she did so, the counselor lifted newspapers from the pile. This was a very graphic way to help this client remember that it is better not to let things pile up by procrastinating.

With another young client, using a tape recorder helped him become less dependent on the counselor and more skilled at solving his own problems. Adam had lots of worries, such as what he should do if someone teased him, what he should do if his mother wasn't home after school, and what he should do if he didn't understand how to do his schoolwork.

Because Adam's father was concerned that Adam might be "inventing" some problems because he really liked coming to counseling, the counselor decided to teach Adam how to be his own counselor. When he arrived for his session, she asked Adam what was bothering him that week. He shared a situation about his friend teasing him, and the counselor helped Adam develop some tease tolerance techniques. Adam was to ask himself if he was what his friend said he was, if names could hurt him, and how he could handle the situation if he couldn't control what came out of the other person's mouth. Next the counselor said that she would pretend to be Adam and that Adam could be the counselor. As the counselor, Adam was asked to help solve a problem similar to his real one. After role-playing this, Adam was given a tape recorder and a blank tape. During the week, whenever he had a problem, he could use the tape recorder and first be the person who has the problem and then switch roles and pretend to be the counselor who helps him solve the problem. When Adam returned for his next session, he played the tape for the counselor. He had recorded several problems and had done a good job of helping himself deal with his problems.

Props were useful in a marriage counseling session when a rope helped a couple see the "tug of war" state of their marriage and to understand how they each felt controlled. Each person held one end of the rope, pulled on it, and verbalized one of the ways she or he felt controlled by the partner. The counselor wrote down each of the statements so the couple could also see what each other said. This simple activity was a good stimulus for mobilizing some energy and illuminating some of the issues that needed to be solved.

Homework Suggestions

To facilitate self-reliance, homework assignments can effectively extend the concepts dealt with during the counseling session. The following ideas can be adapted and expanded on, depending on the client's age:

1. Have clients make a 'mad pillow,' which they decorate with pictures of things or people with whom they feel angry. When they experience anger, they can pound the pillow rather than act aggressively toward another person.
2. Suggest that when clients worry excessively about minor, as opposed to major, problems, they can buy a bubble pipe. As they use it, they can visualize the minor problems "blowing away."
3. Invite clients who are dealing with a lot of anger to write down on separate pieces of paper situations in which they have been angry. They should then collect as many rocks as they have slips of paper and go to a river or open field. As they throw the rock away with force, they can yell out the name of the anger-provoking situation.
4. If clients have difficulty accomplishing tasks because they're overwhelmed with the amount of work to be done, invite them to buy a timer, set it for a given amount of time to work and a given amount of time to relax.
5. Recommend that clients make books of written text and/or illustrations to express their perceptions about a problem and their methods of solving it.
6. For clients who think that the "grass is greener on the other side of the fence" (i.e., spouses who think they would be better off single, adolescents who think they would be better off living with their friends' parents), have them interview people to find out more what it is "really like" on the other side.

GROUP APPLICATIONS

The specialized individual counseling approaches previously described can usually be applied in a group context. Each of the approaches is discussed with a brief explanation of group applicability.

Art

To facilitate group cohesiveness, participants can make a collage to represent their group, using finger paint and scraps from fabric and paper. In a self-awareness group, members could tear a shape out of construction paper that tells something about themselves as a way to introduce themselves to the group. To teach cooperation, group participants could be given paper, tape, and magazines and instructions to design an object of beauty. Roles that members play in developing this project could then be discussed. In a group setting, members might take turns drawing symbols that they feel represent other group members as a way to provide feedback on how they come across to others.

Imagery

Guided imagery can be readily applied to a group setting. In a classroom or small group, students could be led in a guided imagery relative to test taking, task completion, stress management, or cooperative behavior with classmates. Guided imagery has also been used extensively in career development (Gladding, 1998). Heppner, O'Brien, Hinkelman, & Humphrey (1994) described using guided imagery in life planning to spur the imagination of their clients. Jacobs (1992) used projective fantasies in a group setting where participants were encouraged to imagine themselves as a common object and to describe what their lives would be like if they were this object. As a result of this activity, they were able to see their lives differently.

Music

Musical activities facilitate self-awareness and interpersonal relationships. In a classroom setting, students can compose and perform their own compositions related to guidance topics: feelings, self-concept, decision making, friendship, or values. Newcomb (1994) noted that music can be used in classroom guidance as an energizer, to set the mood, to develop group cohesiveness, or as a way of emphasizing the theme of a lesson.

Bowman (1987) described the "feelings ensemble." A group is divided into smaller groups of five or six, and each group is given a feeling word that becomes the title of their composition. They are instructed to make up and perform a song in front of the large group that describes their feeling word. They may use sound makers such as pencils or rulers, or the counselor can provide them with whistles, horns, harmonicas, or kazoos. After several minutes of planning, each group performs while other members attempt to guess what feeling they are expressing.

Music is also a good way to build group identity and cohesiveness. Group members can compose a song or select a recording that expresses who they are. An alternative activity is the musical collage. Each individual group member selects short segments of songs that have meaning, and tapes each of these segments to create a collage. After listening to each person's collage, group members discuss how the music represents that individual (Bowman, 1987).

Writing

Various forms of writing can be adapted for group use. Open-ended sentences can become a get-acquainted activity or prompt discussion and sharing. Questionnaires are also used this way, or they can be adapted to the specific focus of the group. For example, members of a stress management group might be given a questionnaire about ways they deal with stress. As responses are shared, members will benefit from hearing others' ideas.

In a classroom setting, students can be given journal topics related to self-awareness, clarification of values, or feelings about various issues. Examples of topics include:

"Something I like best about myself is . . ."
"Something I feel strongly about is . . ."
"Something I'm good at doing is . . ."
"Something that I value highly is . . ."

Topics of this nature encourage self-exploration. Journal writing can be further shared in student dyads or triads to clarify responses. In such a situation, participants must feel comfortable with the sharing and have the option to pass if they wish.

Bibliotherapy

Borders and Paisley (1992) suggested that bibliotherapy be used not only in problem-centered interventions in individual or small-group counseling, but also with children in classroom guidance, to promote developmental growth. Their research indicated that the use of stories is an effective approach to help children solve problems and enhance personal growth.

Play

For younger children, particularly in a school setting, play can be highly effective in a small group of four or five children to improve socialization skills. One or two children in the group are selected as good models; the targeted individuals may need to develop cooperative versus competitive behavior, learn to control aggression, become more comfortable with group interaction, or learn to share.

In the group setting, the play is generally more structured and the toys used are selected to help children work on the desirable behaviors. For instance, if two of the children in the group have difficulty sharing, the counselor may have only one can of blocks for all group members to use. As the children play with the blocks, the counselor reflects on the interaction and involves the children in discussing how it feels when friends share or don't share, thus seeking to develop behaviors that will transfer to other situations.

Board games can also be developed for group use. For an activity to help children enhance school performance, a game called "Road to Achievement" (Vernon, 2002) helps children identify effective study skills. "The Long and Short of It" (Vernon, 1998) teaches children how to identify short- and long-term consequences in a group setting.

CONCLUSIONS

Creative approaches to counseling offer creative ways to supplement or give an alternative to the traditional verbal approaches. For counseling to be meaningful and effective, it is necessary to engage the client, and specialized approaches facilitate this in an enjoyable, self-motivating way. Gladding (1998) noted that approaches of this nature are "process-oriented, emotionally sensitive, socially directed, and awareness-focused" (preface) and can help clients from diverse backgrounds enhance their development.

The specialized approaches are not limited to the descriptions in this chapter. Movement, dance, drama, humor, and puppetry are other approaches that can meet client needs. No "universal" format exists for application; the creativity of the counselor, and assessment of what would most effectively engage the client guide the implementation. The training needed to use these specialized approaches depends on whether they are used to supplement a verbal approach or constitute the major aspect of the counseling. As Nickerson and O'Laughlin (1982) noted, the issue is perhaps one of degree. In other words, a counselor does not have to be an artist to use some art with clients who are not able to express themselves verbally, but if art were the primary modality, further training would be needed.

Creative approaches have been used successfully with children and adolescents (Bradley, Gould, & Hendricks, 2004; Bush, 1997; Gladding, 1992, 1998; Pardeck, 1994), the borderline client (Silverman, 1991), the elderly (Gladding, 1998), clients with eating disorders (Brown, 1991; Sapp, 2000), and children from violent homes (Malchiodi, 1997). They can be used to treat specific problems or can be applied preventively, particularly in school settings.

The diversity of specialized counseling approaches can help effectively address a wide range of client needs, including clients from diverse backgrounds. These methods move counseling beyond the mental arena, which relies on verbal techniques, to a more comprehensive orientation using a multitude of approaches.

SUMMARY

Although counseling has traditionally been characterized by a verbal orientation, practitioners are now encouraged to explore other methods to help people cope with psychological problems. In this chapter, a variety of creative approaches to counseling were described. These approaches have been found to be effective for a variety of problems presented by both children and adults.

As discussed in this chapter, creative approaches to counseling can be adapted to fit the client's learning style. Art, imagery, and writing were identified as appropriate strategies for clients of all ages. Specific ways to use music, bibliotherapy, and play were also described. Implementing approaches of this nature can enhance the counseling process because they combine theory and practice in flexible ways to focus on the unique aspects of the client and the problem.

CHAPTER TWELVE

COUNSELING USES
OF TESTS

LARRY C. LOESCH, PH.D., N.C.C.
University of Florida

LINDA H. FOSTER, PH.D., N.C.C.
McAdory High School

In the introduction of his historically significant text *Using Tests in Counseling*, Goldman (1971) proposed that testing and counseling are inextricably linked. He wrote, "The types of tests used, and the ways in which testing is conducted, differ to some extent, but all have in common a relationship between counselor and counselee in which the latter's well-being, adjustment, and choices are paramount" (p. 1). Goldman's prophetic words remain true today. Today's counselors have ever increasing needs and requirements for valid and reliable information about their counselees. Thus, the importance of the relationship between counseling and testing continues to increase, perhaps reaching its pinnacle at the point of test interpretation. Goodyear and Lichtenberg (1999) wrote, "Test interpretation can have real consequences. That is, interpretations of test data are used to make decisions related to such matters as psychological diagnosis, treatment planning, hiring, career choice, occupational classification, . . . and so on. In each of these instances, a person's life can be affected, sometimes profoundly" (p. 2). Testing is indeed an important part of the work of professional counselors and a part that requires substantive knowledge and well-honed skills.

Unfortunately, some counselors have been reluctant to accept the proposal that testing is an integral part of counseling, instead viewing it as an "adjunct" to their counseling activities. This perspective ignores the reality that counselors quite routinely, but usually subjectively, gather and interpret information from and about their counselees. Effective counselors acknowledge that subjective information gath-

This chapter is respectfully dedicated to the memory of Dr. Nicholas A. Vacc who co-authored the first three versions of it with Dr. Loesch.

ering and interpretation are important parts of counseling processes, but also recognize that effective assessment and evaluation (i.e., testing) procedures can facilitate and enhance achievement of counseling goals and the efficiency of their counseling.

Some counselors' attitudes toward testing, in part, reflect confusion about semantics. *Measurement* may be considered the assignment of numeric or categorical values to human attributes according to rules (Aiken, 2002). *Assessment* includes measurement and also can be considered the data-gathering process or method (Drummond, 1999). *Evaluation* subsumes assessment and can be considered the interpretation and application of measurement data according to rules (Vacc & Loesch, 2000). *Appraisal* is sometimes considered synonymous to assessment (Vacc & Loesch, 2000), but more frequently with evaluation. Unfortunately, *testing* has been used as a synonym for each and all of these terms!

Testing (particularly when used as a synonym to appraisal/evaluation) can involve value judgments being made about measurement results, and therefore about people. For this reason, testing has become equated with "labeling" people. Most counselors do not want to be viewed as "labeling" people because it connotes being "nonhumanistic" or "uncaring." Therefore, counselors often decry testing based on incorrect understandings of what it really is. However, it is not the act of making judgments that must be avoided, for counseling processes are fraught with counselors' value judgments. Rather it is making unfounded and/or invalid value judgments that must be avoided. Given the substantial evidence that clinicians' subjective judgments correlate poorly with more objective indices of human attributes (Groth-Marnat, 2003), counselors are well advised to seek the best assessment procedures available. Thus testing, when properly understood and used, is a significant aid, not a hindrance, to the counseling process.

USES OF TESTS IN COUNSELING

Anastasi and Urbina (1997) and Gregory (2000) have listed general uses for testing, while others (e.g., Drummond, 1999; Goodyear & Lichtenberg, 1999; Hood & Johnson, 2002; Vacc & Loesch, 2000) have identified more specific counseling applications. The following is a summary of primary counseling-related uses of testing.

Preliminary (Problem) Exploration and/or Diagnosis

For counseling processes to be efficient, counselors must gain accurate information about counselees as rapidly as possible. In fact, counselors typically must make a "diagnosis" soon after initial contact with their respective counselees. Unfortunately, the term *diagnosis* is not interpreted consistently in the counseling profession. In some contexts, it simply means "trying to find out what's going on with the counselee" (i.e., to determine rather general information about a counselee or the counselee's problem). In other contexts, it means to determine a very specific mental health syndrome for the counselee. For example, Gregory (2000) wrote that, "Diagnosis consists of two intertwined tasks: determining the nature and source of a person's . . . behavior, and classifying the behavior pattern within an accepted diagnostic system" (p. 38). How-ever, in either case, one efficient means of gaining accurate information from which to understand a person's behavior is testing.

Testing in this context has several distinct advantages over other types of coun-selor interactions and data gathering with counselees. First, it enhances comprehen-sive and systematic inquiry. Second, testing (in most cases) enables normative com-parison of a counselee's personal data with that of other, similar persons. Third, it typically results in a relatively concise summary of counselee characteristics. Finally, testing *may* "uncover" counselee characteristics about which the counselee is un-aware. Thus, substantive information about counselees' characteristics, behaviors, or problems can be gained expeditiously when testing is an integral part of initial coun-seling activities (Drummond, 1999).

Selection or Screening

Testing in this context means using test results to identify persons who might benefit from counseling or who are eligible for counseling services. For example, in large scale testing programs (such as those conducted in schools), identification of "out-liers" in score distributions *may* suggest persons in need of counseling. In individual-ized situations, test results *may* be used to determine if a person meets particular cri-teria for the receipt of counseling services.

Using test information for selection or screening usually involves measurement and evaluation of applicant attributes for use in educational, business/industry or em-ployment, or counseling agency decision making. Thus, test results often are used to supplement more subjectively obtained information (i.e., personal judgments) so that decision making is improved and more efficient, thereby benefitting all involved.

Testing for selection or screening purposes has advantages similar to those for preliminary exploration or diagnosis. Comprehensive information can be obtained systematically and rapidly. For example, it is common in employment screening situ-ations for applicants to complete a "test battery" as part of the application process. The ability to make normative comparisons of test results is particularly important in selection or screening processes. In this context, counseling professionals often es-tablish "statistical decision-making rules," based on numeric test result criteria, to supplement personal judgment criteria in decision-making processes.

Placement and/or Planning

Test results are often used by counselors to help them determine the most appropriate situations (e.g., educational programs or occupational categories) in which to place peo-ple. This use of testing is closely related to the selection or screening use, except that the focus of placement is typically narrower than that for a selection process. For exam-ple, determining assignment to a particular program of studies within an institution of higher education is usually a narrower focus than determining eligibility for admission to the institution. Similarly, determining an applicant's appropriate job classification may be narrower in scope than determining the applicant's suitability for employment.

Testing for placement usually involves obtaining data about level of aptitude or competency. Tests used for such purposes may assess general attributes (e.g., when intelligence test scores are used as one of the criteria for placement in an academically gifted student program) or relatively specific abilities (e.g., when work sample tests are used to determine the speed with which a person can perform a job-specific task).

Testing for planning also usually involves the assessment of level of an ability or competency, and often the process is indistinguishable from that for placement. However, in this case, tests are used specifically to determine areas of functioning where increased competency is needed. Testing for planning thus involves identifying the best ways to facilitate the necessary improvement.

Facilitation of Self-Understanding

A primary reason counselees seek counseling services is for the facilitation of self-understanding. One of the roles of the counselor in this regard is as an information gatherer, transmitter, and interpreter. This role necessitates the integration of both communication and assessment skills. Whiston (2000) wrote that, "[J]ust as counselors need effective communication skills, they also need effective assessment skills. Assessing clients is an integral part of the counseling process; it is not a distinct area where some counselors administer tests" (p. 6). Counselors' effectiveness in this role is largely contingent upon counselees' trust in the counselor. Counselees must strongly "believe in" their counselors before they will accept exploration into areas of self-understanding. This trust is difficult to achieve in early stages of the counseling process. However, testing is one means by which counselors can obtain information that enhances feedback to counselees. Use of "objective" test information may then serve to increase counselors' "credibility" with their counselees.

The normative aspects of test results also may be useful in facilitating counselees' self-understanding. For example, counselees often wish to know how their characteristics, attributes, abilities, or behaviors compare with those of other people. Test results provided in normative contexts can be a basis for comparison. Another possible use for counselees in this regard is to use test results to identify specific aspects of themselves they may wish to change. Therefore, testing to facilitate self-understanding may serve to help counselees identify counseling goals.

The testing process, when focusing upon characteristic behaviors, also facilitates counselees' self-understanding. Many tests incorporate logical, systematic, and relatively "transparent" approaches to analysis of human behavior. Thus, actually engaging in the testing process may enable counselees to learn new ways of evaluating themselves.

Assessment of Individual Progress

With increasing frequency and urgency, counselors are being required to demonstrate the effectiveness of their counseling activities to others, particularly others outside the counseling profession. Although there are a wide variety of ways that counselors can generate evidence of their counseling effectiveness, use of tests is clearly one of the more accepted and expeditious methods. Effective counseling is synonymous with counselee change, which presumably is perceived by counselees as positive. However, demonstration of counselee change is difficult if left to subjective interpretations by counselees or counselors. Testing can be a more objective way of obtaining counselee change information. For example, pre- and postcounseling assessments of counselee characteristics, attributes, and/or behaviors can provide data for evaluating the degree of change.

Counselors also have a professional obligation to demonstrate their effectiveness to their counselees. Use of tests in this context may have an added, very subtle benefit. One of the more difficult aspects of counseling is maintaining a high level of counselee motivation throughout the counseling process, a difficulty that increases as the length of the counseling process increases. The counselor's provision of "encouraging" feedback, as well as counselee's self monitoring, helps to maintain counselee motivation. However, again, these are subjective processes. Periodic use of tests that yield "objective" indications of counselee change can be a powerful reinforcer of counselee motivation.

Licensure or Certification

Testing has become a significant factor in many professional counselors' personal careers. A greatly increased emphasis on counselor credentialing in the past three decades has resulted in the development of several major national counselor certifications. In addition, counselor licensure laws now exist in forty-seven states and the District of Columbia. All these procedures require some type of performance evaluation and most require successful performance on a credentialing examination. The examinations used encompass a variety of measurement formats including multiple-choice, essay, and simulation tests. Typically, counselors have to exceed a minimum criterion score on an examination to become certified and/or licensed and/or otherwise credentialied. Thus, the counseling profession has embraced testing as an effective and efficient method for obtaining useful information for professional purposes.

BASIC CONCEPTS IN TESTING

Tests used for counseling and related purposes are usually evaluated by three major attributes: validity, reliability, and appropriateness.

Validity

Validity is commonly defined as the extent to which a test measures what it purports to measure (Aiken, 2002; Drummond, 1999; Hood & Johnson, 2002). Messick (1998) provided clarification of that common definition when he wrote, "Validity is an integrated evaluative judgment of the degree to which empirical evidence and theoretical rationales support the *adequacy* and *appropriateness* of *inferences* and *actions* based on test scores or other modes of assessment" (p. 13). Messick's definition emphasizes that, ultimately, validity is based on judgment and is the most important in consideration of how test results are used. It also is the primary criterion upon which any test should be evaluated (Anastasi & Urbina, 1997; Gregory, 2000).

Historically, validity was usually considered as a generalized characteristic of a test. However, the most recent edition of the *Standards for Educational and Psychological Testing* (AERA/APA/NCME, 2000) includes a significant change in how validity is viewed, which in turn has significant implications for how it is established. Validity is now viewed as "contextual," which means that the validity of a test must be specified *for a particular purpose and for use with a particular group of people.* If a test is to be used for a purpose or with a group of people other than those for which current validity information exists, then additional evidence of validity must be generated before the test can be considered valid for use in the new situation.

Three major types of validity typically have been discussed in most of the professional literature on testing. *Content validity* referred to the extent to which a test was an accurate and representative sample of a domain to which inferences would be made (Aiken, 2002). Domains of interest to counselors include human attributes, characteristics, behaviors, attitudes, and abilities. Content validity evaluation was usually associated with measures of cognitive abilities. *Construct validity* was the accuracy with which test scores reflected levels or degrees of psychological constructs (Aiken, 2002). Construct validity was particularly important for evaluating measures of personality dynamics, attitudes, or interests. *Criterion-related validity* referred to the extent to which test scores were predictably associated with other, often behavioral, criteria (Aiken, 2002). Performance and competency measures in particular had to have criterion-related validity.

The newer interpretation of validity emphasizes the importance of substantive documentation and research to establish test validity for a particular use with a particular group of people. Within this perspective, a test's validity must be based on *evidence* of (a) representativeness of a content domain, (b) appropriate response processes, (c) appropriate internal structure, or (d) appropriate relationships to other variables, or some combination of these types of evidence.

Reliability

The consistency of measurement results yielded by a test is known as reliability (Anastasi & Urbina, 1997). Similar to validity, three types of reliability are usually described in the literature. *Stability*, sometimes called test-retest reliability, indicates the likelihood of a group of people achieving the same or similar test scores if the test is administered on two or more occasions. *Equivalence*, sometimes called parallel forms, reliability indicates the extent to which two versions of a measure yield the same or essentially similar results. *Internal consistency* reliability indicates the extent to which items within a test (or subscale) correlate with one another (i.e., are internally consistent). The type of reliability deemed most important depends on the nature of the testing situation (Gregory, 2000).

Appropriateness

A test is appropriate if factors extraneous to the purpose and nature of the test itself (e.g., size of print type used, testing conditions, test delivery format, or reading level of test content) do not influence performance on or responding to the test. Validity, reliability, and appropriateness are interrelated but not necessarily interdependent. A valid test is necessarily reliable and appropriate. However, a test can produce reliable (i.e., consistent) but invalid results. Similarly, an inappropriate test (e.g., one for which the response format is inappropriate for the respondents) can produce reliable but not valid results.

GENERAL TESTING VOCABULARY

Tests have been characterized and/or differentiated through the use of a wide variety of terms. The following are brief clarifications of terms commonly used in the testing literature.

Interpretation Basis

Norm-referenced and *criterion-referenced* are two terms commonly used to describe tests. The distinction between the two types of tests is usually made in regard to the interpretation of the results from each type (Gregory, 2000). In norm-referenced testing, a respondent's test score is reported in comparison to performance on the same test by other persons. Percentiles, or other "standardized" scores such as T scores or deviation IQs (which are different from the original intelligence quotient which was defined as the person's mental age divided by the person's chronological age times 100), are commonly used to indicate *relative* performance. For example, a person whose score is at the eighty-fifth percentile is interpreted to have performed on the test at a level equal to or surpassing 85 percent of the persons in the "norm" group for the test. These persons presumably are similar to the respondent in important ways. Norm-referenced testing necessitates establishment of normative data but not of specific behavioral criteria.

In criterion-referenced testing, a respondent's test score is interpreted in comparison to some specified behavioral domain or criterion of proficiency. A respondent's score indicates how many criterion-specific tasks (i.e., items) the respondent completed successfully and therefore how many of the specific criteria (e.g., identified skills) the respondent has achieved. Criterion-referenced testing involves the development of specific behavioral criteria and careful specification of the relationships of test items to those criteria.

Standardized Tests

Aiken (2002) indicated that *standardized tests* usually are commercially prepared by measurement experts and incorporate uniform sets of items and administration and scoring procedures. In general, a test is "standardized" if it is used in the same way for all respondents. Gregory (2000) also emphasized that "standardized" does not mean that the test *necessarily* accurately measures what it is intended to measure. So-called "nonstandardized" tests frequently are user-prepared and administration procedures may vary depending on the situation. The validity of standardized and nonstandardized tests must be evaluated on an individual basis; a test is not necessarily valid by designation as standardized or invalid by designation as nonstandardized.

Individual and Group Tests

Individual tests are designed and intended to be administered to one person at a time by a single administrator. These tests usually involve the administrator "tailoring" the testing procedure (e.g., determining the time allowed for responding) to a specific respondent and/or testing situation. A group test is one that is designed and intended to be administered to more than one person at a time.

Power and Speed(ed) Tests

In most types of testing, interest is in maximum and/or thorough respondent performance. Therefore, testing time allotments exceed time needed by most respondents to complete the test. Such tests are called power tests. Intellectual ability, aptitude, and achievement tests are common examples of power tests. In contrast, speed(ed) tests involve speed of performance as a dynamic in the assessment process. Task completion tests (e.g., typing or other manual dexterity skills tests) are common examples of speed tests.

Vertical and Horizontal Tests

Tests that have different but conceptually and structurally related forms based on some hierarchy (e.g., age category, developmental level, or grade) are known as vertical tests. Tests conceptually and structurally related that assess within a number of different domains simultaneously within a defined category (e.g., age group or grade level) are known as horizontal tests. Some tests, such as aptitude or achievement "test batteries" commonly used in schools, are both vertical and horizontal tests.

Structured and Unstructured Tests

Tests also differ by response task. In a structured test, the respondent is presented with a clear stimulus (e.g., an item stem) and instructed to select the appropriate response from those presented (e.g., response choices, sometimes known as distractors in a multiple-choice test). In an unstructured test, the respondent is presented with either a clear or an ambiguous stimulus and instructed to construct a response. This differentiation is evident in different types of personality inventories.

Computer-Based Tests

Rapid technologic advancements are being made in the uses of computers for testing. In computer-based testing, the respondent "interacts" with a computer by providing responses (through keyboard, joystick, or "touch screen" input) to stimuli (e.g., questions or graphics) presented on a computer monitor. Both the number and type of tests being transformed to computer application are increasing at an exponential rate.

The major advantages of computer-based testing are that responses are made easily, sophisticated visual and/or graphical effects can be incorporated into testing paradigms, respondents have considerable control over the rate of interaction (i.e., responding), test scoring and data analyses are completed rapidly, and local "data sets" (e.g., local normative data) are easily established. Historically, the major limitations of computer-based testing concerned the "security" of the tests and testing procedures. However, significant recent improvements in computer-based testing have helped to minimize these concerns.

Computer-based testing clearly is the "method of choice" for the future. In particular, the increasing use of the Internet and World Wide Web as a communications modality likely will increase dramatically both the nature and types of computer-based testing. In addition, increasingly sophisticated technologies will allow a diverse array of testing approaches to be used.

Paper-and-Pencil Tests

Currently, a majority of tests are "paper-and-pencil" tests, for example, wherein respondents provide responses directly on tests, test booklets, or accompanying answer or response sheets. However, the connotation of the term "paper-and-pencil tests" has been broadened beyond the restrictive (literal) definition to encompass almost all structured tests, including computer-based versions of those tests.

Performance Tests

Tests that require respondents to complete physical tasks to allow evaluation of skill or competence levels are known as performance tests. They also are sometimes referred to as "work sample" tests. Performance or work sample tests are used most frequently in the context of vocational or vocational rehabilitation counseling. However, they are increasingly becoming part of other assessment procedures. For example, the "in basket" technique used in the context of employee screening procedures calls for prospective employees to actually respond to a sample of what might be found in the person's "in basket" if hired (e.g., the potential employee could be asked to write a letter of response to a customer complaint or to write an informative memo to other employees). The responses of the potential employee are then evaluated by the employer.

High Stakes Testing

Tests are increasingly being used as the bases for decisions about respondents or the persons who prepare them for the tests that are at least significant and in some cases life altering. The testing enterprise in this context is referred to as *high stakes* testing. The most common example of high stakes testing is statewide achievement testing. For example, based on some of these testing processes, students who do not perform well may be denied a diploma, their teachers' employment may not be continued or may be altered significantly, or their schools may receive differentiated funding. Credentialing examinations, such as those for counselors, also fall in the realm of high stakes testing because failure to surpass a score criterion may mean that an applicant may not be able to practice as a counselor. Increasingly sophisticated assessment techniques in combination with increasing societal demand for performance-based evidence of competence are the driving forces behind the rapidly increasing emphasis on high stakes testing.

ADDITIONAL ASSESSMENT METHODS

The following are methods that may be thought of as tests because they yield data for evaluation purposes. However, they differ in that the data are not necessarily provided by the person to whom the data applies.

Structured and Open-Response Interviews

In a structured interview, the interviewer asks the interviewee a predetermined set of questions. Responses from the interviewee are classified (or coded) into predetermined potential response categories. Questions posed in an open-response interview are also predetermined, but categories of potential responses are not. Rather, *post hoc* analyses are made in the attempt to "sort out" respondent information.

Rating Scales

The use of rating scales involves a rater providing an indication of another person's *level or degree* of an attribute, attitude, or characteristic in terms of predetermined stimuli (e.g., items or criteria). Rating scales may be used to assess "live" behavior or through media (e.g., audiotape, videotape, or photographs) that record the behavior.

Behavior Observations

In making behavior observations, an observer views (sometimes on videotape) a person in a situation and records *frequencies* with which predetermined behaviors occur. Behavior observation and rating techniques are often used in the same contexts. For example, counselor trainees' verbal responses in counseling sessions are typically counted by type and rated for level of effectiveness by supervisors. Behavior observations also are used commonly in determination of a diagnostic classification.

Checklists

When used as assessment techniques, checklists contain either sets of behaviors or attributes. For behaviors, responses usually reflect *perceived* frequencies of occurrence. For attributes, responses usually reflect *perceived* presence or absence. Checklist responses can be self-reported, provided by another person (e.g., a counselor, teacher, or parent), or both.

Writing or Essay Examinations

In a composition (usually essay format) examination, respondents are required to create responses to questions or other stimuli and to communicate their responses using written communication skills, including proper use of grammar, spelling, and information organization. These types of examinations have the advantage of allowing each respondent to develop a highly personalized response. However, they have the disadvantage of allowing significant variation in the responses presented, which in turn hinders determination of an effective or successful response to the stimulus presented, which then makes scoring difficult. Standardization in presentation of writing examinations and in "scoring" responses to them is increasingly being achieved through the use of computer-based test formats.

MAJOR TYPES OF TESTS

Specific tests are usually described according to their respective individual characteristics. More commonly, however, tests are grouped according to the general human dynamic being assessed. Therefore, counselors typically use five major types of standardized tests: achievement, aptitude, intelligence, interest, and personality.

Achievement Tests

Achievement tests are developed to measure the effects of relatively specific programs of instruction or training (Aiken, 2002; Gregory, 2000). Accordingly, achievement tests are used widely in educational systems and institutions. However, achievement tests are also used in business and industry settings to determine the need for or effects of "on the job" or other specialized training. In either case, achievement tests are designed to provide information about how much has been learned up to the date of assessment as a result of educational or training experiences.

Structured or guided learning activities, such as school curricula, are intended to enable participants to learn the content of specific knowledge and skill domains. Achievement tests are developed to be related to those domains. Thus, content validity considerations are particularly important in evaluating achievement tests. Because achievement tests are generally administered one time, usually at the end of an instructional period, internal consistency reliability is a primary consideration in their evaluation.

Achievement tests typically are subdivided into three types: single-subject-matter, survey batteries, and diagnostic. The purpose of *single-subject-matter* achievement tests is to assess level of knowledge retention for a specifically defined content domain. This type of test is most commonly used in schools. However, they are sometimes used in other specialized training programs such as construction or trade apprenticeship programs. *Survey battery* achievement tests are collections of single-subject-matter tests. Achievement test batteries contain subtests, each of which is designed to measure achievement in a specific area. Achievement test batteries have several advantages over a collection of single-subject-matter tests. Administration procedures are simplified by the format similarity in each subsection. Testing costs often are less for achievement test batteries because printing, test booklet binding, answer sheet printing, and overall processing costs are usually minimized. The greatest advantage of achievement test batteries, however, is that all subtests in the battery have the same norm group. This commonality facilitates comparisons among a respondent's relative levels of achievement across areas tested.

Diagnostic achievement tests are primarily concerned with measuring skills or abilities. For example, diagnostic tests can be used to determine which reading, writing, or mathematical skills students are able to perform. Diagnostic achievement tests are sometimes referred to as "deficit measurement" tests because they reveal skills that have not yet been mastered. Subsequent instruction can be focused specifically upon the development of these skills. It should be noted that although diagnostic tests identify skills that have not yet been achieved, they do not reveal *why* the skills have not been achieved. Achievement tests yield descriptive but not causal relationship results.

Clearly there is a trend toward the development of criterion-referenced achievement tests paralleling the trend toward development of curricular competency objectives in schools. This latter trend should help clarify the objectives schools are trying to accomplish. However, it may result in greater tendencies to "teach to the test," particularly when curricular and test objectives and competencies are highly similar. Therefore, counselors using achievement tests should consider the instruction underlying results.

Aptitude Tests

Traditionally, aptitude tests have been defined as tests intended for the prediction of an individual's future behavior. For example, aptitude tests have been used to predict future performance in an academic curriculum area or in a specialized vocational activity. The traditionally used definition has the advantage of implying how the tests are to be used (i.e., for prediction). However, the definition does not clarify why aptitude tests have greater predictive power than other types of tests, or how they differ from other types of tests.

The nature and purposes of aptitude testing are best conceived within the global context of evaluation of human abilities. Within that context, intelligence testing is considered to be the measurement and evaluation of potentially generalized human functioning. Aptitude testing within that context is conceived as measurement and evaluation of potential functioning within more specific domains of human behavior. In general, the narrower the domain of human functioning into which prediction is to be made, the easier it is to develop effective predictive tests. Thus, aptitude tests have greater predictive power because they usually focus on specific areas of human functioning.

The physical formats of most aptitude tests are similar to other measures of cognitive functioning (e.g., intelligence or achievement tests). They frequently contain multiple-choice items, with a few tests containing manual or other dexterity tasks. The difference between aptitude and achievement tests lies in the criteria to which the items are theoretically related. Items in achievement tests are presumed to be related to academic and other learning experiences to which respondents have been *previously* exposed. Items in aptitude tests are presumed to be related to learning or occupational tasks that respondents will be *expected* to master or accomplish in the future.

Although theoretical distinctions can be made between aptitude and achievement tests, practical distinctions are difficult to operationalize. All human performance on tests is contingent upon respondents' previous learning and life experiences. For example, there is considerable debate as to whether the Scholastic Assessment Test (SAT; formerly the Scholastic Aptitude Test) is an achievement or an aptitude test. Ostensibly, it is an aptitude test because it is used primarily to predict secondary school students' performance in college curricula. Presumably, individual items are closely related to the types of mental functioning tasks that college students are required to master. However, SAT scores have high positive correlations with students' high school grade point averages (GPAs), which have high positive correlations with secondary school level achievement tests. Further, most students who complete the SAT have been enrolled in "college prep" curricula that focused upon mastery of academic skills (i.e., skills necessary for successful performance in college). School systems publicize increases in the average SAT scores for graduates (as if the SAT was an achievement test) while colleges extol the positive correlations between SAT scores and GPAs (as if the SAT were an aptitude test). The debate will not likely be ended soon.

Aptitude tests are usually categorized into either single-domain or multi-factor batteries. The differentiation is the same as that for achievement tests. Single-domain aptitude tests focus upon a specific aspect of human performance such as a particular type of academic performance or job behavior. Aptitude (multi-factor) test batteries are assemblies of single-domain tests having a common format, administration procedure, and norm group. Regardless of type, criterion-related validity (specifically *predictive* validity) is most important for aptitude tests. Similar to achievement tests, internal consistency reliability is the most important type for aptitude tests. For large-scale testing programs, equivalent forms reliability also is important.

Counselors use aptitude test results primarily in academic and/or vocational counseling contexts. Because of the "faith" many people place in aptitude test results, it is imperative that counselors establish that aptitude tests have validity for the respective contexts in which predictions are made. Erroneous "predictions" of performance can have significant, long-term detrimental effects for counselees.

Intelligence Tests

No area in testing has resulted in more heated debate than the nature and effective measurement of intelligence (Anastasi & Urbina, 1997). Considerable interest exists among professionals in being able to evaluate an individual's "level of mental ability" because of the many significant implications that could be derived from such knowledge. However, while many of these implications serve the benefit of humankind, some can be construed as highly unethical. Therefore, it may be best that neither a definitive explanation nor a fully valid measurement of intelligence has yet been, or will be, conceived.

The voluminous literature on intelligence testing prohibits more than cursory coverage of the topic. Therefore, only a few of the major concepts are addressed here. At the core of intelligence testing is how intelligence is defined. Some, following the lead of Binet, conceive of intelligence as a *unitary* (also called unifactor) construct. In brief, they believe that intelligence is a single, generalized (likely inherited) human ability that underlies all human functioning. The most well-known example of a test based on this conceptualization is the Stanford-Binet Intelligence Test (S-B). In contrast, others, following the lead of Wechsler, believe that intelligence is the sum total of a large and diverse set of more specific (likely inherited) mental abilities. That is, they believe that intelligence is a *multifactor* construct. A variety of intelligence tests have been developed based on this conceptualization, such as the Wechsler Intelligence Scale for Children (WISC) or Wechsler Adult Intelligence Scale (WAIS). Still others, such as the Kaufmans, believe that intelligence is multifactored but inseparable from prior experiences and/or learning, and have developed tests such as the Kaufman Assessment Battery for Children (K-ABC) or Kaufman Adolescent and Adult Intelligence Test (KAIT) to reflect this "integrated" perspective. The pragmatic result is that different intelligence tests yield from one to twenty or more (subscale) scores depending on the definition used as the basis for the respective tests.

Intelligence tests also are classified as *group* or *individual* tests. Group intelligence tests are usually of the "paper-and-pencil" variety. They are heavily dependent on facility in use of language and are designed to be administered to large groups of persons during a single administration. As the name implies, individual intelligence tests are *designed* to be administered to one person at a time. Individual intelligence tests also typically include "performance" tasks to be completed by respondents. The significant advantage of individual intelligence tests over group intelligence tests is that competent administrators can learn much about *how* a person responds to a testing task (i.e., method of problem solving and/or affective reactions) by careful observation during the testing session. The significant disadvantage of individual intelligence testing is the cost of administering tests on an individual basis.

Intelligence tests (or subsections of them) also are described as verbal or nonverbal. A "verbal" intelligence test employs the use of language, such as providing definitions of words in a "vocabulary" subtest. In a "nonverbal" intelligence test, persons can respond without having to interpret written or spoken language. Traditionally, such tests have been composed of a variety of tasks involving figures, diagrams, symbols, or drawings (e.g., the Raven's Progressive Matrices). However, the term also has come to include "performance" tests (or subtests) in which respondents physically manipulate objects (e.g., the Leiter International Performance Scale). Most well-accepted individual intelligence tests include both verbal and nonverbal subtests. Most group intelligence tests are verbal, although a few nonverbal ("culture-fair") group intelligence tests have been developed.

The immense general interest in intelligence assessment has subjected intelligence testing to intense scrutiny, which has resulted in substantial criticism being aimed at intelligence tests. A common criticism is that intelligence tests are really "academic aptitude" tests; items in them seem closely related to the types of abilities needed to be successful in academic systems. Another criticism is that intelligence tests are biased; they favor persons from upper socioeconomic classifications because of the types of values reflected in the tests. However, the most significant criticism for counselors is that intelligence tests are culturally and/or racially biased. Arguments and counterarguments have emerged as to whether, how, or why intelligence tests are racially or culturally biased. At the very least, there is a basis for questioning possible bias in intelligence tests. Therefore, counselors who intend to use intelligence tests should spend considerable time studying available expository and empirical information about intelligence testing.

Interest Inventories

Interest inventories were developed as a means to assess a person's relative preferences for (i.e., feelings about) engaging in a variety of conceptually related activities (Anastasi & Urbina, 1997; Drummond, 1999; Hood & Johnson, 2002). Among the most well-known interest inventories are the Strong Interest Inventory, Kuder Occupational Interest Survey, and Jackson Vocational Interest Survey. Although the vast majority of interest inventories focus upon assessment of vocational interests, leisure (or avocational) interest inventories are sometimes useful to counselors. However, the following discussion relates only to vocational interest inventories because of their predominance.

Vocational interest inventories are intended to provide information on a person's interests in various vocations or occupations. To achieve this goal, respondents indicate their degree of preference on a scale with incremental values for each of a large set of activities. The activities that respondents prefer are obtained and related to types of work activities that are characteristic of various occupations. Noteworthy is that activities for which preference information is obtained may not be obviously related to particular occupations. That is, respondents typically do not know which activities are conceptually and/or empirically related to particular occupations.

Associations between activities and occupations are established by having persons who report being "satisfied" in an occupation indicate their preferences for a variety of activities. Activities that are most frequently preferred by "satisfied" workers become associated with the respective occupations. Thus, vocational interest assessment typically is a comparison of a respondent's pattern of activity preferences with those of persons reporting satisfaction in various occupations. Vocational interest assessment has reached a degree of sophistication such that interests levels in a wide variety of occupations are achieved through responses to a relatively small number of items (i.e., activities).

For counseling purposes, the basic assumption underlying interest assessment is that people are prone to engage in activities they prefer. Thus, a *very* simplistic view of "vocational" counseling is that of pairing people's interests with activities inherent in occupations, with interest assessment as a major component of the process. However, such a simplistic view belies the limitations of vocational interest assessment.

Chief among the limitations of interest assessment is that "high interest in" an occupation is not necessarily synonymous with "aptitude for" an occupation. Unfortunately, counselees who are poorly counseled often erroneously assume that interest and aptitude are equivalent, and may subsequently make misinformed decisions. Another limitation of interest assessment is susceptibility to response sets. For example, some people report high levels of interest in particular activities because they believe it is socially acceptable to do so. Perhaps this explains why many young people "over-select" the "higher" professions as occupational goals although they do not have the requisite aptitudes for those professions. A third limitation is reliability. Interests often fluctuate because of the influences of life experience, maturation, social context, and/or economic need. Thus, even the best vocational interest inventories have low stability reliability coefficients. Finally, there is the potential for gender bias in interest assessment. Clearly gender roles and situations in the workplace are changing. These changes result in gender-specific or non–gender-specific normative data for interest inventories. Development costs restrict frequencies of instrument and/or normative refinements. Therefore, the continuing possibility exists that vocational interest inventory results can be misinterpreted because of gender bias.

These limitations notwithstanding, assessment of vocational interests is used frequently by counselors. Several reasons underlie this trend. One is that counselees seek the most expedient means of finding satisfying and rewarding work. A second reason is that interest assessment is nonthreatening to counselees; it is acceptable to lack interest in an area. A third is that counselees view interest assessment as a way to understand themselves without fear of disclosing their "deficiencies." In summary, counselors and counselees favor interest assessment because it provides information that is easily obtained and accepted in counseling processes.

Personality Inventories

A definition of personality assessment is difficult because of its multifaceted nature. However, in general, personality inventories are designed to yield information about a person's characteristics, traits, behaviors, attitudes, opinions, and/or emotions (Anastasi & Urbina, 1997; Gregory, 2000; Hood & Johnson, 2002). Personality assessment is particularly germane to the work of counselors, but it is the most complex type of assessment; counselors must be knowledgeable in both psychometric principles and personality theory. Additionally, they should have substantive supervised practice before using personality assessment instruments.

Personality inventories are classified as *structured* or *unstructured*. Structured personality inventories contain a set of items that are interpreted in the same way by all respondents. These inventories also contain a set of potential item responses from among which a respondent selects one as most appropriate (i.e., pertinent to or characteristic of self). Structured personality inventories are sometimes referred to as self-report inventories (Anastasi & Urbina, 1997). Responses are selected by respondents, not interpretations of administrators. Structured personality inventories yield quantitative scores based on predetermined scoring criteria. They are intended to be interpreted in comparison to normative data. The Myers-Briggs Type Inventory, Minnesota Multiphasic Personality Inventory–2, Sixteen Personality Factor Questionnaire, and California Psychological Inventory are among the more well-known self-report personality inventories.

Unstructured personality inventories contain stimuli that can be interpreted in different ways by different respondents. Unstructured personality inventories are sometimes referred to as "projective" tests because in many of them respondents are required to "project" thoughts or feelings onto the stimuli presented. The Rorschach Inkblot Test, Thematic Apperception Test, House-Tree-Person, and Kinetic Family Drawing Test are well-known examples of projective personality inventories. Although "scoring" procedures have been developed for some unstructured personality inventories, results are more commonly "clinical interpretations" of responses made.

Personality inventories have a number of limitations, many of which are similar to those for interest inventories. For example, personality inventories are susceptible to "faking." In these instances, counselees subvert the validity of the assessment by providing responses they believe will make them "look good" or "look bad." Personality inventories also are susceptible to invalidity through contextual bias. What is a "perfectly normal" response in one context may be evaluated as an exceptionally deviant response in another (Dana, 1993; Whiston, 2000). Counselees also may perceive the use of personality inventories as threatening. While counselees may be intrigued about the nature of their personalities, fear of "negative" attributes often outweighs curiosity-based motivation to respond openly and honestly.

The use of personality inventories can be beneficial in helping counselees gain insights into their functioning. However, most counselors do not receive extensive training in personality assessment. Therefore, they should restrict the use of personality inventories to persons who are functioning normally, but who have areas of concern they want to address. In general, most counselors will derive most benefit from use of structured or self-report inventories.

Test Bias

No discussion of basic concepts in testing would be complete without some reference to test bias. Anastasi and Urbina (1997) wrote that, "The principal questions that have been raised regarding test bias pertain to validity coefficients . . . and to the relationship between the group means on the test and on the criterion . . ." (p. 165).

Test bias *appears* evident when at least two distinctly identifiable groups achieve different results on a test. These differences may be attributed to factors (e.g., gender, race, or physical condition) that, theoretically, *should not* be bases for the differences. It is important to note that while test bias is usually thought of as a characteristic of test items, its most significant (and usually detrimental) impact concerns interpretations of test data and the actions taken on the basis of those interpretations.

A variety of methods have been developed to alleviate test bias, including empirical means. Test developers are conscientiously striving to produce nonbiased tests. Nonetheless, there remain some tests that are biased. Therefore, counselors must be sensitive to test results that may be biased and should strive to ensure that their interpretations of test results are not flawed by being based on biased data.

Documents Pertinent to Testing

There are at least five types of informational documents pertinent to testing with which counselors should be familiar. The first type is sections of relevant ethical standards pertaining to testing (see Chapter 3). In particular, counselors should be thoroughly familiar with the measurement and evaluation sections of the ACA *Code of Ethics and Standards of Practice* and the NBCC *Code of Ethics*. These standards are available in written form from the parent organizations and in electronic form at their respective websites (*http://www.counseling.org* and *http://www.nbcc.org*). The second type, documents related to *appropriate practices for test users*, is covered later in this chapter.

The third type is *test manuals*. A good test manual contains the theoretical bases of the test; evidence of validity, reliability, and appropriateness; normative or criterion data; and other information necessary for proper use of the test. Good tests have good test manuals, and good counselors make good use of those manuals. Indeed, maximum benefit cannot be derived from a test unless the test user is familiar with the material presented in the test manual.

Specific information about tests, such as that usually found in test manuals, increasingly is being conveyed from test publishers' websites. Typically, this information can be found by first visiting the appropriate publisher's home page and then linking to the needed information for a particular test.

The fourth type is a single document, the *Standards for Educational and Psychological Testing* (AERA/APA/NCME, 2000). The *Standards* were developed initially, and subsequently revised, through collaborative effort of the American Psychological Association (APA), American Educational Research Association (AERA), and National Council on Measurement in Education (NCME), and are now published by AERA. The *Standards* are the recognized criteria against which tests, testing procedures, test manuals, and other test information should be evaluated. Counselors should become thoroughly familiar with these standards in order to critique, select, and use tests effectively for counseling purposes.

The fifth type is the set of documents that have to do with broad-scale professional practices pertinent to testing. For example, both the Fair Access Coalition for Testing in the United States and the International Test Commission headquartered in Paris have developed documents clarifying appropriate professional practices for test use, including qualifications of various types of test users. The documents and other information provided by organizations such as these frequently are focused upon specific problematic situations such as ideological conflicts about tests and/or their use among professional groups interested in testing or perspectives on cross-cultural testing practices. These types of documents most commonly are presented as a link off the home page of a sponsoring organization. Counselors should be familiar with the contents of these types of documents because they suggest boundaries and guidelines for the appropriate uses of tests.

RECENT TRENDS IN TESTING

A recent and highly significant trend in testing is application of *Item Response Theory* (IRT) in test development practices. McKinley (1989) wrote:

> The attractiveness of IRT as both a research and measurement tool is derived primarily from its *parameter invariance* properties. The property of invariance means that the item statistics that are obtained from the application of the IRT model are independent of the sample of examinees to which a test (or other instrument) is administered. Likewise, the personal statistics obtained for examinees are independent of the items included in the test. This is in marked contrast to more traditional statistics, such as item and examinee proportion-correct or number-correct scores (p. 37).

In classical (i.e., "traditional") test theory and practices based on it, resultant test statistics are, technically, applicable only to the norm group from which the response data were derived; other groups would have other item and/or test statistics. Thus, item and test statistical data in traditional analyses are unique to the set of items included and to the particular norm group. In comparison, use of IRT models yields data that are, theoretically, invariant with regard to both the sample of examinees and the sample of items.

Thorough discussion of IRT models is beyond the scope of this chapter. However, interested readers are referred to McKinley (1989) for a good overview of IRT or to Hambleton (1998) for a complete discussion. The important point is that the use of IRT models has resulted in significant improvement in the development of tests, particularly in testing for achievement, aptitude, and credentialing (Anastasi & Urbina, 1997; Gregory, 2000).

A related recent trend is use of so-called *adaptive testing* models. Adaptive testing is quite literally what the term implies: each test is "adapted" for each respondent. Currently, adaptive testing is used almost exclusively for ability testing (although other applications are possible). In a typical adaptive testing situation (e.g., the SAT or GRE), the first item to which the examinee responds is a relatively arbitrarily selected starting point, usually based on a generalized presumption about the examinee (e.g., based on the examinee's age or grade level). However, selection of the next and all subsequent items is based on performance on the preceding item. For example, if the examinee provides an incorrect response to the first item, the examinee is next presented with an item of lesser difficulty. Conversely, if the examinee provides the correct response to an item, the examinee is next presented with an item having a higher difficulty level.

Adaptive testing is theoretically sound because of advances in the use of IRT models and computers. That is, IRT models allow development of item difficulty indices that are *theoretically* sample and item set free. The use of computer-based formats for adaptive testing allows the determination of the next item to which the examinee should respond to be made rapidly.

An examinee's experience with adaptive testing is significantly different than that for traditional testing. For example, in adaptive testing, not all examinees respond to the same items or even the same number of items for a given test; each response pattern is individualized. Examinees responding to adaptive tests also are not permitted to go "backwards" in the item sequence, which means that test respondents are not permitted to "skip" an item and then go back to it later.

It is clear that adaptive testing yields a highly personalized test for each examinee, reduces testing time (and therefore costs), and facilitates more rapid provision of feedback (which in some cases is immediate upon completion of the test). Adaptive testing is becoming much more common even though many persons find the unidirectional task sequencing to be disconcerting. Nonetheless, it is likely that adaptive testing will continue to be used more frequently as computer-based testing becomes more common.

Another recent trend in testing that appears to be being rapidly embraced by members of the testing community is "generalizability theory." In generalizability theory, a test score is considered as a single sample from a universe of possible scores for the respondent. "The reliability of that score is the precision with which it estimates a more generalized universe value of the score (the 'true score')" (Aiken, 2002, p. 91). Both a *generalizability coefficient* (which is similar to a traditional reliability coefficient) and a *universe value of the score* can be calculated. The primary application of generalizability theory is exploration of how factors such as the nature of the items; administration, motivational, and environmental conditions; and other facets of performance influence the generalizability coefficient (and therefore reliability of measurement).

So-called *authentic assessment* is actually a subtype within the more general category of performance assessment. Authentic assessment also is sometimes referred to as alternative assessment to emphasize that it is different from traditional paper-and-pencil testing (Aiken, 2002). In brief, performance assessment involves evaluation of the products of some behavior or action (such as the use of an identified skill). The most common representation of authentic assessment is the use of *portfolios* in educational systems. As an alternative to traditional written tests, students are asked to create a portfolio and to fill it with "products" or "physical evidence" that represent their "best" work in a number of different areas (e.g., math, science, art, or language arts). The contents of the portfolio are then examined and evaluated by the instructor.

The use of portfolios and other authentic assessment techniques was heralded as a more caring, individualized, and outcome-based alternative to traditional assessment practices during the late 1980s and throughout much of the 1990s. Whether this popularity will continue is unknown. However, it appears to be waning in at least the scientific community because authentic assessment procedures simply have not faired well when reasonable psychometric scrutiny has been applied. For example, both intra- and interrater (e.g., teacher) reliability coefficients for portfolio evaluations are astonishingly low. Further, there remains considerable debate as to how much structure should be imposed on the composition of the portfolio materials. That is, to what extent should students be told what has to be included in their respective portfolios? Authentic assessment is an alternative to traditional assessment, but it is far from an equivalent alternative.

Clearly the most significant current trend in assessment is what might be called multicultural sensitivity. Historically, assessment has been mired in an *etic* perspective, for example, a "perspective that emphasizes universals among human beings by using examination and comparison of many cultures from a position outside those cultures" (Dana, 1993, p. 21). The alternative is to adopt an *emic* perspective, which is one that is "culture specific and examines behavior from within a culture, using criteria relative to the internal characteristics of that culture" (Dana, 1993, p. 21). The emic perspective suggests that test results must be considered in the context of the cultural characteristics of the person(s) from whom the results were obtained. A particularly striking example of the need for multicultural sensitivity in testing is when tests are used to support or confirm a diagnosis of mental illness. Clearly the "appropriateness" of behavioral reactions to life stressors is determined in part by the cultural context in which the reactions are manifest. If testing is done without due consideration to potentially influential and/or important cultural factors, how can the test results possibly be valid (Dana, 1993; Lee, 2001; Whiston, 2000)?

APPROPRIATE PRACTICES FOR TEST USERS

Counselors' effective use of tests is directly related to the degree of responsibility they assume for using the tests. Historically, guidelines for responsible uses of tests had to be extrapolated from statements of ethical standards. A vast majority of counselors have attempted to use tests ethically and, therefore, responsibly. However, their effort was limited by lack of specificity in ethical standards statements. In response to this situation, in 1989, the American Counseling Association (ACA; formerly the American Association for Counseling and Development, AACD), through its Association for Assessment in Counseling and Education (AACE; formerly the Association for Measurement and Evaluation in Counseling and Development, AMECD) division, developed the guidelines entitled *Responsibilities of Users of Standardized Tests* (RUST). The following are comments on major sections of those guidelines.

With regard to test decisions, counselors (as test users) are responsible for determination of information assessment needs and clarification of the objectives for and limitations of testing for each circumstance. Thus, counselors (not counselees or others) have the final authority for decisions about test use in their profession. Qualifications of test users also are an important factor in the testing process. They should be considered with regard to the purposes of testing, characteristics of the tests, conditions of test use, and the roles of other professionals.

Emphasized in the test selection guidelines is that careful consideration should be given to each test's validity, reliability, appropriateness, and other technical characteristics and psychometric properties. Also, respondent participation in the test selection process is desirable, if appropriate and/or possible. Test administration procedures should be conducted by qualified administrators who give proper test orientation and directions in appropriate testing conditions. Test scoring should be conducted only by fully qualified persons to ensure accurate results.

Provided within the guidelines are test interpretations in the contexts of uses for placement, prediction, description, assessment of growth, and program evaluation. The importance of appropriate norms, technical factors, and the effects of variations in administration and scoring are emphasized. Guidelines for communicating test results in individual or group contexts also are presented.

Unfortunately, only these brief comments on the RUST statement can be provided here. Counselors who use tests should carefully read the entire document, which is available through the Resources link at *http://aac.ncat.edu*.

Another document of significance to counselors in using tests is the *Code of Fair Testing Practices in Education*. This non-copyrighted document was developed by the Joint Committee on Testing Practices (JCTP). The JCTP includes member representatives from a variety of professional organizations, notably including the ACA and AACE. The code is distinct in that it delineates responsibilities of both test users and test developers. Major sections of the code present guidelines for topics such as test development or selection, test score interpretation, fairness in testing, and informing test takers of results. The code is available as a link from *http://aac.ncat.edu*.

Although the code was developed specifically to address testing practices in educational settings, the important points in it extend beyond that limitation. That is, the code contains useful information and sound suggestions for use of tests in any circumstance. Counselors should use the code both for guidance about good testing practices and for clarification of responsibilities among test users and developers.

TESTING IN PROGRAM EVALUATION

Counselors should be familiar with the "counseling program evaluation literature." However, many counselors erroneously believe that generating and reporting test results is synonymous with program evaluation. Testing is an aspect of program evaluation, but a "testing program" does not replace program evaluation. Effective program evaluation involves gathering a wide variety of both objective (empirical) and subjective information about program impacts (Loesch, 2001). Test results are just one part of this process.

Formative and *summative* are the two major types of program evaluation processes. In formative program evaluation, data are gathered while the program is in progress so that process adjustments and modifications can be made to maximize the program's (eventual) effectiveness. Summative program evaluation involves gathering data at the conclusion of a program in order to determine the extent of the program's overall impact. Carefully and effectively designed program evaluation processes usually encompass both types.

Testing and test results can be used in either type of program evaluation process. For example, test data derived while counseling and/or other programmatic activities are being conducted can be used to identify needed changes in those activities. Test data obtained after a program has been concluded can be used for analysis and evaluation of which activities were effective. In either case, if tests are used within appropriate guidelines they can be invaluable resources in program evaluation processes.

Just as program evaluation is not synonymous with testing, neither is it synonymous with research. However, research designs and principles often are incorporated into program evaluation processes. Specifically, summative program evaluation processes typically involve "pre-post" testing, which includes tests being administered before a program begins and the same (or equivalent) tests being administered at the program's end. In addition to any concern about test validity, this type of procedure requires concern for the appropriateness and reliability of tests used. Thus, the major concerns regarding test use for counseling purposes are at least equally important for research and program evaluation purposes.

The need for counselors to be accountable for their activities has been widely publicized. Program evaluation processes should be a part of counselors' accountability efforts because these processes reflect the full scope of services rendered by counselors. However, counselors need to be involved in program evaluation activities because competent counselors know about tests and testing, and therefore should serve as resources for development of program evaluation procedures.

SUMMARY

Testing is an integral and legitimate part of a counselor's professional functioning. However, counselors have a choice about the attitudes they adopt toward testing. They can view it as a "necessary evil" and employ minimal effort toward testing functions, or they can do what they need to do to gain understanding of psychometric principles, tests, and testing processes and therefore reap the benefits of effective testing practices. Counselors who adopt this latter perspective will find that testing is a valuable resource, and one that enhances many of their professional activities.

Note that almost all testing companies have their own Website; search by company name, test name, or type of test.

CHAPTER THIRTEEN

DIAGNOSIS IN COUNSELING

LINDA SELIGMAN, PH.D., L.P.C.
George Mason University

Alice, age twenty consulted a counselor at her college because of feelings of depression. She told the counselor that she has barely been able to get out of bed for the past month. She has been eating little, has strong feelings of unexplained guilt, has not attended most of her classes, and has thought about committing suicide. She could offer no explanation for her mood change and said she has never felt like this before.

Michael, age twenty-eight, sought help for depression from a community mental health center. Although he has been going to work and fulfilling his family obligations, he has felt hopeless for over a month. Michael reported a 10-year history of unstable moods with long periods of depression as well as episodes of elation, high energy, and distractibility.

Susan, age 11, was brought to her pediatrician by her mother who stated that Susan has been sad and tearful for the past month, since her parents separated. Although Susan does become much more cheerful when her father visits and has been going to school regularly, she was moody and irritable much of the time.

Robert, age 45, sought help from a psychiatrist for long-standing depression, coinciding with a history of alcohol and drug abuse. He has multiple physical complaints and had several alcohol related accidents. He has begun several treatment programs but has not been able to remain drug- or alcohol-free for more than a few weeks.

Cheryl, too, sought counseling for depression. At 35, she had achieved a great deal. Married with two children, she was a successful writer and photographer. However, she has been troubled by feelings of sadness of at least two years' duration that she has been unable to dispel on her own. Although she has been able to function relatively well and conceal those feelings from others, she finally decided to seek help.

All five of these people sought help for depression. However, their depressions differ in several respects: presence of an apparent precipitant, duration, frequency, severity, and accompanying symptoms. Similarly, the diagnoses, the treatments, and the prognosis for each person's disorder differ.

Alice probably is experiencing a Major Depressive Disorder, Single Episode, with Melancholic Features. This form of depression tends to respond fairly quickly to several types of counseling (e.g., cognitive, brief psychodynamic), often in combination with antidepressant medication. Michael is suffering from a Bipolar I Disorder, Most Recent Episode Depressed. This disorder is frequently chronic without treatment but is amenable to treatment through a combination of counseling and medication. Susan has experienced a recent loss and is reacting to that loss with an Adjustment Disorder with Depressed Mood. Family counseling seems most likely to alleviate Susan's sadness. Robert, on the other hand, may be suffering from a Substance-Induced Mental Disorder, caused by his long-standing substance use. Prognosis here is far less favorable and treatment may entail hospitalization. Dysthymic Disorder probably is the diagnosis for Cheryl's symptoms. Medication and hospitalization are usually not needed for treatment of this disorder but its response to counseling varies and is difficult to predict.

The importance of diagnosis can be seen from these examples. Without an accurate diagnosis, counselors will probably have difficulty determining the proper treatment for a disorder and assessing whether a person is likely to benefit from counseling. In the previous examples, Susan, and probably Cheryl, are good candidates for counseling. Alice and Michael are also likely to benefit from counseling, but as part of a team effort, with counselors and psychiatrists working together to ameliorate the depression. Robert's case is too complicated by physiological concerns for counseling to be a primary focus of treatment at present. Perhaps once he has been medically evaluated and detoxified, counseling can facilitate his adjustment to a healthier lifestyle and complement other forms of treatment.

BENEFITS OF DIAGNOSIS

Estimates indicate that 40–50 million Americans have mental or addictive disorders (Maxmen & Ward, 1995). According to Hinkle (1994, p. 174), "At the foundation of effective mental health care is the establishment of a valid psychodiagnosis." An accurate diagnosis is essential in determining the appropriate treatment for a mental disorder and in indicating when counseling is likely to be effective and when a referral is necessary. These are not the only reasons why diagnosis is a fundamental skill in the counselor's repertoire (Seligman, 1996; Seligman, in press).

- A diagnostic system provides a consistent framework as well as a set of criteria for naming and describing mental disorders.
- Knowing the diagnosis for a client's concerns can help counselors anticipate the course of the disorder and develop a clearer understanding of the client's symptoms.
- Knowledge of diagnosis enables counselors to make use of the literature on treatment effectiveness (Seligman, 1998) (e.g., what types of interventions are most likely to ameliorate a given disorder) and to formulate a treatment plan that is likely to be effective.

- The process of counseling employs a common language, used by all mental health disciplines, thereby facilitating parity, credibility, communication, and collaboration.
- Diagnoses are linked to several standardized inventories (e.g., the Minnesota Multiphasic Personality Inventory, the Millon Clinical Multiaxial Inventory), enabling counselors to use inventories as a source of information on their clients.
- Counselors can more easily demonstrate accountability and effectiveness and are less vulnerable to malpractice suits if they make diagnoses and treatment plans according to an accepted system.
- Using a standardized system of diagnosis helps counselors obtain third-party payments for their services, thereby making counseling affordable to many people who would not otherwise be able to receive help.
- The use of standard diagnostic terminology helps counselors to research the nature and effectiveness of their practice and improve their treatment skills.
- Sharing diagnoses with clients, when appropriate, can help them to understand their symptoms, and experience less guilt and take more appropriate responsibility for themselves. Knowing that others have experienced similar symptoms and that information is available about their conditions can also be reassuring.
- Explaining to clients that they have a diagnosable mental disorder can unbalance previously established views of their difficulties and can help them to take a fresh look at their issues and perhaps increase their openness to treatment.
- The use of diagnosis helps counselors determine those clients they have the skills and training to help as well as those who would benefit from a referral.

RISKS OF DIAGNOSIS

Although many benefits come from the use of a standard diagnostic system, some risks also are inherent in the use of such a system (Seligman, in press, p. 64).

- Attaching a diagnostic label to someone can be stigmatizing, if misused, and can lead to negative perceptions of that person at school, at work, or in the family.
- In some cases, knowing the diagnostic term for a person's symptoms can be more discouraging and threatening than viewing the problem in lay terms. For example, parents may be more comfortable dealing with a child they view as behaving badly than with one who has a conduct disorder.
- Diagnosis can lead to overgeneralizing, to viewing clients as their mental disorders (e.g., a Borderline, a Depressive) rather than as a person with a particular set of concerns, and can promote a focus on pathology rather than on health.
- Although the process of diagnosis can facilitate information gathering and treatment planning, it also can make it more difficult to think about people in developmental and systemic terms and to take a holistic view of clients and their environments.
- Similarly, attaching a diagnostic label to one person puts the focus of treatment on the individual rather than on a family or social system. This can reinforce

the family's perception of that person as its only problem and can make it more difficult for a family to work together on shared issues and concerns.

■ The diagnosis of some mental disorders can have a negative impact on peoples' ability to obtain health or disability insurance and can affect their employment if they are in high-risk or security-related positions.

■ In addition, the widely accepted systems of diagnosis have all grown out of a Western concept of mental illness and may not be as relevant to people from other cultures.

Although some risks clearly are inherent in the process of diagnosis, most of the risks can be avoided by skillful counseling, judicious presentation of diagnostic information to avoid misunderstanding by clients and their families, and maintenance of the clients' confidentiality whenever possible. Particularly important in reducing risks is counselors' knowledge of diagnosis as well as their multicultural competence and sensitivity. "Barriers to effective counseling in the postmodern era lie more within the counselor than between the pages of a book. The *DSM*, when used properly, can enhance rather than detract from skills and culturally sensitive counseling" (Seligman, 1999a, p. 6). Resources such as *Diagnosis in a Multicultural Context* (Paniagua, 2001) and *Diagnosis and Treatment Planning in Counseling* (Seligman, 1996; Seligman, in press) can help counselors to maximize the benefits and minimize the risks of diagnosis.

GROWING IMPORTANCE OF DIAGNOSIS

Some counselors and students in counseling, particularly those who are primarily interested in school or business settings, may feel uncomfortable with the idea of making diagnoses. They may view their role as emphasizing support, crisis-intervention, and information giving and may refer people who have mental disorders to other mental health practitioners. Consequently, they may feel little need to learn about diagnosis. Other counselors may have a strongly humanistic, multicultural, or family systems emphasis in their counseling and may believe that the process of labeling clients is antithetical to their conception of the counselor's role.

However, changes in the field of counseling make it important for all counselors to be familiar with the process and tools of diagnosis and most counselors seem to recognize that. A study by Mead, Hohenshil, and Singh (1997), in which 334 Certified Clinical Mental Health Counselors were surveyed on their use of the *Diagnostic and Statistical Manual of Mental Disorders (DSM)*, reflected the importance of this resource to counselors. Mead and her colleagues found that 91 percent of respondents "indicated that the *DSM* is their most frequently used professional reference" (p. 394). Most believed they were skilled in the use of the *DSM* and 93 percent reported that they believed they were usually able to provide accurate diagnoses using the *DSM*. Although respondents did note shortcomings in the *DSM*, including bias, labeling, and difficulty of use, they found the *DSM* particularly helpful with case conceptualization, treatment planning, billing, communication with other professionals, education, and meeting employers' requirements. Mastery of diagnosis can not only improve the effectiveness of mental health counselors but also is required by many places of employment where diagnoses are needed for accountability, determination of treatment effectiveness, record-keeping, and third-party payments.

Although knowledge of diagnosis is essential to mental health counselors, counselors in schools and businesses also should be familiar with the process of diagnosis for somewhat different reasons. Knowledge of diagnosis enables those counselors to determine whether they can provide services that will help a client or whether a referral is needed; it can help them to select the most appropriate referral; and it can help them anticipate the client's probable response to treatment. Making a diagnosis also can help counselors in schools and businesses to assess whether clients should remain in that setting, possibly with some extra help, or whether the client needs an environment providing more support and assistance. Diagnosis, therefore, is an important skill for all counselors.

THE *DSM-IV-TR* AND OTHER DIAGNOSTIC SYSTEMS

The most widely used diagnostic system in the United States is the *Diagnostic and Statistical Manual of Mental Disorders, (DSM)*. The most recent edition of this volume, the *DSM-IV-TR*, was issued in 2000 by the American Psychiatric Association. The first edition of the *DSM*, containing 108 categories of mental disorders, was published in 1952 (Hohenshil, 1993). Developed primarily by and for psychiatrists, it presented a psychobiological view of the nature of emotional disorders. It was replaced in 1968 by the *DSM-II*, a landmark publication in the field of mental health that looked at mental disorders primarily in terms of psychoses, neuroses, and personality disorders.

The *DSM-III* was introduced in 1980. Field tests involving over 500 clinicians were used to maximize the validity of that volume. In addition, psychologists, as well as a small number of social workers and counselors, worked along with psychiatrists to develop this revision of the *DSM*. The *DSM-III* was more comprehensive and detailed than its predecessor and was designed to be more precise and less stigmatizing in its language. The *DSM-III* made some major changes in definitions and terminology used for mental disorders. For example, the term "neurosis," which had become a pejorative and common term in the language, was no longer used. Schizophrenia was defined more narrowly and was used to describe only severe disorders involving evident loss of contact with reality.

A revised version of the *DSM-III*, the *DSM-III-R*, was published in 1987. The *DSM-III-R* reflected changes arising from increased knowledge of mental disorders as well as from changes in attitudes and perceptions. For example, the diagnosis of homosexuality was excluded from this edition, reflecting greater understanding as well as increased acceptance of homosexuality.

The primary justification for a change from the *DSM-III-R* to the *DSM-IV*, published in 1994, was compelling empirical support. Three criteria were used to determine revisions: extensive literature reviews, clinical trials, and two drafts of the

DSM-IV that invited feedback to determine whether support was available for a suggested change. The *DSM-IV*, like the *DSM-III* and *DSM-III-R*, was deliberately atheoretical. The *DSM-IV* included over 300 categories of mental disorders, as well as extensive descriptive information, much of which focused on gender, ethnicity, and cultural patterns in mental disorders. This reflects great progress in making the *DSM-IV* sensitive to differences related to group membership. The current edition, the *DSM-IV-TR*, is called a text revision of the *DSM*; further text was added describing diagnoses and their manifestations. No substantive changes in diagnostic criteria were made in the *DSM-IV-TR*. A more detailed discussion of the development of the *DSM* can be found in "Twenty Years of Diagnosis and the *DSM*" (Seligman, 1999b). Work is already underway on the *DSM-V* with publication currently anticipated in 2010.

The frequent revisions of the *DSM* demonstrate that knowledge of mental disorders is a vital and changing body of information. New material is constantly discovered about biochemistry, the emotions, and their interaction and impact. In many ways, we are still novices in our understanding of the psychology of people. As a result, our current information is often inadequate and imprecise. Although the *DSM* makes an important contribution to clarifying and organizing mental disorders, it is a complex publication whose skillful use requires sound clinical judgment as well as experience (Seligman, 1999a). A subsequent section of this chapter provides an introduction to the major types of mental disorders and gives readers some familiarity with the *DSM-IV-TR*. Browsing through the volume, reading about diagnoses of interest, and making diagnoses of case studies will increase comfort and familiarity with this sometimes intimidating volume. However, true ease of use with the *DSM* rarely comes without considerable clinical experience.

Although the *DSM-IV-TR* is the standard for diagnostic nomenclature in the United States, another system of diagnosis is also used, particularly in medically oriented settings. The *ICD-10 Classification of Mental and Behavioural Disorders* (World Health Organization, 1992), known in the United States as the *ICD-10*, is an international publication of the World Health Organization. The code numbers of the *ICD-10* are coordinated with the *DSM-IV-TR* and clinicians may refer to Appendix H of the *DSM-IV-TR* to determine the appropriate *ICD-10* diagnosis if required by a managed care organization.

DEFINITION OF A MENTAL DISORDER

The *DSM-IV-TR* defines a mental disorder as "a clinically significant behavioral or psychological syndrome or pattern that occurs in an individual" (American Psychiatric Association, 2000, p. xxxi). Responses that are expectable or culturally sanctioned are not considered mental disorders. According to the *DSM-IV-TR*, at least one of three features, distress, impairment and/or significant risk, must be present in order for a person to be diagnosed as having a mental disorder. Although these features are often present in combination, illustrations are provided of the features in isolation to clarify their nature.

Beth sought counseling after her fiancé broke their engagement for the third time. She was a successful lawyer who continued to perform well at her job despite her turmoil. A very private person, Beth continued to see friends and family and go to work every day showing little or no apparent evidence of her distress. However, every night she cried herself to sleep and even had some fleeting suicidal thoughts. Although Beth manifested no impairment nor was she really at risk, she was certainly experiencing considerable distress and met the criteria for a mental disorder, Adjustment Disorder with Depressed Mood.

On the other hand, Frank, a 14-year-old who was brought to counseling by his parents, reported that life was great; he saw his only problem as his parents' nagging. For the past year, Frank had cut classes frequently and spent several days each week hanging out at the neighborhood shopping center with his friends, he disobeyed his parents' rules, he had frequent arguments with family and teachers, and usually seemed angry and annoyed. Frank had little distress about his situation and was not yet at risk. Frank's diagnosis, Oppositional Defiant Disorder, was characterized primarily by impairment.

Hilda reported neither distress nor impairment when she consulted a counselor at the suggestion of her family physician. At 5′6″ tall, Hilda weighed 100 pounds and was quite pleased with her figure, estimating that she had only another 5 to 10 pounds to lose. Hilda had the diagnosis of Anorexia Nervosa, Restricting Type, and had dieted herself into a life-threatening physical condition.

Some symptoms that do not cause significant distress, impairment, or risk and are expectable responses are not viewed as mental disorders. For example, Jessica consulted a counselor after the birth of her third child within the past five years. Although she was a caring and knowledgeable parent, she had difficulty asking for help and managing her time. Counseling could certainly help Jessica handle the many demands on her and her husband, but Jessica did not have a mental disorder. Her reactions caused no risk to herself or the children, did not reflect impairment, and were characterized by appropriate, understandable, and manageable distress. Jessica would be described as experiencing a Phase of Life Problem rather than a mental disorder.

MULTIAXIAL ASSESSMENT

Whether or not people who present for counseling have mental disorders, a multiaxial diagnosis offers counselors a way to organize information on clients' symptoms, their physical conditions, their levels of coping, and the stressors they are experiencing. A full multiaxial assessment involves viewing a person according to five axes.

Axis I includes what the *DSM* calls Clinical Disorders and Other Conditions That May Be a Focus of Clinical Attention. All disorders and conditions in the *DSM-IV-TR* are included in Axis I with the exception of the Personality Disorders and both Mental Retardation and Borderline Intellectual Functioning that are listed on Axis II. These Axis II listings may actually involve less severe symptoms than some of the diagnoses on Axis I but they have a pervasive and enduring impact on a person's life.

People may have one or more diagnoses or conditions on Axis I and Axis II or one or both of these axes may have no diagnosis or condition listed. Each diagnosis has a code number provided in the *DSM*. When a diagnosis is listed, both the name and the code number are specified (e.g., 307.51 Bulimia Nervosa). In addition, clinicians generally describe the severity of a mental disorder, using the terms *mild, moderate,* and *severe.* Three additional specifiers describe disorders a person had previously that no longer meet the full criteria for the disorder. *In partial remission* describes symptoms that once met the criteria for a mental disorder but now are manifested in more limited ways. *In full remission* describes disorders whose symptoms no longer are evident but which remain clinically relevant, perhaps because the person still receives medication for the disorder. *Prior history* characterizes past disorders, no longer treated or in evidence, but which remain noteworthy, perhaps because they have a tendency to recur under stress. Disorders characterized as prior history would be one step removed from those described as in full remission but both would be viewed as important to keep in mind. The *DSM* also provides terminology to be used when no diagnoses are listed on Axis I or on Axis II (e.g., V71.09 No Mental Disorder on Axis II). When more than one diagnosis is listed on an axis, they are listed in order of treatment priority. The *Principal Diagnosis* is assumed to be the first diagnosis on Axis I unless otherwise specified. The *DSM-IV-TR* also offers the optional use of the descriptor *Reason for Visit,* used if the presenting concern is not the principal diagnosis.

Axis III includes *General Medical Conditions.* On this axis, clinicians list physical disorders that may be relevant to a person's emotional condition. This would include such conditions as migraine headaches that might be related to stress as well as conditions such as cancer or diabetes that might have an impact on a person's emotional adjustment. Although clinicians may informally list physical signs and symptoms on Axis III in their own notes, an official multiaxial assessment should include only medically verified physical conditions on Axis III. Until that verification is obtained, clinicians should state on Axis III that the medical symptoms and conditions are provided *by client report.*

On Axis IV, clinicians list *Psychosocial and Environmental Problems* that may be having an impact on a client. Clinicians may use their own labels for these stressors and also can organize them according to the *DSM* categories of stressors. These categories include problems with one's primary support group; problems related to the social environment; problems related to educational, occupational, or housing concerns; economic problems; and problems related to access to health care services or to interaction with the legal system. Counselors generally list on Axis IV only stressors that have occurred within the past year, unless an earlier stressor is especially relevant to the current diagnosis such as combat experiences related to a diagnosis of Posttraumatic Stress Disorder.

Axis V includes a *Global Assessment of Functioning* rating on a scale ranging from 1 to 100. Here, counselors rate clients' current functioning, paying particular attention to symptoms associated with mental disorders and conditions listed on Axes I and II. (Highest level of functioning also can be rated if the clinician chooses.) Ratings below 50 indicate people with severe symptoms who need close monitoring and probably medication and even hospitalization. Ratings above 50 indicate higher levels of functioning. Most people who are seen for counseling in outpatient settings seem to have ratings between 50 and 70.

Axes IV and V are particularly useful in treatment planning. Clients with many stressors listed on Axis IV and low ratings on Axis V are experiencing considerable stress and have poor levels of functioning. They typically require a multifaceted treatment plan, including counseling, medication, and possibly hospitalization. On the other hand, clients with an opposite profile, few stressors on Axis IV, and high ratings on Axis V, are experiencing more manageable stress and probably have good coping mechanisms. Such clients are likely to make good use of brief counseling.

The following example of a multiaxial assessment illustrates how such a diagnosis can quickly provide a broad and rich picture of a client:

Axis I:	V71.01 Adult Antisocial Behavior
	315.2 Disorder of Written Expression, Mild
Axis II:	301.20 Schizoid Personality Disorder
Axis III:	346.20 Headaches, cluster
Axis IV:	Psychosocial stressors: Arrest
Axis V:	Current global assessment of functioning (GAF): 45
	Highest GAF in the past year: 60

The previous multiaxial assessment was made on a 37-year-old man, Dennis Roth, who had been arrested and charged with assault and battery. Mr. Roth lived alone and earned a living by raising dogs. One of his dogs had escaped to a neighbor's yard where he damaged some plants and frightened the neighbor's son. The neighbor dealt with this by shooting and killing the dog. When Mr. Roth discovered this, he smashed the window of his neighbor's car and physically attacked the neighbor.

Prior to this, Mr. Roth had no legal problems and was viewed by his neighbors as a loner but as someone who was always available to help when cars or other machinery broke down. Mr. Roth had left high school when he was 16, reporting poor grades and discouragement. He had lived on a small farm, raising dogs, since that time. He had little contact with others, except that necessitated by his business and other daily activities, but reported being contented with his life.

His primary source of success and gratification and the focus of his life were his dogs. Consequently, Mr. Roth's strong response to the shooting of his dog reflected the impact this event had on his life. He had no history of criminal or violent behavior and was unlikely to present a danger to others in the future.

The multiaxial assessment provides insight into the dynamics of this client's attack on his neighbor. Axis I reflects the current incident (Adult Antisocial Behavior) and this client's long-standing learning disorder that limited his success in school as well as his career opportunities. Axis II lists his Schizoid Personality Disorder, reflected in his lack of interest in interpersonal relationships, his preference for solitary activities, and his usual detached state. Mr. Roth's medically diagnosed headaches are listed on Axis III, contributing to his constricted lifestyle. The primary stressor was his arrest and the threat of incarceration that would prevent him from caring for his dogs. Axis V indicates that this man's highest and usual level of functioning (60) is moderately impaired, particularly in terms of relationships. Current GAF of 45 reflected his aggressive behavior toward his neighbor and his continued rage. This multiaxial assessment was instrumental in obtaining probation for Mr. Roth, with the condition that he seek counseling to help him with impulse control and communication skills.

REVIEW OF THE *DSM-IV-TR*

The mental disorders and conditions described in the *DSM-IV-TR* are divided into seventeen broad categories. Although this chapter is not designed to teach or interpret the *DSM*, a brief review of the seventeen sections is provided here to give readers some familiarity with the major types of mental disorders. Many specific mental disorders and conditions included in each broad category are not cited here. Readers planning to use the *DSM* with their clients should study that book and probably complete courses or training in the use of the *DSM*. Professional organizations offer professional workshops related to the *DSM* and the American Counseling Association offers a home study program to teach diagnosis and treatment planning (Seligman, 1995). In addition, study guides and other texts are available to facilitate mastery of the *DSM*. These include *Study Guide to DSM-IV-TR* (Fauman, 2002), *DSM-IV Made Easy* (Morrison, 1995), the *DSM-IV-TR Case Studies* (Frances & Ross, 2001), *Diagnosis and Treatment Planning in Counseling* (Seligman, 1996; Seligman, in press), and *Selecting Effective Treatments* (Seligman, 1998).

Disorders Usually First Diagnosed in Infancy, Childhood, or Adolescence

This is the largest and most comprehensive category in the *DSM* and includes disorders that typically begin during the early years, although some may persist into adulthood. Many of the other diagnoses in the *DSM* also can be applied to children and adolescents but most of the disorders young people experience are included in this first category. Categories of disorders in this section include Mental Retardation, Learning Disorders, Motor Skills Disorder, Pervasive Developmental Disorders such as Autism, Attention-Deficit/Hyperactivity Disorder, Disruptive Behavior Disorders (e.g., Conduct Disorder and Oppositional Defiant Disorder), and Communication Disorders (e.g., Stuttering, Phonological Disorder). Also included in this category are Feeding and Eating Disorders of Infancy or Early Childhood such as Pica, Tic Disorders including Tourette's Disorder, and the Elimination Disorders (Encopresis and Enuresis). Other disorders in this section include Separation Anxiety Disorder, Selective Mutism, Reactive Attachment Disorder, and Stereotypic Movement Disorder.

Of the disorders in this section, Learning Disorders, Attention-Deficit/Hyperactivity Disorder, Conduct Disorder, Oppositional Defiant Disorder and Separation Anxiety Disorder are particularly important to school counselors and others working with children of elementary school age. Children with learning disorders typically have both social and academic impairment. Although they are usually of normal intelligence, they have inordinate difficulty mastering a particular area of learning such as reading or mathematics and, consequently, may experience teasing, criticism, and frustration. They usually need both counseling and academic help. Children diagnosed with Attention-Deficit/Hyperactivity Disorder also tend to have academic, social, and often family problems as a result of their symptoms such as a high level of motor activity, distractibility, and impulsivity which impair their efforts to concentrate and engage in rewarding activities with family and friends. Conduct Disorder, involving repeated violations of laws and rules (e.g., stealing, vandalism, truancy), is sometimes the precursor of adult antisocial or criminal behavior. Consequently, rapid treatment of this disorder is important although client resistance and mistrust may be high. Oppositional Defiant Disorder involves angry, defiant, and argumentative behavior and sometimes accompanies Attention-Deficit/Hyperactivity Disorder and Conduct Disorder. Family counseling is especially important in treatment of Oppositional Defiant Disorder. Separation Anxiety Disorder has been known as school phobia and typically involves difficulty separating from care givers, accompanied by an avoidance of school. Early intervention is critical here, too, because the longer this disorder persists, the more difficult it is for the child to return to school. Additional information on disorders in this section of the *DSM* can be found in books such as *Counseling Treatment for Children and Adolescents with DSM-IV-TR Disorders* (Erk, 2004).

Delirium, Dementia, and Amnestic and Other Cognitive Disorders

These cognitive disorders all involve some type of transient or permanent damage to the brain. Causes can include an injury, drug or alcohol use, exposure to a toxic chemical or other substance, disease such as AIDS or Parkinson's, or an abnormal aging process as in Alzheimer's disease.

Counselors rarely are qualified to diagnose or treat either the cognitive disorders listed previously or the Mental Disorders Due to a General Medical Condition that follow. However, they should be familiar with the nature and typical symptoms of these disorders so that they can refer clients whom they suspect of having such disorders to a psychiatrist or neurologist for a conclusive diagnosis. Counselors may work with clients with these disorders as part of a treatment team; the counselor may provide therapy to the family of the affected person or may counsel the client to facilitate social and occupational adjustment in light of any limitations that may be imposed by the disorder. Primary treatment, however, will come from a physician.

Mental Disorders Due to a General Medical Condition

This section in the *DSM* includes disorders that directly and physiologically result from medical conditions listed on Axis III. Examples include Personality Change Due to a General Medical Condition, such as that caused by temporal lobe epilepsy, and Catatonic Disorder Due to a General Medical Condition that might result from encephalitis.

Substance-Related Disorders

This section includes psychological and behavioral disorders associated with substance use (Substance Abuse and Substance Dependence), as well as the induced or physiological disorders resulting from drug or alcohol use such as Intoxication, Substance-Induced Sexual Dysfunction, and Substance-Induced Mood Disorder. Counselors should specify whether a person with Substance Abuse or Dependence is experiencing Physiological Dependence, is in remission, is on agonist therapy such as Antabuse, or is in a controlled environment such as a halfway house.

The Substance Use Disorders are divided into Substance Abuse and Substance Dependence (usually the more severe and pervasive of the two). These diagnoses describe people who use alcohol or any other substances (e.g., amphetamines, cannabis, cocaine, hallucinogens, inhalants, nicotine, opioids, sedatives) in a self-damaging way, usually with the knowledge that they are being harmed by their substance use. Although these people may continue to maintain employment and present a positive facade to friends and family, their performance and relationships usually are adversely affected by their substance use, and they may be endangering their lives by their substance misuse. Counselors in nearly all settings should be familiar with the diagnosis and treatment of these prevalent disorders, particularly counselors working in employee assistance programs. Treatment for substance use disorders typically involves a multifaceted approach including group, individual, and family counseling; education; and participation in a self-help group such as Alcoholics Anonymous.

Schizophrenia and Other Psychotic Disorders

The disorders included in this section all are characterized by symptoms of loss of contact with reality. Schizophrenia involves a severe, pervasive loss of contact with reality, often including auditory hallucinations, and lasting at least six months. Types of Schizophrenia include Paranoid, Disorganized, Catatonic, Undifferentiated, and Residual. Schizophreniform Disorder has the same criteria as Schizophrenia but the symptoms are less than six months in duration. Delusional Disorders are characterized by nonbizarre delusions lasting at least one month. An example is a man who became convinced, without reason, that his wife was having a series of affairs. Delusional Disorders typically are circumscribed and are more likely than Schizophrenia to have an apparent precipitant and to begin abruptly. Brief Psychotic Disorder is characterized by symptoms of Schizophrenia or Delusional Disorder that are less than one month in duration. When psychotic symptoms have a precipitant, for example the loss of one's family in an accident, and when the symptoms begin suddenly rather than gradually, the prognosis for recovery is generally good. This usually is the case with Brief Psychotic Disorder. Schizoaffective Disorder includes criteria for both the diagnosis of Schizophrenia and a Mood Disorder (Major Depressive Disorder or Bipolar Disorder). Shared Psychotic Disorder involves two people, usually in a close relationship, who have a shared delusional belief. Psychotic Disorders Due to a General Medical Condition are included in this section, such as psychosis resulting from Lupus.

Mood Disorders

This section of the *DSM* includes disorders characterized primarily by manic or depressive features. Manic features are less commonly presented by clients than are depressive ones. Mania is typified by an elevated, expansive or irritable mood; grandiosity; distractibility and agitation; and excessive pleasure seeking. One client, a man in his mid-20s, employed as a teacher and planning to get married, reported during a manic episode that he realized he was destined to be a Hollywood film star. He resigned from his job, bought an expensive sports car, enrolled in three acting classes, and prepared to move to California. Clearly, manic features can be very disruptive and self-destructive. Their treatment usually involves both medication and counseling.

Clients experiencing depression present quite different symptoms. They may feel helpless, discouraged, and even suicidal; experience excessive guilt and self-blame; and have little interest or pleasure in anything. Sleeping and eating problems as well as fatigue are also common. Irritability may also reflect depression, especially in children and adolescents. Cognitive-behavioral and brief psychodynamic approaches to treatment are often used to treat depression, frequently in combination with medication.

Diagnoses in the Mood Disorders category include Major Depressive Disorder (severe depression of at least two weeks duration), Dysthymic Disorder (long-standing moderate depression), and Bipolar I and II Disorders and Cyclothymic Disorder that combine depressive and manic or hypomanic symptoms. Specifiers such as Seasonal Pattern, Postpartum Onset, or Melancholic Features indicating the patterns and features of the disturbance further describe each diagnosis. This section is an important one for counselors because of the prevalence of Mood Disorders, especially Major Depressive Disorders, in both inpatient and outpatient settings.

Anxiety Disorders

Anxiety is another symptom that is frequently presented in counseling. Several of the anxiety disorders in the *DSM* involve a phobia, a persistent and exaggerated fear of an object or situation, leading to impairment through avoidance of the feared stimulus. Examples of these disorders include Social Phobia (fear of social embarrassment), Agoraphobia (fear of places from which escape is difficult, such as crowds or public transportation), and Specific Phobia (fear of a specific object or situation such as heights or snakes). Panic Disorder, characterized by unexpected feelings of physical and emotional panic; Obsessive-Compulsive Disorder, characterized by recurrent unwanted thoughts or impulses; Posttraumatic Stress Disorder and Acute Stress Disorder, triggered by exposure to traumatic experiences such as rape and natural disasters; and Generalized Anxiety Disorder (pervasive and excessive anxiety and worry lasting at least six months) also are included in this section. Acute Stress Disorder and Posttraumatic Stress Disorder are frequently encountered by counselors on hotlines or in crisis centers; these disorders involve a cluster of symptoms (e.g., withdrawal, reexperiencing the trauma, anxiety) following a traumatic event. Anxiety symptoms sometimes mimic those of physical conditions, and a thorough diagnostic evaluation of people experiencing anxiety is important. Properly diagnosed, most anxiety symptoms respond well to a multifaceted treatment plan including improving coping mechanisms, desensitization, relaxation, and, in some cases, medication (Seligman, 1998).

Somatoform Disorders

People with Somatoform Disorders are commonly referred for counseling by their physicians. These clients strongly believe they are experiencing a physical ailment; however, medical examinations fail to find any medical cause for their complaints. People with these disorders typically have difficulty managing stress and expressing themselves verbally; their physical complaints often reflect their emotional upset. Types of Somatoform Disorders include Somatization Disorder, characterized by many unverified physical complaints; Conversion Disorder, involving impairment in motor or sensory function such as paralysis or blindness without medical cause; Pain Disorder; Hypochondriasis, typified by preoccupation with the idea of having a serious illness; and Body Dysmorphic Disorder, characterized by an imagined or exaggerated flaw in one's appearance.

Factitious Disorders

People with Factitious Disorders rarely present for counseling in a straightforward fashion (Seligman, 1998). These people enjoy the role of patient and deliberately feign physical or psychological symptoms so that they can assume a sick role. A subtype of Factitious Disorder is Factitious Disorder by Proxy which involves causing another person, usually a child, to feign or experience medical complaints. Often, the histories of people with Factitious Disorders involve experiencing illness as rewarding, and they learn this dysfunctional way of getting attention. Little is known about treatment for this disorder because people with this disorder tend to resist treatment and typically leave treatment prematurely. Building a therapeutic alliance and promoting motivation to change is essential to successful treatment of people with Factitious Disorders.

Dissociative Disorders

The best known of these disorders is Dissociative Identity Disorder (DID), previously called Multiple Personality Disorder. This disorder was exemplified on television and film through the cases of Eve and Sybil. Dissociative Amnesia, Dissociative Fugue and Depersonalization Disorder are also included in this section. All of these disorders involve an alteration in consciousness (e.g., memory loss, alternate personality states) that is neither organic nor psychotic. Until recently, these disorders were believed to be rare. New information on their prevalence is providing a different picture, although DID remains a controversial diagnosis.

Sexual and Gender Identity Disorders

The *DSM-IV-TR* divides these disorders into three groups: Sexual Dysfunctions, Paraphilias, and Gender Identity Disorders. The three are very different in terms of their nature and treatment. People with Sexual Dysfunctions, such as a Sexual Desire Disorder, an Arousal Disorder, an Orgasmic Disorder, or a Sexual Pain Disorder, usually are eager for help. They may be encouraged to seek treatment by an unhappy partner. Paraphilias, on the other hand, involve sexual urges or behaviors that interfere with social adjustment and relationships. Examples are Exhibitionism, Fetishism, Sexual Sadism, Voyeurism, and Pedophilia (sexual activity with children). People with these disorders are often reluctant to change but may seek treatment because of a court mandate or the insistence of an unhappy partner. Gender Identity Disorders are characterized by strong and persistent cross-gender identification accompanied by discomfort with one's assigned sex. Prognosis for treatment of Sexual Disorders is related to motivation.

Eating Disorders

Eating Disorders are especially prevalent among adolescent females and, if left untreated, can be physically harmful and even fatal. A body weight that is 85 percent or less than expected as well as an intense fear of weight gain primarily characterize Anorexia Nervosa (Restricting, Binge Eating, or Purging Type). Bulimia Nervosa (Purging or Nonpurging Types) entails frequent consumption of large quantities of food, often accompanied by self-induced vomiting or excessive use of laxatives or diuretics to avoid weight gain. Treatment of Eating Disorders often is conducted in a group setting and involves both cognitive-behavioral and psychodynamic interventions.

Sleep Disorders

Sleep Disorders may be described as Primary (not related to other medical or mental disorders) or as related to other specific diagnoses. Emotions, environment, lifestyle, and physiology all can be causative factors in these disorders. Sleep Disorders include Insomnia; Hypersomnia, characterized by excessive sleeping or fatigue; Narcolepsy, in which a person suffers from sudden and irresistible sleep; Breathing-Related Sleep Disorder; Circadian Rhythm Sleep Disorder, usually caused by an irregular or unusual sleep schedule; and Nightmare, Sleep Terror, and Sleepwalking Disorders. Sleep disorder clinics are available to facilitate diagnosis of these disorders by tracing the client's brain wave activity during sleep while monitoring sleep patterns.

Impulse-Control Disorders Not Elsewhere Classified

Disorders in this section typically involve a repetitive cycle in which people have a buildup of tension and anxiety linked to a craving to engage in some harmful behavior. They release the tension via the behavior, then may be apologetic and promise change, only to repeat the cycle. Disorders described in this section of the *DSM* include Intermittent Explosive Disorder (describing people who repeatedly engage in impulsive aggressive or destructive behaviors such as spouse abuse), Kleptomania (stealing objects that are not needed), Pathological Gambling, Pyromania (fire setting), and Trichotillomania, a disorder that involves pulling out the hairs on one's head or body. Treatment for these disorders typically involves behavioral counseling as well as help with stress management and interpersonal relationships.

Adjustment Disorders

People who respond to a stressor with mild to moderate, but clinically significant, impairment within three months of the stressor are described as having an Adjustment Disorder. The type of Adjustment Disorder (e.g., With Depressed Mood, With Anxiety, With Disturbance of Conduct) is specified when the diagnosis is made. This diagnosis can be maintained for a maximum of six months following the termination of the stressor. If symptoms persist beyond that time, the diagnosis must be changed. These disorders, among the mildest mental disorders found in the *DSM-IV-TR*, are common in people going through negative life experiences (e.g., a divorce, illness, being fired from a job) but also can be found in people experiencing positive life changes (e.g., marriage, the birth of a child, graduation). Adjustment disorders generally respond well to crisis intervention and solution-focused brief counseling.

Personality Disorders

Personality Disorders, listed on Axis II of a multiaxial assessment, are long-standing, deeply ingrained disorders, typically evident at least by adolescence or early adulthood. Although most of these disorders are not as severe as such disorders as Schizophrenia and Bipolar I Disorder in terms of the impairment they cause, they are among the most treatment-resistant disorders. Personality Disorders typically are manifested by pervasive patterns of dysfunction that show up in all areas of a person's life. People with Personality Disorders usually do not have a clear and positive self-image, a set of effective coping mechanisms, or an array of healthy peer relationships. Consequently, counseling for people experiencing Personality Disorders is often either a lengthy and challenging process or is terminated prematurely by the client.

Personality Disorders take many forms. For example, they can be characterized by patterns of suspiciousness, isolation, antisocial behavior, mood instability, grandiosity, dependence, or perfectionism. Many people with histories of criminal and irresponsible behavior, dating back to childhood, are diagnosed as having Antisocial Personality Disorder, often seen by counselors working in corrections or substance abuse settings. Other Personality Disorders frequently treated in counseling include Dependent, Borderline, Histrionic, and Narcissistic Personality Disorders. Less often seen in counseling are people with Paranoid, Schizoid, Schizotypal, Avoidant, and Obsessive-Compulsive Personality Disorders. For more information on personality disorders, readers are referred to Millon (1996).

Other Conditions That May Be a Focus of Clinical Attention

These conditions are not viewed as mental disorders, but may be a focus of attention in counseling. Conditions listed in the *DSM* may be used alone to describe a person who does not have a mental disorder, or they may be used along with one or more mental disorders on a multiaxial assessment to indicate important areas to be addressed in treatment. Included among the conditions are Psychological Factors Affecting Medical Condition, in which emotional or behavioral patterns adversely affect a medical disorder; Medication-Induced Movement Disorders such as Neuroleptic-Induced Tardive Dyskinesia; Relational Problems including Partner, Parent-Child, Sibling, and other interpersonal difficulties; and Problems Related to Abuse or Neglect. Additional conditions include Acculturation Problem, Age-Related Cognitive Decline, Identity Problem, Religious or Spiritual Problem, Occupational Problem, Phase of Life Problem, and Borderline Intellectual Functioning (listed on Axis II) among others. Although people who present with Conditions and who do not have accompanying mental disorders may seek counseling and may derive considerable benefit from that process, they typically are emotionally healthy people with good resources who have encountered a difficult period in their lives. Often people such as these, like people with Adjustment Disorders, learn and grow considerably from the counseling process.

DIAGNOSIS IN CONTEXT

This chapter has focused primarily on diagnosis. However, diagnosis is only one of three steps counselors should take before counseling a person. The other two steps, intake interviews and treatment planning, are discussed briefly here.

Intake Interviews

Intake interviews precede diagnosis and provide much of the information needed to make an accurate diagnosis. Some agencies have a formal intake process in which a prospective client goes through a structured interview, completes some forms and inventories, and possibly even meets with more than one clinician (e.g., a counselor and a psychiatrist). In other settings, such as private practices and college counseling settings, the first counseling session usually serves as an intake interview. In a less structured way, the counselor gathers information about a client in order to assess the urgency of the client's situation, orients the client to the counseling process, determines the client's suitability for counseling in that setting, formulates a diagnosis, and develops a treatment plan.

Intake interviews vary widely in terms of their duration and thoroughness. They may be as brief as 15 minutes, focusing on presenting concerns and their development, or they may extend over several sessions of an hour or more in length, to provide a comprehensive and in-depth picture of the client. Topics typically included in an intake interview include identifying information (e.g., client's age, occupation, relationship status), presenting concerns, previous emotional difficulties, treatment history, present life situation, information on family of origin and present family, developmental history, cultural and spiritual background, leisure activities, relationships, education, career, and medical history (Seligman, 1996). While conducting an intake interview, counselors should gather information not only from the clients' words but also from their appearance, their behavior during the interview, their interactions with the counselor, their mood and display of emotion, their contact with reality, and their thinking process. That information can be summarized in a mental status evaluation and is important in helping counselors develop a full picture of their clients and make an accurate diagnosis.

Treatment Planning

Treatment planning is the third step in the process that begins with the intake interview, continues with a multiaxial assessment according to the *DSM-IV-TR*, and culminates in the treatment plan. This three-step process has been compared to the shape of an hourglass (Hershenson, Power, & Seligman, 1989). The information collected during the intake interview provides a broad picture of the client. This information is processed and condensed into a diagnosis, analogous to the narrow part of the hourglass. The focus is then expanded once again with treatment planning. Beginning with the establishment of mutually agreed upon objectives, the treatment plan provides counselors with a map to guide their work with their clients.

Many models have been developed for treatment plans. One developed by the author, the DO A CLIENT MAP, is presented here (Seligman, 1996; Seligman, 1998; Seligman, in press). The title of the model is a mnemonic device with each letter in the name reflecting one of the twelve important areas to be addressed in treatment planning:

1. Diagnosis according to the *DSM-IV-TR*
2. Objectives of treatment
3. Assessment procedures
4. Clinician characteristics
5. Location of treatment
6. Interventions (both theoretical framework and specific interventions)
7. Emphasis of treatment (e.g., supportive, probing)
8. Numbers (individual, group, or family counseling)
9. Timing (duration and scheduling of sessions)
10. Medication
11. Adjunct services
12. Prognosis

By responding to each item in the outline of a treatment plan, counselors can develop a comprehensive and useful guide for working with a client. Of course, effective treatment planning requires that counselors become knowledgeable not only about diagnosis but also about the other elements in the MAP. For example, counselors should be well informed on empirically supported treatments when determining interventions (Messer, 2001).

Illustration of the Three-Step Process

The following case provides an abbreviated version of the three-step process of intake interview, multiaxial assessment, and treatment plan. The case begins with a short summary of information obtained from the intake interview with the client, continues with a multiaxial assessment, and finishes with a brief treatment plan.

Intake Information. Amber, a 15-year-old African American female, requested some help from her school counselor, who referred her and her family to a community mental health center. Amber lived with her mother, her 12-year-old brother, and her stepfather of two months. Amber's father died three years ago in an automobile accident. Amber stated that she was very angry with her mother for remarrying and could not understand what attracted her to her new husband, Jeff. Amber reported that her mother expected Amber to call Jeff "Dad" and to participate in family outings. Amber spent as much time away from home as she could and reported sadness and loss of interest in academic and social activities since her mother's marriage.

Before that event, Amber had been a quiet and capable student, earning satisfactory grades and participating in several school clubs. She had a small circle of girlfriends and had recently begun to date. Other than some expectable grief and withdrawal around the time of her father's death, Amber had been well adjusted, and no history of problem behavior was reported. She was in good health and rarely missed school. She was above average in intelligence and was well oriented to reality.

1. **D**iagnosis according to the *DSM-IV-TR*
   Axis I: 309.0 Adjustment Disorder with Depressed Mood, Acute
   Axis II: V71.09 No diagnosis on Axis II
   Axis III: No physical disorders or conditions reported
   Axis IV: Psychosocial stressors: Problems with primary support group
                (Death of father, mother's remarriage)
   Axis V   Current GAF: 65
2. **O**bjectives of treatment
   a. Reduce Amber's level of sadness as measured by the Beck Depression Inventory.
   b. Improve her relationships with her mother and stepfather as reflected in increased amounts of rewarding time spent together and on improved scores on the Family Functioning Scale.
   c. Increase Amber's interest and involvement in academic and social activities reflected by a daily journal of activities and ratings of mastery and pleasure.
3. **A**ssessment procedures: Beck Depression Inventory, Family Functioning Scale.
4. **C**linician: No specific counselor variables are indicated here; arguments could be made for assigning Amber to either a male or a female counselor. Her preference for counselor's gender and ethnicity will be considered.
5. **L**ocation: Outpatient private practice or community mental health center.
6. **I**nterventions: A cognitive-behavioral orientation will be emphasized; Amber is telling herself that she must not allow anyone to usurp her father's position in

the family, and this is causing dysfunction. Affect (sadness, anger) and behavior (avoidance of family, destructive patterns of communication) also need to be addressed. Such techniques as cognitive restructuring, practicing improved communication skills, monitoring mood levels, and planning activities would be used in individual counseling. Family counseling will follow a communications approach such as that of Virginia Satir, helping Amber's parents to allow a more gradual development of the stepfather/stepdaughter relationship, helping Amber to reestablish her close tie to her mother, understand her mother's decision to remarry.

7. **E**mphasis of treatment: Counseling will initially be supportive and accepting but will encourage Amber to address her grief and develop her coping skills.
8. **N**umbers: Individual counseling will be combined with family counseling with the whole family as well as with Amber and her mother and Amber and her stepfather, and Amber and both parents.
9. **T**iming: Weekly 45- or 50-minute counseling sessions will be scheduled for approximately 3–4 months.
10. **M**edication: A referral for medication is not indicated.
11. **A**djunct services: Involvement in a rewarding and ongoing peer activity will be encouraged. Tutoring might be needed in any school subjects in which Amber has fallen behind.
12. **P**rognosis: Excellent, in light of Amber's relatively mild diagnosis and her previously high level of functioning as well as her family support.

THE FUTURE OF COUNSELING AND DIAGNOSIS

Diagnosis has become an essential skill of the counselor (Seligman, 1999b). According to the American Counseling Association *Code of Ethics and Standards of Practice* (1995, p. 36), "Counselors take special care to provide proper diagnosis of mental disorders."

The 1990s witnessed the growth of private practice and managed care, an increasing emphasis on accountability for counselors, the expansion of the counselor's role to include both relatively well-functioning people and those with severe mental disorders, and the growth of most master's degree programs in counseling to forty-eight or more credits. At the outset of the twenty-first century, these trends have continued, along with increased collaboration between school and mental health counselors and an emphasis on empirically supported treatment and brief solution-focused treatment. These trends suggest that diagnosis and treatment planning will continue to grow in importance and will remain essential skills for counselors in all settings

SUMMARY

This chapter has reviewed the important benefits that knowledge of diagnosis and the *DSM* can bring to counselors and their clients. It also cites some possible pitfalls of the diagnostic process that counselors should try to avoid. An overview was presented of the process of multiaxial assessment according to the *Diagnostic and Statistical Manual of Mental Disorders—Text Revision* (American Psychiatric Association, 2000). The seventeen categories of mental disorders and conditions also were described.

Diagnosis is one piece of a three-step process that facilitates effective counseling. An intake interview and review of any records is the first step, yielding information that is needed for a diagnosis (the second step). A treatment plan then can be developed, based on the diagnosis or multiaxial assessment, and reflecting knowledge of the appropriate use of counseling.

PART III

COUNSELING IN SPECIFIC SETTINGS

This section describes the basic environments in which counselors today are most likely to work. Chapter 14, "School Counseling," begins by providing an overview of historical foundations, comprehensively discusses the many roles and functions that school counseling may involve, and considers new directions for the role of the school counselor given the current needs of students and families. An excellent description of the characteristics and steps in the development of a comprehensive school counseling program, traits of effective school counselors, and role variations in elementary, middle, and high school settings make this an important chapter for anyone considering a school counseling focus in the context of degree completion.

Chapter 15, "Counseling in Mental Health and Private Practice Settings," describes the other major settings in which the counselor may practice. The history of mental health counseling is outlined, and the process of how counseling expanded from its early educational/vocational focus to encompass therapeutic, mental health activities is described. Major events that have influenced this process, such as the Community Mental Health Act of 1963, which provided federal funding for community mental health agencies and programs, are presented, and the possibilities for the future of mental health counseling in the twenty-first century are considered. Mental health counselors have been engaged in a continuing process to earn recognition as mental health professionals similar to social workers, psychologists, and psychiatrists, and this process has supported the movement toward counselor licensure. As more states have passed legislation enabling counselors, both in mental health and other specializations, to be recognized as practicing professionals, more counselors have chosen to go into private practice, either as a full-time career option or as an adjunct to their other work. Both the positive aspects and the negative aspects of starting a private practice are outlined for the counselor. This chapter also depicts the expanding roles and work settings of community/mental health counselors in the twenty-first century.

As these chapters indicate, the role of counselors has continuously expanded and will inevitably continue to do so. As the opportunities for therapeutic mental health professions increase in our society, so will the settings and environments in which counselors may choose to practice.

CHAPTER FOURTEEN

SCHOOL COUNSELING

SUSAN KEYS, PH.D.
ALAN G. GREEN, PH.D.
Johns Hopkins University

Clive

Clive is an 11-year-old sixth-grade African American student at Davis Middle School. Clive lives in a suburban community with his parents, a 17-year-old sister, and her 1-year-old son. Clive attends school regularly.

Two years ago, Clive's pediatrician diagnosed him as having ADHD. The pediatrician prescribed a standard dosage of Ritalin to control acting out behavior in the classroom (i.e., disturbing class, not doing his assignments). School records from the elementary school indicate that the Ritalin was effective in helping Clive manage his behavior in the classroom. Teachers described him as being more focused on classroom tasks and having more favorable interactions among his classmates. School records also indicated his reading and math performance levels are at grade level.

Now in middle school, Clive's English teacher, Mrs. Washington, has begun to raise concerns about his behavior in her afternoon class. According to Mrs. Washington, Clive is not completing his assignments and is disturbing the class with "irrelevant questions" during discussions of class readings. Feeling frustrated about how to get Clive to change his behavior, Mrs. Washington refers Clive to the school counselor.

This type of referral to a school counselor is quite typical. Feeling distressed about a student's performance, a teacher reaches out to the resources at hand. The school counselor represents a valuable and accessible source of help. In this case, how might the school counselor respond to Mrs. Washington's request for help? How do the established roles and functions of a school counselor influence how this counselor responds? Are there other actions a school counselor might take that would enhance problem solving for Clive and Mrs. Washington and would extend the school counselor's role and function beyond how it is commonly conceptualized? This chapter explores these and other questions as a way of discovering more about school counseling.

OVERVIEW

A school system's mission is to educate students. Student achievement is an overarching concern of both the school system and the broader community served by that system. How well students in a particular school perform on standardized tests often becomes the benchmark for measuring a school's success. School systems employ school counselors to support this broader educational mission. School counselors accomplish this by implementing a variety of services that address students' academic, personal, interpersonal, and career needs.

School counselors work in elementary, middle, and high school settings. Generally, elementary schools employ a single, full- or part-time counselor; middle schools or high schools employ a team of counselors. Such teams include anywhere from two to four or more counselors per school. Although the American School Counselors Association (1993) recommends a counselor-to-student ratio of 1/100 (ideal) to 1/300 (maximum), not all school districts are able to maintain this standard. The highest ratios usually exist at the elementary level and the lowest typically exist at the high school level.

This chapter explores in more detail what it means to be a school counselor in a school today. More specifically, the chapter describes the historical foundations of the profession, examines the principal roles and functions of a school counselor, and considers new directions for the role given the current needs of students and families.

HISTORICAL FOUNDATIONS

Vocational Guidance

School counseling claims its roots in the vocational guidance movement initiated in the early 1900s by Frank Parsons. Early methods of working with individuals consisted of matching an individual's personal characteristics with the requirements of an occupation. This later evolved into the use of tests and other measurements as a way of assessing individual aptitude and personality traits. During this early movement, providing occupational information, vocational assessment, and job placement became the core functions of such a specialist. The need for job placement at the end of World War I and during the Great Depression placed an even greater emphasis on these functions.

Testing continued to be a popular way of screening and placing draftees in the military as part of the country's mobilization during World War II. During postwar time, the Veterans' Administration provided funds for graduate training for individuals interested in becoming counselors and psychologists, and as a result the counseling profession grew and expanded.

Personal Counseling

The movement toward urbanization in the 1950s brought with it a host of psychological stresses—increases in crime, divorce, lack of extended family living in close proximity, more crowded living conditions. The need for personal psychological services became apparent. The profession responded to this shift in need for services. Counselors, influenced by these societal changes and by the emerging work of Carl Rogers, began to move away from a strictly testing, vocational practice to a more growth-oriented form of personal counseling. The American Personnel and Guidance Association, the forerunner of the current American Counseling Association, originated at this time.

In 1957, the United Soviet Socialist Republic launched Sputnik. America responded in part by examining the education of its young people and promoting occupations in areas of math and science. The National Defense Act of 1958 provided funds to support school-based counseling and guidance services and to help institutions of higher education establish counselor education programs (Schmidt, 1999). Some suggest that this Act was the single most influential event in the history of school counseling. As a result of this funding support, the number of full-time school counselors increased 126 percent from 1958 to 1963 (Schmidt, 1999). Unfortunately, this influx of money came at a time when the profession itself was not clearly defined and counselor education programs were limited in scope. Since the school counseling profession was in the process of defining itself, training programs typically emphasized what had become traditional counselor roles and functions—hence an emphasis on tests and measurements and occupational information, and counseling theories to support personal change. Programs usually included a course in guidance services, but again, since the field itself was evolving, such courses at best offered only a general introduction. Field experiences or internships did not always exist as requirements.

As a result, many new counselors were added to school staffs without a clear understanding of what their role should be and, in many cases, without adequate training to effectively deliver counseling services in a school setting. If one believes that people end up doing what they feel most comfortable doing, it was inevitable that counselors would drift away from the less clearly defined counseling functions to the more readily accessible quasi-administrative tasks such as scheduling, test coordination, record keeping, and the more vocationally oriented functions of academic and career advising.

State requirements of classroom teaching experience as a prerequisite for certification also restricted entry into the profession to those who had been classroom teachers. Although this teaching prerequisite continues today in some states, other states have established policies that allow those who have not taught to enter the school counseling profession, usually after additional field placements or work-related experiences.

Developmental Guidance and Counseling

Concerned about a deteriorating image of school counseling, in 1962 the American Personnel and Guidance Association (the precursor of today's American Counseling Association) appointed a commission to study the role and function of the school counselor and school counselor preparation. Gilbert Wrenn chaired this committee. The committee's findings, summarized in Wrenn's (1962) *The Counselor in a Changing World*, was the forerunner of much of what we think of today as important elements of the school counselor's role and function. In brief, this report recommended that counselors (a) emphasize developmental rather than crisis needs in their counseling work with students; (b) provide consultation to teachers, administrators, and parents; (c) be aware of the changing character of student populations and the world culture into which a student will move; and (d) coordinate counseling resources within the school and between the school and community.

During the late 1960s and early 1970s, influenced by Wrenn's report, the school counseling profession underwent a major transformation with the emergence of the comprehensive developmental guidance and counseling movement. As a result of this movement, the focus of a school counselor's work shifted from a crisis-oriented, reactive service delivery model with services designed to help the more "at-risk" student, to a more proactive, developmental approach aimed at helping all students in the building. Primary prevention became a principal component of the school counselor's work, with the healthy development of all students as a central part of the school counseling program's mission (Paisley & Borders, 1995; Wittmer, 1993). To achieve this mission, school counselors worked to establish comprehensive developmental guidance and counseling *programs* as opposed to a more limited emphasis on developmental counseling *services* (Gysbers & Henderson, 2001).

Elementary school counseling emerged concurrently with this new movement. As a result, elementary school counselors have more easily adopted a comprehensive, developmental program focus than their middle and high school counterparts.

In 1989, feeling that the term *guidance* no longer accurately represented the school counselor's specialized training, the American School Counselors Association agreed to eliminate the term from the school counselor's title (N. Perry, personal communication, February 18, 1998). Today, most schools and school systems are moving toward establishing comprehensive developmental school counseling programs. Some, however, continue to operate in a more limited and fragmented fashion. Unfortunately vestiges of the history of school counselors assuming administrative roles and tasks remain. Many school counselors continue to refer to themselves as school "guidance" counselors, and many continue to perform excessive administrative and clerical responsibilities.

NATIONAL STANDARDS

In 1997, the American School Counselor Association (ASCA) published National Standards for School Counseling Programs (ASCA, 1997). These standards complement the features of comprehensive developmental programs and promote what ASCA considers to be the essential foundations for program content (Dahir, 2001). The standards support the academic, career, and personal/social development of students through defined student competencies. (For more information see *http://www .schoolcounselor.org/content.cfm?L1=1&L2=9.*)

STATE REQUIREMENTS FOR PRACTICE

State law requires school counselors to obtain a state-issued credential in order to be employed by a public school system. Some states call this credential "certification;" some refer to it as "licensure" or "endorsement" (Farrell, 1997, p. 1). Requirements such as teaching experience, course work, practicum and internship, provisional employment, and written or oral exams vary from state to state (Farrell, 1997; Paisley & Hubbard, 1989). All states require graduate education in school counseling as an entry-level prerequisite to obtain a school counselor credential (Farrell, 1997). Forty states and the District of Columbia require a master's degree in school counseling or related field (Farrell, 1997). Most states have implemented continuing professional development requirements for practicing school counselors (Farrell, 1997).

A national school counselor (NCSC) certification also exists. Applicants for this credential must first be certified as a national certified counselor (NCC) with additional training focusing on school counseling. The NCSC certification, however, does not supplant the state certification for eligibility to practice in public schools.

COMPREHENSIVE DEVELOPMENTAL PROGRAM CHARACTERISTICS

The primary task of an effective school counselor is to develop and implement a comprehensive school counseling program that promotes the emotional, social, cognitive, and career development of students. Comprehensive developmental programs have the following features in common.

Primary Prevention

The principal mission of a comprehensive developmental program is to help students achieve academic success. The program accomplishes this by focusing on students' developmental needs. School counselors who function within a developmental program paradigm may provide crisis intervention services for individual students as well as groups of students and teachers affected by a large-scale traumatic event. The majority of the school counselor's time, however, is directed toward activities that help all students acquire the skills and knowledge necessary to master age-appropriate developmental tasks.

Distinct and Independent

The comprehensive developmental program is a distinct and independent program that has (1) an identified mission related to the broader school mission; (2) specific goals and objectives, often articulated as student competencies; and (3) an organized curriculum. The curriculum is a set of sequential activities and interventions that extend across different grade levels and are organized around age-appropriate topics related to academic, personal, interpersonal, and career development. Many commercially available materials—kits, manuals, videos, and computer software—are available to support curriculum development and implementation.

Integrated

Comprehensive developmental programs exist as an integral part of the overall educational process. Although the program has a distinct curriculum, the implementation of this curriculum can occur as a part of the larger educational program. School counselors often team with teachers to create interdisciplinary projects and assignments so that the content of the developmental program is taught and reinforced within the broader curriculum. For example, literature classes may include reading and writing assignments that focus on mental health topics and problem solving; science classes may address the physiological aspects of stress as well as techniques for managing stress; and group projects in any course might emphasize communication and social skills.

Systematic Program Development Process

Direction for the development of a comprehensive program at the school level in some school systems comes from the central administrative office. Some school systems have identified general goals and core objectives by school level and grade and expect that all counselors in the system will work to accomplish these outcomes. In other systems, the school counselor is responsible for developing his or her own program plan without a larger system blueprint. Regardless of whether the school counselor operates from a larger system plan or independently, the school counselor must be certain that what is developed and applied in his or her particular school is based on the needs of the population served by that school. The following steps guide the program planning, implementation, and evaluation phases of the program development process. (See Gysbers & Henderson, 2000, for further discussion of school counseling program development and program components.) These steps relate to program planning at either the system or school level.

Step One: Obtaining Administrative Support.   Anyone who has ever worked in a school knows that administrative support is critical to the success of any program. Whether developing a new program or revamping an existing program, the school counselor will need to acquire the support of his or her principal. Linking what the school counselor hopes to accomplish to the broader school mission, in particular student achievement, is a useful strategy for helping an administrator recognize the value in what the counselor proposes. Before committing time and resources to the development of a new program initiative, up-front administrative support is critical.

Step Two: Establishing an Advisory Committee.   School and community support is also needed for successful program development. Many school counselors find it helpful to have an advisory committee assist with all phases of the program development process. The purpose of this committee is to offer advice and assistance; in some cases the advisory committee exists as a decision-making body. Committee membership generally includes teachers and family members, while some may also include representatives from community agencies and other groups such as the local library, churches, and parks and recreation. Members of the committee assist the counselor in (a) understanding student, family, and community needs; (b) establishing program priorities; (c) generating and selecting strategies; and (d) acquiring resources to support program initiatives. The advisory committee also serves as a communication link between the school counseling program and the stakeholders represented by committee members.

Step Three: Assessing Needs.   In order to assure program relevancy, the school counselor works to identify the needs of the population to be served by the school-counseling program. A need is defined as a gap between what exists and what is desired. For example, one school counselor might decide to target social skills as a need area for first graders since the teacher reports high levels of fighting on the playground. In this case, a gap exists between "what is" (fighting on the playground) and "what needs to be" (students who play well together). Deciding whose needs to assess is an important decision at this point in the process. Is the program interested in student needs? Parent needs? Teacher needs? Or all three? Keeping the focus more narrow (focusing on just one group's needs at a time) results in a more manageable needs assessment process. Some counselors initiate a large scale needs assessment process as part of a two- or three-year program development cycle; other counselors conduct needs assessments more frequently, targeting a limited area of concern.

The needs assessment process itself may use informal or formal procedures, or a combination of both. Informal methods might include (a) focused conversations with teachers, administrators, and family members; (b) monitoring reasons for referrals to the counselor; and (c) observations of students' behavior. Formal methods could include (a) a review of incident data normally collected by the school such as number of suspensions, number of fights, and attendance patterns; and (b) a paper and pencil survey in which the target population is asked to report about concerns or worries. When using the survey method, counselors may also ask students, family members, and teachers to report their perceptions of the target group's needs. Generally, the counselor surveys different members of the school community at the same time about the needs of the same target group—students, or teachers, or family members. Some counselors choose to address student needs in one program cycle, and teacher or family needs in another.

Also relevant to the needs assessment process is the school counselor's use of achievement data collected by the school and school system. The recently passed No Child Left Behind Act (U.S.D.E., 2001) targets closing the achievement gap between students who are socially or economically disadvantaged and students who are culturally diverse, and other groups of students. School counselors need to be familiar with school achievement data that are disaggregated according to race, gender, and other criteria that distinguish subgroups of students who need more focused interventions that remove barriers to learning and support increased academic success. Later in the program development process as counselors plan interventions, it is also important that counselors be familiar with the research-based practices proven to be effective with these subgroups of students.

The advisory committee assists the school counselor in analyzing and interpreting the data collected as part of the needs assessment process. The committee may also help to prioritize and make decisions about which needs to address first.

Step Four: Specifying Goals and Objectives. After targeting a particular need area, goals are specified in general terms (to increase social skills for first graders) and objectives are stated as specific, measurable outcomes (first-grade students will be able to demonstrate taking turns during playground games). One goal could have several different but related objectives. Planning for evaluation also occurs at this step to assure that objectives can be measured in a reasonable fashion.

Step Five: Developing and Implementing Strategies. Once goals and objectives have been established, the school counselor, along with the advisory committee, can begin to develop strategies to accomplish desired program outcomes. Creativity is highly valued at this phase of the process. Strategies should include ways to integrate the school counseling program's objectives within the broader school curriculum.

After deciding which strategies to implement, the school counselor devises an implementation plan. This plan identifies (a) persons responsible for certain tasks, (b) resources necessary to accomplish the task, (c) a time line, and (d) steps to monitor progress.

Step Six: Evaluating Progress. Program evaluation is the final step in the program development process. School counselors assess program effectiveness by ascertaining the extent to which objectives have been achieved. Positive outcomes bring a sense of accomplishment and success and assist the counselor in demonstrating program accountability. Evaluation outcomes also include important information that assists with program revision—how strategies might need to be fine-tuned or adapted differently.

The program development process is continuous. Once the evaluation phase is completed, the program is revised and reinitiated, or if all objectives have been successfully accomplished, the program development cycle begins again.

PROGRAM INTERVENTIONS

Today's school counselor assumes multiple responsibilities in the interest of fulfilling the mission of the comprehensive, developmental school counseling program. The actual program strategies provided by a school counselor can be thought of as direct services (those that affect and involve the student directly with the counselor) and indirect services (those that indirectly affect the student, generally as a result of the counselor's direct work with a significant other person in the student's life [teacher, parent] or as the result of implementing another type of program initiative). Direct

	Direct	Indirect
Counselor	*	
Teacher (Classroom Guidance)	*	
Consultant		*
Coordinator		*

FIGURE 14.1   Counselor Role and Type of Service.

services are typically counseling and classroom guidance; indirect services include consultation and coordination. Figure 14.1 describes each of these functions in more detail.

Counseling

Counselors implement their counseling role when they work with individual students or small groups of students related to career and vocational issues, personal and interpersonal problems, behavior problems, and academic concerns. School counselors use traditional theoretical paradigms and more newly developed short-term models of intervention. Brief counseling models are particularly attractive to school counselors since a responsibility for large numbers of students limits the time available to work in long-term individual counseling relationships. Students usually see a school counselor for counseling either as a result of referring themselves, or through a referral made by a teacher, parent, or administrator. Areas of concern typically addressed in counseling include school attitudes and behavior, absenteeism, test-taking and study skills, low self-esteem, peer relationships, family transitions, career and educational planning, decision making, and coping, communication, and problem-solving skills. Student appraisal is an important part of the counseling process and can take the form of administering standardized achievement tests, aptitude tests, interest inventories, or personality inventories (Schmidt, 1999). Direct observation of students and reviewing student records are other methods of appraisal used by the school counselor.

Although most of the school counselor's counseling work is developmental in nature, some counselors do provide counseling services that are more clinically focused. This is particularly so with counselors who conduct groups for students with chronic concerns such as eating disorders, school phobia, post-traumatic stress, and substance abuse. In such cases it is important for school counselors to work closely with a supervisor. Such groups may be co-led with a mental health professional from an agency on contract with the school to provide school-based mental health services.

It is important for school counselors to help identify those students for whom the preventative components of the school counseling program are insufficient. Students with more pervasive needs may require additional counseling services beyond what the school counselor can provide. In such cases the school counselor may refer the student to a school-based team for further assessment. The school counselor may also assist the student and family with a referral to an outside-of-school agency.

Counselors also provide counseling services to individual students facing a particular crisis and to students and other members of the school community who are recovering from a large-scale traumatic event.

In addition to lack of sufficient time for counseling services, the school counselor may have difficulty gaining adequate access to students. The pressure to achieve results on standardized achievement tests that meet school system goals and that satisfy the expectations of parents places an enormous stress on teachers. This can result in an unwillingness on the part of teachers to release students from academic time so that they may see the school counselor. This underscores the importance of acquiring administrative and community support for the school counseling program and communicating to the school community how the school counseling program, including counseling services, can enhance student achievement.

Classroom Guidance

One of the central components of a comprehensive, developmental program is classroom guidance. Classroom guidance consists of an organized set of lessons designed to increase student knowledge and skill in a particular area related to a developmental need. Such topics might include "Making and Keeping Friends" at the elementary level, "Managing Anger" in the middle school, and "The College Selection Process" at the high school level. School counselors deliver the series of lessons in a classroom format using developmentally appropriate teaching strategies. Needs assessment data provide direction for the selection of themes for classroom guidance units. Likewise, classroom guidance units can be one of several strategies used to accomplish the goals and objectives of the comprehensive developmental program.

Consultation

Consultation is the process by which teachers, parents and other family members, and administrators receive problem-solving assistance from the school counselor regarding the student's well-being and academic progress. The process is generally thought of as triadic, that is, it involves three key members: the client (student), the consultee (teacher, parent, administrator), and the consultant (counselor). Generally, the consultee perceives the counselor as an expert and approaches the counselor for assistance with the client or student. Consultation is an indirect service to the client because the counselor "works through" the consultee rather than working directly with the client. In some cases the counselor may also provide direct counseling services to the student but this would be within the counselor as opposed to consultant role. This triadic process is depicted in Figure 14.2.

Recently, consultation has expanded beyond this more traditional triadic process to a process that emphasizes the collaborative relationship between the counselor, consultee, and other helpers. Rather than functioning as a solitary expert, a

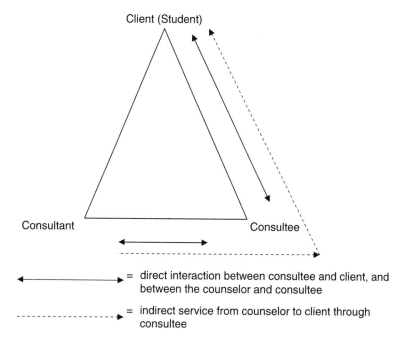

FIGURE 14.2   **Consultation as Triadic, Indirect Relationship Between the Counselor and the Client.**

consultant that works more collaboratively functions as an "expert among experts," explicitly recognizing that all members of the problem-solving team have something of value to contribute to the problem-solving process (Keys, Bemak, Carpenter, & King-Sears, 1998). This collaborative approach to consultation is particularly useful when the problem to be solved is too complex for a single institution or service provider to solve alone. Through collaborative consultation, multiple experts, including family members and representatives from community agencies, come together with school representatives to (a) identify problems, (b) transfer knowledge and information, (c) determine strategies and the role each person will play in implementing these strategies, (d) carry out their roles interdependently, and (e) monitor progress (Keys et al., 1998). A collaborative consultation model (see Figure 14.3) is effective when addressing a particular student's needs or when planning broader prevention initiatives. Collaborative consultation results in a more comprehensive treatment plan for the individual or comprehensive prevention program for the school or larger group of service recipients.

School counselors function frequently as members of varied school teams such as crisis intervention, school improvement, admission, review, and dismissal teams as part of the procedures for special education, and pupil services teams. A collaborative consultation process supports a school counselor's teamwork. Counselors' contributions to the team's efforts include an expertise in human growth and development,

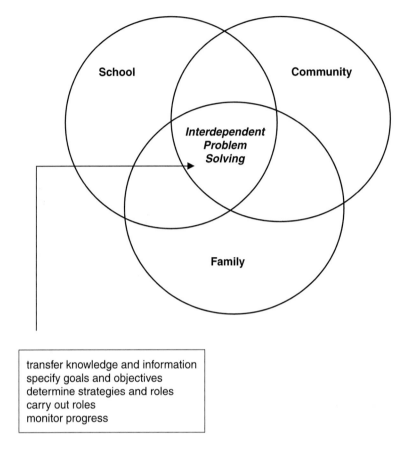

FIGURE 14.3 Consultation as a Collaborative, Interdependent Relationship Between the Counselor and Other Problem Solvers.

skills in group process, group dynamics, problem solving and conflict resolution, and knowledge of theoretically based methods of personal and systemic change.

Consultation within a school setting may focus on change in the client, change in the consultee, and change in the system or context surrounding the client (Parsons, 1996). Client-focused consultation results in problem-solving strategies targeted directly at the student. Consultee-focused consultation focuses on changes in the consultee's knowledge, skills, or ability to be objective. System-focused consultation addresses change at the subsystem level, including classroom, school, peer group, family, or neighborhood subsystems. All types of consultation occur because of a concern the consultee or counselor has about a student; thus, even consultee-focused and system-focused consultations ultimately result in change for the student. Figure 14.4 summarizes sample problem-solving strategies that could result from each type of consultation focus.

There are many topics for which the counselor can provide consultation. Recent acts of terrorism and the repercussions of these actions on the mental health

Problem: Student fails to complete homework assignments.

	Strategies
Client-focused	The counselor and the teacher each agree to work with the student on developing better study skills related to making a written record of assignments, selecting a study time, and increasing study time duration.
Consultee-focused	The counselor works with the teacher to increase the teacher's skills in behavior management, particularly around the delivery of positive reinforcement of the student's appropriate behavior.
System-focused	The counselor works with the teacher to change the pattern of how homework is assigned so that students receive assignments earlier in the week.

FIGURE 14.4   Problem-Solving Strategies Related to Type of Consultation Focus.

of students and others makes it imperative that the school counselor be well in-formed about the emotional reactions to terrorism and other world events along with the best practices for helping a school community reestablish equilibrium in the event of such actions.

Coordination

The coordination of comprehensive programs requires that the counselor creatively integrate program development activities with counseling and consultation services. Without effective coordination of services, counselors may use their time inefficiently and may end up providing services that remain disconnected from each other and the larger program mission. Effective coordination also assures the integration of needs assessment and program evaluation data in program decision making. Examples of specific activities involving this function include coordinating communication be-tween outside-of-school service providers with school-based service providers, man-aging special school projects such as career day or a depression screening, overseeing the collection of needs assessment data and survey development, and establishing a time line for the delivery of classroom guidance units across a particular grade level.

Standardized test coordination is another function assigned to many school counselors. As a part of this function, the counselor coordinates all aspects of the school's testing program. This could include overseeing that tests are kept in a secure location, preparing the schedule for test administration, training of test administra-tors to assure adherence to standardized testing procedures, and providing inservice activities for teachers to learn about test interpretation.

Often school counselors are called upon to perform noncounseling duties in the course of their day, such as course scheduling, attendance record keeping, and lunchroom/hall supervision duty. These tasks, as a part of the school counselor's official job duties, or over time, have been informally assigned by the school principal. While it is often necessary for education professionals to step beyond their primary roles on behalf of student needs and the mission of the school, school counselors must be careful when they perform noncounseling duties. Once a school counselor is viewed as someone who is available to keep track of attendance, or monitor the bus stop in the afternoon, it becomes easier for that counselor to be seen as an extra hand on campus, a perception that will pull the counselor away from his or her more primary roles of counselor, teacher, consultant, and coordinator.

There are strategies that can be employed to handle this type of situation professionally, producing outcomes that are satisfactory to both the principal and the school counselor. For example, implementing and publicizing a comprehensive school counseling program that is developmental, preventive, and proactive in scope allows leaders to respect the counselor's role in the school and not burden them with additional unrelated duties. Another solution would be to present program evaluation data to the school principal as evidence for how counseling, classroom guidance, consultation, and coordination activities benefit the school's mission. Working collaboratively with school administrators and parents can lead to creative solutions to staffing shortages and the reassignment of administrative duties.

A "TYPICAL" DAY IN THE LIFE OF A SCHOOL COUNSELOR

The following example could occur at an elementary, middle, or high school. The tasks performed by Jane, the school counselor, illustrate how in this case the school counselor implements the counselor, educator (classroom guidance), consultant, and coordinator roles.

7:30 A.M.

Jane arrives early at school, about 45 minutes before students begin to arrive. Classes begin at 8:40. Jane uses this as an opportunity to confirm with teachers that the times she will be meeting with students remain a convenient time for teachers to release students from classes. Before leaving for home the previous day Jane had placed reminder notes in each teacher's box asking them to verify times before the beginning of second period. As she checks in with the central office, she notices a note in her box indicating that a teacher has scheduled a make-up test for that morning and cannot release a student as planned. Jane passes this teacher's classroom on the way to her office and she indicates to the teacher that she will make the change. Jane also gives the teacher a note for the student to let the student know that she will be given a new time. (Coordination)

As Jane moves down the hallway from the central office to her counseling office a teacher stops to ask if she has time to discuss a student later that day. The teacher has a free period at 2:00 and Jane checks her schedule and decides to make whatever adjustments are necessary in order to be able to see the teacher. Jane learned early on the value of always walking the halls with a clipboard containing blank paper for notes and a copy of her daily and weekly schedule. (Consultation)

In one last stop before reaching her office, Jane stops at another teacher's door to quickly ask how a particular student is doing in this teacher's class. Both the teacher and student have been working with Jane on increasing homework completion. The teacher gives a thumbs up and Jane makes a mental note to follow up later for more details. This is a student Jane plans to see later in the day so this informal check will provide a reference point for that meeting. (Consultation)

8:15 A.M.

Jane greets a grandparent who has come to talk about his grandchild's failing grades and disruptive behavior. One decision they make is to meet with the larger team of teachers to develop a more multidimensional plan for improving behavior and achievement. Silently, Jane thinks about the other grandparents in her school community who are raising grandchildren and wonders if they might find it helpful to be part of a support group of grandparents in similar circumstances. (Consultation)

9:00 A.M.

Jane begins to make the necessary shifts in her schedule so that she might notify teachers and students of new times for meetings based on the changes she had to make that morning. She also pulls together materials for the classroom guidance session she is to do next period. (Coordination)

9:20 A.M.

Jane enters a classroom to begin the first class in a five-week unit on stress management. Between now and the end of the first quarter, Jane will have worked in a classroom setting on this topic with all students in one grade level. Helping students reduce stress is part of Jane's overall program plan for this academic year. Jane is also very cautious about making any changes in her schedule that would infringe upon this classroom time. Teachers have been very generous in setting aside time for Jane to integrate her guidance curriculum within their broader curriculum and they expect Jane to arrive promptly. Jane knows last-minute changes can strain this relationship. (Classroom Guidance)

10:00 A.M.

Jane meets with an individual student related to completing homework. The student indicates things are improving and Jane conveys that his teacher seems to agree. The student's time gets interrupted by a call from the principal asking Jane to meet with him at noon. Jane checks her schedule and asks if 12:30 would work just as well. They agree on 12:30. Jane finishes her session with the student, makes a few notes, and uses the rest of the period to return phone calls. (Counseling, Consultation)

10:40 A.M.

Jane meets with a group of students as part of a weekly ongoing group on self-esteem. (Counseling)

11:20 A.M.

Jane slips into a PE class to observe a student who the PE teacher referred for aggressive and rude behavior. Jane has not yet met with this student. Both the PE teacher and Jane agreed that some observation time before meeting with the student would be helpful. Jane witnesses a near fight brought on by the student's insistence that he did not step out of bounds. Jane notes that the other students seem to have little patience for this student's behavior. (Consultation, Counseling)

Jane returns to her office and completes her portion of the forms that are part of the permanent records of a student who is transferring to another school. She also looks ahead in her calendar and sets a tentative time to see the student she has just observed. (Coordination)

NOON
Jane meets over lunch with two students who were caught skipping classes and leaving the building without authorization during the school day. Jane works hard to get to the bottom of the problem, being careful not to be perceived as a disciplinarian. (Counseling)

12:30 P.M.
Jane meets with the principal who shares with Jane his concerns about a particular teacher's inability to manage classroom behavior. Apparently several parents came to see the principal this morning and want their children removed from this teacher's class. The teacher is new this year. The principal asks Jane to work with this teacher. Jane feels like she is between a rock and a hard place. She can't say no to her boss, the principal, yet she also feels an allegiance to her colleague, the teacher. Jane shares the principal's concerns, yet does not acknowledge this concern out loud. Jane knows responding to this request will require trust building with the teacher, recognition of the teacher's strengths, and sensitivity to how stressful this must be for the teacher. Jane gets the principal to agree to an initial problem-solving meeting between the three of them. (Consultation)

1:00 P.M.
Jane joins peer mediators who meet on a daily basis at this time to mediate conflicts brought to their attention by either students or faculty. Today, the students work with two students who are in conflict over rumors each accuses the other of spreading. Jane and a teacher trained students as peer mediators earlier in the school year. (Counseling)

2:00 P.M.
Jane meets with the teacher who had requested an appointment that morning. The teacher shares concerns about a student who appears to be depressed. The teacher is worried that the student could be suicidal. Based on the information conveyed by the teacher, Jane decides to meet with this student before school is dismissed for the day. Jane checks the student's schedule with the teacher, finishes their conversation, and goes to locate the student. (Consultation)

2:30 P.M.
Jane meets with the student and does a risk assessment for suicide. No imminent danger seems to exist; however, the student does seem depressed and in need of counseling support. Jane lets the student know that she will be contacting her parents for a conference. Despite the student's objections, Jane persists with her need to speak to the student's parents. Jane also lets the student know that she will be asking the student's teachers for feedback about her school performance. (Counseling)

3:00 P.M.

Jane contacts the student's parents by phone and arranges for a meeting the next day. Jane has a checklist that she had already developed to tap the type of information needed from teachers. She places this in each teacher's box, asking for a return by the end of the next school day. (Consultation)

3:30 P.M.

Jane participates in the monthly School Improvement Team meeting. Jane knows that this is an important committee since this team makes many of the site-based decisions about program changes, school goals, and budget. (Consultation, Coordination)

4:30 P.M.

Jane reviews her schedule for the next day, leaves any messages for teachers in their mailboxes, and returns the last of her phone calls. She makes one phone call to the local YMCA to inquire about support groups for grandparents raising grandchildren. She invites the mental health counselor at this agency to meet with her to discuss how they might jointly offer such a service. (Coordination)

CHARACTERISTICS OF AN EFFECTIVE SCHOOL COUNSELOR

School counselors will tell you that they are never bored. Jane's day gives some insight into why that is true. Ask school counselors to list the important characteristics of an effective school counselor and they will most likely indicate that a counselor must be warm, empathic, genuine, and nonjudgmental—all things we learn early on are important core conditions of a counseling relationship. Yet Jane's day suggests the need for some additional qualities. Flexibility is one of the first that comes to mind. Jane provides an excellent example of what this means for a school counselor. Rarely does a school counselor's day begin and end as the counselor expected. Change in what a counselor expects to do on a certain day, as well as change in the times established to do those things, is inevitable as the counselor strives to meet an unending diversity of student, teacher, administrator, and family needs.

Our example also illustrates that a school counselor needs to be well organized. Many people's expectations place heavy demands on a school counselor's time. Being well organized maximizes what a school counselor is able to accomplish.

Unlike a teacher who has a responsibility for a certain number of students and a certain subject matter, the school counselor oversees a program that touches each student in the building. School counselors work with a variety of people (students, teachers, administrators, family members, members of the community) in a variety of contexts (individual counseling, group counseling, classroom guidance, consultations, team meetings). This wide array of potential "clients" and systems for service delivery requires a school counselor to acquire a multidimensional knowledge base and multiple areas of expertise.

A final quality that describes a school counselor is the ability to maintain objectivity. It would be very easy and natural for a counselor to feel angry or upset if a teacher fails to acknowledge the counselor as an equal member of the school team. Just as Jane adjusts her schedule to accommodate teachers' needs, Jane could begin to resent a teacher who always expects accommodation yet never accommodates for Jane. The objective counselor is able to keep personal feelings from interfering with the execution of his or her role and function. The objective counselor enters the school with no preconceived notion of how teachers, family members, or students "should" act or not act toward the counselor.

At this point, we have provided some sense of what happens during the day in the life of a school counselor and some of the personal qualities that contribute to a counselor's ability to be effective. The next section looks at variations of a counselor's role and function depending on school level.

SCHOOL COUNSELING AT THE ELEMENTARY, MIDDLE, AND HIGH SCHOOL LEVELS

School counselors at all school levels, elementary, middle, and high school, deliver similar services—counseling, classroom guidance, consultation, and coordination. The balance and proportion of services varies across school levels, and in some cases may be directly related to administrative support of the school counselor's role. The goals and objectives for programs at each school level are closely connected to developmental needs.

Elementary School Counseling

As an elementary school counselor, Jane's day will consist of activities that center around helping children, ages 5–11, adjust to the expectations of the school environment and form new relationships beyond the immediate family. Significant changes in one's social environment and emotional maturity characterize development during childhood. Students enter the elementary school with a need for basic social and academic skills, and leave for middle school immersed in complexity of the early stages of puberty.

Group counseling is a popular intervention at the elementary school level that allows students to explore personal and interpersonal problems in a safe environment. Most counselors conduct structured groups that focus on skill development such as problem solving, communication, conflict resolution, and study skills. Groups for children undergoing transitions in their family are also common. These same themes may be addressed in classroom guidance sessions. In both the group and classroom context, interventions and lessons are interactive and action-oriented. Role-play, literature, puppetry, art, music, and games are typical mediums for engaging students in the learning process.

The school counselor also helps the school identify students who need additional counseling services. The school counselor usually participates on the school's admission, review, and dismissal team for special education, and would also be a member of any other school-based team that assesses student strengths and weaknesses and designs appropriate interventions. Different school systems have unique organizational structures and names for such teams; however, most have some type of team process for supporting student learning. School counselors at the elementary level are typically a part of such a process.

Classroom management is a common topic for teacher–counselor consultation at the elementary school level. Elementary school counselors need to be adept at behavior management principles and how to design behavioral contracts that are theoretically sound. Consultations with parents also frequently revolve around behavior management issues.

Middle School Counseling

Middle schools typically include sixth to eighth grades, with some school systems defining middle school as seventh and eighth grades only. Helping students cope with transition would be a central task for Jane if she worked in a middle school. Students in sixth (seventh) grade are busy adjusting to the expectations of multiple teachers, daily schedules that are more complex, larger classes, new friends, and new social and academic experiences. Eighth grade students, on the other hand, must adjust to leaving the familiar for the even more complex system of high school.

Early adolescence is a time of marked physical, emotional, and cognitive changes. Probably the one thing that most distinguishes this period of time is the diversity with which early adolescents move through this stage of development. Some achieve physical changes that make them appear older than their years, while others remain more childlike in physique. Others develop an interest in members of the opposite sex, become more able to think abstractly, and have an interest in developing more opportunities to socialize away from the school or home settings. Talking on the telephone and sending electronic instant messages becomes an important link between friends outside of school.

The middle school counselor must not only be sensitive to the breadth of change within an individual student, but also must be cognizant that not all early adolescents undergo changes at the same rate or within the same time frame. All of these developmental considerations set the context for what the school counselor does at the middle school level. Teamwork with teachers and other school-based professionals is particularly important. Some middle schools organize the school around teaching teams, with counselors assigned to different teams. Each team works in a concentrated fashion with a particular set of students, overseeing all academic and social concerns. Coordination of activity becomes increasingly important for the middle school counselor since teachers and schedules are not as easily accessible or flexible as the elementary school. Middle school counselors conduct group counseling sessions, classroom guidance lessons, and work with individual students. Topics addressed in these activities include decision making, conflict resolution, peer relationships, study skills, and issues such as use of alcohol and other controlled substances, sexuality, and managing anger. Academic advising and early career development also become important parts of the services provided by the middle school counselor.

Parents and other family members rely on the middle school counselor for assistance with setting boundaries for appropriate behavior for the middle school child. Reaching for increased autonomy, yet not ready for independence, conflicts between parents and children are common. The middle school counselor provides parents with an understanding of early adolescent development as well as concrete strategies for maintaining communication and setting age-appropriate limits. School counselors also mediate conflicts between students and teachers, parents and teachers, and parents and students.

High School Counseling

If Jane was a high school counselor, her day may have started out with the same coordinating activities suggested in our example. The content of her prevention and intervention activities, however, is distinct. Academic pressures exist at a new level in high school since this experience is a critical link to career choices and plans for post-secondary school employment and training. The high school counselor devotes much time to meeting individually with students around academic advising and career development issues. Career concerns are paramount for adolescents and high school counseling programs need to provide opportunities for students to explore interests, gather information about different occupations, make decisions, and complete applications and entrance exams for post-secondary school options. School counselors also provide consultation to parents and other family members around these transition issues.

Students in high school are particularly concerned about their social surroundings and how they fit within their social milieu. Peer relationships are of utmost importance to the adolescent. It is also a time when adolescents experiment with new behavior and test limits set by the school and family. Developing a self-identity is another important developmental task for this age.

These needs influence how a school counselor approaches student problems. For example, in Jane's consultation with the teacher regarding a student's completion of homework, in addition to assessing the student's academic skills, the teacher and Jane will address how to help the student prioritize social activities with schoolwork. When working with students who have been missing class, Jane would work directly with the students to find out why they missed class and to develop an intervention that would increase attendance. Maintaining communication with teachers and parents would be important; however, Jane would be careful to protect student confidences. How Jane, as a high school counselor, approaches the problem may be different than how an elementary school counselor might respond. In an elementary student's situation, the absenteeism may result from issues at home that are beyond the student's control rather than from causes such as peer pressure or feelings of inadequacy. In such a case, the elementary school counselor may be more apt to work directly with the family to resolve the problem.

Typically, high school counselors spend a larger percentage of time on program management, academic advising, and administrative tasks usually revolving around the scheduling of courses than their elementary or middle school counterparts. Elementary school counselors generally have the most time and flexibility to provide direct counseling services.

A RETURN TO THE CASE OF "CLIVE"

A discouraged Mrs. Washington has approached Clive's school counselor for assistance. Given what has been described about the school counselor's role and function, what actions might the school counselor take to assist Mrs. Washington and Clive?

Assessment

After receiving Mrs. Washington's referral, the school counselor will take several steps to develop a more complete understanding of Clive and the reason for referral. These could include:

- A consultation with Mrs. Washington in order to find out more about Clive's behavior in the classroom, Mrs. Washington's response to this behavior, Clive's academic skills, and any other background information about Clive that Mrs. Washington is able to share
- A review of Clive's records from elementary school to determine his academic history
- A consultation with the school nurse regarding the current status of Clive's medication
- A consultation with Clive's parents to better understand family dynamics and to acquire parental perceptions of Clive as a learner
- An observation of Clive by the counselor in Mrs. Washington's classroom in order to assess classroom dynamics
- Consultations with Clive's other teachers to determine patterns of behavior
- A counseling session with Clive to acquire his perception of the reason for referral

After completing this assessment phase, the school counselor will begin to make some decisions about how to proceed with helping Clive based on the information collected. In this particular case, the school counselor's consultation yielded a variety of pertinent information, including the fact that Clive's medication had not been reevaluated in the past year, that his brother had died recently, and that Clive had not felt permitted by his family to mourn his brother's loss.

Interventions

Bringing Clive's teacher and parents together to share concerns and figure out together how best to help Clive is a first step in developing and coordinating a comprehensive action plan. The school counselor realizes that his or her independent actions cannot sufficiently address Clive's problems. At this meeting it is important to develop a consensus about the problem and the desired outcome. Interventions that result from this meeting might include:

- Counseling sessions with Clive to address his sense of loss. Although the school counselor cannot commit to a long-term counseling relationship due to time constraints and other responsibilities, the counselor may commit to working with Clive on this personal issue for six to eight counseling sessions. If this does not appear to be sufficient, a referral to an outside-of-school mental health professional would be appropriate.
- Further consultation with Clive's parents to help them understand how they might be more supportive to Clive. This could include further exploration of the need for some short-term family therapy to help the whole family adjust to their loss. Again, the school counselor could coordinate a referral.
- Further consultation with Mrs. Washington to develop behavior management strategies for responding to Clive's inappropriate classroom behavior and for helping Clive complete homework assignments. Through consultation, the school counselor can also share with Mrs. Washington the typical effects of loss and grief on early adolescents.
- Establishing a communication link between Mrs. Washington and Clive's parents pertaining to homework assignments.
- Recommending a referral to Clive's physician for a medication reevaluation.
- Obtaining written permission from Clive's parents for the school counselor to discuss the school's concerns with Clive's physician.

Generally, the school counselor takes responsibility for coordinating these action steps and maintaining communication with all involved.

Evaluation

At the conclusion of the parent-teacher-counselor meeting, the school counselor would establish a date for all involved to evaluate the status of all interventions and to determine progress toward helping Clive adjust to his loss and improve his school performance. If at that time sufficient progress has not been made, the school counselor may recommend that Clive's case be placed on the agenda of the school's student support team. This would integrate into the problem-solving process additional school-based resources and assessment possibilities.

EXPANDING THE VISION: SOME THOUGHTS ON THE FUTURE OF SCHOOL COUNSELING

The needs of students in today's schools are often too complex for a single institution or solitary service provider to solve alone. In fact, such problems challenge service providers within and outside the school building to think more creatively about how to deliver services, exactly what services should be provided, and how their roles and functions need to adapt to be responsive to changing needs. The school counselor is not exempt from this discussion. The following describes three new roles for counselors working in today's schools.

Collaborator

School counselors have long perceived themselves to be collaborators with teachers and families. By expanding their counseling, consultation, and coordinating functions to include collaboration as the fourth "C," collaboration takes on a new sense of importance. If school counselors are to develop truly comprehensive programs, they must begin to connect what happens in school programs with prevention efforts in the larger community. This suggests that the goal of integrating the school counseling program within the larger educational program is not sufficient. School counselors cannot afford to remain isolated from broader community initiatives. This will require school counselors to become familiar with other service agencies and community organizations such as juvenile justice, child and family welfare, and managed care groups, and to work collaboratively with these groups in the planning and implementing of programs for children, youth, and families. It is also important for school counselors to be knowledgeable about state-level system reform initiatives that affect services for children and families (Lockhart & Keys, 1998).

System-Change Agent

The school counseling model as currently designed focuses on individual change through counseling, consultation, coordination, and classroom instruction. Successful prevention efforts, however, require not only strategies directed at the individual, but also strategies aimed at changing the developmental context that surrounds the individual (Dryfoos, 1990; Lerner, 1995). This means that school counselors must begin to perceive their role more broadly and conceptualize problems more systemically. Appropriate targets for intervention in addition to the individual might include the family, the peer group, the neighborhood, the work environment, and the school and classroom environments (Dryfoos, 1990). This would be consistent with the earlier mentioned system-focused model of consultation.

Systemic change may include changes in practices, policies, or attitudes. For example, school counselors as system change agents may take a leadership role in their school building for creating new service delivery systems. One way a school counselor might do this would be to expand and redefine the school counseling program advisory committee. A change in policy would occur when the group membership is reconstituted with a new mission and function. A change in practice would occur when the actual practices of the group are modified. Creating a school-based, school-family-community mental health team presents a new possibility for both change in policy and practice. This team would expand upon the program development functions of the advisory committee by bringing within its purview all support programs and mental health initiatives that operate within the building (change in policy). This team would also include a broader representation from the community than the advisory committee (change in policy). It would also work to prevent duplication and fragmentation of services across all school-based programs of this type by reviewing all school-based programs and meeting with program coordinators (change in practices).

Intervening to change attitudes is the most difficult type of system change and often necessary to build support for innovations. The new team structure for the school-family-community mental health team described above may meet with teacher resistance, particularly if a teacher perceives participation on this team an intrusion on his or her time. School counselors need to use their communication skills to listen to stakeholder concerns, and be responsive to concerns. It is also important to encourage and reinforce small steps toward the innovative practice.

Family Specialist

It is a known fact that students achieve in school at higher rates when families are involved in the student's education. As a family specialist, the school counselor gives priority to working with all families—nuclear, extended, foster, single-parent, or blended. In this role, the school counselor helps connect families with the school in general and teachers specifically, and works to assure that family members feel comfortable entering the building and participating in school conferences.

The school counselor, as family specialist, is knowledgeable about diverse cultures. Many school counselors work in urban and suburban settings with populations that reflect many different cultures. An understanding of how culture affects family attitudes about school, mental health, discipline, and the role of counselors is important when trying to make connections between families and the school.

School counselor–family specialists also need to have knowledge of family systems theory and need to have skills for implementing short-term family counseling. In addition, the school counselor–family specialist advocates for other needed school-based and community services and works to connect families with other service providers. This may mean creating a different "typical day" structure. The school counselor–family specialist may work a more flexible day, with early morning and evening hours available to accommodate family schedules. This new role may also mean that the counselor works out of the building on some days, attending meetings and case management conferences at agency sites.

SUMMARY

The kinds of complex student problems facing today's schools require comprehensive solutions that integrate the expertise of multiple service providers and diverse helping institutions. School counselors present a viable link between schools, families, and the larger outside-of-school network of service providers. A school counselor, who integrates the roles of collaborator, system change agent, and family specialist within the already established roles of counselor, consultant, and coordinator, is a valuable resource for schools striving to increase student achievement.

CHAPTER FIFTEEN

COUNSELING IN MENTAL HEALTH AND PRIVATE PRACTICE SETTINGS

REBECCA T. BROWERS, ED.D.
Eastern Washington University

During the 1960s, as counselors began to look for professional opportunities in addition to the traditionally held positions in educational settings, they moved into various settings within the community. Initially, community counseling focused on the needs of individuals (and occasionally couples and families) who were essentially healthy, but struggling with normal conflicts, uncertainties, or developmental transitions. Following the Community Mental Health Centers Act of 1963, counselors were employed to provide service to clients who had previously been hospitalized for various mental disorders. The last three decades of the twentieth century brought rapid and remarkable change to the practice of community mental health counseling.

Today, professional mental health counselors respond to clients facing a more complex world, a pluralistic society, changing views on families, and a shifting economic structure. Many clients may be burdened by troubling circumstances within their home, on the job, or in their communities. Some face situations such as parenting grandchildren, caring for incapacitated older parents, or living with domestic violence, and seek assistance from counselors for needs of varying severity.

Community mental health counselors provide counseling in a wide variety of settings. Government funded agencies, clinics, and programs can be found in most communities, where various services are usually supported by state or county funds, or a combination of the two. In recent years, it has become typical for community mental health care to focus on the more severe needs of adults and children in a community or a region, frequently being the primary resource for the chronically mentally ill, those diagnosed with a substance abuse, or more severely troubled adults and youth. Some communities are also fortunate enough to have public or private nonprofit agencies, primarily dependent on monies from grants, contributions, or public campaigns like the United Way (Nugent, 2000).

Counselors in private practice receive payment either directly from their clients or from their clients' insurance companies. Clients seek counseling services for many different reasons and may turn to practitioners in independent private practice, group practices, or for-profit clinical settings for assistance. Counseling is provided to individuals, couples, families, or groups, and addresses normal concerns associated with stresses in daily living such as decision making, transitions, developmental concerns, building communication skills, and others. Some clients may deal with issues of a more severe nature requiring longer term counseling, as well. Some counselors in private practice specialize in specific problems or a particular client population such as depression, anxiety, phobias, substance abuse, post-traumatic stress disorder (PTSD), eating disorders, or children with attention deficit disorder.

Professional mental health counselors hold master's degrees and may pursue a variety of professional credentials. In most states, counselors must have a license regulated by the state in order to be in private practice and to qualify for third-party payments. Licensed professional counselors are sometimes called upon to testify in court, may receive contracts to conduct assessments and evaluations, write psychological reports, and consult with other mental health care professionals. Depending on areas of specialty, they may also be referral sources for physicians, other health care professionals, and managed health care systems.

A counselor in private practice, in addition to being a competent practitioner who is able to assess and effectively treat a broad range of client needs, must also possess, or be able to hire someone who possesses, skills in managing a business. The demands of a practice include promoting the practice, scheduling appointments, maintaining accurate client records, handling the financial details of billing, bookkeeping, filing tax reports, and communicating with insurance providers.

The relatively short, dynamic, and rich history of the counseling profession is an interesting one. Mental health counselors have diversified from their roots in educational and vocational guidance, have adapted to the demands of the clinical environment, and have responded to the needs of the community. It's been an exciting ride, and there is more to come.

OUT OF THE SCHOOL YARD AND INTO THE COMMUNITY: A RETROSPECTIVE

Prior to the 1960s, those pursuing graduate education in order to become counselors generally went on to provide counseling services in traditional educational settings such as public and private schools, colleges, and universities. School counselors were almost guaranteed a secure position in the nation's elementary, junior high, and high schools as a result of federal funding which accompanied the passage of the National Defense Education Act of 1958 and the subsequent Secondary Education Act of 1964.

During the 1960s and 1970s, counselors were also employed in colleges, universities, and junior colleges (which later evolved into community colleges). Traditionally, the role of the counselor was associated with student affairs and was quite diverse, including career development, academic planning, academic assessment, advising, and residence life support, while also responding to the mental health needs of residential and commuter students. Counselors on a campus responded to the mental health needs of the campus, as well. Occasionally, counselors in higher education filled a more narrowly defined function, with student counseling services being distributed among several offices (Levine, 1980).

However, as the 1960s neared an end, the escalating war in Vietnam reduced the amount of federal dollars available for many human services programs, including school counseling programs (Brooks, 1997). Similar reductions in state funding soon followed and positions decreased for school counselors, as well as counselors in postsecondary settings, leading to a bleak job market for several graduating classes and limiting the necessity for new hires in counselor education.

SUPPLY AND DEMAND: A NEW JOB MARKET

The difficulties faced by counselors in traditional educational settings, and struggles faced by new graduates with ambitions to enter the ranks of school counselors, led to a growing interest in mental health counseling opportunities outside school settings. Fortunately, community awareness, employment opportunities, and emerging sources of funding began to evolve around the same time. The Community Mental Health Centers Act of 1963 signaled a significant shift in attitudes about counseling and the delivery of mental health care services. The intent of the act was to establish community-based treatment centers as alternatives to the overstressed, marginally effective state hospital system that had prevailed since the nineteenth century. The transition to community mental health care was believed to be more humane and effective than the mental health "warehouses" that many state hospitals had become (Brooks, 1997; Brooks & Weikel, 1986).

Community mental health care centers were to be staffed by multidisciplinary treatment teams that included the four "core provider" professions of psychiatry, psychology, social work, and nursing, as well as a variety of paraprofessionals whose training was unspecified. As the centers began hiring staff, master's level counselor education graduates filled many of the undesignated "paraprofessional" positions. Counselors trained at the doctoral level, but increasingly denied licensure as psychologists by state boards, also found receptivity from the community mental health centers, which were frequently exempt from licensure requirements (Brooks, 1997).

The sudden increase in demand for mental health care providers from multiple disciplines and compatible perspectives presented both a challenge and an opportunity for the counseling profession. It was clear that to compete in a shifting job market, counselor education programs needed to expand their training, and counselors would need to reassess their professional goals to include community-based mental health counseling, an opportunity welcomed by many.

EMERGING OPPORTUNITIES IN COMMUNITY COUNSELING

The social concerns and the political movements of the decades of the sixties, seventies, and even the eighties contributed to a need for more community-based counseling services. The civil rights movement, the women's movement, returning Vietnam veterans, anti-war activism, the sexual revolution, changing demographics in the home and the workplace, and the counseling profession's increased emphasis on human growth and development all raised public awareness of the value of counseling for individuals, couples, and families. The emerging needs reflected a continuum of care to include supportive services, crisis intervention and response, assessment and referral, and short- or long-term counseling. In response to the growing trend for community mental health care services, counselor education programs revised the curricula and graduate students broadened their training in some cases, became more specialized in other cases, and increased their credentials to better prepare them to work in community mental health care, both public and private.

PROFESSIONAL GROWING PAINS

As the counseling profession was undergoing a period of rapid change and productive growth, it understandably experienced some professional growing pains. In 1978, the American Mental Health Counselors Association (AMHCA) became the thirteenth division of the American Counseling Association (ACA), which was then known as the American Personnel and Guidance Association (APGA). From the beginning, and well into the 1980s, AMHCA's rapidly growing membership paralleled the tremendous increase in numbers of counselors working in public and private community mental health care. From the very beginning, AMHCA consistently assumed an active role in the professionalization of the mental health counseling field by proposing and supporting standardization of counselor education programs, state licensure, and certification requirements. A primary goal of AMHCA has always been to professionally and politically advocate for the recognition of counselors as equal to that of other nonmedical mental health disciplines: clinical psychology, social work, and psychiatric nursing (Brooks, 1997).

Historically, APGA had devoted most of its legislative efforts to an educational agenda, corresponding with the majority of the members up until the late 1970s. Almost as soon as it became an APGA division, there was disagreement between AMHCA and the parent organization, based on concerns that the increasingly diverse needs of counselors were being neglected. APGA was becoming more diversified with members representing interests in community mental health counseling, rehabilitation counseling, vocational counseling, religious values in counseling, and college student personnel, to name a few.

At one point, in 1986, with a membership that exceeded 10,000, AMHCA became the largest division of the parent organization, which had adopted its new name, the American Association for Counseling and Development in 1983. The philosophical and fiscal struggles between ACA and AMHCA continued well into the nineties, but a compromise was reached toward the end of the 1990s when AMHCA and ACA separated their financial affairs and took actions that permitted counselors to join the division with or without joining ACA.

Although membership has declined, AMHCA continues to be a powerful voice at the local, state, and national levels, remaining actively involved in efforts to promote and secure gains in public policy and legislation that ensures professional status for mental health counselors. ACA and its divisions work together to educate the public regarding the role of counselors in community mental health care and to advocate for the needs of the consuming public. The basis for some of the earlier organizational conflicts, ironically, reflects one of the major strengths of the counseling profession. Namely, included among the professional ranks are counselors who fill many distinctly different roles in community settings, but respectfully collaborate to serve the needs of those in the community. ACA, with its eighteen divisions, is a reflection of that diversity.

THE NEED FOR COMMUNITY-BASED MENTAL HEALTH COUNSELING

Professional mental health counselors face greater demands and have correspondingly more opportunities for practice in today's market. Community-based mental health care providers are striving to serve the priorities of a broader client population who present with clinical issues of a more severe nature than a generation ago. While some agencies are responding to increasing budget demands and a reduction in crucial programs and services, community needs are not diminishing and it is clear that the necessity for competent and accessible mental health counseling services will continue to grow.

Mental health providers, counselor educators, and community mental health care agencies all engage in the process of examining clinical issues and client concerns that affect the profession in general, and their community, in particular. All share the responsibility to identify the most ethical and effective ways to respond. It is realistic to say that an accurate assessment of those needs permits counselors to be better prepared to provide the most competent and ethical treatment for clients. It also indirectly determines the focus and setting of their work, and it is directly related to the availability of professional opportunities for practitioners.

COUNSELING CONCERNS AFFECTING COMMUNITIES

In 2002, the President's New Freedom Commision on Mental Health confirmed that, while common to the population, many who suffer from mental health problems have unmet needs. It went on to say that no community is untouched by this mental illness, young or old; African American, Native American, Pacific American,

Hispanic American, Alaska Native, Asian American, or White American. The challenges are found in schools, homes, and the workplace. In any given year, 5 to 7 percent of adults have a serious mental illness, with 5 to 9 percent of children experiencing a serious emotional disturbance. In fact, mental illnesses rank first among illnesses that cause disability in the United States, Canada, and Western Europe, taking a serious toll on the health and well-being of families and communities, while creating a major economic dilemma related to the direct and indirect costs in the workplace—reportedly as much as $79 billion in the United States alone. Included in that figure is almost $12 billion in mortality costs and $4 billion in productivity costs due to incarcerated individuals and for the time of those who provide family care. It is a public health challenge to be taken seriuosly (SAMSHA, 2003).

According to ACA, the most frequent occurrences are anxiety disorders (12.6 percent), followed by affective disorders (including depression) (9.5 percent) and cognitive impairment (2.7 percent). Although fewer individuals are affected by more serious conditions such as schizophrenia (1.1 percent) and antisocial personality disorder (1.5 percent), the disruption to the individual is more severe, and counseling interventions are likely to be longer in duration. It is worth noting that while individuals may have more than one disorder in a year, less than 7 percent of the population experience symptoms for a full year or longer (ACA, 1999).

Depression affects the sufferer by limiting his or her opportunity to function comfortably in the world, it can complicate other medical conditions, and can be serious enough to lead to suicide, approximately 30,000 per year (SAMSHA, 2003). With 15 million Americans experiencing depression in their lifetime, and about 10 percent of the population each year (Department of Health and Human Services [DHHS], 2002), it is also true that the illness affects families, productivity, and communities. In fact, according to the National Mental Health Association, unipolar depression is considered the leading cause of disability in the world (Mrazek, 1998).

The Substance Abuse and Mental Heath Services Administration (SAMSHA), a division of the Department of Health and Human Services, states that 52 million Americans have some type of alcohol, drug, or mental health disorder each year (DHHS, 1995). Individuals with substance abuse problems frequently are assessed with a dual diagnosis, meaning that they are affected by a disorder in addition to an addiction (Seligman, 1997). Just as individuals suffering from depression, those who interact with or are affected by someone with a substance abuse problem may also experience stress, anxiety, depression, or related concerns that are alleviated by counseling.

Members of the communities experience circumstances that, while psychological and emotional in nature, are exacerbated by economic, social, and political conditions, and require intervention and support from the mental health care community. Professional counselors provide assistance to families affected by domestic violence, people living with AIDS, and hospice clients and their families, to name a few.

Mental Health Needs of Children and Adolescents

David Satcher, the United States Surgeon General, issued a press release indicating that one in ten children suffer from mental illness to a degree that they experience some level of impairment. According to records, he estimated that fewer than half of those received needed treatment. This, of course, carries implications for costly, and potentially tragic consequences for those not treated. Satcher urged the adoption of science-based prevention and treatment and continued research, while also identifying the need to "better educate frontline providers—teachers, health care workers, school counselors and coaches, faith-based workers, and clinicians" (2001).

But the fact is, school counselors will continue to have caseloads and responsibilities that make it unlikely that they can sufficiently respond to the number of needs and the severity of problems experienced by children and adolescents, without the support and collaboration of mental health counselors in the community. The current trend is for more integration of services between schools and community mental health care services. On occasion, individual schools or school districts contract with community services for student needs that are specialized in nature or exceed the resources of the school. School counselors and community mental health counselors work together in an atmosphere of mutual respect to meet the needs of the children and adolescents, link with families, and consult regarding environmental and situational concerns of the school.

The statistics suggest that children and adolescents are currently underserved, indicating a critical need for even further support for community-based programming to supplement the strained school-based resources and to better address severe and long-term needs. The Institute of Medicine, in *Schools and Health* (1997), estimated about 4 million children between the ages of 9 and 17 have serious emotional disturbances. Similarly, the National Institute on Mental Health stated that up to one in five children and young people have psychological problems which are severe enough to require some form of professional help, whereas only 20 percent of youth with mental disorders, or their families, receive help (Hoagwood, 1999). A major concern is the potential for tragic consequences when the urgent needs of youth are neglected—the increased risk for suicide, homicide, or other forms of violence. An estimated 2,000 teenagers in the United States commit suicide each year, making it the third leading cause of death, after accidents and homicide (ACA, 1999).

Approximately 90 percent of teenagers who commit suicide have a psychiatric diagnosis, most often a form of a mood disorder (depression) and have problems with alcohol or other substances (ACA, 1999). These statistics do not reflect the young people who attempt suicide, and those who seriously contemplate the act, and are in need of mental health counseling to move them out of such a high-risk state.

The consequences of failing to provide adequate mental health counseling and related services to children and adolescents with severe emotional needs are significant and affect not only the individual, but his or her family, their school, and all of our communities. Communities must continue to support and increase the mental health resources available to young people. In addition to school counselors, professional counselors outside of the educational system must be prepared to respond to the psychological and emotional needs of the young people they serve.

Older Adults: A New Arena

Gerontological counseling, a new specialty area, is relatively new, but given the rapidly changing demographics, it is not surprising that it merits its own chapter in most introductory counseling textbooks (including this one). It is being infused into counselor education programs and proposed as a specialty area by the Council for the Accreditation of Counseling and Related Educational Programs (CACREP). According to the American Association of Retired Persons, people over the age of 65 currently make up more than 13 percent of the population, with an estimated 71.5 million older persons by the year 2030 (AARP, 2003). Residents of the United States are anticipating longer life spans and the population is predicted to include "20 percent over the age of 65 before 2050." The 85 and over group is the fastest growing segment of our society (Newman & Newman, 1999).

As the life span increases, there are implications for various areas of community counseling practice. Counselors who focus on families, careers and lifestyles, and addictions will experience changes in their client base to include more older adults. Older persons are already affected by major depression (more than 6 million), have a suicide rate greater than the general population (six times the general population rate for elderly white males), and suffer from substance abuse (Lebowitz, 1999; Myers & Schiebert, 1996). Using data from a current study (Folson, Gfroerer, Pemberton & Penne, 2002), the number of adults needing treatment for substance abuse problems will grow to 4.4 million in 2020 compared to 1.7 million in 2000 and 2001.

Disappointingly, the recent passage of a Medicare and prescription drug and reform bill did not include reimbursement for licensed professional counselors. It is logical and necessary that the counseling profession and community mental health counselors continue their efforts to insure access for older adults to comprehensive mental health care and increase their emphasis on individuals in later life in addition to the traditional focus on adults, children, and adolescents.

Mental Health Counseling in Community Settings

Counseling in private practice and for-profit settings will be addressed in a subsequent section; this portion of the chapter is devoted to public and nonprofit community-based mental health care settings. Initially, when counselors began to seek counseling positions outside of traditional educational institutions, most positions were to be found in publicly funded, community mental health centers. Many professional counselors still find challenging and rewarding opportunities in such agencies today. The agencies fulfill a necessary and important function in communities. Counselors who work in community agencies gain experience working with very diverse client populations who present with problems from moderate to severe and often enjoy the variety afforded them in such a setting. Because there are a significant number of clients with acute needs, counselors working in community agencies must be competent in diagnosis and treatment planning and must be knowledgeable about psychotropic medications (Nugent, 2000). The work is demanding, fast paced, and never boring.

Most communities have a municipally funded mental health care facility. In addition to a broad-based agency, there are usually many other agencies or programs that are more narrowly focused on a specific need or population. These agencies may collaborate with a community system of care, may serve as referral sources, or may function completely independent of other programs within the community. The agency, by virtue of its location, its affiliation, or its source of funding, may serve particular population or community needs (e.g., county funded court diversion programs, county youth services, or a community halfway house). Counselors who have a specialty, or want to increase their experience in a specific area of practice, may work in one of these programs or agencies.

Public and Private Nonprofit Support for Mental Health Counseling

Other than services available from counselors in private practice many, if not most, community-based mental health care services are nonprofit and it is not always readily apparent what the source of funding is. While both categories may be nonprofit, the origins of the funding often determines what is available. Either category can be broad or specific in its focus, and clients may pay a set fee, a fee based on a sliding scale, or may receive service for free.

Public Nonprofit Agencies.   In many cases, state, local, or county funds, or government grants, or some combination of those sources supports agencies or programs. Government funded or sponsored services tend to be multipurpose and available to the general public. As alluded to previously in the chapter, even with the prevalence of a major publicly supported community mental health care center in most communities, mental health care services are found in many different programs scattered throughout the community and are not necessarily coordinated in the most efficient manner. Those seeking services are likely to find different requirements for eligibility depending on their particular need, a diagnosis, their ability to pay, or limitations associated with insurance or managed care companies. Accessing counseling services can be a complicated and frustrating process at a time when the individual may have a diminished capacity to navigate the maze.

In spite of the obvious challenges to be overcome, there are some clear advantages to utilizing a community-based "system" of mental health care. Individuals seeking counseling will find many different areas of specialization available among practitioners in the community. Not only are different clinical needs addressed, but an array of treatment options offered, different theoretical perspectives respected, flexible delivery systems utilized, and diverse counseling environments represented. Services may be interdisciplinary or certain specialty areas are focused on that are not available elsewhere in community settings. Community mental health care agencies and counselors usually are strong advocates for their clients. Examples of community mental health services other than centralized community mental health centers include the following:

- Drop-in crisis centers
- Outpatient substance abuse treatment and support programs

- Day treatment programs for severely and persistently mental ill individuals
- Support services for Alzheimer's patients and their caregivers
- Counseling services aimed toward ethnic and culturally diverse communities
- Child and family agencies
- Homeless shelters
- Anger management groups

Private Nonprofit Agencies.   Nonprofit agencies include those supported by the United Way, religiously affiliated nondenominational organizations (e.g., Catholic Family Services, Samaritan Counseling Centers, Lutheran Social Services), charities, private endowments, or grants. There is occasionally overlap, or even a duplication of service provided by public and private nonprofit mental health counseling services, but private nonprofit agencies tend to include some programs that would otherwise be absent from the community.

Because of the diverse sources of funding, private nonprofit agencies reflect the greatest range of services, employment opportunities, and wages in the professional counseling community. Mental health counseling professionals with less traditional interests, or those dedicated to working with a specific population or clinical interest, may be drawn to opportunities with private counseling services.

Whether public or private, nonprofit programs often function more independently and more autonomously, and therefore, are sometimes not bound by institutional policies and restrictions. Finally, due to increased credentialing requirements (namely licensing and certification), consumers of nonprofit services can feel confident that mental health counselors have been professionally trained and are receiving professional supervision and consultation.

For-Profit Mental Health Care

The concept of community mental health care conjures up a myriad of community-based services in both centralized and specialized programs that offer an alternative to hospitalization; in truth, the majority of mental health care services are provided in the community. Very few clients receive hospitalization, inpatient treatment, or residential treatment today, and in most cases, this is considered preferable (Brooks & Weikel, 1986). Whereas many services are provided through nonprofit agencies, a considerable number of others are accessed by clients from mental health counselors in private, for-profit settings. Clients receiving mental health counseling services pay a fee for service, either out of pocket, or paid by their insurance provider. The private agency or counselor in private practice intends to make a profit, and the fee structure is usually quite different from that of nonprofit services. An advantage of private practice includes the freedom to be as broad or as narrow in the services offered, or the clients served.

Private Agencies.   Services provided by professional counselors in private agencies range from individual, group, marital, or family counseling, to programs offered through contractual arrangements for other private companies, or occasionally, public institutions (Male, 1990). An example of this is a contracted employee assistance program (EAP) provided to a corporation or an industry by a private counseling agency. Specific time-limited service might be enlisted from a private agency to provide counseling and support to employees during a time of major or unanticipated layoffs.

Some private mental health care agencies specialize in specific areas of clinical need (e.g., eating disorders, substance abuse, sex abuse) and may "market" their services to public or private concerns that offer general counseling services but are unprepared to respond to certain client needs requiring special knowledge, training, or resources. In the case of private agencies that operate for profit, the mental health counselor is generally employed by the agency and receives a salary. In some arrangements, the counselor receives a percentage of the fees collected from their clients.

Private Practice.   Professional counselors in private practice may work independently, affiliate with other private practitioners to share administration and supervision services and costs, and may have part-time or full-time practices. It should be stressed that it is neither typical, nor advisable for mental health counselors to go into independent practice without significant postgraduate experience in working with a range of clients and counseling concerns. To do so without sufficient preparation is a violation of quite a few professional ethical standards, but most clearly would not meet the ACA standard that states, "Counselors practice only within the boundaries of their competence, based on their education, training, supervised experience, state and national professional credentials, and appropriate professional experience" (1997a, C.2.). Most counselors in private practice have spent time in community or agency practice and have acquired an appropriate license prior to pursuing an independent practice. Whether working in an independent private practice or affiliating with other private mental health care providers, it is essential to have a well-developed resource and referral network and a system in place for assessing and responding to clients in crisis. That system should include a process for admitting a client to a hospital or treatment facility, should it become necessary.

Depending on your point of view, mental health counselors in private practice have either maximum freedom and flexibility, or maximum limitations in their professional work. In the extreme, private practice affords the freedom of choosing to whom service will be provided, and the ability to work with those clients using whatever theoretically sound methods and interventions considered most effective, without external influences on the format or duration of treatment.

Some counselors feel when they are not dependent on third-party payment, they can be more responsive to the needs of the client, determining (with the client) how frequently to schedule appointments and the duration of the counseling process. It should be noted that mental health counselors who exercise this "maximum freedom" generally are limited to the white upper-middle class (Nugent, 2000); although in theory, the independent counselor in private practice could offer services to the most diverse client population, depending on their range of competency and their flexibility in setting fees.

Successful mental health counselors in private practice are more likely to be financially successful if they are eligible for third-party reimbursement (i.e., insurance payments) and are recognized as core providers by managed health care systems.

Their client roster includes some clients that pay "out-of-pocket," and the counselor is effective in counseling different clients with a variety of concerns. Professional mental health counselors who are trained in group counseling techniques may provide effective services and increase their income by offering counseling groups. Most counselors in private practice are generalists, but some counselors with advanced training and experience are identified as especially effective or expert in treating certain conditions and disorders, and may develop lucrative practices because of those specialties. In addition to a general practice, counseling specialties may include the following:

- Marital and family counseling
- Child and adolescent counseling
- Treatment of eating disorders
- Counseling for clients with borderline personality disorder
- Gerontological counseling
- Addictions and substance abuse counseling
- Rehabilitation counseling
- Divorce mediation
- . . . and many more

Other Roles in Private Practice: Supervision, Consulting, and Teaching.
Most mental health counselors engage in professional responsibilities in addition to direct service to their client. Although the primary emphasis is often placed on counseling, counselors in private practice may also provide clinical supervision, professional consultation, teaching and training to other professional counselors or counselors-in-training.

The ACA *Code of Ethics*, and the states that issue licenses to professional mental health counselors, require that they receive appropriate supervision and consultation (1997a). Counselors must also participate in ongoing continuing educational experiences to maintain their professional credentials, as well as to strengthen their skills. While all counselors, regardless of their years of experience or their level of competence, must continue to meet these professional obligations, those who are more experienced or who have knowledge in an area of specialization sometimes use that knowledge and experience to offer service to other mental health professionals. This is a service to the profession and a means of increasing income in a private practice. Counselors must meet stringent qualifications to become licensed and certified as professional counselors and in areas of specialization. Part of the process requires counselors to accrue a specific number of hours of clinically supervised postgraduate counseling practice. Experienced counselors often meet the qualifications specified by accrediting boards to provide that supervision and enjoy providing such service. This supervision is conducted in both one-on-one arrangements and with small groups of counselors and the counselor receives a fee for this contracted service—usually the same as the hourly rate charged for counseling services in their private practice. Counselors who are competent in supervision, but not in private practice, also occasionally offer supervision (and consultation) services on a contractual basis.

Like counseling, effective supervision requires specific knowledge and skills. Counselors who provide supervision may hold the relatively recently established credential, Approved Clinical Supervisor, established by the National Board for Certified Counselors (NBCC). Counselors who engage in supervision must be clear about any acquired risk of liability that accompanies their supervisory role and should verify that they have sufficient coverage in professional liability insurance policies.

Consultation is a form of supervision and occurs in several different contexts. Peer consultation takes place on a regular basis and can be either formal or informal. Informal consultation describes the activity whereby counselors communicate, respecting the ethical principles of confidentiality (ACA, 1997a), regarding the well-being of their clients. The communication may be oriented toward case management or in order to address a specific client issue or need. The consultation is sometimes intended to "bounce ideas off each other" and other times to seek professional advice from someone with an area of expertise. Although it is a professional responsibility to engage in consultation, in most cases, there is usually not an associated fee for the service and none of the participants in the consultation have any increased responsibility based on the communication.

A different method of consultation is when, as a professional counselor, one provides a contracted service to another mental health professional, mental health agency, or to those in a different field seeking counseling or other human services. This is described as *expert* or *process* consultation. Some examples of consultation services that might be enlisted from a mental health counselor include coming to a job site to facilitate a conflict resolution process, or for a period of time, being available for counseling and support to employees following a violent incident resulting in loss of life and injuries to workers on the job.

Teaching or *training* provides those in private practice with another, often rewarding professional activity and an additional means of enhancing their income. Of course, through the formal and informal consultation process counselors always, in a sense, engage in teaching and learning. However, professional mental health counselors may be asked, or seek opportunities to teach, particularly if they are recognized as having a relevant or unusual area of special knowledge or practice. Professional counselors may teach counselors-in-training by accepting appointments as adjunct faculty members in counselor education programs. It is quite valuable to bring the perspective of field-based or community mental health counseling into the classroom environment, because the "hands-on" experience of the practitioner enhances the academic component of the counselor education program.

Counselors teach courses for other counseling professionals and those working in related fields, usually offered in association with an educational institution or professional association, available for credit as continuing professional education. Additionally, mental health counselors are sometimes called upon to teach courses, provide skills training, offer workshops and seminars, prepare materials, or make professional speeches for businesses, agencies, and community organizations. Popular topics include stress management, effective parenting skills, and communication training. In addition to supplementing income, counselors who consult, train, and teach experience the added benefit of becoming more recognized in the community.

To a large degree, the success of a private practice depends on effective marketing strategies. Word of mouth is usually the most valuable marketing tool and a respected reputation in the community is good advertising.

Some Final Thoughts on Private Practice.   The entrepreneurial opportunities afforded counselors who have a private practice are considerable. Counselors who work independently can create a practice that utilizes their own professional and personal strengths, allows them to respond to individuals and counseling and clinical issues which most interest them, and removes many of the restrictions associated with being part of a system of care.

On a personal level, counselors in private practice must enjoy working with all kinds of people, maintain a fascination with human behavior, be tolerant of very diverse lifestyles, and be accepting of ambiguity. They must be creative, energetic, and comfortable with risk taking.

Maintaining clinical competence is a professional, ethical, and in the case of the private practice, essential responsibility in order to be successful. Conditions may sometimes conspire to make those previously listed responsibilities difficult to meet. For example, because the private practitioner's income is tied directly to how much work they do, they cannot depend on a regular or predictable salary and often work extremely long hours, sometimes as much as 50–60 hours per week, while establishing a practice (Male, 1990). Challenges such as these run counter to what is considered best practice, can become a stressor, and constitute a block to therapeutic effectiveness (Brooks, 1997). Professional mental health counselors must take responsibility for self-care and must take measures to remedy such a situation in order to provide competent counseling for their clients.

Because a private practice is a business, the mental health counselor in independent practice must be able to attend to the development and operating needs of the practice. In most cases, this means handling those responsibilities himself or herself. Like any other business, managing a private counseling practice means arranging for and maintaining office space, paying bills, and hiring and supervising any employees. Counselors promote their services, communicate with referral sources, consult with other professionals, and navigate the maze of insurance and managed health care systems. Some responsibilities idiosyncratic to the counseling profession are maintaining client records, remaining current in therapeutic practice developments, and keeping abreast of frequently changing licensing, insurance, and tax regulations that affect the counselor and the client. Professional mental health counselors who succeed in private practice enjoy the opportunity to be independent, find the tasks exciting, and especially enjoy the incredible variety that comes with the territory.

Other Settings in the Community

With the increase in integrated services and wrap-around care, it is sometimes difficult to draw clear distinctions between community-based counseling and that meeting a different description. The author would like to briefly address two major resources in the provision of community mental health care services, which, if not strictly defined as community-based mental health care, certainly interface with community services. Those resources are hospitals or health care facilities and managed health care systems (frequently referred to as health maintenance organizations, or HMOs).

Hospitals and Health Care Facilities.   Hospitals and other comprehensive health care facilities may operate for-profit, or nonprofit and may be private or public. While the majority of the services are provided inpatient, some are provided on site or in communities. In either case, hospitals and health care facilities are a major component of most community health care systems—medical and psychological. Opportunities for counselors may be found in general hospitals, psychiatric facilities, Veterans' Administration facilities, rehabilitation centers and substance abuse treatment programs. While some hospitals may not include any counseling programs, usually called behavioral medicine in hospital settings, many provide preventative and maintenance programs. Traditionally, medical care facilities relied on clinical psychologists, social workers, psychiatric nurses, and occupational therapists to address counseling and psychological needs of the patients in hospitals. In the past twenty or thirty years, hospitals and related health care facilities have expanded to include services to clients whose medical conditions may be complicated by psychological conditions, or conversely, whose medical diagnosis may cause or contribute to emotional problems. As a result, many mental health counselors are now finding employment in hospitals and medical settings where they collaborate with health care professionals to provide comprehensive treatment which includes counseling.

Counselors in hospital and health care settings focus on crisis work, preventative counseling, remediation, or supportive counseling with patients or clients (outside of medical settings, it is not considered appropriate to refer to clients as patients). Many health care facilities provide services to patients oriented toward wellness, especially for patients with cardiac disease, diabetes, injuries, and those who have had strokes. Counselors can effectively assist clients in identifying and changing behaviors or patterns of thinking, which may have complicated their medical concerns, and can contribute to their recovery. Additionally, counselors may assist clients in addressing the emotional issues of fear, anxiety, anger, or depression that often accompany or resulted from a medical diagnosis.

Other wellness and prevention programs found in hospitals, and employing mental health care counselors, are often available to patients in the hospital and open to the community as well. Those include programs and education focused on smoking cessation, nutrition, exercise, stress reduction, pain management, and sleep disorders.

Counselors have long been part of the medical team that provides counseling for clients or patients in treatment for alcohol and substance abuse and for eating disorders. More recently, health care facilities have begun to offer counseling and support services to patients, and their loved ones, who are critically or chronically ill, are facing or recovering from major surgery, or have a terminal illness.

Managed Health Care (HMOs).   Managed health care systems, or HMOs, are more difficult to define, but clearly influential in the access to services and the quality of care available to communities. A health management organization is a large, privately run comprehensive system of health care that usually includes mental health care services. Several states have also developed systems that resemble HMOs as a means of providing comprehensive health care services to lower income populations. The emergence of these systems of care is an effort to curb escalating health care costs, primarily by restricting access to care or the amount of care that can be utilized. HMOs do not restrict contracts to mental health counselors with Ph.D.s, but also include state-licensed master's degree counselors. Professional mental health counselors may be employed directly by a managed care system or may be an approved contractor. Relatively speaking, managed health care systems are new on the scene, but most health care providers believe that they are here to stay (Corey, Corey, & Callanan, 1998).

There are obvious disadvantages to such systems. The most frequently cited concern is the fear that determinations regarding clients' care will be made by nonclinical personnel, although treatment decisions are best made by mental health professionals in consultation with their clients (Nugent, 2000). There is anxiety that quality of care may be negatively affected by cost-cutting measures now in place or established in the future. Understandably, many health care providers, including mental health counselors, have reacted to the real and perceived threat of limitations to service with resentment, frustration, and legitimate concerns about potential neglect of clients' needs based on limited access to appropriate services.

While it is true that when a managed health care system determines access to and the nature and duration of mental health care service, a client faces potential risks, it has also served to motivate mental health counselors to become more accountable. Counselors are responsible for assessing client needs and developing effective (and consistent with managed health care directives—efficient) treatment plans.

Accountability is good for the client; however, having access to care, and control over the nature of treatment and the duration of service determined by individuals who are not trained as mental health care providers or knowledgeable about diagnosis, treatment, and effective counseling practices is very disturbing.

Having stated that, if managed health care is a reality of life for community mental health counselors, practitioners must be competent in rapid assessment, identifying client needs and establishing goals, and pairing the client with the counselor and intervention most likely to provide assistance. Counselors working as part of a managed health care system should be highly skilled in the use of brief therapy models and also must be well informed about additional community resources, should their client require service beyond or different from what is approved by their HMO.

MENTAL HEALTH COUNSELING AND MENTAL HEALTH COUNSELORS: A NEW IDENTITY

A considerable amount of space in this chapter has been devoted to reviewing the likely settings where professional mental health counselors are providing services. Even a cursory reading of the material should make it very clear that the counseling profession has been in an evolutionary process and that professional mental health counselors have an important role in a cluster of disciplines that make up the professional community of mental health care providers. While the profession has been evolving, there have been profound changes in government policies and a restructuring of comprehensive health care delivery systems (including mental health care). Those changes make it clear that mental health counseling, while necessary and important, must be provided in ways that are compatible with current systems and structures. Current revisions in public policy influence the nature of the work of counselors, the client populations served, the counseling needs that can be addressed, and the settings where they work.

It may seem misplaced to address the issue of professional identity *after* focusing on the settings and opportunities for counseling practice, but the reality is the counseling profession has a history of examining and refining the definition of its professional role. With today's climate of change, the ability to adapt is a valuable and necessary skill. To prepare to be a counselor in community and private practice settings, it is crucial to have a clear understanding of what services are consistent with the description of mental health counseling and how mental health counselors view their role in that process. Ascertaining a clear definition is not as easy as it may seem. In the last thirty-five years, the counseling profession, counselor educators, and counselors in particular have entered a brave new world. Today, counselors can be found in public or private agencies, clinics, residential, and outpatient treatment facilities. They provide a broad range of general counseling services, work in settings that focus on specific clinical issues, or specialize to better meet a particular need. The rapid changes in the mental health counseling profession necessitate a reexamination of the identity of the mental health counselor and the definition of mental health counseling.

Mental Health Counselors and Mental Health Counseling

As a relatively young and dynamic profession, the definition of mental health counseling and counselors continues to evolve and be refined to accurately reflect the needs of the mental health community and the clients being served, while also describing the roles and functions of the mental health practitioner. In 1997, the Governing Council of the American Counseling Association adopted the following definition of professional counseling:

> The Practice of Mental Health Counseling: The application of mental health, psychological, or human development principles, through cognitive, affective, behavioral or systemic intervention strategies that address wellness, personal growth, or career development, as well as pathology. (ACA, 1997b, p. 8)

The governing counsel further defined a professional counseling specialty as:

> A professional counseling specialty is narrowly focused, requiring advanced knowledge in the field founded on the premise that all Professional Counselors must first meet the requirements for the general practice of professional counseling. (ACA, 1997, p. 8)

TABLE 15.1   Definitions of Mental Health Counseling and Mental Health Counselors

. . . the process of assisting individuals or groups, through a helping relationship, to achieve optimal mental health through personal and social development and adjustment to prevent the debilitating effects of certain somatic, emotional, and intra- and/or interpersonal disorders. (AMHCA, 1978)

. . . helps persons to manage specific problems, prevent difficulties, and accelerate development. (Vacc and Loesch, 1987)

. . . (a) someone seeking help, (b) someone willing to help who is (c) capable of, or trained to help (d) in a setting that permits help to be given and received. (Cormier & Hackney, 1992, p. 2)

. . . simply stated, the art of helping people. Professional counselors are individuals trained to share knowledge and skills with those who need help. (Oregon Counseling Association, 1995)

These are the most current definitions provided by the American Counseling Association. A review of the counseling literature reveals the inconsistent manner in which mental health counselors and mental health counseling have been described by respected sources. Note some of the differences and similarities in definitions. The definitions are summarized in Table 15.1. It is important, as mental health counselors, to operate out of a common understanding of how the professionals define the task of counseling and the roles and responsibilities of counselors in that task. It is equally important that professionals are in agreement when presenting that definition to other related disciplines in the mental health practice community and especially to the public. However, the definition is likely to be revised periodically as the profession changes along with the rapidly changing systems that deliver mental health care systems to our communities.

PROFESSIONAL IDENTITY

Rather than engaging in the occasionally frustrating efforts to revise the definitions of mental health counseling and mental health counselors to best reflect the current political and clinical situation in the mental health community, many professionals are more comfortable focusing on the issue of a professional *identity*. The consideration of professional identity accommodates the broader view of the characteristics of a good counselor (see Chapter 2), the importance of the helping relationship, the understanding of what is unique to the mental health counseling profession, and the appreciation of the similarities with other mental health professionals

Unlike other professions in the mental health care arena, the mental health counseling profession may actually resemble a group of professions. Contributing to that perception is the tradition of counselor education programs admitting applicants from many different academic disciplines. Another factor in that perception is that the counseling profession embraces practitioners representing a broad array of counseling specialties; counselors may focus on group counseling, families, be certified as school counselors or mental health counselors, work in substance abuse treatment, and so on, and still be a professional counselor. Although occasionally a bit confusing, the interdisciplinary history counselors share and the integrated methods used in practice create a broader perspective through which counselors can consider the individuals they serve.

A similarity that professional mental health counselors share with other mental health care providers is that all offer counseling that is intentionally therapeutic in nature. The distinctions are more apparent in the methods and approaches employed. Professional counselors retain the historical roots of responding to client needs using a strength model, that is, accessing existing and underlying strengths to help clients make positive changes in functioning. But, similar to other mental health care professions, the profession of mental health counseling has clearly become more clinically oriented during the last twenty or thirty years. This is both necessary and consistent with increased community-based treatment for individuals who traditionally were treated in inpatient facilities. Whereas, in the early days of the profession counselors worked primarily with individuals considered more mentally healthy, today's professional counselor is prepared to respond to mental health needs ranging from individuals suffering from severe and persistent mental illness to clients who are considered to be mentally healthy. Fortunately, counselor education programs, accreditation and licensing boards, the American Counseling Association and its divisions, and professional mental health counselors themselves reflect this transition.

PROFESSIONAL PREPARATION AND CREDENTIALS FOR MENTAL HEALTH COUNSELORS

Although addressed in several other chapters in this book, it is appropriate to cover the subject of counselor education and professional credentials relative to mental health counselors. Professional counselors have master's or a doctorate degree in counseling from a counselor education or closely related program. The academic and supervised clinical experiences that comprise counselor education programs create the foundation from which mental health counselors draw throughout their professional life. The professional credentials that they hold help to clarify the parameters of the education and skills counselors bring to the many and varied roles they fill in the mental health care arena. Furthermore, clients seeking service from a counselor who has earned professional credentials as a mental health counselor can feel confident that the practitioner has received advanced training and abides by the ethics and standards consistent with the credential held.

Council for the Accreditation of Counseling and Related Educational Programs (CACREP)

The Council for the Accreditation of Counseling and Related Educational Programs (CACREP) was established in 1981 and is a corporate affiliate of ACA. Its purpose is to establish educational standards and evaluate master's- and doctoral-level degree programs for accreditation. It evaluates counselor education programs at the master's level in the areas of school counseling, community counseling, student affairs practice in higher education, marriage and family counseling, and mental health counseling. It also accredits doctoral-level programs in counselor education and supervision.

Although a voluntary process, the numbers of accredited counselor preparation programs are increasing, and the trend is continuing (Hollis, 1997). At the end of 2003, there were almost 400 individual programs accredited (all categories) at the master's level, housed in more than 136 institutions CACREP, and 45 at the doctoral level. Faculty and administrators recognize that CACREP accreditation is respected as a standard of excellence in the preparation of counselors.

Graduates of CACREP accredited counselor education programs gain advantages in addition to assurance of a quality education. Forty-seven states specify CACREP accredited or CACREP-like counseling programs when specifying the educational requirements for obtaining a state license. By completing the rigorous and standardized CACREP curriculum, counselors have more ease in securing a professional counseling license when they must move across state lines (Nugent, 2000). Entrance into accredited counselor education doctoral programs may be enhanced by graduation from CACREP master's programs (Gladding, 2000).

Licensing and Certification for Mental Health Counselors

Licensure is a state regulated process, created by statute, and regulates the activities of the professional and occupational activities of the holder of the license. At the time of this writing, forty-five states and the District of Columbia have licensing laws for professional counselors. Unfortunately, there is currently very little consistency in the licensing laws across the nation that regulate counseling. Thirty-nine states and the District of Columbia have *practice acts or practice and title acts*, an act that does not permit one to practice as a counselor without holding a license. Seven states have a *title act*, protecting only the title, and allowing anyone to practice counseling, as long as he or she does not represent themselves as licensed. Five states (Minnesota, California, Nevada, New York, and Hawaii) do not have a specific credential for professional mental health counselors. For obvious reasons, a practice act is preferable; it assures a more professional community of mental health counselors and is a clearer designation for the community to understand. Although not a guarantee of third-party reimbursement, it is highly unlikely that an unlicensed counselor would qualify for payment.

Certification is a rather generic term or designation, potentially referring to a status granted by a state, an agency, a professional organization, or a professional board. Counselors can earn a variety of certifications, including designations that attest to their knowledge in areas of specialized practice. The most common and easily recognized certification in the counseling profession is available from the National Board for Certified Counselors (NBCC). Nationally certified counselors (NCCs) have earned master's or doctorate degrees that meet the academic requirements and have satisfied the experiential and supervision requirements designated by NBCC. Those seeking certification in a specialty area from NBCC may pursue a credential in the areas of mental health counseling, school counseling, career counseling, substance abuse counseling, and supervision.

One might ask, "Why seek a license and certification?" There are several good reasons. Like those who graduate from CACREP programs, nationally certified counselors experience some advantages should they seek a counselor's license in more than one state during the course of a new career. Many states having licensing laws require the National Counselor Exam (NCE) or accept the NCE as partial fulfillment of the standards for obtaining a license. Professional certification is another means of demonstrating to the public that qualified counselors practice according to the high standards established by the counseling profession.

Those in the counseling profession have experienced increasing opportunities, and not so subtle pressure, to continually upgrade their professional status by seeking standard and specialized credentials. In the field of mental health care, professional credentials help to clearly identify the niche occupied by professional mental health counselors. The maintenance of credentials ensures the public that mental health counselors are continuing to upgrade their knowledge, collaborate with other professionals, and strictly adhere to the accepted standards of the profession.

THE FUTURE IS NOW: COUNSELING IN A NEW CENTURY

A great deal of time and energy was devoted to anticipating the twenty-first century, and suddenly—it is *now*. But of course much change still lies ahead for the counseling profession. Individuals, partners, families, and communities will continue to struggle with experiences that are part of the human condition—loss, grief, transition, conflict, and self-doubt—and counselors will continue to respond to the emotional, psychological, and psychosocial needs that arise as a result. In some cases, the changes are a reflection of shifts in society, and in other cases may be a result of those changes. Mental health counselors can expect transitions in the profession that are philosophical in nature, some that are technical, a continuing evolution of mental health care delivery systems, and optimistically, growth in the understanding of how to best use counseling skills to assist others in improving their quality of life.

Technology and Counseling

Once an anathema for anyone who worked in human services, as in other professions, computers figure prominently in the work of mental health counselors. In recent years, many mental health counselors have become proficient in the use of computer assisted diagnostic programs. Community agencies and managed health care systems maintain some or all of clients' records in computer files. Counselors regularly go online to connect with other professionals, to access their professional organizations, and to search the Internet for the most current information and resources to better serve their clients.

The subject of satire only a few years ago, web-based online counseling is now a reality, with the promise of becoming an important means of providing access to mental health services. This provides greater access to rural clients, those who may be housebound or disabled, and those with particular needs not available in their own community, such as non-English speakers. Recognizing the potential risks, the ACA Governing Council (personal communication, H. B. Smith, November 29, 1999) approved ethical standards for online counseling. The standards address the issues of secured sites, confidentiality and its limits, record keeping, and the counseling relationship. Counselors providing information or engaging in counseling and counseling-related activities via the Internet should seek appropriate legal, professional, and technical consultation to be certain that they are not in violation of any state, federal, or professional regulations or statutes, and to ensure that the activities are included in their liability coverage.

Another significant event in the increased use of technology is the implementation of HIPAA (Health Insurance Portability and Accountability Act of 1996). It is designed to protect the privacy of all client health data, including mental health records. It had resulted in mental health practitioners becoming knowledgeable in all the new regulations and revisions in record maintenance and transfer procedures for many.

Health Management Organizations: Here to Stay

Although no longer a new concept, managed health care systems will exert considerable influence on the practice of mental health counseling for the foreseeable future, regardless of whether a professional counselor elects to work within or outside of health maintenance organizations. To work as part of the system, counselors are going to professionally and politically advocate for full recognition as core providers of mental health care. To work outside of managed care, counselors again must advocate and collaborate to develop creative ways to provide counseling services to the community that serve the needs of all clients, while meeting the income requirements of the practitioner.

Ethics for a New Millennium

The counseling profession is at a crossroads. Graduate training assures a solid preparation for entry into the field, increased credentialing options define for the public what they can expect from mental health counseling, and professional counselors have gained recognition and status as professionals in mental health care. With a bright future, it is important to not lose touch with the rich history of the profession. First and foremost, counselors care about those they serve, respecting the dignity of each human being.

In a new age, those roots will serve the profession well. The nature of advocacy is descriptive of the challenges faced by counselors in a new century. The pluralistic nature of America makes it imperative that the profession be mindful of its own biases, increases the knowledge and understanding of differing systems (especially families), and broadens counseling approaches to be more useful to more of the community. Along the same lines, the counseling profession itself would be well served to increase the diversity within its own ranks.

The concept of advocacy expands to include the responsibility of speaking on behalf of the clients we serve and those we don't, seeking services and resources for those who may otherwise fall through the cracks. As economic diversity continues to create greater disparity between the "haves and the have-nots," professionals must lend their clout to improving the conditions of their communities.

SUMMARY

Mental health counselors have a specific role in the larger profession of counseling. The role has evolved out of a rich history and is supported by specific academic and clinical training. Mental health counselors collaborate with other mental health care professionals and have opportunities to practice counseling in many diverse settings. Some of these settings include community agencies (public and private), hospitals and health care facilities, government sponsored programs and services, and private practice. Some counselors have private practices.

Professional counselors have available to them many different professional credentials, which helps to define for the public what counselors do and increases their professional recognition in the mental health care community. Forty-six states offer some form of professional counseling license and all counselors who qualify can seek certification as a National Certified Counselor (NCC). Some professional counselors hold credentials in counseling specialities.

Mental health counselors have made many advances during the relatively brief history of the counseling profession. That history reflects ongoing efforts to make sure the definition of counseling accurately reflects the competencies of counseling practitioners, as well as the roles fulfilled in the mental health profession. The future of mental health counseling promises exciting challenges as mental health counselors use new resources in their work, gain greater access to managed health care systems, and engage with a more diverse society.

■ ■ ■ ■ ■

PART IV

COUNSELING SPECIAL
POPULATIONS

In the previous sections, the basic skills and theoretical bases for counseling were described. In Part Four, "Counseling Special Populations," these skills are applied to a number of specific groups with whom a counselor may work. Each of these special populations demands different combinations of skill, knowledge, and experience from the counselor.

Demographic statistics predict that the percentage of individuals over the age of fifty-five will be increasing in the coming decades. A knowledge of the specific counseling needs of older individuals will become increasingly more important as our society moves into the twenty-first century and beyond. Chapter 16, "Counseling the Older Adult," presents a detailed description of the field of gerontological counseling. The specialized needs and social realities of older individuals are presented. The importance of viewing older clients as individuals, and not from the basis of cultural stereotypes about aging and the elderly, is stressed. Specific developmental challenges with which older individuals must cope are also outlined. The current therapeutic approaches most widely used with older clients, such as reality orientation, reminiscence groups, and remotivation therapy, are described.

Family therapy assumes a systems approach to counseling, and stresses the overall interpersonal context in which the client's problems are occurring. Chapter 17, "Counseling Couples and Families," provides a historical framework for viewing the development of marriage and family counseling and outlines the central concepts of family systems theory. The author presents an overview of the different schools of family therapy and stresses the importance of maintaining an integrative and eclectic approach to understanding and learning from these approaches. Core issues that often emerge in family counseling, such as boundary problems, low self-esteem, and inappropriate family hierarchies, are described. Stages in marriage and family counseling are outlined, with descriptions of appropriate interventions for each particular level. This chapter concludes with discussions of professional issues connected with couples and family counseling and research in family therapy.

Chapter 18, "Counseling Gay, Lesbian, and Bisexual Clients," surveys a field of growing importance to counselors. Issues involving gay individuals are becoming more visible in our society. While clients who happen to be gay should be viewed as individuals first and as gay persons second, the importance for the counselor to maintain a sensitivity to the special concerns of gay clients is stressed. Self-identity, self-esteem, and relationship concerns may take on an enhanced intensity with gay clients, owing to the significant social, psychological, and interpersonal stresses they may experience.

Most counselors, regardless of their particular work setting or client population, will need to confront the issue of effective multicultural counseling. Chapter 19, "Counseling People of Color," presents a twenty-first century paradigm for responding to the challenges of and opportunities for counseling people of color. Demographics, history, race and ethnicity, an exploration of the "cross-cultural zone," ethical considerations, and guidelines for ethnically responsive counseling are presented and discussed and provide the beginning professional with an excellent introduction to the topic.

Finally, this section concludes with Chapter 20, "Counseling Clients with Disabilities," in which an overview of both the goals and the major interventions for working with disabled clients are discussed. Physical, cognitive, and emotional factors in understanding disability are reviewed, with emphasis on helping clients to improve the overall quality of life and to come to terms with the conditions of their particular disability. Counseling clients with psychiatric disorders and the professional qualifications and necessary training for counselors wishing to pursue rehabilitation as a career choice are described to complete a realistic depiction of the scope and practice of the rehabilitation counselor.

Although Part Four of the text introduces the reader to only five selected special populations, the possibilities for roles and responsibilities of the professional counselor are well presented and illustrative of the growth and maturation of the counseling profession. Individuals preparing to enter the profession can expect to be part of a demanding and exciting career field requiring continuing education and supervision beyond the confines of the university and completion of graduate requirements.

CHAPTER SIXTEEN

COUNSELING THE OLDER ADULT

DOUGLAS R. GROSS, PH.D.
Professor Emeritus Arizona State University

DAVID CAPUZZI, PH.D.
Johns Hopkins University
Professor Emeritus Portland State University

Paul was in the final semester of his master of counseling program and was just beginning his internship. With the advice of his program chairperson, Paul had purposely selected a clinic setting that served people 65 years of age and older. He had been interested in working with older adults and had taken several courses designed to provide him with information and experience in working with this population. His orientation to the setting had been completed two days ago; today he was to see his first client.

As he prepared for the session, Paul reviewed many of the things he had learned in his university coursework. His office had been arranged so that the client, a 72-year-old widow, would have both easy access and a comfortable chair. The time scheduled for the appointment had been arranged to accommodate both the client's concerns regarding transportation and an appointment with a physician in the same complex. He knew that she was somewhat resistant to seeking help and that he would need to reassure her of the benefits of counseling. He was also aware that their age difference—he was 29 and she was 72—might be a barrier to communication, and he would need to take this into consideration.

An initial interview and an orientation meeting had been conducted by the intake person in the clinic, and the schedule of fees had been explained to the client, who agreed to it. Paul had reviewed the material collected during the intake interview and knew that she was contemplating moving from her home into a residential setting. The case material revealed that she did not accept this move. Paul's role was to explore with the client her feelings regarding the move and alternatives she might consider.

The client arrived at the clinic a few minutes prior to the scheduled time. She was accompanied by her son and asked that he be allowed to join her in her counseling session with Paul. Paul had not anticipated this but, wishing to make the client feel more comfortable, agreed. Paul's office was quickly rearranged to accommodate the son, and the session began.

During the session, the son told Paul that his mother's health no longer allowed her to live alone. Based upon his mother's physician's recommendation and with his mother's agreement, arrangements had been made to move her to a full care facility. In the past two weeks, however, his mother had become very disturbed about this move. She now felt that with more assistance from her son and his family she could remain in her home. Based upon her physical condition, however, this would not be possible. Her son stated that his mother was aware of this and was denying the reality of the situation. Tears were obvious as the client discussed how much she loved her home and its memories and how she needed to remain independent as long as possible. The session had reached a stalemate with both parties holding to their positions. Paul decided to talk with each person separately, and the son said that he would wait outside.

In the session that followed, Paul explored the fear and anger that the client was feeling. She was afraid of losing her independence and angry that her son was not willing to take care of her as she had always taken care of him. She felt that she was being placed in the facility to die. She knew that she needed a good deal of special care but she felt that with her son's help she could remain in her own home. Paul understood her strong need for independence rather than dependence, and he wanted to do what he could to make this a possibility.

During his session, the son explained that the move had been discussed at length, and he felt that his mother was accepting the fact that she could no longer remain alone. He was surprised by her current reaction and was at a loss as to what could be done to make the transition as positive as possible. He stated that he loved his mother and would do nothing to hurt her. The move was both supported and encouraged by her physician.

Paul brought the client and her son together and shared with them his perceptions of the situation. He encouraged them to talk with each other, as each had talked with him, and asked if they would be willing to return to the clinic to continue to discuss the situation. The client seemed somewhat hesitant, but did agree to return the following Tuesday.

Paul sat for a short time after the client and her son left his office reviewing what had taken place. He decided that he needed to talk with his supervisor regarding the session and what he had done. Perhaps he should have done more to resolve the situation. He could see both sides of the issue, but his feelings were more strongly on the side of the client. He wanted her to be able to remain independent and felt that he needed to develop more of an advocacy role in assisting the client and her son to bring a more positive solution to the situation.

This scenario is one that is occurring more and more in various mental health settings. Counselors and mental health workers are being called on to work with a clientele for whom many are ill prepared. The clientele are older adults who, owing to the lengthening of the life span, are increasing in numbers and will continue to have a profound impact on all areas of counseling and therapy. Today, there are more than 35 million people 65 years of age or older. Based on the projections of the Administration on Aging (AOA), in its 2001 report entitled "A Profile of Older Americans, 2001," this figure will climb to more than 70 million by the year 2030. The impact of this growing population has been addressed by numerous authors (Durodye & Ennis-Cole, 1998; Glover, 1998; Gross and Capuzzi, 2001; Myers, 1995; Thomas & Martin, 2002). According to Gross and Capuzzi (2001), "The growing body of literature in the area of counseling and intervention strategies for the elderly addresses the emerging recognition that this population will continue to represent itself in growing numbers to the counseling professional" (p. 343).

The purpose of this chapter is to present information relative to counseling the older adult. This information will enable the reader to develop an understanding of the demographics, the general and unique nature of the problems presented, research into individual and group counseling approaches that have proven to be effective, and recommendations that should aid the counseling/mental health professional to serve this population more effectively. In this chapter, the term *older adult* refers to people 65 years and older.

DEMOGRAPHY OF AGING

To understand the demographics of the aging population in the United States, it is important that the reader understand this numerical increase and its growing diversity in relation to age, sex, and marital status; geographic distribution; race and ethnicity; retirement, employment, and income; and physical and mental health status. It is not the purpose of this chapter to present an in-depth analysis of these diverse factors. Each is presented to provide the reader with an overview that should aid counselors and other mental health professionals to better understand this growing population that is and will continue to become an ongoing part of their caseloads.

The growing number of older adults within the United States constitutes an escalating portion of our total population. According to Toseland (1990), "The population of older persons in the United States is growing in the 1990s at a more rapid rate than other segments of society. This growth is expected to continue well into the twenty-first century" (p. 3). Projecting these figures into the twenty-first century, the AOA 2001 report indicates that this population will reach 70 million by the year 2030, more than twice their number in 2001. This number would represent approximately 20 percent of the total population and reflect a 7 percent increase over the 13 percent this population currently constitutes.

A COMPOSITE PICTURE

Older adults are too often viewed as a fairly homogeneous group of individuals (Thornton, 2002). A closer look at variations in this grouping will prove this view to be far from the truth. This population is quite diverse and parallels the diversity found in other segments of our population. The following discussion of these demographic variations highlights this diversity and the data reported is taken from "A Profile of Older Americans" AOA (2001).

AGE, SEX, AND MARITAL STATUS

The older adult population itself is aging. One of the most rapidly growing age categories is that of people 85 years and older (the old-old). This population (4.2 million) will increase to 8.9 million by the year 2030. This population was 32 times larger in 2001 than in 1900. Within this same time frame, the 75–84 age group (middle-old) was 16 times larger, and the 65–74 age group (young-old) was 8 times larger than their counterpart in 1900.

Variation is also noted in the percentage of males to females. In 2001, there were 20.6 million older women and 14.4 million older men, or a sex ratio of approximately 143 women for every 100 men. The sex ratio increased with age ranging from 117 women for every 100 men for the 65–69 group to a high of 245 women for every 100 men for persons 85 and over.

These figures are probably not too surprising, given the data related to the greater life expectancy of women. What is surprising, however, is the fact that older men tend to remarry if they lose a spouse and women do not. In 2001, older men were much more likely to be married than older women—74 percent of men, 41 percent of women. Almost half of all older women in 2001 were widows (46 percent). There were four times as many widows (8.49 million) as widowers (2.0 million). Although divorced and/or separated older persons represented only 10 percent of all older persons in 2001, this represents a 4 percent increase since 1990.

GEOGRAPHIC DISTRIBUTION

There is a degree of similarity between the distribution of older adults and the distribution of the general population. States with the largest populations tend to have the largest number of older adults. In 2001, about half (52 percent) of persons 65+ lived in nine states. California had over 3.4 million, Florida 2.8 million, New York 2.4 million, Texas and Pennsylvania each had almost 2 million, and Ohio, Illinois, Michigan, and New Jersey each had over 1 million.

Persons 65 and older were slightly less likely to live in metropolitan areas in 2001 than younger persons (75 percent of the elderly, 80 percent of persons under 65). About 27 percent of older persons lived in central cities and 48 percent lived in the suburbs. The belief that a majority of older adults uproot themselves and move is not supported by the data. The majority of older adults continue to live in the same location. In 1999, only 4.2 percent of persons 65 and older had moved since 1998 compared to 16.5 percent of persons under 65.

RACE AND ETHNICITY

Racial and ethnic differences provide yet another variation within this population (Harris, 1998). In 2001 about 16.4 percent of persons 65 and older were minorities—8.0 percent were Black, 2.4 percent were Asian or Pacific Islander, 5.6 percent were of Hispanic origin, and less than 1 percent were American Indian or Native Alaskan. Only 6.16 percent of racial and ethnic minority populations were 65 and older in 2001. Comparing this to the total population within the United States, these percentages contrast to the general population breakdown, in which 85 percent are White and 15 percent are non-White. Minority populations are projected to represent 25.4 percent of the elderly population in 2030, up from 16.4 percent in 2001.

RETIREMENT, EMPLOYMENT, AND INCOME

Retirement, which at one point in our history was considered a luxury, is today the norm. According to the Special Committee on Aging (SCOA, 1983), 66 percent of older males were employed in the labor force in 1900. Today, less than 16–18 percent of this population is employed, and the projections are that this percentage will continue to decline. The percentages for females for this same period show a much more stable pattern: 10 percent in the labor force in 1900, and 10.8 percent in 2001. The percentage for females has been around 8 to 10 percent since 1988. The people who tend to remain in the labor force after they are 70 are those classified as professionals and those who are craftspeople. Both these categories are descriptive of the self-employed.

Retirement brings with it a set of unique circumstances surrounding the older adult and is related to employment and income. According to Butler, Lewis, & Sunderland (1991), a majority of those who retire do so with incomes stemming from pensions (16 percent), Social Security (38 percent), savings (26 percent), employment (17 percent), and assistance from relatives (3 percent). For the most part, this income is "fixed" and generally represents approximately 40 percent of the income the individual was receiving prior to retirement. With inflation generally on the rise in this country, the reductions, coupled with the "fixed" nature of the income, place the individual in a position of having to manage more carefully his or her income to meet not only the basic costs of living, but also the added costs, specifically those that deal with increasing taxes and expenses associated with health care, that come with retirement (Taylor-Carter, Cook, & Weinberg, 1997).

In 2001, the median income of older persons was $19,688 for males and $11,313 for females. Households containing families headed by persons 65+ reported a median income of $33,936 ($34,661 for Whites, $26,610 for Blacks, and $24,287 for Hispanics). Approximately one of every nine (10.7 percent) family households with an elderly head had incomes less than $15,000 and 40.1 percent had incomes of $35,000 or more.

PHYSICAL AND MENTAL HEALTH

One of the stereotypical pictures of older adults is the view of individuals as frail, weak, and suffering from a myriad of chronic disorders. As with all stereotypes, nothing could be farther from the truth (Thornton, 2002). According to Lemme (1995), "Most adults are in good health and experience few limitations or disabilities. Nearly 71 percent of adults over age 65 living in the community (that is, not in institutions) report their health as excellent, very good, or good" (p. 374). Based on findings such as these, a high percentage of older adults are able to maintain the activities of daily living without the necessity of medical assistance.

In 2001, older people had about four times the number of days of hospitalizations (1.8 days) as did the under 65 aged population (0.4 days). The average length of a hospital stay was 6.4 days for older people, compared to only 4.6 days for all people. In 2001, older consumers averaged $3,493 in out-of-pocket health care expenditures, an increase of more than half since 1990. In contrast, the total population spent considerably less, averaging $2,182 in out-of-pocket costs. Older Americans spent 12.6 percent of their total expenditures on health, more than twice the proportion spent by all consumers (5.5 percent).

The mental health picture for older adults indicates that even though 27 percent of all admissions to public mental hospitals are over 65, only 2 to 4 percent are represented in outpatient mental health treatment facilities (Myers & Schwiebert, 1996; Tice & Perkins, 1996). These percentages may reflect a variety of factors. It could be that, based on values and attitudes, they do not see the benefit in seeking such treatment. They may not understand the concepts that underlie counseling and therapy. It could be that the mental health facility, based on personnel and facilities, is not prepared to work with this population or that older adults place more emphasis on physical versus mental health. Regardless of the reasons, older adults, like their younger counterparts, can benefit from such assistance and need to receive information and encouragement from the mental health professional.

PROBLEMS AND CONCERNS OF OLDER ADULTS

From a psychological viewpoint, the emotional and psychological problems of older adults differ slightly from the emotional and psychological problems of their younger counterparts (Burlingame, 1995; Tueth, 1995). For example, feelings of anxiety, frustration, guilt, loneliness, despair, worthlessness, and fear are prevalent across all age levels. Substance abuse, suicide, depression, violence, AIDS, and domestic abuse are not limited to the young but find equal applicability across the older adult population (Kleinke, 1998; Tueth, 1995; Woods, 1996). The young, as well as the old, must learn to cope daily with a multitude of life situations that test their emotional stability. The process of aging, however, brings with it a set of changing life situations not only unique, but also telescoped into a brief period of years. These life situations—physiologic, situational, and psychological in nature—when viewed in terms of the previously identified problems—force older adults into changing patterns of behavior and lifestyles that have been developed and ingrained over long periods of time. The following are examples of the changing life situations older adults are forced to confront.

Loss of Work Role Identity, Increased Amount of Leisure Time, and Decreased Financial Support

For older adults, the onset of retirement, either by choice or law, removes them from activities that for many years have been the focus of their self-identity. This work/career identity shaped not only their family life and their interactions with family members, but also their social life outside the family. What they did for a living was so much a part of who they were and how they were valued both by self and by others that this loss often creates an identity crisis. The degree of severity that surrounds this issue is related to the older adult's ability to create a new identity.

With retirement comes increased amounts of leisure time—time for which many older adults are ill prepared. Leisure time, the dream of the full-time employee, often becomes the nightmare of retirees. What will they do with this time? What will be done to replace the daily routines so much a part of their working years? How will they relate to significant others now that they are together for extended periods of time? These and other questions need to be addressed, and education and planning are necessary if older adults are to make a positive transition from work to leisure (Gee & Baillie, 1999).

Retirement also brings a significant reduction in income. The majority of older adults enter this period of life on fixed incomes representing approximately 40 percent of their incomes prior to retirement. With increasing inflation, added expenses for health care, and rising taxes, they often move from a financially independent state to a financially dependent state, needing greater support from family, friends, and state and federal agencies. They may also find their lifestyles restricted so that they may better conserve their fixed resources today to meet the continually escalating financial world of tomorrow (Hershey, Mowen, & Jacobs-Lawson, 2003).

Loss of Significant Person(s) and Increased Loneliness and Separation

The aging process brings with it a series of negative life events and the reality of the terminal nature of relationships (Kraaij & de Wilde, 2001). Loss of significant people, due to geographical relocation or death, occurs often during this period of life. Marital and social relationships on which much of the significance of life centered end, and older adults are called on to cope and to find meaning in other aspects of their life. Sometimes this can be done with the support of family and friends. Sometimes it requires the intervention of helping processionals trained to work with this aspect of the aging process. In either case, the loss and its accompanying separation from the secure and familiar are issues that aging people must confront.

Geographic Relocation and Peer and Family Group Restructuring

Although the majority of older adults do not relocate during this period of life, those who do by choice or by extenuating circumstances find themselves adjusting both to new environments and to the building of new family and social relationships. The reasons for such relocations vary with the individual. Often they represent movements to areas that are more climatically conducive to leisure lifestyles, areas that are less demanding based on physical and physiologic disabilities, or areas that are closer to significant family members. Even when the relocation is by choice, the reconstruction process that follows is never easy and often brings with it stress, frustration, loneliness, separation, and regret.

Increased Physiologic Disorders and Increasing Amounts of Dependence

Health often becomes a major issue for older adults. Even though, as reported earlier, the majority report their health as good to excellent, it is a period marked by physiological decline. The body, like any complex machine, is beginning to wear down. The stress, anxiety, and frustration of this process takes a heavy toll. Older people are often called on to cope with health-related situations, both their own and those of loved ones, that demand both personal stamina and financial resources. Either or both of these may not be in great abundance during this period of life.

To compensate, older adults are often forced to depend on others both for support and financial resources. Such dependence, following a life characterized by productivity and independence, is often difficult for them to accept. The resulting anger, depression, and loss of self-esteem need to be addressed if the individual is to cope effectively with the situation (Baltes, 1996).

When these major life changes are viewed in terms of the rapidity of their onset, the lack of preparation for their encounter, and society's negative attitudes regarding older adults, the prevalence of emotional and psychological problems is brought into clear focus. Any one of these changing life situations can produce emotional and psychological difficulties for the individual. In combination, they place the individual in an "at risk" situation in which he or she must develop coping strategies to survive (Whitty, 2003).

THE IMPACT OF AGEISM AND THE INCREASING ABUSE AND MALTREATMENT OF OLDER PERSONS

Ageism, society's negative attitudes regarding older persons, impacts many aspects of the daily life of the elderly. Ageism, which is often presented in terms of age-based expectations, stereotypes, myths, and prejudices, sets forth an image of older persons as being in poor health, disabled, lacking mental sharpness, depressed, lonely, sexless, lacking vitality, and unable to learn or change. Such beliefs, which are biased, unfounded, and untrue, serve to discriminate against older adults and displace and prevent their active involvement within society (Gladding, 2003; Thornton, 2002).

Elder abuse is a growing problem in the United States. The National Center on Elder Abuse (NCEA, 1998) presented data that indicates that nearly 600,000 cases of abuse and maltreatment were reported in 1996. Projecting this figure to the year 2030 when the older population will reach nearly 70 million individuals, the incidence of abuse and maltreatment should reach into the millions. According to Reynolds-Welfel, Danzinger, and Santoro (2000), the abuse and maltreatment of older adults takes at least five major forms. These are neglect, physical violence, psychological abuse, financial exploitation, and violation of inalienable or legal rights. Any one of these forms of abuse and maltreatment may result in physiological, situational, and/or psychological problems for the older person. In combination, they may prove to be life threatening.

In seeking to deal with the myriad of physiological, situational, and psychological changes that are part of the aging process, older adults turn for assistance to family, friends, the church, physicians, counselors, and state and federal agencies. In doing so, they encounter both personal and societal barriers. These barriers include but are not limited to the following:

- Lack of recognition of the need for help
- Personal values and fears regarding seeking assistance
- Ageism on the part of helping professionals
- Society's negative attitudes regarding older adults
- Practical problems such as transportation and financial limitations
- Lack of awareness of existing support services
- Family pressure to keep problems within the family
- Separation from family members who could provide assistance
- Personal mistrust and fear based on abuse and maltreatment

COUNSELING PRINCIPLES

A basic premise of this chapter is that there is a common core of counseling approaches that are applicable across the life span. Skills in rapport building, active listening, ability to demonstrate caring, support, respect, and acceptance are as applicable to the 80-year-old client as the 8-year-old client (Warnick, 1995). According to Waters (1984):

> Regardless of the age of your client, you as a counselor need to communicate clearly, respond both to thoughts and feelings, ask effective questions, and confront when appropriate. It also is important to help people clarify their values and their goals in order to make decisions and develop action plans to implement these decisions (p. 63)

The basic goals and approaches of counseling are not age related. These goals and approaches assist the individual in problem resolution and behavior change, regardless of age. When working with older adults, counselors need not put aside their basic skills and techniques and adopt a new set. What they need to do is to develop an awareness of the aging process and the factors within it that may necessitate adapting existing skills and techniques to more effectively meet the needs of this population (Zucchero, 1998).

Such adaptations are best understood in terms of a set of general counseling recommendations that are more applicable to the older adult than, perhaps to the younger client (Altekruse & Ray, 1998). Such recommendations are directed at compensating for some of the "changing life situations" and "barriers" discussed earlier. The following recommendations have general applicability to both individual and group counseling.

- *Counselors should expend more effort in enhancing the dignity and worth of the older adult.* Given ageist attitudes within society and often within the helping professions, these clients are often led to believe that they are less valuable than younger people. Counselors need to devote time and energy in restoring self-esteem and encouraging clients to review their successes, accomplishments, and positive aspects of their changing lifestyles. Further support for this recommendation can be found in Falk and Falk (1997), Gross and Capuzzi (2001), McWhirter (1994), Warnick (1995), and Strawbridge, Wallhagen, and Cohen (2002).
- *Counselors need to expend more effort in "selling" the client on the positive benefits to be derived from counseling.* Given long-established values and attitudes, the client may well view counseling and the seeking of such assistance as a sign of weakness and place little value on the positive results of such a process. The counselor needs to reinforce the client's seeking assistance and to demonstrate, through actions, the positive results that are possible through counseling. Further support for this recommendation can be found in Burlingame (1995), Hoyt (1993), and Sherman (1993).
- *Counselors must attend more to the "physical environment" of counseling than might be necessary with a younger client.* Because of decreasing physical competencies, attention needs to center on factors such as noise distractions and counselor voice levels due to hearing loss, adequate lighting for those with visual impairments, furniture that will enhance the physical comfort of the client, thermostatic control to protect against extremes in temperatures, office accessibility, and the removal of items that impair ease of movement. Shorter sessions may also be appropriate, because older adults may experience difficulty sitting in one position for a long time. Further support for this recommendation can be found in Gross (1991) and Gross and Capuzzi (2001).
- *Counselors should address counselor-client involvement and the role of the counselor as advocate.* The counselor in this situation needs to take a much more active/doing role to better serve the client. This active/doing role may involve contacting agencies, family, attorneys, and other support personnel for the client. It may also entail serving as advocate for the client, to represent effectively the needs and grievances of the older adult. It might also entail transporting the client or taking the counseling services to the client, as would be the case with "shut-ins" or those who are incapacitated. Further support for this recommendation can be found in Gladding (2003) and Gross and Capuzzi (2001).

- *Counselors need to think in terms of short-term goals that are clear-cut and emphasize the present life situation for the client.* Many of the problems the client presents deal with day-to-day living situations. The counselor, in helping the client find solutions to these problems, not only reinforces the positive aspects of the counseling process, but also encourages the client to continue seeking assistance. Further support for this recommendation can be found in Burlingame (1995), and Myers and Schwiebert (1996).

- *Counselors should pay attention to the dependence/independence issue characteristic of work with older adults.* Changing life situations often force the older adult into a more dependent lifestyle. The reasons vary from client to client but may be centered around health, finances, and family. The counselor needs to realize that a certain degree of dependence may well benefit the client and needs to be encouraged until the client is ready once again to assume an independent role. The majority have functioned somewhat independently most of their adult lives. They often need assistance in seeing that it is still possible. Further support for this recommendation can be found in Baltes (1996) and Brody and Semel (1993).

- *Counselors must be sensitive to the possible age differential between themselves and the clients and to the differing cultural, environmental, and value orientations that this difference in age may denote.* With the exception of peer counseling, the counselor generally is younger than the client. This age difference can generate client resistance, anger, or resentment. It is important that the counselor be aware of this and learn to deal with it in an appropriate manner. The counselor, depending on his or her attitudes regarding aging, may also experience feelings of resistance, anger, or resentment toward the client. Dealing with this at the beginning should enhance the probability of success. Further support for this recommendation can be found in Gross (1991), and Gross and Capuzzi (2001).

- *Counselors need to have some perspective on the client's "place in history" and the significance this place holds in determining values and attitudes.* People whose significant developmental period took place during the Depression years of the 1930s or the war years of the 1940s may well be espousing values characteristic of that era. The counselor needs to accept this and not expect this person to easily incorporate values and attitudes descriptive of the year 2004. Further support for this recommendation can be found in Gross (1991), and Gross and Capuzzi (2001).

- *Counselors should be cautious in the use of diagnostic tools (tests) with this population.* Unlike their younger counterparts, older adults have limited recent experience with such instruments, and tests may create undue anxiety. It is also important to keep in mind that many diagnostic instruments used in mental health do not have norm groups for this population, and, therefore, the results obtained have questionable degrees of reliability and validity. It is important that the counselor, prior to using such tools, determine whether tests are the best means of gaining the types of data needed. Discussions of the numerous problems associated with this recommendation can be found in Birren and Schaie (1996) and Gintner (1995).

COUNSELING PROCEDURES

Because the basic goals and approaches of counseling are not age related, all theoretical systems, techniques, and intervention styles are applicable to this older adult population and are currently being used. One of the most comprehensive reviews of outcome research in counseling older people in the past twenty years was conducted by Wellman and McCormack (1984). They reported the results of more than ninety studies. In this report, a myriad of approaches, including psychoanalytic (Brink, 1979), developmental (Kastenbaum, 1968), brief task-centered therapy (Saferstein, 1972), behavior management (Nigl & Jackson, 1981), peer counseling (Hayes & Burk, 1987), and cognitive behavioral (Meichenbaum, 1974) were cited. The results varied, but all approaches appear to support the use of psychological intervention with this population. According to the authors, much of the research reviewed suffered from methodological weaknesses centering on controls, sampling, and sound theoretical rationales. They indicate, however, that procedures such as (1) regular continued contact, (2) brief psychotherapy approaches, (3) task-oriented and structured activities, (4) high levels of client involvement, (5) multidisciplinary team and peer counseling, and (6) group work all seem to hold promise in working with older adults. The authors further indicated that, given their review, the following goals for counseling older adults appear often:

- To decrease anxiety and depression
- To reduce confusion and loss of contact with reality
- To increase socialization and improve interpersonal relationships
- To improve behavior within institutions
- To cope with crisis and transitional stress
- To become more accepting of self and the aging process (p. 82)

Authors such as Birren and Schaie (1996), Butler et al. (1991), Burlingame (1995), and Warnick (1995) also address the issues of counseling and differing theoretical approaches in working with older adults. According to Butler et al. (1991),

All forms of psychotherapy—from "uncovering" to "supportive" to "reeducative" and from Freudian to Jungian to Rogerian—can contribute to both a better understanding of the psychology and psychotherapy of old age. Further integration and eclectic utilization of all contemporary personality theories and practices, including the life-cycle perspective of human life along with the use of medication, when appropriate, are needed. (p. 407)

Both individual and group approaches to working with older adults are supported in the literature (Brody & Semel, 1993; Gladding, 2003; Gross & Capuzzi, 2001; Thomas & Martin, 2002; Toseland, 1990). Which is the most appropriate depends on the client, the nature of the presenting problem, the resources available to both the client and the counselor, and the setting in which the counseling takes place. Along with the changing life situations identified earlier, it is important to keep in mind that treatment for older clients presents the same variety of problems presented by younger clients. Issues dealing with alcohol and drug usage, abuse, loss, family, marriage, divorce, suicide, crime victimization, and career and avocational areas are often found to be continuing concerns. Both individual and group approaches to this population are applicable.

Individual Approaches

In providing individual counseling or therapy to older adults, counselors have a variety of techniques, intervention strategies, and theoretical systems available to them. The only limitations seem to be those related to the skills and expertise of the counselor. Keeping in mind the nine counseling recommendations mentioned previously, the following counseling skills are highly applicable to this population. Further support for these skills can be found in Burlingame (1995) and Gladding (2003).

ACTIVE LISTENING SKILLS

Older adults, as with their younger counterparts, need to be heard. Use of such techniques as visual contact, encouragers, reflection of both content and feeling, paraphrasing, clarifying, questioning, and summarizing are all appropriate. Such techniques, when used appropriately, serve as encouragers, demonstrate caring, concern, and interest, and provide the client with an opportunity to share, vent feelings, be understood, and gain self-respect.

Nonverbal Skills

Counseling older adults will be enhanced if the counselor is aware of and able to use effectively his or her knowledge of nonverbal communication patterns. Attention paid to body posture, eye contact, tone level, and rate of speech, although not the "royal road" to a person's inner self, is one road that aids the counselor in better understanding the client's communication more completely.

Relationship Variables

Relationship building with older adults may demand more effort on the part of the counselor. The active listening and nonverbal skills mentioned in this section should aid in facilitating this process, but it is important to keep in mind that establishing trust with a much older person may require the counselor to give consideration to his or her language, appearance, solicitous attitude, and values and attitudes related to aging.

A second factor related to relationship building centers on the client's need for both support and challenge. Counselors working with this population need to understand that their view of older adults as fragile may temper their ability to provide the challenge. If challenge is not part of the counseling process, the client may be denied the opportunity for change and growth.

COUNSELING STRATEGIES

The following strategies are not presented in any priority listing. Each needs to be given careful consideration in working individually with this population.

- Take into consideration the longevity of the client's life. In doing so, stress the positive accomplishments and encourage the client to use the many coping skills that he or she has demonstrated in reaching this stage of life.
- Stress the benefits that counseling can provide. Often older adults view such assistance as a weakness on their part and believe counseling carries with it a stigma. Perhaps the words used to describe the service will need to be changed to attract this population. It might be more acceptable for the person to attend a discussion group rather than a therapy group.
- Give attention to the physiologic needs of the client as these relate to mobility, hearing loss, visual acuity, and physical condition (for example, sessions may need to be of shorter duration owing to the clients' inability to sit for extended periods of time).
- Work to establish a more collaborative relationship depending on the various professionals who may be working with the client, for example, physician, social worker, and agency personnel.
- Do not rule out problem areas that you believe are applicable only to a younger population. Drugs, alcohol, and relationships are all viable issues in dealing with older adults. Also, keep in mind that loss, and its impact, are more often experienced by this population.
- Use what is most workable in the selection of intervention techniques based on the special needs and attitudinal set of the client. Certain techniques, owing to their physical nature or affective emphasis, may not be appropriate for this population.
- Keep in mind the "historical period" that has shaped the thinking, behavior, and moral development of the client. Understand that current reactions, behaviors, and general outlook have historical antecedents. Shmotkin and Eyal (2003) present an intriguing approach to this in their article dealing with "psychological time."
- Revisit the ethical standards related to working with older adults. A recent publication (Schwiebert, Myers, & Dice, 2000) identified three unique areas for which few or inadequate ethical guidelines exist. These are (l) older adults with cognitive impairments, (2) victims of abuse, and (3) those with a terminal illness. The authors propose a model for ethical decision making that has application to these unique areas and suggest that this model has applicability to other unique situations faced by counselors working with older adults.

GROUP APPROACHES

Counselors who decide to use a group approach with the older adult can gain a great deal of information and direction from reviewing such authors as Capuzzi and Gross (2002), Thomas and Martin (2002), and Toseland (1990). These authors not only offer special considerations that need to be made for working with older adults in groups such as time parameters, member selection, and group size but also specify the types of groups that have proven to be particularly helpful with this population. Some of the advantages of the group approach mentioned by these authors include (1) discovering common bonds, (2) teaching social skills, (3) aiding in decreasing feelings of loneliness, (4) giving mutual assistance, (5) sharing feelings, and (6) providing shared purposes.

Whether selecting an individual or group modality for working with older adults, it is important to keep in mind that certain approaches to both individual and group work have been designed specifically to deal with this population from a rehabilitative perspective. The needs of the individual in a life care facility may be quite different from the individual who maintains an independent lifestyle. In working with the individual in the life care facility, the following selected approaches have proven to be helpful.

Reality Orientation Therapy Groups

Reality orientation therapy, which combines both individual and group work, is directed at the individual who has experienced memory loss, confusion, and time-place-person disorientation. The thrust of reality orientation therapy is the repetition and learning of basic personal information such as the individual's name, the place, the time of day, day of the week and date, the next meal, time of bath, and so on. If done on an informal basis within the care facility, it should be done on a twenty-four hour basis, and it should be used by all people who have contact with the person. On a formal basis, this is done in a class setting.

Milieu Therapy Groups

Milieu therapy, which may make use of both individual and group work, is based on the concept that the social milieu of the care facility itself can be the instrument for treatment. The environment is organized to provide a more homelike atmosphere, with the individual taking more responsibility, trying new skills, and being involved in decision making in a somewhat safe environment. Levels of activity, self-care, and self-worth have increased using this approach.

Reminiscence Therapy Groups

These groups are designed to encourage the sharing of memories with groups of six to eight members and are conducted in both institutional and noninstitutional settings. This approach is similar to the "life review" process and in a group setting enhances a cohort effect, helping members identify and share accomplishments, tribulations, and viewpoints, while at the same time increasing opportunities for socialization. Music, visual aids, and memorabilia are often used to aid in stimulating group discussion.

Remotivation Therapy Groups

Remotivation therapy, which can be done in either a group or individual setting, seeks to encourage the moderately confused person to take a renewed interest in his or her surroundings by focusing attention on the simple, objective features of everyday life. Common topics are selected such as pets, gardening, and cooking, and people are encouraged to relate to these topics by drawing on their own life experiences.

In working with the greater percentage of older adults who continue to live independent lives, self-help groups, assertiveness training groups, growth groups, support groups, and the variety of special topic groups find equal applicability in work with this population as they do with a younger client population. Is counseling with older adults different from work with younger clients? The answer seems to be one of selective emphasis. In both individual and group work, all counseling interventions have applicability. The counselor needs to adapt his or her approach to accommodate the unique factors that parallel the aging process.

Topic and Theme-Focused Support Groups

Although these types of groups may be provided in institutionalized settings, they are often directed at the portion of the older population that is living independently. According to Thomas and Martin (2002), these groups that have a specific focus have proliferated with the increase in these types of groups for other populations. These groups target such areas as loss, health issues, retirement, career skills, sexuality, and care giving, and focus on skill building related to assertiveness training, social interaction, independent living competencies, stress, and intrafamily communication. Most topic and theme-focused support groups can be offered in a variety of settings. The size, composition, duration, and meeting frequency depend upon the needs of the group and the member competencies.

SUMMARY

As older adults increase in number, more will be seen in counseling. Counselors whose preparation has primarily focused on working with a younger population need to adapt this preparation to work more effectively with these clients. Counselor educators need to revise existing preparation programs to provide a curriculum that incorporates both didactic and experiential programming related to this population (Durodoye & Ennis-Cole, 1998; Myers, 1995).

The counseling needs of older adults are very similar to those of the younger client. When differences exist, they are best described in terms of a set of changing life situations that are characteristic of the aging process. The following recommendations can help the beginning counselor better understand what he or she needs to do to prepare for this clientele:

- Counselors need to secure information regarding the aging process and physiological, sociological, and psychological factors that have an impact on this process.
- Counselors need to understand the negative effects of "ageism" and clarify their values regarding aging from both self- and other-person perspectives. These values and attitudes will either enhance or impede their success with the older adult.
- Counselors need to be aware of the client's "place in history" and the significance this place holds in formulating values and attitudes that impact the client's view of the counseling process.
- Counselors need to emphasize short-term goals with older adult clients. These goals need to be clearly understood and accepted by the client and should place emphasis on the present life situation of the client.
- Counselors need to be aware of some of the drawbacks to using various diagnostic tools with an older adult population. Counselors may need to seek out more creative ways of data gathering.
- Counselors need to pay more attention to the physical setting in which counseling takes place. This environment needs to encourage, not discourage, the older adult's participation.
- Counselors need to view their role with the client more from an advocacy perspective. They need to be more actively involved with the day-to-day life of the client. Based upon the increasing incidence of abuse/maltreatment, older persons represent a population "at risk." As with any "at risk" population, efforts to reduce this risk call for more active participation.
- Counselors need to be willing to go to the client and not always expect the client to come to them. It may be necessary to take counseling to the client's home or to other settings due to the physical limitations of the older adult.
- Counselors need not fear or be apprehensive about involvement with older adults. They differ from their younger counterparts generally in increased life experiences and the rapidity of change descriptive of the aging process.
- Counselors need to use the longevity and the developed coping strategies that accompany the aging process to enhance the clients' present life situation. These clients have an advantage inasmuch as they have proven qualities of survival, that the counselor can use to improve self-esteem, interpersonal relations, family problems, loneliness, dependence versus independence, and a myriad of other concerns representative of this population.

The common theme of these recommendations is that counselors must pay more attention to and show more concern for the older adult. They must recognize their unique needs and, more importantly, treat them as fully deserving of the care counselors provide to younger people.

In the case that introduced this chapter, Paul did his best to apply what he had learned regarding working with the older adult client. He had paid attention to the physical environment and time considerations. He had studied the intake interview information and felt prepared to work with the client's concerns regarding her relocation. Paul had not anticipated the two clients who arrived but was flexible in attempting to deal with the situation. Both the individual sessions with the client and her son and the joint meetings left Paul questioning what he had done and felt perhaps he should have done more. A meeting with his supervisor was scheduled to address some of these questions.

It is our hope that the information contained in this chapter will provide answers to some of these questions and that counselors such as Paul will enter the counseling relationship with more assurance that they have both the information and the skills necessary to deal with the older adult client.

CHAPTER SEVENTEEN

COUNSELING COUPLES AND FAMILIES

CASS DYKEMAN, PH.D.
Oregon State University

The placement of this chapter in a section called "Counseling Special Populations" confirms Duncan Stanton's (1988) contention that, "Non-family therapists often view family therapy as (a) a modality, that (b) usually involves the nuclear family" (p. 8). He goes on to point out the inaccuracy of this conception, explaining that family therapy is based on a point of view that emphasizes the contextual nature of psychological problems.

> More fundamentally, it (family therapy) is a way of construing human problems that dictates certain actions for their alleviation. Its conceptual and data bases differ from most other (especially individually oriented) therapies in that the interpersonal context of a problem and the interplay between this context and the symptoms are of primary interest. An index patient is seen as responding to his or her social situation; those around the patient are noted to react to this response; the patient then reacts "back," and so on, in an on-going, give and take process. Interventions designed to alter this process derive from such interactional formulations. (p. 8)

It is, of course, possible for a counselor who is oriented to the treatment of individuals to interview the members of a client's family in the course of treatment. However, this rarely occurs, since the individual orientation places the source of dysfunction within the client rather than focusing on the context in which the symptoms occur. Table 17.1 illustrates some of the other differences in perspective between a psychodynamic and a family therapy point of view. The psychodynamic approach is based in Freudian theory, and emphasizes internal constructs such as the id, ego, and superego; in contrast, family therapy is primarily based in systems theory and emphasizes interpersonal behavior. To further illuminate this paradigm shift, several concepts from systems theory will be illustrated within a human behavioral context.

TABLE 17.1   Two Contrasting Views of Therapy: Psychodynamic and Family Systems

	PSYCHODYNAMIC	FAMILY SYSTEMS
Causality	linear	recursive
Time Focus	past	present
Pathology	intrapsychic	interpersonal
Assessment	individual	systemic
Therapy	long-term catharsis transference abreaction insight	brief reframing restructuring problem-solving behavior change
Therapist	passive	active

Fundamental Unity. The universe is one system with infinite levels of subsystems; analysis at any level needs to consider the levels above and below. To understand the individual, it is essential to analyze both the inter-individual context and the intra-individual subsystems. A person's strange behavior may be due to dysfunctional family interactions or may be due to a chemical imbalance in the individual's blood.

System Change. Change in any part of a system will impact the whole system. If therapy with an individual is successful, the system of which the client is a part will be affected. Unfortunately, we will know of those changes only through the selective filter of our client, and that our chances of success are diminished by the homeostatic drag of the system.

Recursive Causality. Inherent in the first two concepts is a nonlinear epistemology. Thus our observation that A causes B is due only to our punctuation of a behavioral sequence that fails to see what follows from B or what preceded A. Every act (or nonaction) provokes feedback, which alters the nature of the next act. In a family, "Does he drink because she nags?" (his punctuation); or "Does she nag because he drinks?" (her punctuation).

Homeostasis. Systems use negative feedback to maintain a steady state; positive feedback creates change in the system. If one member of a family begins to change, perhaps as the result of individual therapy, the usual routine interactions of the family will be disrupted, and the family will send messages designed to bring the person in therapy back into line.

Viability. The viability of a system is based on order and structure; entropy is disorder. In addition to structure, which is a static quality, the system must also be open to new input if it is to be capable of accommodating to its changing environment. A family with young children needs a generational hierarchy, but the hierarchy must also be open to modification as the children mature. (Adapted from Sieburg, 1985)

With this brief description of systems concepts, perhaps the following definition of family therapy, as stated by Wynne (1988), can be presented:

> Family therapy is a psychotherapeutic approach that focuses on altering interactions between a couple, within a nuclear family or extended family, or between a family and other interpersonal systems, with the goal of alleviating problems initially presented by individual family members, family subsystems, the family as a whole, or other referral sources. (pp. 250–251)

THE HISTORY OF FAMILY THERAPY

The history of family therapy is relatively brief. It begins in the 1950s, with the seminal contributions of Nathan Ackerman, Theodore Lidz, Lyman Wynne, Murray Bowen, and Carl Whitaker. All of these psychiatrists, originally trained in the prevailing psychodynamic model, broke away from its restrictive influence and began to see that dysfunctional behavior was rooted in the individual's past and present family life. Each of these pioneers arrived at this insight relatively independently: Ackerman through his research on the mental health problems of the unemployed in Pennsylvania; Lidz studying the families of schizophrenics at Yale; Wynne treating patients with psychosis and ulcerative colitis in Massachusetts, and later doing research on the families of schizophrenics at the National Institute of Mental Health (NIMH); Bowen through his work with families at the Menninger Foundation and later with Wynne at NIMH; and Whitaker through seeing families at Oak Ridge and his later work with families with a schizophrenic member at Emory. In his preface to *The Psychodynamics of Family Life* (1958), the first book-length treatment of this point-of-view, Ackerman said:

> This approach attempts to correlate the dynamic psychological processes of individual behavior with family behavior in order to be able to place individual clinical diagnosis and therapy within the broader frame of family diagnosis and therapy. It has been necessary, therefore, to explore a series of interrelated themes: the interdependence of individual and family stability at every stage of growth from infancy to old age; the role of family in the emotional development of the child; the family as stabilizer of the mental health of the adult; the family as conveyor belt for anxiety and conflict and as a carrier of the contagion of mental illness; the interplay of conflict between family and community, conflict in family relationships, and conflict within individual family members; and breakdown in adaptation and illness as symptoms of the group pathology of the family. (p. viii)

With this statement he did much to set the agenda for the next three decades.

During this same period, an unusual group of people assembled in Palo Alto to study the communication processes of schizophrenics. The project was headed by Gregory Bateson, an anthropologist, who hired Jay Haley, a recent graduate in communications theory; Don Jackson, a psychiatrist; and John Weakland, whose initial training was in chemical engineering. Early in the project, Haley began consulting with Milton Erickson who was known at that time primarily as a hypnotherapist. From this rich melange emerged the beginnings of strategic family therapy. In 1959,

Jackson founded the Mental Research Institute (MRI) in Palo Alto and invited Virginia Satir to join him. When the Bateson project ended in 1961, Haley and Weakland also joined the staff at MRI.

Satir diverged from the pragmatic approach of strategic therapy when she left MRI to join the human potential movement at the Esalen Institute. With the publication of her book *Conjoint Family Therapy* in 1964, she established her own approach to family treatment, which incorporated elements of the thinking of the group at MRI within a framework of Gestalt and experiential therapy.

Structural family therapy emerged on the east coast in the work of Salvador Minuchin and his colleagues at Wyltwick School and later the Philadelphia Child Guidance Clinic (PCGC). At Wyltwick, Minuchin worked with the families of delinquent boys and at PCGC he did research on families with a member who was psychosomatic. Each of these projects resulted in a book that enriched our understanding of family functioning (Minuchin, Montalvo, Gurney, Rosman, & Schumer, 1967; Minuchin, Rosman, & Baker, 1978). He was joined by Haley in 1967, and they worked together for ten years. As might be expected, the concepts of strategic and structural therapy have much in common. Haley, who met his second wife, Cloe Madanes at the PCGC, left with her in 1977 to found the Family Therapy Institute of Washington, D.C.

Murray Bowen began his career at the Menninger Foundation and focused his research on families with a schizophrenic member. He continued this at the NIMH where, in 1954, he had the families of schizophrenic youngsters actually live in the hospital so that he could observe their interactions. In 1959, he moved to Georgetown University Medical Center where he worked for the rest of his career.

Last, but not least, is Carl Whitaker, who is often referred to as the "clown prince of family therapy." Whitaker began his career as a gynecologist, but soon switched to psychiatry. He was chief psychiatrist at Oak Ridge, Tennessee, where he first began bringing the family into treatment with his patients. He moved from Oak Ridge to the chair of the Department of Psychiatry at Emory University in 1946. The publication of his first book, *The Roots of Psychotherapy* (Whitaker & Malone, 1953), led to his dismissal, and he went into private practice for ten years. The book, which he co-authored with his colleague, Thomas Malone, challenged much of traditional psychodynamic thinking and was resoundingly condemned by the psychiatric establishment. In 1965, Whitaker began teaching at the University of Wisconsin. He would remain at this institution through the rest of his professional life. He referred to his work as Symbolic-Experiential Family Therapy.

For a more complete treatment of the history of family therapy see Becvar and Becvar's Family Therapy (2002) or Gladding's *Family Therapy: History, Theory, and Practice* (2002).

CHAPTER OVERVIEW

While it would be possible to follow this brief historical introduction with a detailed description of each of the major therapeutic approaches, I have elected to take a different approach. It is my contention that family therapy has moved beyond the "schools of therapy" orientation and that a systematic eclecticism is now possible. For the reader who is interested in a comparison of the various approaches, Table 17.2 presents a comparative assessment of some of the relevant aspects of family therapy.

The present attempt to reduce the emphasis on the differences between various approaches to family therapy has the support of at least one of the major figures in the field. Salvador Minuchin, writing as early as 1982, also decried the tendency to fragment the field into schools of therapy:

> In early explorations of family therapy, the field increased its sophistication and expanded its territory. Naturally, the early explorers staked the unmarked corners with their trade names: strategic, systemic, structural Bowenian, experiential, and so on. The old-timers knew that their private truths were only partial, and when they met around a cup of coffee, they gossiped about the beginnings and shared their uncertainties and hopes. But, lo and behold, their institutions grew, and they needed large buildings to accommodate all their students. Slowly, before anybody realized it, the buildings became castles, with turrets and drawbridges, and even watchmen in the towers. The castles were very expensive and they needed to justify their existence. Therefore, they demanded ownership of the total truth. . . . But the generation of elders is becoming older. The castles are becoming very expensive to run and, like the English aristocracy, the lords of the manor will soon be opening them only on Sunday for the new generation of tourists. Those who come to my castle will not find me there. (p. 662)

In what follows, I have attempted to synthesize what I regard as some of the most useful of the ideas of the several therapists referred to above. I will begin first with a family systems perspective on the diagnosis of family dysfunction. This will be followed by sections on how to conduct the initial interview, family therapy techniques, legal and ethical questions, and research.

DIAGNOSIS OF FAMILY DYSFUNCTION

Tolstoy said in the opening line of *Anna Karenina*, "All happy families resemble one another, but each unhappy family is unhappy in its own way." Family therapists tend to reverse this position, believing that good family functioning is based in diversity, while family dysfunction is due to narrowness and rigidity. Haley (1987) goes so far as to argue that therapies that have a picture of "ideal" functioning are in fact limiting, in that they impose "a narrow ideology, thus preventing the diversity that human beings naturally display. To put the matter simply, if the goal of therapy is to introduce more complexity, then imposing on clients psychological explanation of their own and other people's behavior is antitherapeutic" (p. 233).

When a system's orientation is applied to psychological problems, the diagnosis of the difficulty is very different from that presented in the *Diagnostic and Statistical Manual of Mental Disorders-IV-TR* (American Psychiatric Association, 2000). Rather than focusing on the internal state of the individual, the family systems approach looks for pathology in the interactions that occur between people who have significance for each other.

TABLE 17.2   A Comparison of Family Therapy Approaches

	STRATEGIC (HALEY)	STRUCTURAL (MINUCHIN)	TRANSGEN-ERATIONAL (BOWEN)	EXPERIENTIAL (WHITAKER)	CONJOINT (SATIR)
Who is included in therapy?	Everyone involved in the problem	Whoever is involved and accessible	The most motivated family member(s)	Who he decides should come	The pattern is flexible
What is the theory of dysfunction?	Confused hierarchy; communica-tion; rigid behavioral sequences	Boundaries (enmeshed or disengaged); stable coalitions; power	Fusion (emotions control; symbiosis with family of origin); anxiety; triangulation	Rigidity of thought and behavior	Low self-esteem; poor communi-cation; triangulation
What are the goals of therapy?	Solve the problem; restore hierarchy; introduce flexibility	Solve the problem; change the structure; increase flexibility	Greater differentiation of self; reduced anxiety	Increase family creativity; greater sense of belonging and individuation	Improved communication; personal growth
What is the method of assessment?	Structured initial interview; intervene and observe the reaction; focus on the present	Joining the family to experience its process; chart the family structure; focus on the present	Detailed family history over several generations using the genogram; focus on the past	Informal; not separated from treatment; focus on both past and present	Family life chronology is used to take history and assess present functioning
What are the intervention procedures?	Directives are used to change behavior; they may be straightforward, paradoxical, or ordeals	Reframing is used to change the perception of the problem; structure is changed by unbalancing and increasing stress	Reducing anxiety by providing rational, untriangulated third party; coaching to aid in differen-tiation from family of origin	Increasing stress to force change; reframing symptoms as efforts at growth; affective confrontation	Modeling and coaching clear communica-tion; family sculpting; guided interaction
What is the stance of the therapist?	Active, directive, but not self-revealing; planful, not spontaneous	Active, directive, personally involved; spontaneous; humorous	Interested but detached; reinforces calmness and rationality	Active, personally involved; encourages and models "craziness," co-therapy	Active, directive, matter-of-fact, nonjudgmental; models open communication

Rather than adopting a linear model of causality, the family systems approach perceives causality as circular or recursive. It's not that a child is rebellious because his or her father is too authoritarian, or that the father is authoritarian because the child is rebellious, but that both are caught up in a chronic repetitive sequence of behavior: the "game without end."

Rather than focusing on the way people think or feel, the family systems therapist tends to focus on what they do. The purpose of family therapy is not insight, but behavior change. Within the broad commonality of the systems orientation, each of the major family therapists has emphasized different aspects of human functioning as the source of symptomatic behavior. The following sections provide a compilation of the thinking of a number of family therapists regarding symptomatic behavior.

Family Life Cycle

Family dysfunction is often the result of a failure to accomplish the developmental tasks demanded by the family life cycle (Table 17.3). The fullest conceptualization of a stage approach to family development is generally attributed to Carter and McGoldrick (1999), although the concept dates back to the 1950s (Gerson, 1995). Since Carter and McGoldrick, most of the major family therapists have acknowledged the significance of family life cycle changes as a major source of stress and disequilibrium for the family. Inherent in the life cycle concept is the idea that there are certain developmental tasks that must be accomplished during periods of transition from one stage to another. Successful movement to the next development stage requires changes in the roles and structure of the family. If the family is unable to accommodate to the need for change, stress and symptomatology will occur.

The demand for change is a normal part of family development. It is not these normal difficulties that create the problem, but rather the chronic mishandling of them. It is the attempted solution that is the problem. Denying the need for change, treating a normal developmental change as if it were a problem, and striving for perfection are all likely to result in family distress. In general, the reaction of a dysfunctional family to a demand for change is met by doing "more of the same." For example, a girl becomes a teenager and exerts more autonomy; parents become concerned for her safety and morality; they introduce or increase their control over her behavior; the girl resents their attempt to control her autonomy and rebels; the parents increase their control; and so on (Gerson, 1995; Micucci, 1998). In a family with young children, a problem might arise when the grandparents have difficulty in giving up their parental role with their own children, thus interfering with the discipline of their new grandchildren.

The problems associated with family life cycle changes are exacerbated in remarried families. This exacerbation occurs because an individual's development is out of synchronization with the developmental stage of his or her family. For example, a newly remarried family is focused on issues of inclusion and forming of a viable entity; if that family contains an adolescent, he or she is focused on issues of separation and individuation.

TABLE 17.3 Stages of the Family Life Cycle

FAMILY LIFE CYCLE STAGE	EMOTIONAL PROCESS OF TRANSITION: KEY PRINCIPLES	SECOND ORDER CHANGES IN FAMILY STATUS REQUIRED TO PROCEED DEVELOPMENTALLY
1. Leaving home: single young adults	Accepting emotional and financial responsibility for self	a. Differentiation of self in relation to family of origin b. Development of intimate peer relationships c. Establishment of self in respect to work and financial independence
2. The joining of families through marriage: the new couple	Commitment to new system	a. Formation of marital system b. Realignment of relationships with extended families and friends to include spouse
3. Families with young children	Accepting new members into the system	a. Adjusting marital system to make space for children b. Joining in child rearing, financial, and household tasks c. Realignment of relationships with extended family to include parenting and grandparenting roles
4. Families with adolescents	Increasing flexibility of family boundaries to permit children's independence and grandparents frailties	a. Shifting of parent/child relationships to permit adolescent to move in and out of system b. Refocus on midlife marital and career issues c. Beginning shift toward caring for older generation
5. Launching children and moving on	Accepting a multitude of exits from and entries into the family system	a. Renegotiation of marital system as a dyad b. Development of adult-to-adult relationships between grown children and their parents c. Realignment of relationships to include in-laws and grandchildren d. Dealing with disabilities and death of parents (grandparents)
6. Families in later life	Accepting the shifting of generational roles	a. Maintaining own and/or couple functioning and interests in face of physiologic decline: exploration of new familial and social role options b. Support for a more central role for middle generation c. Making room in the system for the wisdom and experience of the elderly, supporting the older generation without overfunctioning for them d. Dealing with loss of spouse, siblings and other peers and preparation for death

Source: From *The Changing Family Life Cycle: Individual, Family, and Social Perspectives* (3rd ed., p. 2), by B. Carter and M. McGoldrick, 1999. Needham Heights, MA: Allyn & Bacon. Copyright (©) 1999 by Allyn & Bacon. Reprinted by permission.

Fusion in the Nuclear Family and/or the Family of Origin

Bowen (1994) conceived a scale of differentiation of self from 0 to 100. At the low end of the scale, people are fused or enmeshed with their families to the extent that they are unable to think or act independently. Their lives are ruled by emotional reactivity. According to Bowen, people diagnosed as schizophrenic would be extremely fused.

At the upper end of the scale, people have achieved emotional separation from their families, are able to act autonomously, and can choose to be rational in emotionally charged situations. The individual's level of differentiation is closely related to the differentiation of his or her parents, and the process is transgenerational in nature. People with low levels of differentiation (fusion) are particularly reactive to environmental stressors and when under stress are likely to resolve it by (a) withdrawal, (b) conflict, (c) dysfunction of one spouse, or (d) triangulation of a child that results in dysfunction. When the latter occurs, that child, who is caught in the tug of war between the parents, will be even less differentiated than the parents. This is the basis of the intergenerational transmission of dysfunction (Bowen, 1991, 1994).

Boundary Problems

According to Minuchin, family boundaries are created by implicit rules that govern who talks to whom about what (Minuchin, Colapinto, & Minuchin, 1998; Minuchin & Fishman, 1990). When no rules exist, everyone is privy to everyone else's thoughts and feelings. Thus, family boundaries become diffuse and individuals become enmeshed (fused). When the rules are too strict and communication breaks down, the boundary is said to be rigid and the individuals disengaged. The preferred state is to have clear rules that allow for both individuation and togetherness. The similarity of this concept to Bowen's idea of differentiation of self is obvious, but Minuchin has developed it to refer to both extrafamilial boundaries and intrafamilial boundaries that separate subsystems (i.e., holons).

Family dysfunction can occur because the family is either disengaged from or enmeshed with the external environment. This is frequently a problem with remarried families where rules regarding contact with ex-spouses may be either rigid or lacking. Dysfunction can also occur when internal subsystems of the family are enmeshed or disengaged. The classic dysfunction in our culture is the mother who is enmeshed with a child (i.e., cross-generational coalition) and the father who is disengaged from both.

Dysfunctional Sequences

Haley (1987) believes family dysfunction is often caused by behavioral sequences that are rigid, repetitive, and functionally autonomous. He describes such a sequence as follows:

1. One parent, usually the mother, is in an intense relationship with the child. By *intense* is meant a relationship that is both positive and negative and where the

responses of each person are exaggeratedly important. The mother attempts to deal with the child with a mixture of affection and exasperation.

2. The child's symptomatic behavior becomes more extreme.
3. The mother, or the child, calls on the father for assistance in resolving their difficulty.
4. The father steps in to take charge and deal with the child.
5. Mother reacts against father, insisting that he is not dealing with the situation properly. Mother can react with an attack or with a threat to break off the relationship with father.
6. Father withdraws, giving up the attempt to disengage mother and child.
7. Mother and child deal with each other in a mixture of affection and exasperation until they reach a point where they are at an impasse. (pp. 121–122)

Such patterns can repeat ad infinitum unless some new behavior is introduced into the sequence. It perhaps needs to be pointed out that the dysfunctional behavior should not be "blamed" on any of the individuals; all are equally involved and each could change the sequence by introducing a new incompatible element. Unfortunately, the family members are not usually aware of the complete sequence and in any case punctuate the sequence in such a way as to hold themselves blameless.

Hierarchy Problems

Haley (1987) and Minuchin (Minuchin & Nichols, 1993) both stress the importance of hierarchy problems in family dysfunction. Problems can occur when the hierarchy is either absent, ambiguous, or culturally inappropriate; that is, when no one is in charge, when it is unclear who is in charge, or when the person wielding the power is not sanctioned by cultural mores. Dysfunction may also be due to coalitions that cut across generational boundaries. An example of the latter would be when a father and child collude to avoid what they feel are the mother's overly rigid rules. Another common example would be in a family where there is marital conflict and both parents try to enlist the children on their side of the argument.

Communication Problems

Virginia Satir (1983) placed special emphasis on the ways that people in a family communicate as a source of dysfunction. Communication may be inadequate owing to lack of clarity (e.g., information is deleted; "People get me down." Which people? How do they do that?). Communication can also be confusing because of a lack of topic continuity. This occurs when people are not really listening and their responses to the other become non-sequiturs. When people are unwilling to reveal themselves or commit themselves to a statement or request, communication falters (e.g., "I don't suppose you would like to go to my mother's with me?" rather than "I would like you to go with me to my mother's.").

Sometimes communication is problematic because it is incongruent; either the nonverbal behavior or vocal tone communicates a message that contradicts the verbal content. Such incongruency is often the basis for irony and humor, but when it is unintentional and the message is not clarified, the receiver does not know how to respond. In the extreme case, this is the classic "double bind," described by Bateson, Jackson, Haley, and Weakland (1956). Satir (1983) describes this, and the effect that such incongruent communication can have on a child:

> How do mates unconsciously induce a child to behave in such a way that he eventually gets identified as a "patient?" . . . What conditions must be present for a child to experience the pressures associated with a double bind?
> a. First, the child must be exposed to double-level messages repeatedly and over a long period.
> b. Second, these must come from persons who have survival significance for him. . . .
> c. Third, perhaps most important of all, he must be conditioned . . . from an early age not to ask, "Did you mean that or that?" but must accept his parents conflicting messages in all their impossibility. He must be faced with the hopeless task of translating them into a single way of behaving. (pp. 45–46)

Low Self-Esteem

Satir (1983) also posits low self-esteem as the basis of much family difficulty. She describes a process similar to Bowen's (1994) intergenerational transmission process to reveal how low self-esteem not only affects the individuals and couples, but also is "inherited" by their children. Description of the entire process is beyond the scope of this chapter. The essential elements include low self-esteem in both marital partners, intolerance of each other's differences, and seeking to improve their sense of self-esteem through their children. If the parents don't agree on how the children should behave, the children are confronted with the impossible task of pleasing both parents (another type of double-bind). Since they cannot please both parents, the children develop low self-esteem and may become symptomatic.

Conflict Over Which Family of Origin to Model

Whitaker says, "We assume that dysfunction is related to the struggle over whose family of origin this new family is going to model itself after. One way to view etiology asserts there is no such thing as a marriage; it is merely two scapegoats sent out by families to perpetrate themselves" (Whitaker & Keith, 1981, p. 196). Young people who come from a common cultural background may be less likely to experience this problem, but in our polyglot society, the appropriate behaviors for "wife" or "husband" are often unclear, or represent role conflicts. When a child enters the picture before these roles are synchronized, the new roles of "mother" and "father" further complicate the picture. Often the young couple find themselves acting just like their parents, although they are reluctant to admit it.

Narrow Rigid Beliefs and Self-Percepts

In a sense, this brings us full circle. To the extent that one's beliefs are narrow and unchanging, adaptation to the demands of a changing environment or the developmental demands of the family life cycle will be difficult. Milton Erickson held "... that individuals with a symptom were constricted by their own certainties, their own rules, whether these rules guided their belief system, their perceptions of self, their patterns of physiological response or relational habits, or their own ideas of contingency (i.e., if A, then B)" (Ritterman, 1986, p. 37). The symptom, per se, is not the problem, but instead is "a metaphorical expression of a problem and attempt at resolution . . . the underlying problem is understood to be inflexibly patterned behavior resulting from internal and/or interactional rules that proscribe available choices and prevent the resolution of developmentally routine or unusual life dilemmas" (Ritterman, 1986, p. 36).

When an individual or a family is unable to resolve a difficulty, it is assumed that the conscious mind is imposing a narrow, restrictive mind-set that does not allow the creative recovery of the resources necessary to solve the problem. From this point of view, the conscious, rational mind must be diverted to allow the creative potential of the unconscious to function. This is done through hypnosis or the use of indirect methods such as metaphor.

THE INITIAL INTERVIEW

In order to gain a better understanding of how family therapists work, let us look at how the initial interview is conducted. The following description owes a great deal to Jay Haley (1987), but also incorporates ideas from other therapists.

Presession Planning

Whenever possible, the therapist should determine in advance who will attend the session, and have at least a general idea of the nature of the presenting problems. Whitaker and Bumberry (1988) call this the "battle for structure," and place great emphasis on the importance of the therapist determining who will attend the first session. It is their belief that if the therapist does not have control at this stage, therapeutic leverage is lost and the family is less likely to be helped. This may entail a presession telephone call or the use of an intake form. On the basis of the data derived from this initial contact, a presession plan should be developed that will include the counselor's hypotheses about the underlying basis of the presenting problem, areas of inquiry that must be addressed to reject or confirm the hypotheses, and a general plan for the session.

The Joining Stage

The most important task of the initial interview is to join with the family, accommodating to their affective tone, tempo, language, and family structure. This is done through mimesis (Walsh & McGraw, 2002). Mimesis is a therapeutic skill "used by the therapist to join with the family and become like family members in the manner or content of their communications" (Sauber, L'Abate, Weeks, & Buchanan, 1993, p. 255). Foreman and Cava (1993) advocate matching the family's style even to the extent of matching breathing, body movements, and representational system predicates (visual, auditory, kinesthetic). Care needs to be taken, however, that this matching does not cross the line into parody.

Tracking is another joining technique and consists of little more than Rogers-like "uh-huhs," reflection of content, and asking for clarification. During this time, the therapist should avoid comment or interpretation (Haley, 1987).

A third aspect of joining is maintenance. This aspect of joining refers to the therapist sensing the family's structure and acting in such a way as to be included within it (Minuchin & Nichols, 1993). If Dad acts as the "central switchboard" in this family, the therapist accommodates to that and contacts other members through him.

During the joining stage, the therapist should not allow the introduction of material related to the family problem. Only after some social contact has been made with every family member should the next stage begin (Haley, 1987). Joining, of course, is not finished at the end of this stage, but must be of concern throughout the therapy.

More structured approaches to joining include the use of family chronologies and genograms (McGoldrick, Gerson, & Shellenberger, 1999). McAllister (1998) shares valuable information on joining with conservative Christian families. Both McGoldrick (1998) and Minuchin, Colapinto, and Minuchin (1998) present a wealth of information on joining with economically and/or ethnically diverse families.

The Problem Statement Stage

When significant contact has been made with all family members in the social or joining stage, the therapist introduces the problem stage. During the joining stage, the therapist has learned something of the family structure and hierarchy and uses this information to decide to whom the first question should be directed. Haley (1987) recommends that "the adult who seems less involved with the problem be spoken to first, and the person with the most power to bring the family back be treated with the most concern and respect" (p. 22). He also says that, in general, it is unwise to begin with the identified patient (IP).

Don't attempt to force a mute member to speak. This member is often the IP who has lots of practice in resisting adult coercion. Instead, ask another family member, "What would Johnny say if he chose to talk?" This can be repeated in a round robin if necessary, and in most instances, the mute member will feel the need to defend himself or clarify his real feelings.

The second decision the therapist must make is how the problem question should be framed. Obviously, the question can be as vague as, "What brings you here today?" or as specific as "What is the problem for which you are seeking help?" It can also be framed to elicit etiologic information or be future-focused on the kinds of changes that are desired. I generally prefer ambiguity and a focus on the future: "When this therapy is successful, how will your family be different?"

When everyone has had an opportunity to express what they see as the "pain in the family" (Satir, 1983), the therapist can begin to flesh out the details that will help to clarify the function that the problem serves in the family. The following series of questions may prove helpful.

1. Who has the problem?
2. Where else have you sought help and how did it work for you? What has been tried, by whom, and for how long? Is there anything you have tried that you feel could have been done more?
3. Why is the symptom a problem? Does anyone in the family not consider the symptom a problem? Who in the family is most upset by the problem?
4. How often does it occur? When? Where? Who reacts to it? In what way? What happens just before it occurs? What happens next?
5. When did the symptom begin? Why did you come in now?
6. How do you account for the problem?
7. Do the parents agree or disagree about the problem, its cause, and the best solution?
8. What would happen if the symptom got better or worse?
9. What do you hope will happen as the result of coming here? What is your ideal goal? What would you settle for? How optimistic are you about improvement? What do you want to see the identified patient doing two weeks from now that would show progress? (Bergman, 1985)

The Interaction Stage

When the problem has been reasonably clarified or when it has become clear that the family is not in agreement regarding the nature of the problem, it is time for the therapist to introduce the interaction stage. During the earlier two stages, the therapist has maintained his or her centrality in the communication network, speaking in turn to each of the family members and blocking interruptions and attempts at dialogue between family members. This procedure tends to reduce tension and provide order and relatively clear communication, and establishes the therapist's power and leadership in the therapeutic process. The focus in the problem phase has been on clarifying how the family views the problem. In the interaction stage, the therapist's focus will be on determining the patterns of interaction that sustain the problem. In order to get this information the therapist asks the family to "dance" in his or her presence (Kershaw, 1992).

This occurs most easily and naturally when the family is not in agreement regarding the problem. When this is true, the therapist can encourage them to discuss their differences and try to reach agreement. During this phase, it is crucial that the therapist abdicate the center of the communication network. All attempts to communicate with the therapist should be referred back to a family member. The therapist does not, however, completely abandon the leadership position; instead the role changes to being the director of the family drama, introducing a third party when two seem to reach an impasse, or asking family members to change their seating patterns to facilitate new encounters (Grove & Haley, 1993; Minuchin & Nichols, 1993).

If family members are in agreement regarding the problem that brings them to therapy (usually focusing on one person as the cause of the difficulty), they can be asked to perform the problem. "When Johnny doesn't take out the garbage, what happens? Who is first to notice? Show me how it works." In order to get the family to act, rather than talk about the problem, it will be necessary for the therapist to get to his or her feet, help the family to build an appropriate stage set (in fantasy), and set the scene into action.

Interactions that are developed from the idiosyncratic information presented by the family are most likely to reveal the information needed to understand the problem. Unfortunately, some families are so uncommunicative that the therapist is unable to elicit enough information to stage an appropriate interaction. When this occurs, it is well to have a few preplanned interaction situations available. One that is often useful, particularly in families with young children, is to ask the family to enact a day in their lives. Establish who sleeps where, move them into the appropriate places, and then have the alarm go off. If it is to be successful, the therapist will need to coach this interaction, slowing it down and focusing on the most simple, concrete details of family life. In a large family, who has access to the bathroom at what time is often a major source of conflict. Care must also be taken to ensure that all family members become involved. Other generic interactions might be to plan a family vacation together, or decide how to spend a free Saturday. Or, using building blocks or crayon and paper, have the family draw their living quarters and discuss who spends the most time with whom in what part of the house.

The purpose of the interaction stage is to determine the family hierarchy, to reveal any stable coalitions, to locate diffuse or rigid boundaries between family subsystems, and hopefully to reveal the chronically repeating interactional sequence that sustains the problem behavior. When this information has been obtained, the therapist is in a position to develop the interventions that will lead to beneficial change.

In-Session Conference

When the therapist is working with an observing team, or even when working alone, it is useful at this point to leave the family and take a few minutes to think about what has been observed in order to abstract from the concrete interactions the patterns that need correction. When working with an observing team, it is often true that the observers are more able to perceive these patterns than the therapist who is immersed in the hypnotic pull of the family dance. Moran et al. (1995) contains an excellent description of the use of such a team. The purpose of the in-session conference is to assess the accuracy of the presession hypotheses and to reformulate them in light of the new data gathered during the session. When this has been done, it is possible to design directives (homework) that will begin to change the family's dysfunctional interactions. In some instances the appropriate homework is not clear, but it is my contention that some homework should still be assigned. Family therapy, or any kind of therapy for that matter, is unlikely to be successful if the therapy is encapsulated in the therapeutic hour. The therapist needs to make an assignment that will establish an ongoing process that keeps the therapy salient throughout the week. When the therapist makes a homework assignment without being sure of its relevance, it is comforting to keep Jeff Zeig's dictum in mind. Zeig, who is an Ericksonian hypnotherapist, says his approach to therapy is "ready-shoot-aim" (personal communication, 1988). In other words, if you wait until you are sure of your interventions, therapy will be a long, drawn-out process. If you go with your hunches, and learn from the results, you will probably hit the bull's-eye much sooner.

Goal-Setting Stage

As Haley (1987) has said, "If therapy is to end properly, it must begin properly—by negotiating a solvable problem and discovering the social situation that makes the problem necessary" (p. 8). The purpose of the goal-setting stage is to reach agreement with the family on a solvable problem and to initiate a process that will alter the social situation in such a way that the problem is no longer necessary. It is essential that the problem to be solved be stated in behavioral terms so that one will know when it has been solved. It is equally essential that the problem be one that the therapist believes is capable of solution. Often the process of operationalizing the complaint will be sufficient to produce a solvable problem. When a "rebellious child" problem is operationalized to "staying out after curfew," we have a specific concern upon which one can focus. However, some problems, and this would include most of the categories of the DSM-IV-TR (2000), are not capable of solution. With ambiguous problems, the therapist must reframe the problem in such a way that it can be solved, and in such a way that the family will accept it. This is not an easy task and sometimes taxes the therapist's creative resources. A notable example would be a case in which Haley reframed a case of schizophrenia as "pseudo-schizophrenia" and then went on to help the family specify how the IP's behavior might be improved. It cannot be emphasized enough that the problem to be solved must be stated in behavioral terms (i.e., never negotiate to "improve communication," "raise self-esteem," or "make our family more cohesive").

When agreement has been reached regarding the problem, the therapist should assign homework that will have face validity with regard to the problem, but will also address the underlying structural or sequential changes that are necessary. In the case of "pseudo-schizophrenia" mentioned above, one might assume that the family is obsessively monitoring the patient, watching for abnormal behavior. An assignment that would utilize the obsessive nature of the family (i.e., pacing) and still institute a change would be to ask the family to keep an elaborate baseline measure of the "normal" behavior of the patient and bring it to the next session.

In a family with a daughter who is not keeping an assigned curfew, it might appear that the rebelliousness is being secretly (and perhaps unconsciously) reinforced by the father. An intervention might be to put dad in charge of the daughter's behavior for a week, asking him during the session to negotiate with his daughter the expectations and consequences of noncompliance.

Initial sessions, particularly with large families, often cannot be conducted within the usual 50-minute hour. If it is not possible to schedule a longer session, it is likely that it will take more than one session to establish the therapeutic contract.

When this is true, one should still attempt to give some kind of homework assignment that will increase the power of the therapy. When in doubt, asking family members to each keep a baseline of the behavior that they see as problematic is a good first step.

Ending Stage

The therapist should end the session by setting a second appointment and specifying who should be present. The family should not be asked if they want to return; this should be assumed unless someone indicates otherwise.

Postsession

When working with a team, there should be a postsession debriefing to give an opportunity to share various perceptions of the family and the response to the interventions. When working alone, it is essential to record your impressions of the presenting problem, the family structure, hypotheses regarding needed changes and, most importantly, the homework that was assigned. The latter should be recorded verbatim, if possible, in order to check on the family compliance.

FAMILY THERAPY TECHNIQUES

In the preceding section, the focus was on the process of conducting the initial interview. In this section, I will focus on the techniques utilized by the therapist throughout the therapy. The techniques offered here are derived from several therapeutic points of view.

Circular Questioning

Following Bateson's dictum that "information is a difference; difference is a relationship (or a change in the relationship)," the Milan group developed a technique they refer to as circular questioning (Benson, Schindler, & Martin, 1991; Walsh & McGraw, 2002). The "circular" referred to here is epistemological; their questions are intended to uncover the complementarity of family relationships that make the presenting symptom necessary for family homeostasis. Each member of the family is invited to tell how he or she sees the relationship between two other family members, or between two different periods, or any other difference likely to be significant to the family. For example:

1. In terms of family relationships: "Tell us how you see the relationship between your sister and your mother."
2. In terms of specific interactive behaviors: "When your father gets mad at Bill, what does your mother do?"
3. In terms of differences in behavior: "Who gets most upset when Jimmy wets the bed, your father or your mother?"

4. In terms of ranking by various members of the family of a behavior or interaction: "Who is closest to your grandmother? Who is next, and next?"
5. In terms of change in the relationship before and after a precise event: "Did you and your sister fight more or less before your mother remarried?"
6. In terms of differences in respect to hypothetical circumstances: "If one of you kids should have to stay home, not get married, who would be best for your mother? Your father?" (Fleuridas, Nelson, & Rosenthal, 1986)

Perhaps it should be mentioned here, parenthetically, that this procedure would be anathema to some other therapists, including Virginia Satir, who specifically proscribes "gossiping" and "mind-reading." However, the Milan group has demonstrated that often more can be obtained by asking a person what he or she thinks about others than by asking questions that are more personal. When this is done in the family context, where all can hear and respond, the result is quite different than it would be in an interview with an individual.

Reframing

Haley (1987) says, "It cannot be emphasized enough that the problem the therapist settles on must be a problem which the family wants changed but which is put in a form that makes it solvable" (p. 38). While some problems presented by families lend themselves readily to therapeutic intervention, frequently it is necessary for the therapist to reframe the problem. Reframing may include the following:

1. Operationalizing—casting the problem in observable, behavioral terms. The problem of "a child who is driving us crazy" is reframed by specifying the specific behaviors that are problematic and asking the parents to keep a record of their frequency of occurrence.
2. Emphasizing complementarity—describing the problem in an interactional context, rather than as the property of one member of the family. A father who is depressed is asked, "Who makes you depressed?"
3. Denominalizing—removing a reified diagnostic label and replacing it with a behavior that can be consciously controlled. Anorexia might be reframed as "a girl who refuses to eat."
4. Positive connotation—describing the symptomatic behavior as positively motivated in the service of the family system. A defiant, delinquent boy is described as particularly sensitive to family conflict and his behavior as a sacrificial act designed to keep the parents from divorce.

Giving Directives

Giving directives refers to creating or selecting an intervention that will attack the hypothesized basis of the presenting problem. According to Haley (1987), giving directives has several purposes:

. . . the main goal of therapy is to get people to behave differently and so to have different subjective experiences. Directives are a way of making those changes happen. . . . directives are used to intensify the relationship with the therapist. By telling people what to do, the therapist gets involved in the action . . . directives are used to gather information. When a therapist tells people what to do, the ways they respond give information about them and about how they will respond to the changes wanted. Whether they do what the therapist asks, do not do it, forget to do it, or try and fail, the therapist has information she would not otherwise have. (p. 56)

Directives can be categorized as either compliance- or defiance-oriented. Compliance-oriented directives are offered to families who may be expected to carry out the assignment as given. When the therapist wants the family to carry out the directive, the following should be considered:

1. The directive should be framed in such a way as to use the language and imagery of the family and be focused on solving the problem presented by the family.
2. Avoid asking the family not to do something; ask them to do something different.
3. Ask everyone to do something.
4. Be extremely concrete and repetitive (unless you have reason to be otherwise).
5. Arrange for concrete, specific feedback.
6. Practice the homework during the session, or at least ask the family to tell you in their own words what the assignment includes.
7. Use antisabotage techniques: brainstorm reasons why they might not be able to comply; suggest probable problems that might interfere with compliance; discuss how they can overcome the problems.

Compliance-oriented directives can be either straightforward or paradoxical; the main idea is that you want them to be carried out. An example of a straightforward directive would be to ask Dad to be in charge of the discipline, and ask Mom to keep a record of problem behaviors and report them for his consideration. An example of a compliance-oriented paradoxical directive would be to prescribe the symptom to occur at a special time and place.

The following are some examples of compliance-oriented directives:

1. Caring days: Ask a hostile couple to act as if they care for each other by daily performing five minor behaviors requested by his or her spouse. (LeCroy, Carrol, Nelson-Becker, & Sturlaugson, 1989)

2. Role reversal: Ask a disengaged husband to give his enmeshed wife a vacation from responsibility for the children. He is to be responsible for the meting out of discipline; she may consult with him, but is not to be in charge.

3. Safe practice: Ask a man who is afraid of job interviews to apply for jobs that he would not take if they were offered.

4. Surprise: Ask a couple who are hostile and out of touch with each other to plan a surprise that will please the other, but would be so out of character that the other could never guess what it would be. Each should attempt to guess what the other will do, making a written record of his or her guesses.

5. Symptom prescription: Ask a single mother with two boys who are disrespectful to their mother and constantly fighting to hold a daily wrestling match where she is the referee and will enforce fair fighting; boys are to agree to reserve their fighting to these bouts. Mother is to insist on "the bouts" even if the boys are unwilling.

Defiance-oriented directives are offered to families whom one assumes to be resistant. The intention is to have the family defy the therapist in such a way as to eliminate the problem behavior. Defiance-oriented directives are always paradoxical. They should only be used by therapists who have considerable supervised experience with the use of such directives; they should never be used if there is a risk the family would be harmed if the directive was followed rather than defied. When the therapist wants the family to defy the directives the following should be considered:

1. Do this only with families that have demonstrated their resistance.
2. Use this only after you have joined the family sufficiently to make noncompliance a significant issue. Your relationship to the family should be clearly defined as one of bringing about change.
3. The problem to be solved should be clearly defined and agreed on.
4. The rationale for the directive must utilize the family language and imagery and provide an acceptable rationale for the directive. Haley (1987) says that designing paradoxical directives is easy; you simply observe how the family members are behaving and ask them to continue. How you make the directive appear reasonable and how you react to changes that occur are the hard parts.
5. Give the directive and ask for a report.
6. When the family reports that they did not carry out the homework, condemn the noncompliance and be puzzled and surprised by the symptom reduction. Don't take credit for the change!
7. Repeat the directive and warn against relapse.

The following are some examples of defiance-oriented directives:

1. Positive connotation. Reframe the problem behavior in positive terms and indicate that it would be dangerous for the family to change.
2. Symptom increase. Recommend that the problem behavior be increased in order to get a better understanding of it.
3. Restraining. Recommend that the family slow down in its attempts to solve the problem.
4. Symptom retention. Advise the family to retain a certain percent of the problem in order to remember how awful it was.
5. Predict relapse of a symptom that has been brought under control.

Ordeals

Ordeals are offered to families who are highly motivated to change but can't seem to accomplish their purpose. An ordeal is a behavior that is more obnoxious, frustrating, and time consuming than the symptomatic behavior. The family must agree to perform the ordeal whenever the symptom occurs. Haley (1993b) noted that in order to be successful, the ordeal should contain the following elements:

1. The problem must be clearly defined.
2. The person must be committed to getting over the problem.
3. An ordeal must be selected with the client's collaboration ". . . the ordeal should be voluntary by the person and good for the person experiencing it, but not necessarily for the person imposing it . . . to inadvertently cause a person to suffer is one thing; to arrange it deliberately is quite another." (Haley, 1984, p. 13)
4. The directive must be given with a rationale.
5. The ordeal must continue until the problem is solved.
6. The ordeal is in a social context. The therapist must be prepared to assist in the systemic reorganization that the elimination of the symptom will require.

An example of an ordeal might be a bulimic woman with a stingy husband. The woman has been bingeing and forcing herself to vomit for years. Her husband becomes aware of the symptom and they come to therapy. After establishing a relationship with them and ensuring the couple's commitment to solving the problem, the therapist might offer the following ordeal. When the wife feels she can no longer avoid a binge, she and her husband should go to the store and buy all the foods that the wife prefers to binge on, spending at least $25.00. They are then to return home and together they are to unwrap all of the food and stuff it down the garbage disposal. This is to continue until the wife no longer feels the need to binge.

Jay Haley developed the concept of ordeal therapy as the result of his experience with Milton Erickson. He presents some of Erickson's cases that use the ordeal in *Uncommon Therapy: The Psychiatric Techniques of Milton H. Erickson, MD* (Haley, 1993c); his further development of the concept is presented in his books: *Conversations with Milton H. Erickson, MD: Volume II Changing Families* (Haley, 1985), and *Jay Haley on Milton H. Erickson* (Haley, 1993b).

Rituals

Rituals can be used in therapy to help an individual or family move from one status or state to another. Rituals are particularly helpful in closing off past anger and guilt. The following examples illustrate their use:

> *Closing off the past.* A couple who couldn't resist fighting over wrongs done by the other in the past were asked to write down all their complaints, put them in a box, wrap them carefully, and bury them outside the therapist's window.

They were told that the past was buried there and if they wanted to fight over it, they would have to come to the therapist's office. (Coppersmith, 1985)

Rites of passage. A gentile couple was having difficulty dealing with their 13-year-old son. They were overinvolved and too restrictive; he was increasingly rebellious. They were asked to plan a "Christian bar mitzvah" to symbolize his coming of age.

Ambiguous Assignments

Assignments that are mysterious and apparently unrelated to the presenting problem can be helpful in encouraging a family to find its own solution to its problems. While what is to be done should be clear, the purpose for doing it should be completely obscure at least to the clients. The purpose of the assignment is to depotentiate conscious, linear thinking about the problem and allow creativity in reframing to take place. Milton Erickson often asked people to climb Squaw Peak. The peak, located in north Phoenix near his home, offered a considerable, but not unreasonable, challenge and provided plenty of time to think about why the task was assigned (Lankton, 1988).

Another example would be a task a therapist assigned to a 30-year-old son who was having trouble leaving home: "I'd like you to go to the store and buy a goldfish and everything you will need to take care of it." Interestingly, he defied the directive and instead bought a Christmas cactus because, "It will be easier to take with me when I leave after the holidays."

Assigning Directives

When a directive has been determined, the therapist must also decide how to present it to the family in a way that it will be accepted (or in the case of paradox, rejected). It is important to allow plenty of time to seed the intervention, assign it, clarify it, and practice it. It is also important to couch the task in the family's language and to tie task completion to the presenting problem. Whenever possible, dramatize the assignment by delaying the actual presentation as you ruminate on whether the family is ready for it. The extreme of this dramatization is the "devil's pact" where the assignment is delayed for several sessions and offered only after the family has agreed to comply without knowing what the assignment will be.

Haley (1993a) decries the fact that most clinical training does not include the development of skill in the area of assigning directives and hence that most clinicians must learn it on their own. He indicates most of his own skill in this area was learned from Milton Erickson (Haley, 1993b).

Collecting the Homework

A cardinal rule of this sort of therapy is to be sure to collect the homework, and to take either compliance or noncompliance very seriously. If the homework is ignored or not given sufficient attention, it signals very clearly to the family that compliance is not necessary. The reaction (or nonreaction) of the family to the assignment allows one to aim more carefully on the second attempt. When family members have carried out the task, congratulate them and encourage them to process the experience. Do not explain why the assignment was given or interpret the outcome.

When the family has only partially complied or did not carry out the task, it is often best for the therapist to take the blame for the noncompliance. This assumption of blame indicates to the family that either (a) the assignment was not sufficiently concrete and specific enough for this family to understand or (b) the therapist has miscalculated and the family was not ready for such a task at this time. In either case, in order to demonstrate its capacity for understanding or its readiness for change, the family will be motivated to complete the next task that is assigned (Haley, 1987).

The techniques offered in the section above are, of course, only a brief introduction to the procedures used by various family therapists. Unfortunately, space does not allow a more complete discussion. I am particularly conscious of having omitted the in-session techniques of Virginia Satir (1983) and Carl Whitaker (Connell, Whitaker, Garfield, & Connell, 1990) and the coaching techniques associated with the transgenerational work of Murray Bowen (Kerr & Bowen, 1988). Useful sources for family therapy techniques are the *Procedures in Marriage and Family Therapy* (Brock & Barnard, 1999), *101 Interventions in Family Therapy* (Nelson & Trepper, 1993), and *101 More Interventions in Family Therapy* (Nelson & Trepper, 1998).

PROFESSIONAL ISSUES

Specialization or Profession?

At present there exists a strong debate as to whether family therapy is a professional specialization or a distinct profession (Gladding, Remley, & Huber, 2001). Members of a number of different professions (i.e., psychiatry, nursing, psychology, counseling, and social work) practice family therapy as a professional specialization. In addition, there are mental health practitioners who practice family therapy exclusively and view this work as distinct from the activity of other professions. These practitioners go by the title of Marriage and Family Therapists (MFTs). Who is going to win the above noted debate? Gladding, Remley, and Huber (2001) suggested that this debate most likely will be resolved as a "both-and." That is, *both* MFTs and other mental health professionals will practice family therapy *and* Marriage and Family Therapy will be viewed as a distinct profession.

Professional Associations

A number of professional associations serve mental health practitioners who work with families. The professional association for MFTs is the American Association for Marriage and Family Therapy (AAMFT). Founded in 1942, the goal of this 23,000 member-strong organization is the promotion of Marriage and Family Therapy as a distinct mental health discipline (Shields, Wynne, McDaniel, & Gawinski, 1994).

The professional home for counselors is the American Counseling Association (ACA). Since 1986, the ACA has maintained a division for those members whose professional practice involves family therapy. This division is the International Association of Marriage and Family Counselors (IAMFC). The IAMFC's goals include:

1. Promote skill development in systems theory, couple counseling, and family counseling.
2. Promote standards in marriage and family counseling.
3. Promote public policy and legislation for marriage and family counseling.
4. Promote research and knowledge in marriage and family counseling.
5. Promote awareness of multiculturalism and diversity in marriage and family counseling.
6. Promote the use of technology in marriage and family counseling. (International Association of Marriage and Family Counselors, 2003)

Currently, the IAMFC has approximately 7,500 members. Other organizations with a family therapy focus include the American Family Therapy Academy (AFTA), Division 43 of the American Psychological Association (APA), and the Family Therapy Section of the National Council on Family Relations (NCFR).

Licensure/Certification

Currently, forty-two states have enacted certification or licensure laws for mental health professionals who practice family therapy (American Association for Marriage and Family Therapy, 2003a). A growing trend is state-to-state licensure reciprocity and licensure uniformity (Gladding, 2002). At the federal level, regulations recognizing family therapy as a "core" mental health profession were set forth in the early 1990s (Shields et al., 1994). National certification as a marriage and family therapist is available to professional counselors through the National Academy for Certified Family Therapists (NACFT).

Program Accreditation

Two organizations accredit programs that train persons to practice family therapy. The Commission on Accreditation for Marriage and Family Therapy Education (COAMFTE) accredits programs that prepare MFTs. COAMFTE accreditation covers both degree granting programs and post-graduate training institutes. Currently, sixty-nine programs possess COAMFTE accreditation (American Association for Marriage and Family Therapy, 2003b). In their study of MFT training, Touliatos and Lindholm (1992) found COAMFTE accredited programs and non-accredited programs to be similar.

The other accrediting body is the Council for Accreditation of Counseling and Related Educational Programs (CACREP). This organization accredits programs that prepare persons to serve as professional counselors with the following specializations: (a) school counseling, (b) mental health counseling, (c) community agency counseling, (d) student affairs, and (e) marriage and family therapy. CACREP only accredits degree-granting programs. Currently, there are sixteen CACREP accredited marriage and family therapy programs (Council for Accreditation of Counseling and Related Educational Programs, 2003).

Ethical and Legal Issues

The ethical codes of the AAMFT (1998), ACA (1995), and APA (1992) are applicable to the practice of family therapy, but the IAMFC code (2003) is perhaps the most relevant to professional counselors practicing family therapy. Elsewhere in this text (Chapter 3), Stauffer and Kurpius present the legal and ethical issues related to counseling. However, when one assumes a family systems orientation, some special issues arise. Common issues that are especially problematic for the family therapist include:

Responsibility—Who is the client? Is it possible to serve all members of a family even-handedly? Can you define the family system or the relationship as the client? Does insisting on seeing the whole family before treatment can begin deny treatment to those who are motivated? Is it ethical to coerce reluctant members into therapy?

Confidentiality—Is the promise of confidentiality given to the family as a unit, or does it apply to individual family members? What should be done about information obtained from an individual prior to the involvement of other family members? Can you offer confidentiality to children when seen in a family therapy context? If family members are seen separately during family therapy, should they be promised confidentiality? Does privileged communication exist for a family? Will a written agreement not to subpoena hold up legally? Can one member of the family waive privileged communication for all?

Therapist control—Is it appropriate for the therapist to increase the family stress in order to bring about change? Should the therapist use indirect (hypnotic, metaphoric) or paradoxical procedures that bypass conscious processes? Is the use of such techniques a violation of the concept of informed consent? In dealing with "inappropriate hierarchies" may the therapist impose his or her own values on the family? Is family therapy antithetical to the feminist perspective?

Informed consent—Who should consent to treatment? What needs to be disclosed? How can a therapist utilize defiance-oriented directives or paradox and provide full disclosure?

Third-party payments—Is it ethical for a family therapist working within a systems perspective to assign a diagnostic label to an individual in order to obtain payment? Is not such labeling antithetical to a systems therapist's core beliefs? (Adapted from Becvar & Becvar, 2002; Gladding, Remley, & Huber, 2001; Margolin, 1982; Patten, Barnett, & Houlihan, 1991).

The current context does not allow space for resolution of these issues, and in fact, several of them cannot be readily resolved. The counselor who is interested in working within a family therapy perspective should, however, be aware of these issues and be prepared to grapple with them.

RESEARCH IN FAMILY THERAPY

Background

The history of family therapy research is filled with contradictions. On one hand, this specialization/profession emerged from research projects such as Bateson's work on schizophrenia (Bateson et al., 1956). On the other hand, empirical research has been largely ignored in family therapy (Diamond, Serrano, Dickey, & Sonis, 1996; Gladding, 2002; Lebow & Gurman, 1995; Shields et al., 1994). In a major review of family therapy research, Lebow and Gurman (1995) noted that:

> In reviewing the research base of couple and family therapy, one faces a basic dilemma. Traditional empirical research has not been the foundation for the development of these modes of practice, nor has it been the fabric of much of this work. . . . Alternative modes of investigation such as inductive reasoning, clinical observation, and deconstruction have dominated in the development of methods and treatment models. Some couple and family therapists have even been reluctant to acknowledge that empirical research has an important role. At one discouraging point, now fortunately past, there was considerable debate about whether traditional research had any relevant role in the development of family therapy. (p. 29)

In the past decade, the growth of empirical research in family therapy has been remarkable. Thus, now mental health practitioners, health insurers, and the public at large possess the ability to compare and contrast family therapy with other types of interventions.

In terms of family therapy research, three questions that any future professional counselor should address are:

1. Does family therapy work?
2. What are the professional practice patterns of family therapists?
3. How does one access family therapy research in order to enhance one's professional practice?

Each of these questions will be addressed below separately.

Does Family Therapy Work?

Research that examines whether an intervention works is known as *outcome* research. In family therapy, a dearth of outcome research left the above question unanswered until the late 1980s. Only at that time had a sufficient number of studies been published to allow researchers to conduct meta-analyses of the family therapy research literature. Meta-analysis is a research technique by which multiple individual studies can be grouped together to empirically analyze the overall effectiveness of a particular intervention approach. Hazelrigg, Cooper, and Borduin (1987) conducted the first meta-analysis of family therapy outcome research. In their meta-analysis of twenty studies, they found that family therapy had a positive effect on clients when

TABLE 17.4   Research Support for Efficacious Treatment

ISSUE
Adolescent Drug Abuse
Agoraphobia
Alcoholism
Anxiety
Conduct/Oppositional Disorders
Delinquency
Depression
Eating Disorders
Parenting Skills
Pediatric Psychopathy
Schizophrenia

Note: Table based upon research reported in Alexander and Barton (1995), Diamond et al. (1996), Kazdin (1997), and Lebow and Gurman (1995).

compared to either no treatment or an alternative treatment. Subsequent meta-analyses have confirmed that family therapy is indeed an efficacious mental health treatment approach (Hahlweg & Markman, 1988; Markus, Lange, & Pettigrew, 1990; Shadish, 1992; Shadish et al., 1993).

In addition to knowledge concerning the overall effectiveness of family therapy, strong evidence exists in the research literature concerning the effectiveness of this type of therapy with a wide range of problems. Table 17.4 lists a variety of issues where treatment by family therapy has been proven efficacious. Overall, it is known that families treated with family-based interventions improved more than at least 67 percent of families treated with alternative treatments or no treatment (Diamond et al., 1996).

What Are the Professional Practice Patterns of Family Therapists?

Within the mental health service provider community, there exists a prejudice that family therapists do nothing more than "interminable marriage counseling for trivial problems" (Simmons & Doherty, 1995, p. 5). Surprisingly, little research on the practice patterns of family therapists has been conducted. Thus, research evidence that could challenge the above prejudice has not existed until recently. The groundbreaking studies on this topic were conducted by the research team of Bill Doherty and Deborah Simmons.

Doherty and Simmons (1996) studied the professional practice patterns of a random sample of MFTs drawn from fifteen states. The practice variables they examined included (a) caseload, (b) presenting problem, (c) diagnosis, and (d) length of treatment. They found that MFTs, on average had twenty-four clients in their active caseload and completed twenty client contact hours per week. The clients served by the MFTs presented a multitude of problems at the commencement of treatment. These problems included (a) depression (44 percent), (b) marital problems (30 percent), (c) anxiety (21 percent), and (d) parent-child problems (13 percent). Adjustment Disorder was the modal diagnostic category (25 percent). Other prevalent diagnostic categories included Depressive Disorder (23 percent) and Anxiety Disorders (14 percent). The median number of sessions per client was 12. Interestingly, almost one-half (49.4 percent) of the treatment provided by the national sample of *marriage and family* therapists was individual counseling. Doherty and Simmons's research studies suggest that family therapists *do* serve clients with serious problems.

In 1996, Doherty and Simmons noted that median fee per hour charged by MFTs was $80. The AAMFT (2003c) reports that 58 percent of MFTs in private practice make less than $50,000 per year. In addition, Todd (1998) reports that managed care organizations (MCOs) are driving down the fees MFTs can charge. Todd stated that "it is quite likely that reimbursement rates could reach $25–$30 per hour (or lower) for outpatient services. For sure, fees will not keep up with the cost of living" (p. 2). The other factors Todd identified for declining fees included (a) the MCOs' tight reign on approved provider lists and (b) the over-supply of mental health practitioners.

Simmons and Doherty (1998) also studied whether the practice patterns of MFTs differed in reference to training background. They examined whether clinical members of the AAMFT from four disciplinary groups (i.e., counseling, marriage and family therapy, social work, psychology) differed in terms of clinical practice or client satisfaction. Simmons and Doherty found that "results showed highly similar practice patterns and client outcomes across all four disciplinary groups" (p. 321).

How Does One Access Family Therapy Research in Order to Enhance One's Professional Practice?

The vast majority of family therapy research can be found in professional journals. Both the IAMFC and the AAMFT sponsor such journals that they send to their members. These journals are *The Family Journal* (IAMFC) and the *Journal of Marital and Family Therapy* (AAMFT). Easy access to research is one of the major benefits of membership in a professional association. Other family therapy journals include *American Journal of Family Therapy, Child and Family Behavior Therapy, Family Process, Family Therapy, Journal of Family Psychology, Journal of Family Psychotherapy, Journal of Feminist Family Therapy*, and *Journal of Systemic Therapies*.

SUMMARY

This chapter has attempted to introduce the reader to the contextual thinking that is the essence of family therapy. I have tried to illustrate this perspective through descriptions of family therapy diagnosis, interviewing, and treatment. In family therapy, diagnosis focuses on interpersonal rather than intrapersonal dysfunction. Sound family therapy interviewing follows a distinct eight-stage process beginning with presession planning and ending with postsession debriefing. Family therapy treatment is rich with powerful techniques. These techniques include circular questioning and ordeal prescription among others.

In addition to diagnosis, interviewing, and treatment, professional issues that are of concern to family therapists were addressed. These issues include licensure, training, professional development, and ethics. Finally, the evidence for the efficacy of family therapy was reviewed. It is my hope that this brief introduction to the concepts and techniques of family therapy will whet the reader's appetite for further exploration.

CHAPTER EIGHTEEN

COUNSELING GAY, LESBIAN, AND BISEXUAL CLIENTS

JENNIE L. MILLER, PH.D.
Healing Plains Mental Health

REESE M. HOUSE, ED.D.
Readers Digest Foundation

There are at least 20 to 25 million gay, lesbian, and bisexual individuals in the United States, based on the estimate that approximately 10–15 percent of the adult population is gay (Betz & Fitzgerald, 1993; Brown, 1996; Fassinger, 1991; Kinsey, Pomeroy & Martin, 1948; Kinsey, Pomeroy, Martin, & Gebhard, 1953; Schlager, 1998; Singer & Deschamps, 1994). These figures may actually underestimate the true number of gay, lesbian, and bisexual individuals in society as many individuals do not report same gender activity due to the stigma attached to being gay in our society. Recently, some studies have questioned the 10–15 percent figure and found the number of reported gay individuals closer to 5 percent (Singer & Deschamps, 1994). However as Singer and Deschamps stated: "gross underreporting in many studies, especially those that involve face-to-face interviews with researchers, is pervasive" (p. 9).

Whatever the exact number of gays, lesbians, and bisexuals in the United States, they are becoming more visible and active in their pursuit of equal rights. Before the 1970s, sexual orientation was a fairly invisible part of the American population. This invisibility was, to a large extent, by choice. The stigmatization of homosexuality in our society caused most gays, lesbians, and bisexuals to avoid the risks associated with disclosing their sexual orientation. "Hostility and discrimination at the hands of an unaccepting society created a climate of secrecy that did not permit challenges to the prevailing stereotypes" (Blumstein & Schwartz, 1983, p. 9). In the last thirty years, great numbers of gays developed a community identity to counter negative reactions from society. This "coming out" of gays has provoked considerable backlash and antigay sentiment throughout the United States. Sexual prejudice continues to be pervasive in the United States despite a decrease in moral condemnation in the 1990s and an increase in reported opposition to antigay discrimination (Herek, 2000).

As more and more people identify themselves as gay and become more visible, all members of society, including counselors, will be forced to address issues involving sexual orientation. All counselors have clients who are gay. Some of these clients will be self-identified as gay and some will hide their gay identity and pass as heterosexual. Some counselors may say, "I don't know anyone who is gay or lesbian," or "No gay people will come to me as a high school counselor or pastoral counselor," or " I have no gay clients on my caseload." These perceptions are inaccurate. Whether a counselor has a private practice, works for an agency, school, church, business, or in the military, he or she will have gay, lesbian, and bisexual clients. This chapter provides an introduction to basic facts and issues about being gay that will help counselors become effective when working with gay clients and their families and friends.

Who Is Gay, Lesbian, or Bisexual?

The initial challenge for counselors may be in determining a client's sexual orientation. There is no typical gay, lesbian, or bisexual. Contrary to prevailing stereotypes, all gay males are not hairdressers with platform shoes and excessive jewelry. Neither do all lesbians wear flannel shirts and blue jeans. There is no description that is completely inclusive and describing the "typical" gay male, lesbian, or bisexual is impossible. Gay, lesbian, and bisexual people come from a cross-section of races, nationalities, religions, socioeconomic levels, family backgrounds, geographical locations, and cultures. There are gay parents, spouses, children, teenagers, couples, grandparents, uncles, aunts, and cousins. Similarly, the sexual orientation of an individual cannot be determined by occupation. Gays are business owners, ministers, teachers, lawyers, truck drivers, members of the armed services, and industrial workers. The following examples illustrate the diversity of gay clients.

1. Sally and Jennifer are a lesbian couple who have been living as partners in the same small community for ten years. They are 31 and 34. Sally is a nurse and Jennifer works as a counselor in a drug treatment program. Sally and Jennifer decided they wanted to have a child together and Sally was artificially inseminated. Their son Kevin is now 7 and attends public school. As co-parents, the two women attend school functions and work with Kevin's teachers on his academic and social progress. Sally and Jennifer face the same issues as any couple in raising a child. However, some teachers are uncomfortable working with Sally and Jennifer as co-parents and some children tease Kevin about having two mothers.

2. Chet is a 33-year-old male lawyer who has entered a 28-day treatment program for cocaine abuse. He is a successful attorney, practicing in a large law firm. He is gay and lives with his lover of 3 years. No one at work knows that he is gay. As a closeted individual, he is reluctant to discuss his sexual orientation in the treatment program. However, the issue of being gay and closeted, which requires leading a "double" life, causes stress and exacerbates his abuse of cocaine. Chet must face his abuse issues in treatment and also needs to address the issues surrounding his gay life, or the treatment is not likely to be successful.

3. Joe is a 19-year-old freshman in college who was a star football player in high school. Joe confronts the usual stresses of all college freshmen. In addition, he has discovered that he is attracted to men. On a visit back home, he tries to discuss his feelings with his high school football coach, whom he trusts and respects. The football coach is unclear about how to respond to Joe and seeks the advice of the high school counselor.

4. Rosalind dated boys throughout high school and college and always imagined that she would get married and have children. She was engaged at one time, but things did not work out. After college graduation, Rosalind developed a close friendship with a woman at work. The friendship moved to a more intimate level and they engaged in a consensual sexual relationship. Rosalind did not identify as a lesbian and found that she was still attracted to both men and women. After struggling with this dual attraction, Rosalind sought counseling to explore the issue of being bisexual.

A Word About Words

Language is important for what it communicates as well as what it implies. Gay, lesbian, and bisexual individuals hear biased and offensive street language such as "queer," "faggot," "homo," "dyke," and "queen" throughout their lives. This language affects self-esteem, stigmatizes gays and lesbians, and is just as offensive to them as ethnic slurs are to ethnic populations. Thus, gays, lesbians, and bisexuals are sensitive to terminology.

Many reject the term "homosexual" because it is the term used by the dominant and often oppressing class in our culture. Though it is commonly used in the professional literature, media, and popular fiction, the term "homosexual" reflects an inaccurately narrow, clinical focus on sexual conduct. It is seen by many as archaic, imprecise, and misleading (Miller, House, & Tyler, 2001). The term "homoerotic" is another clinical term that is similarly narrow and is frequently rejected as a noninclusive term. Another term frequently questioned is "sexual preference." Preference implies that individuals choose to be gay, lesbian, or bisexual. There is increasing evidence that sexual predisposition is biologically innate; thus the term "sexual orientation" is now considered the more acceptable term ("Avoiding Heterosexual Bias in Language," 1991; Ritter & O'Neill, 1989).

As counselors work with clients, they need to be aware that clients may strongly object to certain terms. Though *gay* is often used as a general term for both men and women, not everyone will be comfortable being called "gay." Most women who use an identifying term prefer to be called lesbian or gay women, and most men who identify as gay men prefer to be called gay rather than homosexual. Some individuals prefer the term bisexual. Recently the term "queer" is being used more by gays, lesbians, and bisexuals as a way of shifting its meaning from a derogatory sense to a position of empowerment (Guiterrez, 2004; Tierney & Dilley, 1998). Language is fluid and changes depending on the context and the individual. Counselors need to simply ask clients their terminology preference rather than use language that might be offensive to some individuals.

Why Are People Gay, Lesbian, or Bisexual?

What causes people to be gay, lesbian, or bisexual is currently a matter of controversy. The causes of sexual orientation have not yet been determined and it seems increasingly clear that no one factor can explain so complex and variable a trait as sexual orientation (Byne, 1997; Levay, 1996; Levay & Hamer, 1994; Rosario, 1997). The most recent studies suggest that biological factors are involved in the determination of sexual orientation (Hershberger, 1997; Turkheimer, 1998; Wright, 1999). Genetic patterns, pre- and postnatal hormonal activity, environmental/biological toxins, and brain structure differences are areas being explored as possible causes of sexual orientation (LeVay & Hamer, 1994; Pillard, 1996). Several researchers support the idea that genes may influence or predispose individuals, but emphasize that environmental cues and social learning play a key role in creating the broad continuum of sexual orientation (Bailey & Dawood, 1998; Bailey, Dunne, & Martin, 2000; Johnston & Bell, 1995; LeVay & Hamer, 1994; Pattatucci, 1998).

Whatever the causes of sexual orientation, counselors need to recognize "that persons with diverse sexual orientations exist and that the existence of this diversity is not pathological" (Dworkin & Gutierrez, 1989, p. 7). Same gender sexual orientation is a "valid developmental outcome for many adults" (Morin & Rothblum, 1991, p. 947) and counselors need to assist gays, lesbians, and bisexuals in a nonbiased and professional manner.

Definition of Gay, Lesbian, and Bisexual

Stein and Cohen (1986) define homosexuality as "an attraction for a person of the same sex within one or more of the dimensions of affection, fantasy, or erotic desire" (p. 28). However, it is not always easy to define who is gay, lesbian, or bisexual. A significant number of people in society have same-sex relations. How do we know which of these individuals is lesbian, gay, or bisexual? What about the adolescent male who fantasizes about another boy in the classroom? Or the individual who has had a few same-sex experiences as a teenager? What about the woman who feels an occasional attraction to another woman? Or the person who has sexual desires for a person of the same gender but never acts upon the desire? What about the married man with children who identifies as heterosexual, but has sex with men outside of marriage?

The answers to these and many other questions about sexual orientation are often confusing and unclear. Terminology used in professional writing about homosexuality has often been imprecise (Bohan, 1996; Krajeski, 1986). Part of the confusion results from the "popular misconception that homosexuality and sex are one and the same" (Blumenfeld & Raymond, 1988, p. 85). The fact that an individual engages in specific sexual conduct does not define that person's sexual orientation.

Kinsey et al. (1948) were the first to indicate that the labels "homosexuality" and "heterosexuality" do not describe most people. They concluded that people's

TABLE 18.1   **The Kinsey Scale of the Continuum of Human Sexual Experience**

KINSEY RATING	DESCRIPTION
0	Exclusively heterosexual in psychological response and behavior
1	Predominantly heterosexual; incidental homosexual behavior
2	Predominantly heterosexual; more than incidental homosexual behavior
3	Equally heterosexual and homosexual in psychological response and behavior
4	Predominantly homosexual; more than incidental heterosexual behavior
5	Predominantly homosexual; incidental heterosexual behavior
6	Exclusively homosexual in psychological response and behavior

orientations were not exclusive and that homosexuality and heterosexuality are poles on a continuum (see Table 18.1). This continuum suggests that people have a range in both sexual attractions and sexual behaviors. Some people are always attracted to a person of the opposite gender. Others are always attracted to a person of the same gender. However, many people are attracted to and act sexually with both genders.

The term "bisexual" has existed as a concept since the process of psychosexual development was conceptualized by Freud and his contemporaries, but not until recently have bisexuals been included in theory or research about sexual orientation (Bohan, 1996; Fox, 1995; Fox 2000; Weinberg, Williams, & Pryor, 1994). "Bisexuality has been continually attacked as a nonentity, a transitional stage from heterosexuality to homosexuality or vice-versa, and as a denial of one's homosexuality" (Wolf, 1992, p. 175).

Klein (1993) found that the Kinsey continuum did not adequately explain the complexity of sexual orientation, and in addressing the issue of bisexuality, asked such questions as "what does it mean to be a Kinsey 2 or 3?" (p. 15). He developed seven distinct variables (Table 18.2) that can be used with clients to help clarify the complexity of sexual orientation.

It is important to understand that *sexual attraction* is not synonymous with *sexual behavior*. A person can be attracted to one gender and yet have sex with another. This may or may not be the case with Rosalind, described earlier in this chapter, who is questioning her sexual behavior with both men and women. Asking about *sexual fantasies* is often a helpful tool in counseling and many believe that one's fantasies and dreams are the most important criterion in determining sexual orientation (Klein, 1993). Sexual fantasies can change over the life span and these changes provide important information for counselors. The fourth variable, *emotional preference*, focuses on which gender an individual prefers to be emotionally involved with. *Social preference* addresses the degree to which a person likes to socialize with members of his or her own gender, or the opposite gender. *Heterosexual or homosexual lifestyle*, the sixth variable, asks whether the person lives in the heterosexual or homosexual social world. Does he or she have mostly bisexual, lesbian, or gay friends or mostly heterosexual

TABLE 18.2   Seven Variables of Sexual Orientation

1. Sexual Attraction
2. Sexual Behavior
3. Sexual Fantasies
4. Emotional Preference
5. Social Preference
6. Heterosexual or Homosexual Lifestyle
7. Self-identification

friends and acquaintances? *Self-identification* asks the individual to state whether they identify themselves as gay, lesbian, bisexual, or heterosexual. Using these seven variables, Klein developed the Sexual Orientation Grid to help develop a profile in clarifying sexual orientation. Using the grid, individuals rate themselves on a 7-point scale indicating their sexual orientation in the past, the present, and the ideal situation.

It is important to differentiate between "act" and "identity" when discussing sexual orientation. Individuals who focus only on the "act" believe that sexual acts or behaviors define the person. When using this concept, labels are given to the behaviors in question rather than to the person engaging in the behavior (Blumenfeld & Raymond, 1988). However, this behavior-based definition fails to recognize a holistic view of the person. For example, a male teenager who experiments with same-sex behavior does not necessarily have a gay identity. The experimental behavior is just that and to label someone as "homosexual" or "gay" because of such experimentation does not take into account the developmental nature of sexuality.

Palma & Stanley (2002) point out that counselors should emphasize sexual identity formation as a process that acknowledges personal and cultural factors interacting reciprocally in self-identification. Under this approach, being gay is associated with a lifestyle, not just sexual desires or behavior.

> Being gay is not merely the ability and willingness to engage in homosexual behavior. Indeed, being gay is being different, having a distinct identity, frequently in a way that is felt even before it is consciously or sexually expressed. Gayness is a special affinity and a special feeling toward people of the same gender; it is not the inability to love and to relate to others, nor is it a denial of the opposite sex. Rather it is a special capacity and need to love and to express one's love for people of the same gender in all the meanings of the term "love." (Woodman & Lenna, 1980, p. 11)

When society categorizes an individual using only one dimension of humanness, a significant part of that person is omitted. This omission leads to stereotyping and labeling which have a significant and detrimental impact on the individual. Examples of such stereotyping and labeling include "He is a dumb jock; what is he doing with a philosophy major?" "She's a woman; she shouldn't do that kind of work." "He's gay; he should not be working with children." "She is married; she couldn't possibly be bisexual." All of these statements focus on only one aspect of the individual. By focusing on an isolated aspect, the person in each of these examples is minimized and reduced to that one aspect—an unfair and inaccurate characterization of the whole person. The more holistic approach to human behavior focuses on the integration of all aspects of the individual, including the emotional, social, intellectual, spiritual, and physical dimensions of each person. This approach recognizes that individuals are unique and emphasizes the importance of looking at the whole person rather than determining someone's worth based on a single characteristic.

Counselors who work with gays, lesbians, and bisexuals need to consider the more holistic view and realize that while sexual activity is a part of many relationships, it is frequently not the primary focus of relationships. Not all gay, lesbian, and bisexual clients will come to counseling to address issues related to sexual orientation. Counselors need to address the issues that are presented and not make sexual orientation the problem.

HOMOPHOBIA AND HETEROSEXISM

Cultural Homophobia

We live in a homophobic culture. The term *homophobia* was first defined by Weinberg (1973) as a fear, dread, or loathing of gays and lesbians. Perhaps it would be more accurate to describe homophobia as a fear of individuals who are "perceived" to be gay, lesbian, or bisexual. People who are homophobic rely upon their own preconceived ideas of sexuality and often make a point of condemning, punishing, and even outlawing gays and lesbians (Forstein, 1986; Rothblum & Bond, 1996; Rubenstein, 1993). It is important to note that individuals are not born with homophobia and heterosexism; these are attitudes learned and acquired by interaction with other individuals (Yep, 1997).

People who are homophobic downgrade, deny, or stereotype the existence of gays, lesbians, and bisexuals. These phobic and negative responses range from individuals who tell "fag" or "queer" jokes to the extreme examples of violence against and murder of gays, lesbians, and bisexuals. Documented hate crimes including physical violence and harassment against gays and lesbians have increased dramatically over the past few years (National Gay & Lesbian Task Force [NGLTF], 2003). As Mel White (1995) stated: "there is a war raging against gay and lesbian people in our country right now. Our civil rights are on the line. Our freedom is at stake. The homophobic lies of the religious right are murdering the souls and threatening the civil rights of gay and lesbian Americans" (p. 284).

Public figures have fueled the flames of bigotry through their public comments. Jerry Falwell and Pat Robertson, fundamentalist Christian pastors, continue to bash gays as a part of their fund-raising campaigns. The "Family Research Council" and "Focus on the Family" are only two of the more prominent organizations that are committed to waging war against what they call "the homosexual agenda." Radio talk show hosts and authors, such as Rush Limbaugh and Dr. Laura Schlessinger, rail against the "homosexual lobby" and "biological mistakes." Fred Phelps, a minister from Kansas, who maintains a website "godhatesfags.com" pickets the funerals of people who have died of AIDS with signs that say "sodomites," "fags," and "You are damning souls and dooming America" (White, 1995). He and his followers were protestors at the 1998 funeral of Matthew Shepard, a University of Wyoming student, who was pistol-whipped, tied to a fence, and left to die by two individuals who knew that because Shepard was gay he would be an easy target for robbery (Lopez, 1998). These examples of homophobia by public figures perpetuate homophobia, giving it the credibility of public statement without societal retribution. One need only imagine the response to similar statements about racial or religious minorities to see clearly the societal acceptance of public expressions of homophobia. Such comments create a polarization between gays and the members of society who purport and tolerate such homophobic comments.

Cultural homophobia is also manifested in the widespread discrimination faced by gays. Gay individuals are discriminated against in employment, housing, and within religious and community organizations. Certain career positions like teaching, the military, police, and public office are frequently available only to those who keep their sexual orientation hidden. The Boy Scouts have successfully upheld their right through the Supreme Court to exclude gay people from being members of their organization (Penn, 2003). Likewise, those who are known or perceived to be gay are frequently denied housing. In fact in 1998, Maine reversed a statewide gay-rights law prohibiting housing and employment discrimination (Peyser, 1998). In twelve states and a number of municipalities it is legal to dismiss employees or to not allow individuals to purchase or rent property simply because they are gay (National Gay & Lesbian Task Force [NGLTF], 2003). Gays, lesbians, and bisexuals are also denied the sanctuary of religious organizations on the basis of their sexual orientation. The Catholic church continues to denounce homosexual activity and same-sex marriage through a recent published position paper "Homosexuality and Hope" (Georgemiller & Stevenson, 2003).

Cultural Heterosexism

Cultural heterosexism assumes that heterosexuality is or should be the only acceptable sexual orientation. Heterosexism "is so ubiquitous that it is hardly noticeable. Even a cursory survey of American society reveals that homosexuality is largely hidden and when publicly recognized, it is usually condemned or stigmatized" (Herek, 1993, p. 90). As Sears pointed out, "there is a subtle pervasive uneasiness with persons whose sexual identity is nonheterosexual" (Sears, 1997, p. 16). Though closely aligned with homophobia, it is less blatant and overt, and does not usually involve active aggression against gays and lesbians. This type of oppression creates a climate where "it is not necessary, most of the time, to beat us up or to murder or torture us to ensure our silence and invisibility" (Kitzinger, 1996, p. 11). However, heterosexism demands heterosexuality in return for first-class citizenship. There are a myriad of subtle and indirect ways that the system reinforces heterosexuality as the only acceptable and viable life option, for example: (1) parental expectations that their children will marry a person of the opposite sex; (2) media portrayals of positive and satisfying relationships as exclusively heterosexual; (3) the presumption by teachers that all of their students are straight; and the exclusion of any discussion of homosexuality in most classes (Blumenfeld & Raymond, 1988). Cultural heterosexism is a more insidious form of discrimination, and occurs by neglect, omission, and/or distortion while homophobia is discrimination by intent and design (Blumenfeld & Raymond, 1988).

Heterosexism, along with homophobia, are societal norms in the United States against which gays, lesbians, and bisexuals must struggle and result in prejudice, discrimination, harassment, and antigay violence (Pearson, 2003; Rothblum & Bond, 1996; Sears & Williams, 1997). These societal norms exclude openly gay, lesbian, and bisexual individuals from social, religious, and political power and force them into silence concerning their lives (Herek, 2000; Mollenkott, 1985). Gay youth and their families are constantly battling issues within the educational system regarding safety and equality. Gays are also denied legal recognition as couples, leading to limitations on visitations in hospitals, custody rights, survivorship benefits, and the denial of the right to participate in a variety of other benefits available only to married couples.

In spite of these efforts to blame and silence them, lesbians, gay men, and bisexuals have made tremendous social and political gains in the past thirty-five years. These advances include securing passage of protective state and local legislation and gaining considerable status as a minority community in American society (Herek, 2000; Lacayo, 1998; Peyser, 1998). Congress finally passed a Hate Crimes Statistics Bill, which mandates collection of statistics on bias crimes of all kinds, including antigay crimes ". . . this has been heralded by activists as a significant victory for gay rights" (Fassinger, 1991 p. 163). According to the most recent report released by the FBI in 2001, there were 1,317 reported antigay hate crimes in 1999, with sexual orientation bias-motivated crimes being third and with religion and race as second and first; there is also a reported trend since 1996 that antigay violence has been increasing steadily (PFLAG, 2003).

As counselors work with gays, lesbians, and bisexuals, they need to be sensitive to the effects of homophobia and heterosexism on their clients. Individuals may question their sexual orientation and experience it as a source of pain, danger, and punishment rather than love, intimacy, and community. Herek (2000) notes that sexual prejudice remains widespread in the United States; even though moral condemnation seems to have decreased in the 1990s, opposition to antigay discrimination has been increasing. Many counselors are beginning to realize that gay individuals are at a higher risk for problems due to society's oppressive and hostile reactions rather than attributing them to one's sexual orientation (Pearson, 2003; Reynolds & Hanjorgiris, 2000).

Internalized Homophobia

Internalized homophobia represents an internalization of the negative attitudes and assumptions of societal homophobia by an individual (Sophie, 1987). Internalized homophobia results from the combination of negative attitudes apparent in cultural homophobia and an individual's own fear of being gay, lesbian, or bisexual. Gay individuals learn to fear their sexual orientation from the negative attitudes expressed by others in society. "Bisexuals, lesbians, and gay males live in a world that teaches that same-sex activity is morally repulsive, psychologically damaging, or that it does not exist at all" (Blumenfeld & Raymond, 1988, p. 264). This negative information about their sexuality comes from credible sources like friends, family, church, school, and mass media. When this information is internalized, it creates substantial dissonance. Such dissonance often results in low self-esteem, threatens the development of identity, and becomes a major source of distress for gay clients. Gay clients have reported higher levels of depression, anger, anxiety, as well as symptoms of posttraumatic stress (Herek, Gogan, Gillis, & Glunt, 1998).

Homophobia and Heterosexism in Counselors

Counselors are raised in the same homophobic and heterosexist culture as everyone else. Counselors may believe that they are not afflicted with homophobia or heterosexism and that they are immune from negative responses toward gays. However, such immunity seems unlikely. Counselors who have not confronted their homophobic beliefs and behaviors provide inadequate, improper, and harmful services to gay clients and those related to or dependent on them (Carroll & Gilroy, 2001; Matthews & Bieschke, 2001; Pearson, 2003). Ethical codes of the counseling profession emphasize that discrimination on the basis of sexual orientation is not ethical or acceptable. As Buhrke (1989) states "it is the ethical counselor who respects the worth, dignity, potential, and uniqueness, of heterosexual, bisexual, and lesbian and gay people" (p. 77).

Table 18.3 identifies personal homophobia assessment questions, developed by the National Association of Social Workers [NASW], (1985, pp. 153–154) to help counselors identify and address their own homophobia. The questions may also be used in counseling sessions with clients who are dealing with homophobia issues.

Changing Attitudes

The struggle for equality by gays is currently at the center of political and social struggles in American life. This struggle will likely continue. When President Bill Clinton directed the change in military policy toward lesbians and gays, a heated backlash and debate erupted. This is only one example of the emerging presence of gay issues that are increasingly visible in newspapers, radio, TV, magazines, and movies. Interestingly enough, from 1994 to 1997 there was a 67 percent increase in discharges of gay military personnel (Peyser, 1998). Americans are being forced to take a stand on an issue that they previously had ignored or denied. With this attention, there have been an increased number of surveys and opinion polls asking Americans their views on gay issues.

General trends in these surveys indicate that the American public is becoming more accepting of gays and lesbians. In 1983, a survey by *Newsweek* magazine reported that 66 percent of the U.S. population felt that homosexuality was an unacceptable lifestyle (Blumenfeld & Raymond, 1988). *Newsweek* conducted a similar poll in 1992 and found that 53 percent of the public thought homosexuality was an unacceptable

TABLE 18.3   Personal Homophobia Assessment Questions

1. Do you stop yourself from doing or saying certain things because someone might think you are gay, lesbian, or bisexual? If yes, what kinds of things?

2. Do you ever intentionally do or say things so that people will think you are not gay? If yes, what kinds of things?

3. Do you believe that gays or lesbians can influence others to become gay or lesbian? Do you think someone could influence you to change your sexual orientation?

4. If you are a parent, how would you (or do you) feel about having a lesbian, gay, or bisexual daughter or son?

5. How do you think you would feel if you discovered that one of your parents or parent figures, or a brother or sister, were gay, lesbian, or bisexual?

6. Are there any jobs, positions, or professions that you think lesbians, gays, and bisexuals should be barred from holding or entering? If yes, why so?

7. Would you go to a physician whom you knew or believed to be gay, lesbian, or bisexual if that person were of a different gender from you? If that person were of the same gender as you? If not, why not?

8. If someone you care about were to say to you, "I think I'm gay," would you suggest that the person see a therapist?

9. Have you ever been to a gay or lesbian bar, social club, party, or march? If not, why not?

10. Would you wear a button that says "How dare you assume that I'm heterosexual"? If not, why not?

11. Can you think of three positive aspects of a gay, lesbian, or bisexual lifestyle? Can you think of three negative aspects of a heterosexual lifestyle?

12. Have you ever laughed at a "queer" joke?

lifestyle (Wilson, 1992). *Time* reported in their 1998 survey that 52 percent of the population believed that homosexual relationships were "acceptable for others, but not for self" compared to 35 percent in a similar poll conducted in 1978; that 12 percent thought homosexual relationships were "acceptable for others and self" in 1998 compared to only 6 percent in 1978; that 33 percent said homosexual relationships were "not acceptable at all" in 1998 compared to 59 percent in 1978 (Lacayo, 1998).

Also, there is a growing consensus that gays, like other minorities, deserve protection from job discrimination. Yang (1999) reported that 70 percent of Americans from 1970 to 1984 reported that homosexual relations were wrong, and in a 1996 National Opinion Research Center Survey only 56 percent of Americans continued to hold the same opinion. He also noted that from 1992 to 1999, 80 percent of Americans believed in equal employment; and, from 1994 to 1999, 70 percent of Americans believed that equal housing should also be available for gay individuals (Yang, 1999). *Time* asked if individuals were opposed to openly gay individuals teaching in local schools finding 51 percent were in favor with 42 percent opposed (Lacayo, 1998). Individuals were also asked about gays serving in the military with 52 percent favoring service and 39 percent opposed. *Newsweek* reported in 1998 that

83 percent of the population believed that gays should have equality in obtaining jobs and 75 percent believed gays should have equal rights in acquiring housing (Peyser, 1998). In the same survey though, 54 percent believed that homosexuality was a sin. *Newsweek* reported that young adults (18–30 years) were much more accepting of gay issues including marriage and adoption than individuals over the age of 30; and that the baby boomer group (30+ years) were more accepting of gay issues than individuals over 50 years of age (Peyser, 1998). The NGLTF (2003) most recently reported thirty-six states with anti-same-sex marriage laws. The current trend sees the greatest increase in acceptance of gay individuals in the areas of employment and housing (Yang, 1999). Despite these increases in acceptance of gays, there still remain sizable minorities that advocate against the rights of gays and lesbians and believe that gay lifestyles are improper. Homophobia and heterosexism remain at the core of these negative attitudes in our society.

DEVELOPING AN IDENTITY

In human development theories, the development of a distinct identity, and positive self-worth are primary tasks identified as necessary for a healthy state of being. People develop and define their identities and sense of self-worth through an interactive process between themselves and their environment. The ability to give and accept affirmation and love accompany this positive view of identity and self-worth.

Coming Out

This process of developing an identity as a gay person is called "coming out." Coming out and identifying oneself as gay is frequently a reason that gay individuals find themselves in counseling. There are many stages in the coming out process. The first step in the coming out process is to acknowledge feelings of attraction for the same gender. Then, individuals will need to decide whether to share their sexual orientation with others such as parents, friends, children, employers, and coworkers. Clients need to understand why they wish to share information with others and the possible consequences.

Several "coming out" models provide a framework for understanding this process of identity development (Cass, 1984; Coleman, 1985; Falco, 1987; Lewis, 1984; Reynolds & Hanjorgiris, 2000; Sophie, 1987; Troiden, 1989). The authors' model in Table 18.4 draws on each of these systems to identify the client's experiences and counselor's tasks for six coming out stages. It is important to remember that these stages will not necessarily occur in the order listed. After going through one stage, individuals frequently find themselves circling back to the same stage again when new thoughts, feelings, or actions occur.

The coming out process may occur at any age. Some individuals have indicated that they knew they were attracted to the same sex as early as age 6 or 7. If people come out during the teenage years, then development of sexual identity is congruent with adolescent development. However, coming out as a teenager can be particularly

TABLE 18.4 The Coming Out Stages

PRE-DISCLOSURE: Pre-coming out [Coleman]; Being different [Lewis]; Identity confusion [Cass]; Recognizing and accepting lesbian feelings [Sophie]; Sensitization [Troiden].

Client experience: Awareness of being different—may be vague. May not be able to talk about feelings. Confused, alienated, defensive, and beginning to wonder about the possibility of being gay. Probably has not disclosed feelings of being different to anyone.

Counselor task: Helps client identify both internal and external conflicts. Assists client in talking about thoughts and feelings without judging or labeling. Helps client understand that feelings and thoughts are acceptable. Helps client look at consequences of acting on thoughts and feelings. Is open to the client's awareness.

DISCLOSURE: Coming out [Coleman]; Dissonance [Lewis]; Identity Comparison [Cass]; Coming out to self [Sophie]; Identity confusion [Troiden].

Client experience: Acknowledges same gender feelings and identifies self as possibly gay. Faces and copes with resultant conflict with heterosexual lifestyle including homophobia and heterosexism. Experiences confusion, questions values, roles, and self-concept. Concerned about possible loss of friends and family. Expresses strong attraction to individuals of the same gender.

Counselor task: Accepts client's acknowledged feelings and thoughts. Helps client understand that same-sex feelings and thoughts are acceptable. Helps client through grieving process, work through denial, shame, anxiety, anger, alienation, and self-esteem issues. Encourages client to re-evaluate expectations and goals. Helps client develop positive image of gays and lesbians. Helps client value their personhood. Helps client sort through issues of sex role identification. Provides client with gay community resources, such as publications, support groups, spiritual groups, etc. Asks client questions about coming out like: How will people react to your coming out? Who in your life will be affected by your coming out? Have you acted on your sexual thoughts?

EXPLORATION/EXPERIMENTATION: Exploration [Coleman]; Relationships [Lewis]; Identity tolerance [Cass]; Coming out to others [Sophie].

Client experience: Experiments with social and sexual relationships. Decides who to come out to, in what setting, to how many people, how much and what to say. Feels intense emotion and is uncertain of social skills. Needs to find supportive community and gain a positive self-concept.

Counselor task: Helps client decide about coming out. Helps cope with the consequences of coming out. Helps client establish support network while continuing to accept feelings and thoughts. Helps client develop self-esteem and interpersonal skills. Assists client in understanding the intensity of feelings and the awkwardness in social relationships. Helps client develop a model for pursuing relationships including dating, courtship, and sexual behavior.

TABLE 18.4   Continued

IDENTITY DEVELOPMENT: First relationships [Coleman]; Stable identity [Lewis]; Identity acceptance [Cass]; Identity assumption [Troiden].

Client experience: Develops and learns to live in same-sex relationships. Begins to attribute value to being gay by taking part in gay subculture. Develops skill of "passing" as heterosexual and decides when it is appropriate to be "out." Feels more positive about being gay.

Counselor's task: Helps client with continuing issues of self-esteem. Helps client with frustration and pain of being rejected by some people. Is supportive of relationship issues. Helps client with communication skills and role development in relationships. Helps client understand that some relationships may not last and to learn from the loss.

IDENTITY PRIZING: Identity pride [Cass].

Client experience: Values the gay, lesbian, or bisexual experience above the heterosexual. Accepts self as valuable and contributing member of society. Enjoys and values gay subculture and friends gained as a gay person. Comes out to more people. Experiences anger and rejection from members of society, yet maintains a positive sense of self.

Counselor task: Assists client in continuing decisions about self-disclosure. Helps client express thoughts and feelings and understand actions in addressing the conflicts and joys in life. Finds ways to support client in maintaining a positive self-image in spite of some continuing societal rejection.

IDENTITY INTEGRATION: Integration [Coleman, Lewis]; Identity synthesis [Cass]; Commitment [Troiden].

Client experience: Integrates internal and external experiences into a healthy self-view. Being gay or lesbian takes much less energy and attention. Public and private identities merge into one unified and integrated self-image. Relationships are more successful and are characterized by honesty, mutual trust, and intimacy. Client proceeds on with age-appropriate issues and developmental tasks.

Counselor task: Affirms view that being gay is only one aspect of total self. Helps client continue to adapt to new identity. Assists with continuing self-disclosure and self-labeling. Helps client with ongoing development of personal relationships.

difficult because adolescents seek and need approval and support from both peers and adults. Some researchers suggest that we are currently seeing the first "out" generation of adolescents that implies a totally different dynamic in the issues and concerns they experience (Bass & Kaufman, 1996; Herdt & Boxer, 1993; Reynolds & Hanjorgiris, 2000). Teenagers take the risk of being both thrown out of their homes by parents if they identify themselves as gay and experiencing rejection from their friends (Bass & Kaufman, 1996; Blumenfeld, 1992; D'Augelli, Hershenberger, & Pilkington, 1998; Silberman & Hawkins, 1988). Many individuals do not come out until later years and may not "enter their true adolescence until their chronological adolescence has long passed" (Coleman, 1985, p. 36). Some individuals "come out" as senior citizens.

Whenever gays come out they will be addressing an identity crisis and will need assistance in sorting through the coming out issues and developing a positive sense of self.

Because gays are not usually born into gay families, the process of coming out is more difficult than it otherwise would be. Most gays and lesbians have few role models and no self-validating and visible culture on which to pattern themselves (Fassinger, 1991; Forstein, 1986; Garnets & Kimmel, 1993; Rothblum & Bond, 1996; Sears & Williams, 1997). Bisexuals have even fewer role models and are caught in the middle of two worlds (Wolf, 1992). Generally, gays, lesbians, and bisexuals who have not come out suffer oppression alone, without benefit of advice or emotional support from relatives or friends. Since the development of a defined and positive gay identity is frequently not encouraged or supported by friends and family or by society, it is essential for counselors to be positive and supportive as clients work through the coming out process.

There are many issues to be addressed in the development of identity and the coming out process. The alternatives open to the individual and the ramifications of choices must be explored and clarified. It is important that the counselor remain aware of the process and the interrelationship between developing an identity and coming out. Clients may need assistance in looking at both the positive and negative aspects of coming out. Counselors will need to use personal history assessment techniques to determine how to assist the client in the decision-making process about coming out. The client who is anticipating self-disclosure concerning sexual orientation may benefit from practicing the disclosure through role-playing. Use of the empty chair technique, allowing the client to play different parts, will help the client experience expected reactions such as fear, abuse, and abandonment.

Deciding Whether to Come Out

Each person must decide whether to identify oneself as gay, lesbian, or bisexual. Not identifying oneself and living a secret life is termed living in the "closet." Secrecy about feelings and self-perceptions supports internalized homophobia. Closeted gays blanket their entire lives with self-constriction, constantly monitoring their thoughts, emotions, and responses. Such hiding does irreparable harm to their sense of integrity and leaves them in a stressful and dissonant position, detracting from their mental health and well-being.

Coming out is a never-ending process and decisions about whether to come out occur on a daily basis. The stresses of addressing the issue of sexual orientation will affect the function and quality of life no matter how far out of the closet gays are, or how carefully cloistered and defended they are about their lifestyle (Riddle & Sang, 1978; Weston, 1991). Gays, lesbians, and bisexuals experience constant pressure both to stay in and to come out of the closet. For example, after a weekend when coworkers are discussing what they did, does the gay person share with whom he or she spent time, or make up an appropriate other-gender partner? At holiday times does the gay person bring his or her partner to the family dinner, or go alone and feign being unattached? Does a bisexual married women come out to her family and friends?

As counselors work with clients who are addressing coming out issues, they need to remember that self-disclosure is necessary for self-acceptance and self-

TABLE 18.5 The Consequences of Coming Out—Questions to Consider

1. What kind of reactions do you expect when you tell family members, friends, co-workers, etc.?
2. How can you determine what the reactions might be?
3. What would be the worst possible reaction?
4. What can you do to prepare yourself against that reaction?
5. What happens when or if you tell your parents?
6. Should you tell your parents together or individually?
7. Should you tell both of your parents?
8. What happens if you do not tell certain people?
9. Is it necessary to tell everyone?
10. What are the best ways to tell people?
11. Can you think of alternative ways to tell people?
12. Are you aware that responses may change over time?

regard. Disclosing your sexual orientation and perceived identity is necessary for affirmation of self-worth and enhancement of personal integrity (Bass & Kaufman, 1996; Garnets & Kimmel, 1993). Thus, choosing to stay in the closet and not identifying oneself as gay frequently supports shame and guilt and perpetuates a negative self-image. However, it is important that each person decide whether to identify as gay and how far to come out of the closet. Counselors need to counsel about this question, rather than give answers (Norton, 1995). Circumstances vary and counselors need to assist clients in this difficult decision-making process by assessing the issues involved. Counselors who are not familiar with the emotional constellation involved in coming out can give clients some very inappropriate advice (Markowitz, 1991). Joe, the college freshman identified earlier in the chapter, faces some difficult choices. What will be the effect on his relationships with family and friends? If he comes out, will his parents continue financial support for college? If they do not, does he have alternatives to finance his education? If the decision is to stay in the closet, how will this effect Joe? Questions listed in Table 18.5 can help clients determine the consequences of coming out.

Identity Dysfunctions

Individuals who do not develop a positive self-view in the coming out process frequently develop an identity dysfunction. Identity dysfunctions lead the person to initiate friendships or work relationships that support the continuation of a negative self-view. The resulting behaviors manifest themselves in difficulties with intimacy and maintaining relationships. Dysfunctions of identity are confusion, conflict, and denial. Counselors need to understand and identify the dysfunctional roles taken on by the client and explore with the client alternative ways of enhancing the self rather than denying the self.

Identity Confusion. When people are not accepted by the culture, they experience rejection. For example, teenagers are expected to attend high school dances with members of the opposite sex. If gay teenagers want to take someone of the same gender to a senior prom, they do not conform to the expectations of parents and peers. The majority of gay teenagers are reared in nongay families, which seldom provide the support needed in accepting and affirming a nonsanctioned identity (Fassinger, 1991; Rothblum & Bond, 1996). The resulting rejection may be perceived as rejection of the self or emotional abandonment, and thus disaffirms an individual's sense of worth (Colgan, 1987). The rejection and resulting low self-worth create identity confusion for the individual.

Bisexuals may experience even more identity confusion than gay men and lesbians because of the inherent complexity of bisexuality. The following questions are often asked by individuals who are confused about identity issues: Who am I in this society? Why don't I fit into the roles defined by society? What can I do to be accepted in society? Where can I find support? Counselors need to assist clients in responding to such questions about how to fit into a society that is nonaccepting. Answering questions like these will help clients address the confusion that they are experiencing.

Identity Conflict. Gay, lesbian, and bisexual clients with identity conflicts often have low self-worth and place the needs of others above their own. Identity conflict frequently involves over-attachment or over-identification with another person. An individual may become lost in the self of others. This response stems from previous rejection and emotional isolation. An individual may become obsessed with another person and do whatever the partner wants to avoid further rejection. As a result, the individual may become victimized and possibly sexually dysfunctional (Colgan, 1987; Island & Letellier, 1991; Reynolds & Hanjorgiris, 2000). Individuals in identity conflict may experience feelings of unworthiness and blame themselves each time a relationship is terminated. Another common feature of over-identification is for a person to immerse him or herself in community organizations, thus placing the needs of the community above self needs. Counselors need to address the low self-esteem issues of such clients, help them learn to value themselves and seek balance in their relationships.

Identity Denial. When individuals deny their sexual orientation and negate their identity they sometimes detach from their emotions. For example, they might disconnect their emotions during sexual performance, insulate themselves from feelings by drug and alcohol abuse, or adopt the role of "rejector" or "suitor" in relationships. The rejector acts from a sense of anger and hostility while the suitor is constantly in search of the right man or woman who will bring immediate fulfillment (Silverstein, 1981). All of these behaviors are forms of self-denial and deaden the pain the individual is feeling from the loss of the self.

Community Identity. As counselors work with gay, lesbian, and bisexual clients, especially those addressing identity issues, it would be helpful to have knowledge of gay and lesbian community organizations. Gays and lesbians have established communities to support each other because of their invisibility and oppressed status (D'Augelli & Garnets, 1994). Both social and professional groups have been established in most urban areas and many individuals find folks in kindred communities away from home. Social organizations are formed around common interests like hiking, bowling, bridge, and square dancing. Other local and national organizations have been established to serve political and advocacy functions for gays. Groups exist that address a wide range of issues like health, legal concerns, aging, youth, religious, and political needs. Bookstores, with gay and lesbian periodicals, books, and newspapers exist in most large cities. Most large cities have gay, lesbian, and bisexual counseling centers that serve as a community resource.

Counselors need to be aware of the gay community resources and make this information available to their clients. It should be noted that there are not as many resources available for the bisexual community and counselors need to take extra care to find appropriate resources for their bisexual clients. Counselors located in rural communities need to be aware of national resources available by mail and the resources in the nearest large city. A sample of community and national sources are listed in Appendix 1.

SPECIAL SITUATIONS IN COUNSELING

Relationships

Unlike ethnic minorities, lesbians and gay men were not measured by the U.S. census until 1992, making it extremely difficult to obtain accurate demographic information on living patterns in the gay community. The studies that have been conducted contradict the popular perception that the majority of gays and lesbians do not live with a partner or maintain a monogamous relationship. In studies conducted between 1977 and 1983, 40 to 60 percent of gay men indicated they were in a steady relationship. A 1992 study found that 56 percent of gay men and 71 percent of lesbians were in steady relationships (Singer & Deschamps, 1994). A more recent survey of gays and lesbians found that 45 percent and 80 percent of women and 40 percent and 65 percent of men were in monogamous relationships (Kurdek, 1995; Ossana, 2000).

With increased attention being paid to homosexuality in the popular media, there is more awareness of lesbian and gay couples (Kurdek, 1995; Ossana, 2000; Peplau, 1993). This, along with studies by social scientists, have begun to provide a few models on which gay and lesbian couples can base their relationships. However, lesbian and gay couples frequently base their expectations on heterosexual modeling that may include one partner taking care of the other, or one partner being more feminine or masculine (McWhirter & Mattison, 1984). As products of society, gay men and women share the expectations and rules of opposite-sex couples and assume roles in relation to each other that are most often based on sex role expectations for heterosexual couples (Murphy, 1992).

> Lesbians are socialized as women first, and gay men are socialized as men first. Men are taught to be assertive, competitive, and aggressive and to initiate sexual activity.

> Women are taught to be compliant, passive, and sexually exclusive. Given this conditioning, it is not uncommon for gay male couples to experience competition as a difficulty in relationships or for lesbian couples to have trouble with fusion and difficulty in separating. (Silberman & Hawkins, 1988, p. 106)

There are still only a few visible role models on which gay and lesbian couples can base their relationship. Gay and lesbian couples frequently express curiosity about how other same-sex couples deal with their everyday lives and address issues such as finances, outside relationships, family, and sex. While the lack of modeling for gay and lesbian couples creates uncertainty about how to behave as a couple, the lack of societal guidelines for same-sex couples allows for creativity in establishing the ground rules in the relationship.

Most often, gay and lesbian couples will bring concerns to counseling that are no different from the issues in heterosexual relationships. These may include differences in socioeconomic and family backgrounds, level of education, religious and value differences, communication problems, previous relationships, illness, financial issues, individual emotional problems, sexual dysfunction, and jealousy. Even though gay and lesbian couples confront the very same day-to-day concerns as any two people living together, "they do not have the social, legal or moral sanctions that sustain opposite-sex couples. Thus, the development and maintenance of same-sex couples involves a commitment to a difficult process with many destructive internal and external forces in its path" (Forstein, 1986, p. 105).

Lesbian and gay male couples who live together as same gender partners do experience relationship problems unique to sexual orientation. McWhirter & Mattison (1984) identify ignorance, prejudice, oppression, and homophobia as issues that every gay couple must address. To fight these, counselors must assess the depth of these issues and the effect on the self-concept of the individuals involved. It may be helpful to suggest to clients that they gain accurate information about homosexuality through reading, videotapes, attendance at lectures, and other sources to help them fight these issues in society. As a corollary to these concerns, couples frequently disagree about how open to be about their sexual orientation. If one member of the couple is more out of the closet than the other, it will present problems for the relationship that need to be addressed in counseling.

Lesbian Couples

Lesbians typically seek out relationships that are characterized by deep emotional bonds and the sharing of intimacy at various levels. It is common for lesbian couples to go through a developmental process with each stage representing a continued commitment to generativity and collaboration (Clunis & Green, 1993; Slater, 1995). Partners strive to develop equity within the relationship, which is viewed by them as atypical in heterosexual relationships (Slater, 1995). These relationship-nurturing traits of lesbian relationships may be because of the cultural messages women receive about the value of coupling and relationship bonding (Clunis & Green, 1993), the lack of sex role definition within lesbian relationships, and the freedom to establish roles without prescription.

Although there are many positive aspects regarding lesbian couples, there are also negative aspects that the counselor needs to be aware of when dealing with lesbian couples. Since lesbian relationships are not recognized socially or legally, problems are magnified when a lesbian couple has children (Browning, Reynolds, & Dworkin, 1991; Slater, 1995). Sally and Jennifer may face teachers who are uncomfortable working with or hostile toward two mothers. When couples break up, custody disputes arise and the nonbiological mother may not be allowed visitation rights even though the couple had been together for several years.

One of the major difficulties lesbian couples experience is the issue of intimacy versus autonomy (Browning et al., 1991; Ossana, 2000). Lesbian couples can become so close that they experience fusion, and conflicts may arise regarding individual needs as opposed to relationship needs. Another common problem lesbian couples may experience is dealing with stage differences in "coming out" or individual development of identity. When one partner is totally open and the other one has not told her family, many conflicts can arise. Other stressors include monogamy versus nonmonogamy issues, sexual issues regarding desire and absence of, racial/cultural differences, and parenting issues (Browning et al., 1991).

Gay Male Couples

The custody issues, the degree of "outness," and the stresses identified for lesbian couples also apply for gay male couples. Another issue for gay male couples is the common fear that the relationship will not last and that gay men are incapable of intimacy. The lack of societal support for gay male relationships may be one reason that some relationships end prematurely. However, surveys have found that these stereotypes are not true and that indeed gay male couples do establish lasting intimate relationships (Blumstein & Schwartz, 1983; LaSala, 2001; McWhirter & Mattison, 1984).

McWhirter and Mattison (1984), in their pioneering effort, developed a descriptive and developmental model of gay male relationships in which they identify six stages that describe the tasks a male couple encounters as the relationship develops.

1. Stage One—Blending (year one)
2. Stage Two—Nesting (years two and three)
3. Stage Three—Maintaining (years four and five)
4. Stage Four—Building (years six through ten)
5. Stage Five—Releasing (years eleven through twenty)
6. Stage Six—Renewing (beyond twenty years)

This model provides a basis for understanding that, although each relationship has a life of its own, there are predictable developmental stages that a gay male relationship passes through. Counselors might use this model in counseling with gay couples to assess whether the couple is on "task" or whether one member of the couple has moved at a faster pace than the other. The accumulation of data and development of concepts pertinent to working with gay male couples are a recent phenomena, and counselors would benefit from a careful perusal of the data as they develop.

Violence in Lesbian and Gay Male Couples

One serious problem that is being recognized in lesbian and gay couples is physical violence, abuse, and battering. There is limited research on this phenomena, but some suggest that there is approximately the same amount of battering in gay and lesbian couples as there is in heterosexual couples (Font, 1995; Ossana, 2000). The dynamics within the abusive gay or lesbian relationship are similar to heterosexual relationships in that there is a loss of personal power, self-esteem, and control (Clunis & Green, 1993; Island & Letellier, 1991; Ossana, 2000). However, violence between same gender couples seems to concern authorities less and due to the invisibility and lack of social support, it is difficult for those involved to seek interventions (Carl, 1995; Conley, 1995).

Gay men and lesbians batter because they want to exercise power over their partners. Individuals who batter have learned that violence is effective in getting their partners to comply with their wishes (Hart, 1989). The impact of battering on the victim can be profound as a sense of fear, mistrust, and disillusionment takes over and closeness and equality in the relationship disappears. As in any issues of violence, the safety of the victim takes precedence over supporting the relationship or taking care of the current emotional needs (Hammond, 1989). Counselors need to be sensitive to these issues and help restore the integrity and self-worth of the victim in addition to examining issues with the abuser. Island and Letellier (1991) outline the following guidelines in helping victims of partner abuse:

1. Couple counseling is inappropriate and dangerous.
2. The counselor must understand domestic violence issues.
3. The counselor must be gay-sensitive and/or gay-affirmative.
4. The counselor must not use any theories to excuse or justify battering behavior.
5. The counselor must not view violence (especially male) as innate and natural.

Gay and Lesbian Families

Gays and lesbians are coupling, creating new families, having and rearing children, and challenging society's definition of what "family" means. Sally and Jennifer, identified at the beginning of this chapter, are examples of a growing phenomena in the United States. Gay men and lesbians are choosing to have children and to raise them in redefined families. The result is a "lesbian and gay baby boom" (Martin, 1993; Patterson, 1995). It is estimated that 6–12 million children have lesbian, gay, bisexual, or transgendered parents or families in the United States (Lamme & Lamme, 2002).

Most of the difficulties of gay and lesbian parenting are similar to the stresses felt in heterosexual marriage and may include such issues as jealousy, time spent with children, privacy, and communication. However, gay and lesbian parents often confront added stressors (Matthews & Lease, 2000). Co-parenting a child is frequently exacerbated by the couple's inability to become legal stepparents. Gay and lesbian couples who wish to adopt children will find it difficult; currently very few gay or lesbian couples in the United States have been granted legal adoptions of children. In some divorce situations, concerns arise about custody and visitation rights of the gay parent to his or her child. Many states discriminate against gay individuals in awarding child custody, and in some states being gay is reason enough to be considered an unfit parent. Counselors, at the least, need to be aware of the statutes in their states and help clients find supportive legal assistance. Some counselors may want to consider being more proactive and assist gay and lesbian clients to obtain more legal rights.

Other issues that arise for gay parents include concerns about coming out to the wife or husband, to children, and to other family members. Issues of coming out are also pertinent to the children of gay and lesbian parents. These children will need to grieve the loss of their heterosexual parent, resolve conflicts between their love for their parent and social standards, examine their own fears about being gay or lesbian, and decide whether to tell their friends. Some children may choose to hide their parent's sexuality from friends because they fear a negative response. These issues of coming out are very delicate and intricate, as described in an earlier section, and must be considered in the framework of the developmental history of the individual.

Religious Issues

Gays and lesbians who are raised in families affiliated with a religious denomination are often confronted with conflicting values between their sexual orientation and their religion. Since the twelfth century, there has been hostility directed toward individuals of same gender orientation (O'Neill & Ritter, 1992). Frequently, religions believe that sex between people of the same gender runs counter to God's plan. Such religious doctrine makes it difficult for the gay person to live authentically in the religious world. If a gay person is unable to actively participate in the spiritual and religious dimensions of life without oppression and confusion, then this issue may need to be addressed in counseling (Davidson, 2000; Fortunato, 1983; Palma & Stanley, 2002).

Gay clients frequently come to counseling with the belief that there is no place for them in their religion and that they are "sinners," "black sheep," or "unwanted." Some have been excommunicated from the church; others have not been allowed to be married; some have been denied ordination. Client distress manifests itself in anger toward the church, and feelings of personal shame and guilt. Clients will need an opportunity to discuss the options available to them and decide whether to remain affiliated with the religion of their family, seek a new religious affiliation, or pursue other avenues to meet their spiritual needs. Gays who remain in a nonaccepting church need to learn how to balance the negative views of the church and their sexual orientation.

Most major denominations now have gay church groups affiliated with them or are revisiting doctrine to be more inclusive. These groups include Dignity (Catholic), Integrity (Episcopal), Affirmation (United Methodist), Affirmation (Mormon), Evangelicals Concerned, Friends for Lesbian and Gay Concerns (Quakers), Kinship (Adventist), Lutherans Concerned (Lutheran), Seventh Day Adventist Kinship International, Gay Synagogue (Jewish), and Unitarian Universalists for Lesbian/Gay Concerns. The Metropolitan Community Church is a nondenominational gay church that has services nationwide. Also, many individuals in church groups are striving to rectify the homophobia within their church by establishing "affirming" or "welcoming" congregations that are inclusive of gays, lesbians, and bisexuals.

As counselors work with clients about religious beliefs and sexual orientation, they must be aware of their own religious value system and beliefs. Counselors who have been raised in a denomination that discriminates against gays will have to either move beyond these homophobic and heterosexist beliefs or refer to counselors who are gay-supportive to help clients address these difficult issues.

Drug and Alcohol Abuse

There is a widely held assumption by mental health professionals that drug and alcohol abuse is quite high in the gay and lesbian community. Some have stated that alcoholism is the number one health problem among gay men and lesbians (Kus, 1987). The research in this area is sparse and contains methodological limitations (Anderson, 1996; Bux, 1996; Mays & Cockran, 2001; Paul, Stall, & Bloomfield, 1991). However, the available research does suggest that approximately 20–30 percent of gay men and lesbians are chemically dependent on alcohol or drugs (Anderson, 1996; Clunis & Green, 1993; Kus, 1990; Lohrenz, Connely, Coyne, & Spare, 1978; Mays & Cochran, 2001; Paul et al., 1991).

Research has shown that internalized homophobia may explain the etiology and the high incidence of alcoholism in gay American men (Fisher & Harrison, 2000; Kus, 1987) and lesbians (Browning et al., 1991; Fisher & Harrison, 2000; Mays & Cochran, 2001). Gays and lesbians tend to misuse alcohol or drugs to ameliorate their feelings related to societal rejection, alienation, and stress (Deevey & Wall, 1992; Fisher & Harrison, 2000; Hicks, 2000). Although the substance abuse may result from a lack of a positive identity, counselors cannot assist with resolution of the underlying problem until the substance abuse has stopped. Chet, the lawyer who entered a treatment program for cocaine abuse, must be clean and sober in order to address the issues that surround leading a double life.

The sexual orientation of the client should not affect the quality of treatment services provided by chemical dependency professionals. With such a high incidence of chemical abuse among gay, lesbian, and bisexual clients, treatment centers need to address sexual orientation issues with clients. One suggested method is to ask clients in a routine and nonjudgmental manner during the treatment intake session about their sexual orientation. Asking gives the clients the choice about whether to reveal sexual orientation. Asking the question also allows clients to be less worried about when they will be "found out" because it sends a message that sexual orientation is a legitimate issue (Finnegan & McNally, 1987). Gay, lesbian, and bisexual clients who come to treatment may be experiencing heightened shame and guilt. Therefore, it is important to approach questions about sexuality in routine ways that indicate to clients that any answers are acceptable. "If the question is not posed, the gay or lesbian client may feel heterosexuality is assumed and homosexuality is possibly unacceptable in this setting" (Finnegan & McNally, 1987, p. 61). Not asking about sexual orientation may indicate that the agency is not sensitive to gay issues and the underlying feelings of gay clients.

Too often, lesbians, gay men, and bisexuals have sought treatment for relationship difficulties, depression, or anxiety and never reported their chemical abuse nor have they been asked (Faltz, 1992). Intake and assessment procedures with all gay clients should include questions about drinking and using.

Self-help groups, a necessary adjunct to counseling chemically dependent individuals, are available for gays and lesbians in most cities. These include Alcoholics Anonymous, Narcotics Anonymous, Valium Anonymous, and Cocaine Anonymous. Counselors need to know about local gay- friendly self-help groups and make appropriate referrals.

HIV/AIDS

There is clear evidence that human immunodeficiency virus (HIV), which causes AIDS (acquired immunodeficiency syndrome) continues to spread in the United States and the rest of the world. The HIV/AIDS pandemic continues to have a tremendous social and psychological impact on individuals, families, schools, and communities. To date, there is no cure for HIV, but, because treatment in recent years has been promising and mortality rates have dropped, there seems to be a false sense of security among those engaging in high risk behavior. It is predicted that an effective vaccine will be available in 7 to 10 years (Makgoba, Solomon, & Tucker, 2002). It is still important to remember that although vaccines to prevent HIV infection are being developed, a vaccine will only prevent new infections, not offer a cure for those already infected.

AIDS, first identified in 1981, is a usually fatal disease for which there is no known cure or immunization. Gay men were initially the hardest hit group in the United States. As a result, homophobia and stigma became intertwined with the first responses to HIV/AIDS. Initially, HIV/AIDS was popularly referred to as the "gay disease" and as the Wrath of God (WOG) (McLaughlin, 1989). One writer said "in some quarters the misapprehension exists that HIV/AIDS is caused by homosexuality, not a retrovirus" (Brandt, 1988, p. 165). Early in the pandemic, the association of HIV/AIDS with gay men created a secondary epidemic of prejudice, fear, and ignorance (House, Eicken, & Gray, 1995). These continuing associations have led to discrimination against those with HIV/AIDS and those who are suspected of having HIV/AIDS.

Counselors need to recognize that these external factors continue to have a profound impact on all gays while understanding the individual behavioral manifestations caused by HIV/AIDS. Significant psychological reactions like depression, anxiety, and anger often result from finding out that you are HIV-positive. Fears of death and dying, isolation, disclosure of sexual orientation to family and community, contagion issues, hopelessness, loss of self-esteem, and an increase in internalized homophobia are common responses to the diagnosis of HIV/AIDS.

Counselors are in a pivotal position to address the current issues related to HIV/AIDS by acting as agents of change in schools, churches, community agencies, government programs, treatment centers, and private practice. They can assess and assist with the needs of the friends and family of persons living with HIV/AIDS (PLWAs) (Kain, 1998). Counselors can also provide accurate information about

HIV/AIDS to clients and family members, professional colleagues, and the communities where they live and work. For those infected, we must help them continue to live their lives fully and in the ways they choose. Kain (1998) asks us to be mindful about understanding the difference of what it means to counsel HIV-positive clients in the 1980s and now. Instead of helping HIV-positive individuals face their diagnosis and death, we must avoid counseling people living with the disease as if their illness separates them from their lives.

Since information about HIV/AIDS changes rapidly, it is important for counselors to familiarize themselves with community-based HIV/AIDS service organizations that provide services, education, and advocacy for people whose lives are affected by HIV/AIDS. These organizations are an ideal place for counselors to both learn current information about HIV/AIDS issues themselves as well as refer clients for services. Not all counselors will be able to start a support group or provide needed information to every client concerned about HIV/AIDS, but they do need to know that group support, financial advocacy, recreational opportunities, and crisis intervention services are available at nearby HIV/AIDS organizations. Frequently, legal services are also provided to ensure that people with HIV infection can live full, productive lives in the face of possible legal difficulties. These organizations use many avenues to reach its audiences: publications, videos, safer sex workshops, outreach into communities of color, information tables on city streets, distribution of condoms and safer sex guidelines to bars and clubs, and educational programs for mental health professionals and employers (Gay Men's Health Crisis, 2003).

Counselors must be prepared to take risks as advocates for PLWAs and their families in order to guarantee competent and compassionate treatment. Such risks include: (1) non-judgmental confrontation of beliefs based on ignorance and behavior grounded in prejudice and bigotry; (2) taking the leadership in HIV/AIDS education and prevention strategies; (3) challenging misstatements about HIV/AIDS and gays whenever they occur; (4) providing accurate factual information; (5) encouraging the reconsideration of uninformed opinions; and (6) educating clients by discussing safer sex practices and the dangers of sharing needles during drug use (Gray, House, & Champeau, 2004).

HIV/AIDS has caused people to talk about sex and death, two subjects that people in our society avoid. It has helped bring gays, sex, and death out of the closet. The multiple threats of significant health problems, issues of death and dying, coping with the fear associated with HIV/AIDS, and social backlash related to HIV/AIDS present complex and difficult issues for which counselor support is critical. Compassionate and gay-affirmative counselors can help sort through the myriad of issues presented by HIV/AIDS.

Loneliness, Guilt, Depression, Suicide

Many gays experience loneliness, depression, anxiety, guilt, anger, and/or suicidal thoughts as a result of the dissonance between their feelings and society's proscriptions. These conflicts are much the same as those experienced by all members of society. But, many gays experience a greater depth of feeling and an absence of hope of resolving the conflicts (Fortunato, 1983). Great anxiety and loneliness come from realizing that there may never be support from parents, siblings, family members, or loved ones. Life can be extremely painful to gays who have lost friends or a job or their church membership because of their sexual orientation. These feelings of loss must either be avoided, fought, or worked through. Counselors need to assist gay clients in working through the stages of loss that are inherent to being gay in a heterocentric culture. The following stages provide a structure when assisting clients with these issues.

Denial/Bargaining.   Gay clients in this stage remain closeted and secretive. Frequently, they have feelings of paranoia, are depressed, have phobic reactions, and are alcohol or drug abusers. They may recognize societal oppression, but refuse to deal with it. They will bargain with themselves about being gay, make excuses for their behavior, and deny their sexual orientation even though they may be engaging in same-sex behavior. They are caught in a codependent phase, making excuses for their behavior and defending the people who are oppressing and rejecting them. Counselors need to confront the denial and direct the focus to the source of the oppression.

Anger.   Clients who are in the anger stage frequently address their anger outwardly in the form of protests, marches, letter writing, or circulating petitions. This can be a very positive use of anger. However, if they simply express their anger without addressing the source of the anger, the individual may become rigid, defensive, and closed. Anger can also be directed toward oneself and is often related to the shame and guilt that the individual feels about being gay. This inward expression of anger is often associated with loneliness and suicidal ideation. Counselors need to work carefully with clients in this stage, help them express their anger in appropriate ways, and eventually work through the anger.

Depression.   Individuals who are in extreme denial and live totally in the closet isolate themselves from other gays and have minimal social and sexual contacts. These individuals have ingested the fear of being gay and internalized the oppression of society. Gays who are depressed may be suicidal, drink and use drugs too much, and engage in self-pity. They see society as "right" and themselves as "wrong." Counselors need to address the feelings of shame and guilt, and encourage clients to take responsibility for themselves rather than blaming society and the people in their life for the awful state of "their world." It is also important to note that the depression may not be related to sexual orientation and may be caused by other issues or events in the client's life.

Acceptance/Integration.   In this stage, individuals begin to accept and integrate sexual orientation into their life. In this process, individuals need to stop asking the question "Why me?", stop denying their sexual orientation, and relate to others in an open and caring manner. Individuals in this stage begin to look beyond the expectations that other people will affirm them, and look for self-affirmation. This involves taking a public step and proactively assuming responsibility for their lives. When these steps are taken, "energy that has been locked within can be released and rein-vested elsewhere" (O'Neill & Ritter, 1992, p. 145). Counselors need to be encourag-ing and supportive in this process.

Reformulating/Transformation.   Individuals, after taking a public step, will often experience a newfound freedom. The energy that has been consumed by their main-taining a false public self is now available for more creative endeavors. This new cen-teredness permits individuals to live more spontaneously and move beyond their loss (O'Neill & Ritter, 1992). This reformulating and transformation expands insight and vision and allows individuals to lead more productive and fulfilling lives.

Moving from a lonely or depressed state to healing and productivity is a complex process, and counselor support is critical. Counselors need to be warm, accepting, and nonjudgmental as gay, lesbian, and bisexual clients work through these processes.

PROFESSIONAL DIRECTIONS

The attitudes of counseling professionals toward gay men and lesbians have changed dramatically over the years. In 1973, the American Psychiatric Association stopped labeling homosexuality as a form of mental illness. The American Psychological As-sociation did the same in 1975. The assumption associated with these changes was that counseling practices would be modified to reflect a view of homosexuality as an acceptable lifestyle (Corey, Corey, & Callanan, 1988). Today, more and more coun-selors hold positive attitudes toward gays, lesbians, and bisexuals, but a 1990 study found that a large and diverse sample of psychologists held negative biases and misin-formation about gays and lesbians (Garnets & Kimmel, 1993). Some counselors be-lieve "that homosexuality necessarily indicates the presence of psychopathology" (Hancock, 1994, p. 400). Brown (1996) indicated several factors continue to exist in the training and experiences of counselors that lead to ignorance and bias in counsel-ing with gay, lesbian, and bisexual individuals. Brown also stated that there seems to be a failure in integrating accurate information into curriculums. These negative stances toward gays, lesbians, and bisexuals oppose the current ethical standards and practices of the profession.

Counselors should deliberately create a gay-affirmative approach that validates sexual orientation, recognizes the oppression of gays, lesbians, and bisexuals, and ac-tively helps them overcome its external and internal effects (Brown, 1996; Fassinger, 1991; Palma & Stanley, 2002; Pearson, 2003). To be gay-affirmative is to value ho-mosexuality and heterosexuality equally as natural or normal attributes (Carroll & Gilroy, 2001; Fassinger, 1991; Kocarek & Pelling, 2003; Krajeski, 1986). This ap-proach is proactive in nature and helps to restore options to our clients.

Many professional organizations have developed a gay and lesbian task force, committee, or division to provide support for counseling professionals and a positive direction for counseling with gays and lesbians. Division 44, the Society of the Psy-chological Study of Lesbian and Gay Issues of the American Psychological Associa-tion (APA), and the Association of Gay, Lesbian and Bisexual Issues in Counseling

(AGLBIC), a division of the American Counseling Association (ACA), are examples of efforts to support gay and lesbian concerns within professional organizations.

Until recently it was assumed that heterosexuality was the only suitable orientation for counselors (Rochlin, 1985). However, publicly identified gay male and lesbian mental health professionals are growing in number. Gay professionals who come out serve as an important resource both for the gay community and for other counselors. They also provide a role model for gays, lesbians, and bisexuals and security for those who want to see a gay professional (Woodman & Lenna, 1980). Since identification with the therapist is one of the key elements that produces change in clients, it is important for gay, lesbian, and bisexual counselors to publicly identify themselves.

SUMMARY

Before counselors can work effectively with gay, lesbian, and bisexual clients they must confront the cultural homophobia and heterosexism in our society. Many counselors have absorbed misinformation and myths about homosexuality. For example, many counselors function under the myth that all clients are heterosexual. A question like "When did you first know that you were gay?" has a heterosexual bias. It could just as easily be asked "When did you first know that you were straight?" When counselors believe and act on myths about gays, they provide a disservice to gay, lesbian, and bisexual clients.

The lack of practical knowledge about gays and the gay lifestyle is a major obstacle to satisfactory counseling. Therefore, the first responsibility for counselors is to educate themselves about the unique concerns of gays, lesbians, and bisexuals. This step includes learning about laws, policies, and practices that affect lesbian, gay, and bisexual persons and educating yourself about gay and lesbian culture and community norms. Counselors can do this most easily by meeting and talking with gay people. Such face-to-face meetings will likely dispel the myths and preconceived ideas about gays. It is also important for counselors to read gay-affirmative books and periodicals and know about available resources for gays. The websites, the reference list at the end of this chapter, and the resource list in Appendix 1 offer current sources of information.

It is crucial that counselors recognize that they may be seen as the representative of a hostile society, or as an authority figure with a heavily weighted opinion. Some gay men, lesbians, and bisexuals avoid counseling because they fear rejection if they reveal their sexual orientation. Each counselor must counter these expectations with an expressed awareness of the issues facing the gay or lesbian client and an openness to the concerns expressed. Counselors have the responsibility to let clients know that they will listen. They can do this by having gay books visibly placed on bookshelves, posting supportive articles about gay issues on bulletin boards, seeing that gay articles get placed in the school newspaper, and by rejecting and challenging antigay language and jokes.

It is also important to be an ally for gays, lesbians, and bisexuals by promoting the acceptance and understanding of gays and lesbians (Dworkin & Gutierrez, 1992;

Washington & Evans, 1991). Counselors, as allies in the communities in which they live, can support public and institutional policy decisions that affect gays, lesbians, and bisexuals. They can encourage tolerance in educational and religious settings, and advocate for nondiscriminatory measures. Counselors must not ignore the cultural and societal context in which their clients live, and they need to be supportive of clients in their struggles to transcend cultural homophobia and heterosexism.

Professional counselors are in a powerful position to help gays recognize and accept their sexual identity, improve their interpersonal and social functioning, and value themselves while living in a predominately heterocentric society. Counselors who are sensitive to sexual orientation issues, who have examined and challenged the heterosexist and homophobic assumptions of our culture, and who have confronted their own values, can assist all clients, whatever their sexual orientation.

GAY, LESBIAN, AND BISEXUAL RESOURCES

PROFESSIONAL ORGANIZATIONS

Association for Gay, Lesbian, and Bisexual Issues in Counseling (AGLBIC)
www.aglbic.org
5999 Stevenson Ave.
Alexandria, VA 22304-3300

National Committee on Lesbian, Gay, and Bisexual Issues
National Association of Social Workers
750 1st Street, NE
Washington, DC 20002-4241
(202) 408-8600 Ext. 390

National Association of Lesbian and Gay Alcoholism Professionals (NALGAP)
1911 Fort Myer Dr., # 900
Arlington, VA 222209
(703) 741-7686 Ext. 123

Office for Gay, Lesbian, and Bisexual Concerns
c/o American Psychological Association
750 First Street, NE
Washington, DC 20002
(202) 336-5500

INFORMATION AND REFERRAL

Family Pride Coalition
POB 34337
San Diego, CA 92163
(202) 583-8029

Federation of Parents and Friends of Lesbians and Gays, Inc. (PFLAG)
1101 14th St. NW, Suite 1030
Washington DC 20005
(202) 638-4200

Gay and Lesbian Outreach to Elders
1853 Market Street
San Francisco, CA 94103
(415) 255-2937

Gay and Lesbian Alliance against Defamation (GLAAD)
1825 Connecticut Ave, NW, 5th Flr.
Washington, DC 20009
(202) 986-1360

The Gay, Lesbian, and Straight Education Network
www.glsen.org
121 West 27th St. Ste. 804
New York, NY 10001
(212) 727-0135

Gay Men's Health Collective
2339 Durant
Berkeley, CA 94704
(650) 548-2570

Gay Men's Health Crisis
Box 274
132 West 24th Street
New York, NY 10011
(212) 367-1000

Human Rights Campaign
919 18th St. NW
Suite 800
Washington, DC 20006
(202) 628-4160

Lambda Legal Defense and Education Fund
120 Wall St., Suite 1500
New York, NY 10005
(212) 809-8585

National Gay and Lesbian Task Force
1700 Kalorama Rd. NW
Washington, DC 20009
(202) 332-6483
www.ngltf.org/ngltflink.html#national

National Gay and Lesbian Families Project
1700 Kalorama Rd. NW
Washington, DC 20009
(202) 332-6483

RELIGIOUS ORGANIZATIONS

Affirmation (Gay and Lesbian Mormons)
Box 46022
Los Angeles, CA 90046
(213) 974-1080

Affirmation (United Methodists for Gay and Lesbian Concerns)
Box 1021
Evanston, IL 60204
(847) 475-0499

Dignity, USA
1500 Massachusetts Avenue, NW
Suite 11
Washington, DC 20005
(202) 861-0017

Evangelicals Concerned
c/o Dr. Ralph Blair
311 East 72nd, #1G
New York, NY 10021
(212) 517-3171

Friends for Lesbian and Gay Concerns (Quakers)
143 Campbell Ave.
Isica, NY 14850
(215) 234-8424

GLAD (Gay and Lesbian Affirming Disciples)
Christian Church (Disciples of Christ)
Box 19223
Indianapolis, IN 46219-0223
(206) 324-6231

Integrity (Episcopalian)
P.O. Box 19561
Washington, DC 20036-0561
(201) 868-2485

Lutherans Concerned/North America
Box 10197
Fort Dearborn Station
Chicago, IL 60610-0197

National Gay Pentecostal Alliance
P.O. Box 1391
Schenectady, NY 12301-1391

Presbyterians for Gay/Lesbian Concerns
Box 38
New Brunswick, NJ 08903-0038
(732) 249-1016

Seventh Day Adventists-Kinship International, Inc.
Box 3840
Los Angeles, CA 90078
(323) 876-2076

Unitarian Universalists for Lesbian/Gay Concerns
25 Beacon Street
Boston, MA 02108
617/742-2100

United Lesbian and Gay Christian Scientists
Box 2171
Beverly Hills, CA 90212-2171

World Congress of Gay and Lesbian Jewish Organizations
POB 23379
Washington, DC 20026-3379
(202) 452-7424

Metropolitan Community Church
Usually listed in the white pages of the local telephone directory
or
Universal Fellowship of Metropolitan Community Churches
5300 Santa Monica Boulevard #304
Los Angeles, CA 90029
(323) 464-5100

BOOKSTORES

A Different Light
New York, San Francisco, West Hollywood
(800) 343-4002

Chosen Books
940 West McNichols
Detroit, MI 48203
(313) 864-0458 or (800) 225-5300

Giovanni's Room
345 South 12th Street
Philadelphia, PA 19107
(215) 923-2960

Glad Day Bookshop
673 Boylston Street
Boston, MA 02116
(617) 267-3010

Lambda Rising
1625 Connecticut Avenue
Washington, DC 20009
(800) 621-6969

Oscar Wilde Memorial Bookstore
15 Christopher Street
New York, NY 10014
(212) 255-8097

The Naiad Press, Inc.
P.O. Box 10543
Tallahassee, FL 32302
(800) 533-1973

PUBLICATIONS

The Advocate
6922 Hollywood Boulevard, 10th Floor
Los Angeles, CA 90028
(800) 827-0561

Children of Lesbians and Gays Everywhere (COLAGE)
3543 18th St., #17
San Francisco, CA 94110
(415) 861-5437

Gay Community News
167 Tremont Street, Fifth Floor
Boston, MA 02111
(617) 426-4469

Gayellow Pages
Renaissance House
Box 292, Village Station
New York, NY 10014
(212) 674-0120

In the Family
(A magazine for lesbians, gays, bisexuals and their relations)
P.O. Box 5387
Takoma Park, MD 20913
(301) 270-4771

Children of Lesbians & Gays Everywhere
2300 Market St. #165
San Francisco, CA 94114
(415) 861-5437

Anything That Moves
The Magazine for the Family Bisexual
2261 Market St., No. 496
San Francisco, CA 94114-1600
(415) 626-5069

HOTLINES

Gay Men's Health Crisis, Inc. (New York)
(212) 367-1000

National Center for Missing and Exploited Children
(800) 843-5678

U.S. Public Health Service AIDS HOTLINE
(800) 342-AIDS

■ ■ ■ ■ ■

CHAPTER NINETEEN

COUNSELING PEOPLE OF COLOR

COURTLAND C. LEE, PH.D.
University of Maryland

BESSIE CHUANG, M.ED.
Suffolk University

As the twenty-first century begins to unfold, demographic realities make it imperative that the profession of counseling reconsider its traditional definition of and responses to ethnic diversity. Population projections for the new century suggest that those U.S. citizens from historically minority racial/ethnic groups will supplant those citizens of European origin, identified racially as "White," as the majority of the country's population (Campbell, 1996). This chapter presents a twenty-first century paradigm for responding to the challenges of and maximizing the opportunities inherent in counseling people of color. The chapter begins with an overview of the demographics of people of color. Next an historical perspective traces the evolution of the theory and practice of counseling with people of color. This is followed by a contemporary exploration of the distinction between the terms *race* and *ethnicity*. The chapter then considers a potential pitfall and the promise inherent in counseling people of color. Next are an exploration of the "cross-cultural zone" in counseling intervention and an examination of dynamics to consider when counseling with people of color. Ethical considerations for counseling people of color are next discussed. The chapter ends with important guidelines for ethnically responsive counseling.

WHO ARE PEOPLE OF COLOR?—DEMOGRAPHIC REALITIES OF THE TWENTY-FIRST CENTURY

For purposes of establishing a common reference point, it is important to delineate client groups of color. In this chapter, "clients of color" refers to people of African American, Asian Pacific American, Hispanic/Latino, and Native American cultural backgrounds. It is impossible to detail the complexity of each ethnic group. The following descriptions of the ethnic groups are by no means exhaustive. Instead, they should serve as a starting point for counseling-related issues with each group of people.

African Americans

African Americans are currently the largest ethnic group of color in the United States, comprising 13 percent of the U.S. population (U.S. Bureau of the Census, 2000). Within the social sciences literature, the African American experience has traditionally been viewed as a monolithic entity. It is important to understand that there are many aspects and facets to this cultural experience. Among African Americans are distinct ethnic groups such as Jamaican Americans, Caribbean Americans, Nigerian Americans, as well as Black Americans who have been in the United States for almost four centuries as a result of the slavery experience. While these groups share discrimination and other related issues, they also have their own histories and cultural realities. For example, the abominable history of slavery, the Jim Crow era, and contemporary discrimination have shaped life experiences for generations of Black Americans. These experiences, however, vary dramatically from those who have immigrated in more recent decades.

Despite differences among African American ethnic groups, an examination of this culture will reveal that Americans of African descent have developed a worldview that is grounded in African-oriented philosophical assumptions. These assumptions have been identified by scholars as the principle of *Afrocentricity* (Ahia, 1997; Lee, 2004). This philosophical orientation emphasizes the centrality and love of Africa and Africanness as a means to deal with one's past, present, and future. Afrocentricity includes concepts such as perceptions of time, spirituality, human relations, family membership, and holism (Ahia, 1997; Lee, 2004).

Asian Pacific Americans

Asian Pacific Americans include people whose ethnic heritage originates in East Asia (e.g., Chinese, Japanese, Korean), Southeast Asia (e.g., Vietnamese, Cambodian, Burmese), South Asia (e.g., Indian, Pakistani, Nepali), West Asian (e.g., Iranian, Afghan, Turkish), and from the Middle East (e.g., Iraqi, Jordanian, Palestinian). This population has doubled with each passing decade and currently constitutes approximately 4 percent of the U.S. population (U.S. Bureau of the Census, 2000). The largest ethnic group within Asian Pacific American culture is the Chinese, followed by Filipinos, Japanese, Asian Indians, and Koreans. The first Asian Pacific Americans to arrive in the United States were the Chinese immigrants who came for the construction of the transcontinental railroad and the Gold Rush in the nineteenth century. Since then, others have followed suit and contended with discriminatory immigration laws, labor exploitation, and large-scale incarceration in the form of the Japanese internment during World War II.

Each Asian American ethnic group has its own unique cultural history and traditions. However, some dynamics are rooted in centuries-old Asian religious traditions of Buddhism, Confucianism, Islam, Christianity, Hinduism, ancestor worship, and animism. These play a major role in shaping the cultural values of Asian Americans regardless of ethnic background. These dynamics include factors such as moderation in behavior, self-discipline, patience, and humility. Many of these behaviors and values are dictated by family relationships that emphasize honor and respect for elders (Chung, Bemak & Okazaki, 1997; Sue, 1997; Toarmino & Chun, 1997).

Latino/Hispanic Americans

Demographers have projected that the Latino/Hispanic community will be the largest ethnic group of color within the century. Currently representing 12 percent of the U.S. population, the numbers of Latino/Hispanic Americans continue to rise rapidly as a result of continuing immigration and high birthrates (U.S. Bureau of the Census, 2000).

The largest Latino/Hispanic ethnic groups in the United States are Mexicans, followed by Puerto-Ricans and Cubans (U.S. Bureau of the Census, 2000). Not only do these groups differ in terms of ethnicity, but variations also exist among them based on racial characteristics, as there are Latinos of African, Asian, European, and Indian heritage. Furthermore, there is also significant diversity with respect to levels of acculturation, rural/urban lifestyles, educational attainment, English/Spanish proficiency, socioeconomic status, and relationship with the United States. Whereas Mexican Americans, for example, have struggled with European and American colonization and forced displacement, many Cuban refugees were invited into the United States to escape Communist tyranny.

Although Mexicans and Cubans are the more prominent groups, Latino/Hispanic Americans also include Central Americans (e.g., Dominicans, Nicaraguans, and Salvadorians) and South Americans (e.g., Chileans, Argentineans). Again, each group possesses a distinct historical and contemporary relationship with the United States, thereby affecting worldviews.

Latino/Hispanic culture developed as a result of the fusion of Spanish culture, brought to the Americas by missionaries and soldiers with American Indian and African (the result of the slave trade) cultures in Mexico, South America, and the Caribbean Basin. Commonality among Latino/Hispanic American ethnic groups is found in the use of the Spanish language, the influence of Roman Catholic religious traditions, and the strong bonds between family members (Constantine & Barón, 1997; Lopez-Baez, 1997).

Native Americans

Contemporary Native Americans are the descendants of the original inhabitants of the North American continent. Native Americans currently represent less than 1 percent of the U.S. population and include more than 500 different cultural communities defined as sovereign entities. The U.S. government recognizes approximately 250 nations, but another 250 Native American groups go without the formal acknowledgment from the government (U.S. Bureau of the Census, 2000). Most Native Americans first identify with a specific ancestral community, then to the larger

American Indian group (Herring, 1997). Native Americans range from those who are very traditional, speaking their indigenous language, living on the reservations, and practicing long-standing customs, to those who are very acculturated living in metropolitan areas.

As a cultural group Native Americans have had both a long and troubled history. The basis of their trouble has been their relationship with the U.S. government—a relationship often marked by conflict and oppression. As diverse as this cultural group is, there is a shared history of displacement, matched with collective resistance. Moreover, there are a few common values that are characteristic of Native Americans. These include spirituality, a strong reverence for nature, and a deep respect for one's people (Garrett & Garrett, 1994; Herring, 1992).

A New Perspective on People of Color

The beginning of the twenty-first century has brought with it a changing face of ethnic America. In recent years, the concepts of race and ethnicity have been continuously reinterpreted. Because of this, it has been suggested that the country has entered what can be considered a "post-ethnic" era (Kotkin & Tseng, 2003). Largely spearheaded by young people, long-standing notions of ethnicity and race are being reconsidered. Old racial and ethnic distinctions are blurring and being redefined. This new period is characterized by the evolution of a new reality in which individual identity is shaped more by cultural preference than ethnic heritage.

This evolutionary process has been impacted by the abolition of anti-miscegenation laws and the Civil Rights Movement, which have promoted an increase in the number of interracial marriages resulting in growing numbers of biracial and multiracial individuals (Kenney, 2000). The process has also been influenced by young people interacting in ever-growing numbers across traditional racial and ethnic lines.

The result of this process has been to push the American public to reexamine its racial and ethnic boundaries and norms. No longer can race and ethnicity be easily defined or explained—lines are blurred and identities have begun to shift. In fact, there is new nomenclature that indicates the blending of two cultures. This includes, for example, "Blasian" representing individuals of Asian and African heritage, "Hinjew"—Indian and Jewish, and "Blaxican"—African American and Mexican (Kotkin & Tseng, 2003).

Counselors today must, therefore, reexamine the traditional ethnic categories that have traditionally been used to identify client groups. These must now be expanded to include individuals whose cultural outlooks and worldviews include multiple ethnic realities.

AN HISTORICAL PERSPECTIVE: THE EVOLUTION OF THE THEORY AND PRACTICE OF COUNSELING PEOPLE OF COLOR

The concept that counseling people of color requires awareness, knowledge, and skills that differ from the traditions of counseling practice is still evolving within the profession. Much of what is known about counseling clients from ethnic groups of color has its origins in the study of African Americans (Lee, 2004). Jackson (1977), in tracing the emergence of an African American perspective in counseling, suggests that although rudimentary notions on differential therapeutic approaches for Black people appeared in the 1940s, the bulk of the knowledge base on counseling Blacks was developed in the 1960s and 1970s. These decades, a period of social and political ferment in America, saw the rise of a generation of Black scholars who made major contributions to the profession. Many of these thinkers (Banks, 1972; Harper, 1973; Nobles, 1972; Vontress, 1969; White, 1970), African American counterparts to Carl Rogers, Albert Ellis, and Fritz Perls, stated that Black culture with its African origins was qualitatively different from European-based White culture. Therefore, the validity of theories and techniques grounded in European/European American cultural traditions had to be questioned when applied to counseling interactions with African Americans. These pioneering scholars established new theoretical and practical directions for counseling with African Americans.

The 1970s also saw Black and White scholars initiate attempts to empirically validate new theoretical notions on and models of counseling with ethnic minority people. A body of research evidence began to emerge aimed at providing answers to questions on race as a variable in the counseling process (Harrison, 1975; Sattler, 1977). While this research often yielded confusing and conflicting results, it served the purpose of stimulating thinking and continued investigation about the dynamics of counseling with Black and other client groups of color.

During the 1980s and 1990s, the knowledge base developed by African American scholars in the 1960s and 1970s contributed to an important professional trend in counseling. Because of the contributions Black scholarship has made, the total profession has come to recognize the importance of considering cultural diversity in the counseling process. This has led to a profusion of counseling professionals from diverse cultural and ethnic backgrounds advancing the notion of "multicultural counseling."

Multicultural counseling places the emphasis for counseling theory and practice equally on the cultural impressions of both the counselor and the client (Axelson, 1993). The ideas on counseling theory and practice advanced by scholars from diverse cultural backgrounds in the past two decades have generated an important new knowledge base. This base includes the fundamental concept that cultural differences are real and must be actively considered in counseling. The awareness emerging from this area of thought has generated a realization that counseling must be inclusive of a variety of ways of thinking, feeling, and behaving as well as responsive to diverse worldviews (Pope-Davis, Coleman, Liu, & Toporek, 2003; Roysircar, Arrendondo, Fuertes, Ponterotto, & Toporek, 2003).

PRELUDE TO PRACTICE

Before examining counseling practice with people of color, it is important to consider several issues that must be understood if effective therapeutic intervention is to take place.

Race Versus Ethnicity: A Contemporary View

The terms "race" and "ethnicity" (ethnic group) are generally used interchangeably. They are often both used to refer to groups of people who share similar physiological traits and/or personality characteristics. These traits and characteristics are either genetically transferred or have become reinforced through group association over long periods of time. However, these terms are not synonymous. Webster's dictionary (1998) defines race as, "any of the different varieties or populations of human beings distinguished by (a) physical traits such as hair, eyes, skin color, body shape, etc.: traditionally the three primary divisions are Caucasoid, Negroid, and Mongoloid, although many subdivisions of these are also called races, (b) blood types, (c) genetic code patterns, (d) all their inherited characteristics which are unique to their isolated breeding population." Whereas Webster (1998) defines the term *ethnic* in the following manner, "designating or of a population subgroup having a common cultural heritage, as distinguished by customs, characteristics, language, common history, etc."

It can be argued that "race" has become an archaic anthropological/biological classification of human differences that historically has been used as part of political, social, cultural, and economic brutality and exploitation in many parts of the world. A classic example of this is Adolf Hitler's classifying Judaism (a religion and cultural experience) as a "race" and perpetrating the Holocaust in the last century. This definition of race forms the core of the heinous phenomenon known as "racism" (Lee, 2001).

What is most important from a counseling perspective, however, are not genetically transferred physiological/biological traits, but rather, personality characteristics among people that become reinforced through association over time. It is these longstanding dynamics of thinking, feeling, and behaving that form the cultural basis of "ethnicity" or an "ethnic group." This makes implicit the importance of the concept of ethnicity as a significant counseling construct. In considering a new counseling paradigm for changing population dynamics, therefore, it is important that the focus is on the importance of ethnicity and ethnic diversity in the relationship between counselor and client (Lee, 2001). This chapter focuses on counseling issues that must be considered when counseling clients from ethnic groups of color in the contemporary American social context.

The Pitfalls of a Monolithic Perspective

In discussing the whole concept of counseling people of color, there is a danger of assuming that all people from an ethnic group are the same and that one methodological approach is universally applicable in any counseling intervention with them. Indeed, if one reviews much of the psychological or counseling literature related to the counseling issues of people of color, he or she might be left with the impression that there is an all-encompassing ethnic reality and that all people from a specific group act, feel, and think in a homogenous fashion. Such an impression invariably leads to a monolithic perspective on the African American, Asian American, Hispanic American, or Native American experience in the United States, as well as stereotypic thinking in which individuals from these groups are considered indistinguishable from one another in terms of attitudes, behaviors, and values. Counseling professionals possessing such a perspective run the risk of approaching clients of color not as distinctive human beings with individual experiences, but rather merely as stereotypes.

People of color differ from one another in terms of experiences. Each African American, Asian American, Hispanic American, or Native American is a unique individual who is the sum total of his or her common human experiences, specific cultural experiences, and personal life experiences. Indeed, it has been asserted that attempting to identify common experiences among people of color is a precarious enterprise, because ethnic groups of color are not homogeneous (Lee, 2004). The counseling process with people of color, therefore, must incorporate the notion that there is a high degree of intragroup variability and that interventions must be client- and situation-specific. It is incumbent upon professional counselors to approach intervention with clients of color in an individualistic as opposed to a monolithic manner.

The Promise of a Proactive Perspective

Far too often, counseling intervention with people of color is designed to counteract the negative effects of extreme environmental stress on intra- and interpersonal functioning. Counseling is generally a reactionary process that focuses on the remediation of educational, economic, or social deficiencies which are the results of negative transactions between people of color and their environments. Counseling outcomes, therefore, are in many cases reconstructive in nature. The goal of counseling people of color traditionally has been rehabilitation as opposed to prevention.

However, if counseling is to be a comprehensive and effective discipline for helping people of color, then the scope of services offered should be proactive in nature. Counseling practice must move beyond merely assisting clients of color to react to negative environmental forces, to a point where the goal of intervention is helping them become empowered through the development of mastery skills. Promoting environmental mastery skills among clients of color would enable them to confront challenges in a competent and proactive manner.

ENTERING THE "CROSS-CULTURAL ZONE": THE DYNAMICS OF CULTURALLY RESPONSIVE COUNSELING WITH PEOPLE OF COLOR

Entering a counseling relationship with a person of color brings with it certain unique challenges and inherent opportunities. Engaging in such a relationship entails entering an important and potentially problematic zone of helping. This helping space can be conceptualized as the "cross-cultural zone." A counselor enters the cross-cultural zone whenever he or she differs from a client in terms of ethnic background and cultural realities. Traditionally conceptualized, this helping space has been entered whenever a White counselor enters a helping relationship with a client from an ethnic group of color.

What has been clearly evident in the cross-cultural zone is that the cultural and ethnic differences between counselor and client can be a significant impediment to the counseling process. Metaphorically, these counselor-client differences in the cross-cultural zone can hang between them like an impenetrable brick wall, impeding or negating counseling. This brick wall emphasizes the cultural distance between the counselor and the client. In many instances, the cultural and ethnic differences in the cross-cultural zone are ignored thereby widening the distance between helper and helpee.

The goal, therefore, when entering the cross-cultural zone is to scale the brick wall and decrease the cultural and ethnic distance between counselor and client. It is important that ethnic and cultural differences are acknowledged and factored into the counseling relationship. In order to accomplish this and increase counseling effectiveness in the cross-cultural zone, important dynamics must be considered. Responsive counseling practice in the cross-cultural zone with clients of color must be predicated on an understanding of these dynamics. Implicit in these dynamics are the beliefs, social forms, and material traits that constitute distinct client worldviews. These dynamics also significantly impact the psychosocial development of clients. Dynamics that may need to be considered in culturally responsive counseling with clients of color include the relationship between ethnic identity development and degree of acculturation, language, kinship influences, gender role socialization, religious/spiritual influences, immigration experience, help-seeking attitudes and behavior, and historical hostility.

The Relationship Between Ethnic Identity Development and Degree of Acculturation.   Counseling effectiveness in the cross-cultural zone may ultimately hinge upon an understanding of the concepts of ethnic identity and acculturation and the relationship between them. An appreciation of this relationship, and its influence on psychosocial development, is fundamental to culturally responsive counseling (Lee, 1997).

Ethnic identity refers to an individual's sense of belonging to an ethnic group and the part of one's personality that is attributable to ethnic group membership (Rotheram & Phinney, 1987). Ethnic identity may be considered as the inner vision that a person possesses of himself or herself as a member of an ethnic group. It forms the core of the beliefs, social forms, and personality dimensions that characterize distinct cultural realities and worldview for an individual.

The development of ethnic identity has traditionally been conceptualized as an evolutionary linear stage process (Atkinson, Morten, & Sue, 1993; Cross, 1995) or, more recently, as a dynamic personality status process in which racial information is simultaneously interpreted and internalized at a variety of levels (Helms, 1995). It is important to point out that most models of ethnic identity development in the United States have been developed in a context where people of European origin have been in a position of social and cultural dominance with respect to other groups. In this country, European Americans have generally enjoyed cultural privilege in their relationships with other ethnic groups (McIntosh, 1989). This cultural privilege has profoundly influenced the attitudes of European Americans toward members of ethnic minority groups (Helms, 1995). Likewise, the perceptions of this cultural privilege held by people from ethnic minority groups has profoundly influenced attitudes they hold of themselves and European Americans as racial beings (Atkinson, Morten, & Sue, 1993; Helms, 1995).

Ethnic identity development, therefore, occurs in a milieu characterized by complex social interaction among individuals from ethnic minority groups and the European American majority in the United States. The essence of this interaction for ethnic minority individuals is found in the concept of acculturation.

Acculturation, within the context of contemporary American society, refers to the degree to which an individual identifies with or conforms to the attitudes, lifestyles, and values of the European American-based macroculture (Lee, 1997). For individuals of color, it is generally a process of willing or unwilling attitudinal and behavioral changes brought about by overt and covert pressure from social, educational, or economic institutions within the macroculture (Lee, 1997).

Psychosocial development is greatly influenced by a sense of ethnic identity and the degree of acculturation among people of color. The relationship between these two concepts shapes attitudes, behaviors, and values. This relationship between ethnic identity development and acculturation may be conceptualized in the following four categories:

- *Strong sense of ethnic identity/High degree of acculturation.* This category characterizes the relationship between ethnic identity and acculturation for those individuals considered to be "bicultural." In other words, they have a strong sense of belonging to their particular ethnic group, while possessing a high degree of identification with or conformity to the macroculture. Bicultural individuals can move comfortably, both physically and psychologically, between their ethnic culture and the macroculture.

    A concrete example of such movement is language competency. Bicultural individuals tend to be bilingual. They have generally mastered the "standard" English characteristic of the macroculture, while still maintaining fluency in their ethnic language or linguistic traditions. They are usually capable of moving from the English of the macroculture to the language of their ethnic group with relative ease.

- *Weak sense of ethnic identity/High degree of acculturation.* Individuals in this category have a limited sense of belonging to their ethnic group and little in the dynamics of their personality is reflective of ethnic group membership. These individuals, however, have a high degree of identification with the macroculture. People with these experiences tend to be marginal to the culture of their ethnic group. This marginalization may result from a conscious choice to adopt exclusively the attitudes, behaviors, and values of the macroculture. Often such a choice is motivated by overt or subtle macroculture messages about the unacceptability or undesirability of significant aspects of ethnic minority cultural practices. Many individuals represented in this category internalize the idea that the key to social, educational, or economic advancement in American society is predicated on a complete rejection of an ethnic minority worldview and total conformity to macroculture values.

However, such marginalization may also be the result of a lack of contact with one's ethnic group culture. This is often the case, for example, when children are raised with little sense of their ethnic heritage, due to cross-cultural adoption, or other factors that may remove them from contact with the experiences of their ethnic group. In such cases the marginalization from ethnic group experiences is not by choice but rather from lack of exposure.

- *Strong sense of ethnic identity/Low degree of acculturation.* Individuals in this category have a strong ethnic identity. On the other hand, they have little identification with or are marginal to the macroculture. An excellent example of this experience is found among those people who are recent immigrants. While many new immigrants may learn the language and adopt the practices of the macroculture, many others continue to nurture the cultural customs of the "old country."

  Likewise, this may represent the reality of members of ethnic groups of color who, although born in the United States, have had limited social or economic opportunities due to systemic barriers such as racism. Effectively barred from all but superficial participation in the macroculture, many of these individuals find cultural validation exclusively within their ethnic group.

- *Weak sense of ethnic identity/Low degree of acculturation.* People with experiences in this category are marginal to both their ethnic group and the macroculture. They have a limited sense of belonging to any group and very little of their personality is attributable to specified group membership. Such a person would be considered physically, mentally, and spiritually ill in any culture. This person would be highly dysfunctional.

Importantly, the relationship between a sense of ethnic identity and the degree of acculturation for any person may be influenced by a number of variables such as age, gender, ethnic group, length of residence in the United States, level of education, extent of experience with racism, and socioeconomic status. It is also necessary to consider that the dynamic nature of human development and behavior make it impossible to neatly place individuals into any one of these four categories. Both ethnic identity development and acculturation are dynamic processes suggesting that an individual may experience ongoing movement across the categories. Such shifts might be due to a combination of intrapersonal and environmental factors at any given point in an individual's life.

The dynamics of ethnic identity and acculturation and the important relationship between them need to be factored into culturally responsive counseling in the cross-cultural zone. Psychosocial development is greatly influenced by an individual's sense of ethnic identity and degree of acculturation. Similarly, the relationship between these two concepts is a crucial aspect of mental health. Assessing ethnic identity and acculturation processes, therefore, can serve as an important vehicle for understanding the reality and issues confronting clients of color. Counselors need to be sensitive to issues of ethnic identity and carefully explore the degree of cultural similarity or dissimilarity between themselves and clients. Analysis of ethnic identity or acculturation levels should provide the focus of any counseling intervention with clients of color.

Language Preference.   Counseling is an activity that relies on communication between counselor and client. It is known as the "talking cure." Language, therefore, is an important variable in all counseling interactions, but it can assume complex dimensions in counseling with people of color. This is because the practice of counseling is predicated on an understanding of Standard English, while many clients from ethnic groups of color do not necessarily value this language tradition as a primary means of communication.

Language is culture. It is the cornerstone of ethnic identity. Language structures meaning, determines perception, and transmits culture. It communicates thought and subjective cultural experiences at deep and subtle levels (Sue & Sue, 2002; Westwood & Ishiyama, 1990). Acquisition and use of language is a primary aspect of psychosocial development and socialization in all cultures. Mastery of language generally implies mastery of culture.

Verbal and nonverbal communication is a cultural phenomenon involving the use of symbols of meaning that are culturally defined. The same words or gestures can have different meanings depending on the cultural context in which they are used (Gudykunst & Kim, 1984; Westwood & Borgen, 1988).

Culturally responsive counseling, therefore, must be based on an appreciation of and sensitivity to possible language differences between counselor and client. These include differences in language fluency, accent, dialect, and the use of nonverbal communication (e.g., eye contact, body language, facial expressions, emotional expressions). Failure to respect language differences in a counseling relationship invariably leads to misunderstanding and the possible alienation of clients.

An appreciation for language dynamics must be a central theme in the cross cultural zone. Clients of color must be able to tell their stories in a manner that is most comfortable and appropriate for them (Roysircar, Arrendondo, Fuertes, Ponterotto, & Toporek, 2003; Westwood & Ishiyama, 1990).

Kinship Influences.   Immediate and extended kinship networks must be considered as primary sources for promoting mental health and normal development among many ethnic groups of color. Such networks may include immediate and extended family, friends, or community cultural resources. Within these networks can be found hierarchical structures and carefully defined age and/or gender roles that promote a collective unity among people. This collective unity provides the basis for a worldview that emphasizes communalism rather than individualism (Lee, 1997).

Kinship support networks are crucial in providing resolution to both situational and developmental problems related to educational, career, or personal-social matters. In many instances, the supportive dynamics of these indigenous networks may keep an individual from needing to seek outside decision-making or problem-resolution assistance. Culturally responsive counseling practice, therefore, must include an understanding of and appreciation for the role of kinship dynamics in mental health and well-being. As appropriate, counselors should find ways in which to make use of the kinship system in the counseling process (Lee, 1997, 2001).

Gender Role Socialization.   Gender role socialization may need to be an important dynamic to consider when counseling across ethnic gaps. Many ethnic groups of color have developed different perceptions of the roles of men and women. These differential gender perceptions can influence the expectations considered normal for psychosocial development. Such expectations, therefore, can account for fundamental differences in personality development for men and women (Arredondo, Psalti, & Cella, 1993; Lee, 1997).

When necessary, gender role socialization and its effects on development should be considered when counseling people of color. Counselors may need to be aware of how gender-based differences in developmental expectations are manifested in decision making and problem resolution among the men and women of a particular ethnic group.

Religious/Spiritual Influences.   While religion and spirituality are universally accepted as major influences on human development, they have only recently been considered as important or appropriate issues in the counseling process (Kelly, 1995; Lee & Sirch, 1994). However, culturally responsive counseling may be enhanced if the influence of religion and spirituality are considered as crucial dynamics in the helping process. This is because for many ethnic groups of color, there is often little distinction made between religious and secular life. The philosophical tenets inherent in religious or spiritual beliefs influence all aspects of human development and interaction.

Within the cultural traditions of many groups, religious institutions or spiritual centers are important sources of psychological support. Likewise, religious or spiritual leaders have been expected to not only provide for spiritual needs, but also offer guidance for physical and emotional concerns. These institutions and their leaders have been an important indigenous source of help for decision making and problem resolution in many cultures for generations (Bond, Lee, Lowe, Malayapillay, Wheeler, Banks, Kurdt, Mercado, & Smiley, 2001). As appropriate, it might be necessary to form consultative relationships with religious/spiritual leaders or other indigenous helpers/healers for the benefit of clients.

Immigration Experience.   Many individuals from ethnic groups of color are relatively recent arrivals to the United States. For these people, the immigration experience may be an important dynamic of culture that merits consideration in the counseling process.

Immigration, in some instances, has been prompted by political or social upheaval in other parts of the world. Many recent immigrants arrive here as refugees who have escaped repressive governments or political instability. In addition to cultural beliefs and practices, these people bring with them the trauma associated with forced separation from family and homeland. In other cases, individuals have been lured here by the age-old promise of economic and social opportunity. Many times, however, these immigrants enter the country without proper documentation. Two major challenges often confront so-called "undocumented aliens." The first is living with the knowledge that at any time immigration officials might send them back to their country of origin. The second, which is common to all recent immigrants, is reconciling the desire to maintain cultural customs from back home with the pressure to adopt major aspects of the American macroculture.

Whatever the reason for immigration, however, the experience of suddenly finding oneself a stranger in a new land can effect human development in ways that need to be considered in culturally responsive counseling. Counseling professionals, therefore, should be aware of the possible influence immigration experiences have on the attitudinal orientations, behavioral repertoires, and value systems of clients from ethnic groups of color.

Help-Seeking Attitudes and Behavior.   Counselors must recognize the fact that there is great ethnic group variability with respect to help-seeking attitudes and behaviors. Not all ethnic groups traditionally value or understand the nature of formal counseling as a source of help. It might be necessary, therefore, to step outside the confines of the traditional helping setting to offer counseling services. Counselors may need to think creatively in terms of how they provide services to clients for whom the counseling process might be a totally alien experience. As previously mentioned, it might be necessary to form consultative relationships with religious/spiritual leaders or other indigenous helpers/healers for the benefit of clients (Lee, 2001).

Historical Hostility.   Counseling people of color in the United States requires sensitivity to a dynamic that can be labeled *historical hostility* (Lee, 1997; Vontress, Johnson, & Epp, 1999). The essence of this dynamic can be observed anywhere in the world where there has been a long-term pattern of exploitation or oppression between one group of people who is favored on the basis of ethnicity, religion, politics, and so on, and another who is devalued in a common relationship. With respect to the United States, in their collective experience, ethnic minority people harbor conscious and unconscious negative emotions produced by traditions of brutality and frustrations which they and their forbearers suffered at the hands of Europeans and their European American descendants (Vontress, Johnson, & Epp, 1999).

This concept underscores the historical reality of intergroup relations in this country. Sadly, the history of the United States is replete with examples of negative social encounters between European Americans and people from other cultural backgrounds—from the enslavement of Africans, to the systematic destruction of Native American culture, to the internment of Japanese American citizens during World War II. The motivating forces defining these encounters have generally been racism or other forms of social and economic oppression. Over time, the social and political process associated with racism and oppression in the United States has taken a collective physical and psychological toll on ethnic minority groups. This toll is often seen in intense negative feelings that members of ethnic minority groups often possess, either overtly or covertly, toward members of the majority group in the United States. Whether these feelings are justified or warranted at any given point in time is generally rendered moot by the nature of the often exploitative and destructive relationship between European Americans and people from non-European backgrounds in the United States.

With respect to counseling, historical hostility can manifest itself in resistance to the helper and the helping process. It is important to note that counseling has often been a sociopolitical process for many members of ethnic groups of color (Lee, 1997; Sue & Sue, 2002). Mental health services have been perceived as a tool of oppression and social control in many ethnic minority communities (Lee, 1997; Sue & Sue, 2002). Often counseling is a forced, as opposed to a voluntary, experience with a culturally insensitive or unresponsive agent of some aspect of the broad social welfare system (Lee, 1997).

Historical hostility is a cultural dynamic that must be factored into counseling in the cross-cultural zone. This is particularly the case for those clients whose counseling issues relate to the stress of racism, prejudice, discrimination, or socioeconomic disadvantage. Resistance to counseling might include denial of problems, viewing counseling as something that is done to an individual rather than with them, distrust of the counselor and the process, silence, passive aggressive behavior, or premature termination. These phenomena may be symptomatic of generalized negative feelings about the dominant group fostered by generations of negative intergroup relations.

While this list of dynamics is by no means exhaustive, given the demographic realities of American society, even a cursory review of ethnic groups of color suggests that these are some of the more salient influences on psychosocial development. Although the influence of these dynamics may vary across clients, a working knowledge of them and how they may impact the helping process should frame the context of culturally responsive counseling intervention in the cross-cultural zone. An understanding of these dynamics will go far in helping counselors eliminate the brick wall and minimize the cultural distance often inherent in the cross-cultural zone.

ETHICAL CONSIDERATIONS IN THE "CROSS-CULTURAL ZONE"

Confronted with the challenges of the cross-cultural zone, counselors must examine practice to ensure that it is culturally responsive. A major part of such introspective examination involves close scrutiny of the ethical standards that guide practice. Scholars have written extensively on ethical standards as they relate to counseling people of color (Delgado-Romero, 2003; La Fromboise, Foster, & James, 1996; Lee & Kurilla, 1997; Pack-Brown & Williams, 2003; Pedersen, 1995; Ridley, Liddle, Hill, & Li, 2001; Sue, 1996). The literature suggests that counselors who are culturally responsive increase their chances of practicing in an ethical fashion with clients of color. Counselors who are not aware of cultural dynamics and their impact on client development risk engaging in unethical conduct.

Ethical standards are rules and principles of conduct designed to guide counselor practice. The codes of ethics of mental health professions, such as those of the American Counseling Association (ACA, 1995), provide such rules and principles. In a multicultural society such standards have implications for counselor-client interactions in the cross-cultural zone. It has been asserted that counselors have an ethical responsibility to meet the needs of people of color within the context of a multicultural society (Delgado-Romero, 2003; La Fromboise, Foster, & James, 1996; Lee & Kurilla, 1997; Pack-Brown & Williams, 2003; Ridley, Liddle, Hill, & Li, 2001; Sue, 1996).

In view of the dynamics that may effect counseling in the cross-cultural zone, the issue of client welfare warrants examination with respect to the potential harm that may occur when cultural dynamics are not taken into consideration. Ethically, counselors are obligated not only to protect clients from potential harm or prevent harm when possible (beneficence), but also they are equally responsible for not inflicting harm upon clients (nonmaleficence). There can be little doubt that potential harm can be inflicted when counselors do not effectively address the dynamics of culture in the cross-cultural zone.

Counselors must enter the cross-cultural zone in a manner that is both culturally responsive and ethically responsible. With respect to ethical codes (ACA, 1995), therefore, whenever counselors enter the cross-cultural zone in working with a client they must:

- Recognize societal diversity and embrace a cross-cultural approach.
- Respect client dignity and promote client welfare.
- Recognize that kinship units are important and, as appropriate, enlist kinship understanding and involvement in the counseling process.
- Actively attempt to understand the diverse cultural backgrounds of their clients.
- Learn how their own racial/ethnic identity impacts upon the counseling process.
- Avoid imposing their own cultural values on clients.
- Be committed to gaining awareness, knowledge, and skills to work with ethnically diverse populations.
- Consider a client's ethnic experience in clinical diagnoses.
- Recognize the impact of ethnicity on test administration and interpretation.

Questionable or unethical conduct is often due to a lack of multicultural literacy on the part of counselors. However, cultural ignorance should be no excuse for unethical counseling conduct. Providing services to clients of color by professionals not competent in understanding and providing services to such individuals should be considered unethical.

In order to effectively engage in ethical practice across ethnic realities, counselors must participate in an ongoing professional development process. The focus of this process should be the development and upgrading of skills to intervene effectively into the lives of clients from a variety of ethnic backgrounds. In order to become culturally responsive as a counselor, one must become fully aware of his or her own heritage, as well as possible biases that may interfere with helping effectiveness, gain knowledge about the history and culture of people of color, and develop new skills. Counselors who engage in ethical practice with clients of color have an awareness of their own cultural assumptions, values, and biases. They also have developed an understanding of the worldviews of clients of color and they have acquired appropriate intervention strategies and techniques.

Ethical practice is a pervasive challenge for professional counselors. Counselors must be ever vigilant that their interventions are dedicated to promoting the worth, dignity, and potential of all clients. This becomes particularly crucial when clients come from ethnic groups of color. Ethical conduct in a multicultural context is predicated on awareness of and sensitivity to unique cultural realities and their relationship to optimal human development. Professional counselors who practice without such awareness and sensitivity run the danger of engaging in unethical conduct. Ignorance of cultural dynamics can be no excuse for unethical practice.

BEST PRACTICE IN THE "CROSS-CULTURAL ZONE": GUIDELINES FOR ETHNICALLY RESPONSIVE COUNSELING WITH PEOPLE OF COLOR

If counselors are to be effective in the cross-cultural zone with clients of color, then they must approach counseling from a perspective that simultaneously acknowledges human difference and celebrates human similarity. They must adopt a philosophy that views each client as a unique individual while, at the same time, taking into consideration the client's common experiences as a human being (i.e., the universal developmental challenges that face all people regardless of ethnic background) and the specific experiences that come from his or her ethnic background. It is important that counselors consider each client within an ethnic group context and a broader global human perspective (Lee, 2001).

Counselors who are responsive to clients of color have heightened awareness, an expanded knowledge base, and use helping skills in a culturally responsive manner. This premise provides a framework for best practice in the cross-cultural zone (Roysircar, Arredondo, Fuertes, Ponterotto, & Toporek, 2003).

Counselor Self-Awareness

The prerequisite for effective counseling in the cross-cultural zone is counselor self-awareness. It is important that counselors fully experience themselves as racial/ethnic beings. An individual who expects to work with clients of color must first be anchored in his or her own ethnic realities. This process should start with explorations of how one's own ethnic background has influenced his or her psychosocial development. It is of critical importance that a person considers the role that ethnic heritage and customs play in shaping his or her personality characteristics. It is also crucial that a person assess his or her own stage of ethnic identity development. The crucial questions that one must ask in this regard are: "How do I experience myself as a member of Ethnic Group X?" "How do I experience other members of Ethnic Group X?" and "How do I experience people of other ethnic backgrounds?"

As part of this self-exploration process, it is also important that a counselor evaluate the influences that have shaped the development of his or her attitudes and beliefs about people from different ethnic backgrounds. It is important to evaluate the explicit, as well as the often subtle messages one has received throughout his or her life about people who are ethnically "different." A counselor must evaluate how his or her personal attitudes and beliefs about people from different ethnic groups may facilitate or hamper counseling effectiveness.

Ethnically responsive counselors explore personal issues and questions, no matter how uncomfortable, in an attempt to discern how their own ethnic heritage, values, and biases might impact upon the counseling process. Self-exploration leads to self-awareness, which is crucial in developing a set of personal attitudes and beliefs to guide ethnically responsive counseling practice. Ethnically responsive counselors are sensitive to ethnic group differences because they are aware of their own identity as ethnic beings.

Counselor Knowledge

It is imperative that ethnically responsive counselors have a knowledge base from which to plan, implement, and evaluate their services. First they must have an understanding of how economic, social, and political systems operate with respect to their treatment of ethnic groups of color. Counselors should have an understanding of the historical impact of environmental forces such as racism on the psychosocial development of many ethnic groups of color.

Second, counselors who are responsive to diverse ethnic realities acquire working knowledge and information about specific groups of people. This should include general knowledge about the histories, experiences, customs, and values of ethnically diverse groups. From such knowledge should come an understanding of specific ethnic contexts and how they may influence personal and social development.

A counselor should enhance his or her personal growth and professional development by reading the literature and exposing himself or herself to other forms of artistic expression (e.g., television programs, films, artwork) of ethnic groups of color. A great deal of information about lifestyles, customs, traditions, language patterns, values, and histories, as well as their impact on human development and personality, can be gained from such forms of artistic expression. In addition, the Internet can be an important aid in exposing a counselor to information about people of color.

A counselor should also go out and experience ethnic diversity firsthand. There is a limit to how much can be learned about different ethnic groups from books, classes, workshops, and films. Much more can be learned by actually being among people from diverse ethnic backgrounds and interacting with them in their cultural environments. Such in vivo experiences can raise levels of awareness, increase knowledge, and provide important dimensions to empathic style in counseling interventions.

Counselor Skills

It is imperative that ethnically responsive counselors build a repertoire of relevant skills. They should be able to use counseling strategies and techniques that are consistent with the life experiences and cultural values of clients of color.

Ethnically responsive skills should be based on the following premises. First, ethnic group diversity is real and should not be ignored. Second, ethnic group differences are just that—differences. They are not necessarily deficiencies or pathological deviations. This suggests having the ability to meet clients where they are, despite obvious cultural gaps spawned by ethnic differences between helpers and helpees. Third, when working with clients from diverse ethnic groups, it is important to avoid stereotypes and a monolithic perspective. It is crucial that counselors consider clients as individuals within an ethnic group context.

In this ethnically responsive paradigm, a number of theoretical approaches should be included in a counselor's repertoire. It is important that a counselor's style be eclectic enough that he or she can use a variety of helping approaches. These approaches should incorporate diverse ethnic group views and practices with respect to the dynamics of ethnic identity/acculturation, language preference, kinship influences, gender role socialization, religious/spiritual influences, immigration experience, help-seeking attitudes and behavior, historical hostility, racism, and economic disadvantage discussed previously.

In addition to sensitivity to such dynamics in their skill repertoire, it is also important for a counselor to understand and be willing to assume the role of systemic change agent or advocate for many clients of color. When working with such clients, a counselor might need to consider the negative effects of phenomena such as racism or other forms of cultural, economic, or social oppression on development. The etiology of problems is often not in clients but rather in intolerant or restrictive environments. The only way in which clients will be able to solve problems or make decisions is to eradicate these systemic impediments. An ethnically responsive counselor often must assume the role of systemic change agent and help clients to challenge such impediments (Lee, 1998).

The components of this best practice paradigm not only are the basis of ethnically responsive counseling but can also be considered as the foundation of quality counseling in general. As counselors strive to be aware of and responsive to the needs of ethnically diverse client groups, they raise the standard of the profession for all (Lee, 2001).

SUMMARY

This chapter has presented a twenty-first century paradigm for counseling with people of color. It has explored both traditional and contemporary ethnic classifications for people of color along with the complexity of detailing each group. It has also examined the important distinction that must be made between the terms *race* and *ethnicity* when counseling across cultures. The chapter also considered the potential peril and the inherent promise in counseling people of color. The "cross-cultural zone" was introduced along with the dynamics that must be considered if effective counseling is to occur in that important helping space. Ethical considerations for counseling in the "cross-cultural zone" were also considered in the chapter. Finally, important guidelines for developing the awareness, knowledge, and skill for best practice in the "cross-cultural zone" were presented.

The cross-cultural zone can be a challenging place for counselors. It can also be a helping space of great opportunity. Demographic projections make it clear that counselors will be spending more time in this zone in the years to come. It is therefore incumbent upon them to increase their self-awareness, obtain the knowledge, and develop the skills to be effective in counseling with people of color.

The essence of counseling is the ability to help people solve problems and make decisions. Ethnically responsive counselors should have the ability to help people solve problems or make decisions in a manner that is both ethically responsible and consistent with a client's ethnic group realities. The well-being of people of color and the integrity of the profession demand that counselors do no less.

CHAPTER TWENTY

COUNSELING CLIENTS WITH DISABILITIES

MALACHY BISHOP, PH.D.
University of Kentucky

HANOCH LIVNEH, PH.D.
ELIZABETH WOSLEY-GEORGE, PH.D.
Portland State University

The present chapter focuses on the application of various concepts and counseling interventions to working with clients with disabilities. The chapter is organized into three main sections. First, a general overview of the principal goals and interventions for clients with disabilities is provided. Next, specific concerns facing clients with specific disabilities are outlined along with strategies for counseling. Finally, a brief description is offered of recommended academic education for counselors who intend to work with clients with disabilities, followed by a presentation of program accreditation and professional certification and membership issues.

OVERVIEW OF GOALS AND INTERVENTIONS APPLIED TO CLIENTS WITH DISABILITIES

The ultimate goals of rehabilitation counseling are improving the quality of life of persons with disabilities (Bishop & Feist-Price, 2002; Livneh, 2001) and helping people to adapt to life with a disability. Life, however, does not proceed in a vacuum. Therefore, the abstract goal of quality of life improvement must be concretized by anchoring it in terms of psychological, physical, social, and environmental contexts such as emotional well-being, community, and labor force membership and participation. Livneh (2001) recently proposed that "the prism of QOL" can be divided into a hierarchical paradigm based on three functional domains: intrapersonal, inter-personal, and extrapersonal (or community-based). These domains are further re-duced to specific content areas. The intrapersonal domain includes the two primary components of (a) health (health status, biomedical functioning) and (b) psychologi-cal well-being (observed symptoms, subjective appraisal). The interpersonal domain includes (a) family life and (b) peer and social relations. The extrapersonal domain includes (a) work activities, (b) housing and living environments, (c) recreational ac-tivities, and (d) learning or school activities.

The goal in rehabilitation counseling is to assist the individual with a disability to achieve maximal quality of life through the implementation of counseling and other interventions that address the whole person and the many environments in which he/she lives. For example, the goal of community membership, or integration of people with disabilities, encompasses improving life quality via independent living, self-support, or self-sufficiency in both the home and the community at large. The goal of labor force reintegration, on the other hand, pertains to the improvement of life through economic independence as typically manifested in successful gainful em-ployment, job satisfaction and satisfactoriness, competitiveness, and reduced job stress (Szymanski, 1999).

Understanding the process of psychosocial adaptation to disability is also a key research and practice component in rehabilitation counseling (Parker, Schaller, & Hansmann, 2003). The process of adjustment has been described in such terms as reintegration, reassessment, value shift, the development of new cognitive schemas, and striving to achieve life goals (Kendall & Buys, 1998; Linkowski, 1971; Livneh & Antonak, 1997; Wright, 1983; Wright & Kirby, 1999). Rehabilitation goals associ-ated with adaptation to disability, as with those associated with quality of life, may be further divided in terms of the domains physical and psychosocial. The domain of physical adjustment refers to the body's capability to function successfully within its surroundings. It is assessed through the performance of activities of daily living (ADL), mobility, and the negotiation of the physical environment. Psychosocial adaptation, alternatively, refers to the capacity to function appropriately in the per-sonal and interpersonal spheres. It often includes coping with the adverse effects of the disabling conditions and maintaining social competency in the face of negative attitudes and restrictions imposed by others.

Moreover, rehabilitation interventions can be further classified into person-aimed (internal focus) and environment-aimed (external focus) strategies (Livneh, 1989). Person-aimed interventions are those that envision the client as their prime target and seek to modify his or her emotions, perceptions, cognitions, behaviors, and/or skills. Environment-aimed interventions, on the other hand, are those that consider the external environment as the target of interest and, hence, strive to mod-ify it in order to meet client needs and goals. Counseling is just one modality adopted by practitioners who work with clients with disabilities. Personal adjustment counseling strategies occupy a single rehabilitation intervention component, focusing on the psychosocial adjustment domain, and emphasizing client-aimed interventions. The counseling intervention and the application of counseling theories and interven-tions to adjustment to life with a disability is the focus of this chapter. Readers should be aware, however, that rehabilitation counselors are trained in a wide range of skill and knowledge areas, and in practice are often called upon to combine person-aimed with environment-aimed interventions.

APPLICATION OF COUNSELING INTERVENTIONS TO SPECIFIC GROUPS OF CLIENTS WITH DISABILITIES

There are a number of problems that are frequently faced by persons with disabilities, and which can be seen to arise as a result of (1) the disability itself; (2) the environment in which the disability is experienced; (3) the individual's response to the disability; or (4) the response of family members, and others in the social environment. These problems can be characterized as existing in and impacting the personal domain and/or the interpersonal domain.

Problems that may affect the personal domain include: (1) lack of motivation, frequently associated with secondary gain; (2) reluctance to participate in rehabilitation tasks; (3) increased depression and anxiety; (4) impaired body image; (5) insult to self-concept; (6) loss of control; (7) loss of reward and pleasure sources; (8) loss of physical and economic independence; (9) difficulty in accepting and adjusting to disability; and (10) inability to access the environment.

Problems that impact the interpersonal domain include: (1) increased dependency (medical, psychosocial, and/or financial); (2) impaired social and vocational roles; (3) changing family dynamics and relationships; (4) disruption of social life; (5) negative attitudes toward disability; (6) societal rejection and social isolation; (7) disuse or lack of appropriate social skills; and (8) decreased sexual activity (Falvo, 1999; Lubkin, 1998; Thomas, Thoreson, Parker, & Butler, 1998).

In order to cope successfully with these issues, most authors recommend intervention strategies that emphasize the mastery of independent living and coping skills. Training modules aimed at achieving these goals typically stress the need for the client to acquire the physical, social, emotional, and cognitive skills necessary to successfully adapt to the disability. Moos and Tsu (1977) recommend the following adaptive tasks as part of coping with disability: (1) dealing with pain and incapacitation; (2) dealing with the management of stress in both institutionalized and community environments; (3) managing negative feelings elicited by the disability; (4) maintaining a positive self-image; (5) developing a sense of competence and mastery; (6) changing lifestyle; (7) fostering independence; (8) managing relationships with family and friends, and (9) preparing the client for an uncertain future when additional losses are anticipated.

The following sections acquaint the reader with the most paramount disability-associated issues and psychological interventions applicable to counseling clients with disabilities. Given the large number of disabling conditions with which counselors work, only the most common conditions are dealt with in this chapter. The selected disabilities include cancer, blindness, deafness, spinal cord injury, cardiac impairment, epilepsy, traumatic head injury, and psychiatric disorders. Each condition is first considered as related to its impact upon the person's life (functional limitations, psychosocial implications) and then recommendations for counseling and related interventions are provided.

Counseling Clients with Cancer

Impact of Cancer.   Over the life span, cancer will affect between one in two and one in four individuals in the United States (Orr & Orange, 2002). Cancer continues to be the second leading cause of death in the United States, and 1.33 million new cases of cancer will be diagnosed in 2003 (American Cancer Society, 2003). Cancer is not a single disease entity. There are more than 100 different types of diseases termed *cancer* (often referred to as malignancy or neoplastic disease). In men, cancers of the prostate, lung, colon and rectum, and urinary bladder will be diagnosed most often, whereas in women, cancers of the breast, lung, colon and rectum, and uterine corpus will be diagnosed most often (American Cancer Society, 2003). Among females, lung and breast cancers are the chief causes of fatality, while lung and prostate cancers are the most common causes of death among males. Although cancer can strike at any age group, it is more common in older individuals (Falvo, 1999; Freidenbergs & Kaplan, 1999). Among children, leukemia is the most common type of cancer (Bowe, 2000).

Physical Impact.   Because of the variety of cancer types, it is virtually impossible to cogently discuss all the functional limitations associated with the disorder. Hence, only the most prominent physical limitations resulting from the onset of cancer will be delineated. (The interested reader may refer to Falvo, 1999, and Freidenbergs & Kaplan, 1999, for a more detailed treatment of the topic.) Limitations on activities of daily living (grooming, bathing, dressing, feeding, toiletry) are more commonly associated with cancers affecting the brain, the larynx, head and neck, breast, lung, and upper extremities. Ambulation difficulties result more often from cancers of the lower extremities and the brain. Speech and communication are affected by cancers of the brain, the larynx, and the head and neck. Most cancers, with the possible exception of leukemia, lymphoma, and cancers of the lung and spinal cord, have an adverse effect on the person's sexual functioning and cosmesis. Finally, most forms of cancer, as well as many cancer treatments, are at one point or another, associated with organic pain, feelings of fatigue, and general weakness (Orr & Orange, 2002).

Psychosocial Impact.   Of the diseases that affect humans, perhaps none creates more distress within individuals than cancer. Despite significant advances in the diagnosis and treatment of cancer over the last decade, the diagnosis of cancer is associated with considerable fear and anxiety. Considering that the diagnosis of cancer brings with it an unknown prognosis, prolonged treatment, extended hospitalizations, disruptions in lifestyle, and uncertain prospects for cure, the period following initial diagnosis represents a time of significant stress (Ey, Compas, Epping-Jordan, & Worsham, 1998). Indeed, although much less is known of the long-term effects of stress, the prevalence rate of extreme psychological distress (anxiety, depression, etc.)

among individuals first diagnosed with cancer is reported to be anywhere between 30 to 60 percent (Kangas, Henry, & Bryant, 2002), a rate that is approximately 4 to 5 times that found in community samples. This internal state is due to the impact that the disease has on health and life quality, where fundamental beliefs about being a productive member of society, personal control over one's life events, and prospective future goals are challenged.

Recommendations for Intervention.   Medical treatment of cancer is directed at eradicating the tumor(s) and detected metastatic areas, and is accomplished mainly through surgery, radiation therapy, and/or chemotherapy. Additional treatment modalities include immunotherapy (strengthening the individual's own immune system), hormonal therapy (adjuvant hormone treatment to maximize the benefits of chemotherapy), and bone marrow transplantation. Whereas, surgery and radiation therapy are relatively straightforward procedures, chemotherapy, due to its generalized effects on many of the body systems, carries with it a host of related side effects (nausea, appetite loss, hair loss, fatigue, weakness). Counselors who work with clients with cancer should thoroughly familiarize themselves with these added problems and their psychosocial and social-familial implications (Falvo, 1999; Freidenbergs & Kaplan, 1999).

Immediately following the diagnosis of cancer, the counselor's main role is to assist the client with cancer to effectively cope with the ensuing anxiety and stress. The counselor should provide the client with accurate and useful information about the disease, its course, and its prognosis, so that irrational fears and misperceptions may be alleviated and realistic hope instilled. Optimism, or the tendency to induce or maintain a positive state of mind, may mitigate the experience of negative emotions so often noted in patients dealing with cancer (Schnoll, Knowles, & Harlow, 2002). Counselors, however, should be cautious in striking a balance between optimism and realism. The prognosis for persons diagnosed with cancer is increasingly brighter with ongoing medical advances, and counselors should help the client to maintain a positive outlook while at the same time helping clients to prepare to deal realistically with such challenges as may arise in the months and years following diagnosis. Issues of disease recurrence following treatment; the ambiguity surrounding the cause, treatment, and progression of the disease; the effects of treatment and its associated side effects; and the financial burdens of hospital and treatment costs should all be dealt with early in the coping process (McAleer & Kluge, 1978).

Obviously, one of the most painful tasks facing the counselor and client is dealing with the issue of death, dying, and the grieving process. As the disease progresses, if no cure is found, and the certainty of impending death looms larger, counseling sessions should focus on the acceptance of death. Counseling for the acceptance of death should focus on issues such as facing the agony of separation from loved ones, preparation of the family for the separation, and taking pride in one's past accomplishments ("leaving a mark" on this world).

Freidenbergs and Kaplan (1999) recommend a three-prong approach to counseling cancer patients that includes: (1) educational interventions (such as clarifying the patient's medical condition and teaching about cancer and its side effects);

(2) counseling interventions (such as encouraging the patient to vent feelings offering reassurance and verbal support); and (3) environmental interventions (such as referring the patient for further health services).

Of the various counseling approaches, two that seem to address many of the aforementioned issues are Gestalt and cognitive-behavioral therapy. Gestalt therapy may benefit clients in resolving unfinished life issues that, due to the impending death, may never be resolved (saying farewell to loved ones, and in general, gaining awareness of personal feelings toward death and dying, pain and suffering). Gestalt therapy techniques may also be appropriate for dealing with the issues surrounding perceived or real functional or anatomical losses. Cognitive-behavioral interventions include muscle relaxation techniques, systematic desensitization, thought stopping, and guided imagery. These techniques can reduce muscle and cognitive tension associated with anxiety, stress, and pain.

Counseling Clients Who Are Blind

Impact of Blindness.   Visual impairment and blindness represent significant health problems in the United States. There are approximately 10 million blind and visually impaired persons in the United States (American Foundation for the Blind, 2000). Further, because the leading causes of vision impairment and blindness are primarily age-related diseases, as a significant percentage of the U.S. population ages, the number of Americans at risk for age-related eye disease will increase, and is in fact expected to double within the next three decades (Prevent Blindness America, 2002). The following represent the major functional limitations associated with blindness.

Physical Impact.   The chief problem faced by a person who is blind is associated with mobility limitations. Lack of freedom of movement creates considerable obstacles for persons who are blind. These obstacles can compromise the capacity to live independently in the community and have direct implications for physical independence, economic independence, employment, and social integration (Panek, 2002).

Psychosocial Impact.   Psychological adjustment to blindness or visual impairment is affected by a number of factors, including the extent of the visual loss, the age at which the individual becomes visually impaired (Falvo, 1999), and whether sight loss occurs gradually or suddenly (Panek, 2002). Sight loss is frequently associated with depression, fear, and anxiety. The period of greatest emotional stress typically occurs at the onset of vision loss, rather than at the point of complete blindness (Panek, 2002). Further, the level of depression frequently appears to be related to the extent of the visual loss (Livneh & Antonak, 1997).

Blindness has been described as a highly feared condition, and is frequently identified as more feared than other disabilities (Rosenthal & Cole, 1999). For many, blindness is associated with losses across a range of life areas, including loss of physical integrity or "wholeness," loss of visual contact with the environment, and some degree of loss of an aspect of communication ability (Panek, 2002). Socially, a person who develops visual impairment may become increasingly dependent on the environment, yet the person may not be emotionally prepared to accept this dependence. Hence, interpersonal relations are frequently marked by self-restraint, insecurity, and cautiousness (Falvo, 1999). Future goals and aspirations can be strongly affected, as can relationships with the physical and social worlds. In addition, a person who is blind often faces negative societal attitudes (rejection, social stereotyping, pity, fear, patronization) that further impede his or her integration into the community.

Recommendations for Intervention.   The initial and foremost intervention modalities with blind and visually impaired clients include maximization of the use of residual vision and sight substitutes. Important rehabilitation interventions include orientation and mobility training (cane travel and use of a guide dog) and compensatory communication training (large type printer, special magnifying lenses, Braille use, Braille typewriters, scanners, optical character recognition, Kurzweil reading machine). The acquisition of such knowledge and skills brings about renewed positive self-esteem, a sense of independence, and control of the environment (Falvo, 1999; Rosenthal & Cole, 1999).

The following recommendations are noted in the literature concerning the psychosocial adjustment to blindness (Falvo, 1999; Vander Kolk, 1983).

1. Assist the client to view disability functionally (emphasize remaining abilities) rather than anatomically (merely in terms of loss of sight).
2. Help the client to understand the emotional responses (such as anxiety and depression) that follow adventitious blindness and accept this condition.
3. Explore feelings with regard to attitudes held by family and peers.
4. Help the client to understand the feelings of family and peers that result from changes associated with the condition.
5. Be understanding and accepting of client's emotional responses and the use of psychological defenses, and offer supportive counseling accordingly.
6. Avoid fostering unnecessary dependence in the client.
7. Help the client adjust his or her self-concept and personal goals so that realistic limits imposed by the disability are not ignored.
8. Teach the client self-care, socialization, assertiveness, and independent living skills.

Person-centered, Gestalt, and behavioral counseling approaches have been identified as being particularly suited for clients who are blind (Ryder, 2003; Vander Kolk, 1983). Person-centered counseling is characterized by active listening, empathizing, reframing or paraphrasing, and congruence, or being genuine in your response to the client. Behavioral therapy emphasizes modeling of adaptive behaviors via the senses of touch and hearing, reinforcement of appropriate behaviors, and rehearsal of newly acquired behaviors and skills. Gestalt stresses acting out feelings and attitudes and role playing various inner conflicts associated with loss of sight. Finally, counselors must be aware that clients who are blind rely almost exclusively on auditory cues. The customary eye contact with the client is thus rendered ineffective.

Similarly, long periods of silence that traditionally are judged to be constructive in allowing for reflective thinking may be interpreted by the client as signs of disinterest, distress, or rejection on the part of the counselor.

Counseling Clients Who Are Deaf

Impact of Deafness.   Approximately 20 million Americans have some form of unilateral or bilateral hearing impairment, including over 2 million persons who are classified as having profound hearing loss (Kerman-Lerner & Hauck, 1999). As with blindness and visual impairment, the prevalence of hearing impairment increases significantly with age. As a result, the number of persons with significant hearing impairment is expected to increase substantially over the next few decades. The principal functional limitations associated with deafness are discussed here.

Physical Impact.   Since people who are deaf are restricted in their information intake to primarily visual channels, the paramount problem they encounter is communicative. Although fundamentally a social problem, loss of or impaired hearing poses numerous environmental obstacles that might have a direct effect upon the person's safety and security. For example, the inability to readily respond to honking horns, police or ambulance sirens, children crying, a yell for help, a phone ringing, or a tree falling could create decidedly life-threatening situations in the lives of people who are deaf.

Psychosocial Impact.   A number of psychological, social, vocational, and emotional factors should be considered when counseling deaf persons. As mentioned, deafness creates a cardinal communicative handicap. The impact of deafness extends to include sociocultural deprivation, experiential depreciation, and isolation from family and friends. The extent of this impact depends to some extent on whether the deafness or hearing loss is congenital or acquired. Persons with congenital deafness may find support and opportunities for social integration in the deaf community, where a common language is shared. Persons who acquire hearing impairment later in life may feel more socially isolated, as though they fully belong to neither the deaf community nor the hearing world (Falvo, 1999). As a result, acquired hearing loss is frequently associated with social isolation and feelings of loneliness, frustration, anxiety, and depression (Falvo, 1999; Livneh & Antonak, 1997). Regarding vocational implications, the impact of deafness or hearing loss on employment depends on the type of work, the age at onset (congenital or acquired), and the extent of the hearing loss (Harvey, 2002). Deafness and hearing loss have the potential to impact both the ability of the individual to perform work tasks, and the ability to fully participate in the work culture.

Recommendations for Intervention.   When surgical (including cochlear implants) or sound amplification methods (use of a hearing aid) fail to improve auditory functioning, treatment of the person who is deaf must resort to compensatory communication skills training. Among the most commonly used training methods are speech (lip) reading, speech therapy (especially for prelingual hearing loss), finger spelling, sign language, and the use of adaptive equipment (teletypewriters, television decoders, telephone aids such as telecommunication devices for the deaf-TDD). Counselors who work with clients who are deaf should become proficient, yet remain flexible, in the use of these communicative methods (Falvo, 1999; Harvey, 2002). Counselors should also be prepared to communicate through nonverbal mechanisms, such as written materials, and be able to use body language. In addition, the counselor should acquire sufficient knowledge about people who are deaf, their subculture, and the psychosocial, educational, and vocational ramifications of deafness.

The following list presents counseling and communication guidelines it is important to be aware of when serving clients who are deaf (Bolton, 1976; Harvey, 2002):

1. Be aware that deaf people communicate in different ways, depending on the type of deafness or impairment, age at onset, language skills, amount of residual hearing, lip-reading or sign language skills, and familial, cultural, and personality factors. Find out which combination of communication techniques is most effective with each individual.
2. Involve parents and family members in the counseling process, paying special attention to their attitudes toward the person who is deaf.
3. Adopt a situation-specific and practical counseling approach (emphasize the here-and-now).
4. Avoid highly verbal and abstract levels of communication, especially when clients have become deaf prelingually.
5. Allow time and be patient, since clients who are deaf will generally require longer periods of time for services.
6. Become more aware of possible fatigue associated with lengthy communication periods.

Counseling Clients Who Have Spinal Cord Injuries

Impact of Spinal Cord Injury.   Among Americans, the number of persons with a spinal cord injury (SCI) is estimated at 200,000. These figures include individuals diagnosed with either paraplegia or quadriplegia. The incidence of spinal cord injury in the United States is approximately 10,000 new injuries per year (Crewe & Strauss, 2002). Of these injuries, the majority resulted from motor vehicle crashes (44.5 percent), followed by falls (18.1 percent), acts of violence (16.6 percent), sports injuries (12.7 percent), and other causes (8.1 percent) (Heinemann, 1999). Most people with spinal cord injury are, at the time of the accident, young (median age = 26 years) and male. The functional limitations attributed to spinal cord injury are summarized here.

Physical Impact.   Impaired mobility is obviously the cardinal limitation associated with spinal cord injury. However, in addition to restricted ambulation, individuals with spinal cord injury, depending on the degree and severity of their injury, might also be functionally impaired in personal hygiene (e.g., grooming and bathing activities), eating and drinking, dressing, toileting, writing, driving an automobile, and especially in men, performing sexually. Further complications may arise from muscle spasticity, contractures (loss of range of motion), pressure sores, pain, cardiopul-monary and genitourinary system infections, and body temperature regulation (Crewe & Krause, 2002; Falvo, 1999).

Psychosocial Impact.   There is tremendous variation among individuals in terms of the psychological and social response to SCI. This variation appears to depend less on the objective status of the injury than on personal, social, and environmental vari-ables, such as personality, age at onset, level of education, cultural and ethnic back-ground, social support, and other factors (Crewe & Krause, 2002). Spinal cord injury is associated with sudden and unexpected life changes in many areas, and although there is considerable disagreement about the psychological response to SCI, depres-sion is frequently identified as a common psychological problem (Crewe & Krause, 2002; Livneh & Antonak, 1997).

Changes in body image invoke perceptual distortions that may result in dimin-ished ability to acquire new physical skills and adapt to environmental requirements. Since social, occupational, and financial problems are rather common, disruption of family life and social roles may occur. Possible long-term psychological reactions to the traumatization are passivity, dependency (including secondary gain), passive-aggressiveness, frustration, and feelings of social inadequacy and embarrassment (Cull & Hardy, 1975). Increased substance abuse has also been observed among peo-ple with spinal cord injury (Crewe & Krause, 2002; Heinemann, 1999). Finally, atti-tudinal barriers and public misunderstanding may create additional obstacles, imped-ing the person with spinal cord injury from reintegrating into the physical, social, and vocational environments.

Recommendations for Intervention.   For the most part, medical interventions for spinal cord injury include: (1) surgery (to relieve pressure on the cord); (2) stabiliza-tion of the vertebral column; (3) medication (to relieve autonomic disturbances); (4) skin care; (5) bladder and bowel function training; (6) proper dietary control; (7) sexual functioning retraining; and (8) physical and occupational therapy to im-prove ambulation, mobility, and proper use of extremities (Hu & Cressy, 1992).

Counseling with people who have a spinal cord injury should address problems created by the injury in any area of life, including self-concept, acceptance of disabil-ity, independent living issues, sexual and marital or relationship adjustment, social relationships, and vocational concerns (Crewe & Krause, 2002; Hayes & Potter, 1995; Hu & Cressy, 1992). Two important concerns to clients with spinal cord in-jury are sexual functioning and socialization. Spinal cord injury is likely to impact sexual arousal and function, fertility and pregnancy, and in some cases, care of the newborn. Because of the potential impact on family goals, and the close relationship of sexuality and sexual function to self-esteem and personal identity, counseling in this area is essential. Counselors should be prepared to respond to both the emo-tional impact of changes in sexuality and sexual function, and also be aware that sig-nificant advances have been made in recent years in terms of enabling sexual activity (Crewe & Krause, 2002). Counselors should be ready to deal with these and related sexual, and marital, and relationship concerns at any time during the counseling process. Clients may also need to be taught new interpersonal skills (knowing when to refuse unnecessary help or request assistance without feeling inadequate, embarrassed, or guilty).

Other counseling issues to be addressed include coping with the psychological strain associated with loss of independence and needing to rely on others for personal care and daily function; coping with changes in body function, such as occurrences of spasticity, loss of bowel and bladder control, and maintaining skin and muscle health; social isolation; and vocational issues. Substance abuse issues are also important to assess, and are frequently overlooked by counselors and rehabilitation professionals (Crewe & Krause, 2002; Heinemann, 1999).

Counseling Clients with Cardiac Impairment

Impact of Cardiac Impairment.   Cardiovascular diseases are the leading cause of disability and death in the United States. A total of 30 million Americans have some form of heart and blood vessel disease. It is estimated that approximately 1 million Americans annually survive major cardiac events (e.g., heart attacks, coronary artery bypass surgery) annually (Rey, 1999). In addition, almost 6 million Americans experience symptoms of cardiovascular disease (Rey, 1999). The major cardiovascular diseases include: (1) hypertensive heart disease (elevated blood presure); (2) congestive heart failure (the heart's inability to pump sufficient blood to meet the body's requirements); (3) arteriosclerotic heart disease (buildup of lipid deposits on the inner walls of the arteries, leading to narrowing or blocking of the passages and resulting in a heart attack or coronary thrombosis); (4) heart attack or myocardial infarction (complete occlusion of the coronary artery resulting in a portion of the heart muscle being deprived of blood supply); (5) rheumatic heart disease (a childhood disease resulting from rheumatic fever which damages the heart muscle and valves); and (6) various congenital heart defects (Falvo, 1999; Rey, 1999).

Physical Impact.   There are a number of functional limitations associated with cardiac impairment. Chief among them are angina pectoris (chest pain), dyspnea (shortness of breath upon exertion), diet restriction, difficulties in tolerating extremes of temperature, and limitations of vocational pursuits (such as restricted walking, climbing, and lifting ability) and avocational pursuits (such as limited ability to engage in various sports activities). The nature and degree of these limitations are linked directly to the severity and duration of the particular impairment involved (Johnson, Getzen, & Alpern, 2002; Rey, 1999).

Psychosocial Impact.   Individuals affected by cardiac impairments are likely to exhibit reactions of fear and anxiety during the acute illness phase (during and following a heart attack) and long-term depressive reactions. Anxiety and depression are often magnified because of fears of recurrent attacks, forced dependency, other life stresses, sexual dysfunction, marital or relationship conflicts, financial worries, returning-to-work issues, and the reduction in preimpairment activities (Falvo, 1999; Johnson et al., 2002; Rey, 1999). In addition, denial of impairment may be present.

Denial may take one of the following forms: (1) total denial of being ill or disabled; (2) denial of major incapacitation; (3) minimization of effects of disability; or (4) admission of illness in the past, but denial of its present incapacitation. Although denial can represent an adaptive and beneficial response acutely, chronic denial can interfere with medical treatment and efforts to implement behavior modification (Rey, 1999). Other frequent psychological reactions include fear, helplessness, dependency, anger, and frustration (Livneh & Antonak, 1997).

Recommendations for Intervention.   The goals of cardiac rehabilitation are to prolong the patient's life and improve life quality, both psychosocially and vocationally. These goals are accomplished via educating the client on the nature of the impairment and its risk factors, modifying lifestyle (for example, weight loss, exercise, restricted diet, alcohol, and tobacco consumption), maintaining psychosocial integrity, and sustaining existing vocational abilities (Falvo, 1999; Johnson et al., 2002; Rey, 1999). Medical interventions related to cardiac impairment include: (1) surgical procedures (coronary artery bypass grafting, coronary angioplasty, electronic pacemaker implantation, cardiac transplantation); (2) restrictions on existing diet practices (reducing fat intake, restricting salt); (3) building exercise tolerance; (4) avoiding tobacco usage; and (5) medication (such as nitroglycerine, anticoagulants, beta-receptor blockers, calcium channel blockers, diuretics) to manage vessel dilation, chest pain, high blood pressure, heart rate, and so forth (Falvo, 1999; Johnson et al., 2002; Rey, 1999).

Psychosocial management to improve quality of life can be affected by numerous physical, psychological, social, vocational, and financial interventions. It is incumbent upon the counselor who works with heart patients to construct a comprehensive psychosocial rehabilitation program that incorporates the following elements (Backman, 1989; Rey, 1999):

1. Provide the client with information on the nature of and functional limitations linked to heart disease.
2. Train the client in relaxation techniques, such as progressive relaxation and guided imagery, to relieve emotional stress.
3. Encourage the client to ventilate his or her anxieties, concerns, and other negative emotions in a supportive, therapeutic environment.
4. Assist the client in cognitive restructuring, with the goal of modifying irrational and maladaptive emotional reactions and thoughts.
5. Apply behavioral modification procedures to enable the client to acquire appropriate behaviors necessitated by present physical conditions. Clients may be taught new adaptive behaviors through thought stopping of stress-inducing themes, behavioral prescriptions, role-playing exercises, and behavioral rehearsals of new and adaptive behaviors.
6. Pay attention to sexual concerns and misperceptions such as fears about death resulting from sexual activity.
7. Discuss with the client issues related to returning to work. Explore and analyze vocational interests, assets, and limitations, with the goal of achieving successful and functionally appropriate vocational placement.

Counseling Clients with Epilepsy

Impact of Epilepsy.   Epilepsy is one of the most common neurological disorders, with an age-adjusted incidence of between 20 and 70 per 100,000, and a prevalence of 4 to 10 per 1,000 worldwide (Jacoby & Baker, 2000). The incidence of epilepsy in the United States is generally agreed to be between 1 and 2 percent of the population (Livneh & Antonak, 1997). The reported prevalence of active epilepsy in the United States is about 50 per 1,000 persons (Thompson & Trimble, 1996). The word *epilepsy* is a generic term, synonymous with convulsive disorder or seizure disorder. These terms refer to a wide variety of seizure conditions rather than a single condition. Epilepsy may develop from a wide variety of causes, including traumatic brain injury, birth trauma, vascular disease, substance abuse, and numerous others, and a definitive etiology, or cause, is identified in only about one-third of all newly diagnosed cases of epilepsy (Hauser, 1997). Approximately 75 percent of all people with epilepsy have developed seizures prior to the age of 21. With appropriate medication, around 60 percent of those who have epilepsy can become seizure-free and an additional 15–20 percent experience a reduction in their seizure frequency (Fraser, 1999).

Physical Impact.   A seizure involves a disruption of the normal electrical activity of the brain in which neurons become unstable and fire in an abnormally rapid manner. This excessive electrical discharge results in a seizure which may be confined to one area and hemisphere of the brain (partial seizure) or may occur throughout the brain in entirety (generalized seizure) (Fraser, Glazer, & Simcoe, 2002). Thus, the specific functional, cognitive, affective, and behavioral impact of epilepsy depends upon the duration and location in the brain of the seizures (Fraser et al., 2002). As a result, "some seizures impair brain functioning slightly, while others result in a complete cessation of normal activities" (Fraser et al., 2002, p. 339). During the seizure-free periods, people with epilepsy are fully functioning members of society. Although ability to drive an automobile is usually not affected, differing state laws require certain seizure-free periods (that may range from three to twenty-four months) before a driving license is issued or reinstated. Functional limitations often arise as well from the adverse side effects of anticonvulsant medication. These medications, especially when reaching toxic levels, can cause the user to have a wide array of symptoms, ranging from skin rash, gum bleeding, hand tremor, coordination difficulties, weight gain, and vision problems to nausea, vertigo, fatigue, and drowsiness (Fraser, 1999).

Psychosocial Impact.   The impact of epilepsy on a person's life is multidimensional and can span a range of functional and psychosocial domains. Along with the potential physical and cognitive problems associated with seizures, epilepsy has been associated with psychological and emotional problems, social isolation, and with problems concerning education, employment, family life, and leisure activities (Thompson & Oxley, 1993). The impact and psychosocial consequences of epilepsy cannot always be understood as resulting directly or logically from the occurrence of seizures. In fact, because it is at once a medical diagnosis, a social label, and, to some extent, a part of the personal identity, epilepsy "perhaps more than any other disorder, is associated with profound deleterious psychological and sociological consequences that are not directly related to the actual disease process" (Engel, 2000, p. xiii).

Obviously, the anxiety and stress associated with the anticipation of seizures, the lack of cognitively structured environment for the person with epilepsy, and the perceived discrediting attribute of epilepsy can result in an immensely taxing psychosocial world. Attempts at concealing the condition from friends, employers, and others can lead to further stress and anxiety. These, in turn, can be associated with increased seizures, resentful feelings of embarrassment, shame and guilt, and social isolation. Also, due to the side effects of anticonvulsant medications, people with epilepsy may experience periods of impairment in various mental processes, including memory, attention, problem solving, and judgment (Fraser, 1999), all of which can increase the psychosocial impact.

Recommendation for Intervention. Medical treatment of epilepsy consists of drug therapy (anticonvulsant medication), vagus nerve stimulation, and, in an increasing number of cases, brain surgery. Commonly used anticonvulsant medications, such as carbamazepine (Tegretol), phenytoin (Dilantin), Phenobarbital, valproic acid (Depakene), ethosuximide (Zarontin), lamotrigine (Lamictal), topiramate (Topimax), clonazepam (Klonopin), and Primidone (Mysoline), among others, prevent either hypersynchronic neuron discharge or spread of discharge. Surgical intervention generally consists of removal of a portion of the temporal lobe (temporal lobectomy) when seizures are still uncontrollable after medication use (Bowe, 2000; Fraser et al., 2002). The vagus nerve stimulator (VNS) is an implanted device that delivers regular bursts of energy to the brain via the vagus nerve. The VNS appears to have increased effectiveness in seizure reduction over time (Fraser et al., 2002). Also, the ketogenic diet, which is a high fat, low carbohydrate, restricted calorie and no sugar diet may be an effective option for children with hard to control seizures. Because the diet induces chemical changes in the body, it must be prescribed by a physician and monitored by a physician and a dietician (Epilepsy Foundation, 2002).

General counseling goals include: (1) examining the nature of the epileptic seizures and their effect on the client; (2) dispelling the misperceptions held by client and family regarding epilepsy and its functional implications; (3) discussing with client and family ways of coping with the adverse effects of epilepsy; and (4) minimizing the number of areas affected by the existence of epilepsy and assuming responsibility for, and independence of, one's own life. Counselors should encourage clients with epilepsy to become educated about the condition and its management. Denial of epilepsy is not an infrequent occurrence. Because denial is manifested in failure to comply with medication schedules, ignoring requests to avoid alcohol intake, and/or pursuit of hazardous vocational or avocational activities, this repudiation of reality must be dealt with by the counselor.

Counseling Clients with Head Injury

Impact of Head Injury. Each year, approximately 500,000 persons in the United States incur traumatic head injury (THI) requiring hospitalization. Almost 90 percent of these individuals survive the head injury. However, 75,000 to 100,000 of these survivors sustain severe enough mental and physical impairments to render normal life virtually impossible (Kraus & Sorenson, 1994). THI affects primarily young adults in their late teens and twenties. Males outnumber females by a ratio of 2 or 3:1 (Dixon & Layton, 1999; Twelfth Institute on Rehabilitation Issues, 1985). Causes of THI typically include motor vehicle accidents, falls, assaults, sports accidents, and gun shots (Dixon & Layton, 1999). THI is defined as "brain damage from a blow or other externally inflicted trauma to the head that results in significant impairment to the individual's physical, psychosocial and/or cognitive functional abilities" (Twelfth Institute of Rehabilitation Issues, 1985, p. 3). Hence, THI differs from conditions emanating from internal brain traumas such as stroke or brain tumors.

Physical Impact.   Since THI results from either direct and localized damage to the brain, or from more diffuse insult (concussion, brain swelling, intracranial fluid pressure), its physical manifestations are widely varied (Falvo, 1999). Physical correlates of THI typically include various perceptual-spatial deficits, such as visual-motor incoordination, visual dysfunction, muscle spasticity, seizures and aphasia, and might also be associated with headaches, dizziness, lack of energy, and fatigue. These deficits normally affect the ability to read, write, eat, dress, ambulate, and drive (Dixon & Layton, 1999; Schwartz, 2002).

Psychosocial Impact.   The effects of THI on personality may be conveniently classified into three general categories—cognitive, affective, and behavioral. The cognitive consequences of head trauma encompass those intellectual deficits resulting from the injury. These include impairments of verbal processes, learning, memory, recognition, abstract reasoning, judgment, attention, and concentration. Affected are speech and language abilities (communicative and symbolic processing), insight, organizational skills, problem-solving and decision-making skills, and processing of information. Increased suspiciousness, delusional beliefs, and paranoid ideation may also be observed (Cunningham et al., 1999; Dixon & Layton, 1999; Falvo, 1999).

The affective consequences of THI relate to the emotional reactions directly associated with the onset of injury. The most common emotional reactions include anxiety, denial, depression, and agitation. Anxiety is manifested through panic-like and catastrophic reactions to the impairment and persistent irritability (Prigatano, 1989). Denial of the disorder is a common reaction among head-injured people and may include minimizing the consequences of the injury, unawareness of injury-related problems, and failure to acknowledge the injury. Depression, which usually sets in following initial acknowledgment of the injury and its consequences, is manifested by low self-regard, feelings of worthlessness, social withdrawal, and generally diminished or blunted affect. Finally, agitation (usually considered a by-product of lower tolerance for frustration) is typified by emotional lability (frequent and easily triggered changes in temperament), anger, irritability, loss of control over emotions, self-centeredness, lack of concern of others' welfare, and impatience (Cunningham et al., 1999; Falvo, 1999).

The behavioral components of THI include impulsivity, aggressive behavior, behavioral restlessness, social disinhibition (including sexually aggressive remarks), decreased initiative and motivation, and diminished goal-directed behaviors (Falvo, 1999; Prigatano, 1992). These changes may be the result of changes in brain function, psychological reactions to the brain injury, or a combination of these and other factors (Cunningham et al., 1999).

Recommendations for Interventions.   A wide range of interventions is available for helping clients with THI. Since a substantial number of the THI survivors manifest behavioral disorders, the goals of most rehabilitation programs have been geared toward decreasing these behavioral disturbances, increasing socially appropriate behaviors, and preparing the individual to enter the community after the acquisition of independent living and, when feasible, educational and vocational skills.

Behaviorally oriented treatment approaches appear to be particularly useful when counseling clients who sustained head injury. Behavioral management, based on operant conditioning principles such as negative reinforcement (to modify or extinguish maladaptive behaviors), positive reinforcement in the form of social praise and tangible rewards (to increase appropriate social behaviors), behavioral shaping (reinforcing approximations of desired responses), and token economies, is often used with THI clients (Greif & Matarazzo, 1982; McMahon & Fraser, 1988).

Cognitive retraining and cognition remediation are frequently used interventions based on the principles of cognitive therapy. Using intensive teaching, cognitive retraining, and extensive rehearsal, clients are taught to improve their mental functions and gradually ameliorate their perceptual, verbal, thought-processing, and problem-solving deficits (Ben-Yishay & Diller, 1983). In order to achieve these targets, counselors adopt a variety of highly structured activities to facilitate learning. These include the use of memory aids such as written or tape-recorded reminders and diaries, repeated explanations, and multiple examples to gradually instill confidence in the client in the ability to cope with the cognitive challenges of everyday life activities, such as problem solving, money management, and time management (Greif & Matarazzo, 1982; Schwartz, 2002).

Two final approaches, to be briefly mentioned, are family and group counseling. Because THI can have a profound effect on the family, and because the family has significant influence on the individual's reaction to the injury, family counseling is an important component of THI rehabilitation (Falvo, 1999). Group counseling is another beneficial treatment approach to clients with THI. It offers participants several advantages. Notable among them are socialization with persons facing similar problems, expanding one's repertoire of interpersonal behaviors, alleviating isolation and demoralization, learning how others have progressed in overcoming their difficulties, and engaging in supportive, goal-oriented group activities (Cicerone, 1989).

Counseling Clients with Psychiatric Disorders

For the purposes of this chapter, two groups of psychiatric conditions will be discussed: schizophrenia and major depressive disorder. Schizophrenia is one of the most common diagnoses of clients seeking rehabilitation counseling and presents counselors with a number of unique challenges. Depression represents a potentially significantly disabling condition in its own right, and is also frequently associated with other disabilities.

Schizophrenia. Schizophrenia represents a heterogenous group of disorders with certain core clinical features (Hyman, Arana, & Rosenbaum, 1995). Described as the most chronic and disabling of the severe mental disorders, schizophrenia typically develops in the late teens or early twenties. This illness has the potential to curtail career plans, end relationships, and negatively impact not only the people directly affected but also their families and friends. *The Diagnostic and Statistical Manual of Mental Disorders* (DSM), currently in its fourth edition (text revision; APA, 2000) specifies five major subtypes of schizophrenia: Paranoid, Disorganized, Catatonic, Undifferentiated, and Residual. The lifetime prevalence rate for schizophrenia in the general population is approximately 1 percent (Bond, 1999) and more than 2 million Americans are affected by schizophrenia in any given year (NIMH, 1995). Even with available treatment, most people continue to experience symptoms persistently or episodically throughout a large part of their lives. One measure of the anguish of schizophrenia may be inferred from its lethality: an estimated one of every ten people with the illness commits suicide (NIMH, 1995).

Psychosocial Impact of Schizophrenia. Schizophrenia is known to have two main categories of symptoms: the "positive" symptoms, which are prominent during the active phase of the illness, and the "negative" symptoms, which are prominent during the prodromal and residual phases. Both categories of symptoms have significant psychosocial impact. It is, however, the positive symptoms that typically lead to psychiatric treatment or hospitalization. These positive symptoms reflect an excess or distortion of normal functions and include hallucinations, disorganized speech, and grossly disorganized or catatonic behavior (APA, 2000). The negative symptoms of the illness are equally disabling and include affect flattening, alogia, avolition, anhedonia, withdrawal, social isolation, attentional impairment, and a decreased motivation for self-care.

The psychosocial impact of the illness on people with schizophrenia is costly. The behavioral symptoms and significant cognitive deficits impair interpersonal relationships. Common problems in thinking—which include poor memory, concentration difficulties, distorted or inaccurate perceptions, and difficulty grasping concepts—become evident in completion of tasks that were easy to accomplish prior to onset of the disorder. Accompanying this decline are marked impairment in social functioning, vulnerability to stress, and difficulty in coping with normal activities of daily living. It is estimated that persons with schizophrenia account for between one-third and one-half of the U.S. homeless population (Hong, 2002). The incidence of dual diagnosis (i.e., substance dependence) has also been a detrimental factor in the lives of people with schizophrenia (Doughty & Hunt, 1999).

Recommendations for Intervention. There is currently not a cure for schizophrenia, and treatment is aimed at reducing or controlling the symptoms (Falvo, 1999). In the last decade increasing understanding of the biochemical changes associated with schizophrenia has developed, along with identification of changes in the structures that appear to be involved in the development of schizophrenia (Kaplan & Sadock, 1996). It is also known that environmental factors can have an important influence on the development and course of the illness. Current models suggest an individual may have a vulnerability that, when stressful life events occur, leads to the development of symptoms. Stresses may be biological, environmental, or both (Kaplan & Sadock, 1996).

Antipsychotic drugs remain the mainstay treatment for schizophrenia, especially in alleviating the "positive" symptoms of the illness. Unfortunately, the older antipsychotic medications have noxious extrapyramidal and anticholinergic side effects that contribute to noncompliance with treatment. The extrapyramidal (motor-related) side effects, some of which respond to treatment with antiparkinsonian anticholinergic side effect medications such as trihexyphenidyl (artane) and benztropine (cogentin) also have the potential to cause a permanent and physically disfiguring condition known as tardive dyskinesia (involuntary stereotypical movements following prolonged dopamine block).

Newer medications, such as Clozapine (Clozaril) and Risperidone (Risperdal), appear to offer more favorable side effect profiles. Clozapine, originally introduced into the United States in 1990, has been shown to result in few extrapyramidal side effects. People who are prescribed Clozapine, however, need to have their blood monitored on a weekly basis, as the side effect of agranulocytosis (depletion of white blood cells) is potentially lethal. Risperidone (Risperdal), which was introduced after Clozapine, is devoid of anticholinergic side effects, such as dizziness, blurred vision, urinary retention, and fecal impaction; however, Risperdal may produce extrapyramidal side effects at large dosages. Other new antipsychotics on the market have also been found to have favorable side effect profiles. These medications include Sertindole (Serlect) and Olanzapine (Zyprexa), both introduced in 1996, and Seroquel (Quetiapine fumarate), which was approved by the Food and Drug Administration (FDA) in 1997.

Counseling treatment should be individualized, and based on the recognition that the course and impact of schizophrenia is experienced in a unique way by each individual. Treatment should address both the abilities and the deficits of the individual (Kaplan & Sadock, 1996) and focus on helping the individual to understand his/her condition and its impact on social, psychological, and vocational functioning, and on helping the client to cope with this impact. Self-management and treatment compliance is an important counseling concern, as individuals with schizophrenia may deny their need for medication, or simply stop taking it in response to the frequently significant side effects (Falvo, 1999).

Behavioral approaches, such as social skills training, are aimed at increasing social skills, self-sufficiency, practical living skills, and developing interpersonal communication skills (Kaplan & Sadock, 1996). The importance of a counseling relationship in which the individual with schizophrenia feels safe has been emphasized, and the ability of the client to form a therapeutic relationship has been identified as an important predictor of treatment outcome (Kaplan & Sadock, 1996).

Major Depressive Disorder.   Depression, also known as major depressive disorder, is a common and costly mental illness that affects approximately 17.6 million

Americans each year. Estimates for the cost of depression to the nation in 1990 ranged from $30 to $44 billion. Depression also has an astronomical value in lost work, estimated to be as high as 200 million days each year. By the year 2020, it has been estimated that major depression will be the second most important cause of disability worldwide (Davidson & Meltzer-Brody, 1999). The lifetime risk for major depressive disorder in community samples has varied from 10 percent to 25 percent for women and from 5 percent to 12 percent for men (APA, 2000).

Psychosocial Impact of Major Depressive Disorder.   The significant psychosocial impact of major depression is suggested by a review of the symptoms of the illness. These include persistent sad or "empty" mood, loss of interest in pleasurable activities, decreased sexual drive, and increased fatigue. These symptoms often lead to major problems in interpersonal relationships. Very often, the person with depression is misunderstood and blamed for being lazy. On the job, the individual may frequently be tardy or absent, as motivation and energy levels compounded by feelings of hopelessness make work seem meaningless. Irritability, lack of interest, and crying spells make coworkers, family, and friends uncomfortable. Insomnia or hypersomnia and a disturbed sleep pattern, coupled with poor memory and concentration difficulties, often affect decision making and general performance at work and at home. Frequent suicidal ideation and attempts put friends and family on edge, further worsening feelings of guilt already being experienced by the affected individual. In certain cases, the symptoms are accompanied by psychotic features, such as command auditory hallucinations, further increasing the risk for suicide.

Recommendations for Intervention.   Effective pharmacological and psychological treatment for people diagnosed with major depression are available and are frequently used concurrently. Medication includes the traditional tricyclics, heterocyclics, and monoamine oxidase (MAO) inhibitors, which, in addition to causing sedation, weight gain, and orthostatic hypotension, typically have many anticholinergic side effects such as dizziness, blurred vision, constipation, urinary retention, and fecal impaction. The sedation caused by these medications may make it especially difficult to drive or to operate machines on the job. Furthermore, the use of MAO inhibitors calls for a strict avoidance of foods containing tyramine, examples of which are aged cheeses, beer, red wines, smoked fish, dry or fermented sausages, caviar, yeast extracts, liver (beef and chicken), and overripe fruits (Diamond, 2002; Kaplan & Sadock, 1996).

Fortunately, the newer antidepressants fluoxetine (Prozac), fluvoxamine (Luvox), sertraline (Zoloft), citalopram (Celexa), and paroxetine (Paxil), known as Selective Serotonin Reuptake Inhibitors (SSRIs), lack the anticholinergic side effects and potential cardiotoxicity of the tricyclics. In addition, they are less sedating and do not cause weight gain. In addition to the SSRIs other new antidepressants have been introduced. They include mirtazapine (Remeron), nefazodone (Serzone), and trazadone (Desyrel) (Diamond, 2002). Venlafaxine (Effexor), an antidepressant introduced into the United States in 1994, inhibits the uptake of the neurotransmitters, norepinepherine and serotonin. Buproprion (Wellbutrin) is the only antidepressant that works on the dopamine nerve cells, and is reported to have fewer anticholinergic side effects than the tricyclics (Diamond, 2002). Electroconvulsive Therapy (ECT) is usually reserved for acute disabling episodes of depression and for cases that are refractory to other therapies.

The following list presents counseling guidelines to be aware of when serving clients with depression (Bishop & Swett, 2000; Livneh & Antonak, 1999):

1. Encourage clients to vent and verbalize feelings of frustration, grief, loss, guilt, self-blame, and shame.
2. Reinforce the client's strengths and assets by rewarding positive self-statements and participation.
3. Set limited, concrete, and short-term goals to assure success in attaining longer term rehabilitation goals.
4. Interrupt and challenge client's irrational and self-defeating beliefs and statements.
5. Break down problems perceived as unmanageable or overwhelming into smaller, more manageable, and time-bound issues.
6. Reinforce interpersonal contacts, social participation, and the development of social skills.

TRAINING AND QUALIFICATIONS OF COUNSELORS WHO WORK WITH CLIENTS WITH DISABILITIES

Academic Training and Program Accreditation

Academic training of counselors whose interest lies in working with clients with disabilities is accomplished through rehabilitation counselor education (RCE) programs. These training programs are typically graduate (master's level) programs and are offered by counselor education or counseling psychology departments. The programs normally require two years of academic and clinical training to complete when pursued on a full-time basis. Delivery of rehabilitation counseling coursework through distance education options, such as web-based courses and videoconferencing, is increasingly being used by programs around the country.

The curriculum content in most of these training programs has been developed and verified by the Council on Rehabilitation Education (CORE). CORE was established in 1971 as an accreditation body to oversee the academic and clinical training of rehabilitation counselors and to promote effective delivery of rehabilitation services to people with disabilities. Ninety-three RCE programs are currently CORE accredited. These programs must show evidence of a graduate-level curriculum that provides its trainees with a course of study that includes, but is not limited to, the following knowledge and/or skill areas: (1) history and philosophy of rehabilitation; (2) rehabilitation legislation; (3) organizational structure of the rehabilitation system (public and private, nonprofit, and for-profit service delivery); (4) counseling theories, approaches, and techniques; (5) case management; (6) career development and vocational counseling theories and practices; (7) vocational evaluation, occupational information, job analysis, and work adjustment techniques; (8) job development and placement; (9) medical aspects of disability; (10) psychosocial aspects of disability; (11) knowledge of community resources and services; (12) rehabilitation research and program evaluation; (13) measurement, appraisal and testing; (14) legal and ethical issues in rehabilitation counseling; (15) independent living; (16) consultation services; (17) service coordination; and (18) special topics in rehabilitation (such as transition from school to work, supported employment, and rehabilitation engineering). In addition, rehabilitation counseling trainees are required to participate in supervised practicum and internship experiences totalling a minimum of 600 clock hours in approved rehabilitation sites and under the supervision of a certified rehabilitation counselor.

Certification and Licensure

The Commission on Rehabilitation Counselor Certification (CRCC) is the primary certifying body of rehabilitation counselors in the United States. The main purpose of CRCC is to assure that professionals who practice counseling with clients with disabilities (rehabilitation counseling) meet acceptable standards of professional expertise. In accordance with the knowledge and skill areas required by CORE for program accreditation purposes, CRCC tests rehabilitation applicants on a broad range of content subjects. The duration of the certification is five years, at the end of which the Certified Rehabilitation Counselor (CRC) is required to have accumulated a total of 100 approved contact (clock) hours of continuing education to maintain his or her certification.

State-regulated licensure of counselors who work with clients with disabilities is usually accomplished through the enactment of omnibus state legislation that governs the practice of various professional counselor groups (mental health, marriage and family, community, rehabilitation). These state laws regulate individuals in the use of the title ("professional counselor"), as well as the practice of the profession.

Professional Associations

At present, the following national professional organizations offer membership to counselors who seek to specialize in working with clients with disabilities: (1) the American Rehabilitation Counseling Association (ARCA), a Division of ACA; (2) the National Rehabilitation Counseling Association (NRCA), a Division of the National Rehabilitation Association (NRA); (3) the Rehabilitation Psychology Division (Division 22) of the American Psychological Association (APA); and (4) the National Association of Rehabilitation Professionals in the Private Sector (NARPPS).

ARCA and NRCA are organizations representing professional rehabilitation counselors and others concerned with improving the lives of persons with disabilities (educators, researchers, administrators). These two organizations have as their mission the provision of leadership to promote excellence in rehabilitation counseling practice, training, research, consultation, and professional growth. They further emphasize the importance of modifying environmental and attitudinal conditions and barriers so that more opportunities become available to persons with disabilities in employment, education, and community activities. The membership of ARCA and NRCA is composed of rehabilitation counselors and other practitioners employed in both the public and private sectors (divisions of vocational rehabilitation, commissions for the blind and visually impaired, hospitals and rehabilitation units, mental health centers, rehabilitation workshops, university services for students with disabilities, self-help organizations, and private rehabilitation organizations).

The Rehabilitation Psychology Division of the APA represents members (mainly psychologists) who are interested in the psychosocial consequences of disability and rehabilitation (personal adjustment and growth, coping strategies, social and attitudinal barriers) in order to better serve persons with disabilities. This division is equally interested in the development of high standards and practices for professional psychologists who serve clients with disabilities. Most of the division members are educators, researchers, and practicing psychologists whose clientele is comprised mainly of persons with physical, psychiatric, and cognitive impairments.

Finally, NARPPS is an organization whose members are invariably committed to the advancement of rehabilitation practices in the private for-profit rehabilitation sector. Although traditional counseling activities make up only a minor portion of the job tasks performed by private rehabilitation professionals, they, nonetheless, offer individual and group counseling services to clients as may be required for achievement of sound vocational choice and successful job placement. Members of NARPPS typically include rehabilitation counselors, rehabilitation nurses, vocational evaluators, and job placement specialists.

SUMMARY

The purpose of this chapter was to acquaint the beginning counseling student with (1) the impact of various disabling conditions on the client; (2) the intervention strategies most commonly adopted by counselors who work with clients with disabilities; and (3) the academic programs, their accreditation procedures, certification and licensure considerations, and the professional organizations of counselors who serve clients with disabilities. Counselors who intend to pursue the career of rehabilitation counseling and specialize in working with clients with disabilities may find it advantageous to directly contact these organizations through their websites.

REFERENCES

Chapter 1

Altekruse, M., & Wittmer, J. (1991). Accreditation in counselor education. In F. Bradley (Ed.), *Credentialing in counseling* (pp. 53–62). Alexandria, VA: American Association for Counseling and Development.

American Counseling Association (ACA). (1995). *Code of ethics and standards of practice.* Alexandria, VA: Author.

American Counseling Association. (1999a). Special message: Congress approves $20 million for school counseling as part of Omnibus Spending Package for FY2000. *http://www.counseling.org/urgent/special112299a.html*

American Counseling Association.(1999b). Special message: WIIA passes house and senate. Clinton to sign bill into law. *http://www.counseling.org/urgent/special112299a.html*

American Counseling Association (ACA). (1999c). School counselors' caseloads grow 9.3 percent. *Counseling Today, 42*(4), 10.

American Counseling Association (ACA). (1999d). *Ethical standards for Internet on-line counseling.* Alexandria, VA: Author.

American Counseling Association. (2003a). Licensure chart—Requirements for mental health counselor credentials. Retrieved September 15, 2003. *http://www.counseling.org/site/PageServer?pagename=resources_licensure_chart*

American Counseling Association. (2003b). Mission and vision statements. Retrieved August 2, 2003. *http://www.counseling.org/site/PageServer?pagename=about_mission*

American Counseling Association Office of Public Policy and Information. (1996). *Briefing paper: Mental Health Insurance Parity Act passed.* Alexandria, VA: Author.

American Counseling Association Office of Public Policy and Information. (1998a). *Briefing paper: Higher education programs updated.* Alexandria, VA: Author.

American Counseling Association Office of Public Policy and Information. (1998b). *Briefing paper: Congress passes bill recognizing counselors under health professional training programs.* Alexandria, VA: Author.

American Counseling Association Office of Public Policy and Information. (1998c). *Briefing paper: Workforce Investment Act signed into law. Legislation revamps job training, reauthorizes the Rehabilitation Act.* Alexandria, VA: Author.

American Counseling Association Office of Public Policy and Information. (2002a, March). *A guide to state laws and regulations on professional school counseling.* Alexandria, VA: American Counseling Association.

American Counseling Association Office of Public Policy and Information. (2002b, March). *Elementary and secondary school counseling program (ESSCP) FY03 funding request.* Alexandria, VA: American Counseling Association.

American Counseling Association Practice Research Network. (2002, March). Where do professional counselors work? *Research into Practice, Practice into Research, 1*(3).

American Personnel and Guidance Association (APGA). (1968). *Standards for preparation of elementary school counselors.* Washington, DC: Author.

American Personnel and Guidance Association (APGA). (1969). *Guidelines for graduate programs in the preparation of student personnel workers in higher education.* Washington, DC: Author.

American Personnel and Guidance Association (APGA). (1976). *Model for state legislation concerning the practice of counseling, 1976, draft no. 4.* Alexandria, VA: Author.

American School Counselor Association. (2002). *The ASCA national model: A framework for school counseling programs.* Herndon, VA: Author.

Association for Counselor Education and Supervision (ACES). (1967). Standards for the preparation of secondary school counselors. *Personnel and Guidance Journal, 46,* 96–106.

Aubrey, R. F. (1982). A house divided: Guidance and counseling in 20th century America. *The Personnel and Guidance Journal, 61,* 198–204.

Baker, S. B., & Gerler, E. R. (2001). Counseling in schools. In D. Locke, J. Myers, & E. Herr (Eds.), *The handbook of counseling* (pp. 289–318). Thousand Oaks, CA: Sage Publications.

Barstow, S. (1999). *Counselors unfairly treated by TRI-CARE/CHAMPUS.* Briefing paper for the American Counseling Association. Alexandria, VA: American Counseling Association.

Bartlett, W. E., Lee, J. E., & Doyle, R. E. (1985). Historical development of the Association for Religious and Values Issues in Counseling. *Journal of Counseling and Development, 63*(7), 448–451.

Baruth, L. G., & Robinson, E. H., III. (1987). *An introduction to the counseling profession.* Englewood Cliffs, NJ: Prentice Hall.

Beers, C. W. (1908). *A mind that found itself.* NY: Doubleday.

Belkin, G. S. (1988). *Introduction to counseling* (3rd ed.). Dubuque, IA: Wm. C. Brown Publishers.

Bistline, J. (1991, Feb.). Self-insured plans and their impact on the counseling profession. *The Advocate*, p. 10.

Bradley, F. (1991). *Credentialing in counseling.* Alexandria, VA: American Association for Counseling and Development.

Brewer, J. M. (1942). *History of vocational guidance.* NY: Harper.

Brooks, D. K. (1986). Credentialing of mental health counselors. In A. J. Palmo & W. J. Weikel (Eds.), *Foundations of mental health counseling* (pp. 243–261). Springfield, IL: Charles C. Thomas.

Brooks, D. K., Jr. (1988). Finishing the job. In R. L. Dingman (Ed.), *Licensure for mental health counselors* (pp. 4–7). Alexandria, VA: American Mental Health Counselors Association.

Brown, D., & Srebalus, D. (1988). *An introduction to the counseling profession.* Englewood Cliffs, NJ: Prentice Hall.

Brown, L., & Kraus, K. (2003, Sept.). Point Counterpoint: School counselors—Professional counselors in school settings. *Counseling Today, 46*(3), 14–15.

Caplow, T. (1966). The sequence of professionalization. In H. M. Vollmer & D. L. Mills (Eds.), *Professionalization.* Englewood Cliffs, NJ: Prentice Hall.

Cicourel, A. V., & Kitsuse, J. I. (1963). *The educational decision-makers.* Indianapolis, IN: Bobbs-Merrill.

City of Cleveland, Ohio v. Cook, Municipal Court, Criminal Division, No. 75-CRB 11478, August 12, 1975. (Transcript dated August 19, 1975).

Commission on Rehabilitation Counselor Certification (CRCC). (2003). New criteria and dates for certification. *http://www.crccertification.com/cert_popup.html*

Council for Accreditation of Counseling and Related Educational Programs (CACREP). (1987). *Accreditation procedures manual for counseling and related educational programs.* Alexandria, VA: Author.

Council for Accreditation of Counseling and Related Educational Programs (CACREP). (1994). *Accreditation standards and procedures manual.* Alexandria, VA: Author.

Council for Accreditation of Counseling and Related Educational Programs (CACREP). (2001). *Accreditation procedures manual for counseling and related educational programs.* Alexandria, VA: Author.

Council for Accreditation of Counseling and Related Educational Programs (CACREP). (2003, April). Update of accredited programs. Retrieved September 15, 2003. *http://www.counseling.org/cacrep/directory.htm*

Council on Rehabilitation Education (CORE). (2003). New CORE Standards. Retrieved October 1, 2003. *http://www.core-rehab.org/*

Council on Rehabilitation Education (CORE). (1997). *Accreditation manual for rehabilitation counselor education programs.* Rolling Meadows, IL: Author.

Cummings, N. A. (1990). The credentialing of professional psychologists and its implication for the other mental health disciplines. *Journal of Counseling and Development, 68*(5), 485–490.

D'Andrea, M., & Daniels, J. (2001). Facing the changing demographic structure of our society. In D. Locke, J. Myers, & E. Herr (Eds.), *The Handbook of Counseling* (pp. 529–540). Sage Publications.

Danzinger, P. R., & Welfel, E. R. (2001). The impact of managed care on mental health counselors: A survey of perceptions, practices, and compliance with ethical standards. *Journal of Mental Health Counseling, 22,* 137–150.

Davis, J. B. (1914). *Moral and vocational guidance.* Boston: Ginn.

Davis, J. B. (1956). *Saga of a schoolmaster: An autobiography.* Boston: Boston University Press.

Espina, M. (1999). *Licensure chart: Requirements for mental health counselor credentials.* Unpublished paper prepared for members of the American Counseling Association. Alexandria, VA: American Counseling Association.

Everett, C. A. (1990). The field of marital and family therapy. *Journal of Counseling and Development, 68*(5), 498–502.

Fong, M. (1998). Considerations of a counseling pedagogy. *Counselor Education and Supervision, 38,* 106–112.

Foos, J. A., Ottens, A. J., & Hills, L. K. (1991). Managed mental health: A primer for counselors. *Journal of Counseling & Development, 69*(4), 332–336.

Forrest, D. V., & Stone, L. A. (1991). Counselor certification. In F. Bradley (Ed.), *Credentialing in counseling* (pp. 23–52). Alexandria, VA: American Association for Counseling and Development.

Ginzberg, E. (1971). *Career guidance.* New York: McGraw-Hill.

Gladding, S. T., & Ryan, M. (2001). Community counseling settings. In D. Locke, J. Myers, & E. Herr (Eds.), *The handbook of counseling* (pp. 343–355). Thousand Oaks, CA: Sage Publications.

Glosoff, H. L. (1993). An assessment of the career benefits of state statutory credentials and national board certification as perceived by professional counselors. *Dissertation Abstracts International, 55*(09), 2719. (University Microfilms No. AAC95-03041).

Glosoff, H. L. (1998). Managed care: A critical ethical issue for counselors. *Counseling and Human Development, 31*(3), 1–16.

Glosoff, H. L., Benshoff, J. M., Hosie, T. W., & Maki, D. R. (1995). The 1994 ACA model legislation for licensed professional counselors. *Journal of Counseling and Development, 74*(2), 209–220.

Goldenberg, H. (1973). *Contemporary psychology.* Belmore, CA: Wadsworth.

Gross, M. L. (1962). *The brain watchers.* NY: Random House.

Herr, E. (1985). *Why counseling?* Alexandria, VA: American Association for Counseling and Development.

Hollis, J. W. (2000). *Counselor preparation: Programs, personnel, trends* (10th ed.). Muncie, IN: Accelerated Development.

Hosie, T. W. (1991). Historical antecedents and current status of counselor licensure. In F. Bradley (Ed.), *Credentialing in counseling* (pp. 23–52). Alexandria, VA: American Association for Counseling and Development.

Hosie, T. W., & Glosoff, H. L. (2001). Counselor education. In D. Locke, J. Myers, & E. Herr (Eds.), *The Handbook of Counseling* (pp. 393–416). Sage Publications.

Hosie, T. W., West, J. D., & Mackey, J. A. (1993). Employment and roles of mental health counselors in employee assistance programs. *Journal of Counseling and Development, 71,* 355–359.

Hoyt, K. B. (1974). Professional preparation for professional guidance. In E. Herr (Ed.), *Vocational guidance and human development* (pp. 502–527). Boston: Houghton Mifflin.

Humes, C. W. (1987). *Contemporary counseling: Services, applications, issues.* Muncie, IN: Accelerated Development.

Joint Committee on Testing (1962). *Testing, testing, testing.* Washington, DC: American Association of School Administrators.

Kiselicia, M., & Ramsey, M. (2001). Multicultural counselor education: Historical perspectives and future directions. In D. Locke, J. Myers, & E. Herr (Eds.), *The handbook of counseling* (pp. 433–452). Thousand Oaks, CA: Sage Publications.

Lewis, J. A., & Hayes, B. A. (1988). Options for counselors in business and industry. In R. Hayes and R. Aubrey (Eds.), *New directions for counseling and human development.* Denver, CO: Love Publishing.

Loesch, L. C. (1984). Professional credentialing in counseling—1984. *Counseling and Human Development, 17*(2), 1–11.

Marino, T. W. (1995). Facing a challenge to a school counseling program. *Counseling Today, 38*(4), 6, 18.

McDaniels, C. O. (1964). *The history and development of the American Personnel and Guidance Association, 1952–1963.* Unpublished doctoral dissertation. Charlottesville, VA: University of Virginia.

Miller, C. H. (1971). *Foundations of guidance* (2nd ed.). New York: Harper & Row.

National Board for Certified Counselors (NBCC). (1995). *Specialty certification.* Greensboro, NC: Author.

National Board for Certified Counselors (NBCC). (1998). *Standards for the ethical practice of web counseling.* Greensboro, NC: Author.

National Board for Certified Counselors (NBCC). (1999). NCC—The National Certified Counselor Credential. *http://www.nbcc.org/info.htm*

Norris, W. (1954). *The history and development of the National Vocational Guidance Association.* Unpublished doctoral dissertation. Washington, DC: George Washington University.

Ohlsen, M. M. (1983). *Introduction to counseling.* Itasca, IL: F. E. Peacock.

Palmo, A. J., & Weikel, W. J. (1986). *Foundations of mental health counseling.* Springfield, IL: Charles C. Thomas.

Parsons, F. (1894). The philosophy of mutualism. *The Arena, 9,* 738–815.

Parsons, F. (1909). *Choosing a vocation.* Boston: Houghton-Mifflin.

Pedersen, P. B. (1991a). Concluding comments to the special issue. Special Issue: Multiculturalism as a fourth force in counseling. *Journal of Counseling and Development, 70*(1), 250.

Pedersen, P. B. (1991b). Multiculturalism as a generic approach to counseling. Special Issue: Multiculturalism as a fourth force in counseling. *Journal of Counseling and Development, 70*(1) 6–12.

Picchioni, A. P., & Bonk, E. C. (1983). *A comprehensive history of guidance in the United States.* Austin, TX: Texas Personnel and Guidance Association.

Psychotherapy Finances. (1995). Survey report. *Managing your practice and your money, 21*(1), Whole Issue 249.

Reed, A. Y. (1916). *Vocational guidance report 1913–1916.* Seattle, WA: Board of School Directors.

Reed, A. Y. (1920). *Junior wage earners.* New York: Macmillan.

Reed, A. Y. (1944). *Guidance and personnel services in education.* Ithaca, NY: Cornell University Press.

Remley, T. P. (1991). An argument for credentialing. In F. Bradley (Ed.), *Credentialing in counseling* (pp. 23–52). Alexandria, VA: American Association for Counseling and Development.

Richards, L. S. (1881). *Vocophy.* Marlboro, MA: Pratt Brothers.

Rockwell, P. J., Jr. (1958). *Social concepts in the published writings of some pioneers in guidance.* Unpublished doctoral dissertation. Madison, WI: University of Wisconsin.

Rogers, C. R. (1942). *Counseling and psychotherapy.* Boston: Hougton Mifflin.

Rogers, C. R. (1951). *Client-centered therapy.* Boston: Hougton Mifflin.

Rudolph, J. (1986). Third-party reimbursement and mental health counselors. In A. J. Palmo and W. J. Weikel (Eds.), *Foundations of mental health counseling* (pp. 271–284). Springfield, IL: Charles C. Thomas.

Sampson, J. P., Jr., & Bloom, J. W. (2001). The potential for success and failure of computer applications in counseling and guidance. In D. Locke, J. Myers, & E. Herr (Eds.), *The handbook of counseling* (pp. 613–627). Thousand Oaks, CA: Sage Publications.

Sattem, L. (1997). *Mandatory continuing professional education in an emerging field: A prospectus on the counseling profession.* Doctoral Dissertation: The Ohio State University.

Schmitt, S. (1999a). NBCC drops career and gerontology counseling specialties. *Counseling Today, 41*(2), 1, 19.

Schmitt, S. (1999b). FACT still fighting for testing rights. *Counseling Today, 42*(4), 24.

Shertzer, B., & Stone, S. C. (1986). *Fundamentals of counseling.* Boston, MA: Houghton Mifflin.

Shimberg, B. (1982). *Occupational licensing: A public perspective.* Princeton, NJ: Educational Testing Service.

Smith, R. L., Carlson, J., Stevens-Smith, P., & Dennison, M. (1995). Marriage and family counseling. *Journal of Counseling and Development, 74*(2), 154–157.

Stephens, W. R. (1954). *Technical recommendations for psychological tests and diagnostic techniques.* Washington, DC: American Psychology Association.

Stephens, W. R. (1970). *Social reform and the origins of vocational guidance.* New York: Harper & Row.

Stripling, R. O. (1983). Building on the past—A challenge for the future. In G. R. Walls & L. Benjamin (Eds.), *Shaping counselor education programs in the next five years: An experimental prototype for the counselor of tomorrow* (pp. 205–209). Ann Arbor: ERIC/CAPS.

Stone, C. (2003, Sept.). Point Counterpoint: School counselors—Educators first, with MH expertise. *Counseling Today, 46*(3), 15.

Sue, D. W. (1991). A model for cultural diversity training. Special Issue: Multiculturalism as a fourth force in counseling. *Journal of Counseling and Development, 70*(1), 99–105.

Swanson, C. (1988). Historical perspective on licensure for counselors. In R. L. Dingman (Ed.), *Licensure for mental health counselors* (pp. 1–3). Alexandria, VA: American Mental Health Counselors Association.

Sweeney, T. J. (1991). Counselor credentialing: Purpose and origin. In F. Bradley (Ed.), *Credentialing in counseling* (pp. 23–52). Alexandria, VA: American Association for Counseling and Development.

Throckmorton, E. W. (1992). Mental health counselors and reimbursement decisions: How do third-party payers of mental health benefits decide which mental health providers to pay. Dissertation, Ohio University. *Dissertation Abstracts International 53*(03) (University Microfilms No. AAC 9230310).

Vacc, N., & Loesch, L. (1994). *A professional orientation to counseling* (2nd ed.). Muncie, IN: Accelerated Development

Weikel, W. J. ((1985). The American Mental Health Counselors Association. *Journal of Counseling and Development, 63*(7), 457–460.

Weikel, W. J., & Palmo, A. J. (1989). The evolution and practice of mental health counseling. *Journal of Mental Health Counseling, 11*(1), 7–25.

Weldon v. Virginia State Board of Psychologist Examiners. Corporation Court Opinion (Court Order). Newport News, VA: October 4, 1972.

West, J. D., Hosie, T. W., & Mackey, J. A. (1987). Employment and roles of counselors in mental health agencies. *Journal of Counseling and Development, 66,* 135–138.

West, J. D., Hosie, T. W., & Mackey, J. A. (1988). The counselor's role in mental health: An evaluation. *Counselor Education and Supervision, 27,* 233–239.

Williamson, E. G. (1965). *Vocational counseling: Some historical, philosophical, and theoretical perspectives.* NY: McGraw-Hill.

Zimpfer, D. G. (1992, January). *Insurance experience of licensed counselors.* Paper presented at the 1992 National Conference of the Association for Counselor Education and Supervision. San Antonio, TX.

Zunker, V. (1994). *Career counseling. Applied concepts of life planning* (4th ed.). Pacific Grove, CA: Brooks/Cole.

Chapter 2

Bandler, R., & Grinder, J. (1979). *Frogs into princes.* Mob, UT: Real Peoples Press.

Barak, A., Shapira, G., & Fisher, W. A. (1988). Effects of verbal and vocal cues of counselor self-confidence on clients' perceptions. *Counselor Education and Supervision, 27,* 355–367.

Berger, R. L., McBreen, J. T., & Rifkin, M. J. (1996). *Human behavior: A perspective for the helping professions.* White Plains, NY: Longham Publishers.

Brammer, L. M., & MacDonald, G. (1996). *The helping relationship: Process and skills.* Needham Heights, MA: Allyn and Bacon.

Brems, C. (2000). *Dealing with challenges in psychotherapy and counseling.* Belmont, CA: Brooks/Cole.

Carkhuff, R. R. (1969). *Helping and human relations* Vol. I and II. New York: Holt, Rinehart & Winston.

Carkhuff, R. R. (1986). *The art of helping* (5th ed.). Amherst: MA: Human Resources Development Press.

Carkhuff, R. R., & Berenson, B. (1967). *Beyond counseling and therapy.* New York: Holt, Rinehart & Winston.

Combs, A. W. (1986). What makes a good helper? A person-centered approach. *Person-centered Review, 1*(1), 51–61.

Cormier, B., Cormier, L. S., & Cormier, W. H. (1997). *Interviewing strategies for helpers: Fundamental skills and cognitive behavioral interventions.* Pacific Grove, CA: Brooks/Cole.

Cozby, P. C. (1973). Self-disclosure: A literature review. *Psychological Bulletin, 79,* 73–91.

Driscoll, M. S., Newman, D. L., & Seals, J. M. (1988). The effects of touch on perception of counselors. *Counselor Education and Supervision, 27,* 344–354.

Egan, G. (1975). *The skilled helper.* Monterey, CA: Brooks/Cole.

Egan, G. (2002). *The skilled helper: A problem-management approach to helping* (7th ed.). Pacific Grove, CA: Brooks/Cole.

Evans, D. R., Hearn, M. T., Uhlemann, M. R., & Ivey, A. E. (1993). *Essential interviewing: A programmed approach to effective communication.* Pacific Grove, CA: Brooks/Cole.

Gelatt, H. B. (1989). Positive uncertainty: A decision-making framework for counseling. *Journal of Counseling Psychology, 36,*(2), 252–256.

Gladding, S. T. (2000). *Counseling: A comprehensive profession.* Englewood Cliffs, NJ: Prentice-Hall.

Hendrick, S. S. (1988). Counselor self-disclosure. *Journal of Counseling and Development, 66*(9), 419–424.

Ivey, A. E. (1998). *Intentional interviewing and counseling: Facilitating client development in a multicultural society.* Pacific Grove, CA: Brooks/Cole.

Ivey, A. E., Ivey, M. B., & Simek-Downing, L. (1987). *Counseling and psychotherapy: Integrating skills, theory and practice.* Englewood Cliffs, NJ: Prentice-Hall.

Ivey, A. E., & Simek-Downing, L. (1980). *Counseling and psychotherapy.* Englewood Cliffs, NJ: Prentice-Hall.

Keller, D. (1984). *Humor as therapy.* Wauwatosa, WI: Med-Psych Publications.

Levin, F. M., & Gergen, K. J. (1969). Revealingness, ingratiation, and the disclosure of self. *Proceedings of the 77th Annual Convention of the American Psychological Association, 4*(1), 447–448.

McCarthy, P. (1982). Differential effects of counselor self-referent responses and counselor status. *Journal of Counseling Psychology, 29,* 125–311.

Meier, S. T., & Davis, S. R. (1993). *The elements of counseling.* Pacific Grove, CA: Brooks/Cole.

Murphy, B. C., & Dillon, C. (2003). *Interviewing in action: Relationship, process, and change* (2nd ed.). Pacific Grove, CA: Brooks/Cole.

Okun, B. F. (1996). *Effective helping: Interviewing and counseling techniques* (5th ed.). Pacific Grove, CA: Brooks/Cole.

Patterson, C. H. (1985). *The therapeutic relationship: Foundations of eclectic psychotherapy.* New York: Harper & Row.

Peca-Baker, T. A., & Friedlander, M. L. (1987). Effects on role expectations on clients' perceptions of disclosing and nondisclosing counselors. *Journal of Counseling and Development, 66*(2), 78–81.

Pietrofesa, J. J., Hoffman, A., & Splete, H. H. (1984). *Counseling: An introduction.* Boston: Houghton-Mifflin.

Pietrofesa, J. J., Hoffman, A., Splete, H. H., & Pinto, D. V. (1978). *Counseling: Theory, research & practice.* Chicago: Rand McNally.

Prochaska, J. O., & Norcross, J. C. (2003). *Systems of psychotherapy: A transtheoretical analysis* (5th ed.). Pacific Grove, CA: Brooks/Cole.

Rogers, C. R. (1957). The necessary and sufficient conditions of therapeutic personality change. *Journal of Counseling Psychology, 21,* 95–103.

Rogers, C. R. (1958). The characteristics of a helping relationship. *Personnel and Guidance Journal, 37,* 6–16.

Rogers, C. R. (1961). *On becoming a person.* Boston: Houghton-Mifflin.

Rogers, C. R. (1967). *The therapeutic relationship and its impact.* Madison, WI: The University of Wisconsin Press.

Scherer, K. R. (1986). Vocal expression: A review and model for future research. *Psychological Bulletin, 99,* 143–165.

Sexton, T. L., & Whiston, S. C. (1994). The status of the counseling relationship: An empirical review, theoretical implications, and research directions. *The Counseling Psychologist, 22*(1), 6–78.

Sexton, T. L., Whiston, S. G., Bleuer, J. C., & Walz, G. R. (1997). *Integrating outcome research into counseling practice and training.* Alexandria, VA: American Counseling Association.

Shulman, L. (1979). *The skills of helping individuals and groups.* Itasca, IL: F. E. Peacock Publishers.

Strong, S. R. (1968). Counseling: An interpersonal influence process. *Journal of Counseling Psychology, 15,* 215–224.

Suiter, R. L., & Goodyear, R. K. (1985). Male and female counselor and client perceptions of four levels of counselor touch. *Journal of Counseling Psychology, 32*(4), 645–648.

Ward, D. E. (1984). Termination of individual counseling: Concepts and strategies. *Journal of Counseling Psychology, 63*(1), 21–26.

Chapter 3

American Counseling Association. (1995). *Code of ethics and standards of practice.* Alexandria, VA: Author.

American Counseling Association. (1999) *Approved by the ACA governing council, October 1999.* Retrieved September 1, 2003 from *http://www.counseling.org/site/PageServer?pagename=resources_internet*

American Counseling Association. (2002). *Cross cultural competencies and objectives.* Alexandria, VA: Author. Retrieved September 1, 2003 from *http://www.counseling.org/site/PageServer?pagename=resources_competencies*

American Heritage College Dictionary 4th ed. (2002). Boston, MA: Houghton Mifflin Company.

American Psychological Association. (1991). APA Council of Representatives adopts new AIDS policies. *Psychology and AIDS Exchange, 7,* 1.

American Psychological Association. (2002). *Ethical principles of psychologists and code of Conduct.* Washington, DC: Author.

Association of State and Provincial Licensing Psychology Boards. (2001). *Ethics, law, and avoiding liability in the practice of psychology.* Montgomery, AL: Author.

Arizona Revised Statute 46–451.

Atkinson, D. R. (2004). *Counseling American minorities* (6th ed.). NY: McGraw Hill.

Bordin, E. S. (1994). Theory and research on the therapeutic working alliance: New directions. In A. O. Horvath, L. S. Greenberg (Eds.), *The working alliance: Theory, research and practice.* NY: Wiley.

Cooke v. Berlin, Arizona, 735 P.2d 830 (App. 1987).

Cottone, R. R., & Tarvydas, V. M. (2003). *Ethical and professional issues in counseling* (2nd ed.). Columbus, OH: Merrill/Prentice Hall.

Corey, G., Corey, M. S., & Callahan, P. (1998). *Issues and ethics in the helping professions.* (5th ed.). Pacific Grove, CA: Brooks/Cole.

Everstine, L., Everstine, D. S., Geymann, G. M., True, R. H., Frey, D. H., Johnson, H. G., & Seiden, R. H. (1980). Privacy and confidentiality in psychotherapy. *American Psychologist, 35,* 828–840.

Goldfarb v. Virginia State Bar (1975), 421 U.S. 773.

Hammer, M. (1972). To students interested in becoming psychotherapists. In M. Hammer (Ed.), *The theory and practice of psychotherapy with specific disorders* (pp. 1–23). Springfield, IL: Charles C. Thomas.

Herlihy, B., & Corey, G. (1992). *Dual relationships in counseling.* Alexandria, VA: American Association for Counseling and Development.

Herlihy, B., & Corey, G. (1996). *ACA ethical standards casebook* (5th ed.). Alexandria, VA: American Counseling Association.

Horvath, A. O., & Symonds, B. D. (1991). The relation between working alliance and outcome in psychotherapy: A meta-analysis. *Journal of Counseling Psychology, 38,* 139–149.

Koocher, G. P., & Keith-Spiegel, P. (1998). *Ethics in psychology: Professional standards and cases* (2nd ed.). New York: McGraw-Hill.

Jaffee vs. Redmond. 95–266 (U.S.C., June 13, 1996).

Lawrence, G., & Robinson Kurpius, S. E. (2000). Legal and ethical issues involved when counseling minors in a non-school setting. *Journal of Counseling and Development, 78,* 130–136.

Levenson, M. (1989). *Right to accept or refuse treatment: Implications for the mental health profession.* Unpublished manuscript, Arizona State University.

Loewy, M. I. (1998). Obesity in children. *Professional School Counseling,* 1(4). 18–22.

Lustig, D. C., Strauser, D. R., Rice, N. D., & Rucker, T. F. (Fall, 2002). The relationship between working alliance and rehabilitation outcomes. *Rehabilitation Counseling Bulletin,* 46(9), 25.

MacKinnon, B. (1998). *Ethics: Theory and contemporary issues* (2nd ed.). Belmont, CA: Wadsworth.

Meara, N. M., Schmidt, L. D., & Day, J. D. (1996). Principles and virtues: A foundation for ethical decision making, policies and character. *The Counseling Psychologist, 24,* 4–77.

National Board for Certified Counselors (2001a). *National counselor exam.* Alexandria, VA: Author. Retrieved on September 1, 2003 from *http://www.nbcc.org/exams/nce.htm*

National Board for Certified Counselors (2001b). *What can I expect from a counselor.* Alexandria, VA: Author. Retrieved September 1, 2003 from *http://www.nbcc.org/admin/clientrights.htm*

Newman, J. L., & Robinson, S. E. (1991). In the best interests of the consultee: Ethical issues in consultation. *Consulting Psychology Journal, 43,* 23–29.

New Oxford American Dictionary. (2001). Oxford: Oxford University Press.

Pope, K. S., Tabachnick, B. G., & Keith-Spiegel, P. (1987). Ethics of practice: The beliefs and behaviors of psychologists as therapists. *American Psychologist, 42,* 993–1006.

Public Education Work Group of the Task Force on Sexual Exploitation (1988). *It's never ok!* Advocate Web. Retrieved September 1, 2003 from *http://www.advocateweb.org/hope/itsneverok/*

Remley, T. P., and Herlihy, B. (2001). *Ethical, legal, and professional issues in counseling.* Saddle River, NJ: Merrill.

Remley, T. P., Jr., & Huey, W. C. (2002). An ethics quiz for school counselors. *Professional School Counselor, 6,* 3–11.

Rennie v. Klein, 476 F. Supp. 1294 (D. N. J., 1979, modified, Nos. 79-2576 and 70-2577 3rd Cir., July 9, 1981).

Robinson, S. E. (1988). Counselor competency and malpractice suits: Opposite sides of the same coin. *Counseling and Human Development, 20,* 1–8.

Robinson, S. E., & Gross, D. R. (1989). Applied ethics and the mental health counselor, *Journal of Mental Health Counseling, 11,* 289–299.

Robinson Kurpius, S. E. (1997). Current ethical issues in the practice of psychotherapy. *The Hatherleigh Guide to Ethics in Therapy* (pp. 1–16). New York: Hatherleigh Press.

Robinson Kurpius, S. E., & Gross, D. R. (1996). Professional ethics and the mental health counselor. In W. J. Weikel & A. J. Palmo (Eds.), *Foundations of mental health counseling* (pp. 353–377). Springfield, IL: Charles C. Thomas. pp. 353–377.

Rogers v. Orkin, 634 F. 2nd 650 (1st Cir., 1980).

Sattler, H. A. (1990). Confidentiality. In B. Herlihy & L. Golden (Eds.), *ACD Ethical Standards Casebook* (4th ed). Alexandria, VA: American Association for Counseling and Development.

Schwitzgebel, R. L., & Schwitzgebel, R. K. (1980). *Law and psychological practice.* New York: John Wiley & Sons.

Semans, M., & Stone Fish, L. (2000). Dissecting life with a Jewish scapel: A qualitative exploration or Jewish families. *Family Process,* 39(1), 121–139.

Sim, J. (1997). *Ethical decision making in therapy practice.* Oxford: Butterworth, Heineman.

Snider, P. D. (1987). Client records: Inexpensive liability protection for mental health counselors. *Journal of Mental Health Counseling, 9,* 134–141.

Sue, D. W., & Sue, D. (2003). *Counseling the culturally diverse* (4th ed.). New York: John Wiley Sons.

Tarasoff v. Board of Regents of the University of California, 118 Cal. Rptr. 14.551 P.2d 334 (1974).

Tarasoff v. Board of Regents of the University of California, 113 Cal. Rptr. 14.551 P.2d 334 (1976).

Thoreson, R. W., Shaughnessy, P., Heppner, P. P., & Cook, S. (1993). Sexual contact during and after the professional relationship: Attitudes and practices of male counselors. *Journal of Counseling and Development, 71,* 429–434.

U.S. Department of Health and Human Services (2003). *OCR privacy brief: Summary of the HIPAA privacy rule.* Retrieved September 1,

2003 from *http://www.hhs.gov/ocr/privacy summary.pdf*

Welfel, E. R., & Kitchener, K. S. (1995). Introduction to the special section: Ethics eduation—An agenda for the 90's. In D. N. Bersoff (Ed.), *Ethical conflicts in psychology*. Washington DC: American Psychological Association. pp. 126–131.

Wyatt v. Stickney, 325 F. Supp. 781 (1971).

Chapter 4

ACA *Code of Ethics and Standards of Practice*. (1995). Annapolis Junction, MD: ACA Distribution Center.

American Psychological Association. (2001). *Publication manual* (5th ed.). Washington, DC: Author.

Ambert, A., Adler, P. A., Adler, P., & Detzner, D. F. (1995). Understanding and evaluating qualitative research. *Journal of Marriage & Family, 57*, 879–893.

Coelho, R. J., & La Forge, J. (1996). Journal publication as a professional practice activity for rehabilitation counselors. *Journal of Applied Rehabilitation Counseling, 27*(1), 17–21.

Cone, J. D., & Foster, S. L. (1995). *Dissertations and theses from start to finish*. American Psychological Association: Washington, DC.

Creswell, J. W. (1994). *Research design: Qualitative & quantitative approaches*. Thousand Oaks, CA: Sage.

Denzin, N. K., & Lincoln, Y. S. (Eds.). (1994). *Handbook of qualitative research*. Thousand Oaks, CA: Sage.

Flick, U. (1998). *An introduction to qualitative research*. Thousand Oaks, CA: Sage.

Galvan, J. L. (1999). *Writing literature reviews: A guide for students of the social and behavioral sciences*. Los Angeles, CA: Pyrczak.

Herman, K. C. (1997). Embracing human science in counseling research. *Counselor education and supervision, 36*, 270–283.

Hill, C. E., & Gronsky, B. (1984). Research: Why and how? In J. M. Whileley, M. Kagan, L. W., Harmon, B. R., Fretz, F., & Tanny, R. (Eds.), *The coming decade in counseling psychology*, (149–159). Schenectady, NY: Character Research.

Hoshmund, L. T. (1989). Alternative research paradigms: A review and teaching proposal. *Counseling Psychologist, 17*, 3–79.

Lincoln, Y. S., & Guba, E. G. (1985). *Naturalistic inquiry*. Newbury Park: Sage.

Loesch, L. C., & Nicholas, V. A. (1996). *Research in Counseling and Therapy* (Report No. RR93002004). Washington, DC: Office of Educational Research and Improvement. (ERIC Clearinghouse on Counseling and Student Services Co. ED 404611).

Maxwell, J. A. (1992). Understanding and validity in qualitative research. *Harvard Educational Review, 62*, 279–299.

Merchant, N. (1997). Qualitative research for counselors. *Counseling and Human Development, 30* (1).

Miles, M. B., & Huberman, A. M. (1994). Qualitative data analysis. *An expanded sourcebook*. Newbury Park, CA: Sage.

Morse, J. M., & Field, P. A. (1995). *Qualitative research methods for health professionals* (2nd ed.). Thousand Oaks, CA: Sage.

Nicol, A. A. M., & Pexman, P. M. (1999). *Presenting your findings: A practical guide to creating tables*. Washington, DC: American Psychological Association.

Nisenoff, S., & Espina, M. R. (1999, June). The a-b-c's of research in professional counseling.

Peshkin, A. (1988, October). In search of subjectivity—one's own. *Educational Research*, 17–21.

Polkinghorne, D. E. (1991). Qualitative procedures for counseling research. In C. E.,Watkins & L. J. Schneider (Eds.), *Research in counseling* (pp. 163–204). Hillsdale, NJ: Lawrence Erlbaum.

Polkinghorne, D. E. (1994). Reaction to special section on qualitative research in counseling process and outcome. *Journal of Counseling Psychology, 41*(4), 510–512.

Rechtien, J. G., & Dizinno, G. (1997). A note on measuring apprehension about writing. *Psychological Reports, 80*, 907–913.

Reilly, R. (2000). *Trends in academic progress*. Washington, DC: U.S. Department of Education.

Remley, T. P. Jr. & Herlihy, B. (2001). *Ethical, legal, and professional issues in counseling*. Upper Saddle River, NJ: Prentice Hall.

Rubin, J. H., & Rubin, I. S. (1995). *Qualitative interviewing: The art of hearing data*. Thousand Oaks, CA: Sage.

Sexton, T. L. (1996). The relevance of counseling outcome research: Current trends and practical implications. *Journal of Counseling and Development, 74*, 590–600.

Sexton, T. L., & Griffin, B. L. (Eds.). (1997). *Constructivist thinking in counseling, practice, research, and training*. New York: Teachers College Press.

Shank, G. D. (2002). *Qualitative research: A personal skills approach.* Upper Saddle River: NJ: Pearson Education.

Stockton, R., & Toth, P. L. (1997). Applying a general research training model to group work. *Journal for Specialists in Group Work, 22*(4), 241–252.

Strauss, A., & Corbin, J. (1998). *Basics of qualitative research: Techniques and procedures for developing grounded theory* (2nd ed.). Thousand Oaks, CA: Sage.

Szuchman, L. T. (2002). *Writing with style: APA style for counseling.* Pacific Grove, CA: Brooks/Cole.

Zinsser, W., (1990). *On writing well* (4th ed.). New York: Harper Collins.

Chapter 5

Aiken, L. R. (2000). *Psychological testing and assessment* (10th ed.). Needham Heights, MA: Allyn & Bacon.

Alexander, G. J. (1999). Telehealth: Confidentiality in cyberpsych. Therapist-client confidentiality in telehealth. Retrieved June 26, 2003, from the World Wide Web: *http://www.telehealth.net/articles/cyberpsych.html*

Amig, S. (2001). Internet dilemmas. *Behavioral Health Management, 21*(3), 48.

Baltimore, M. L. (2002). Recent trends in advancing technology use in counselor education. *Journal of Technology in Counseling, 2*(2). Retrieved June 24, 2003, from the World Wide Web: *http://jtc.colstate.edu/vol2_2/editor.htm*

Baltimore, M. L., & Jencius, M. (1999). Professional publishing paradigm: Cyberpublication and the Journal of Technology in Counseling. *Journal of Technology in Counseling, 1*(1). Retrieved June 25, 2003, from the World Wide Web: *http://jtc.colstate.edu/vol1_1/cyberpublication.htm*

Barak, A. (1999). Psychological applications on the Internet: A discipline on the threshold of a new millennium. *Applied and Preventive Psychology, 8,* 231–246. Retrieved June 26, 2003 from the World Wide Web: *http://construct.haifa.ac.il/~azy/app-r.htm*

Blair, R. (2001). Psychotherapy online. *Health Management Technology, 22*(2), 24.

Block, A. R. (1994). Computerized diagnosis of psychological factors in medical illness. *Behavioral Health Management, 14*(1), 16–20.

Bower, B. (1990, Jan 20). Computers get a boost as psychotherapists. *Science News,* 37.

Braggerly, J. (2002). Practical technological applications to promote pedagogical principles and active learning in counselor education. *Journal of Technology in Counseling, 2*(2). Retrieved June 25, 2003, from the World Wide Web: *http://jtc.colstate.edu/vol2_2/baggerly/baggerly.htm*

Cabaniss, K. (2001, Feb. 21). Counseling and computer technology in the new millennium: An internet Delphi study. Unpublished doctoral dissertation. Virginia Polytechnic Institute and State University, Blacksburg, Virginia.

Carr, D. (2000, Mar 1). The browser as couch: Can the health care industry bring psychiatric services online? *Internet World,* 69.

Carroll, J. (1995). There are now ways to escape from the paper jungle. *Computing Canada, 21*(24), 45.

Casey, J. A. (1999). Computer assisted simulation for counselor training of basic skills. *Journal of Technology in Counseling, 1*(1). Retrieved June 25, 2003, from the World Wide Web: *http://jtc.colstate.edu/vol1_1/simulation.htm*

Casey, J., Bloom, J. B., and Moan, E. (1994). Use of technology in counselor supervision. ERIC Digest ED372357 Apr 94. ERIC Clearinghouse on Counseling and Student Services, Greensboro, NC. Available online at *http://www.ed.gov/databases/ERIC_Digests/ed372357.html*

CD-ROM record storage has two-year payback. (1995, Dec 1995). *American City & County,* 36.

Childress, C. (1998). Potential risks and benefits of online psychotherapeutic interventions. Retrieved July 3, 2003, from the World Wide Web: *http://www.ismho.org/issues/9801.htm*

Clark, M. A., & Stone, C. B. (2002). Clicking with students: Using online assignments in counselor education courses. *Journal of Technology in Counseling, 2*(2). Retrieved June 25, 2003, from the World Wide Web: *http://jtc.colstate.edu/vol2_2/clarkstone.htm*

Computers, a sympathetic shoulder to cry on. (1999). *The Lancet, 353*(9), 2046.

Davidson, C. (1991, Nov 2). Will computers hold key to mental hospitals? *New Scientist,* 22.

Delmonico, D., Daninhirsch, C., Page, B., Walsh, J., L'Amoreaux, N. A., & Thompson, R. S. (2000). The palace: Participant responses to a virtual support group. *Journal of Technology in Counseling, 1*(2). Retrieved June 25, 2003, from the World Wide Web: *http://jtc.colstate.edu/vol1_2/palace.htm*

Edwards, Y. V., Portman, T. A. A., & Bethea, J. (2002). Counseling student computer competency skills: Effects of technology course in training. *Journal of Technology in Counseling,* *2*(2). Retrieved June 24, 2003, from the World Wide Web: *http://jtc.colstate.edu/vol2_2/edwards.htm*

Engstrom, C. M. (1997, Summer). Integrating information technology into student affairs graduate programs. *New Directions for Student Services, 78,* 59–69.

Gale, A. U., & McKee, E. C. (2002). An information literate approach to the internet for counselors. *Journal of Technology in Counseling, 2*(2). Retrieved June 25, 2003, from the World Wide Web: *http://jtc.colstate.edu/vol2_2/gale.htm*

Goedert, J. (2003). Is the Internet as good as the couch? *Health Data Management, 11*(2), 14.

Gould, M. S., Munfakh, J. H., & Lubell, K. (2002). Seeking help from the Internet during adolescence. *Journal of the American Academy of Child and Adolescent Psychiatry, 41*(10), 1182–1189.

Grohol, J. M. (1997, October 24). Why online psychotherapy? Because there is a need. Retrieved July 4, 2003, from the World Wide Web: *http://www.grohol.com/archives/n102297.htm*

Hackerman, A. E., & Greer, B. G. (2000). Counseling psychology and the Internet: A further inquiry. *Journal of Technology in Counseling, 1*(2). Retrieved June 25, 2003, from the World Wide Web: *http://jtc.colstate.edu/vol1_2/cyberpsych.htm*

Haley, M., & Carrier, J. W. (2002). Psychotherapy groups. In D. Capuzzi & D. Gross (Eds.), *Introduction to group counseling* (3rd ed.). Denver, Colorado: Love Publishing, 291–318.

Hayes, G. (1999). Where's the data: Is multimedia instruction effective in training counselors? *Journal of Technology in Counseling, 1*(1). Retrieved June 24, 2003, from the World Wide Web: *http://jtc.colstate.edu/vol1_1/multimedia.htm*

Heinlen, K. T., Welfel, E. R., Richmond, E. N., & Rak, C. F. (2003). The scope of Web counseling: A survey of services and compliance with NBCC standards for the ethical practice of WebCounseling. *Journal of Counseling and Development, 81*(1), 61–70.

Hines, P. T. (2002). Student technology competencies for school counseling programs. *Journal of Technology in Counseling, 2*(2). Retrieved June 25, 2003, from the World Wide Web: *http://jtc.colstate.edu/vol2_2/hines/hines.htm*

Houser, W. R. (1995). A pretty GILS is like a memory of all an agency's info. *Government Computer News, 14*(25), 21.

Ingram, J. A. (1998). Cybertherapy: Pariah with promise? Retrieved July 3, 2003 from, the World Wide Web: *http://www.selfhelpmagazine.com/ppc/viewpoint/cybparpr.html*

Jedlicka, D., & Jennings, G. (2001). Marital therapy on the Internet. *Journal of Technology in Counseling, 2*(1). Retrieved June 25, 2003, from the World Wide Web: *http://jtc.colstate.edu/vol2_1/Marital.htm*

Jones, K. D., & Karper, C. (2000). How to develop an online course in counseling techniques. *Journal of Technology in Counseling, 1*(2). Retrieved June 25, 2003, from the World Wide Web: *http://jtc.colstate.edu/vol1_2/online.htm*

Kalb, C. (2001, Jan. 22). Seeing a virtual shrink: More therapists are hanging out shingles online. *Newsweek,* 54.

King, S. (1994). Analysis of electronic support groups for recovering addicts. *Interpersonal Computing Technology: An Electronic Journal for the 21st Century, 2*(3), 47–56. Retrieved July 4, 2003, from: *http://www.helsinki.fi/science/optek/1994/n3/king.txt*

Knouse, S. B. (2001). Virtual mentors: Mentoring on the Internet. *Journal of Employment Counseling, 38*(4), 162–170.

LeBeau, C. (2001). Cyberanalyze this. *Family PC, 8*(4), 34.

Locking down windows server 2003. (2003, April 25) *eWeek,* NA.

Lundberg, D. J., & Cobitz, C. I. (1999). Use of technology in counseling assessment: A survey of practices, views and outlook. *Journal of Technology in Counseling, 1*(1). Retrieved June 24, 2003, from the World Wide Web: *http://jtc.colstate.edu/vol1_1/assessment.htm*

McCarty, D., & Clancy, C. (2002). Telehealth: Implications for social work practice. *Social Work, 47*(2), 153–162.

McFadden, J. (2000). Computer-mediated technology and transcultural counselor education. *Journal of Technology in Counseling, 1*(1). Retrieved June 24, 2003, from the World Wide Web: *http://jtc.colstate.edu/vol1_2/transcult.html*

Myers, J. E., & Gibson, D. M. (2003). Technology competence in counselor education: Results of a national survey. Retrieved June 24, 2003, from the World Wide Web: *http://www.cybercounsel.uncg.edu/book/manuscripts/techcomp.htm*

National Board of Certified Counselors (2001, Nov. 3). The practice of Internet counseling.

Retrieved June 24, 2003, from the World Wide Web: *http://www.nbcc.org/ethics/webethics.htm*

National Center for Education Statistics. (n.d.). Distance education at postsecondary education institutions: 1997–98. Retrieved June 24, 2003, from the World Wide Web: *http://www.nces.ed.gov/surveys/peqis/publications/2000013/*

O'Halloran, T. M., Fahr, A. V., & Keller, J. R. (2002). Career counseling and the information highway: Heeding the road signs. *Career Development Quarterly, 50*(4), 371–377.

Pelling, N. (2002). The use of technology in career counseling. *Journal of Technology in Counseling, 2*(2). Retrieved June 25, 2003, from the World Wide Web: *http://jtc.colstate.edu/vol2_2/pelling.htm*

Pelling, N., & Reynard, D. (1999). The use of videotaping within developmentally-based supervision. *Journal of Technology in Counseling, 1*(1). Retrieved June 24, 2003, from the World Wide Web: *http://jtc.colstate.edu/vol1_1/supervision.htm*

Pergament, D. (1998). Internet psychotherapy: Current status and future regulation. *Health Matrix, 8*(2), 233–279.

Powell, T. (1998). Online counseling: A profile and descriptive analysis. Retrieved July 3, 2003, from the World Wide Web: *http://netpsych.com/Powell.htm*

Powers, C. P., Bray, M., Furr, S., & Algozzine, R. F. (2002). Accessibility of counseling education programs' web sites for students with disabilities. *Journal of Technology in Counseling, 2*(2). Retrieved June 24, 2003, from the World Wide Web: *http://jtc.colstate.edu/vol2_2/flowersbray.htm*

Quinn, A. C., Hohenshil, T., & Fortune, J. (2002). Utilization of technology in CACREP approved counselor education programs. *Journal of Technology in Counseling, 2*(2). Retrieved June 24, 2003, from the World Wide Web:*http://jtc.colstate.edu/vol2_2/quinn/quinn.htm*

Riemer-Reiss, M. L. (2000a). Utilizing distance technology for mental health counseling. *Journal of Mental Health Counseling, 22*(3), 189.

Riemer-Reiss, M. (2000b). Vocational rehabilitation counseling at a distance: Challenges, strategies and ethics to consider. *The Journal of Rehabilitation, 66*(1), 11.

Rogers, J. (2001, Jan.). PT links. *Psychology Today*, 79.

Sands, T. (2000). Student-initiated listservices. *Journal of Technology in Counseling, 1*(2). Retrieved June 25, 2003, from the World Wide Web: *http://jtc.colstate.edu/vol1_2/listserv.htm*

Smith, R. C., Mead, E. D., & Kinsella, J. (1998). Direct supervision: Adding computer-assisted feedback and data capture to live supervision. *Journal of Marital and Family Therapy, 24*, 113–125.

Smith, S. (2001a, July). User beware. *Psychology Today*, 15.

Smith, S. (2001b, July/Aug). Technology plus psychology. *Psychology Today*, 15–16.

Stamm, H. (1998). Clinical applications of telehealth in mental health care. *Professional Psychology: Research and Practice, 29*(6), 536–542. Retrieved June 24, 2003, from the World Wide Web: *http://www.apa.org/journals/pro/pro296536.html*

Stover, M. (1993). PsychNet: A niche network for psychology. *Online, 17*(3), 74–79.

Stubbs. P. (2000). Mental health care online. Retrieved June 26, 2003, from the World Wide Web: *http://www.geocities.com/online_form/history-online.htm#onlinehistory*

Suler, J. (1998, March). Mom, dad, computer: Transference reactions to computers. Retrieved July 13, 2003, from the World Wide Web: *http://www.rider.edu/~suler/psycyber/comptransf.html*

Swiss AIDS federation provides online Geneva. (1999, November 29). Xinhua News Agency, 1008329h0200.

Viire, E. (1997). Health and safety issues for VR (Virtual Realtiy). *Communications of the ACM, 40*(8), 40–42.

Wintrob, S. (1995). Climbing off the paper mountain. *Computing Canada, 21*(23), 47.

Wittmer, J. (2000). Managing your school counseling program: K-12 developmental strategies (second edition). Minneapolis, MN: Educational Media Corporation. Retrieved June 24, 2003, from the World Wide Web: *http://coe.fgcu.edu/faculty/sabella/bootcamp/school%20counseling%20and%20technology.pdf*

Woodford, M. S., Rokutani, L., Gressard, C., & Berg, L. B. (2001). Sharing the course: An experience with collaborative distance learning in counseling education. *Journal of Technology in Counseling, 2*(1). Retrieved June 25, 2003, from the World Wide Web: *http://jtc.colstate.edu/vol2_1/Sharing.htm*

Wong, W. (2000). Great ideas get lost in the sea of incomplete documentation. *Electronic Design, 48*(19), 68.

Wyatt, J. (1991, Dec 7). Computer-based knowledge systems. *The Lancet*, 1431–1437.

Chapter 6

Andersen, S. M., Glassman, N. S., Chen, S., & Cole, S. W. (1995). Transference in social perception: The role of chronic accessibility in significant-other representations. *Journal of Personality and Social Psychology, 69*, 41–57.

Bandura, A. (1977). Social learning theory. Englewood Cliffs, NJ: Prentice Hall.

Bandura, A. (1991). Social cognitive theory of self-regulation. Organizational Behavior and Human Decision Processes, 50, 248–287.

Bandura, A. (1993). Perceived self-efficacy in cognitive development and functioning. *Educational Psychologist, 28*(2), 117–148.

Beck, A. T. (1976). Cognitive therapy and the emotional disorders. New York: International Universities Press.

Becker, J., & Schmaling, K. (1991). Interpersonal aspects of depression for psychodynamic and attachment perspectives. In J. Becker, A. Kleiman, et al. (Eds.). *Psychosocial aspects of depression* (pp. 131–168). Hillsdale, NJ: Lawrence Erlbaum Associates.

Benjamin, J. (1998). *Shadow of the other: Intertsubjectivity and gender in psychoanalysis.* New York: Routledge.

Bergin, A. E., & Garfield, S. L. (1994). Overview, trends, and future issues. In A. E. Bergin & S. L. Garfield (Eds.). *Handbook of psychotherapy and behavior change* (4th ed., pp. 821–830). New York: Wiley.

Bordin, E. S. (1976). The generalizability of the psychoanalytic concept of the working alliance. *Psychotherapy: Theory, Research and Practice, 16*, 252–260.

Brodley, B. T. (1996). Uncharacteristic directiveness: Rogers and the "Anger and Hurt" client. In B. A. Farber, D. C. Brink, et al. (Eds.). *The Psychotherapy of Carl Rogers: Cases and commentary* (pp. 310–321). New York: Guilford.

Connor-Green, P. A. (1993). The therapeutic context: Preconditions for change in psychotherapy. *Psychotherapy, 30*, 375–382.

Corey, G. (1991). Person-centered therapy. In *Theory and practice of counseling and psychotherapy* (4th ed.). (pp. 203–229). Pacific Grove, CA: Brooks/Cole.

Dozier, M., & Tyrrell, C. (1998). The role of attachment in therapeutic relationships. In J. A. Simpson & W. S. Rholes (Eds.). *Attachment theory and close relationships* (pp. 221–248). New York: Guilford Press.

Driscoll, R. (1994). *Pragmatic psychotherapy.* New York, NY: Van Nostrand Reinhold Company.

Ellis, A. (1962). *Reason and emotion in psychotherapy.* New York: Stuart.

Ellis, A. (1993a). Fundamentals of rational-emotive therapy for the 1990s. In W. Dryden & L. K. Hill (Eds.), *Innovations in rational-emotive therapy* (pp. 1–32). Newbury Park, CA: Sage.

Ellis, A. (1993b). The intelligent woman's guide to dating and mating. New York: Stuart.

Ellis, A. (1993c). Reflections on rational-emotive therapy. *Journal of Consulting and Clinical Psychology, 61*(2), 199–201.

Ellis, A. (1995). Changing rational-emotive therapy (RET) to rational-emotive behavioral therapy (RETB). *Journal of Rational-Emotive and Cognitive Behavior Therapy, 13*(2), 85–89.

Ellis, A. (1997). Extending the goals of behavior therapy and of cognitive behavior therapy. *Behavior Therapy, 28*(3), 333–339.

Ellis, A. (1999a). Early theories and practices of rational emotive behavior therapy and how they have been augmented and revised during the last three decades. *Journal of Rational-Emotive & Cognitive Behavior Therapy, 17*(2), 69–93.

Ellis, A. (1999b). Rational emotive therapy and cognitive behavior therapy for elderly people. *Journal of Rational-Emotive & Cognitive Behavior Therapy, 17*(1), 5–18.

Ellis, A., & Dryden, W. (1997). The Practice of Rational Emotive Behavior Therapy (2nd ed.). New York: Springer.

Ellis, A., Gordon, J., Nennan, M., & Palmer, S. (1997). *Stress counselling: A rationale emotive behaviour approach.* London: Cassell.

Ellis, A., & MacLaren, C. (1998). *Rational emotive behavior therapy: A therapist's guide.* The Practical Therapist Series. San Luis Obispo, CA: Impact.

Ellis, A., & Whitely, J. M. (1979). *Theoretical and empirical foundations of rational-emotive therapy.* Monterey, CA: Brooks/Cole.

Erikson, E. H. (1968). *Identity: Youth and crisis.* New York: Norton.

Farber, B. A., Lippert, R. A., & Nevas, D. B. (1995). The therapist as attachment figure. *Psychotherapy, 32*, 204–212.

Frank, K. A. (1999). Psychoanalytic participation: Action, interaction, and integration. *Relational Perspectives Book Series* (Vol. 16). Hillsdale, NJ: The Analytic Press.

Freud, A. (1936). *The writings of Anna Freud (Vol. 2), The ego and the mechanisms of defense.* New York: International Universities Press.

Freud, S. (1949). *An outline of psychoanalysis.* New York: Norton.

Freud, S. (1915–1917). Introductory lectures on psychoanalysis. New York: Norton.

Garfield, S. L., & Bergin, A. E. (1994). Introduction and historical overview. In S. L. Garfield & A.E. Bergin (Eds.). *Handbook of psychotherapy and behavior change* (pp. 3–18). New York: John Wiley & Sons, Inc.

Gaston, L. (1990). The concept of the alliance and its role in psychotherapy: Theoretical and empirical considerations. *Psychotherapy, 27,* 143–153.

Gelso, C. J., & Carter, J. A. (1985). The relationship in counseling and psychotherapy: Components, consequences, and theoretical antecedents. *Counseling Psychologist, 13,* 155–243.

Gelso, C. J., & Carter, J. A. (1994). Components of the psychotherapy relationship: Their interaction and unfolding during treatment. *Counseling Psychologist, 41*(3), 296–306.

Gelso, C. J., & Hayes, J. A. (1998). The psychotherapy relationship: Theory, research, and practice. New York: Wiley.

Gelso, C. J., & Woodhouse, S. (2003). Toward a positive psychotherapy: Focus on human strength. In W. B. Walsh (Ed.), *Counseling psychology and optimal human functioning* (pp. 171–198). Mahwah, NJ: Lawrence Erlbaum Associates, Publishers.

Greenson, R. R. (1967). *Technique and practice of psychoanalysis.* New York: International Universities Press.

Hansen, J. T. (2002). Postmodern implications for theoretical integration of counseling approaches. *Journal of Counseling & Development, 80,* 315–321.

Hawtin, S., & Moore, J. (1998). Empowerment of collusion? The social context of person-centred therapy. In B. Thorne, E. Lambers, et al. (Eds.). *Person-centred therapy: A European perspective* (pp. 91–105). London: Sage.

Hayashi, S., Kuno, T., Morotomi, Y., Osawa, M., Shimizu, M., & Suetake, Y. (1998). Client-centered therapy in Japan: Fugio Tomoda and taoism. *Journal of Humanistic Psychology, 38*(2), 103–124.

Horvath, A. O., & Greenberg, L. S. (1989). Development and validation of the working alliance inventory. *Journal of Counseling Psychology, 36*(2), 223–233.

Joyce, D. P. (1995). The roles of the intervenor: A client-centered approach. *Mediation Quarterly, 12*(4), 301–312.

Kelly, E. W., Jr. (1997). Relationship-centered counseling: A humanistic model of integration. Journal of Counseling & Development, 75, 337–344.

Kohut, H. (1985). Self psychology and the humanities: Reflections on a new psychoanalytic approach. New York: Norton.

Lambert, M. J., & Bergin, A. E. (1994). The effectiveness of psychotherapy. In A. E. Bergin & S. L. Garfield (Eds.). *Handbook of psychotherapy and behavior change* (4th ed., pp. 143–189). New York: Wiley.

Lanyado, M., & Horne, A., et al. (Eds). (1999). *The handbook of child and psychotherapy: Psychoanalytic approaches.* New York: Routledge.

Laungani, P. (1997). Replacing client-centred counselling with culture-centred counselling. *Counselling Psychology Quarterly, 10*(4), 343–351.

Lionells, M. (1995). Interpersonal-relational psychoanalysis: An introduction and overview of contemporary implications and applications. *International Forum: Psychoanalysis, 4,* 223–230.

Meichenbaum, D. (1977). *Cognitive-behavior modification.* New York: Plenum Press.

Michael, J. (1991). Historical antecedents of behavior analysis. *Applied Behavior Analysis Newsletter, 14*(2), 7–12.

Morris, E. K. (1992). The aim, progress, and evolution of behavior analysis. *Behavior Analyst, 15,* 3–29.

O'Hara, M. (1996). Rogers and Sylvia: A feminist analysis. In B. A. Farber, D. C. Brink, et al. (Eds.). *The psychotherapy of Carl Rogers: Cases and commentary* (pp. 384–300). New York: Guilford Press.

Petrocelli, J. V. (2002). Process and stages of change: Counseling with the transtheoretical model of change. *Journal of Counseling & Development, 80,* 22–28.

Robbins, S. B. (1989). Role of contemporary psychoanalysis in counseling psychology. *Journal of Counseling Psychology, 36*(3), 267–278.

Rogers, C. R. (1951). *Client-centered therapy.* Boston: Houghton Mifflin.

Rogers, C. R. (1957). The necessary and sufficient conditions of therapeutic personality change. *Journal of Consulting Psychology, 21,* 95–103.

Rogers, C. R. (1961). *On becoming a person.* Boston: Houghton Mifflin.

Skinner, B. F. (1938). *The behavior of organisms.* New York: Appleton-Century-Crofts.

Skinner, B. F. (1953). *Science and human behavior.* New York: Macmillan.

Sue, D. W., & Constantine, M. G. (2003). Optimal human functioning in people of color in the United States. In W. B. Walsh (Ed.). Counseling psychology and optimal human functioning (pp. 93–122). Mahwah, NJ: Lawrence Erlbaum Associates, Publishers.

Strolorow, R. D. (1992). Closing the gap between theory and practice with better psychoanalytic theory. *Psychotherapy, 29*(2), 159–166.

Ursano, R. J., Sonnenberg, S. M., & Lazar, S. G. (1991). *Concise guide to psychodynamic psychotherapy.* Washington, DC: American Psychiatric Press.

Walsh, W. B. (2003). Person-environment psychology and well-being. In W. B. Walsh (Ed.). *Counseling psychology and optimal human functioning* (pp. 93–122). Mahwah, NJ: Lawrence Erlbaum Associates, Publishers.

Wheeler, S., & Izzard, S. (1997). Psychodynamic counsellor training: Integrating difference. *Psychodynamic Counselling, 3*(4), 401–417.

Wolpe, J. (1982). *The practice of behavior therapy* (3rd ed.). Elmsford, NY: Pergamon Press.

Worrel, J., & Remer, P. (2003). *Feminist perspectives in therapy* (2nd ed.). Hoboken, NJ: John Wiley & Sons.

Zeman, S. (1999). Person-centered care for the patient with mid- and late-stage dementia. *American Journal of Alzheimer's Disease, 14*(5), 308–310.

Suggested Readings

Psychodynamic Approach

Becker, J., & Schmaling, K. (1991). Interpersonal aspects of depression from psychodynamic and attachment perspectives. In J. Becker, A. Kleinman, et al. (Eds.), *Psychosocial aspects of Depression* (pp. 131–168). Hillsdale, NJ: Lawrence Erlbaum Associates.

Brenner, C. (1974). *An elementary textbook of psychoanalysis* (Rev., ed). Garden City, NY: Doubleday (Anchor).

Freud, A. (1946). *The ego and the mechanisms of defense.* New York: International Universities Press.

Freud, S. (1949). *An outline of psychoanalysis.* New York: Norton.

Gelso, C. J., & Carter, J. A. (1994). Components of the psychotherapy relationship: Their interaction and unfolding during treatment. *Counseling Psychologist, 41*(3), 296–306.

Kohut, H. (1985). *Self psychology and the humanities: Reflections of a new psychoanalytic approach.* New York: Norton.

McWilliams, N. (1994). *Psychoanalytic diagnosis: Understanding personality structure in the clinical process.* New York: Guilford.

Robbins, S. B. (1989). Role of contemporary psychoanalysis in counseling psychology. *Journal of Counseling Psychology, 36*(3), 267–268.

Storolow, R. D. (1992). Closing the gap between theory and practice with better psychoanalytic theory. *Psychotherapy, 29*(2), 159–166.

Teyber, E. (1997). Interpersonal process in psychotherapy: A relational approach (3rd ed.). Pacific Grove, CA: Brooks/Cole.

Ursano, R. J., Sonnenberg, S. M., & Lazar, S. G. (1991). *Concise guide to psychodynamic psychotherapy.* Washington, DC: American Psychiatric Press.

Cognitive-Behavioral Approach

Bandura, A. (1986). *Social foundations of thought and action: A social cognitive theory.* Englewood Cliffs, NJ: Prentice Hall.

Bandura, A. (1993). Perceived self-efficacy in cognitive development and functioning. *Educational Psychologist, 28*(2), 117–148.

Beck, A. T. (1976). *Cognitive therapy and the emotional disorders.* New York: International Universities Press.

Dryden, W. (1994). Reason and emotion in psychotherapy: Thirty years on. *Journal of Rational-Emotive and Cognitive-Behavior Therapy, 12*(2), 83–99.

Dryden, W., & Hill, L. K. (1993). Innovations in rational-emotive therapy. Newbury Park, CA: Sage.

Ellis, A. (1995). Changing rational-emotive therapy (RET) to rational emotive behavior therapy (REBT). *Journal of Rational-Emotive and Cognitive Behavior Therapy, 13*(2), 85–89.

Ellis, A. (1997). Extending the goals of behavior therapy and of cognitive behavior therapy. *Behavior Therapy, 28*(3), 333–339.

Heward, E. L., & Cooper, J. O. (1992). Radical behaviorism: A productive and needed philosophy for education. *Journal of Behavioral Education, 2*(4), 345–365.

Michael, J. (1991). Historical antecedents of behavior analysis. *Applied Behavior Analysis Newsletter, 14*(2), 7–12.

Morris, E. K. (1992). The aim, progress, and evolution of behavior analysis. *Behavior Analyst, 15,* 3–29.

Person-Centered Approach

Boy, A. V., & Pine, G. J. (1999). *A person-centered foundation for counseling and psychotherapy* (2nd ed.). Springfield, IL: Charles C. Thomas Publisher.

Ford, J. G. (1991). Rogers's theory of personality: Review and perspectives. *Journal of Social Behavior and Personality, 6*(5), 19–44.

Graf, C. (1994). On genuineness and the person-centered approach: A reply to Quinn. *Journal of Humanistic Psychology, 34*(2), 90–96.

Orlov, A. B. (1992). Carl Rogers and contemporary humanism. *Journal of Russian and East European Psychology, 30*(1), 36–41.

Rogers, C. R. (1951). *Client-centered therapy.* Boston: Houghton Mifflin.

Rogers, C. R. (1961). *On becoming a person.* Boston: Houghton Mifflin.

Rogers, C. R. (1980). *A way of being.* Boston: Houghton Mifflin.

Rogers, C. R., & Sanford, R. C. (1985). Client-centered psychotherapy. In H. I. Kaplan, B. J. Sadock, & A. M. Friedman (Eds.), *Comprehensive textbooks of psychiatry* (4th ed.) (pp. 1374–1388). Baltimore: Williams & Wilkins.

Stolorow, R. D. (1992). Closing the gap between theory and practice with better psychoanalytic theory. *Psychotherapy, 29*(2), 159–166.

Tobin, S. A. (1991). A comparison of psychoanalytic self psychology and Carl Rogers's person-centered therapy. *Journal of Humanistic Psychology, 31*(1), 9–33.

Chapter 7

Amatea, E. S. (1989). *Brief strategic intervention for school behavior problems.* San Francisco: Jossey-Bass.

Asay, T. P., & Lambert, M. J. (1999). The empirical case for common factors in therapy: Quantitative findings. In M. A. Hubble, B. L. Duncan, & S. D. Miller (Eds.). *The heart and soul of change: What works in therapy* (pp. 23–55). Washington, DC: American Psychological Association.

Bergin, A. E., & Garfield, S. L. (Eds.). (1994). *Handbook of psychotherapy and behavior change* (4th ed.). New York: John Wiley & Sons.

Bertolino, B. (1999). *Therapy with troubled teenagers: Rewriting young lives in progress.* New York: John Wiley & Sons.

Bertolino, B., & O'Hanlon, B. (2002). *Collaborative, competency-based counseling and therapy.* Boston: Allyn and Bacon.

Binder, J. L., Strupp, H. H., & Henry, W. P. (1995). Psychodynamic therapies in practice: Time limited dynamic psychotherapy. In B. Bongar & L. E. Beutler (Eds.). *Comprehensive textbook of psychotherapy,* pp. 48–63. New York: Oxford University Press.

Cade, B., & O'Hanlon, W. H. (1993). *A brief guide to brief therapy.* New York: W. W. Norton.

Claxton, G. (1997). *Hare brain, tortoise mind: Why intelligence increases when you think less.* Hopewell, NJ: Ecco Press.

Cooper, J. F. (1995). *A primer of brief psychotherapy.* New York: W. W. Norton.

Crosby, A. W. (1997). *The measure of reality: Quantification and western society, 1250–1600.* Cambridge, UK: Cambridge University Press.

Cummings, N., & Sayama, M. (1995). *Focused therapy: A casebook of brief intermittent psychotherapy throughout the life cycle.* New York: Brunner/Mazel.

de Shazer, S. (1985). *Keys to solution in brief therapy.* New York: Norton.

de Shazer, S. (1990). What is it about brief therapy that works? In J. K. Zeig & S. G. Gilligan (Eds.). *Brief therapy: Myths, methods, and metaphors* (pp. 90–99). New York: Brunner/Mazel.

de Shazer, S. (1991). *Putting difference to work.* New York: Norton.

DeJong, P., & Berg, I. K. (1998). *Interviewing for solutions.* Pacific Grove, CA: Brooks/Cole Publishing.

DeJong, P., & Berg, I. K. (2002). *Interviewing for solutions* (2nd ed.). Pacific Grove, CA: Brooks/Cole Publishing

Durrant, M. (1995). Creative strategies for school problems: Solutions for psychologists and teachers. New York: Norton.

Durrant, M., & Kowalski, K. (1993). Enhancing views of competence. In S. Friedman (Ed.). *The new language of change: Constructive collaboration in psychotherapy* (pp. 107–137). New York: Guilford Press.

Efran, J. S., Lukens, M. D., & Lukens, R. J. (1990). *Language, structure, and change: Frameworks for meaning in psychotherapy.* New York: Norton.

Ellis, A. (1989). Rational-emotive therapy. In R. J. Corsini & D. Wedding (Eds.). *Current psychotherapies* (4th ed.) (pp. 197–238). Itasca, IL: Peacock Publishers.

Ellis, A. (1990). How can psychological treatment aim to briefer and better?—the rational-emotive approach to brief therapy. In J. K. Zeig & S. G. Gilligan (Eds.). *Brief therapy: Myths, methods, and metaphors* (pp. 291–302). New York: Brunner/Mazel.

Ellis, A. (1996). *Better, deeper, and more enduring brief therapy: The rational emotive behavior therapy approach.* New York: Brunner/Mazel.

Epston, D., & White, M. (1995). Termination as a rite of passage: Questioning strategies for a therapy of inclusion. In R. A. Neimeyer & M. J. Mahoney (Eds.). *Constructivism in psychotherapy* (pp. 339–354). Washington, DC: American Psychological Association.

Fisch, R. (1990). Problem-solving psychotherapy. In J. K. Zeig & W. M. Munion (Eds.). *What is psychotherapy?: Contemporary perspectives* (pp. 269–273). San Francisco: Jossey-Bass.

Fisch, R. (1994). Basic elements in the brief therapies. In M. F. Hoyt (Ed.). *Constructive therapies* (pp. 126–139). New York: Guilford Press.

Fisch, R., Weakland, J. H., & Segal, L. (1982). *Tactics of change: Doing therapy briefly.* San Francisco: Jossey-Bass.

Friedman, S. (Ed). (1993). *The new language of change: Constructive collaboration in psychotherapy.* New York: Guilford Press.

Haley, J. (1973). *Uncommon therapy: The psychiatric techniques of Milton H. Erickson.* New York: Norton.

Hart, B. (1995). Re-authoring stories we work by situating the narrative approach in the presence of the family of therapists. *Australian and New Zealand Journal of Family Therapy, 16,* 181–189.

Herman, E. (1995). *The romance of American psychology: Political culture in the age of experts.* Berkeley, CA: University of California Press.

Hoyt, M. F. (Ed.). (1994). *Constructive therapies.* New York: Guilford Press.

Hoyt, M. F. (1995). *Brief therapy and managed care: Readings for contemporary practice.* San Francisco: Jossey-Bass.

Hoyt, M. F. (Ed.). (1996). *Constructive therapies* (Vol. 2). New York: Guilford Press.

Hoyt, M. F. (2000). *Some stories are better than others: Doing what works in brief therapy and managed care.* Philadelphia, PA: Brunner/Mazel.

Hoyt, M. F., & Combs, G. (1996). On ethics and the spiritualities of the surface: A conversation with Michael White. In M. F. Hoyt (Ed.), *Constructive therapies (Vol. 2)* (pp. 33–59). New York: Guilford Press.

Hubble, M. A., Duncan, B. L., & Miller, S. D. (1999). *The heart and soul of change: What works in therapy.* Washington, DC: American Psychological Association.

Koss, M. P., & Butcher, J. N. (1986). Research on brief psychotherapy. In S. L. Garfield & A. E. Bergin (Eds.). *Handbook of psychotherapy and behavior change* (3rd ed., pp. 627–670). New York: John Wiley.

Koss, M. P., & Shiang, J. (1994). Research on brief psychotherapy. In A. E. Bergin & S. L. Garfield (Eds.). *Handbook of psychotherapy and*

behavior change (4th ed., pp. 664–700). New York: John Wiley.

Lakoff, G., & Johnson, M. (1999). Philosophy in the flesh: The embodied mind and its challenge to western thought. New York: Basic Books.

Lambert, M. J. (1992). Implications of outcome research for psychotherapy integration. In J. C. Norcross & M. R. Goldstein (Eds.). *Handbook of psychotherapy integration* (pp. 94–129). New York: Basic Books.

Levenson, H. (1995). *Time-limited dynamic psychotherapy.* New York: Basic Books.

Lipchik, E. (2002). *Beyond technique in solution-focused therapy: Working with emotions and the therapeutic relationship.* New York: Guilford Press.

Mahoney, M. J. (1997). Brief moments and enduring effects: Reflections on time and timing in psychotherapy. In W. J. Matthews & J. H. Edgette (Eds.). *Current thinking and research in brief therapy: Solutions, strategies, narratives.* New York: Brunner/Mazel.

Mann, J. (1981). The core of time-limited psychotherapy: Time and the central issue. In S. H. Budman (Ed.). *Forms of brief therapy* (pp. 25–43). New York: Guilford Press.

Mann, J. (1991). Time limited psychotherapy. In P. Crits-Christoph, & J. P. Barber, (Eds.). *Handbook of short term dynamic psychotherapy* (pp. 17–44). New York: Basic Books.

Matthews, W. J., & Edgette, J. H. (Eds.). (1997). *Current thinking and research in brief therapy: Solutions, strategies, narratives.* New York: Brunner/Mazel.

McCloskey, K. A., & Fraser, J. S. (1997). Using feminist MRI brief therapy during initial contact with victims of domestic violence. *Psychotherapy, 34,* 433–446.

McKeel, A. (1996). A clinician's guide to research on solution-focused brief therapy. In S. D. Miller, M. A. Hubble, & B. L. Duncan (Eds.). *Handbook of solution-focused brief therapy* (pp. 251–271). San Francisco: Jossey-Bass.

McWhorter, J. (2001). *The power of Babel: A natural history of language.* New York: Perennial.

Metcalf, L. (1995). *Counseling toward solutions: A practical solution-focused program for working with students, teachers, and parents.* West Nyack, NY: Center for Applied Research in Education.

Miller, G. (1997). *Becoming miracle workers: Language and meaning in brief therapy.* New York: Aldine de Gruyter.

Miller, S. D., Hubble, M. A., & Duncan, B. L. (Eds.). (1996). *Handbook of solution-focused brief therapy.* San Francisco: Jossey-Bass.

Monk, G., Winslade, J., Crocket, K., & Epston, D. (Eds.). (1997). *Narrative therapy in practice: The archaeology of hope.* San Francisco: Jossey-Bass.

Mostert, D. L., Johnson, E., & Mostert, M. P. (1997). The utility of solution-focused, brief counseling in schools: Potential from an initial study. *Professional School Counseling, 1,* 21–24.

Murphy, J. J. (1997). *Solution-focused counseling in middle and high schools.* Alexandria, VA: American Counseling Association.

Neimeyer, R. A., & Mahoney, M. J. (Eds.). (1995). *Constructivism in psychotherapy.* Washington, DC: American Psychological Association.

O'Hanlon, W. H. (1987). *Taproots: Underlying principles of Milton Erickson's therapy and hypnosis.* New York: Norton.

O'Hanlon, W. H. (1990). A grand unified theory for brief therapy: Putting problems in context. In J. K. Zeig & S. G. Gilligan (Eds.). *Brief therapy: Myths, methods, and metaphors* (pp. 78–89). New York: Brunner/Mazel.

O'Hanlon, W. H. (1999) *Do one thing different: And other uncommonly sensible solutions to life's persistent problems.* New York: William Morrow and Company.

O'Hanlon, W. H., & Weiner-Davis, M. (1989). *In search of solutions: A new direction in psychotherapy.* New York: Norton.

Parry, A., & Doan, R. E. (1994). *Story re-visions: Narrative therapy in the postmodern world.* New York: Guilford Press.

Palmatier, L. L. (1990). Reality therapy and brief strategic interactional therapy. *Journal of Reality Therapy, 9,* 3–17.

Palmatier, L. L. (1996). Freud defrauded while Glasser defreuded: From pathologizing to talking solutions. *Journal of Reality Therapy, 16,* 75–94.

Pransky, G. S. (1998). *The renaissance of psychology.* New York: Sulzburger and Graham.

Pransky, G. S., Mills, R. C., Sedgeman, J. A., & Bleven, J. K. (1997). An emerging paradigm for brief treatment. In L. Vandecreek, S. Knapp, & T. L. Jackson (Eds.). *Innovations in clinical practice: A source book* (Vol. 15, pp. 401–420). Sarasota, FL: Professional Resource Press.

Rosenbaum, R., Hoyt, M. F., & Talmon, M. (1990). The challenge of single-session therapies! Creating pivotal moments. In R. A. Wells & V. J. Giannetti (Eds.). *Handbook of the brief psychotherapies* (pp. 165–189). New York: Plenum Press.

Selekman, M. D. (1993a). *Pathways to change: Brief therapy solutions with difficult adolescents.* New York: Guilford Press.

Selekman, M. D. (1993b). Solution-oriented brief therapy with difficult adolescents. In S. Friedman (Ed.). *The new language of change: Constructive collaboration in psychotherapy* (pp. 138–157). New York: Guilford Press.

Sharf, R. S. (1996). *Theories of psychotherapy and counseling: Concepts and cases.* Pacific Grove, CA: Brooks/Cole.

Shulman, B. H. (1989). Some remarks on brief therapy. Special issue: Varieties of brief therapy. *Individual Psychology: Journal of Adlerian Theory, Research, and Practice, 45*(1–2), 34–37.

Sklare, G. B. (1997). *Brief counseling that works: A solution-focused approach for school counselors.* Thousand Oaks, CA: Corwin Press.

Skolimowski, H. (1994). *The participatory mind: A new theory of knowledge and of the universe.* London: Penguin.

Strupp, H. H. (1981). Toward the refinement of time-limited dynamic psychotherapy. In S. H. Budman (Ed.). *Forms of brief therapy* (pp. 219–242). Guilford Press: New York.

Walter, J. L., & Peller, J. E. (1992). *Becoming solution-focused in brief therapy.* New York: Brunner/Mazel.

Walter, J. L., & Peller, J. E. (2000). *Re-creating brief therapy: Preferences and possibilities.* New York: Norton.

Watzlawick, P., Weakland, J., & Fisch, R. (1974). *Change: Principles of problem formation and problem resolution.* New York: Norton.

Wells, R. A., & Giannetti, V. J. (Eds.). (1990). *Handbook of brief psychotherapies.* New York: Plenum Press.

White, M., & Epston, D. (1990). *Narrative means to therapeutic ends.* New York: Norton.

Winslade, J., & Monk, G. (1999). *Narrative counseling in schools: Powerful and brief.* Thousand Oaks, CA: Corwin Press.

Worchel, J. (1990). Short-term dynamic psychotherapy. In R. A. Wells & V. J. Giannetti (Eds.). *Handbook of the brief psychotherapies* (pp. 193–216). New York: Plenum Press.

Zeig, J. K., & Gilligan, S. G. (Eds.). (1990). *Brief therapy: Myths, methods, and metaphors.* New York: Brunner/Mazel.

Chapter 8

American Counseling Association (1995). *Code of ethics and standards of practice.* Alexandria, VA: Author.

Anchor, K. N. (1979). High-and-low-risk self-disclosure in group psychotherapy. *Small Group Behavior, 10,* 279–283.

Anderson, J. D. (1979). Social work with groups in the generic base of social work practice. *Social Work With Groups, 2*, 281–293.

Anderson, J. D. (1985). Working with groups: Little-known facts that challenge well-known myths. *Small Group Behavior, 16*(3), 267–283.

Arbuckle, D. (1975). *Counseling and psychotherapy: An existential-humanistic view.* Boston: Allyn & Bacon.

Ashkenas, R., & Tandon, R. (1979). Eclectic approach to small group facilitation. *Small Group Behavior, 10,* 224–241.

Association for Specialists in Group Work (ASGW). (1983). *Professional standards for training of group counselors.* Alexandria, VA: Author.

Association for Specialists in Group Work. (1991). *Ethical guidelines for group leaders.* Alexandria, VA: Author.

Association for Specialists in Group Work. (1991). Professional standards for training of group workers. *Together, 20,* 9–14.

Association for Specialists in Group Work. (1992). Professional standards for training of group workers. *The Journal for Specialists in Group Work, 17*(1), 12–19.

Association for Specialists in Group Work. (1999). Principles for diversity-competent group workers. *The Journal for Specialists in Group Work, 24*(1), 7–14.

Association for Specialists in Group Work. (2000). *Professional standards for the training of group workers.* Alexandria, VA. Author.

Bales, R. F. (1950). *Interaction process analysis: A method for study of small groups.* Reading, MA: Addison-Wesley.

Bates, M., Johnson, C. D., & Blaker, K. E. (1982*). Group leadership: A manual for group counseling leaders* (2nd ed.). Denver: Love Publishing.

Bean, B. W., & Houston, B. K. (1978*).* Self-concept and self-disclosure in encounter groups. *Small Group Behavior, 9,* 549–554.

Bednar, R., & Lawlis, G. (1971). Empirical research in group psychotherapy. In S. L. Garfield & A. E. Bergin (Eds.), *Handbook of psychotherapy and behavior change* (2nd ed., pp. 420–439). New York: Wiley.

Berg, R. C., Landreth, G. L., & Fall, K. A. (1998). *Group counseling: Concepts and procedures* (3rd ed.). Philadelphia, PA: Taylor & Francis.

Bertcher, H. J., & Maple, F. F. (1977). *Creating groups.* Newbury Park, CA: Sage.

Berzon, B., Pious, C., & Farson, R. (1963). The therapeutic event in group psychotherapy: A study of subjective reports by group members. *Journal of Individual Psychology, 19,* 204–212.

Bloch, S. (1986). Therapeutic factors in group psychotherapy. In A. J. Frances & R. E. Hales (Eds.). *Annual Review* (Vol. 5 pp. 678–698). Washington, DC: American Psychiatric Press.

Braaten, L. J. (1975). Developmental phases of encounter groups and related intensive groups. *Interpersonal Development, 5,* 112–129.

Bradford, L. P., Gibb, J. R., & Benne, K. D. (Eds.). (1964). *T-group theory and laboratory method: Innovation in re-education.* New York: John Wiley.

Butler, T., & Fuhriman, A. (1980). Patient perspective on the curative process: A comparison of day treatment and outpatient psychotherapy groups. *Small Group Behavior, 11,* 371–388.

Capuzzi, D., & Gross, D. R. (1992). *Introduction to group counseling.* Denver: Love Publishing.

Capuzzi, D., & Gross D. R. (1998). *Introduction to group counseling* (2nd ed.). Denver: Love Publishing.

Capuzzi, D., & Gross, D. R. (2002). Introduction to group counseling (3rd ed.). Denver: Love Publishing.

Carkhuff, R. R. (1969). *Helping and human relations: A primer for lay and professional helpers.* Vol. 2: *Practice and research.* New York: Holt, Rinehart & Winston.

Carkhuff, R. R., & Berenson, B. G. (1977). *Beyond counseling and therapy* (2nd ed.). New York: Holt, Rinehart & Winston.

Clark, A. J. (1992). Defense mechanisms in group counseling. *The Journal for Specialists in Group Work, 17*(3), 151–160.

Cohen, A. M., & Smith, D. R. (1976). *The critical incident in growth groups: Theory and techniques.* La Jolla, CA: University Associates.

Conyne, R. K., Wilson, F. R., Kline, W. B., Morran, D. K., & Ward, D. E. (1993). Training group workers: Implications of the new ASGW training standards for training and practice. *The Journal for Specialists in Group Work, 18*(1), 11–23.

Corey, G. (1985). *Theory and practice of group counseling* (2nd ed.). Pacific Grove, CA: Brooks/Cole.

Corey, G. (2000). *Theory and practice of group counseling* (5th ed.). Belmont, CA: Brooks/Cole.

Corey, G. (2004). *Theory and practice of group counseling* (6th ed.). Belmont,CA: Brooks/Cole.

Corsini, R., & Rosenberg, B. (1955). Mechanisms of group psychotherapy: Processes and dynamics. *Journal of Abnormal and Social Psychology, 51,* 406–411.

Council for Accreditation of Counseling and Related Educational Programs (CACREP). (1988). *Accreditation procedures manual and application.* Alexandria, VA: Author.

Council for Accreditation of Counseling and Related Educational Programs. (1994, 2001). *CACREP accreditation standards and procedures manual* Alexandria, VA: Author.

De Julio, S. J. , Bentley, J., & Cockayne, T. (1979). Pregroup norm setting: Effects on encounter group interaction. *Small Group Behavior, 10,* 368–388.

Dinkmeyer, D. C., & Muro, J. J. (1971). *Group counseling: Theory and practice.* Itasca, IL: Peacock.

Dinkmeyer, D. C., & Muro, J. J. (1979). *Group counseling: Theory and practice* (2nd ed.). Itasca, IL: Peacock.

Donigan, J., & Malanti, R. (1997). *Systemic group therapy: A triadic model.* Pacific Grove, CA: Brooks/Cole.

Dyer, W. W., & Vriend, J. (1973). Effective group counseling process interventions. *Educational Technology, 13*(1), 61–67.

Frank, J., & Ascher, E. (1951). The corrective emotional experience in group therapy. *American Journal of Psychiatry, 108,* 126–131.

Gazda, G. M. (1984). *Group counseling* (3rd ed.). Dubuque, IA: Brown.

Gazda, G. M., Ginter, E. J., & Horne, A. M. (2001). *Group counseling and psychotherapy: Theory and application.* Needham Heights, MA: Allyn & Bacon.

Gazda, G. M., & Peters, R. W. (1975). An analysis of human research in group psychotherapy, group counseling and human relations training. In G. M. Gazda (Ed.), *Basic approaches to group psychotherapy and group counseling* (pp. 38–54). Springfield, IL: Thomas.

George, R. L., & Dustin, D. (1988). *Group counseling: Theory and practice.* Englewood Cliffs, NJ: Prentice-Hall.

Gladding, S. T. (2003). *Group work: A counseling specialty* (4th ed.). Upper Saddle River, NJ: Merrill/Prentice Hall.

Goldstein, E. G., & Noonan, M. (1999). *Short-term treatment and social work practice: An integrative perspective.* New York: The Free Press.

Goldstein, M. J., Bednar, R. L., & Yanell, B. (1979). Personal risk associated with self-disclosure, interpersonal feedback, and group confrontation in group psychotherapy. *Small Group Behavior, 9,* 579–587.

Golembiewski, R. T. (1962). *The small group: An analysis of research concepts and operations.* Chicago: University of Chicago Press.

Hare, A. P. (1973). Theories of group development and categories for interaction analysis. *Small Group behavior, 4,* 259–304.

Hare, A. P., Borgatta, E. F., & Bales, R. F. (Eds.). (1967). *Small groups: Studies in social interaction* (rev. ed.). New York: Knopf.

Herlihy, B., & Corey, G. C. (1997). *Boundary issues in counseling: Multiple roles and responsibilities.* Alexandria, VA: American Counseling Association.

Higgs, J. S. (1992). Dealing with resistance: Strategies for effective group. *The Journal for Specialists in Group Work, 17*(2), 67–73.

Hill, W. F. (1957). Analysis of interviews of group therapists' papers. *Provo Papers, 1,* 1.

Hill, W. F., & Gruner, L. (1973). A study of development in open and closed groups. *Small Group Behavior, 4,* 355–381.

Jacobs, A. (1974). The use of feedback in groups. In A. Jacobs & W. W. Spradline (Eds.). *The group as an agent of change* (pp. 31–49). New York: Behavioral Publications.

Jacobs, E. E., Masson, R. L., & Harvill, R. L. (1998). *Group counseling: Strategies and skills.* Pacific Grove, CA: Brooks/Cole.

Janis, I. L. (1972). *Victims of groupthink: A psychological study of foreign-policy decisions and fiascos.* Boston: Houghton-Mifflin.

Johnson, D. W., & Johnson, F. P. (2000). *Joining together: Group theory and group skills.* Boston: Allyn & Bacon.

Jourard, S. (1971). *The transparent self* (rev. ed.). New York: Van Nostrand Reinhold.

Kalodner, C. R., & Riva, M. T. (1997). Group research: Encouraging a collaboration between practitioners and researchers: a conclusion. *Journal for Specialists in Group Work, 22*(4), 297.

Kottler, J. A. (1983). *Pragmatic group leadership.* Pacific Grove, CA: Brooks/Cole.

La Coursiere, R. (1980). *The life-cycle of groups: Group development stage theory.* New York: Human Sciences.

Leiberman, M. A., Yalom, I. D., & Miles, M. B. (1973). *Encounter groups: First facts.* New York: Basic Books.

Levin, E. M., & Kurtz, R. P. (1974). Participant perceptions following structured and nonstructured human relations training. *Journal of Counseling Psychology, 21,* 514–532.

Levine, N. (1971). Emotional factors in group development. *Human Relations, 24,* 65–89.

Long, L. D., & Cope, C. S. (1980). Curative factors in a male felony offender group. *Small Group Behavior, 11,* 389–398.

Lungren, D. C. (1971). Trainer style and patterns of group development. *Journal of Applied Behavioral Science,* 689–709.

MacKenzie, K. R. (1997). *Time-managed group psychotherapy: Effective clinical applications.* Washington, DC: American Psychiatric Press, Inc.

Martin, L., & Jacobs, M. (1980). Structured feedback delivered in small groups. *Small Group Behavior, 1,* 88–107.

Neukrug, E. (1999). *The world of the counselor: An introduction to the counseling profession.* Pacific Grove, CA: Brooks/Cole.

Ohlsen, M. M. (1977). *Group counseling* (2nd ed.). New York: Holt, Rinehart & Winston.

Ohlsen, M. M., & Ferreira, L. O. (1994). The basics of group counseling. *Counseling and Human Development, 26*(5), 1–20.

Ormont, L. R. (1993). Resolving resistances to immediacy in the group setting. *International Journal of Group Psychotherapy, 43*(4), 399–418.

Parloff, M. B., & Dies, R. R. (1978). Group therapy outcome instrument: Guidelines for conducting research. *Small Group Behavior, 9,* 243–286.

Perls, F. (1969). *Gestalt therapy verbatim.* New York: Bantam.

Reid, C. H. (1965). The authority cycle in small group development. *Adult Leadership, 1,* 308–310.

Remley, T. P., and Herlihy, B. (2005). *Ethical, legal, and professional issues in counseling.* Saddle River, NJ: Merrill.

Roller, B. (1997). *The promise of group therapy: How to build a vigorous training and organizational base for group therapy in managed behavioral healthcare.* San Francisco, CA: Jossey-Bass.

Rowe, W., & Winborn, B. B. (1973). What people fear about group work: An analysis of 36 selected critical articles. *Educational Technology, 13*(1), 53–57.

Shapiro, J. L., & Bernadett-Shapiro, S. (1985). Group work to 2001: Hal or haven (from isolation)? *Journal for Specialists in Group Work, 10*(2), 83–87.

Snortum, J. R., & Myers, H. F. (1971). Intensity of T-group relations as function of interaction. *International Journal of Group Psychotherapy, 21,* 190–201.

Stava, L. J., & Bednar, R. L. (1979). Process and outcome in encounter groups: The effect of group composition. *Small Group Behavior, 10,* 200–213.

Thelen, H., & Dickerman, W. (1949). Stereotypes and the growth of groups. *Educational Leadership, 6,* 309–316.

Truax, C. B., & Carkhuff, R. R. (1967). *Toward effective counseling and psychotherapy: Training and practice.* Chicago: Aldine.

Tuckman, B. W. (1965). Developmental sequences in small groups. *Psychological Bulletin, 63,* 384–389.

Vriend, J. (1985). We've come a long way, group. *Journal for Specialists in Group Work, 10*(2), 63–67.

Yalom, I. D. (1970). *The theory and practice of group psychotherapy.* New York: Basic Books.

Yalom, I. D. (1975). *The theory and practice of group psychotherapy* (2nd ed.). New York: Basic Books.

Zimpfer, D. G. (1967). Expression of feelings in group counseling. *Personnel and Guidance Journal, 45,* 703–708.

Zimpfer, D. G. (1986). Planning for groups based on their developmental phases. *Journal for Specialists in Group Work, 11*(3), 180–187.

Chapter 9

Albion, M. J., & Fogarty, G. J. (2002). Factors influencing career decision making in adolescents and adults. *Journal of Career Assessment, 10*(1), 91–126.

Alston, R. J., Bell, T. J., & Hampton, J. L. (2002). Learning disability and career entry into the sciences: A critical analysis of attitudinal factors. *Journal of Career Development, 28*(4), 263–275.

American Counseling Association. (1995). *Code of ethics and standards of practice.* Alexandria, VA: Author.

American Psychological Association. (2003). Guidelines on multicultural education, training, research, practice, and organizational change for Psychologists. *American Psychologist, 58*(5), 377–402.

Arbona, C. (1990). Career counseling research and Hispanics: A review of the literature. *The Counseling Psychologist, 18*(2), 300–323.

Atkinson, D. R., Morten, G., & Sue, D. W. (1998). *Counseling American minorities: A cross-cultural perspective* (5th ed.). Boston: McGraw-Hill.

Bandura, A. (1986). *Social foundations of thought and action: A social cognitive theory.* Englewood Cliffs, NJ: Prentice-Hall.

Bandura, A. (1997). *Self-efficacy: The exercise of control.* New York: Freeman.

Betz, N. E., & Corning, A. F. (1993). The inseparability of "career" and "personal" counseling. *The Career Development Quarterly, 42*(2), 137–142.

Betz, N. E., & Fitzgerald, L. (1987). *The career psychology of women.* Orlando, FL: Academic Press Inc.

Blake, R. J., & Sackett, S. A. (1999). Holland's typology and the five-factor model: A rational-empirical analysis. *Journal of Career Assessment 7*(3), 249–279

Blanchard, C. A., & Lichtenberg, J. W. (2003). Compromise in career decision making: A test of Gottfredson's theory. *Journal of Vocational Behavior, 62*(2), 250–271

Bolles, R. N. (2003). *What color is your parachute? 2004.* Berkeley, CA: Ten Speed Press.

Bowman, S. L. (1998). Minority women and career adjustment. *Journal of Career Assessment, 6,* 417–431.

Brown, D. (2002). The role of work and cultural values in occupational choice, satisfaction, and success: A theoretical statement. *Journal of Counseling & Development, 80*(1), 48–56.

Brown, D., & Associates (Eds.). (2002). *Career information, career counseling, and career development* (8th ed.). Boston: Allyn & Bacon.

Brown, D., & Brooks, L. (1991). *Career counseling techniques.* Boston: Allyn & Bacon.

Brown, M. T. (2000). Blueprint for the assessment of socio-structural influences in career choice and decision making. *Journal of Career Assessment, 8*(4), 371–378.

Brown, S. D., & Krane, N. E. R. (2000). Four (or five) sessions and a cloud of dust: Old assumptions and new observations about career counseling. In S. D. Brown & R. W. Lent (Eds.), *Handbook of counseling psychology* (3rd ed.). New York: Wiley.

Byars, A. M. (2001). Rights-of-way: Affirmative career counseling with African American women. In W. B. Walsh, R. P. Bingham, M. T. Brown, & C. M. Ward (Eds.). *Career counseling for African Americans* (pp. 27–48). Mahwah, NJ: Erlbaum.

Career assessment for a new millennium. (2000). Special section of the *Journal of Career Assessment, 8*(4).

Career development of women of color and white women. (2002). Special issue of the *Career Development Quarterly, 50*(4).

Chartrand, J. M., Borgen, F. H., Betz, N. E., & Donnay, D. (2002). Using the Strong Interest Inventory and the Skills Confidence Inventory to explain career goals. *Journal of Career Assessment, 10*(2), 169–189.

Chung, B. Y. (1995). Career decision-making of lesbian, gay, and bisexual individuals. *The Career Development Quarterly, 44,* 178–190.

Chung, B. Y. (2002). Career decision-making self-efficacy and career commitment: Gender and ethnic differences among college students. *Journal of Career Development, 28*(4), 277–284.

Chronister, K. M., & McWhirter, E. H. (in press). Applying social cognitive career theory to the empowerment of battered women. *Journal of Counseling & Development.*

Cohen, B. N. (2003). Applying existential theory and intervention to career decision-making. *Journal of Career Development, 29*(3), 195–210.

Comas-Diaz, L., & Greene, B. (1994). *Women of color: Integrating ethnic and gender identities in psychotherapy.* New York: Guilford Press.

Cook, E. P., Heppner, M. J., & O'Brien, K. M. (2002). Career development of women of color and White women: Assumptions, conceptualization, and interventions from an ecological perspective. *Career Development Quarterly, 50*(4), 291–305.

Council for Accreditation of Counseling and Related Educational Programs. (2001). *The 2001 Standards.* Alexandria, VA: Author. Retrieved October 1, 2003 from *http://www.counseling.org/cacrep/2001standards700.htm.*

Crist, P. A. H., & Stoffel, V. C. (1992). The Americans with Disabilities Act of 1990 and employees with mental impairments: Personal efficacy and the environment. *American Journal of Occupational Therapy, 46*(5), 434–443.

Croteau, J. M., Anderson, M. Z., Distefano, T. M., & Kampa-Kokesch, S. (2000). Lesbian, gay, and bisexual vocational psychology: Reviewing foundations and planning construction. In R. M. Perez, K. A. DeBord, K. J. Bieschke, & L. S. Brown (Eds.), *Handbook of counseling and psychotherapy with lesbian, gay, and bisexual clients* (pp. 383–408). Washington, DC: American Psychological Association.

Croteau, J. M., & Thiel, M. J. (1993). Integrating sexual orientation in career counseling: Acting to end a form of the personal-career dichotomy. *The Career Development Quarterly, 42*(2), 174–179.

Crozier, S. D. (1999). Women's career development in a "relational context." *International Journal for the Advancement of Counselling, 21*(3), 231–247.

Day, S. X., Rounds, J., & Swaney, K. (1998). The structure of vocational interests for diverse racial/ethnic groups. *Psychological Science, 9,* 40–44.

Dillard, J. M., & Harley, D. A. (2002). Working with ethnic minority employees in the workplace. In

D. S. Sandhu (Ed). (2002), *Counseling employees: A multifaceted approach* (pp. 131–149). Alexandria, VA: American Counseling Association.

Dipeolu, A., Reardon, R., Sampson, J., & Burkhead, J. (2002). The relationship between dysfunctional career thoughts and adjustment to disability in college students with learning disabilities. *Journal of Career Assessment, 10*(4), 413–427.

Engels, D. W., Minor, C. W., Sampson, Jr., J. P., & Splete, H. H. (1995). Career counseling specialty: History, development and prospect. *Journal of Counseling and Development, 74*(2), 134–138.

Enright, M. S., Conyers, L. M., & Szymanski, E. M. (1996). Career and career-related educational concerns of college students with disabilities. *Journal of Counseling and Development, 75*(2), 103–114.

Fabian, E. S., Lent, R. W., & Willis, S. P. (1998). Predicting work transition outcomes for students with disabilities: Implications for counselors. *Journal of Counseling and Development, 76*(3), 311–316.

Farr, M. J., Ludden, L. L., & Shatkin, L. (Eds.). (2001). Guide for occupational exploration (3rd ed.). Indianapolis, IN: Jist Works.

Fitzgerald, L. F., & Weitzman, L. M. (1992). Women's career development: Theory and practice from a feminist perspective. In H. Daniel Lea & Z. B. Leibowitz (Eds.), *Adult career development: Concepts, issues, and practices* (2nd ed., pp. 124–160). Alexandria, VA: The National Career Development Association.

Flores, L. Y. & O'Brien, K. M. (2002). The career development of Mexican American adolescent women: A test of social cognitive career theory. *Journal of Counseling Psychology, 49*(1), 14–27.

Fouad, N. A. (Chair) (1999, August). *Frank Parsons—Contributions to vocational psychology 90 years later.* Symposium conducted at the meeting of the American Psychological Association, Boston, MA.

Fouad, N. A. (2002). Cross-cultural differences in vocational interests: Between-group differences on the Strong Interest Inventory. *Journal of Counseling Psychology, 49*(3), 283–289.

Fouad, N. A., & Arbona, C. (1994). Careers in a cultural context. *The Career Development Quarterly, 43*(1), 96–104.

Fouad, N. A., & Bingham, R. P. (1995). Career counseling with racial and ethnic minorities. In W. B. Walsh & S. H. Osipow (Eds.). *Handbook of vocational psychology: Theory, research, and practice* (2nd ed., pp. 331–366). Mahwah, NJ: Erlbaum.

Frank Parsons's continuing legacy to career development interventions. (2001). Special section of the *Career Development Quarterly, 50*(1).

Gainor, K. A. (2001). Vocational assessment with culturally diverse populations. In L. A. Suzuki, J. G. Ponterotto, & P. J. Meller (Eds.). *Handbook of multicultural assessment: Clinical, psychological, and educational applications* (2nd ed., pp. 169–189). San Francisco: Jossey-Bass.

Gati, I., & Saka, N. (2001). Internet-based versus paper-and-pencil assessment: Measuring career decision-making difficulties. *Journal of Career Assessment, 9*(4), 397–416.

Gelberg, S., & Chojnacki, J. T. (1995). Developmental transitions of gay/lesbian/bisexual-affirmative, heterosexual career counselors. *The Career Development Quarterly, 43*(3), 267–273.

Ginzberg, E., Ginsburg, S. W., Axelrad, S., & Henna, J. L. (1951). *Occupational choice: An approach to a general theory.* New York: Columbia University Press.

Goldman, L. (1990). Qualitative assessment. *The Counseling Psychologist, 18,* 205–213.

Gore, P. A., & Leuwerke, W. C. (2000). Information technology for career assessment on the Internet. *Journal of Career Assessment, 8*(1), 3–19.

Gottfredson, L. S. (1981). Circumscription and compromise: A developmental theory of occupational aspirations. *Journal of Counseling Psychology, 28*(6), 545–579.

Gottfredson, L. S. (1996). Gottfredson's theory of circumscription and compromise. In D. Brown, L. Brooks, & Associates (Eds.). *Career choice and development* (3rd ed., pp. 179–232). San Francisco: Jossey-Bass.

Gottfredson, L. S. (2002). Gottfredson's theory of circumscription, compromise, and self-creation. In D. Brown & Associates (Eds.), *Career choice and development* (4th ed., pp. 85–148). San Francisco: Jossey- Bass.

Gysbers, N. C., Heppner, M. J., & Johnston, J. A. (1997). *Career counseling: Process issues and techniques.* Boston: Allyn & Bacon.

Hackett, G., & Byars, A. M. (1996). Social cognitive theory and the career development of African American women. *The Career Development Quarterly, 44,* 322–340.

Harmon, L. W., Hansen, J. I., Borgen, F. H., & Hammer, A. L. (1994). *Strong Interest Inventory: Applications and technical guide.* Palo Alto, CA: Consulting Psychologists Press.

Hartung, P. J. (2002). Cultural context in career theory and practice: Role salience and values. *Career Development Quarterly, 51*(1), 12–25.

Hawks, B. K., & Muha, D. (1991). Facilitating the career development of minorities: Doing it differently this time. *The Career Development Quarterly, 39,* 251–260.

Heppner, M. J., O'Brien, K. M., Hinkelman, J. M., & Flores, L. Y. (1996). Training counseling psychologists in career development: Are we our own worst enemies? *The Counseling Psychologist, 24*(1), 105–125.

Heppner, M. J., O'Brien, K. M., Hinkelman, J. M., & Humphrey, C. F. (1994). Shifting the paradigm: The use of creativity in career counseling. *Journal of Career Development, 21*(2), 77–86.

Holland, J. L. (1973). *Making vocational choices: A theory of careers.* Englewood Cliffs, NJ: Prentice Hall.

Holland, J. L. (1991a). *Self-Directed Search (SDS0 Form CP: Computer Version.* Tampa, FL: Psychological Assessment Resources.

Holland, J. L. (1991b). *Self-Directed Search (SDS0 Form CP: Interpretive Report.* Tampa, FL: Psychological Assessment Resources.

Holland, J. L. (1996a). Exploring career with typology: What we have learned and some new directions. *American Psychologist, 51,* 397–406.

Holland, J. L. (1996b). Integrating career theory and practice: The current situation and some potential remedies. In M. L. Savickas & W. B. Walsh (Eds.). *Handbook of career counseling theory and practice* (pp. 1–11). Palo Alto, CA: Davies-Black.

Holland, J. L. (1997). *Making vocational choices.* Tampa, FL: Psychological Assessment Resources.

Holland's Theory. (1999). Special issue of the *Journal of Vocational Behavior, 55*(1).

Hunt, B., Jaques, J., Niles, S. G., & Wierzalis, E. (2003). Career concerns for people living with HIV/AIDS. *Journal of Counseling & Development, 81*(1), 55–60.

Ibrahim, F. A., Ohnishi, H., & Wilson, R. P. (1994). Career assessment in a culturally diverse society. *Journal of Career Assessment, 2*(3), 276–288.

Isaacson, L. E. (1985). *Basics of career counseling.* Boston: Allyn & Bacon.

Isaacson, L. E., & Brown, D. (1999). *Career information, career counseling, and career development* (7th ed.). Boston, MA: Allyn and Bacon.

Kapes, J. T., Mastie, M. M., & Whitfield, E. A. (1994, 2000). *A counselor's guide to career assessment instruments* (3rd ed., 4th ed.). Alexandria, VA: National Career Development Association.

Kinnier, R. T., & Krumboltz, J. D. (1984). Procedures for successful career counseling. In N. Gysbers (Ed.). *Designing careers: Counseling to enhance education, work and leisure.* San Francisco: Jossey-Bass.

Krieshok, T. S. (2001). How the decision-making literature might inform career center practice. *Journal of Career Development, 27*(3), 207–216.

Krumboltz, J. D. (1989, August). *The social learning theory of career decision making.* Paper presented at the annual convention of the American Psychological Association, New Orleans, LA.

Krumboltz, J. D. (1994). Improving career development theory from a social learning perspective. In M. L. Savickas & R. W. Lent (Eds.). *Convergence in career development theories* (pp. 9–31). Palo Alto, CA: Consulting Psychologists Press, Inc.

Krumboltz, J. D. (1996). A learning theory of career counseling. In M. L. Savickas & W. B. Walsh (Eds.), *Handbook of career counseling theory and practice* (pp. 55–80). Palo Alto, CA: Davies-Black.

Krumboltz, J. D., & Vosvick, M. A. (1996). Career assessment and the career beliefs inventory. *Journal of Career Assessment, 4*(4), 345–361.

Lattimore, R. R., & Borgen, F. H. (1999). Validity of the 1994 Strong Interest Inventory with racial and ethnic groups in the United States. *Journal of Counseling Psychology, 46,* 185–195.

Lee, C. C. (Ed.). (1997). *Multicultural issues in counseling: New approaches to diversity* (2nd ed.). Alexandria, VA: American Counseling Association.

Lent, R. W., Brown, S. D., & Hackett, G. (1994). Toward a unifying social cognitive theory of career and academic interest, choice, and performance. *Journal of Vocational Behavior, 45,* 79–122.

Lent, R. W., Brown, S. D., & Hackett, G. (2002). Social Cognitive Career Theory. In D. Brown & Associates (Eds.), *Career choice and development* (4th ed., pp. 255–311). San Francisco: Jossey-Bass.

Leong, F. T. L. (Ed.). (1995). *Career development and vocational behavior of racial and ethnic minorities.* Hillsdale, NJ: Lawrence Erlbaum.

Leong, F. T. L., Austin, J. T., Sekaran, U., & Komarraju, M. (1998). An evaluation of the cross-cultural validity of Holland's theory: Career choices of workers in India. *Journal of Vocational Behavior, 52,* 441–455.

Leong, F. T. L., & Gim, R. H. C. (1995). Career assessment and intervention with Asian-Americans. In F. T. L. Leong (Ed.). *Career development and vocational behavior of racial and ethnic minorities.* Hillsdale, NJ: Lawrence Erlbaum.

Leong, F. T. L., & Hartung, P. (1997). Career assessment with culturally different clients:

Proposing an integrative-sequential conceptual framework for cross-cultural career counseling research and practice. *Journal of Career Assessment, 5*(2), 183–202.

Leung, S. A., & Hou, Z. (2001). Concurrent validity of the 1994 Self-Directed Search for Chinese high school students in Hong Kong. *Journal of Career Assessment, 9*, 283–296.

Levinson, E. M., Ohler, D. L., Caswell, S., & Kiewra, K. (1998). Six approaches to the assessment of career maturity. *Journal of Counseling & Development, 76*(4), 475–482.

Lofquist, L. H., & Dawis, R. V. (1969). *Adjustment to work.* Englewood Cliffs, NJ: Prentice-Hall.

Lofquist, L. H., & Dawis, R. V. (1984). Research on work adjustment and satisfaction: Implications for career counseling. In S. Brown & R. Lent (Eds.). *Handbook of counseling psychology.* New York: John Wiley.

Mael, F. A. (1991). Career constraints of observant Jews. *The Career Development Quarterly, 39*(3), 341–349.

Martin, W. E. Jr., & Farris, K. K. (1994). A cultural and contextual decision path approach to career assessment with Native Americans: A psychological perspective. *Journal of Career Assessment, 2*(3), 258–275.

McMahon, M., Patton, W., & Watson, M. (2003). Developing qualitative career assessment processes. *Career Development Quarterly, 51*(3), 194–202.

McWhirter, E. H. (1994). *Counseling for empowerment.* Alexandria, VA: American Counseling Association Press.

McWhirter, E. H. (1997). Perceived barriers to education and career: Ethnic and gender differences. *Journal of Vocational Behavior, 50*, 124–140.

McWhirter, E. H. (2001, March). Social action at the individual level: In pursuit of critical consciousness. Invited keynote address, 5th Biennial Conference of the Society for Vocational Psychology, Houston, TX.

McWhirter, E. H., Hackett, G., & Bandalos, D. L. (1998). A causal model of educational plans and career expectations of Mexican-American high school girls. *Journal of Counseling Psychology, 45*, 166–181.

McWhirter, E. H., Torres, D., & Rasheed, S. (1998). Assessing barriers to women's career adjustment. *Journal of Career Assessment, 6*, 317–332.

Morrow, S. L., Gore, Jr., P. A., & Campbell, B. W. (1996). The application of sociocognitive framework to the career development of lesbian women and gay men. *Journal of Vocational Behavior, 48*(2), 126–148.

Nagler, M. (1993). *Perspectives on disability* (2nd ed.). Palo Alto, CA: Health Markets Research.

National Career Development Association. (1997). *Career Counseling Competencies.* [Retrieved 9/28/03 from *http://ncda.org/about/polccc.html*].

National Center on Secondary Education and Transition (2002). *Policy Update—Youth with Disabilities and the Workforce Investment Act of 1998.* Minneapolis, MN: National Center on Secondary Education and Transition.

National Vocational Guidance Association, American Vocational Association (1973). *Position paper on career development.* Washington, DC: Author.

Nauta, M. M., Saucier, A. M., & Woodard, L. E. (2001). Interpersonal influences on students' academic and career decisions: The impact of sexual orientation. *Career Development Quarterly, 49*(4), 352–362.

Nevo, O. (1987). Irrational expectations in career counseling and their confronting arguments. *Career Development Quarterly, 35*(3), 239–250.

O'Brien, K. M. (2001). The legacy of Parsons: Career counselors and vocational psychologists as agents of social change. *Career Development Quarterly, 50*(1), 66–76.

Okiishi, R. W. (1987). The genogram as a tool in career counseling. *Journal of Counseling and Development, 66*(3), 139–143.

Oliver, L. W., & Whiston, S. C. (2000). Internet career assessment for the new millennium. *Journal of Career Assessment, 8*(4), 361–369.

Olson, C., McWhirter, E. H., & Horan, J. J. (1989). A decision making model applied to career counseling. *Journal of Career Development, 16*(2), 19–23.

O'Ryan, L. (2003). Career counseling and social justice. *Counselors for Social Justice Newsletter, 4*(1), 1, 3.

Osborne, W. L., Brown, S., Niles, S., & Miner, C. U. (1998). *Career development, assessment, & counseling: Applications of the Donald E. Super C-DAC approach.* Alexandria, VA: American Counseling Association.

Osipow, S. H., & Fitzgerald, L. F. (1995). *Theories of career development* (4th ed.). Englewood Cliffs, NJ: Prentice-Hall.

Osipow, S. H., Leong, F. T. L., & Barak, A. (Eds.). (2001). Contemporary models in vocational psychology: A volume in honor of Samuel H. Osipow. Mahwah, NJ: Erlbaum.

Pace, D., & Quinn, L. (2000). Empirical support of the overlap between career and mental health counseling of university students. *Journal of College Student Development, 14*(3) 41–50.

Parsons, F. (1909). *Choosing a vocation*. Boston: Houghton-Mifflin.

Pearson, S. M., & Bieschke, K. J. (2001). Succeeding against the odds: An examination of familial influences on the career development of professional African American women. *Journal of Counseling Psychology, 48*(3), 301–309.

Pedersen, P. (2000). Handbook for developing multicultural awareness. Alexandria: ACA Press.

Peterson, G. W. (1998). Using a vocational card sort as an assessment of occupational knowledge. *Journal of Career Assessment, 6*(1), 49–67.

Peterson, G. W., Ryan-Jones, R. E., Sampson, J. P., & Reardon, R. C. (1994). A comparison of the effectiveness of three computer-assisted career guidance systems: Discover, SIGI, and SIGI PLUS. *Computers in Human Behavior, 10*(2), 189–198.

Peterson, N., & Gonzalez, R. C. (2000). *The role of work in people's lives: Applied career counseling and vocational psychology*. Belmont, CA: Wadsworth/Thomson Learning.

Pinkney, J. W., & Jacobs, D. (1985). New counselors and personal interest in the task of career counseling. *Journal of Counseling Psychology, 32*(3), 454–457.

Prince, J. P. (1997). Career assessment with lesbian, gay, and bisexual individuals. *Journal of Career Assessment, 5*(2), 225–238.

Prochaska, J. O., & DiClemente, C. C. (1984). *The transtheoretical approach: Crossing the traditional boundaries of therapy*. Homewood, IL: Dow-Jones-Irvin.

Prochaska, J. O., & DiClemente, C. C. (1992). The transtheoretical approach. In J. C. Norcross (Ed.). *Handbook of psychotherapy integration* (pp. 300–334). New York: Basic Books.

Prochaska, J. O., DiClemente, C. C., & Norcross, J. C. (1992). In search of how people change: Applications to addictive behaviors. *American Psychologist, 47*, 1102–1114.

Reiff, H. B. (1997). Academic advising: An approach from learning disabilities research. *Journal of Counseling and Development, 75*(6), 433–441.

Ritter, K. Y., & Terndrup, A. I. (2002). *Handbook of affirmative psychotherapy with lesbians and gay men*. New York: Guilford Press.

Rivera, A. A., Anderson, S. K., & Middleton, V. A. (1999). A career development model for Mexican-American women. *Journal of Career Development, 26*(2), 91–106.

Salomone, P. R. (1988). Career counseling: Steps and stages beyond Parsons. *The Career Development Quarterly, 36*, 218–221.

Seligman, L. (1994). *Developmental career counseling and assessment* (2nd ed.). Thousand Oaks, CA: Sage.

Sharf, R. S. (2002). *Applying career development theory to career counseling* (3rd ed.). Pacific Grove, CA: Brooks/Cole.

Shin, SungLim A. (1999). Contextualizing career concerns of Asian American students. In Y. M. Jenkins (Ed.), *Diversity in college settings: Directives for helping professionals* (pp. 201–209). New York: Routledge.

Slaney, R. B. (1978). Expressed and inventoried vocational interests: A comparison of instruments. *Journal of Counseling Psychology, 25*, 520–529.

Soh, S., & Leong, F. T. L. (2001). Cross-cultural validation of Holland's theory in Singapore: Beyond structural validity of the RIASEC. *Journal of Career Assessment, 9*, 115–133.

Special issue on career assessment with people of color. (1994). Special issue of *The Journal of Career Assessment, 2*(3).

Special issue on career assessment with women of color. (1998). *Journal of Career Assessment, 6*(4).

Special issue on cultural issues in career counseling. (1993). Special issue of *The Career Development Quarterly, 42*(1).

Special issue on gay and lesbian career development. (1995). Special issue of *The Career Development Quarterly, 44*(2).

Special issue on Super's contribution to career development theory. (1994). Special issue of *The Career Development Quarterly, 43*(1).

Special issue on the vocational issues of lesbian women and gay men. (1996). Special issue of *The Journal of Vocational Behavior, 48*(2).

Special issue on theory into practice in career assessment for women. (1997). *Journal of Career Assessment, 5*(4).

Sue, D. W., Carter, R. T., Casas, J. M., Fouad, N. A., Ivey, A. E., Jensen, M., LaFromboise, T., Manese, J. E., Ponterotto, J. G., & Vazquez-Nutall, E. (1998). *Multicultural counseling competencies: Individual and organizational development*. Thousand Oaks, CA: Sage Publications, Inc.

Sue, D. W., & Sue, D. (2002). *Counseling the culturally diverse: Theory and process* (4th ed.). New York: John Wiley & Sons.

Super, D. E. (1957). *The psychology of careers*. New York: Harper & Brothers.

Super, D. E. (1963). Self-concepts in vocational development. In D. E. Super et al. (Eds.), *Career development: Self-concept theory*. New York: CEEB Research Monograph No. 4.

Super, D. E. (1974). *Measuring vocational maturity for counseling and evaluation.* Washington, DC: National Vocational Guidance Association.

Super, D. E. (1990). A life span, life-space approach to career development. In D. Brown, L. Brooks, & Associates (Eds.), *Career choice and development: Applying contemporary theories to practice* (2nd ed.) (pp. 197–261). San Francisco: Jossey-Bass.

Super, D. E., & Neville, D. D. (1986). *The Salience Inventory.* Palo Alto, CA: Consulting Psychologists Press.

Swanson, J. L. (1996). The process and outcome of career counseling. In W. B. Walsh & S. H. Osipow (Eds.). *Handbook of vocational psychology* (2nd ed., pp. 217–259). Mahwah, NJ: Erlbaum.

Szymanski, E. M., & Parker, R. M. (Eds.). (1996). *Work and disability: Issues and strategies in career development and job placement.* Austin, TX: Pro-Ed.

Teideman, D. V., & O'Hara, R. P. (1963). *Career development: Choice and adjustment.* Princeton, NJ: College Entrance Examination Board.

Walsh, W. B., Bingham, R. P., Brown, M. T., & Ward, C. M. (Eds.). (2001). *Career counseling for African Americans* (pp. 27–48). Mahwah, NJ: Erlbaum.

Walsh, W. B., & Osipow, S. H. (1994). *Career counseling for women.* Hillsdale, NJ: Lawrence Erlbaum Associates, Inc.

Ward, C. M., & Bingham, R. P. (2001). Career assessment for African Americans. In W. B. Walsh, R. P. Bingham, M. T. Brown, & C. M. Ward (Eds.), *Career counseling for African Americans* (pp. 27–48). Mahwah, NJ: Erlbaum.

Wehman, P. (2001). Pursuing postsecondary education opportunities for individuals with disabilities. Baltimore, MD: Paul Brookes Publishing.

Worell, J., & Remer, P. (2003). *Feminist perspectives in therapy: Empowering diverse women* (2nd ed.). New York: John Wiley & Sons.

Yang, J. (1991). Career counseling of Chinese American women: Are they in limbo? *Career Development Quarterly, 39*(4), 350–359.

Zunker, V. G. (2001). *Career counseling: Applied concepts of life planning* (6th ed.). Monterey, CA: Brooks/Cole.

Zunker, V. G., & Osborn, D. S. (2001). *Using assessment results for career development* (6th ed.). Pacific Grove, CA: Brooks/Cole.

Zytowski, D. G. (1985). *Kuder DD Occupational Interest Survey manual supplement.* Chicago: Science Research Associates.

Zytowski, D. G. (1994). A super contribution to vocational theory: Work values. *Career Development Quarterly, 43*(1), 25–31.

Chapter 10

American Association for Marriage and Family Therapy. (1985). *Code of ethical principles for marriage and family therapists.* Washington, DC.

American Counseling Association. (1995). *The Code of Ethics and Standards of Practice.* Alexandria, VA.

American Psychological Association. (1992). *Ethical principles of psychologists* (Rev. ed.). Washington, DC.

Aponte, Harry J. (1996). Political bias, moral values, and spirituality in the training of psychotherapists. *Bulletin of the Menninger Clinic 60*(4), 488–502.

Bergin, A. E. (1991). Values and religious issues in psychotherapy and mental health. *American Psychologist, 4,* 394–403.

Bergin, A. E., & Garfield, S. L. (Eds.). (1994). *Handbook of psychotherapy and behavior change* (4th ed.). New York: Wiley.

Bergin, A. E., & Jensen, J. P. (1990). Religiosity of psychotherapists: A national survey. *Psychotherapy, 27,* 2–7.

Borysenko, J. (1987). *Minding the body, mending the mind.* New York: Bantam Book.

Borysenko, J. (1990). *Guilt is the teacher, love is the lesson.* New York: Warner Books.

Burke, M. T., & Miranti, J. G. (Eds.). (1992). *Ethical and spiritual values in counseling.* Alexandria, VA: American Counseling Association.

Burke, M. T., & Miranti, J. G. (Eds.). (1995). *Counseling: The spiritual dimension.* Alexandria, VA: American Counseling Association.

Burke, M. T., Hackney, H., Hudson, P., Miranti, J., Watts, G., & Epp, L. (1999). Spirituality, religion, and CACREP curriculum standards. *Journal of Counseling and Development, 77,* 251–257.

Burke, M. T., & Miranti, J. G. (1998). Spirituality as a force for social change. In C. C. Lee & G. R. Walz (Eds.), *Social action: A mandate for counselors.* Alexandria, VA: American Counseling Association.

Campbell, D. (1992). *Campbell Interest and Skill Survey.* Minneapolis, MN: NCS Assessments.

Carlson, T. D., Kirkpatrick, D., Hecker, L., & Killmer, M. (2002). Religion, spirituality, and marriage and family therapy: A study of family therapists' beliefs about the appropriateness of addressing religious and spiritual issues in therapy. *The American Journal of Family Therapy, 30,* 157–171.

Chandler, C. K., Holden, J. M., & Kolander, C. A. (1992). Counseling and spiritual wellness. *Journal of Counseling and Development, 71,* 168–176.

Clinebell, H. (1992). *Well being: A personal plan for exploring and enriching the seven dimensions of life.* San Francisco: HarperCollins.

Clinebell, H. (1995). *Counseling for spiritually empowered wholeness: A hope centered approach.* New York: The Hearth Pastoral Press.

Curtis, R. C., & Davis, K. M. (1999). Spirituality and multimodal therapy: A practical approach to incorporating spirituality in counseling. *Counseling and Values, 43,* 199–210.

Ellison, C. W. (1994). *Spiritual well-being scale.* Nyack, NY: Life Advance.

Faiver, C. M., & O'Brien, E. M. (1993). Assessment of religious beliefs form. *Counseling and Values, 37,* 176–178.

Fowler, J. (1981). *Stages of faith: The psychology of human development and the quest for meaning.* San Francisco: Harper & Row.

Frame, M. W. (2000). The spiritual genogram in family therapy. *Journal of Marital and Family Therapy, 26,* 211–216.

Frame, M. W. (2003). *Integrating religion and spirituality into counseling.* Pacific Grove, CA: Brooks/Cole-Thompson Learning.

Frame, M. W., & Williams, C. B. (1996). Counseling African Americans: Integrating spirituality in therapy. *Counseling and Values, 41,* 16–28.

Fukuyama, M. A., & Sevig, T. D. (1997). Spiritual issues in counseling: A new course. *Counselor Education and Supervision, 38,* 233–242.

Genia, V. (1995). *Counseling and psychotherapy of religious clients: A developmental approach.* Westport, CT: Praeger.

Grimm, D. W. (1994). Therapist spiritual and religious values in psychotherapy. *Counseling and Values 38,* 154–163.

Helmeniak, D. (1987). *Spiritual development.* Chicago, IL: Loyola University Press.

Hermon, D. A., & Hazler, R. J. (1999). Adherence to a wellness model and perceptions of psychological well-being. *Journal of Counseling and Development, 77,* 339–343.

Hickson, J., Housley, W., & Wages, D. (2000). Counselors' perceptions of spirituality in the therapeutic process. *Counseling and Values, 45,* 58–67.

Hinterkopf, E. (1994). Integrating spiritual experiences in counseling. *Counseling and Values, 38,* 165–175.

Hinterkopf, E. (1998). *Integrating spirituality in counseling.* Alexandria, VA: American Counseling Association.

Ingersoll, R. E. (1994). Spirituality, religion, and counseling: Dimensions and relationships. *Counseling and Values, 38,* 98–111.

Ingersoll, R. E. (1995). Construction and validation of the spiritual wellness inventory. Unpublished doctoral dissertation, Kent State University.

Ingersoll, R. E. (1998). Refining dimensions of spiritual wellness: A cross-traditional approach. *Counseling and Values, 42,* 156–165.

Jensen, J. P. & Bergin, A. E. (1988). Mental health values of professional therapists: A national interdisciplinary study. *Professional Psychology: Research and Practice, 19,* 290–297.

Kelly, E. W., Jr. (1995). *Spirituality and religion in counseling and psychotherapy: Diversity in theory and practice.* Alexandria, VA: American Counseling Association.

Lee, C. C., & Sirch, M. L. (1994). Counseling in an enlightened society: Values for a new millennium. *Counseling and Values 8,* 90–97.

Levinson, D. (1978). *The seasons of a man's life.* New York: Knopf.

Malony, H. N. (1993). The use of religious assessment in counseling. In L. B. Brown (Ed.), *Religion, personality, and mental health* (pp. 16–28). New York: Plenum.

Mattson, D. (1994). Religious counseling: To be used, not feared. *Counseling and Values, 38,* 187–191.

McAuliff, G. J., & Eriksen, K. P. (1999). Toward a constructivist and developmental identity for the counseling profession: The context-phase-stage style mode. *Journal of Counseling and Development, 77,* 267–280.

Moore, T. (1992). *Care of the soul.* New York: Harper Perennial.

Myers, J. E., & Truluck, M. (1998). Health beliefs, religious values, and the counseling process: A comparison of counselors and other mental health professionals. *Counseling and Values, 42,* 106–123.

Pate, R. H., & Bondi, A. M. (1992). Religious belief and practice: An integral aspect of multicultural awareness. *Counselor Education and Supervision, 32,* 108–115.

Pate, R. H., & High, H. J. (1995). The importance of client religious beliefs and practices in the education of counselors in CACREP-accredited programs. *Counseling and Values, 40,* 2–5.

Peck, S. (1987). *The different drum*. New York: Simon and Schuster.

Prest, L. A., & Keller, J. F. (1993). Spirituality and family therapy: Spiritual beliefs, myths, and metaphors. *Journal of Marital and Family Therapy, 19*, 137–148.

Richards, P. S., & Bergin, A. E. (1997). *A spiritual strategy for counseling and psychotherapy*. Washington, DC: American Psychological Press.

Seaward, B. L. (1995). Reflections on human spirituality for the worksite. *American Journal of Health Promotion, 9*, 165–168.

Shafranske, E. P., & Malony, H. N. (1996). *Religion and the clinical practice of psychology: A case for inclusion*. Washington, DC: American Psychological Association.

Siegel, B. S. (1990). *Peace, love, and healing*. New York: Harper and Row.

Smith, D. C. (1993). Exploring the religious/spiritual needs of the dying. *Counseling and Values, 41*, 16–28.

Souza, K. Z. (2002). Spirituality in counseling: What do counseling students think about it. *Counseling and Values, 46*, 213–215.

Stander V., Piercy, F. P., Mackinnon, D., & Helmeke, K. (1994). Spirituality, religion, and family therapy: Competing or complementary worlds? *American Journal of Family Therapy, 22*, 27–41.

Steere, D. A. (1997). *Spiritual presence in psychotherapy*. New York: Brunner/Mazel, Inc.

Summit on Spirituality. (1995). Spiritual competencies for counselors. *Counseling Today*. Alexandria, VA: American Counseling Association, p. 30.

Walsh, F. (1999). Opening family therapy to spirituality. In F. Walsh (Ed.), *Spiritual resources in family therapy*. New York: Guilford Press.

Weil, A. (1995). *Spontaneous healing*. New York: Knopf.

Wilber, K. (2000). *Integral psychology: Consciousness, spirit, psychology, therapy*. Boston: Shambhala.

Witmer, J. M., & Sweeney, T. J. (1992). A holistic model for wellness and prevention over the lifespan. *Journal of Counseling and Development, 71*, 140–148.

Witmer, J. M., Sweeney, T. J., & Myers, J. E. (1993). *Wellness Evaluation of Lifestyle: The WEL Inventory*. Palo Alto, CA: Mind Garden.

Wolf, C., & Stevens, P. (2001). Integrating religion and spirituality in marriage and family counseling. *Counseling and Values, 46*, 66–75.

Worthington, E. L., Jr. (1989). Religious faith across the life span: Implications for counseling and research. *The Counseling Psychologist, 17*, 555–612.

Chapter 11

Allan, J. (1982). Social drawing: A therapeutic approach with young children. In E. T. Nickerson & K. O'Laughlin (Eds.). *Helping through action: Action-oriented therapies* (pp. 25–32). Amherst, MA: Human Resource Development Press.

Amerikaner, M., Schauble, P, & Ziller, R. (1982). Images: The use of photographs in personal counseling. In E. T. Nickerson & K. O'Laughlin (Eds.), *Helping through action: Action–oriented therapies* (pp. 33–41). Amherst, MA: Human Resource Development Press.

Bates, M. (1993). Poetic responses to art: Summoning the adolescent voice. *Journal of Poetry Therapy, 3*, 149–156.

Bauer, M. S., & Balius, F. A. (1995). Storytelling: Integrating therapy and curriculum for students with serious emotional disturbances. *Teaching Exceptional Children, 27*, 24–29.

Borders, S., & Paisley, P. O. (1992). Children's literature as a source for classroom guidance. *Elementary School Guidance and Counseling, 27*, 131–139.

Bourne, E. J. (1995). *The anxiety and phobia workbook*. Oakland, CA: New Harbinger Publications.

Bowman, R. P. (1987). Approaches for counseling children through music. *Elementary School Guidance and Counseling, 21*, 284–291.

Bradley, L. J., & Gould, L. J. (1999). Individual counseling: Creative interventions. In A. Vernon (Ed.), *Counseling children and adolescents* (2nd ed., pp. 66–95). Denver: Love Publishing.

Bradley, L. J., Gould, L. J., & Hendricks, P. B. (2004). Using innovative techniques for counseling children and adolescents. In A. Vernon (Ed.), *Counseling children and adolescents* (3rd ed., pp. 75–110). Denver, CO: Love Publishing.

Brems, C. (2002). *A comprehensive guide to child psychotherapy* (2nd ed.). Boston, MA: Allyn & Bacon.

Brown, M. H. (1991). Innovations in the treatment of bulimia: Transpersonal psychology, relaxation, imagination, hypnosis, myth, and ritual. *Journal of Humanistic Education and Development, 30*, 50–60.

Bush, J. (1997). *The handbook of school art therapy*. Springfield, IL: Charles C. Thomas Publisher, Ltd.

Caple, R. (1985). Counseling and the self-organization paradigm. *Journal of Counseling and Development, 64,* 173–178.

Clarkson, G. (1994). Creative music therapy and facilitated communication: New ways of reaching students with autism. *Preventing School Failure, 38,* 31–33.

Conley, D. (1994). *If you believe in you.* Coco Records: Treehouse Publishing.

Davis, W. B., Gfeller, K. E., & Thaut, M. H. (1999). An introduction to music therapy. *Theory and practice* (2nd ed.). Boston: McGraw-Hill.

Doll, B., & Doll, C. (1997). *Bibliotherapy with young people.* Englewood, CA: Libraries Unlimited.

Dufrene, P. (1994). Art therapy and the sexually abused child. *Art Education, 47,* 6–11.

Dunn, R., & Griggs, S. A. (1995). *Multiculturalism and learning style.* Westport, CT: Praeger.

Gladding, S. T. (1987). The poetics of a "check out" place: Preventing burnout and promoting self-renewal. *Journal of Poetry Therapy, 1,* 95–102.

Gladding, S. T. (1992). *Counseling as an art: The creative arts in counseling.* Alexandria, VA: American Counseling Association.

Gladding, S. T. (1995). Creativity in counseling. *Counseling and Human Development, 28,* 1, 1–12.

Gladding, S. T. (1998). *Counseling as an art: The creative arts in counseling.* Alexandria, VA: American Counseling Association.

Griggs, S. A. (1983). Counseling high school students for their individual learning styles. *Clearing House, 56,* 293–296.

Griggs, S. A. (1985). Counseling for individual learning styles. *Journal of Counseling and Development, 64,* 202–205.

Griggs, S. A., Price, G. E., Kopel, S., & Swaine, W. (1984). The effects of group counseling on sixth-grade students with different learning styles. *California Journal of Counseling and Development, 5,* 28–35.

Guzzetta, C. E. (1991). A method for conducting improvised musical play with children both with and without developmental delays in preschool classrooms. *Music Therapy Perspectives, 9,* 46–51.

Havens, R. A., & Walters, C. (2002). *Hypnotherapy scripts* (2nd ed.). New York: Brunner-Routledge.

Hendricks, P. B. (2000). A study of the use of music therapy techniques in a group for the treatment of adolescent depression. *Dissertation Abstracts International, 62,* 107.

Heppner, M. J., O'Brien, K. M., Hindelman, J. M., & Humphrey, C. A. (1994). Shifting the paradigm: The use of creativity in career counseling. *Journal of Career Development, 21,* 77–86.

Horden, P. (2000). *Music as medicine: The history of music therapy since antiquity.* Aldershot: Ashgate.

Hutchins, D. E., & Cole, C. G. (1992). *Helping relationships and strategies.* Pacific Grove, CA: Brooks/Cole.

Hynes, A. (1990). Poetry: An avenue into the spirit. *Journal of Poetry Therapy, 4,* 71–81.

Jackson, T. (2000). *Still more activities that teach.* Salt Lake City: Red Rock Publishing.

Jacobs, E. (1992). *Creative counseling techniques: An illustrated guide.* Odess, FL: Psychological Assessment Resources.

Jennings, S., & Minde, A. (1993*). Art therapy and dramatherapy: Masks of the soul.* Philadelphia, PA: Jessica Kingsley Publishers.

Kenny, A. (1987). An art activities approach: Counseling the gifted, creative and talented. *Gifted Child Today, 10,* 33–37.

Kohen, D. P. (1997). Teaching children with asthma to help themselves with relaxation/mental imagery. In W. J. Matthews & J. H. Edgette (Eds.), *Current thinking and research in brief therapy: Solutions, strategies, narratives* (Vol. 1) (pp. 169–191). New York: Brunner/Mazel.

Kottler, J. A. (2004). *Introduction to therapeutic counseling: Voices from the field.* Pacific Grove, CA: Brooks/Cole.

Kottman, T. (2001). *Play therapy: Basics and beyond.* Alexandria, VA: American Counseling Association.

Kottman, T. (2003). *Partners in play: An adlerian approach to play therapy.* Alexandria, VA: American Counseling Association.

Kottman, T. (2004). Play therapy. In A. Vernon (Ed.). *Counseling children and adolescents* (3rd ed.). (pp. 111–136). Denver, CO: Love Publishing.

Kramer, E. (1998). *Childhood and art therapy* (2nd ed.). Chicago: Magnolia Street.

Kwiatowska, H. (2001). Family art therapy: Experiments with new techniques. *American Journal of Art Therapy, 40,* 27–39.

LaBaw, J. L., & LaBaw, W. L. (1990). Self-hypnosis and hypnotherapy with children. In R. P. Zahourek (Ed.), *Clinical hypnosis and therapeutic suggestion in patient care* (pp. 127–153). New York: Brunnel/Mazel.

Landreth, G. L. (1993). Child-centered play therapy. *Elementary School Guidance and Counseling Journal, 28,* 17–29.

Landgarten, H. B., & Lubbers, D. (1991). *Adult art psychotherapy: Issues and applications.* New York: Brunner/Mazel.

LeBlanc, M., & Richie, M. (1999). Predictors of play therapy outcomes. *International Journal of Play Therapy, 8* (2), 19–34.

Lev-Weisel, R., & Daphna-Tekoha, S. (2000). The self-revelation through color technique: Understanding client's relationships with significant others through the use of color. *American Journal of Art Therapy, 39,* 35–41.

Maas, J. (1982). Introduction to music therapy. In E. T. Nickerson & K. O'Laughlin (Eds.), *Helping through action: Action-oriented therapies* (pp. 87–100). Amberst, MA: Human Resource Development Press.

Malchiodi, C. A. (1997). *Breaking the silence: Art therapy with children from violent homes* (2nd ed.). Bristol, PA: Brunner/Mazel.

Maranto, C. D. (1993). Music therapy and stress management. In P. M. Lehrer & R. L. Woolfolk (Eds.). *Principles and practice of stress management* (2nd ed., pp. 407–422). New York: Guilford Press.

Mercer, L. E. (1993). Self-healing through poetry writing. *Journal of Poetry Therapy, 6,* 161–168.

Milgram, R. M., Dunn, R., & Price, G. E. (1993). *Teaching and counseling gifted and talented adolescents: An international learning style perspective.* Westport, CT: Praeger Publishers.

Miller, M. E. (1991, July 16). A dose of sound to ease cancer's pain. *News & Observer* (Raleigh, NC), pp. 1E, 6E.

Myrick, R. D. (1997). *Developmental guidance and counseling: A practical approach.* Minneapolis, MN: Educational Media.

Myrick, R. D., & Myrick, L. S. (1993). Guided imagery: From mystical to practical. *Elementary School Guidance and Counseling, 28,* 62–70.

Newcomb, N. S. (1994). Music: A powerful resource for the elementary school counselor. *Elementary School Guidance and Counseling, 29,* 150–155.

Nickerson, E. T., & O'Laughlin, K. (Eds.). (1982). *Helping through action: Action-oriented therapies.* Amherst, MA: Human Resource Development Press.

Nugent, S. A. (2000). Perfectionism: Its manifestations and classroom based interventions. *Journal of Secondary Gifted Education, 11,* 215–221.

Oaklander, V. (1988). *Windows to our children.* Moab, UT: Real People Press.

O'Connor, K. (2000). *The play therapy primer* (2nd ed.). New York: Wiley.

O'Connor, K., & Schaefer, C. (1994). *The handbook of play therapy, Volume II: Advances and innovations.* New York: Wiley.

Olness, K., & Kohen, D. (1996). *Hypnosis and hypnotherapy with children.* New York: Guilford Press.

Omizo, M. M., Omizo, S. A., & Kitaoka, S. K. (1998). Guided affective and cognitive imagery to enhance self-esteem among Hawaiian children. *Journal of Multicultural Counseling and Development, 26,* 52–62.

Orton, G. L. (1997). *Strategies for counseling with children and their parents.* Pacific Grove, CA: Brooks/Cole.

Pardeck, J. T. (1994). Using literature to help adolescents cope with problems. *Adolescence, 29,* 421–427.

Pardeck, J. T. (1998). *Using books in clinical social work practice: A guide to bibliotherapy.* New York: The Haworth Press.

Pardeck, J. T., & Pardeck, J. A. (1993). *Bibliotherapy: A clinical approach for helping children.* New York: Gordon and Breach.

Peters, J. S. (2000). *Music therapy: An introduction* (2nd ed.). Springfield, IL: Charles C. Thomas.

Plummer, D. (1999). *Using interactive imagework with children: Walking on the magic mountain.* Philadelphia: J. Kingsley.

Rubin, J. A. (1988). Art counseling: An alternative. *Elementary School Guidance and Counseling, 22,* 180–185.

Rubin, J. A. (1998). *Art therapy: An introduction.* Philadelphia: Taylor & Francis.

Sapp, M. (2000). *Hypnosis, dissociation, and absorption: Theories, assessment, and treatment.* Springfield, IL: Charles C. Thomas.

Schaefer, C. E. & Reid, S. E. (2000). *Game play: Therapeutic use of childhood games.* New York: Wiley.

Silver, R. (2001). *Art as language.* Lillington, NC: Edwards Brothers.

Silverman, D. (1991). Art psychotherapy: An approach to borderline adults. In H. B. Langarten & D. Lubbers (Ed.), *Adult art psychotherapy.* New York: Brunner/Mazel.

Skovholt, T. M., Morgan, J. I., & Negron-Cunningham, H. (1989). Mental imagery in career counseling and life planning: A review of research and intervention methods. *Journal of Counseling and Development, 67,* 287–292.

Sloan, G. (2003). *Give them poetry!* New York: Teachers College Press.

Thaut, M. H. (1990). Neuropsychological processes in music relevance in music therapy. In R. F. Unkefer (Ed.), *Music therapy in treatment of adults with mental disorders: Theoretical bases and clinical interventions* (pp. 3–32). New York: Macmillan.

Thomas, M. (recording artist). (1979). *Free to be . . . You and me* (record album). Carthage, IL: Good Apple.

Thompson, C., Rudolph, L., & Henderson, D. (2004). *Counseling children.* Belmont, CA: Brooks/Cole.

Vernon, A. (1993). *Developmental assessment and intervention with children and adolescents.* Alexandria, VA: American Counseling Association.

Vernon, A. (1998). *The passport program: A journey through emotional, social, cognitive, and self-development* (grades 1–5). Champaign, IL: Research Press.

Vernon, A. (2002). *What works when with children and adolescents: A handbook of individual counseling techniques.* Champaign, IL: Research Press.

Vondracek, F. W., & Corneal, S. (1995). *Strategies for resolving individual and family problems.* Pacific Grove, CA: Brooks/Cole.

Wagner, W. G. (2003). *Counseling, psychology, and children.* Upper Saddle River, NJ: Merrill-Prentice Hall.

Wayman, J. (composer). (1974). *Imagination and me.* Carthage, IL: Good Apple.

Weitzenhoffer, A. M. (1989). *The practice of hypnotism, Vol. 2: Applications of traditional and semi-traditional hypnotism—Nontraditional hypnotism.* New York: Wiley.

White, V. E., & Murray, M. A. (2002). Passing notes: The use of therapeutic letter writing in counseling adolescents. *Journal of Mental Health Counseling, 24*(2), 166.

Wigram, T., Pedersen, I. N. & Bonde, L. O. (2002). *A comprehensive guide to music therapy: Theory, clinical practice, research and training.* London: Jessica Kingsley.

Winsor, R. M. (1993). Hypnosis—A neglected tool for client empowerment. *Social Work, 38,* 603–608.

Witmer, J. M., & Young, M. E. (1987). Imagery in counseling. *Elementary School Guidance and Counseling, 22,* 5–15.

Woytowich, J. M. (1994). The power of the poem in the counseling office. *School Counselor, 42,* 78–80.

Chapter 12

Aiken, L. R. (2002). *Psychological testing and assessment* (11th ed.). Boston: Allyn & Bacon.

American Educational Research Association, American Psychological Association, & National Council on Measurement in Education. (2000). *Standards for educational and psychological testing.* Washington: American Educational Research Association.

Anastasi, A., & Urbina, S. (1997). *Psychological testing* (7th ed.). New York: Macmillan.

Association for Assessment in Counseling and Education. (1989). *Responsibilities of users of standardized tests* (3rd ed.). Retrieved July 8, 2003 from *http://aac.ncat.edu/resources.html.*

Dana, R. H. (1993). *Multicultural assessment perspectives for professional psychology.* Boston: Allyn & Bacon.

Drummond, R. J. (1999). *Appraisal procedures for counselors and helping professionals* (4th ed.). New York: Macmillan.

Goldman, L. (1971). *Using tests in counseling* (2nd ed.). New York: Appleton-Century-Crofts.

Goodyear, R. K., & Lichtenburg, J. W. (1999). *Scientist-practitioner perspectives on test interpretation.* Boston: Allyn & Bacon.

Gregory, R. J. (2000). *Psychological testing History, principles, and applications* (3rd ed.). Boston: Allyn & Bacon.

Groth-Marnat, G. (2003). *Handbook of psychological assessment* (4th ed.). New York: Wiley.

Hambleton, R. K. (1998). Principles and selected applications of item response theory. In R. L. Linn (Ed.). *Educational measurement* (3rd ed. reprint) (pp. 147–200). New York: American Council on Education & Oryx Press.

Hood, A. B., & Johnson, R. W. (2002). *Assessment in counseling: A guide to the use of psychological assessment procedures* (3rd ed.). Alexandria, VA: American Counseling Association.

Lee, C. C. (2001). Assessing diverse populations. In G. R. Walz & J. C. Bleuer (Eds.). *Assessment issues and challenges for the new millennium* (pp. 115–124). Greensboro, NC: ERIC/CAPS.

Loesch, L. C. (2001). Counseling program evaluation Inside and outside the box. In D. C. Locke, J. E. Myers, & E. L. Herr (Eds.). *The handbook of counseling* (pp. 513–525). Thousand Oaks, CA: Sage.

McKinley, R. L. (1989). An introduction to item response theory. *Measurement and Evaluation in Counseling and Development, 22*, 37–57.

Messick, S. (1998). Validity. In R. L. Linn (Ed.). *Educational measurement* (3rd ed. reprint, pp. 13–104). New York, NY: American Council on Education & Oryx Press.

Vacc, N. A., & Loesch, L. C. (2000). *The profession of counseling* (3rd ed.). Philadelphia: Taylor & Francis.

Whiston, S. C. (2000). *Principles and applications of assessment in counseling*. Belmont, CA: Wadsworth.

Chapter 13

American Counseling Association. (1995, June). Code of ethics and standards of practice. *Counseling Today*, 33–40.

American Psychiatric Association. (1980). *Diagnostic and statistical manual of mental disorders* (3rd ed.). Washington DC: Author.

American Psychiatric Association. (1987). *Diagnostic and statistical manual of mental disorders* (3rd ed.). Washington DC: Author.

American Psychiatric Association. (1994). *Diagnostic and statistical manual of mental disorders* (4th ed.). Washington DC: Author.

American Psychiatric Association. (2000). *Diagnostic and statistical manual of mental disorders—text revision*. Washington DC: Author.

Erk, R. R. (2004). *Counseling treatment for children and adolescents with DSM-IV-TR disorders*. Upper Saddle River, NJ: Pearson Education.

Fauman, M. A. (2002). *Study guide to DSM-IV-TR*. Washington DC: American Psychiatric Association.

Hershenson, D. B., Power, P. W., & Seligman, L. (1989). Mental health counseling theory: Present status and future prospects. *Journal of Mental Health Counseling, 11*(1), 44–69.

Hinkle, J. S. (1994). The *DSM-IV*: Prognosis and implications for mental health counselors. *Journal of Mental Health Counseling, 16*(2), 174–183.

Hohenshil, T. H. (1993). Teaching the *DSM-III-R* in counselor education. *Counselor Education and Supervision, 32*(4) 267–275.

Maxmen, J. S., & Ward, N. G. (1995). *Essential psychopathology and its treatment*. New York: W. W. Norton.

Mead, M. A., Hohenshil, T. H., & Singh, K. (1997). How the DSM system is used by clinical counselors: A national study. *Journal of Mental Health Counseling, 19*, 383–401.

Messer, S. B. (2001). Empirically supported treatments. In B. D. Slife, R. N. Williams, & S. H. Barlow (Eds.), *Critical issues in psychotherapy*, 3–19. Thousand Oaks, CA: Sage.

Millon, T. (1996). *Disorders of personality*. New York: John Wiley.

Morrison, J. (1995). *DSM-IV made easy*. New York: Guilford Press.

Morrison, M. R., & Stamps, R. F. (1998). *DSM-IV Internet companion*. New York: W. W. Norton and Co.

Pachis, B., Rettman, S., & Gotthoffer, D. (2001). *Counseling on the net*. Boston: Allyn & Bacon.

Paniagua, F. A. (2001). *Diagnosis in a multicultural context*. Thousand Oaks, CA: Sage.

Seligman, L. (1995). *DSM-IV: Diagnosis and treatment planning home study*. Alexandria, VA: American Counseling Association.

Seligman, L. (1996). Diagnosis and treatment planning in counseling (2nd ed.). New York: Plenum.

Seligman, L. (1998). *Selecting effective treatments* (rev. ed.). San Francisco: Jossey-Bass.

Seligman, L. (1999a). The *DSM-IV*—an essential tool in the hands of skilled clinicians. *Counseling Today*, November 1999, pp. 6, 37.

Seligman, L. (1999b). Twenty years of diagnosis and the DSM. *Journal of Mental Health Counseling, 21*, 229–239.

Seligman, L. (in press). Diagnosis and treatment planning in counseling (3rd ed.). New York: Kluwer.

Spitzer, R. L., Gibbon, M., Skodol, A. E., Williams, J. B. W., & First, M. B. (1994). *DSM-IV casebook*. Washington DC: American Psychiatric Association.

World Health Organization. (1992). *ICD-10 classification of mental and behavioural disorders*. Geneva: Author.

Chapter 14

American School Counseling Association, (1993). The school counselor and comprehensive counseling [Position Statement]. Alexandria, VA: author.

Dahir, C. (2001). The national standards for school counseling programs: Development and Implementation. *Professional School Counseling, 4*, 320–333.

Dryfoos, J., (1990). *Adolescents at risk: Prevalence and prevention*. New York: Oxford University Press.

Farrell, P. (1997). *A guide to state laws and regulations on professional school counseling*. Office of Public

Policy & Information, American Counseling Association, Alexandria, VA.

Gysbers, N., & Henderson, P. (2000). *Developing and managing your school guidance program* (3rd ed.). Alexandria, VA: American Counseling Association.

Gysbers, N., & Henderson, P. (2001). Comprehensive guidance and counseling programs: A rich history and a bright future. *Professional School Counseling, 4,* 246–256.

Keys, S., Bemak, F., Carpenter, S., & King-Sears, M. (1998). Collaborative consultant: A new role for counselors serving at-risk youth. *Journal of Counseling & Development, 76,* 123–133.

Lerner, R. (1995). *America's youth in crisis: Challenges and opportunities for programs and policies.* Thousand Oaks, CA: Sage.

Lockhart, E., & Keys, S. (1998). The mental health counseling role of the school counselor. *Professional School Counseling, 1,* 3–6.

Paisley, P., & Borders, L. D. (1995). School counseling: An evolving specialty. *Journal of Counseling & Development, 74,* 150–153.

Paisley, P., & Hubbard, G. (1989). School counseling: State officials perceptions of certification and employment trends. *Counselor Education and Supervision, 29,* 60–71.

Parsons, R. (1996). *The skilled consultant: A systematic approach to the theory and practice of consultation.* Boston: Allyn & Bacon.

Schmidt, J. (1999). Counseling in schools: Essential services and comprehensive programs (3rd ed.). Boston: Allyn & Bacon.

U.S. Department of Education. (2001). *No Child Left Behind Act of 2001* (H.R.1). Washington, DC: U.S. Department of Education.

Wittmer, J. (1993). *Managing your school counseling program: K-12 developmental strategies.* Minneapolis, MN: Educational Media Corporation.

Wrenn, G. (1962). *The Counselor in a Changing World.* Washington, DC: American Personnel and Guidance Association.

Chapter 15

American Counseling Association. (1997a). *ACA code of ethics and standards of practice.* Alexandria, VA: Author.

American Counseling Association. (1997b, October). *Governing council minutes.* Alexandria, VA: Author.

American Counseling Association. (1999, March). *The effectiveness of professional counseling services* (Office of Public Policy and Information). Alexandria, VA: Author.

American Mental Health Counselor (AMACA). (1978). Paper. Alexandria, VA: Author.

Brooks, D. K., Jr. (1997). Counseling in mental health and private practice settings. In D. Capuzzi & D. R. Gross (Eds.), *Introduction to counseling* (2nd. ed., pp. 309–327). Needham Heights, MA: Allyn & Bacon.

Brooks, D. K., Jr., & Weikel, W. J. (1986). History and development of the mental counseling movement. In A. J. Palmo & W. J. Weikel (Eds.), *Foundations of mental health counseling* (pp. 5–28). Springfield, IL: C. J. Thomas.

Corey, G., Corey, M. S., & Callanan, P. (1998). *Issues and ethics in the helping professions* (5th ed.). Pacific Grove, CA: Brooks/Cole.

Cormier, L. S., & Hackney, H. (1992). *The professional counselor: A process guide to counseling.* Boston: Allyn & Bacon.

Department of Health and Human Services (DHHS). (2003) Administration on Aging. *A profile of older Americans: 2003.* Retrieved April 22, 2004 from *http://research.aarp.org/general/profiles.html.*

Department of Health and Human Services (DHHS). (1995). *Cost of addictive and mental disorders and effectiveness of treatment.* (SAMSHA publication). Rockville, MD: Author.

Folsom, R., Gfroerer. J., Pemberton, M., & Penne, M. (2003). Substance abuse treatment among older adults in 2020: The impact of the aging baby-boomer cohort. *Journal of Drug and Alcohol Dependence, 61*(2), March 2003, 127–135.

Gladding, S. T. (2000). *Counseling: A comprehensive profession* (4th ed.).Upper Saddle River, NJ: Prentice Hall.

Hoagwood, K. (1999, March 15). *Major research findings on child and adolescent mental health* (Summary sheet). National Institute on Mental Health. Alexandria: VA.

Hollis, J. W. (1997). *Counselor preparation, 1996–1997.* Muncie, IN: Accelerated Development.

Institute of Medicine (1997). *Schools and health.* Washington, DC: National Academy Press: Author.

Lebowitz, B. D. (1999). *Depression in later life: Progress and opportunity.* (paper) National Alliance for the Mentally Ill. Alexandria: VA.

Levine, A. (1980). *When dreams and heroes died: A portrait of today's college student.* San Francisco: Jossey-Bass.

Male, R. A. (1990). Careers in public and private agencies. In B. B. Collison & N. J. Garfield

(Eds.), *Careers in counseling and human development* (pp. 81–89). Alexandria, VA: American Counseling Association.

Mrazek, J. (1998, September). *Preventing mental health and substance abuse problems in managed health care settings* (paper). National Mental Health Association. Alexandria, VA.

Myers, J. E., & Schwiebert, V. L. (1996). *Competencies for gerontological counseling.* Alexandria, VA: American Counseling Association.

Newman, B. M., & Newman, P. R. (1999). *Development through life: A psychosocial approach* (7th ed.). Belmont, CA: Brooks/Cole.

Nugent, F. A. (2000). *Introduction to the professions of counseling* (3rd ed.). Upper Saddle River, NJ: Prentice Hall.

Oregon Counseling Association. (1994). What is counseling? [Brochure]. Salem, OR: Author.

President's new freedom commission on mental health. Retrieved November 5, 2003, from *http://www.samsha.gov/news/cl_mhfinalreport.html*

Seligman. L. (1997). *Diagnosis and treatment planning in counseling* (2nd ed.). New York: Plenum Press.

Vaac, N. A., & Loesch, L. C. (1987). *Counseling as a profession.* Muncie, IN: Accelerated Development, Inc. In M. L. Fong (Ed.). Mental health counseling: The essence of professional counseling. *Counselor Education and Supervision, 30*, 106–113.

Chapter 16

Altekruse, M. K., & Ray, D. (1998). Counseling older adults: A special issue. *Educational Gerontology, 24*, 303–307.

Administration on Aging (AOA). (2001). *A profile of older Americans 2001.* U.S. Department of Health and Human Services, Washington DC: Author.

Baltes, M. M. (1996). *The many faces of dependency in old age.* New York: Cambridge University Press.

Birren, J. E., & Schaie, K. W. (1996). *Handbook of the psychology of aging* (4th ed.). San Diego: Academic Press.

Brody, C. M., & Semel, V. G. (1993). *Strategies for therapy with the elderly.* New York: Springer.

Brink, T. L. (1979). *Geriatric psychotherapy.* New York: Human Sciences.

Burlingame, V. S. (1995). *Gerocounseling: Counseling elders and their families.* New York: Springer.

Butler, R. N., Lewis, M., & Sunderland, T. (1991). *Aging and mental health: Positive psychosocial and biomedical approaches* (4th ed.). New York: Macmillan.

Capuzzi, D., & Gross, D. R. (Eds.). (2002). *Introduction to group counseling* (3rd ed.). Denver: Love Publishing.

Durodoye, B. A., & Ennis-Cole, D. (1998). Empowering counselors to work with senior adult clients in the computer age. *Educational Gerontology, 24*, 359–371.

Falk, U. A., & Falk, G. (1997). *Ageism, The aged and aging in America.* Springfield, IL: Charles C. Thomas.

Gee, S., & Baillie, J. (1999). Happily ever after? An exploration of retirement expectations. *Educational Gerontology, 25*, 109–128.

Gintner, G. G. (1995). Differential diagnosis in older adults: Dementia, depression, and delirium. *Journal of Counseling and Development, 73*(3), 346–351.

Gladding, S. T. (2003). *Counseling: A comprehensive profession* (4th ed.). Englewood Cliffs, NJ: Merrill/Prentice Hall.

Glover, R. J. (1998). Perspectives on aging: Issues affecting the latter part of the life cycle. *Educational Gerontology, 24*, 325–332.

Gross, D. R. (1991). Counseling the elderly. In J. Carlson & J. Lewis (Eds.). *Family counseling: Strategies and issues* (pp. 209–223). Denver: Love Publishing.

Gross, D. R., & Capuzzi, D. (2001). Counseling the older adult. In D. Capuzzi & D.R. Gross (Eds.). *Introduction to the counseling profession* (pp. 348–365). Boston: Allyn & Bacon.

Harris, H. L. (1998). Ethnic minority elders: Issues and interventions. *Educational Gerontology, 1*(24), 309–324.

Hayes, R. L., & Burk, M. J. (1987). Community based prevention for elderly victims of crime and violence. *Journal of Mental Health Counseling, 9*(4), 210–219.

Hershey, D., Mowen, C., & Jacobs-Lawson. (2003). An experimental comparison of retirement planning intervention seminars. *Educational Gerontology, 29*, 339–359.

Hoyt, M. (1993, Fall). Brief therapy can be the best therapy. *The Provider, MCC Behavioral Care*, pp. 1–3.

Kastenbaum, R. (1968). Perspectives on the development and modification of behavior in the aged: A developmental field perspective. *Gerontologist, 8*, 280–283.

Kleinke, C. (1998). Coping with life's challenges (2nd ed.). Pacific Grove, CA: Brooks/Cole Publishing Co.

Kraaij, E., & de Wilde, J. (2001). Negative life events and depressive symptoms in the elderly: A life span perspective. *Aging and Mental Health, 5*(1), 84–91

Lemme, B. H. (1995). *Development in adulthood.* Boston: Allyn & Bacon.

McWhirter, E. H. (1994). *Counseling for empowerment.* Alexandria, VA: American Counseling Association.

Meichenbaum, D. (1974). Self-instructional strategy training: A cognitive prosthesis for the aged. *Human Development, 17,* 273–280.

Myers, J. E. (1995). From "forgotten and ignored" to standards and certification: Gerontological counseling comes of age. *Journal of Counseling and Development, 74*(2), 143–149.

Myers, J. E., & Schwiebert, V. L. (1996). *Competencies for gerontological counseling.* Alexandria, VA: The American Counseling Association.

National Center on Elder Abuse (1998). *National Elder Abuse Incidence Study: Final Report.* Author.

Nigl, A. J., & Jackson, B. (1981). A behavior management program to increase social responses in psychogeriatric patients. *Journal of the Geriatrics Society, 29,* 92–95.

Reynolds-Welfel, E., Danzinger, P., & Santoro, S. (2000). Mandated reporting of abuse/maltreatment of older adults: A primer for counselors. *Journal of Counseling and Development, 78*(3), 284–292.

Saferstein, S. (1972). Psychotherapy for geriatric patients. *New York State Journal of Medicine, 72,* 2743–2748.

Schwiebert, V., Myers, J., & Dice, C. (2000). Ethical guidelines for counselors working with older adults. *Journal of Counseling and Development, 78*(2), 123–136.

Sherman, E. (1993). Mental health and successful adaptation in later life. *Generations, 17*(1), 43–46.

Shmotkin, D., & Eyal, N. (2003). Psychological time in later life: Implications for counseling. *Journal of Counseling and Development, 81*(3), 259–267.

Special Committee on Aging (SCOA). (1983). *Developments in aging: 1983* (Vol. 1). Washington, DC: U.S. Government Printing Office.

Strawbridge, W., Wallhagan, M., & Cohen, R. (2002). Successful aging and well-being: Self-rated compared with Rowe and Kahn. *Gerontologist, 42,* 727–733.

Taylor-Carter, M. A., Cook, K., & Weinberg, C. (1997). Planning and expectations of the retirement experience. *Educational Gerontology, 23,* 273–288.

Thomas, M. C., & Martin, V. (2002). Group counseling with the elderly and their caregivers. In D. Capuzzi & D. R. Gross (Eds.), *Introduction to group counseling* (3rd ed., pp. 407–433). Denver, CO: Love Publishing.

Thornton, J. (2002). Myths of aging or ageist stereotypes. *Educational Gerontology, 28,* 301–312.

Tice, C. J., & Perkins, K. (1996). *Mental health issues and aging: Building on the strengths of older persons.* Pacific Grove, CA: Brooks/Cole.

Toseland, R. W. (1990). *Group work with older adults.* New York: New York University Press.

Tueth, M. J. (1995). DSM-IV disorders most commonly seen in the elderly. *Clinical Gerontologist, 16,* 74–76.

Warnick, J. (1995). *Listening with different ears: Counseling people over 60.* Fort Bragg, CA: QED Press.

Waters, E. (1984). Building on what you know: Techniques for individual and group counseling with older people. *Counseling Psychologist, 12*(2), 63–74.

Wellman, R., & McCormack, J. (1984). Counseling with older persons: A review of outcome research. *Counseling Psychologist, 12*(2), 81–96.

Whitty, M. (2003). Coping and defending: Age differences in maturity of defence mechanisms and coping strategies. *Aging and Mental Health, 7*(21), 123–132.

Woods, R. T. (Ed.). (1996). *Handbook of clinical psychology of aging.* Chichester, NY: Wiley & Sons.

Zucchero, R. A. (1998). A unique model for training mental health professionals to work with older adults. *Educational Gerontology, 24,* 265–278.

Chapter 17

Ackerman, N. W. (1958). *The psychodynamics of family life.* New York: Basic Books.

Alexander, J., & Barton, C. (1995). Family therapy research. In R. H. Mikesell, D. Lusterman, S. H. McDaniel (Eds.), *Integrating family therapy* (pp. 91–112). Washington, DC: APA.

American Association for Marriage and Family Therapy. (1998). *AAMFT code of ethics.* Washington, DC: Author.

American Association for Marriage and Family Therapy. (2003a). *Directory of MFT licensing/certification boards* [Online]. Available: *http://www.aamft.org/resources/onlinedirectory/boardcontacts.htm*

American Association for Marriage and Family Therapy. (2003b). *Directory of MFT training programs* [On-line]. Available: *http://www .aamft.org/resources/onlinedirectory/coamfte.htm*

American Association for Marriage and Family Therapy. (2003c). *Studies on fees and salaries of marriage and family therapists* [Online]. Available: *http://www.aamft.org/resources/career_practiceinformation/salaries.htm*

American Counseling Association. (1995). *Code of ethics*. Alexandria, VA: Author.

American Psychiatric Association. (2000). *Diagnostic and statistical manual of mental disorders* (4th ed.). *Text Revision*. Washington, DC: Author.

American Psychological Association. (1992). *Ethical principles of psychologists and code of conduct*. Washington, DC: Author.

Bateson, G., Jackson, D. D., Haley, J., & Weakland, J. (1956). Toward a theory of schizophrenia. *Behavioral Science, 1,* 251–264.

Becvar, D. S., & Becvar, R. J. (2002). *Family therapy: A systematic integration*. Boston, MA: Allyn & Bacon.

Benson, M. J., Schindler, T., & Martin, D. (1991). Accessing children's perceptions of their family: Circular questioning revisited. *Journal of Marital and Family Therapy, 17,* 363–372.

Bergman, J. (1985). *Fishing for barracuda*. New York: W. W. Norton.

Bowen, M. (1991). Alcoholism as viewed through family systems theory and family psychotherapy. *Family Dynamics of Addiction Quarterly, 1,* 94–102.

Bowen, M. (1994). *Family therapy in clinical practice*. New York: Aronson.

Brock, G. W., & Barnard, C. P. (1999). *Procedures in marriage and family therapy*. Boston, MA: Allyn & Bacon.

Carter, B., & McGoldrick, M. (1999). *The expanded family life cycle: Individual, family, and social perspectives* (3rd ed.). Needham Heights, MA: Allyn & Bacon.

Connell, G. M., Whitaker, C., Garfield, R., & Connell, L. (1990). The process of in-therapy consultation: A symbolic-experiential perspective. *Journal of Strategic and Systemic Therapies, 9,* 32–38.

Coppersmith, E. (1985). We've got a secret. In A. Gurman (Ed.), *Casebook of marital therapy* (pp. 369–386). New York: Guilford.

Council for Accreditation of Counseling and Related Educational Programs. (2003). *Accreditation directory* [Online]. Available: *http://www.counseling.org/cacrep/directory.htm*

Diamond, G. S., Serrano, A. C., Dickey, M., & Sonis, W. A. (1996). Current status of family-based outcome and process research. *Journal of the American Academy of Child and Psychiatry, 35,* 6–16.

Doherty, W. J., & Simmons, D. S. (1996). Clinical practice patterns of marriage and family therapists: A national survey of therapists and their clients. *Journal of Marital and Family Therapy, 22,* 9–25.

Fleuridas, C., Nelson, T., & Rosenthal, D. (1986). The evolution of circular questions: Training family therapists. *Journal of Marital and Family Therapy, 12,* 113–127.

Foreman, B. D., & Cava, E. (1993). Neuro-linguistic programming in one-person family therapy. In T. S. Nelson & T. S. Trepper (Eds.), *101 interventions in family therapy* (pp. 50–54). New York: Haworth Press.

Gerson, R. (1995). The family life cycle: Phases, stages and crises. In R. H. Mikesell, D. Lusterman, & S. H. McDaniel (Eds.), *Integrating family therapy* (pp. 91–112). Washington, DC: APA.

Gladding, S. T. (2002). *Family therapy: History, theory, and practice* (3rd ed). Upper Saddle River, NJ: Prentice-Hall.

Gladding, S. T., Remley, T. P., & Huber, C. H. (2001). *Ethical, legal, and professional issues in the practice of marriage and family therapy* (3rd ed). New York: Prentice Hall.

Grove, D. R., & Haley, J. (1993). *Conversations on therapy*. New York: W. W. Norton.

Hahlweg, K., & Markman, H. J. (1988). The effectiveness of behavioral marital therapy: Empirical status of behavioral techniques in preventing and alleviating marital distress. *Journal of Consulting & Clinical Psychology, 56,* 440–447.

Haley, J. (1984). *Ordeal therapy*. San Francisco: Jossey-Bass.

Haley, J. (1985). *Conversations with Milton H. Erickson, MD: Volume II Changing Couples*. New York: Triangle Press.

Haley, J. (1987). *Problem solving therapy* (2nd ed.). San Francisco: Jossey-Bass.

Haley, Jay. (1993a). How to be a therapy supervisor without knowing how to change anyone. *Journal of Systemic Therapies, 12,* 41–52.

Haley, J. (1993b). *Jay Haley on Milton H. Erickson*. New York: Brunner/Mazel.

Haley, J. (1993c). *Uncommon therapy: The psychiatric techniques of Milton H. Erickson, M.D.* New York: W. W. Norton.

Hazelrigg, M. D., Cooper, H. M., & Borduin, C. M. (1987). Evaluating the effectiveness of family therapies: An integrative review and analysis. *Psychological Bulletin, 101,* 428–442.

International Association of Marriage and Family Counselors. (2003). Ethical code for the International Association of Marriage and Family Counselors. Available: *http://www.iamfc.com/ethical_codes.html*

International Association of Marriage and Family Counselors. (2003). *International Association of Marriage and Family Counseling 2000–2002 Strategic plan.* Available: *http://www.iamfc.com/strategic_plan.html*

Kazdin, A. E. (1997). Parent management training: Evidence, outcomes, and issues. *Journal of the American Academy of Child and Psychiatry, 36,* 1349–1357.

Kerr, M., & Bowen, M. (1988). *Family evaluation.* New York: W. W. Norton.

Kershaw, C. J. (1992). *The couple's hypnotic dance.* New York: Brunner/Mazel.

Lankton, C. (1988). Task assignments: Logical and otherwise. In J. Zeig & S. Lankton (Eds.), *Developing Ericksonian therapy* (pp. 257–279). New York: Brunner/Mazel.

Lebow, J. L., & Gurman, A. S. (1995). Research assessing couple and family therapy. *Annual Review of Psychology, 46,* 27–57.

LeCroy, C. W., Carrol, P., Nelson-Becker, H., & Sturlaugson, P. (1989). An experimental evaluation of the Caring Days technique for marital enrichment. *Family Relations, 38,* 15–18.

Margolin, G. (1982). Ethical and legal considerations in marital and family therapy. *American Psychologist, 37,* 788–801.

Markus, E., Lange, A., & Pettigrew, T. F. (1990). Effectiveness of family therapy: A meta-analysis. *Journal of Family Therapy, 12,* 205–221.

McAllister, E. W. C. (1998). Family therapy with conservative Christian families. *Family Therapy, 25,* 169–179.

McGoldrick, M. (1998). *Re-visioning family therapy.* New York: Guilford.

McGoldrick, M., Gerson, R., & Shellenberger, S. (1999). *Genograms: Assessment and intervention.* New York: W. W. Norton.

Micucci, J. A. (1998). *The adolescent in family therapy.* New York: Guilford.

Minuchin, P., Colapinto, J., & Minuchin, S. (1998). *Working with families of the poor.* New York: Guilford.

Minuchin, S. (1982). Reflections on boundaries. *American Journal of Orthopsychiatry, 52,* 655–663.

Minuchin, S., & Fishman, C. (1990). *Family therapy techniques.* Cambridge, MA: Harvard University Press.

Minuchin, S., Montalvo, B., Gurney, B., Rosman, B., & Schumer, F. (1967). *Families of the slums.* New York: Basic Books.

Minuchin, S., & Nichols, M. P. (1993). *Family healing.* New York: The Free Press.

Minuchin, S., Rosman, B., & Baker, L. (1978). *Psychosomatic families.* Cambridge, MA: Harvard University Press.

Moran, A., Brownlee, K., Gallant, P., Meyers, L., Farmer, F., & Taylor, S. (1995). The effectiveness of reflecting team supervision: A client's experience of receiving feedback from a distance. *Family Therapy, 22,* 31–47.

Nelson, T. S., & Trepper, T. S. (Eds). (1993). *101 interventions in family therapy.* New York: The Haworth Press.

Nelson, T. S., & Trepper, T. S. (Eds). (1998). *101 more interventions in family therapy.* New York: The Haworth Press.

Patten, C., Barnett, T., & Houlihan, D. (1991). Ethics in marital and family therapy: A review of the literature. *Professional Psychology: Research and Practice, 22,* 171–175.

Ritterman, M. (1986). Exploring relationships between Ericksonian hypnotherapy and family therapy. In S. de Shazer & R. Kral (Eds.), *Indirect approaches in therapy* (pp. 35–47). Rockville, MD: Aspen Publications.

Satir, V. (1964). *Conjoint family therapy.* Palo Alto, CA: Science & Behavior Books.

Satir, V. (1983). *Conjoint family therapy* (3rd ed.). Palo Alto, CA. Science & Behavior Books.

Sauber, S. R., L'Abate, L., Weeks, G. R., & Buchanan, W. L. (1993). *The dictionary of family psychology and family therapy* (2nd ed.). Newbury Park, CA: SAGE.

Shadish, W. R. (1992). Do family and marital psychotherapies change what people do? A meta-analysis of behavioral outcomes. In T. D. Cook, H. M. Cooper, D. S. Cordray, H. Hortmann, L. V. Hedges, J. Light, T. A. Louis, & F. Mosteller (Eds.), *Meta-analysis for explanation: A Casebook* (pp. 129–208). New York: Russell Sage Foundation.

Shadish, W. R., Montgomery, L. M., Wilson, P., Wilson, M. R., Bright, I., & Okwumabua, T. (1993). Effects of family and marital therapies: A meta-analysis. *Journal of Consulting & Clinical Psychology, 61,* 992–1002.

Shields, C. G., Wynne, L. C., McDaniel, S. H., & Gawinski, B. A. (1994). The marginalization of family therapy: A historical and continuing problem. *Journal of Marital and Family Therapy, 20,* 117–138.

Sieburg, E. (1985). *Family communication.* New York: Gardner Press.

Simmons, D. S., & Doherty, W. J. (1995). Defining who we are and what we do: Clinical practice patterns of marriage and family therapists in Minnesota. *Journal of Marital and Family Therapy, 21,* 3–16.

Simmons, D. S., & Doherty, W. J. (1998). Defining who we are and what we do: Clinical practice patterns of marriage and family therapists in Minnesota. *Journal of Marital and Family Therapy, 24,* 321–336.

Stanton, D. (1988). The lobster quadrille: Issues and dilemmas for family therapy research. In L. Wynne (Ed.), *The state of the art in family therapy research: Controversies and recommendations* (pp. 5–32). New York: Family Process Press.

Todd, T. (1998, November). The business of marriage and family therapy: Updates and projections. *The Academy News, 2,* 2–3.

Touliatos, J., & Lindholm, B. W. (1992). The marriage and family therapist: Graduate preparation of a mental health professional. *Psychological Reports, 71,* 1195–1201.

Walsh, W. M., & McGraw, J. A. (2002). *Essentials of family therapy.* Denver, CO: Love Publishing.

Whitaker, C., & Bumberry, W. (1988). *Dancing with the family: A symbolic-experiential approach.* New York: Brunner/Mazel.

Whitaker, C., & Keith, D. (1981). Symbolic-experiential family therapy. In A. Gurman & D. Kniskern (Eds.), *Handbook of family therapy* (pp. 187–225). New York: Brunner/Mazel.

Whitaker, C., & Malone, T. (1953). *The roots of psychotherapy.* New York: Blakiston.

Wynne, L. (1988). An overview of the state of the art. In L. Wynne (Ed.), *The state of the art in family therapy research: Controversies and recommendations* (pp. 249–266). New York: Family Process Press.

Chapter 18

Anderson, S. C. (1996). Substance abuse and dependency in gay men and lesbians. In J. K. Peterson (Ed.), *Health care for lesbians and gay men: Confronting homophobia and heterosexism* (pp. 59–76). New York: Harrington Park Press/Haworth Press.

Avoiding heterosexual bias in language. (1991). *American Psychologist, 46,* 973–974.

Bailey, M. J., & Dawood, K. (1998). Behavioral genetics, sexual orientation, and the family. In C. J. Patterson & A. R. D'Augelli (Eds.), *Lesbian, gay, and bisexual identities in families: Psychological perspectives* (pp. 3–18). New York: Oxford University Press.

Bailey, M. J., Dunne, M. P., & Martin, N. G. (2000). Genetic and environmental influences on sexual orientation and its correlates in an Australian twin sample. *Journal of Personality and Social Psychology, 78,* 524–536.

Bass, E., & Kaufman, K. (1996). *Free your mind: The book for gay, lesbian, and bisexual youth and their allies.* New York: Harper Collins.

Betz, N. E., & Fitzgerald, L. F. (1993). Individuality and diversity: Theory and research in counseling psychology. *Annual Review of Psychology, 44,* 343–381.

Blumenfeld, W. J. (1992). *Homophobia: How we all pay the price.* Boston: Beacon.

Blumenfeld, W. J., & Raymond, D. (1988). *Looking at gay and lesbian life.* Boston: Beacon.

Blumstein, P., & Schwartz, P. (1983). *American couples.* New York: William Morrow.

Bohan, J. S. (1996). *Psychology and sexual orientation: Coming to terms.* New York: Routledge.

Brandt, A. M. (1988). AIDS: From social history to social policy. In E. Fee & D. M. Fox (Eds.), *AIDS: The burdens of history* (pp. 147–171). Berkeley: University of California.

Brown L. S. (1996). Preventing heterosexism and bias in psychotherapy and counseling. In E. D. Rothblum & L. A. Bond (Eds.), *Preventing heterosexism and homophobia* (pp. 36–58). Thousand Oaks, CA: Sage.

Browning, C., Reynolds, A. L., & Dworkin, S. H. (1991). Affirmative psychotherapy for lesbian women. *The Counseling Psychologist, 19,* 177–196.

Buhrke, R. A. (1989). Incorporating lesbian and gay issues into counselor training: A resource guide. *Journal of Counseling & Development, 68,* 77–80.

Bux, D. A., Jr. (1996). The epidemiology of problem drinking in gay men and lesbians: A critical review. *Clinical Psychology Review, 16,* 277–298.

Byne, W. (1997). Why we cannot conclude that sexual orientation is primarily a biological phenomenon. *Journal of Homosexuality, 34,* 73–80.

Carl, D. (1992). *Counseling same-sex couples.* New York: W. W. Norton.

Carroll, L., & Gilroy, P. J. (2001). Teaching "outside the box": Incorporating queer theory in counselor education. *Journal of Humanistic Counseling, Education and Development, 40,* 49–57.

Cass, V. C. (1984). Homosexual identity formation: A concept in need of definition. *Journal of Homosexuality, 10,* 105–126.

Clunis, D. M., & Green, G. D. (1993). *Lesbian couples*. Seattle: Seal Press.

Coleman, E. (1985). Developmental stages of the coming out process. In J. C. Gonsiorek (Ed.), *A guide to psychotherapy with gay and lesbian clients* (pp. 31–43). New York: Harrington Park.

Colgan, P. (1987). Treatment of identity and intimacy issues in gay males. *Journal of Homosexuality*, *14*, 101–123.

Conley, B. (1995, October). Battering in same-sex couples. *In the Family*, *1*(2), 23–24.

Corey, G., Corey, M. S., & Callanan, P. (1988). *Issues and ethics in the helping profession* (3rd ed.). Pacific Grove, CA: Brooks/Cole.

D'Augelli, A. R., & Garnets, L. D. (1994). Lesbian, gay, and bisexual communities. In A. R. D'Augelli & C. J. Patterson (Eds.), *Lesbian, gay, and bisexual identities over the lifespan: Psychological perspectives*. New York: Oxford University Press.

D'Augelli, A. R., Hershenberger, S. L., & Pilkington, N. W. (1998). Lesbian, gay, and bisexual youth and family: Disclosure of sexual orientation and its consequences. *American Journal of Orthopsychiatry*, *68*, 361–371.

Davidson, M. G. (2000). Religion and spirituality. In R. M. Perez, K. A. DeBord, & K. J. Bieschke (Eds.), *Handbook of counseling and psychotherapy with lesbian, gay, and bisexual clients* (pp. 409–434). Washington, DC: American Psychological Association.

Deevey, S., & Wall, L. J. (1992). How do lesbian women develop serenity? *Health Care for Women International*, *74*, 239–247.

Dworkin, S. H., & Gutierrez, F. (1989). Introduction to special issue. Counselors be aware: Clients come in every size, shape, color, and sexual orientation. *Journal of Counseling and Development*, *68*, 6–8.

Dworkin, S. H., & Gutierrez, F. (1992). Epilogue: Where do we go from here? In S. Dworkin & F. Gutierrez (Eds.), *Counseling gay men and lesbians: Journey to the end of the rainbow* (pp. 335–339). Alexandria, VA: American Counseling Association.

Falco, K. (1987). *Psychotherapy with lesbian clients: A manual for the psychotherapist*. Unpublished doctoral dissertation. Oregon Graduate School of Professional Psychology, Pacific University, Forest Grove.

Faltz, B. G. (1992). Counseling chemically dependent lesbians and gay men. In S. Dworkin & F. Gutierrez (Eds.), *Counseling gay men and lesbians: Journey to the end of the rainbow*

(pp. 245–258). Alexandria, VA: American Counseling Association.

Fassinger, R. E. (1991). The hidden minority: Issues and challenges in working with lesbian women and gay men. *The Counseling Psychologist*, *19*, 157–176.

Finnegan, D. G., & McNally, E. B. (1987). *Dual identities: Counseling chemically dependent gay men and lesbians*. Center City, MN: Hazelden Educational Materials.

First state supreme court rules boy scouts' ban on gays illegal. (1999, August 5). *New York Times*, p. A1.

Fisher, G. L., & Harrison, T. C. (2000). *Substance abuse* (2nd ed). Boston, MA: Allyn & Bacon.

Font, R. (1995, October). Commentary on battering in same-sex couples. *In the Family*, *1*(2), 24–25.

Forstein, M. (1986). Psychodynamic psychotherapy with gay male couples. In T. S. Stein & C. J. Cohen (Eds.), *Contemporary perspectives on psychotherapy with lesbians and gay men* (pp. 103–137). New York: Plenum.

Fortunato, J. E. (1983). *Embracing the exile: Healing journey of gay Christians*. New York: Seabury.

Fox, R. C. (1995). Bisexual identities. In A. R. D'Augelli & C. J. Patterson (Eds.), *Lesbian, gay, and bisexual identities over the lifespan: Psychological perspectives* (pp. 48–86). New York: Oxford University Press.

Fox, R. C. (2000). Bisexuality in perspective: A review of theory and research. In B. Greene & G. L. Croom (Eds.), *Education, research, and practice in lesbian, gay, bisexual, and transgendered psychology: A resource manual* (pp. 161–206). Thousand Oaks, CA: Sage.

Garnets, L. D., & Kimmel, D. C. (1993). Introduction: Lesbian and gay male dimensions in the psychological study of human diversity. In L. D. Garnets & D. C. Kimmel (Eds.), *Psychological perspectives on lesbian and gay male experiences* (pp. 1–51). New York: Columbia University Press.

Gay Men's Health Crisis (2003, August 22). *Missions and Departments*. Retrieved August 22, 2003, from *http://www.gmhc.org/aboutus/gmhc.html*

Georgemiller, R., & Stevenson, M. R. (2003, Summer). "Homosexuality and hope" revisited. *DignityUSA Journal*, pp. 11–12.

Gray, L. A., House, R. M., & Champeau, D. A. (2004). A future in jeopardy: Adolescents and AIDS. In D. Capuzzi & D. R. Gross (Eds.), *Youth at risk: A prevention resource for counselors, teachers, and parents*. Alexandria, VA: American Counseling Association, 243–274.

Gutierrez, F. J. (2004). Counseling queer youth: Preventing another Matthew Shepard Story. In

D. A. Capuzzi & D. R. Gross (Eds.), *Youth at risk: A prevention resource for counselors, teachers, and parents* (pp. 331–352). Alexandria, VA: American Counseling Association.

Hammond, N. (1989). Lesbian victims of relationship violence. In E. D. Rothblum & E. Cole (Eds.), *Lesbianism: Affirming nontraditional roles*. New York: Haworth.

Hancock, K. A. (1994). Psychotherapy with lesbians and gay men. In A. R. D'Augelli & C. J. Patterson (Eds.), *Lesbian, gay, and bisexual identities over the lifespan: Psychological perspectives*. New York: Oxford University Press.

Hart, B. (1989). Lesbian battering: An examination. In K. Lobel (Ed.), *Naming the violence: Speaking out about lesbian battering*. Seattle: Seal Press.

Herdt, G., & Boxer, A. (1993). *Children of horizons: How gay and lesbian teens are leading a new way out of the closet*. Boston: Beacon Press.

Herek, G. M. (1993). The context of antigay violence: Notes on cultural and psychological heterosexism. In L. D. Garnets & D. C. Kimmel (Eds.), *Psychological perspectives on lesbian and gay male experiences* (pp. 89–107). New York: Columbia University Press.

Herek, G. M. (2000). The psychology of sexual prejudice. *Current Directions in Psychological Science, 9*(1), 19–22.

Herek, G. M., Gogan, J. C., Gillis, J. R., & Glunt, E. K. (1998). Correlates of internalized homophobia in a community sample of lesbian and gay men. *Journal of the Gay and Lesbian Medical Association, 2*, 17–25.

Hershberger, S. L. (1997). A twin registry study of male and female sexual orientation. *Journal of Sex Research, 34*, 212–222.

Hicks, D. (2000). The importance of specialized treatment programs for lesbian and gay patients. *Journal of Gay and Lesbian Psychotherapy, 13*, 81–95.

House, R. M., Eicken, S., & Gray, L. A. (1995). A national survey of AIDS training in counselor education programs. *Journal of Counseling and Development, 74*, 5–11.

Island, D., & Letellier P. (1991). *Men who beat the men who love them: Battered gay men and domestic violence*. New York: Haworth Press.

Johnston, M. W., & Bell, A. P. (1995). Romantic emotional attachment: Additional factors in the development of the sexual orientation of men. *Journal of Counseling and Development, 73*, 621–625.

Kain, C. T. (1998). Counseling HIV-positive clients: The tenets of HIV affirmative counseling.

ACAeNews, 1(9). Retrieved September 3, 2002, from *http://www.counseling.org/enews/volume_1/0109a.htm*

Kinsey, A., Pomeroy, W. B., & Martin, C. E. (1948). *Sexual behavior in the human male*. Philadelphia: W. B. Saunders.

Kinsey, A., Pomeroy, W. B., Martin, C. E., & Gebhard, R. H. (1953). *Sexual behavior in the human female*. Philadelphia: W. B. Saunders.

Kitzinger, C. (1996. Speaking of oppression: Psychology, politics, and the language of power. In E. D. Rothblum & L. A. Bond (Eds.), *Preventing heterosexism and homophobia* (pp. 3–19). Thousand Oaks, CA: Sage.

Klein, F. (1993). *The bisexual option*. New York: Harrington Park Press.

Klotz, D. E. (1995). Safer sex maintenance and reinforcement for gay men. In W. Odets & M. Shernoff (Eds.), *The second decade of AIDS: A mental health practice handbook*. New York: Hatherleigh Press.

Kocarek, C. E., & Pelling, N. J. (2003). Beyond knowledge and awareness: Enhancing counselor skills for work with gay, lesbian, and bisexual clients. *Journal of Multicultural Counseling and Development, 31*, 99–113.

Krajeski, J. P. (1986). Psychotherapy with gay men and lesbians: A history of controversy. In T. S. Stein & C. J. Cohen (Eds.), *Contemporary perspectives on psychotherapy with lesbians and gay men* (pp. 9–25). New York: Plenum.

Kurdek, L. A. (1995). Lesbian and gay couples. In A. R. D'Augelli & C. J. Patterson (Eds.), *Lesbian, gay, and bisexual identities over the lifespan: Psychological perspectives* (pp. 243–261). New York: Oxford University Press.

Kus, R. J. (1987). Alcoholics Anonymous and gay American men. *Journal of Homosexuality, 14*, 253–276.

Kus, R. J. (1990). *Keys to caring: Assisting your gay & lesbian clients*. Boston, MA: Alyson Publications.

LaSala, M. C. (2001). Monogamous or not: Understanding and counseling gay male couples. *Families in Society, 82*(6), 605–612.

Lacayo, R. (1998, October). The new gay struggle. *Newsweek*, pp. 32–36.

Lamme, L. L., & Lamme, L. A. (Dec 2001/Jan 2002). Welcoming children from gay families into our schools. *Association for Supervision and Curriculum Development, 59*(4), 65–69.

Levay, S. (1996). *Queer science: The use and abuse of research into homosexuality*. Cambridge, MA: MIT Press.

Levay, S., & Hamer, D. H. (1994, May). Evidence for a biological influence in male homosexuality. *Scientific American, 270*, 44–49.

Lewis, L. A. (1984). The coming out process for lesbians: Integrating a stable identity. *Journal of the National Association of Social Workers, 29*, 464–469.

Lohrenz, L. J., Connely, J. C., Coyne, L., & Spare, K. E. (1978). Alcohol problems in several midwestern homosexual communities. *Journal of Studies on Alcohol, 39*, 1959–1963.

Lopez, S. (1998, October 26). To be young and gay in Wyoming. *Time*, pp. 38–40.

Makgoba, M. W., Solomon, N., & Tucker, T. J. P. (2002). The search for an HIV vaccine. *British Medical Journal, 324*, 211–213.

Markowitz, L. M. (1991, January/February). Homosexuality: Are we still in the dark? *The Family Networker, 15*(1), 27–35.

Martin, A. (1993). *The lesbian and gay parenting handbook: Creating and raising our families*. New York: Harper Collins.

Matthews, C. R., & Bieschke, K. J.(2001). Adapting the ethnocultural assessment to gay and lesbian clients: The sexual orientation enculturation assessment. *Journal of Humanistic Counseling, Education and Development, 40*, 58–73.

Matthews, C. R., & Lease, S. H. (2000). Focus on lesbian, gay, and bisexual families. In R. M. Perez, K. A. DeBord, & K. J. Bieschke (Eds.), *Handbook of counseling an psychotherapy with lesbian, gay, and bisexual clients* (pp. 249–273).Washington, DC: American Psychological Association.

Mays, S. D., & Cochran, S. D. (2001). Mental health correlates of perceived discrimination among lesbian, gay, and bisexual adults in the United States. *American Journal of Public Health, 11*, 1869–1877.

McLaughlin, L. (1998). AIDS: An overview. In P. O'Malley (Ed.), *The AIDS epidemic: Private rights and the public interest* (pp. 15–35). Boston: Beacon.

McWhirter, D. P., & Mattison, A. M. (1984). *The male couple: How relationships develop*. Englewood Cliffs, NJ: Prentice-Hall.

Miller, J. L., House, R. M., & Tyler, V. (2001). Group counseling with gays and lesbians. In D. Capuzzi & D. Gross (Eds.), *Introduction to group counseling* (3rd ed., pp. 469–504). Denver, CO: Love Press

Mollenkott, V. R. (1985). *Breaking the silence, overcoming the fear: Homophobia education*. (Available from the Program Agency, United Presbyterian Church, U.S.A., 475 Riverside Drive, Room 1101, New York, NY 10015.)

Morin, S. F., & Rothblum, E. D. (1991). Removing the stigma: Fifteen years of progress. *American Psychologist, 46*, 947–949.

Murphy, B. C. (1992). Counseling lesbian couples: Sexism, heterosexism, and homophobia. In S. Dworkin & F. Gutierrez (Eds.), *Counseling gay men and lesbians: Journey to the end of the rainbow* (pp. 63–79). Alexandria, VA: American Counseling Association.

National Association of Social Workers. (1985). *Lesbian and gay issues: A resource manual for social workers*. Washington, DC: Author.

National Gay & Lesbian Task Force. (2003). *Hate crimes against gay, lesbian, bisexual, and transgendered Americans*. Retrieved September 4, 2003, from *http://www.ngltf.org*

Norton, J. (1995). The gay, lesbian, bisexual populations. In N. A. Vacc, S. Devaney, & J. Wittmer (Eds.), *Experiencing and counseling multicultural and diverse populations* (3rd ed., pp. 147–177). Bristol, PA: Accelerated Development.

O'Neill, C., & Ritter, K. (1992). *Coming out within: Stages of spiritual awakening for lesbians and gay men*. San Francisco, CA: Harper.

Ossana, S. M. (2000). Relationship and couples counseling. In R. M. Perez, K. A. DeBord, & K. J. Bieschke (Eds.), *Handbook of counseling and psychotherapy with lesbian, gay, and bisexual clients* (pp. 275–302).Washington, DC: American Psychological Association.

Palma, T. V., Stanley, J. L. (2002). Effective counseling with lesbian, gay, and bisexual clients. *Journal of College Counseling, 5*, 74–89.

Parents, families and friends of lesbians and gays (2003). *Hate crimes*. Retrieved September 4, 2003, from *http://www.pflag.org/education/hatecriems.html*

Pattatucci, A. M. L. (1998). Biopsychosocial interactions and the development of sexual orientation. In C. J. Patterson & A. R. D'Augelli (Eds.), *Lesbian, gay, and bisexual identities in families: Psychological perspectives* (pp. 19–39). New York: Oxford University Press.

Patterson, C. J. (1995). Lesbian mothers, gay fathers, and their children. In A. D'Augelli & C. Patterson (Eds.), *Lesbian, gay, and bisexual lives over the lifespan* (pp. 262–290). New York: Oxford University Press.

Paul, J. P., Stall, R., & Bloomfield, K. A. (1991). Gay and alcoholic: Epidemiologic and clinical issues. *Alcohol Health & Research World, 15*(2), 151–160.

Pearson, Q. M. (2003). Breaking the silence in the counselor education classroom: A training seminar on counseling sexual minority clients. *Journal of Counseling and Development, 81,* 292–300.

Penn, D. (August, 2003). Philadelphia Boy Scouts revert back to anti-gay policy. *Lesbian News,* 15–16.

Peplau, L. A. (1993). Lesbian and gay relationships. In L. D. Garnets & D. C. Kimmel (Eds.), *Psychological perspectives on lesbian and gay male experiences* (pp. 395–419). New York: Columbia University Press.

Peyser, M. (1998, August 17). Battling backlash. *Newsweek,* pp. 50–52.

Pillard, R. C. (1996). Homosexuality from a familial and genetic perspective. In R. P. Cabaj & T. S. Stein (Eds.), *Textbook of homosexuality and mental health* (pp. 115–128). Washington, DC: American Psychiatric Press.

Reynolds, A. L., & Hanjorgiris, W. F. (2000). Coming out: Lesbian, gay, and bisexual identity development. In R. M. Perez, K. A. Debord, & K. J. Bieschke (Eds.), *Handbook of counseling and psychotherapy with lesbian, gay and bisexual clients* (pp. 35–55). Washington, DC: American Psychological Association.

Riddle, D. I., & Sang, B. (1978). Psychotherapy with lesbians. *Journal of Social Issues, 34*(3), 84–100.

Ritter, K. Y., & O'Neill, C. W. (1989). Moving through loss: The spiritual journey of gay men and lesbian women. *Journal of Counseling & Development, 68,* 9–15.

Rochlin, M. (1985). Sexual orientation of the therapist and therapeutic effectiveness with gay clients. In J. C. Gonsiorek (Ed.), *A guide to psychotherapy with gay and lesbian clients* (pp. 21–29). New York: Harrington Park.

Rosario, V. A. (Ed.). (1997). *Science and homosexualities.* New York: Routledge.

Rothblum, E. D., & Bond, L. A. (1996). Introduction: Approaches to the prevention of heterosexism and homophobia. In E. D. Rothblum & L. A. Bond (Eds.), *Preventing heterosexism and homophobia* (pp. ix–xix). Thousand Oaks, CA: Sage.

Rubenstein, W. B. (Ed.). (1993). *Lesbians, gay men, and the law.* New York: The New Press.

Schlager, N. (Ed.). (1998). The St. James Press gay and lesbian almanac. New York: St. James Press.

Sears, J. T. (1997). Thinking critically/intervening effectively about heterosexism and homo-phobia: A twenty-five-year research retrospective. In J. T. Sears & W. L. Williams, (Eds.), *Overcoming heterosexism and homophobia* (pp. 13–47). New York: Columbia University Press.

Sears, J. T., & Williams, W. L., (Eds.) (1997). *Overcoming heterosexism and homophobia.* New York: Columbia University Press.

Silberman, B. O., & Hawkins, R. O., Jr. (1988). Lesbian women and gay men: Issues for counseling. In E. Weinstein & E. Rosen (Eds.), *Sexuality counseling: Issues and implications* (pp. 101–113). Pacific Grove, CA: Brooks/Cole.

Silverstein, C. (1981). *Man to man: Gay couples in America.* New York: William Morrow.

Singer, B., & Deschamps, D. (Eds.). (1994). *Gay and lesbian stats: A pocket guide of facts and figures.* New York: The New Press.

Slater, S. (1995). *The lesbian family life cycle.* New York: The Free Press.

Sophie, J. (1987). Internalized homophobia and lesbian identity. *Journal of Homosexuality, 14,* 53–65.

Stein, T. S., & Cohen, C. J. (1986). *Contemporary perspectives on psychotherapy with lesbians and gay men.* New York: Plenum.

Tierney, W. G., & Dilley, P. (1998). Constructing knowledge: Educational research and gay and lesbian studies. In W. F. Pinar (Ed.), *Queer theory in education* (pp. 49–72). Mahwah, NJ: Lawrence Erlbaum Associates.

Turkheimer, E. (1998). Heritability and biological explanation. *Psychological Review, 105,* 782–791.

Troiden, R. R. (1989). The formation of homosexual identities. In G. Herdt (Ed.), *Gay and lesbian youth* (pp. 43–73). New York: Harrington Park Press.

Washington, J., & Evans N. J. (1991). Becoming an ally. In N. J. Evans & V. A. Wall (Eds.), *Beyond tolerance: Gays, lesbians and bisexuals on campus* (pp. 195–204). Alexandria, VA: AACD Press.

Weinberg, G. (1973). *Society and the healthy homosexual.* Garden City: Anchor.

Weinberg, M. S., Williams, C. J., & Pryor, D. W. (1994). *Dual attraction: Understanding bisexuality.* New York: Oxford University Press.

Weston, K. (1991). *Families we choose: Lesbians, gays, kinship.* New York: Columbia University Press.

White, M. (1995). *Stranger at the gate: To be gay and Christian in America.* New York: Penguin.

Wilson, J. D. (1992, September 14). Gays under fire. *Newsweek, 120,* 35–41.

Wolf, T. J. (1992). Bisexuality: A counseling perspective. In S. Dworkin & F. Gutierrez (Eds.), *Counseling gay men and lesbians: Journey to the end of the rainbow* (pp. 175–187). Alexandria, VA: American Counseling Association.

Woodman, N., & Lenna, H. (1980). *Counseling with gay men and women.* San Francisco: Jossey-Bass Publishers.

Wright, W. (1999). *Born that way: Genes—behavior—personality.* New York: Alfred A. Knopf.

Yang, A. (1999). *From wrongs to rights: Public opinion on gay and lesbian Americans moves toward equality.* Washington DC: Policy Institute of the National Gay and Lesbian Task Force.

Yep, G. A. (1997). Changing homophobic and heterosexist attitudes: An overview of persuasive communication approaches. In J. T. Sears & W. L. Williams, (Eds.), *Overcoming heterosexism and homophobia* (pp. 49–64). New York: Columbia University Press.

Chapter 19

Ahia, C. E. (1997). A cultural framework for counseling African Americans. In C. C. Lee (Ed.), *Multicultural issues in counseling: New approaches to diversity* (2nd ed., pp. 73–80). Alexandria, VA: American Counseling Association.

American Counseling Association (1995). *Code of ethics and standards of practice.* Alexandria, VA: Author.

Arredondo, P., Psalti, A., & Cella, K. (1993). The woman factor in multicultural counseling. *Counseling and Human Development, 25,* 1–8.

Atkinson, D. R., Morten, G., & Sue, D. W (1993). *Counseling American minorities: A cross-cultural perspective* (4th ed.). Madison, WI: Brown and Benchmark.

Axelson, J. A. (1993). *Counseling and development in a multicultural society* (2nd ed.). Pacific Grove, CA: Brooks/Cole.

Banks, W. M. (1972). The Black client and the helping professional. In R. L. Jones (Ed.), *Black psychology.* NY: Harper and Row.

Bond, T., Lee, C. C., Lowe, R., Malayapillay, A. E. M., Wheeler, S., Banks, A., Kurdt, K., Mercado, M. M., & Smiley, E. (2001). The nature of counselling: An investigation of counselling activity in selected countries. *International Journal for the Advancement of Counselling, 23,* 245–260.

Campbell, P. R. (1996). Population projections for states by age, sex, race, and Hispanic origin: 1995–2025 (PPL-47, U.S. Bureau of the Census, Population Division). Washington, DC: Government Printing Office.

Chung, R. C., Bemak, F., & Okazaki, S. (1997). Counseling Americans of Southeast Asian descent: The impact of the refugee experience. In C. C. Lee (Ed.), *Multicultural issues in counseling: New approaches to diversity* (2nd ed., pp. 207–231). Alexandria, VA: American Counseling Association.

Constantine, M. G., & Barón, A. (1997). Assessing and counseling Chicano(a) college students: A conceptual and practical framework. In C. C. Lee (Ed.), *Multicultural issues in counseling: New approaches to diversity* (2nd ed., pp. 295–314). Alexandria, VA: American Counseling Association.

Cross, W. E. (1995). The psychology of Nigrescence: Revising the cross model. In J. G. Ponterotto, J. M. Casas, L. A. Suzuki, & C. M. Alexander (Eds.), *Handbook of multicultural counseling* (pp. 93–122). Thousand Oaks, CA: Sage Publications.

Delgado-Romero, E. (2003). Ethics and multicultural competence. In D. B. Pope-Davis, H. L. K. Coleman, W. M. Liu, & R. L. Toporek (Eds.), *Handbook of multicultural competencies in counseling and psychology* (pp. 313–329). Thousand Oaks, CA: Sage Publications.

Garrett, M. W., & Garrett, J. T. (1994). The path of good medicine: Understanding and counseling Native Americans. *Journal of Multicultural Counseling and Development, 22,* 134–144.

Gudykunst, K. B., & Kim, K. Y. (1984). *Communicating with strangers: An approach to intercultural communication.* Reading, MA: Addison-Wesley.

Harper, F. (1973). What counselors must know about the social sciences of Black Americans. *Journal of Negro Education, 42,* 109–116

Harrison, D. K. (1975). Race as a counselor–client variable in counseling and psychotherapy: A review of the research. *Counseling Psychologist, 5,* 124–133.

Helms, J. E. (1995). An update of Helm's White and People of Color racial identity models. In J. G. Ponterotto, J. M. Casas, L. A. Suzuki, & C. M. Alexander (Eds.), *Handbook of multicultural counseling* (pp. 181–198). Thousand Oaks, CA: Sage Publications.

Herring, R. (1997). Counseling indigenous American youth. In C. C. Lee (Ed.), *Multicultural issues in counseling: New approaches to diversity* (pp. 53–72). Alexandria, VA: American Counseling Association.

Herring, R. D. (1992). Seeking a new paradigm: Counseling Native Americans. *Journal of Multicultural Counseling and Development, 20,* 35–43.

Jackson, G. G. (1977). The emergence of a Black perspective in counseling. *Journal of Negro Education, 46,* 230–253.

Kelly, E. W. (1995). *Spirituality and religion in counseling and psychotherapy: Diversity in theory and practice.* Alexandria, VA: American Counseling Association.

Kenney, K. (2000). Multiracial families. In J. Lewis & L. Bradley (Eds.), *Advocacy in counselors: Counselors, clients, community* (pp. 22–70). Greensboro, NC: ERIC/CASS.

Kotkin, J., & Tseng, T. (2003, June 8). Happy to mix it all up. *The Washington Post,* pp. B1–B2.

LaFromboise, T. D., Foster, S., & James, A. (1996). Ethics in multicultural counseling. In P. B. Pedersen, J. G. Draguns, W. J. Lonner, & J. E. Trimble (Eds.), *Counseling across cultures* (4th ed., pp. 47–72). Thousand Oaks, CA: Sage Publications.

Lee, C. C. (1997). Cultural dynamics: Their importance in culturally responsive counseling. In C. C. Lee (Ed.), *Multicultural issues in counseling: New approaches to diversity* (2nd ed., pp. 15–30). Alexandria, VA: American Counseling Association.

Lee, C. C. (1998). Counselors as agents of social change. In C. C. Lee, & G. Walz (Eds.), *Social action: A mandate for counselors.* Alexandria, VA: American Counseling Association and ERIC Counseling and Student Services Clearinghouse.

Lee, C. C. (2001). Defining and responding to racial and ethnic diversity. In D. C. Locke, J. E. Myers, & E. L. Herr (Eds.), *The handbook of counseling* (pp. 581–588). Thousand Oaks, CA: Sage Publications.

Lee, C. C. (2004). Counseling African Americans. In R. L. Jones (Ed.), *Black psychology* (4th ed.). Hampton, VA: Cobb & Henry.

Lee, C. C., & Kurilla, V. (1997). Ethics and multiculturalism: The challenge of diversity. In Hatherleigh Editorial Board (Ed.), *The Hatherleigh guide to ethics in therapy* (pp. 235–248). Long Island City, NY: Hatherleigh Press.

Lee, C. C., & Sirch, M. L. (1994). Counseling in an enlightened society: Values for a new millennium. *Counseling and Values, 38,* 90–97.

Lopez-Baez, S. I. (1997). Counseling interventions with Latinas. In C. C. Lee (Ed.), *Multicultural issues in counseling: New approaches to diversity* (2nd ed., pp. 257–267). Alexandria, VA: American Counseling Association.

McIntosh, P. (1989). White privilege: Unpacking the invisible knapsack. *Peace and Freedom, 2,* 10–12

Nobles, W. (1972). African philosophy: Foundations for a Black psychology. In R. L. Jones (Ed.), *Black psychology.* NY: Harper & Row.

Pack-Brown, S. P., & Williams, C. B. (2003). *Ethics in a multicultural context.* Thousand Oaks, CA: Sage Publications.

Pedersen, P. B. (1995). Culture-centered ethical guidelines for counselors. In J. G. Ponterotto, J. M. Casas, L. A. Suzuki, & C. M. Alexander (Eds.), *Handook of multicultural counseling* (pp. 39–49). Thousand Oaks, CA: Sage Publications.

Pope-Davis, D. B., Coleman, H. L. K., Liu, W. M., & Toporek, R. L. (2003). *Handbook of multicultural competencies in counseling and psychology.* Thousand Oaks, CA: Sage Publications.

Ridley, C. R., Liddle, M. C., Hill, C. L., & Li, L. C. (2001). Ethical decision making in multicultural counseling. In J. G. Ponterotto, J. M. Casas, L. A. Suzuki, & C. M. Alexander (Eds.), *Handook of multicultural counseling* (2nd ed., pp. 165–188). Thousand Oaks, CA: Sage Publications.

Rotheram, M. J., & Phinney, J. S. (1987). Introduction: Definitions and perspectives in the study of children's ethnic socialization. In J. S. Phinney & M. J. Rotheram (Eds.), *Children's ethnic socialization* (pp. 10–31). Newbury Park, CA: Sage.

Roysircar, G., Arredondo, P., Fuertes, J. N., Ponterotto, J. G., & Toporek, R. L. (2003). *Multicultural counseling competencies 2003: Association for Multicultural Counseling and Development.* Alexandria, VA: Association for Multicultural Counseling and Development.

Sattler, J. M. (1977). The effects of therapist-client racial similarity. In A. S. Gurman & A. M. Razin (Eds.), *Effective psychotherapy: A handbook of research* (pp. 252–290). NY: Pergamon Press.

Sue, D. W. (1996). Ethical issues in multicultural counseling. In B. Herlihy & G. Corey (Eds.), *ACA ethical standards casebook* (5th ed., pp. 193–197). Alexandria, VA: American Counseling Association.

Sue, D. (1997). Counseling strategies for Chinese Americans. In C. C. Lee (Ed.), *Multicultural issues in counseling: New approaches to diversity* (2nd ed., pp. 173–187). Alexandria, VA: American Counseling Association.

Sue, D. W., & Sue, D. (2002). *Counseling the culturally different* (4th ed.). NY: John Wiley & Sons.

Toarmino, D., & Chun, C. (1997) Issues and strategies in counseling Korean Americans. In C. C. Lee (Ed.), *Multicultural issues in counseling: New approaches to diversity* (2nd ed., pp. 233–254). Alexandria, VA: American Counseling Association.

U.S. Bureau of the Census (2000). *National Population Estimates—Characteristics.* Washington, DC: Government Printing Office.

Vontress, C. E. (1969). Cultural differences: Implications for counseling. *Journal of Negro Education, 37*, 266–275.

Vontress, C. E., Johnson, J. A., & Epp, L. R. (1999). *Cross-cultural counseling: A casebook.* Alexandria, VA: American Counseling Association.

Webster's Tenth New Collegiate Dictionary (1998). Springfield, MA: Merriam-Webster Inc.

Westwood, M. J., & Borgen, W. A. (1988). A culturally embedded model for effective intercultural communication. *International Journal for the Advancement of Counselling, 11,* 115–125.

Westwood, M. J., & Ishiyama, F. I. (1990). The communication process as a critical intervention for client change in cross-cultural counseling. *Journal of Multicultural Counseling and Development, 18,* 163–1717.

White, J. L. (1970) Toward a Black psychology. *Ebony, 25,* 44–45, 48–50, 52.

Chapter 20

American Cancer Society (2003). *Cancer facts and figures, 2003.* Retrieved August 15, 2003, from *http://www.cancer.org/docroot/STT/stt_0.asp.*

American Foundation for the Blind (2000, October 16). *Statistics and sources for professionals.* Retrieved July 30, 2003, from *http://www.afb.org/info_document_view.asp?documentid=1367.*

American Psychiatric Association. (2000). *Diagnostic and statistical manual of mental disorders* (rev. 4th ed.). Washington, DC: Author.

Backman, M. E. (1989). *The psychology of the physically ill patient: A clinician's guide.* New York: Plenum.

Ben-Yishay, Y., & Diller, L. (1983). Cognitive deficits. In M. Rosenthal, E. Griffith, M. Bond, & J. Miller (Eds.), *Rehabilitation of the head injured adult* (pp. 167–182). Philadelphia, PA: Davis.

Bishop, M., & Feist-Price, S. (2002). Quality of life assessment in the rehabilitation counseling relationship: Strategies and measures. *Journal of Applied Rehabilitation Counseling, 33*(1), 35–47.

Bishop, M., & Swett, E. (2000). Depression: a primer for rehabilitation counselors. *Journal of Applied Rehabilitation Counseling, 31*(3), 38–45.

Bolton, B. (Ed.). (1976). *Psychology of deafness for rehabilitation counselors.* Baltimore, MD: University Park Press.

Bond, G. R. (1999). Psychiatric disabilities. In M. G. Eisenberg, R. L. Gleuckauf, & H. H. Zaretsky (Eds.), *Medical aspects of disability: A handbook for the rehabilitation professional* (2nd ed., pp. 412–434). New York: Springer.

Bowe, F. (2000). *Physical, sensory, and health disabilities: An introduction.* Upper Saddle River, NJ: Merrill.

Cicerone, K. D. (1989). Psychotherapeutic interventions with traumatically brain injured patients. *Rehabilitation Psychology, 34,* 105–114.

Crewe, N. M., & Krause, J. S. (2002). Spinal cord injuries. In M. G. Brodwin, F. Telez, & S. K. Brodwin (Eds.), *Medical, psychosocial and vocational aspects of disability* (2nd ed., pp. 279–292). Athens, GA: Elliott & Fitzpatrick.

Cull, J. G., & Hardy, R. E. (1975). *Counseling strategies with special populations.* Springfield, IL: Charles C. Thomas.

Cunningham, J. M., Chan, F., Jones, J., Kamnetz, B., Stoll, J., & Calabresa, E. J. (1999). Brain injury rehabilitation: A primer for case managers. In F. Chan & M. J. Leahy (Eds.), *Healthcare and disability case management* (pp. 475–526). Lake Zurich, IL: Vocational Consultants Press.

Davidson, J. R., & Meltzer-Brody, S. E. (1999). The underrecognition and undertreatment of depression: What is the breadth and depth of the problem? *Journal of Clinical Psychiatry, 60*(7), 4–9.

Diamond, R. J. (2002). *Instant psychopharmacology: A guide for the nonmedical mental health professional* (2nd ed.). New York: Norton.

Dixon, T. M., & Layton, B. S. (1999). Traumatic brain injury. In M. G. Eisenberg, R. L. Gleuckauf, & H. H. Zaretsky (Eds.), *Medical aspects of disability: A handbook for the rehabilitation professional* (2nd ed., pp. 98–120). New York: Springer.

Doughty, J. D., & Hunt, B. (1999). Counseling clients with dual disorders: Information for rehabilitation counselors. *Journal of Applied Rehabilitation Counseling, 30*(3), 3–10.

Engel, J., Jr. (200). Foreward. In G. A. Baker & A. Jacoby (Eds.), *Quality of life in epilepsy: Beyond seizure counts in assessment and treatment* (pp. xiii–xiv). London: Harwood Academic Publishers.

Epilepsy Foundation (2002). *Medicines for epilepsy* [Brochure]. Landover, MD: Author.

Ey, S., Compas, B. E., Epping-Jordan, J. E., & Worsham, N. (1998). Stress responses and psychological adjustment in cancer patients and their spouses. *Journal of Psychosocial Oncology, 16,* 59–77.

Falvo, D. R. (1999). Medical and psychosocial aspects of chronic illness and disability (2nd ed.). Gaithersburg, MD: Aspen Publishers, Inc.

Fraser, R. T. (1999). Epilepsy. In M. G. Eisenberg, R. L. Gleuckauf, & H. H. Zaretsky (Eds.), *Medical aspects of disability: A handbook for the rehabilitation professional* (2nd ed., pp. 225–244). New York: Springer.

Fraser, R. T., Glazer, E., & Simcoe, B. J. (2002). Epilepsy. In M. G. Brodwin, F. Telez, & S. K. Brodwin (Eds.), *Medical, psychosocial and vocational aspects of disability* (2nd ed., pp. 339–350). Athens, GA: Elliott & Fitzpatrick.

Freidenbergs, I., & Kaplan, E. (1999). Cancers. In M. G. Eisenberg, R. L. Gleuckauf, & H. H. Zaretsky (Eds.), *Medical aspects of disability: A handbook for the rehabilitation professional* (2nd ed., pp. 137–153). New York: Springer.

Greif, E., & Matarazzo, R. G. (1982). *Behavioral approach to rehabilitation.* New York: Springer.

Harvey, E. (2002). Hearing disabilities. In M. G. Brodwin, F. Telez, & S. K. Brodwin (Eds.), *Medical, psychosocial and vocational aspects of disability* (2nd ed., pp. 143–156). Athens, GA: Elliott & Fitzpatrick.

Hauser, W. A. (1997). Incidence and prevalence. In J. Engel, Jr. & T. A. Pedley (Eds.), *Epilepsy: A comprehensive textbook.* Philadelphia: Lippincott-Raven.

Hayes, R. L., & Potter, C. G. (1995). Counseling the client on wheels: A primer for mental health counselors new to spinal cord injury. *Journal of Mental Health Counseling, 17*(1), 18–31.

Heinemann, A. W. (1999). Spinal cord injury. In M. G. Eisenberg, R. L. Gleuckauf, & H. H. Zaretsky (Eds.), *Medical aspects of disability: A handbook for the rehabilitation professional* (2nd ed., pp. 499–527). New York: Springer.

Hong, G. K. (2002). Psychiatric disabilities. In M. G. Brodwin, F. Telez, & S. K. Brodwin (Eds.), *Medical, psychosocial and vocational aspects of disability* (2nd ed., pp. 107–118). Athens, GA: Elliott & Fitzpatrick.

Hu, S. S., & Cressy, J. M. (1992). Paraplegia and quadriplegia. In M. G. Brodwin, F. Telez, & S. K. Brodwin (Eds.), *Medical, psychosocial and vocational aspects of disability* (pp. 369–391). Athens, GA: Elliott & Fitzpatrick.

Hyman, S. E., Arana, G. W., & Rosenbaum, J. F. (1995). *Handbook of psychiatric drug therapy* (3rd ed.). Boston: Little, Brown.

Jacoby, A., & Baker, G. A. (2000). The problem of epilepsy. In G. A. Baker & A. Jacoby (Eds.), *Quality of life in epilepsy* (pp. 1–12). London: Harwood Academic Publishers.

Johnson, J., Getzen, J., & Alpern, H. L. (2002). Cardiovascular disease. In M. G. Brodwin, F. Telez, &

S. K. Brodwin (Eds.), *Medical, psychosocial and vocational aspects of disability* (2nd ed., pp. 237–250). Athens, GA: Elliott & Fitzpatrick.

Kangas, M., Henry, J. L., & Bryant, R. A. (2002). Posttraumatic stress disorder following cancer: A conceptual and empirical review. *Clinical Psychology Review*, 499–524.

Kaplan H. I., & Sadock, B. J. (1996). *Concise textbook of clinical psychiatry.* Baltimore, MD: Williams & Wilkins.

Kendall, E., & Buys, N. (1998). An integrated model of psychosocial adjustment following acquired disability. *Journal of Rehabilitation, 64,* 16–20.

Kerman-Lerner, P., & Hauck, K. (1999). Speech, language, hearing and swallowing disorders. In M. G. Eisenberg, R. L. Gleuckauf, & H. H. Zaretsky (Eds.), *Medical aspects of disability: A handbook for the rehabilitation professional* (2nd ed., pp. 245–272). New York: Springer.

Kraus, J. F., & Sorenson, F. B. (1994). Epidemiology. In J. M. Silver, S. C. Yudofsky, & R. E. Hales (Eds.), *Neuropsychiatry of traumatic brain injury* (pp. 3–41). Washington, DC: American Psychiatric Association.

Linkowski, D. C. (1971). A scale to measure acceptance of disability. *Rehabilitation Counseling Bulletin, 14,* 236–244.

Livneh, H. (1989). Rehabilitation intervention strategies: Their integration and classification. *Journal of Rehabilitation, 55,* 21–30.

Livneh, H. (2001). Psychosocial adaptation to chronic illness and disability: A conceptual framework. *Rehabilitation Counseling Bulletin, 44*(3), 151–160.

Livneh, H., & Antonak, R. F. (1997). *Psychosocial adaptation to chronic illness and disability.* Gaithersburg, MD: Aspen.

Lubkin, I. M. (Ed.). (1998). *Chronic illness: Impact and intervention* (4th ed.). Boston: Jones & Bartlett.

McAleer, C. A., & Kluge, C. A. (1978). Counseling needs and approaches for working with a cancer patient. *Rehabilitation Counseling Bulletin, 21,* 238–245.

McMahon, B. T., & Fraser, R. T. (1988). Basic issues and trends in head injury rehabilitation. In S. E. Rubin & N. M. Rubin (Eds.), *Contemporary challenges to the rehabilitation counseling profession* (pp. 197–215). Baltimore, MD: Paul H. Brooks.

Moos, R. H., & Tsu, V. D. (1977). The crisis of physical illness: An overview. In R. H. Moos (Ed.), *Coping with physical illness* (pp. 3–21). New York: Plenum.

National Institute of Mental Health (1995). *Mental illness in America: The National Institute of Mental Health agenda.* Mental Health Fax 4U

Document No. 955005. Available From Rockville, MD, Ph#1-301-443-5158.

Orr, L. E., & Orange, L. M. (2002). Cancer. In M. G. Brodwin, F. Telez, & S. K. Brodwin (Eds.), *Medical, psychosocial and vocational aspects of disability* (2nd ed., pp. 171–184). Athens, GA: Elliott & Fitzpatrick.

Panek, W. C. (2002). Visual disabilities. In M. G. Brodwin, F. Telez, & S. K. Brodwin (Eds.), *Medical, psychosocial and vocational aspects of disability* (2nd ed., pp. 157–170). Athens, GA: Elliott & Fitzpatrick.

Parker, R. M., Schaller, J., & Hansmann, S. (2003). Catastrophe, chaos, and complexity models and psychosocial adjustment to disability. *Rehabilitation Counseling Bulletin, 46*(4), 234–241.

Prevent Blindness America (2002). *Vision problems in the U.S.: Prevalence of adult vision impairment and age-related eye disease in America.* Retrieved August 15, 2003, from *http://www.nei.nih.gov/eyedata/pdf/VPUS.pdf*

Prigatano, G. P. (1989). Bring it up in milieu: Toward effective traumatic brain injury rehabilitation interventions. *Rehabilitation Psychology, 34*, 135–144.

Prigatano, G. P. (1992). Personality disturbances associated with traumatic brain injury. *Journal of Consulting and Clinical Psychology, 60*, 360–368.

Rey, M. J. (1999). Cardiovascular disorders. In M. G. Eisenberg, R. L. Gleuckauf, & H. H. Zaretsky (Eds.), *Medical aspects of disability: A handbook for the rehabilitation professional* (2nd ed., pp. 154–184). New York: Springer.

Rosenthal, B. P., & Cole, R. G. (1999). Visual impairments. In M. G. Eisenberg, R. L. Gleuckauf, & H. H. Zaretsky (Eds.), *Medical aspects of disability: A handbook for the rehabilitation professional* (2nd ed., pp. 565–585). New York: Springer.

Ryder, B. E. (2003). Counseling theory as a tool for vocational counselors. *Journal of Visual Impairment & Blindness, 97*(3), 149–156.

Schnoll, R. A., Knowles, J. C., & Harlow, L. (2002). Correlates of adjustment among cancer survivors. *Journal of Psychosocial Oncology, 20*(1): 37–59.

Schwartz, S. H. (2002). Traumatic brain injury. In M. G. Brodwin, F. Telez, & S. K. Brodwin (Eds.), *Medical, psychosocial and vocational aspects of disability* (2nd ed., pp. 363–374). Athens, GA: Elliott & Fitzpatrick.

Szymanski, E. M. (1999). Disability, job stress, the changing nature of careers, and the career resilience portfolio. *Rehabilitation Counseling Bulletin, 42*, 279–289.

Thomas, K. R., Thoreson, R. W., Parker, R. M., & Butler, A. (1998). Theoretical foundations of the counseling function. In R. M. Parker & E. M. Szymanski (Eds.), *Rehabilitation counseling: Basics and beyond* (3rd ed., pp. 225–268). Austin, TX: Pro-Ed.

Thompson P., & Oxley, J. (1993). Social aspects of epilepsy. In J. Laidlaw, A. Richens, & D. Chadwick (Eds.), *A textbook of epilepsy* (4th ed., pp. 661–704). London: Churchill Livingstone.

Twelfth Institute of Rehabilitation Issues (1985). *Rehabilitation of the traumatic brain injured.* Menomonie, WI: University of Wisconsin-tout, Vocational Rehabilitation Institute, Research and Training Center.

Vander Kolk, C. J. (1983). Rehabilitation counseling with the visually impaired. *Journal of Applied Rehabilitation Counseling, 14*(3), 13–19.

Wright, B. A. (1983). *Physical disability: A psychosocial approach.* New York: Harper & Row.

Wright, S. J., & Kirby, A. (1999). Deconstructing conceptualizations of "adjustment" to chronic illness: A proposed integrative framework. *Journal of Health Psychology 4*(2), 259–272.

Livneh, Hanoch, 484
Lloyd, Henry D., 6
Locke, Frank, 5
Loesch, Larry C., 286–308

MAC. *See* Masters Addiction Counselor
Machina mundi (world machine), 176
Maladaptive interpersonal problems, 175
Malpractice torts, 77
Managed care, 52–53, 371
  brief counseling and, 175
  See also Health maintenance
    organizations
Mandatory ethics, 76
Manson, Charles, 195
Marital status, of older adults, 386
Marks, Isaac, 129
Marriage and Family Therapists
  (MFTs), 423
Masters Addiction Counselor (MAC), 35
McWhirter, Benedict T., 155–172
McWhirter, Ellen Hawley, 217–239
Measurement
  defined, 287
  See also Testing
*Measurement and Evaluation in Counseling
  and Development*, 109
Medicaid, 51
Medicare, 51–52, 364
Menninger Foundation, 403–404
Mental health counseling, 372–379
  definitions of, 374
  ethics, 378–379
  health management organizations
    (HMOs), 378
  major depressive disorder, 501–503
  professional identity, 374–375
  professional preparation and credentials
    for, 375–377
  schizophrenia, 500–501
  technology and, 377–378
  See also Community mental health
    counselors
Mental health counseling movement
  background, 8–9
  early psychologists, 9–10
  WWI and the development of testing,
    10–11
Mental hygiene movement, 4

Mental illness, 44
Mental Measurements Yearbook (Buros), 229
Mental Research Institute (MRI), 404
Mental Research Institute (MRI) brief
  therapy approach, 178–183
Metcalf, Henry C., 5
Metropolitan Life Insurance, 5
MFTs. *See* Marriage and Family Therapists
Miars, Russell D., 56–74
Micro SKILLS (Eureka), 231
Middle school counseling, 351–352
Midwest (ACA), 28
Milieu therapy groups, 397
Miller, Jennie L., 430–464
Millon Behavioral Health Inventory, 132
Mind-body-spirit connection, 240, 246
Mind That Found Itself, A (Beers), 8
Mind's eye, 263
  See also Imagery
Mini-Mental Status Exams, 133
Minnesota Multiphasic Personality
  Inventory (MMPI), 132, 302
Minorities, career counseling and, 223,
  225–226, 230
Minuchin, Salvador, 179, 405, 406
Miranti, Judith G., 240–257
MMPI. *See* Minnesota Multiphasic
  Personality Inventory
Modal personal orientations, 220
Model legislation, licensure and, 37,
  46–47
Mood disorders, 321
Moral philosophy, 76
  See also Ethics
Morality, 253
MRI. *See* Mental Research Institute
Multiaxial assessment, 315–318
  See also Diagnosis; DSM-IV
Multicultural counseling, 44–46, 80–83
  See also Headings under specific groups;
    People of color
Multicultural sensitivity, testing and, 306
Multiple relationships, 78–79
  with clients, 78–79
Munich Olympics killings, 195
Music therapy, 268–271
  group counseling and, 283
Myers-Briggs Type Inventory, 302
Myths, about group work, 210–214